FREDERICK JACKSON TURNER (1861-1932) was born in Portage,
Wisconsin, and graduated from the University of Wisconsin
in 1884. He took his Ph. D. at Johns Hopkins and returned
to the University of Wisconsin as Assistant Professor of History in 1889, from which position he rose to full Professor.
He left Wisconsin for Harvard in 1910, where he was Professor of History until 1924. From his early college days he had
been familiar with the unique archival materials collected
by Lyman C. Draper and housed in the Wisconsin State Historical Society. These attracted him to the scientific study
of American life at its beginnings. In 1893 he addressed the
American Historical Association with a paper on "The Significance of the Frontier in American History." This essay
was to open a new period in the interpretation of United
States history. For the rest of his life he tested this hypothe-
sis by applying it to limited regions and periods and recon-
ciling it with larger views of American development.

THE UNITED STATES
1830–1850

THE NATION AND ITS SECTIONS

BY

FREDERICK JACKSON TURNER

WITH AN INTRODUCTION
BY
AVERY CRAVEN

The Norton Library
W · W · NORTON & COMPANY · INC ·
NEW YORK

First published in the Norton Library 1965
by arrangement with Holt, Rinehart & Winston, Inc.

Books That Live
The Norton imprint on a book means that in the publisher's
estimation it is a book not for a single season but for the years.
W. W. Norton & Company, Inc.

PRINTED IN THE UNITED STATES OF AMERICA
1 2 3 4 5 6 7 8 9 0

INTRODUCTION

The sudden death of Professor Turner on March 14, 1932, cut short his labors on this volume. It was unfinished. One chapter, at least, was unwritten; another was incomplete; all awaited final revision. Yet, even in its broken form, the work takes high rank in the field of American scholarship and renders unjustifiable any effort at completion by another.

Professor Turner did not relish the making of books. His eager mind was bent on exploration. New approaches fascinated him, and new materials lured him from routine efforts. He disliked to find his researches halted and his ideas crystallized by publication. There were new facts to be unearthed; new findings might alter old conclusions. Until the evidence was all in, the time had not come for the last word. His personal copies of published articles are interspersed with " red ink " and the margins filled with suggestions to be followed out at some future time. His manuscripts are sometimes almost undecipherable by another. They were written and rewritten; question marks are scattered about to indicate uncertainty of conclusions; the pages are interlined, and often notes and suggestions for revision are attached on separate sheets. He probably never would have completed this volume — at least to his own satisfaction. A mind too keen for finality, a spirit too eager for cold print, a pioneer pressing ever outward beyond established trails — he found it hard to reach the end of his writing. In such a case incompleteness is not a weakness.

Professor Turner had long contemplated a volume on this period. In 1907 or 1908 he had written Professor Carl Becker:

My plans for the future are limited at present to cleaning up some of the obligations I have undertaken for a textbook; but I am interested very much in the period 1820–1850. It is the best opportunity for a new work in a period, and it happens to fall in a period when the West needs especial study — which as yet it hasn't received. But I find it very hard to write, and suspect that I need to break for the wilderness and freshen up — rather than tie myself to the chair.

The wilderness had its way. The textbook was never written, although fragments of the effort are scattered through his papers. Introductions and conclusions — charming bits of interpretation — took form easily enough, but the bodies of the chapters were never added and time softened the pressure of obligations. " My craft goes tramping about so many ports," he wrote in October, 1909, " that I feel unable to chart out a sailing route, as a well ordered ocean liner ought."

Meanwhile research, carried on alone and with his seminars, went forward on a wide front. The approach to American history as a series of social evolutions recurring in differing geographic basins across a raw continent not only involved the study of frontiers of many kinds but also the interplay of sections, varying in age, sources of settlement, and environmental influences. Political history had to be restudied to reveal " party ties working nationally, like elastic bands, to hold the sections together, but yielding and breaking in times of especial stress." The close relations between economic, political, and cultural history had to be traced out in a society which began on a crude frontier and shaded back into the complexities of an urban-industrial life. Geography, sociology, economics, and political science were again the provinces of the historian.

The work of Turner's students in those days reflected the breadth of his approach. They wrote in economic and social fields which ranged from agriculture to industry, from the migrations of primitive Indian tribes to the efforts of mature societies to end war or to solve their labor problems. They investigated political developments which began and ended within narrow localities or again broadened out to national or international scope. They knew no sectional boundaries. Some contributed to the history of the South, some to that of the West, some to that of New England. A few turned to European fields. They found his suggestions applicable to all times and all places. They were studying the evolution of human society in peculiar geographic settings as it moved along its devious courses from isolated simplicity to modern international complexities.

Those who have thought that Frederick Jackson Turner had a fixed formula or thesis for American history do not know the man as he worked with his students. He did not believe that the American experience was entirely unique; he did not think that the frontier was the sole factor in producing democracy or that only good came from frontier experiences. He knew that the greater completeness achieved in the older society of the East was as much a part of the American story as were beginnings in the West. His analyses of the rise of " monopolistic capitalism and imperialism " were the more penetrating because he understood the part which frontier attitudes, thrust into radically different endeavors, played in creating both the problems and the American reactions to them. His approaches were never narrow. He recognized the ties which ran unbroken to the old world and the remote past. " No one could have been less of a doctrinaire." No one could have abhorred oversimplification more, even though the essay form of presentation which he so generally adopted forced a degree of surrender from which he has suffered not only at the hands of his critics but at the hands of his followers as well. His chief characteristic was an impelling desire to know all the facts, and a keen appreciation of the significance of all kinds of facts. His genius lay in the capacity to throw the local and unique into its universal setting. He knew how to combine intensity with breadth.

Professor Turner's chief weaknesses lay in an uneven knowledge of the varied units which made up and contributed to American life. In spite of widest research and experience, his native Middle West tended to furnish the materials from which he generalized. He recognized divergent qualities but his mind was so much a part of his own West that unconsciously he found, there, that which was " typical." Furthermore, he shared the boundless optimism of the prairies and, regardless of the logic of facts and, sometimes, of minor conclusions, he invariably ended on a rising note of faith in the future, not always justified.

And so the great years of inspiration and study slipped by. Professor Turner was developing a distinct school of American history, but he was not filling library shelves with new books. This was not the orthodox way and he knew it, and worried about it even more than did his friends.

The acceptance of an invitation to deliver a course of lectures at the Lowell Institute in Boston, in 1918, brought the necessity for producing a concrete piece of work and offered an opportunity, through expansion into book form, to satisfy the waning hopes of the publisher and the growing expectations of many followers.

With this in mind, he prepared his lectures and then set about the task of expansion. The last years at Harvard and those immediately following his retirement, in 1924, saw the chapters on the sections and on " Jacksonian Democracy " drafted. These were sharply revised after his removal to California in 1927, and the chapter on New England reworked for prepublication in the *Huntington Library Bulletin.*

After the summer of 1929, illness constantly interfered with his progress and, in the end, forced him to dictation. By this method he produced the first drafts of the Presidential chapters and then painfully revised them by hand. He made more rapid progress because he did not have the opportunity for further investigations, and might have finished his volume in rough form had he not recovered sufficiently in the spring of 1932 to return regularly to the Huntington Library collections and to his books. When death overtook him, he had temporarily turned aside from his writing to make a further study of John C. Calhoun.

The writing of this volume, therefore, extended over a period of some fifteen years. It was inevitable that during that time new facts would modify his interpretations and new procedures develop. This resulted in some inconsistencies which only a careful final revision could have eliminated. For instance, he used different statistics in his earlier work from those employed in his later studies. In converting exact quantities into round figures, he sometimes used the next higher figure and sometimes the next lower one. In his earlier work he used the sectional groupings of the 1850 census; later he adopted the groupings of today. Although he concluded that there was no " South " in the earlier days of the nation, he made no attempt, except in Chapter II, to avoid the use of the terms which implied that fact. These inconsistencies have not been removed.

Furthermore, the author intended before publication to verify all statements, dates, names, quotations, etc. He expected to elaborate the treatment given certain subjects and to interpolate discussion of certain others omitted in his first drafts. He hoped to improve the style of the work and the clarity of his statements. He planned to eliminate all duplications.

These things he did not have the opportunity to do, and it has seemed both wiser and fairer to leave them undone, except for the correction of obvious errors in statement, names and dates, etc. Even the maps, which are sometimes rather crudely drawn, are reproduced in the original form.

In scattered notes, written on scratch paper at various times, Professor Turner indicated a few of the things he would have included in his Preface. He described his work as based on his own researches and those of his seminary students. He acknowledged his indebtedness to many monograph studies but indicated that citation in notes did not necessarily mean that he had derived his material or his conclusions from them. He desired to thank Professors Frederick Merk, Godfrey Davies, and Marcus Hansen for reading certain chapters of his manuscript. He noted the part which both the Lowell Lectures and the Dowse Lectures (delivered at Cambridge in 1924) had played in giving form to his earlier work. He expressed his deep gratitude to Mr. Merrill H. Crissey, his secretary, for devoted services in research and writing. The dedication to Dr. Max Farrand had already been written and thanks given to The University of Wisconsin, Harvard University, The State Historical Society of Wisconsin, the Carnegie Institution, and the Huntington Library for aid in his studies.

The manuscript has been put in final form for publication by Mr. Crissey, with the assistance of Max Farrand and the writer. It has been a labor of love on the part of all.

AVERY CRAVEN

Huntington Library
San Marino, California
March, 1934

CONTENTS

MAPS

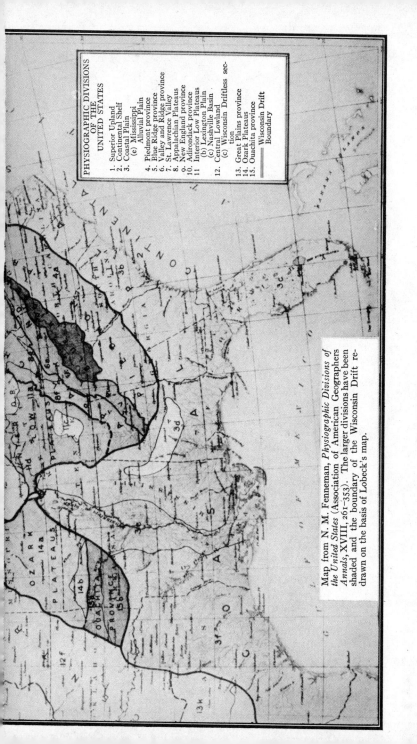

PHYSIOGRAPHIC DIVISIONS
OF THE UNITED STATES

1. Superior Upland
2. Continental Shelf
3. Coastal Plain
   (e) Mississippi
   Alluvial Plain
4. Piedmont province
5. Blue Ridge province
6. Valley and Ridge province
7. St. Lawrence Valley
8. Appalachian Plateaus
9. New England province
10. Adirondack province
11. Interior Low Plateaus
   (b) Lexington Plain
   (c) Nashville Basin
12. Central Lowland
   (c) Wisconsin Driftless section
13. Great Plains province
14. Ozark Plateaus
15. Ouachita province
   ——— Wisconsin Drift
   Boundary

Map from N. M. Fenneman, *Physiographic Divisions of the United States* (Association of American Geographers *Annals*, XVIII, 261–353). The larger divisions have been shaded and the boundary of the Wisconsin Drift re-drawn on the basis of Lobeck's map.

CHAPTER I

SECTIONS AND REGIONS

The purpose of this volume is to set forth and interpret the outstanding features in the development of the United States from 1830 to 1850. It does not seem possible to understand this development without devoting particular attention to the sections of which the nation was composed, for they were as clearly marked as they were influential in their relations with each other and with the Union as a whole.

In these years, new sections were formed as new geographic provinces were occupied. Regional geography played a significant rôle in the economic, political, and social life of a nation whose territory came to equal Europe in size and whose various sections were comparable in resources and extent to the greater nations of that continent. They were, indeed, potentially, nations in themselves.

In the case of such a vast and varied country, changing as it grew and expanding decade after decade, generalizations upon the United States as a whole, in the absence of a survey of the changes in the separate sections, would be misleading. But, acquainted with the background of their life and quality in the period, it should become easier for us to understand the statesmen who went from these various regions to represent them in the halls of legislation and who sought national influence and a national career by negotiating adjustments among the sections.

It will not be the aim to present an exhaustive account of the life and traits of the different sections, but rather to suggest some of their important developments and characteristics.[1]

---

[1] The magazines and newspapers of the period afford material for later investigators to make useful contributions to the history of the several sections. See, for example, Frank Luther Mott's suggestive work, *A History of American Magazines, 1741–1850* (New York, 1930), for indications of the richness of the

The relations between the advance of the frontier and the formation of sections and regions in the United States, will first be considered. Then attention will be directed to the conditions which marked the beginning of the epoch, about 1830. Each of the sections will next be treated in its evolution during the two decades. It should then be possible to describe the interactions of the sections — their rivalries and combinations (particularly in Congressional legislation during these years), and the fundamentally important service of political parties in mitigating these rivalries. Finally, an estimate may be made of the United States in 1850, at the close of the two decades, and a summary of the reasons for considering the period from 1830 to 1850 a distinct era.

Of course, no sharply marked lines can be drawn in the history of any nation: there is a stream of tendency, a continuity of events and institutions, which refuses to yield to artificial divisions. But, so far as any era in the history of the Union can be studied by itself, this one has a marked individuality.

Basing their mappings on geological data, the geographers [2] have laid down the provinces which make up the territory of the United States. These provinces, in general, trend northerly and southerly in great belts. But in the northeastern corner of the country lie the *New England Province,* made up of the New England states with the eastern edge of New York, and the neighboring *Adirondack Province.* The New England section is glaciated, abounding in drowned valleys (which made excellent harbors), in

---

magazines as a means of understanding the taste of the popular reader of the time and the numerous phases of life — many of them now forgotten. On the newspapers, see Lucy M. Salmon, *The Newspaper and the Historian* (New York, 1923); also Frederic Hudson, *Journalism in the United States, from 1690 to 1872* (New York, 1873); and Jas. M. Lee, *History of American Journalism* (Boston, 1917).

[2] I have generalized from the report of N. M. Fenneman, *Physiographic Divisions of the United States* (Association of American Geographers *Annals,* XVIII, 261-353), and A. K. Lobeck, *Physiographic Diagram of the United States* (Madison, Wis., 1922). The map in the former has been reproduced, with slight modifications, in the determination of which assistance was derived from Lobeck. An older, and still useful, analysis is J. W. Powell, "Physiographic Regions of the United States," in *National Geographic Monographs,* I, No. 3 (New York, 1895). See also F. J. Turner, "Sectionalism in the United States," in *Cyclopedia of American Government* (ed. A. C. McLaughlin and A. B. Hart; New York, 1914), III, 280-85, and "Sections and Nation," *Yale Review,* XII, 1-21 [the latter essay reprinted in Turner, *The Significance of Sections in American History* (New York, 1932), as Chap. XII].

waterfalls, in hills, and in intramontane valleys or " intervales." Its boundaries are the Atlantic, the valleys of Lake Champlain and the Hudson River, and the Canadian boundary line running south of the St. Lawrence Valley along the " height of land."

The *Atlantic* (or eastern *Coastal*) *Plain* is subdivided into: (*a*) the " embayed section," running through southern New Jersey and including Delaware, tidewater Virginia, and North Carolina through Pamlico Sound to Cape Lookout; (*b*) the " Sea Island " section, made up of the rest of the tidewater, south from the remaining coastal region of North Carolina to Florida; and (*c*) the Floridian region.

The *Piedmont Province* parallels the Atlantic Plain, and is bounded on the east by the " fall line," where the rivers break in waterfalls from the harder rocks to the coastal plain, and on the west by the rampart of the Blue Ridge. It is the plateau that nurtured the " Westerners " of the first half of the eighteenth century, and constitutes the " upland South." Its northern extension runs across southeastern Pennsylvania and northern New Jersey, the original home of the Quakers and the center of dispersal for the Scotch-Irish and German migration which united with the frontier English to colonize this province between 1700 and 1760.

The *Blue Ridge Province,* divided into northern and southern halves, runs in a narrow band from southern Pennsylvania to northern Georgia, widening at the south along the lofty masses of the Great Smoky Mountains and the Unakas, in the Asheville region of North Carolina. It was the mountain barrier that the western advance had to cross.

West of this province lies the *Appalachian Valley Province,* a broad depression through the Appalachian system, extending from central Alabama to the Hudson and Champlain valleys as far as the Canadian border. Within it lie the upper Tennessee Valley, the Shenandoah Valley of Virginia, the Cumberland Valley of Maryland, and the Great Valley of Pennsylvania, as well as the basin of the Susquehanna River beyond the Blue Ridge. It was the scene of those frontier migrations that moved westward from the Piedmont just before the Revolution.

Extending from south of the Adirondacks, in New York, to central Alabama, in a zone that broadens north of Tennessee into a wide expanse, lie the *Appalachian Plateaus,* reaching an elevation above three thousand feet near their middle portion. This province includes the Catskills, western New York and Pennsylvania to the watershed of the Great Lakes, eastern Ohio, eastern Kentucky, and eastern Tennessee beyond the Tennessee Valley. At this period it was still the home of the descendants of the pioneers who settled on the " Western Waters." Pittsburgh was the economic mistress of the northern half of the region.

The *Interior Low Plateau,* west of this province, is made up of central Kentucky and middle Tennessee. Its rough Highland Rim walled-in the fertile blue-grass basins of the Lexington and Nashville regions.

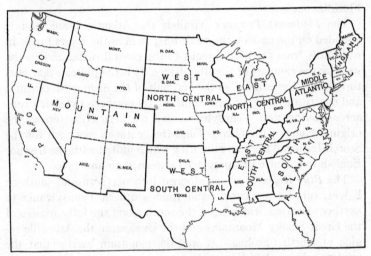

GEOGRAPHIC DIVISIONS, 1910

On either side of this plateau opens up a vast agricultural province: the *Central Lowlands* on the north, including most of the Great Lakes Basin and the prairies of the Middle West; and the *Gulf Plains* division of the Coastal Plain on the south, embracing the southern half of the Mississippi Valley. Beyond the prairies lay the *Great Plains.* The *Ozark Plateaus* occupied southern Missouri and northwestern Arkansas. The provinces of the " Far West " in 1830 were Indian country, or outlying possessions of Mexico or of England — the field of adventurous American explorers, Indian traders and trappers, and the Yankee ships visiting the Pacific ports.

The Census Office, influenced primarily by the statistician, enumerates another set of divisions or sections — namely, the *North Atlantic* (subdivided into *New England* and the *Middle Atlantic States*), the *South Atlantic*, the *North Central* (north of the Ohio River) and the *South Central* (south of the Ohio River) — each subdivided into eastern and western divisions by the Mississippi — the *Mountain Division*, and the *Pacific Division*. Popular usage roughly conforms to these divisions. We speak of New England, the Middle States, the Old South, the Old Northwest (or the Middle West), the Southwest, and the Far West. Each of these divisions developed a life of its own.

On the whole, there is a resemblance between the divisions of the Census Office and those of the geographers.

The human factor has also been at work upon the geological provinces. Whereas the latter arrange themselves in vertical columns, the former respond, also, to a horizontal system. For across the geographical provinces extended the migration of population from the various Atlantic sections and complicated the pattern. But New England is recognized as an independent section by geographer and statistician as well as in popular speech. The Middle Atlantic States are more variously taken, but have come to include only New York, Pennsylvania, and New Jersey. The geographer's analysis, as we have seen, divides this section into parts of various provinces, and these facts are in truth reflected in the social and party, as well as economic, divisions within the states of the section. It is its mixed aspect which has given it a special position as a section in American history. The South Atlantic is, generally speaking, made up of the major portion of the Atlantic Plains, the Piedmont, the Blue Ridge, and the Appalachian Valley south of the Potomac to the Tennessee boundary. The South Central Division includes most of the Gulf Plains, the Interior Low Plateau province, and the eastern-Tennessee portion of the Appalachian Valley. The facts of geology and topography did not prevent this section from having a real unity, but they do explain the interior subdivisions of the section in party policy, economic characteristics, and society.

By 1830 the United States had spread from the seaboard to the Appalachian Mountains, and, broadly based upon the Atlantic and the Gulf of Mexico, had thrust a wide zone of settlement along the lower Great Lakes, the Ohio, and its tributary, the Tennessee, to the Mississippi and the Gulf of Mexico. Significant indications

DISTRIBUTION OF THE POPULATION EAST OF THE 100th
MERIDIAN: 1830

I Up to 6 inhabitants to the square mile
II 6–18 inhabitants to the square mile
III 18–45 inhabitants to the square mile
IV 45–90 inhabitants to the square mile
V Over 90 inhabitants to the square mile

of a further westward advance were seen in the zone of settlement in Missouri, along the river to the western confines of the state.

Between 1830 and 1850 the North Central States, including the prairies of the Old Northwest and the Great Lakes Basin, became a new American section. The most considerable portion of its settlers were of New England ancestry, especially derived from those descendants who had migrated to the West from New York; but there was a large element from other Middle Atlantic states,

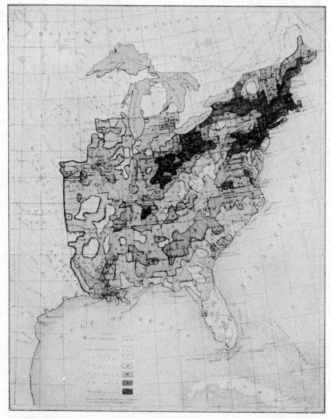

DISTRIBUTION OF THE POPULATION EAST OF THE 100th
MERIDIAN: 1840

I Up to 6 inhabitants to the square mile
II 6–18 inhabitants to the square mile
III 18–45 inhabitants to the square mile
IV 45–90 inhabitants to the square mile
V Over 90 inhabitants to the square mile

and from Germany, Ireland, and the rest of the British Isles, reinforced by immigrants from British America. There was also
the beginning of Scandinavian migration, destined deeply to shape
the society of the northwestern states of this province. These
pioneers of the Great Lakes region and the prairies settled, for the
most part, north of the forested lands of the Ohio Valley into
which Southern pioneers had gone in the years before 1830.

In these two decades, also, the South Central Division, includ-

DISTRIBUTION OF THE POPULATION EAST OF THE 100th
MERIDIAN: 1850

I Up to 6 inhabitants to the square mile
II 6–18 inhabitants to the square mile
III 18–45 inhabitants to the square mile
IV 45–90 inhabitants to the square mile
V Over 90 inhabitants to the square mile

ing Texas, was occupied by men of Southern extraction, and the
basis was laid for the Cotton Kingdom, lying south of the older
trans-Allegheny settlements of Kentucky and Tennessee. Contemporaneously with the Old Northwest, but increasingly contrasting with it, this became another American section. Neither
was a mere emanation from the Eastern states; both possessed a
marked Western quality and an individuality; but the presence of
the negro slave, as well as climatic and geographic conditions and

differences in the colonizing stocks, made it clear, as the years went on, that the upper and lower halves of the Mississippi Valley were to be in conflict over the type of society to be developed in that vast geographic area.[3]

By 1850 both of these sections had strengthened and extended their settlements. The Indians had been removed from the most desired arable lands, and the frontier was pressing against the Indian country along the western borders of Missouri and Arkansas. A broad but sparsely settled zone had been added on the eastern side of newly admitted Texas. In the deserts of Utah the Mormon church had planted its new settlement, led by descendants of New England pioneers; the Oregon country had passed from the domain of the Hudson's Bay Company of fur traders, protected by the flag of Great Britain, to that of the oxcart pioneer farmers of the United States; and a rush of gold seekers from all quarters of the Union and from many other countries had transformed the state of California, recently won from Mexico.

In 1830 Mexico ruled with feeble hand over all the territory south of the forty-second parallel and the diagonal line, from the Rockies to the Gulf, which followed the upper Arkansas and middle Red rivers and the western border of Louisiana. By 1850 this imperial region, south to the present boundary of Mexico (except for the fragment later acquired below the Gila River), was included in the Union.

By the march of the pioneer farmers, by diplomacy, and by war, a territory had been gained equal to the combined area of the United Kingdom, France, Spain, Italy, the Scandinavian countries, Belgium, Holland, and Germany as it was before the World War. An era of marked prosperity, partly the result of the new gold of California, had succeeded the hard times that followed the Panic of 1837. The United States doubled its population between 1830 and 1850, and was teeming with new life, new projects, a belief in " manifest destiny," and confidence in " Young America."

This enlargement of the area of the United States, accompanied by the advance of the frontier and by the spread of settlement into the West, resulted in the formation of new sections as the tide of population flowed into new geographic provinces. A realization of this is a necessary condition for understanding the form

[3] See map of Interstate Migration (at end of volume).

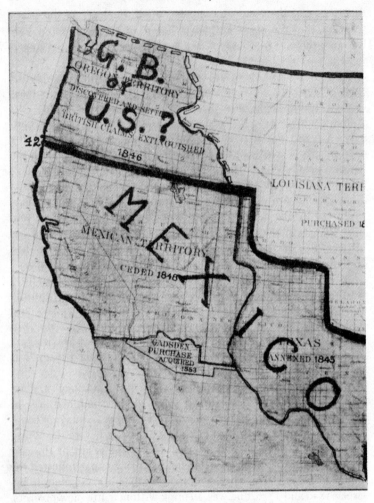

taken in the development of each of the old seaboard sections,
because the influence of this expansion was felt in their economic,
political, and social life. This influence was even more notable in
the relations of the sections with each other. New fields of rivalry
between sections were offered as these new provinces revealed
their natural resources and their power to turn the scale in political conflicts. Sectional contests and sectional alliances in party
history were modified as these new sections arose.

ORIGINAL TERRITORY DEFINED BY THE TREATY OF 1783

FLORIDA

PURCHASED 1819

ACCESSIONS OF TERRITORY
from the
TREATY OF PEACE TO THE GADSDEN PURCHASE

Inevitable in such a changing country were sectional interests, sectional antagonisms, and sectional combinations. Each great area was evolving in its own way. Each had its own type of people, its own geographic and economic basis, its own particular economic and social interests. This fact is often lost sight of in the division of attention between the history of national legislation and national parties, on one side, and state history, on the other. The states did, indeed, constitute definite units, with their own pride and their own jealousy of their constitutional rights. But it is also true that they acted in sectional groups.

Within each of the main geographic provinces of the United States were *regions,* or subdivisions of the section, which were important in molding the history of the separate states and of the section as a whole. Sometimes these regions crossed sectional boundaries, thus creating ties between portions of different sections. Within the section, and even within the states, such regions constituted the basis for separate economic, political, and social types. For example, in the South Central Division, regions like the Lexington Basin, the Nashville Basin, the Black Prairie, and the alluvial lands of the Mississippi Embayment, were favored localities, within which land values, white education, slave concentration, and the residence of men of ability were far higher than in other portions of the section. These differences were marked in the distribution of political-party preponderance, also, though the leaders of all the different parties usually came from these favored regions. The votes by counties in Presidential elections bring out clearly the place of these regions in determining the geographic pattern of party predominance. But, not only in party politics, and the economic and social fields noted above, did regionalism show itself: even in the distribution of religious denominations and literary types, the design made by physical geography was reflected in human geography. Regionalism within the South Central Division finds its counterparts in every other section.

If, to these considerations, we add the fact of the national extension of political parties, we better understand the complex interplay of these factors in the history of the period we are considering. For party loyalty served to mitigate the impact of section upon section, and the strength of each party lay in contrasting regions in the various sections. At times, as we shall see, party allegiance yielded to sectional interests. Particularly was this the case in important Congressional legislation. But, even here, party loyalty moderated sectional antagonism and resulted in compromises. The statesmen who led the various sections and who, at the same time, had Presidential aspirations, found it necessary to aim at such adjustments between sections as would promote their careers in the nation as a whole and at the same time enable them to retain their followings in the sections from which they came. Thus, party proved a flexible bond of union, giving way when sectional interests became compelling, but tending to hold sections together. Moreover, in general, party majorities were not overwhelming. The political maps must not deceive the reader into the belief that areas marked as Democratic were completely Democratic, or Whig, completely Whig. The margin was sometimes very narrow, so that the party must so moderate its policies as not to incur the danger of losing its majority.[4]

But, while regional antagonisms determined the geography of party distribution, the quality of the region did not consistently determine the party complexion. Not all regions of property and prosperity voted Whig, and not all the poor regions of rough country were predominantly Democratic. There were exceptions that prevent the historian from formulating a law of political distribution on physical or economic grounds. It can be said, however, that different physical regions usually voted in opposition to each other and that there was a tendency, falling short of the inevitable, for the Democrats to control the less prosperous areas and for the Whigs to rule in the regions of greater wealth and vested interests.

By 1830 the growth of population in the West, and the development of the frontier type of society, had gone forward to such an extent as to give these sections the balance of political power and bring about the triumph of Jacksonian Democracy. At the beginning of our survey, therefore, we must take account of the ascendancy of rural America under the leadership of a man of the people.

[4] See Franklin H. Giddings, "The Nature and Conduct of Political Majorities," *Political Science Quarterly*, VII, 116–32.

CHAPTER II

THE UNITED STATES IN 1830
JACKSONIAN DEMOCRACY

The United States had, in 1830, a population of nearly thirteen millions. All but three per cent of its people lived between the Mississippi and the Atlantic, and even in this area northern and interior Maine, almost all of Michigan and Wisconsin, northern Indiana, and northern Illinois were practically wilderness. Great islands of Indian country interposed between the settled parts of Georgia and Alabama. Northern Mississippi was likewise in the hands of the red men. But this condition was soon to pass.

Beyond the frontier lay the unwon wilderness stretching to the Pacific — over half the present United States — a land of far reaching prairies and plains, then lofty and forbidding mountain ranges, and, finally, the shores of the ocean that washed the edges of Asia.

The census map of 1830 shows in darker shades the areas of greater density of population. Like successive waves of an advancing tide, these shadings move forward from decade to decade. They represent successive stages of industrial society, the denser settlements being those in which the population exceeds forty-five persons to the square mile, and where manufactures, commerce, and city life are predominant. Such regions were not only deepening in intensity by 1830, but extending laterally into newer zones, like peaceful invaders of the agricultural domains. As these successive frontiers of society advanced, they changed the economic, political, and social interests of the lands they entered. In these transformations lies the explanation of much of our party history and of our ideals. The leaders who lived through these changes shifted their policies to suit the new conditions. New combinations were made and a new political balance of power was effected. As these zones of greater density extended, they brought the people within them into more sympathetic relations.

In 1830 three-fourths of the nation still lived in the states of the Atlantic seaboard; but, if we include their western mountain counties with the Mississippi Valley (as men of the time did in thinking of the West), we find that over a third of the population lived beyond the eastern edge of the Appalachian belt. Of the nearly 13,000,000 Americans,[1] about 5,500,000 were in the North Atlantic Division, 3,500,000 in the South Atlantic, 1,500,000 in the North Central, and 2,000,000 in the South Central. The slave states had less than half the total population of the nation and not much over a third of the white people.

The number of the foreign-born of the United States was not much over 100,000. Nearly three-fourths of them resided in the Middle Atlantic States. But there were unmistakable evidences that the lull in immigration, which had lasted for two generations after the close of the great influx of the eighteenth century, was itself coming to an end. Moreover, the new immigration was to arrive at a time when the rise of urban industrialism and new sections made it a force in American development.

But in 1830 the negroes were a much more considerable factor in all parts of the nation than the foreigners. There were two and one-third million negroes, two-thirds of whom were in the South Atlantic States. They outnumbered the aliens even in New England, in the Middle Atlantic States, and in the North Central Division.

The United States of 1830 was a rural nation. In 1920 over half the population lived in places of 2,500 or more inhabitants, and two-fifths of the people lived in cities of 8,000 or more inhabitants. There were only twenty-five such cities in 1830, and hardly more than one-twentieth of the people lived in them. New York, with about 200,000; Baltimore and Philadelphia, with 80,-000 each; Boston, with 60,000; New Orleans, with 46,000; Charleston, with 30,000; and Cincinnati, with 24,000 — were the largest. Some of the greatest cities of today, like Chicago, were hamlets.

It was a period when cities were practically without water systems, gas, electric light, well-paved streets, paid fire departments, or effective police forces. The first horse-drawn street cars ran

---

[1] Negro population included.

in New York in 1832, and the pictures of the cities at the time
show little to remind us of the present. Postage cost over twelve
and one-half cents for any distance. Hardly two dozen miles of
railroad had been constructed; it took thirty-six hours to go
from Boston to New York by stage and steamboat, and to go
overland from Boston to the Pacific required as many months as
it now takes days by train. Two weeks were occcupied in the
journey from New Orleans to Louisville. There were no ocean-
going steamships.

Anthracite coal was beginning to be used for fuel; but there
were, in general, no furnaces, and coal stoves were a rarity. The
ordinary household light was the tallow dip or the whale-oil lamp.
Friction matches were new and hardly in use. As Senator Hoar
tells us of his boyhood days in Concord, the lighting of the hearth
fire on a New England winter morning was exactly as in the days
of Homer — " a man hides a brand in a dark bed of ashes, at
some outlying farm where neighbors are not near, hoarding a seed
of fire to save his seeking elsewhere." [2] The farmer still used the
scythe and cradle as he had in Egypt. The sewing machine was
not in use. Household spinning, weaving, and shoemaking still survived over much of the country; but the factory system was taking definite form, and with it arose the labor question. Modern
medicine and anesthesia were yet to come.

The regular army consisted of about six thousand men, in seven
regiments of infantry and four of artillery, guarding over six
thousand miles of coast and frontier.[3] The militia training was
a joke. The navy had less than forty vessels of war, a large share
of them old and laid up, " in ordinary," or used as receiving ships.
It was not a military nation of which the " military hero " became
the President, and any suggestions of an increase of the standing
army met with violent attack. The local heroes of the War of
1812 still reaped political rewards, but they were honored as proof
of the efficiency of the volunteer soldier.

Albert Gallatin estimated the capital in banking, in 1830, at

---

[2] Geo. F. Hoar, *Autobiography of Seventy Years* (New York, 1903), I, 43.
[3] See *The American Almanac* (Boston), 1831, p. 146, and *American State
Papers, Military Affairs*, IV. Interesting surveys of the army on the frontier,
with bibliographies, are in: Louis Pelzer, *Marches of the Dragoons in the Mississippi Valley* (Iowa City, 1917); Marcus L. Hansen, *Old Fort Snelling, 1819-
1858* (Iowa City, 1918); and A. J. Turner, " The History of Fort Winnebago,"
Wisconsin Historical Collections, XIV, 65-102.

over $145,000,000, the circulation at over $61,000,000, and the specie in banks at about $22,000,000. Toward the end of 1829, money became plentiful and there were evidences of a tendency to overbanking.

Taking the nation as a whole, the common schools were in a deplorable condition. In the southern sections, private family tutors and academies constituted the means of education for sons of planters of means; but the common people were left without adequate instruction. In Massachusetts, by 1826, a statute had been enacted requiring towns of five hundred families to maintain a free English high school, but the law was not enforced. Organized efforts for better school conditions were undertaken by educational reformers like James G. Carter and Horace Mann, in Massachusetts. By 1829 the American Institute of Instruction met in Boston, and this national conference of teachers, together with labor's agitation in the Middle Atlantic States for really free and democratic schools, marked the inauguration of a period of improvement. A movement began which was to build up the American type of tax-supported, free public common and high schools in place of the pay and pauper schools prevalent in many sections outside of New England. White illiteracy was most notable in the regions of the poor whites and of the southern-upland pioneers in the North Central States, and least in New England and the areas colonized by that stock. So late as 1840, nearly one in twenty of the white population of the United States was recorded as " illiterate " — that is, persons over twenty years of age unable to read and write.

Higher education was but a modest, though important, element in the country's intellectual assets in 1830. There were some sixty colleges, four hundred instructors, and five thousand undergraduate students (many of whom, however, would today be reckoned as preparatory students). Thus, there was one undergraduate to about twenty-five hundred people. In 1922 there were about ten times as many colleges and probably nearly one hundred times as many actual undergraduates, or one to less than two hundred and fifty people. Something like thirteen students to an instructor, and an average of seven or eight instructors to a faculty, in 1830, contrast with the present day. Emphasis was laid upon preparation for the ministry. The curricula were rather rigidly required and of the old classical type. For women, there was little that could be called higher education. State universities of the modern type could hardly be said to have begun. Such colleges as existed exerted a wide influence, and the attendance of southern students in colleges in the North was a significant change from the colonial days when they went to England.

The National Academy of Design was established in 1828, with S. F. B. Morse (later the inventor of the telegraph) as its first president. But, on the whole, the early thirties were marked by little real American art of definite promise. American literature was taking on a new form, and will be considered by sections in the following chapters.

Of the religious denominations, the Methodists easily led, with about 1,900 ministers and 476,000 communicants, followed by the Baptists proper, with nearly 3,000 ministers and over 300,000 communicants, the Presbyterians, with about 1,500 ministers and 173,-000 communicants, and the Congregationalists, with 800 ministers and 120,000 communicants. The Roman Catholic clergy was estimated at 230.[4] The sects which were most flourishing were those that best adjusted themselves to the rural conditions of an expanding people and represented its democratic and emotional spirit.

Prior to 1830 the larger part of the interior of the Union had been colonized from the back country of the South Atlantic section.[5] It was not the tidewater planter who furnished the mass of these settlers, but the nonslaveholding upcountry farmer of the Piedmont region. In an earlier generation, these uplands had been settled by a combined stream of Scotch-Irish and Germans from Pennsylvania and by the yeoman pioneers who had pressed forward the Virginia and Carolina frontiers. Mingled with them were the gentry, but these were far outnumbered by the pioneers, with ax and rifle, who crossed the mountains and cut out new homes on the " Western Waters."

By 1830 they gave the tone to the society of a vast region stretching west from the Appalachian system and including, with some exceptions, the southern counties of Ohio, Indiana, and Illinois, north of the Ohio River, and all the rest of the West to the Gulf of Mexico. Over most of Pennsylvania and interior Virginia and North Carolina, the same type was preponderant.

---

[4] Statistics from the *American Almanac*, 1831, p. 170.
[5] Cf. map of Distribution of Population, 1830 (p. 6, *ante*), with map of Interstate Migration, 1850 (at end of volume).

The ideas and the leaders of this interior-valley society were profoundly to influence the political issues of the nation in the interval between the loss of power by the Old Dominion and the seizure of control by the Cotton Kingdom.

In the period of the Revolution, the " men of the Western Waters " or " men of the Western World," as they called themselves, had forced their way into the Ohio and Tennessee valleys through the passes of the Allegheny Mountains, and in the years that followed they steadily increased their numbers and their power. Thus, the Mississippi Valley of 1830 became the home of forest pioneers. These men, shut off by the mountains from the coast, were the first Americans to break decisively with the Europeans, and to a large extent with the tidewater people.

Composed of various stocks, the special element of Andrew Jackson's [6] people was the Scotch-Irish — the contentious Calvinistic advocates of liberty. Wherever the Calvinist went, he fought arbitrary rule and substituted the doctrine of government by covenant — the free consent of the governed people. Of the Calvinists, none were more strenuous in insistence upon these ideas than the North-of-Ireland folk who came to America. Along with them were the descendants of the English-speaking colonists who had moved away from conventional society to the frontier, and German settlers who in the course of the eighteenth century had drifted from Pennsylvania into the back country of the southern colonies. The Scotch-Irish had been accustomed to the life of cattle-raisers and fighters. The Germans brought with them less of the militant spirit and more of a thrifty, balanced agricultural life. The backwoods families made their ten- or twenty-acre clearing in the surrounding forest with the woodsman's tool, the American ax. They developed an individualism and with it a certain narrowness of view, and emphasized the doctrine of equality. Land was almost free, for, when the pioneer could not purchase, he could settle in his clearing as a squatter and either find the means for paying for it by his later crops or sell his improvements and pass on to a new region, for he was pre-eminently " on

---

[6] For the earlier years of Jackson, see Thos. P. Abernethy, " Andrew Jackson and the Rise of Southwestern Democracy," *American Historical Review*, XXXIII, 64–77; and J. S. Bassett, *The Life of Andrew Jackson* (New York, 1925). Bassett's edition of the *Correspondence of Andrew Jackson* (Carnegie Institution of Washington, 1926–31) has at this writing reached the close of 1838. [Vol. VI, covering the period from 1839 to Jackson's death in 1845, was published in 1933.]

the move." His " neighbor's smoke vexed his eyes "; long before the bark began to dry upon his fence rails, he felt the call to new clearings.

He did not raise extensive crops for a market, but primarily for the subsistence of his family, and he lived to a large extent upon the " hog and hominy " furnished by the swine which fed upon the acorns about the clearing and the corn which made his earliest and chief crop. He had few or no grist- or saw-mills and his log house was the center of a simple and primitive life.

Along with individualism, self-reliance, and equality, went antagonism to the restraints of government. His own gun defended him. Population was sparse and there was no multitude of jostling interests, such as accompanied dense settlement and required a complicated system of government. There were no intricate business relations to need the intervention of the law. Society itself seemed to have dissolved into its individual atoms, at the same time that tradition, precedent — in a word, the past — lost its power by this migration into the new world beyond the mountains.

It was not only a society in which the love of equality was prominent: it was also a competitive society. To its socialist critics it has seemed not so much a democracy as a society whose members were " expectant capitalists." And this, indeed, is a part of its character. It was based upon the idea of the fair chance for all men, not on the conception of leveling by arbitrary methods and especially by law. But, while this is true, it must also be remembered that the simplicity of life in this region and these years, together with the vast extent of unoccupied land and unexploited resources, made it easy for this upcountry democrat to conceive of equality and competitive individualism as consistent elements of democracy. Just in proportion as competition increased, new fields for activity opened and artificial inequalities were checked. The self-made man was the ideal of this society.

As a part of the same conditions, men readily took the law into their own hands. A crime was more a personal affront to the victim than an outrage upon the law of the land. Substantial justice secured in the most direct way was its aim. It had little patience with fine-drawn legal or constitutional distinctions, or even scruples of method. If the thing was in itself proper to be done, then the most immediate, rough-and-ready, effective way was the best way.

From the first, it was evident that these men had means of supplementing their individual activity by informal combinations. One of the things that impressed all early travelers in the United States was the capacity for extra-legal association. This was natural enough, for in America we can study the process by which social customs form and crystallize into law. We can even see how the personal leader becomes the governmental official. This power of the pioneers to join together for a common end, without the intervention of governmental institutions, was one of their marked characteristics. The logrolling, the house raising, the husking bee, the apple paring, the squatters' associations whereby they protected themselves against the speculators in securing title to their clearings on the public domain, the camp meeting, and the courts of " Judge Lynch," are a few of the indications of this attitude.

It is well to emphasize this American trait, because in a modified way it has come to be one of the most characteristic and important features of the United States of today. America does, through informal association and understandings on the part of the people, many of the things which in the Old World are and can be done only by governmental intervention and compulsion. The actions of these associations had an authority akin to that of law. They were usually, not so much evidences of a disrespect for law and order, as the only means by which real law and order were possible in a region where settlement and society had gone in advance of the institutions and instrumentalities of organized society.

Because of these elements of individualistic competition and the power of spontaneous association, leadership, based upon the qualities most serviceable to this young society, easily developed. In the first generation of these pioneers, military companies chose their own officers, each palisaded village had its own natural commander, every community had its hero. And these local leaders, good haters and firm friends, were, like the chiefs whom Tacitus describes, bound to reward their followers. After the War of 1812, Andrew Jackson became the hero of the Mississippi Valley and of the democracy of the less densely settled regions in general.

If we add to these aspects of backwoods democracy its spiritual qualities, we shall more easily understand the significance of the background of Jackson. These men were emotional. As they wrested their clearings from the woods and from the savages who surrounded them, as they expanded those clearings and saw the beginnings of commonwealths where only little communities had been, and as they saw these commonwealths touch hands with each other along the great course of the Mississippi River, they became enthusiastically optimistic and confident of the continued expansion of this democracy. They had faith in themselves and their destiny. And that optimistic faith, that belief in the worth and possibility of the common man, was responsible both for their confidence in their own ability to rule and for their passion for expansion. They looked to the future. " Others appeal to history: an American appeals to prophecy; and with Malthus in one hand and a map of the back country in the other, he boldly defies us to a comparison with America as she is to be," said a London periodical in 1821. They made of their task almost a religion. Just because, perhaps, of the usual isolation of their lives, when they came together in associations — whether of the camp meeting or of the political gathering — they felt the influence of a common emotion and enthusiasm. Lord Bryce aptly said that the southern-upland folk have a " high religious voltage." Whether Scotch-Irish Presbyterians, Baptists, or Methodists, these people saturated their religion and their politics with emotion. Both the stump and the pulpit were centers of dynamic energy, electric cells capable of starting far-flowing currents. These men *felt* both their religion and their democracy. They were not tolerant of " new-fangled " doctrines.

This democracy was one that involved a real feeling of social comradeship among its widespread members. Justice Catron, who came from Tennessee to the Supreme Court in the Presidency of Jackson, said: " The people of New Orleans and St. Louis are next neighbours. . . . if we desire to know any thing [about] a man in any quarter of the.Union, we enquire of our next neighbour, who but the other day lived by him." [7] Exaggerated as this is, it nevertheless had a surprising measure of truth. For the Mis-

---

[7] John Catron to Jackson, Mar. 21, 1835 (*Jackson Correspondence*, V [Washington, 1931], 331). See also Timothy Flint, *The History and Geography of the Mississippi Valley* (Cincinnati, 1833), I, 141–46. So late as 1848 the editor of the *Western Journal*, published in St. Louis, writes (I, 154): " The Valley of the Mississippi, from south to north, constitutes one community of interest."

sissippi River was the great highway down which groups of pioneers like Abraham Lincoln, on their rafts and flatboats, brought the little neighborhood surplus. After the steamboat came to the Western Waters, the voyages up and down, by merchants and by farmers shifting their homes, brought people into contact with each other over wide areas.

All of southern Indiana and southern Illinois, together with Missouri, Arkansas, and the northern parts of Mississippi and Alabama, were but the periphery of the expanding upcountry society which found its center in Kentucky and Tennessee. This enlarged neighborhood democracy was determined, not by a reluctant admission that under the law one man was as good as another : it was based upon a " genuine feeling of good fellowship," sympathy, and understanding. This was important in the region into which so many different commonwealths were pouring their populations. It was by no means the case that these men lost their prejudices : they had the universal antipathies for different customs and different regions. But the very newness of their society made these prejudices less obstinate than in older sections. Therefore, the Mississippi Valley was the region in which the process of mixture of peoples, ideas, and institutions was most easily effected.

This meant nationalism as well as friendly intercourse. Communities were too new and varied in their composition to have the historical state-feeling of the Old Thirteen. All of their experiences, moreover, tended to make them appeal to the general government for protection and advantages. This government was too remote to lay much restraint upon daily life ; at the same time, it was able to furnish them the backing for their designs of building up this region into which the nation was expanding.

De Tocqueville, early in the thirties, wrote :

To evade the bondage of system and habit, of family-maxims, class-opinions, and, in some degree, of national prejudices; to accept tradition only as a means of information, and existing facts only as a lesson to be used in doing otherwise and doing better; to seek the reason of things for one's self, and in one's self alone; to tend to results without being bound to means, and to aim at the substance through the form; — such are the principal characteristics of what I shall call the philosophical method of the Americans.

But if I go further, and seek amongst these characteristics the principal one which includes almost all the rest, I discover that, in most of the operations of mind, each American appeals only to the individual effort of his own understanding.[8]

De Tocqueville was, in fact, describing American pioneer democracy in the days of Jackson. But the best expression of frontier democracy which I have ever seen is in the petition [9] of the frank, rude frontiersmen of western Virginia, at the close of the Revolution, in their demand for statehood separate from the Old Dominion:

> Some of our fellow citizens may think we are not yet able to conduct our affairs, and consult our interest; but if our society is rude, much wisdom is not necessary to supply our wants, and a fool can sometimes put on his clothes better than a wise man can do it for him. We are not against hearing council; but we attend more to our own feelings than to the argumentation of others.

They add that the whole authority of the state rests ultimately upon the opinions and judgments of men who are generally as void of experience as themselves. This is the authentic voice of his people at the time when Andrew Jackson, of Tennessee, won the Presidency. And, because of the large proportion of the country that had recently undergone frontier conditions or was still on the frontier, it was at that time also the voice of the average American democrat.

In order to understand the means by which this leader, trained on the frontier, expressing its militant quality and its democracy, won the Presidency, we must draw a distinction between the Jackson men and the Jacksonian Democrats in 1828. The " Jackson men " included, not only the trans-Allegheny followers of the " Old Hero," and the kindred people of Pennsylvania, but also the New York democracy and the tidewater aristocracy of the southern seaboard. Nevertheless, Jacksonian Democracy was based primarily upon the characteristics of the back country. Jackson was himself a product of the frontier West — that West which was born of the southern upland in the days when a sharp

---

[8] Alexis de Tocqueville, *Democracy in America* (New York, 1898), II, 1–2.
[9] See F. J. Turner, "Western State-Making in the Revolutionary Era," *American Historical Review*, I, 252–53, citing Draper Collections (in State Historical Society of Wisconsin), Newspaper Extracts III, *Maryland Journal*, Dec. 19, 1783. ["Western State-Making" has been reprinted in Turner, *The Significance of Sections in American History* (New York, 1932), in which the passage concerning the petition is on pages 113–15.]

contrast existed between the interior farmers and the tidewater planters.

Although he grew up in this frontier society, he had become a man of property, a cotton planter, a leader who used his leadership to protect the interests of himself and conservative friends in days when all men on the frontier, in the midst of abundant opportunities, strove to build up their fortunes. He had even found himself, in Tennessee, in opposition to political groups whose policies were later to become his own. Among his earlier friends were men to whom the stigma of " Federalists " was attached. " Opportunist " in his politics, as he has been described, he was none the less the national leader to whom frontier democracy turned, who bore in his own personal experiences and qualities many of the frontiersmen's fundamental characteristics. This by no means prevented, in his own state of Tennessee, bitter factional rivalries, and resentments when he gave to statesmen from other sections his confidence and his political rewards. He sometimes purchased national leadership at the cost of losing his own state.[10]

The widening of the suffrage in the older states, by statute and by constitutional change, had been in active progress, and the newer states had, almost from their birth, reposed political power in the hands of the people, either by white manhood suffrage or by so low a tax qualification as to amount to the same thing. By 1830 there were few states that, in practice, had not come to this. The Western states had also based representation, in both houses of their legislatures, on numbers rather than on a combination of property and population. This marked a revolt, characteristic of the period, against the idea that property was entitled to a special representation, against the planter conviction, voiced by John Randolph, that the mere majority, " King Numbers," was tyrannous.

But Randolph's doctrine was ascendant in the tidewater counties of the South Atlantic States, and the terms of the Declaration of Independence which were inconsistent with the alleged primary

---

[10] The foregoing characterization of the society of the region which was the basis of Jacksonian Democracy is taken largely from Chapter XIII of my *The Frontier in American History* (New York, 1921). The chapter was originally prepared for the present work. See also Chapter VI, *post*, on the South Central States. In addition, see Abernethy, as cited on pp. 19, 234.

purpose of government to protect the property-holding class, were repudiated. When, in previous years, the flood of Scotch-Irish, Germans, and other newcomers had passed into the backcountry from the North and had cut across the old lines of slow expansion from the eastern shores, the small counties of the tidewater refused to subdivide the large interior counties as the increased population entered them. They refused to reapportion legislative representation and to make adequate changes in the franchise to meet the changed conditions. Fearing that their historic social structure, and their political control, would be endangered and that the poor and rude but ambitious democracy of the non-slaveholding farmers of the interior would exploit the coast by taxing its property for the building of their roads, the development of their schools, and like expenditures, the tidewater planters determined that the coastal minority must retain its power. They even feared the antislavery sentiment of the western counties and their responsiveness to national, rather than to state, leadership. Gradual abolition had many friends in these counties.

Property's defense of its special privileges, by means of legislative apportionments and the limitation of the franchise, had been exhibited in the constitutional conventions of New York and Massachusetts in 1820. In Massachusetts, however, where the small towns in the interior of the state had a long established advantage in representation proportionate to population, it was the rapidly increasing urban population which sought to secure political power in proportion to its numbers. In New York the argument had been made that an enlargement of the franchise would increase the actual power of the master of industry by his control over the votes of his workmen. Thus, while the contest in the South Atlantic section was that of a Western democracy seeking adequate political recognition, in these Northern states the struggle was made by the growing coastal cities, seeking more adequate representation. In both cases there resulted regional struggles within the state.

To many Americans, Jackson's election seemed a humiliating catastrophe. John Quincy Adams refused to attend the ceremonies when Harvard bestowed the degree of Doctor of Laws upon his successor, explaining that he would not be present to witness her disgrace in conferring her highest literary honors upon a barbarian who could not write a sentence of grammar and hardly could spell his own name. Jackson's penmanship was not clerkly, his spelling was at times modern in the directness with which he reached the desired result, and the grammarian can often find flaws in his sentences. But Adams's description does injustice to the manuscripts of Jackson. The political judgment and foresight which were imperfectly clothed in orthographic garments soon make one forget these aspects.

" General Jackson's manners," said Webster in 1824, " are more presidential than those of any of the candidates. He is grave, mild, and reserved." [11] Harriet Martineau, who visited him in the early thirties and who was sufficiently familiar with the highest English official society to be a good judge, said that he did the honors of his house with gentleness and politeness. He seemed to her " a man made to impress a very distinct idea of himself on all minds." [12] She noted that his countenance commonly bore an expression of melancholy gravity, but from his eyes, when aroused, the fires of passion flashed and his whole person then looked formidable enough. We have a pen portrait from Thomas Hamilton, another English traveler of the time:

Tall and thin, with an erect, military bearing, and a head set with considerable *fierté* upon his shoulders. A stranger would at once pronounce upon his expression, on his frame and features, voice and action, on a natural and most peculiar warlikeness. He has, not to speak disrespectfully, a *game cock* all over him. His face is unlike any other. Its prevailing expression is energy; but there is, so to speak, a lofty honorableness in its worn lines; his eye is of a dangerous fixedness, deep set and overhung by bushy gray eyebrows; his features long with strong, ridgy lines running through his cheeks, his forehead a good deal seamed and his white hair stiff and wirey, brushed obstinately back.

Here we perceive a man of prejudice, passion, and will, born to fight, and carrying a commission from the populace.[13]

[11] *The Writings and Speeches of Daniel Webster* (" National Edition "); Boston and New York, 1903), XVII, 346.

[12] *Society in America* (London, 1837), I, 81.

[13] Jackson's gentler side is touchingly shown in the manuscript correspondence with his wife and other members of his family, contained in the Huntington Library, San Marino, California [printed in *The Huntington Library Bulletin*, No. 3 (Feb., 1933), pp. 109–34], and in " Andrew Jackson at Home," by his granddaughter, Rachel Jackson Lawrence, in *McClure's Magazine*, IX, 792–94. In Jackson's correspondence with Donelson (particularly that in *Jackson Correspondence*, IV [Washington, 1929], *passim*), is revealed the struggle between his fondness for his family and his firm conviction that he must support Mrs. Eaton's attempt to secure social recognition. (See pp. 384–85, *post*.) Gerald W. Johnson, *Andrew Jackson* (New York, 1927), dwells on the romantic side of his domestic life. See also W. H. Sparks, *The Memories of Fifty Years* (Philadelphia, 1872), pp. 151–56.

His triumph constituted an epoch in American history. To the late historian, Professor von Holst, it appeared the beginning of a downward path for the body politic, the rejection of the rule of the better classes, of the intelligent and well-to-do, and the substitution of the feelings and will of the masses for the organized and disciplined direction of the more efficient.[14]

But the " reign of Andrew Jackson " is a test of men's attitude toward the problem of government. On the whole, it must be said that Jackson's Presidency was more representative of the America of his time than would have been that of any of his rivals. The instincts of the American people in supporting him conformed to the general drift of the tendencies of this New World democracy — a democracy which preferred persons to property, an active share by the people in government to the greater system and efficiency of a scientific administration by experts or by an established élite who dealt with the people from above.

In the Presidential election of 1828, Jackson's victory was decisive. Calhoun, who had withdrawn as a candidate for the Presidency in the election of 1824, had then been accepted by both Adams and Jackson for the Vice-Presidency and was elected to that office, which he won again in 1828, although he had expressed apprehension as to the course of some of the adherents of Jackson with regard to the tariff of that year and had urged his South Carolina followers to support " Old Hickory " as a southerner and slaveholder and as a preferable alternative to Adams.[15]   Jackson secured 178 electoral votes against 83 for Adams, and a popular vote of 647,000 against Adams's 508,000. In Jackson's vote, moreover, there is no record for South Carolina, where the electors were chosen for him by the legislature without significant opposition. In Delaware, where likewise the legislature chose the electors, the parties were fairly evenly divided.

As the map shows,[16] Adams carried all the counties of New

[14] H. von Holst, *The Constitutional and Political History of the United States . . . 1828–1846* (Chicago, 1881), pp. 30–31.

[15] *Correspondence of John C. Calhoun*, ed. J. Franklin Jameson (American Historical Association *Annual Report*, 1899, II; Washington, 1900), pp. 268–69, 270; and W. M. Meigs, *The Life of John Caldwell Calhoun* (New York, 1917), I, 374, 387.

[16] By the courtesy of Dr. Jameson, I have used the map of the vote of 1828, by counties, in the Carnegie Institution's historical atlas, now in preparation [by Chas. O. Paullin; published jointly with the American Geographical Society

England except a few in Maine and New Hampshire, as well as
those counties of New York in which the people of New England
origin were powerful, and the similar counties of the Western
Reserve along the shore of Lake Erie in Ohio. These regions, with
the connecting triangle of northwestern Pennsylvania, constituted
the zone of Greater New England. Adams also won counties in the
coastal extension of the old Federalist area in New Jersey and

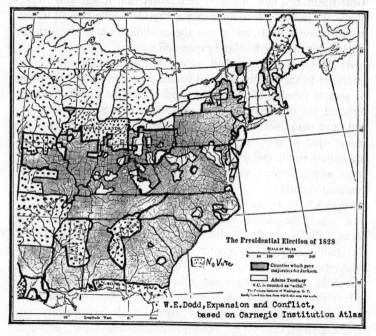

The Presidential Election of 1828

SCALE OF MILES

Counties which gave majorities for Jackson.

Adams Territory

W.E.Dodd, Expansion and Conflict,
based on Carnegie Institution Atlas

Delaware, counties interested in internal improvements along the
Potomac River, and parts of the Ohio Valley, as well as the strongholds of Clay in Kentucky. Taken as a whole, the traditionally
Democratic portions of New York, practically all of Pennsylvania,
the South Atlantic and South Central states (except Kentucky),
and the almost unbroken area of Indiana, Illinois, and Missouri,
gained the victory for Jackson over Greater New England and the

of New York, 1932, under the title, *Atlas of the Historical Geography of the
United States*]. The map has since been published in W. E. Dodd, *Expansion
and Conflict* (Boston, 1915), p. 18. I have also used Edwin Williams, *Politicians
Manual* (New York, 1832), for the election of 1828.

groups of counties which had followed the leadership of Henry Clay, in Kentucky, Ohio, and Virginia.

The election of Andrew Jackson was significant in American history for many reasons. It meant that, in the expansion of the American people, the rural society which had first occupied Pennsylvania, then spread beyond the tidewater country of the South Atlantic States, and, finally, passed into the Ohio Valley and the Gulf Basin, had now achieved such power that it was able to persuade the politicians to nominate a President who proved to represent its own ideals, as against the candidate whose strength lay in the zone of New England expansion.

As the outcome showed, it meant that an agricultural society, strongest in the regions of rural isolation rather than in the areas of greater density of population and of greater wealth, had triumphed, for the time, over the conservative, industrial, commercial, and manufacturing society of the New England type. It meant that a new, aggressive, expansive democracy, emphasizing human rights and individualism, as against the old established order which emphasized vested rights and corporate action, had come into control.

Superficially, this was not so clear. To one distinguished historian,[17] using the geographical classifications of our own time, it has seemed that a " solid South " had united upon a " Southern " slaveholder and cotton planter and, aided by the Democracy of Pennsylvania and New York, had brought him to the Presidency. But these classifications of today do not fit the facts of 1828.

It is obvious that, if one conceives of the " West " of that time as limited to Ohio, Indiana, and Illinois, with their twenty-four electoral votes, the " West " could not have elected Jackson. But what was the " West " of the period? And was there a " solid South "? By 1820 the states beyond the Alleghenies had come to number nine, and their population had grown so rapidly that it was about one-fourth of the total for the Union. A decade later, this region had nearly thirty per cent of the nation's population. The election, however, was held under the census of 1820, and these newer states thus suffered by an apportionment which took no account of eight years of astonishing growth in population. Even so, the trans-Allegheny states had one-fourth of the electoral

[17] Edward Channing (*A History of the United States,* V [New York, 1921], 375–76).

college. By the apportionment under the census of 1830, the proportion rose to nearly thirty per cent.[18] In these reckonings, no account is taken of the kindred society in the western counties of the old states.

What is common to most of this great interior area, is that its society was extemporized in a single generation of pioneering. Even the old French life of Louisiana and parts of Missouri had been engulfed and subjected by the tide of newcomers. By 1828, with the exception of parts of Ohio, the settled portions of the Mississippi Valley were colonized largely by the people of the *interior* of the South Atlantic States, and their children. The upland area of this section must be sharply distinguished, in the sources of its population, its economic and social life, and its political ideals, from the lowland. There was no " solid South " in 1828. The Mississippi Valley's psychology and politics were shaped by its pioneering experience to such an extent that it had a sectional attitude of its own. It would be impossible to understand the events of Jackson's administration if we regarded that portion of the Mississippi Valley which lies south of the Ohio River, reinforced by the slaveholding state of Missouri, as a part of a " solid South," dominated by slaveholding cotton planters in 1828.

Fundamentally, the whole interior — the land of the " Western Waters " — was still a distinct section, even if a changing and unstable one. Through the entire region from Pittsburgh to New Orleans, the Mississippi River and its affluents (the Ohio, the Tennessee, and the Missouri) constituted the great artery of trade and intercourse. Flatboats, rafts, and steamboats carried the agricultural surplus to New Orleans.

The Westerners made a creed of innovation, and emphasized the right of the individual man to equal opportunity, unfettered by custom and as little checked by government as possible. The frontier's rough-and-ready impatience with technicality, and its preference for directness and vigor of action, as well as its ideals of democracy and simplicity and its distrust of government by a trained and established class, all combined to unite the support

[18] The united demand of the West for an increase of power in the federal judiciary had also been a subject of sectional controversy. See the paper by Curtis Nettels, " The Mississippi Valley and the Federal Judiciary, 1807–1837," *Mississippi Valley Historical Review*, XII, 202–26.

of the Mississippi Valley upon Jackson, its hero. He was not so much a cotton planter and slaveholder as a personification of Western wishes and Western will.

The men of the time still thought of this region as the " West," though already the designation " Southwest " was gradually coming into use for the southern half of the Mississippi Valley. For example, Clay's correspondence of this period shows that " Harry of the West " thought of Kentucky as in the " West," [19] as did J. D. Breckenridge (a member of Congress from that state), who spoke in 1823 of the " nine Western States and Territories." [20] Similarly, in 1825, Thomas Ritchie, the editor of the Richmond *Enquirer*, wrote of " 8 western states " which might be expected to vote for Jackson in the House of Representatives. Illinois being conceded to Adams, in that election, this implies that the Southwestern as well as Northwestern states were included in the list.[21] In his first cabinet, Jackson refused the advice of the South Carolina delegation and, while he included some members friendly to Calhoun, the representation from the southern sections was chiefly selected on the recommendations of J. H. Eaton, of Tennessee. Van Buren, who was chosen Secretary of State, complained: " The best known and most influential politicians . . . in Virginia and in South Carolina," who had supported Jackson, were dissatisfied with the cabinet choices.[22] In 1831, on the break-up of this first cabinet, Calhoun lamented that his " old, talented and virtuous section " would have " but one member in the Cabinet, . . . while the west will have the President [Jackson, of Tennessee], the Secretary of State [Edward Livingston, of Louisiana], the Secretary of war [he thought that Hugh Lawson White, of Tennessee, was slated] and the Post Master General [W. T. Barry, of Kentucky]." [23] Jackson himself, in his message vetoing the United States Bank in 1832, uses the expression " the nine Western States." [24]

[19] E.g., Calvin Colton, *The Life, Correspondence, and Speeches of Henry Clay* (New York, 1857), IV, 245; see also p. 242.

[20] Speech in the House of Representatives, Feb. 4. (*Annals of the Congress of the United States*, 17th Cong., 2d Sess., p. 809.)

[21] Chas. H. Ambler, *Thomas Ritchie* (Richmond, Va., 1913), p. 98.

[22] *The Autobiography of Martin Van Buren*, ed. John C. Fitzpatrick (American Historical Association *Annual Report*, 1918, II; Washington, 1920), p. 231. See also pp. 383–84, *post*.

[23] *Calhoun Correspondence*, p. 291; see also p. 393.

[24] Jas. D. Richardson (compiler), *Messages and Papers of the Presidents*,

So late as 1850, the census classified Kentucky and Missouri with the "Northwest"; and Alabama, Mississippi, Louisiana, Texas, Arkansas, and Tennessee constituted the "Southwest."[25] A gradual change was in progress, and it is no more important to dwell upon the Western aspect of the election of 1828 than it is to realize that, before long, the Mississippi Valley became conscious that its unity was yielding to the influence of rival interests which tended to draw its upper half toward a connection with the North Atlantic states and its lower half toward a connection with the South Atlantic section. This will demand consideration in later chapters.

Viewing the growing power of the South Central section, and willing to avail themselves of one of its favorite sons in order to defeat the combined forces of Adams, of New England, and Clay, of the Ohio Valley, the leaders of the tidewater planters in 1828 threw their forces to Jackson, whom they expected to use as their instrument to destroy the nationalistic, loose-construction policy of Clay as embodied in the "American System" of protective tariff and internal improvements. The Virginia and South Carolina state-rights leaders, fearing for the safety of slavery under this system, thought they saw in Jackson a better alternative than Adams.

But their apprehensions, as well as their hopes, were clearly in evidence. Governor Floyd, of Virginia, made it clear that this group had expected Jackson to rely upon a cabinet including orthodox Virginia state-rights politicians and such South Carolinians as Langdon Cheves, James Hamilton, Jr., and Robert Y. Hayne.[26] In consultation with Vice-President Calhoun (" the one

---

1789–1897, II (Washington, 1896), 579. The same classification is implied in Albert Gallatin, *Considerations on the Currency and Banking System of the United States* (Philadelphia, 1831), p. 52.

[25] See also Geo. Tucker, *Progress of the United States in Population and Wealth in Fifty Years*, . . . (New York and Boston, 1843), pp. 58, 195. His classification gains importance from the fact that he was a professor in the University of Virginia. Note also the connotation of the word "West" in *Jackson Correspondence*, V, 331.

[26] Chas. H. Ambler, *The Life and Diary of John Floyd* (Richmond, Va., 1918), pp. 124, 79, 80, 131, 186–87. See also: L. G. Tyler, *The Letters and Times of the Tylers*, I (Richmond, Va., 1884), 375, 377–78; *Van Buren Autobiography*, pp. 229–31 and Chap. xxi; letter of Francis Baylies, in Massachusetts Historical Society *Proceedings*, XLVI, 328–33; Bassett, *Jackson*, II, 408–21; Henry H. Simms, *The Rise of the Whigs in Virginia, 1824–1840* (Richmond, Va., 1929), pp. 27–28; and p. 28, *ante*.

on which we placed the highest value "[27]) they were expected to dominate the policy of the administration. John Tyler, of Virginia, one of the strictest of the sect of state-rights men, flattered himself that Jackson would "come in on the shoulders of the South, aided and assisted by New York and Pennsylvania," and that he must "in the nature of things . . . surround himself by a cabinet composed of men advocating, to a great extent, the doctrines so dear to us," and that, in the strong opposition which he would encounter, he would require the active support of the Virginia group. But he added: "Should he abuse Virginia, by setting at naught her political sentiments, he will find her at the head of the opposition."[28]

The mistaken ideas, followed by rude disillusionment, of the planting interest of the coast are probably expressed by Governor Floyd, who wrote in his "Diary" in 1832:

At this juncture the Southern Party brought out[?] Jackson who was thought to be a States Rights politician . . . When he was elected, to our utter consternation, we found him without principle and of very feeble intellect. He gave himself up to the opposite party, was willing to take any course which would keep him in a majority . . . I did act for the best but we failed to effectuate the good desired because our instrument was vicious though this we did not know when we embraced his cause.[29]

Jackson's age and health were such that, even if he survived four years, he was not expected to seek a second term, and Calhoun was regarded by the state-rights men as his natural successor. How deeply the Virginia and South Carolina statesmen, who thought they saw in Jackson a convenient instrument of their policy, were deceived, events were soon to show. They were deceived, also, by failing to recognize the Western self-consciousness and its determination to carry its own ideals into the conduct of the government. These ideals were, in reality, in conflict with those of the seaboard southern states. It was to take many years before the policy of the South Atlantic prevailed in the South Central section, and the change will form one of the important topics of this volume.

While they hoped, the seaboard planters considered, also, the possibility of disappointment. In 1827 Van Buren had been in

27 Ambler, *Floyd,* p. 124.
28 Tyler, *op. cit.,* pp. 377–78.
29 Ambler, *Floyd,* pp. 186–88; see also pp. 123, 124.

correspondence with Thomas Ritchie concerning plans for an alliance between " the planters of the South and the plain Republicans of the North," based on party principles instead of personal and sectional preferences. Otherwise, Van Buren said, " geographical divisions founded on local interests, or what is more, prejudices between free and slaveholding states will inevitably take their place." He saw in nonsectional adjustment of party an antidote for sectional prejudices. In discussing the propriety of selecting a newspaper organ in Washington, Van Buren, and L. W. Tazewell of Virginia, agreed that Ritchie would be the desirable editor. But Tazewell, in his correspondence with Ritchie, looked forward beyond the inauguration of a Democratic President in 1829. He apprehended that an overwhelming success in the election would involve the danger of party dissensions and felt " solicitous that a Southern Editor should have acquired and established the reputation of the proposed Journal before that day " arrived.[30] Evidently the South Atlantic section regarded the alliance as experimental and of doubtful strength.

This not only shows a foresight which was interesting, but it aids in understanding the distrustful attitude of the seaboard southern men who entered into combination with the Middle Atlantic States and the West. The importance of a national journal, to give the keynote to the party organs of the various sections, was recognized by the friends of both Adams and Jackson and is an indication of the new forces of public opinion which had arisen in the nation. Later events, as we shall see, emphasized the significance of contests for the control over the party organ at the seat of government.

The election of 1828 could not, of course, be decided by any one section, for no section controlled a majority of the electoral college. It was determined by a combination of the West, the South Atlantic States, and the Middle Atlantic section, agreeing upon little more than common opposition to John Quincy Adams of New England. It was not the work of the " solid South," conceived of as the slaveholding states, for no such " solid South " existed. The South Atlantic and the South Central states were at this time separate sections, and upcountry and tidewater South

[30] Van Buren to Ritchie, Jan. 13, 1827 (Van Buren MSS, Library of Congress) ; and Tazewell to Ritchie, quoted in Ambler, *Ritchie*, pp. 108–9.

Atlantic were far from " solid." Moreover, Delaware gave its vote to Adams, and Maryland was divided.

In the free states as a whole, Jackson had a larger popular vote than Adams, and lacked but one electoral vote of equality with him.[31] Of the slaveholding states, Missouri and Kentucky, at least, thought of themselves as " Western " and normally joined the Ohio Valley states north of the river in the important Congressional issues, such as land legislation, internal improvements, and tariff. Missouri's slaves constituted less than one-fifth of her population, and Kentucky's, less than one-fourth (located in the counties of the Blue Grass Basin, which normally followed the leadership of Henry Clay). If these two states be removed from the so-called " Southern " group, Jackson's electoral vote, as well as his popular vote, outside of the slaveholding states, was decisively greater than that of Adams. Moreover, it is a striking fact that, in the slaveholding states of the South Central section, the strength of the vote for Adams, rather than for Jackson, lay, generally, in the counties which possessed the larger proportion of slaves and raised the larger amount of cotton. Only slowly, and toward the close of the period, were they won to the Democratic party.

Nor was Jackson's election achieved by " over-representation of the South," [32] on the assumption that only the free white population should have been considered in the apportionment of power in the electoral college. Among the various arbitrary compromises which had made the Constitution possible, was the provision for representation of three-fifths of the slaves in the states which held such property. But had this provision not existed, Jackson would have won without it, for the number of votes so secured could not have turned the scale.

On the other hand, the Constitution included other artificial arrangements inconsistent with the idea that representation in the electoral college ought to be according to free population. The more populous states were placed at a disadvantage by the provision assigning two electors to each state as a state, regardless

[31] The figures in Channing, *United States*, V, 375, need revision. The eighty-three Adams electors received only about 306,000 votes on the basis there used. Delaware's vote was cast by the legislature, and notice should be taken of the fact that Maine, New York, and Maryland, of the states in which the votes received by the Adams electors are enumerated, voted by districts.

[32] *Ibid.*, p. 376.

of population. New England, with its numerous small states, gained by this provision. Had it not existed, Jackson would have won the electoral vote decisively in the region that had no slaves at all.

Jackson would have been victorious in the free-state area, with no help from the slaveholding states, had the electoral college been based on the actual population. If it is true that the nine states called " Western " by the men of the time could not alone have elected Jackson, it is also true that the states which raised nine-tenths of the cotton of the United States could not have elected him.

If we consider the influence of particular groups of states, the Middle Atlantic, and especially Pennsylvania, had a position of pivotal importance. It was the opinion of Van Buren, an excellent judge, that the influence of Pennsylvania in bringing forward Jackson for the Presidency controlled the result.[33] The outcome in this state could not be attributed to " unjustifiable methods by his partisans," as has been alleged,[34] for Pennsylvania gave a two-to-one vote for Jackson. Henry Clay believed that, if the three great states of Virginia, Pennsylvania, and New York should unite on any one candidate, opposition to that candidate would be unavailing, in all probability.[35]

But the real question, whether a man of " Southern," Western, or Middle Atlantic States affiliations had been chosen, would be answered by the history of his administration. It depended upon the psychology and actions of Andrew Jackson himself, as shown by his earlier career and as exhibited in his choice of men and policies after his election. Here, as we shall see, there can be little doubt. In joining with the West and Pennsylvania in preferring Jackson, the South Atlantic section had deceived itself. It had aided in placing in the White House a man of the frontier, and as a result the West took the reins of authority.

Political power, which had earlier reposed in the South Atlantic section, was in the process of transfer to the trans-Allegheny states, and particularly to Tennessee, whose children had already

[33] *Van Buren Autobiography*, p. 314.

[34] Channing, *op. cit.*, p. 376. The bitterness of the campaign, and the unfair charges against the morals of both men, are illustrated in *Jackson Correspondence*, III (Washington, 1928), and Claude G. Bowers, *The Party Battles of the Jackson Period* (Boston, 1922), pp. 31–34.

[35] Colton, *Clay*, IV, 261; cf. pp. 263, 265.

spread into the northern portions of the Gulf Basin, into the southern counties of Illinois, and across the Mississippi into Missouri and Arkansas, carrying with them political and social ideals of the type of the parent state and thus constituting a great Tennessee area, from which came the Western following of Jackson, Hugh Lawson White, and, later, James K. Polk and John Bell. The rival state of Kentucky, likewise, was still spreading its people into the counties north of the Ohio River — the political domain of Henry Clay and, later, of William Henry Harrison.

CHAPTER III

NEW ENGLAND

Geographically, New England is a clearly defined section — a corner of the Union, pinched out to the northeast between Canada and the Atlantic. Cut off from interior expansion by the Canadian boundary line and the northern watershed, on the one side, and by the mountain system and old New York settlements, on its western border, its early field of adventure beyond the home section was on the Atlantic Ocean.

Within this " New England Plateau," [1] made up for the most part of glaciated lands, were long and narrow strips of valleys and intervales or " fields " between the hills. Most important of these, of course, was the Connecticut Valley, paralleled toward the west by the valley of the Housatonic. The Merrimac River ran its course from the interior of New Hampshire to the sea. Up these valleys the early settlers had spread.[2] By the early twenties, the waterfalls along the lower regions of the Merrimac had become the scene of activity of a manufacturing development which was to revolutionize the region. Boston Bay, the historic nucleus, still maintained its ascendancy as the center of New England capital, shipping, and commerce, as well as the " hub " of its culture and the citadel of its politics.

Between the Connecticut Valley and the coast lay a plateau, now known as the " drumlins " or " orchard lands." It extends

[1] Physiographic descriptions of New England, useful for the reader, are: W. M. Davis, in H. R. Mill (ed.), *The International Geography* (New York, 1909), pp. 721–26; *idem*, " Physical Geography of Southern New England," in *National Geographic Monographs*, I (New York, 1895) ; *idem*, *Geographical Essays* (Boston, 1909), pp. 514–86; and A. P. Brigham, *Geographic Influences in American History* (Boston, 1903), Chap. II. With the industrial New England of 1830 to 1850 may be compared the New England of the present time, as described in Geo. French (ed.), *New England* (Boston, 1911).

[2] See the maps in Lois K. Mathews, *The Expansion of New England* (Boston, 1909).

from New Hampshire through western Rhode Island and eastern Connecticut. Earlier, it was the theater of such agrarian discontent as had been shown in Shays's Rebellion in the days of the Confederation.

The " Old Colony " of southeastern Massachusetts, narrowing into the long projection of Cape Cod, was a land of fisher and farmer folk, much of it sandy wastes.

The " drowned valleys " of the rivers, and the inlets of the sea, made such harbors as Portland, Portsmouth, Salem, Beverly, Boston, the towns of Narragansett Bay, and New London and other Connecticut ports, with the whaling ports of New Bedford and Nantucket.

Rhode Island was divided between the commercial and navigating region of Narragansett Bay and the waste lands of the western half. Long Island skirted the rest of the southern shore of New England, where towns like New Haven, and its little sisters on either side, were active in those varied industries of sea life, small manufactures, and " Yankee notions," which produced the type of the Connecticut Yankee and prepared the way for large manufactures.

To the west, the Berkshires, running northward and connecting with the Green Mountains of Vermont, made a land of hills and intervales which had produced the strong stock that occupied the narrow Housatonic Valley and its lateral tributaries. Forced by the pressure of large, pioneer families in a land cramped for agricultural expansion, these people had moved to make new Western homes, had felt the lure of the cities of the coast, or had remained to deal with hillside farms when Western competition overcame the grain farmer. It was the more conservative who stayed in the farming region of western New England during the decades of our survey. This sturdy, educated, and resourceful stock had not yet lost its vigor; but, in the process of selection by migration, a large proportion of the discontented, the daring, and the innovating had left. The poorer folk, and the young men who constituted so large a portion of the movers, were especially responsive to the innovating impulse in their new communities.

The northeastern region of New England, including New Hampshire and Maine, outside of the cities, was still occupied by a pioneer people — fisher-farmers along the coast and axmen and backwoods farmers in the interior. The pine forests of Maine were attracting speculative purchasers, and in spots there were manufacturing centers and shipbuilding harbor towns. But northeastern New England, in its geography and in its society, contrasted with southern New England and had much in common with the western edge of the section and with the Yankee element in the Middle Atlantic States and the West. These geographic facts were reflected in party politics, as well as in society.

Except for the urban centers of the coast, New England's physical geography, therefore, had fostered the growth of a simple, thrifty, inventive folk who struggled bravely with the rigorous climate, grew strong in experience, increased in numbers beyond the capacity of the arable lands to sustain them under the conditions of the time, and spread leaders and Yankee ideas into the West.

By 1830 the harbors were yielding in importance to the waterfalls. Shipping and commerce were giving way to manufacturing, and the rural towns of New England, which had been the foundations of so much of her society and culture, were passing into a decline as the growing families moved to the manufacturing towns, to the cities, or to the West.[3]

The sectional psychology of the New England people — their morale — was quite as important as the physical conditions. To a very large extent, New Englanders were still the descendants of English colonists, comparatively unaffected by the variety of stocks which had occupied other parts of the country. Puritanism still laid a deep impress upon the people. Calvinistic conceptions, a blend of individualism and social responsibility, were still at work. Men not only placed themselves under a rigorous self-examination to determine whether or not they were among the saved, but they also felt the community sense of responsibility for sin. It was a part of the Calvinistic doctrine and of the New England conscience, that man was his brother's keeper. Herein lies the explanation of much of New England's restraint, her intellectuality, and her reforming instinct. The reading of the pure and strong English of the Bible helped her authors achieve literary pre-eminence; theological discussion sharpened

[3] I am here speaking, of course, of the relative decline, in the period of this book, of the economic well-being and the culture and morale of the rural towns as compared with those of other sections. Later, the rise of industrial cities and the improvement of transportation modified the rural conditions.

their wits. They were accustomed to restraint in speech, and to drawing careful distinctions. The New England conscience and New England thrift went hand in hand. The Puritans listened to Duty, " stern daughter of the voice of God." Understatement was a characteristic even of rural New England's humor; her reserve was an aspect of her Puritanism. In the period of this volume, business men as well as statesmen and ministers took frequent stock, in their diaries, of their moral condition and were mindful of death and the final reckoning. These traits of the later Puritan revealed a self-consciousness and a cool mentality with which foreigners and men of other sections did not always sympathize. For example, the English traveler, Thomas Hamilton,[4] thought the New Englanders

a cold, shrewd, calculating, and ingenious people, of phlegmatic temperament, [with perhaps] less of the stuff of which enthusiasts are made, than any other in the world. In no other part of the globe, not even in Scotland, is morality at so high a premium. . . . The only lever by which people of this character can be moved, is that of argument. A New Englander is far more a being of reason than of impulse. Talk to him of what is high, generous, and noble, and he will look on you with a vacant countenance. But tell him of what is just, proper, and essential to his own well-being or that of his family, and he is all ear. His faculties are always sharp; his feelings are obtuse.

And yet this section proved to be a center from which reforms and ideals spread, energized by the very firmness and narrowness which the Puritan intellect produced.[5] The New England sense of exact justice, and the frugality which the rigorous struggle for existence under harsh conditions entailed, seemed, elsewhere, evidences of hard bargaining and even of meanness. But the traveler from South or West was impressed by the tidiness of the New England villages and the evidences, on all sides, of thrift and morality.

Wherever New Englanders went, they carried the community idea, expressed in such institutions as the town, the common

---

[4] *Men and Manners in America* (Philadelphia, 1833), I, 94–95, 117–30. See also T. C. Grattan, *Civilized America* (London, 1859), I, 82; James Fenimore Cooper, *Notions of the Americans* (Philadelphia, 1828), I, 64, 91 ff.; and Michel Chevalier, *Society, Manners and Politics in the United States* (Boston, 1839), pp. 115–19.

[5] A. B. Darling, *Political Changes in Massachusetts, 1824–1848* (New Haven, 1925), p. 39, concludes that " the history of Massachusetts from 1824 to 1848 is a story of political liberalism and social reform."

school, and the church. But they also carried the instinct for inquiry. From colonial days, the " goers " were often of the " come-outer " class — people who, searching the way of salvation, had come to differ from the community, and who had sought new homes in the wilderness, wherein they could carry out their own conceptions. The " stayers " tended, therefore, increasingly to be the conservative class, respectful of the established order and impatient of the spirit of innovation.

Here was a fructifying section, unable to extend itself contiguously into the West, but destined to scatter seeds of a special kind of society and ideals. By the beginning of the period, New England was particularly in ferment. New migrations of her people were accelerated by profound changes in rural conditions; capital was transferred from ocean-going commerce to manufacture and railroad transportation; industrial urban centers were rising; labor was diverted from household industry to manufacture under the factory system; the Irish began to swell the city population as the country declined.

New social and religious conceptions arose. The laws of New Hampshire, Connecticut, and Massachusetts were so amended, between 1820 and the close of the thirties, as to break the power of the established Congregational church; Unitarianism grew influential; new educational activities, new humanitarian movements, and a new literature began. All of these in some measure reflected the general economic and social tendency of the time, and were due partly to the industrial revolution, partly to the rise of the West, partly to the spread of Jacksonian Democracy, partly to European contacts, but in a large measure were indigenous to the section itself and expressive of its peculiar spirit.

From New England's beginnings, its folk had been a moving population. Narrating the beginnings of migration to that " little Nilus," the Connecticut Valley, Cotton Mather likened the New England of 1634 to " an hive over-stocked with bees "; yet in 1694 this conservative Boston minister lamented that men " *Go Out* from the Institutions of God, Swarming into New Settlements " and finding to their cost " that they were got unto the *Wrong side of the Hedge*." [6] Those reprobated " New Settlements " are now suburbs of Boston.

It is estimated that, between 1790 and 1820, southern New

[6] F. J. Turner, *The Frontier in American History* (New York, 1921), p. 64.

England lost something like 800,000 of its people by migration out of the section.[7] According to the normal increase of population at the time, these 800,000 lost to New England should have at least doubled in the next thirty years. Thus, by 1850, there would have been 1,600,000 New Englanders from these states, including the descendants of those who removed before 1820, living outside of the parent section (ignoring those who migrated between 1820 and 1850). By the census of 1850 there were over 450,000 people born in, but residing out of, New England. At that date the native population living in New England was less than 2,500,000. Assuming 2,000,000 for the New Englanders and their descendants outside of the section, the total population of this origin would be around 4,500,000, of which nearly forty-five per cent resided outside of New England itself.

These figures enable us to measure some of the losses to the section by migration. In 1830 its population was about 2,000,000; in 1850, only 2,700,000 (and of this number 300,000 were foreign-born, chiefly Irish). Thus, although there had been partial compensation by immigration for the more recent losses to the interior by emigration, the total gain was relatively small. More significant still, is the fact that New Hampshire, Vermont, and Connecticut gained only between four and six per cent between 1830 and 1840; and, in the decade after 1840, Maine, New Hampshire, and Vermont were distinctly slow in growth. They were, in proportion to their population, the states most active in sending settlers to the West. By 1850, in successive periods from the close of the eighteenth century, parts of New York and Pennsylvania, the Western Reserve of northern Ohio, northern Indiana and Illinois, southern Michigan and Wisconsin, and northeastern Iowa, had become a Greater New England — the sphere of influence of

[7] *Idem*, "Greater New England in the Middle of the Nineteenth Century," American Antiquarian Society *Proceedings*, N.S., XXIX, 222–41. The basis of the computation is there given in detail. I have drawn freely upon this paper, which was prepared for use in the present work. In an independent investigation, subsequent to the paper, Dr. R. S. Tucker ("The Expansion of New England," *New England Historic Genealogical Register*, Oct., 1922, pp. 301–7) reached a somewhat more conservative result by a different method. He estimates that over a million and a half persons of New England descent were living outside the section in 1850. For the estimate of a loss of 800,000 people by southern New England, 1790 to 1820, see Percy W. Bidwell, *Rural Economy in New England at the Beginning of the Nineteenth Century* (Connecticut Academy of Arts and Sciences *Transactions*, XX, 241–399), pp. 386–87. Compare the figures in Jesse Chickering, *Immigration into the United States* (Boston, 1848), pp. 30 ff.

the combined New England and New York stock of New England origin.[8]

The opening of the Erie Canal in 1825, the extension of steam navigation on the Great Lakes in the thirties, and the railroad connections between Boston and the lake ports early in the forties, opened to New England movers the rich and vacant lands of the North Central States, and, at the same time, poured a competitive and destructive flood of agricultural surplus from these cheap, rich, virgin soils upon the farmers of New England. Home production of wool, wheat, and pork was discouraged by the low prices of the Western products. Between 1840 and 1850 the number of sheep [9] in New England diminished by over 1,500,000 (in excess of 40 per cent), and in the North Central States increased by almost 4,200,000 (more than 117 per cent). By the middle fifties more than half of the beef supply of Massachusetts came from without the state. In 1850 New England produced but thirteen quarts of wheat per capita, in place of the required five or six bushels. Bounties offered by various states for raising wheat proved unavailing.[10] The section raised only three and seven-tenths bushels of corn per capita.

The Commissioner for the Agricultural Survey of Massachusetts wrote in 1840:

Popular manners in this matter have undergone considerable change in the last quarter of the century. Bread made of rye and Indian meal was then always to be found upon the tables in the country; and in parts of the State was almost exclusively used. Wheat-flour was then comparatively a luxury. Now brown-bread, as it is termed, is almost banished from use. . . . The poorest family is not satisfied without their wheat or flour bread.

It was not only in diet that changes occurred. Western competition forced the farmer into new types of agriculture, and contemporaneously the factory of southern New England furnished

---

[8] See map of Interstate Migration (at end of volume). [It will be noted on this map, as well as in a statement made on pages 269–70, *post*, that Indiana received fewer emigrants from New England than the other states mentioned.]

[9] See the statistics in Chester W. Wright, *Wool-Growing and the Tariff* (*Harvard Economic Studies*, V; Boston, 1910), p. 337, chart iv, and comments in Chap. v. Maps of the distribution of sheep, showing the migration westward, are in an article by H. C. Taylor, in University of Wisconsin Agricultural Experiment Station *Bulletin*, No. 16 (1911).

[10] See documents listed in Adelaide R. Hasse, *Index of Economic Material in Documents of the States of the United States* (Carnegie Institution of Washington, 1907———), for the separate states.

him substitutes for many of the things formerly made on the farm by the household industry of his family. It became cheaper, or at least more attractive, to buy than to make. The age of homespun gradually gave way, first in the regions nearer to the factories. There was, as a writer of the time said, a " transition from mother and daughter power to water and steam-power." [11] The daughters, released from the spinning wheel and loom, flocked to the factories, became " hired help," or school-teachers, or sewed the shoes, plaited the straw hats, and made the ready-to-wear garments, parceled out by the neighboring manufacturers under the " putting-out system." [12] As women turned to new industries, a feminist movement could be foreseen. There was a revolution in the social and spiritual life of the section as well as in its economic conditions.

Particularly in southern New England, the growing mill towns furnished temporary home markets, and the farmers changed from raising supplies for the household to raising crops for sale. To the Brighton market came the droves of northern cattle for slaughter for the Boston region, and in its stockyards were trained the men who later became managers of the industry in Western cities like Chicago and Kansas City. The downfall of the old rural New England life was, therefore, a gradual one. But it was felt severely in the regions which were the largest relative contributors to the Western states.

[11] Horace Bushnell, *Work and Play; or Literary Varieties* (New York, 1864), p. 376, and R. M. Tryon, *Household Manufactures in the United States, 1640–1860* (Chicago, 1917), p. 359. A speech of Senator Isaac Hill, of New Hampshire, Feb. 1, 1832 (*Register of Debates in Congress*, VIII, Pt. 1, 230), gives interesting evidence of the regrets of a Democratic Senator over the replacement of household industry.

[12] The monographs of Dr. Percy W. Bidwell are helpful on the agricultural transition: *Rural Economy in New England* (as cited *ante*); " Population Growth in Southern New England, 1810–1860," American Statistical Association *Publications*, XV, 813–39; and especially " The Agricultural Revolution in New England," *American Historical Review*, XXVI, 683–702. In Percy W. Bidwell and John I. Falconer, *History of Agriculture in the Northern United States, 1620–1860* (Carnegie Institution of Washington, 1925), these papers are incorporated in a revision. See also: O. E. Baker, " The Increasing Importance of the Physical Conditions in Determining the Utilization of Land for Agricultural and Forest Production in the United States," Association of American Geographers *Annals*, XI, 23–29, 38; R. M. Harper, " Changes in the Forest Area of New England in Three Centuries," *Journal of Forestry*, XVI, 442–52 (Apr., 1918); Victor S. Clark, *History of Manufactures in the United States* (New York, 1929), I; and Tryon, *op. cit.*

Nevertheless, New England's agricultural handicap may have stimulated that interest in the chemistry of agriculture which was so advanced, both in the section and in the nation as a whole, by the work of Professor John P. Norton, of Yale. The county fair, promoted by Elkanah Watson, at Pittsfield, Massachusetts, and the agricultural societies and press, extended this influence upon scientific agriculture to other sections.

To estimate New England's economic loss through the loss of population, we may apply the tests used by the South in the appraisal of its losses through migration to the West. Madison assumed an average value of two hundred dollars per person, in family lots, for Virginia's slaves. The Old Dominion economist, Professor Thomas R. Dew, writing in the thirties, pointed out, however, that the emigration of slaves was compensated by their higher prices and by the encouragement to raise more of such property; but he argued that the emigration of the whites was a dead loss to the South, for the cost of rearing the emigrant to about the age when he was self-supporting, fell upon the parent state, and thereafter his productive capacity was lost to the state. In addition, the emigration carried off free capital, injured agriculture, prevented improvements, and reduced the value of lands within the state by reducing the number of competitors for them.

If we take the test of the contemporary authorities on foreign immigration, estimate the value of an adult at $1,000, and reckon as adults about one-fifth of the *natives* of New England living outside the section in 1850, there was a loss of over $90,000,000. But, in view of the disproportionate number of young men who migrated, this is an underestimate. On the basis of estimating the value of slaves at $200 average, in family lots, the total would be the same. Supposing that each migrating family carried as little as $250 in cash or movables, the total would be more than $20,000,000 for the natives of New England living outside the section in 1850. The loss from abandoned farms must also have been very large, if we accept the usual estimate that it had cost $150 to clear ordinary woodland in the regions thus abandoned.

The wanderer among the out-of-the-way old hill towns of western and northern New England occasionally comes upon tragic reminders of departed excellence: a house or two on a hill where once a village furnished to the commonwealth some of its distinguished men; forests which overgrow the sites of laboriously tilled fields, now revealed only by the lesser height of the trees which cover them; commodious dwelling houses (often dating back to colonial days), dignified in architecture, but with roofs now falling in, paneled fireplaces in ruins, stripped of finely wrought hardware — pathetic pictures of a departed society. On such abandoned acres, the wealthy summer resident has sometimes made an estate, or foreign-born laborers have replaced the native farmers. The multitude of humbler, isolated homesteads, decayed and deserted, tell a story of the new forces which entered the section, in the years between the War of 1812 and the Civil War, to modify that old, rural civilization of Puritan New England from which was recruited much of the strength and initiative of cities like Boston, New York, and Chicago.

The drain upon the initiative of New England's rural population is emphasized in a volume published by the Boston Chamber of Commerce in 1911, entitled *New England*. The editor, commenting on the exodus of the agricultural population, says:

The result was that there came over New England an era of halting effort, due to loss of primal vigor to the West, and the other newer sections. . . . a drain of New England energy and initiative. . . . there has been a constant exhaustion of New England's vitality comparable only to the giving of her own life to her children by a mother. . . . The wholesale and continued transfusion of her best blood to the veins of the newer states could only mean the weakening of her own constitution and the limiting of her own development.[13]

This is obviously an exaggeration, for New England retained many of the farmer-boys, who migrated to the mill towns and cities and rose in the ranks of masters of industry; and she gained new power in the Union by her colonizing beyond the section and by the consequent dissemination of her economic and political influence and of her ideals.

In the field of shipping and commerce, New York City was indebted to the New England stock for such men as Junius S. Morgan and Edwin D. Morgan, A. A. Low, Moses H. Grinnell, W. E. Dodge, A. G. Phelps, Gideon Lee, William B. Crosby, H. B. Claflin, Preserved Fish, and Joshua Bates (later a partner of the Barings, in London). To those familiar with the mercantile and financial history of New York City, these names are distin-

[13] Pp. 5–6.

guished, and illustrate how important was this migrated Yankee element.[14]

In journalism, when the young Horace Greeley came from his New Hampshire farm to New York, a New England influence was added, upon politics and ideals, at least equal to that of the masters of finance. With Greeley, in the Whig " Triumvirate " (which replaced the Democratic " Albany Regency " as the controlling factor in New York politics), were Thurlow Weed, editor of the *Albany Evening Journal,* who grew up among the Yankees of western New York, and William H. Seward, whose father was of Connecticut birth, and whose home was in the Military Tract in New York, which was so largely settled by New England folk. Millard Fillmore, of Buffalo, afterwards President of the United States, was of New England parentage, and Silas Wright, one of the most influential of United States Senators in this period, was born in Amherst, Massachusetts. In the Albany Regency were such other leading Democrats as W. L. Marcy (later the famous Secretary of State), born in Southbridge, Massachusetts, John A. Dix, of New Hampshire birth, and Azariah C. Flagg.

Out of one hundred and twenty-six members of the New York Constitutional Convention of 1821, forty-one were of New England birth, not to speak of those of New England parentage. Horace Bushnell estimated that a majority of that convention were of Connecticut origin, and he reported a remark of Calhoun that he had seen the time when the natives of Connecticut, together with the graduates of Yale College, in Congress, constituted within five votes of a majority of that body.

In Pennsylvania were such aggressive leaders as Thaddeus Stevens, from Vermont, and Galusha A. Grow, the champion of the Homestead Bill, who came from Connecticut to the " northern tier " of counties, so largely peopled by New Englanders.

Ohio's political leaders in this period included Salmon P. Chase, of New Hampshire birth (later Lincoln's Secretary of the Treas-

14 Geo. Wilson (compiler), *Portrait Gallery of the Chamber of Commerce of the State of New York* (New York, 1890); Jos. A. Scoville [Walter Barrett, pseud.], *The Old Merchants of New York City* (New York, 1863); Freeman Hunt, *Lives of American Merchants* (New York, 1858); [M. Y. Beach] *The Wealth and Biography of the Wealthy Citizens of the City of New York* (New York, 1846); Norcross, *Old New York Swamp;* and John Moody and G. K. Turner, " Masters of Capital in America," *McClure's Magazine,* XXXVI, 2–24, XXXVII, 73–87.

ury, sponsor for the national-bank system, and Chief Justice of
the United States Supreme Court), Senator Benjamin Tappan,
born in Northampton, Massachusetts, and " Ben " Wade, born in
western Massachusetts. A native of New Hampshire, Lewis Cass,
of Michigan, walked from Delaware to Ohio, at the end of the
eighteenth century — to a career as territorial governor of Michigan, Secretary of War, Secretary of State, minister to France, and
Democratic candidate for the Presidency in 1848. Stephen A.
Douglas, who preceded Lincoln as a favorite son of Illinois, was
a Vermonter. Even Abraham Lincoln was himself of New England seventeenth-century ancestry, and, in spite of the wanderings
of the family through Pennsylvania into the upland South, Boston papers, although ignorant of his origins, commented, just before his election to the Presidency, on the strong Yankee quality
in his physiognomy.[15]

Governor Henry Dodge, of Wisconsin Territory, who refused a
nomination for the Vice-Presidency on the Free Soil ticket in 1848,
and who was an influential Senator, was of Rhode Island descent.
A long list of the governors of Wisconsin were of Yankee — especially Vermont — origin.

In Wisconsin's Constitutional Convention of 1846, one-third of
the delegates were of New England birth and one-third came from
those counties of New York where the New England element was
strong. Probably from one-half to two-thirds of the delegates to
this convention were of New England descent. In the Iowa convention of the same year, a third of the members were of New
England birth, although the tide of Northern settlement had just
begun to be important in that state. In all the political leaders of
New England stock, the qualities of the section are clearly marked
— modified, however, by the social environment presented in their
successive homes.

As New England saw her people contributing to the West and
as she saw it growing in power in the Union, she attempted to
bind her sons to the traditional ideals and culture of her own section, by collecting funds for churches and schools founded by descendants of the Puritans. Home missions, and organizations for
promoting education, engaged much attention in New England.
In all the North Central states, New England men were leaders

[15] Massachusetts Historical Society *Proceedings*, XLII, 73.

in these fields. Lawyers, doctors, educators, politicians, merchants, bankers, and ministers were all taken disproportionately from New England folk, and especially from the Yankee youth who were seeking opportunities which the parent land, dominated by older men, did not afford.

Nor was it only to New York, to the prairies, and to the Great Lakes Basin that these " goers " from New England passed: the contributions to other parts of the United States were striking. Amos Kendall, Postmaster-General under Jackson and a directing politician in his group of advisers, came from New Hampshire to act as a tutor in the family of Henry Clay, in Kentucky, and then became one of the leading editors of the state. Maine gave to Mississippi her most eloquent Whig orator, S. S. Prentiss, and Connecticut furnished Louisiana with J. S. Johnston, one of her United States Senators.[16]

Even to the Far West that reached toward the Orient, the Yankee stock sent its adventurers. New England missionaries made the Hawaiian Islands American, and, led by Nathaniel J. Wyeth, the Cambridge iceman, opened the transcontinental route at the beginning of the thirties to the settlement of the Oregon country. To that land, a Boston school teacher, Hall J. Kelley, had long been calling his countrymen. Yankee trading ships were familiar with the California coast, and they left behind them men who were baptized into the Roman Catholic church, took Spanish names, and married into noted Spanish families. When, in 1841, the first considerable Middle Western emigrant train arrived in California, led by John Bidwell, of Yankee stock, it was greeted at Mount Diablo by " Dr." John Marsh, a Harvard graduate.[17] A Massachusetts man, Thomas O. Larkin, was the first United States consul in California, and William B. Ide, a Massachusetts carpenter, took command of the California " Bear Flag Insurrection " and wrote its proclamation. The Oregon oxcart migrations of the forties received supplies and a welcome from Marcus Whitman, a man of Yankee descent, in his mission at Walla Walla.

The Mormon church was founded by the Vermont-born prophet, Joseph Smith. Another Vermonter, Brigham Young, his leonine

---

[16] See Chapter vi, *post*, for other Yankee leaders in the South Central States.
[17] Geo. D. Lyman, *John Marsh, Pioneer* (New York, 1930).

successor, established in the deserts of Utah a commonwealth of which the elders and rulers were New Englanders, and adapted the New England town to meet the needs of a theocracy and an irrigation community in the Great Basin of the interior. New England furnished no more striking evidence of her ability to produce administrators and leaders of a great migration, than in the case of Brigham Young. Such explorers as Jedediah Smith, who opened up to American trade the trails through the Great Basin into California, and the Bent brothers, who carried on a fur trade in Colorado, were of New England ancestry.[18] So, also, were Stephen F. Austin, colonizer of Texas, and Samuel M. Williams, who was for many years important in the economic and political life of Texas. Anson Jones, the last president of the Lone Star Republic, was once a country doctor in the Berkshire Hills of Massachusetts.

These New Englanders in the Far West were, in general, exceptional adventurers, characteristic neither of the section from which they came nor of their old home; but they were striking examples of what the Yankee element could achieve in the way of leadership, and in the case of Utah they furnished a considerable share of the population.

The press and leading public speakers tried in vain to stem this tide of migration of the farmers. Horace Bushnell in 1846 remarked:

To stay here and delve among the snows and rocks and worn-out, sour, old fields of Connecticut, is supposed to indicate a degree of verdancy, or, at least, a want of manly determination, not altogether worthy of respect. . . . We seem even to have it in question in our hearts, whether, at some future day, when the Paradise of the west is beginning to be set in order, the people of old Connecticut will not adjourn bodily and go clear, leaving its bleak hills and flinty fields to themselves.[19]

But he argued that, if the same privations existed in Connecticut and the labor required for Western pioneering were applied there, the farms would show the greater profit. The rugged climate was at least healthful; manufacturing centers afforded a better market close at hand; the country was of superior beauty.[20]

[18] A. H. Bent, *The Bent Family in America* (Boston, 1900).
[19] *Work and Play*, pp. 228–29.
[20] *Ibid.*, pp. 230–32.

The great west . . . will be known as . . . the Poland of the United States. New England, meantime, will be sprinkled over with beautiful seats and bloom as a cultivated garden. . . . The first generation [in the West] can hardly be said to live. They let go life, throw it away, for the benefit of the generation to come after them. And these will be found, in most cases, to have grown up in such rudeness and barbarity, that it will require one or two generations more to civilize their habit. . . . Whatever man or family removes to any new country should understand that he makes a large remove also towards barbarism . . . he has gone beyond the pale of society.[21]

But the " pale " had advanced in the generations since Cotton Mather warned his readers that " the *Angel of the Lord* " became the enemy of those who departed beyond the " *Hedge.*"

Such movements as those which we have been describing, meant a period of adversity for the farming classes in New England generally. Harriet Martineau found that Massachusetts farmers were obliged to mortgage their property when they wished to settle a son or daughter or to make up for a deficient crop; that Boston insurance companies were among their principal creditors; and that an antagonism to the city exhibited itself in many ways. She adds: " With the exception of some Southerners, ruined by slavery, who cannot live within their incomes, I met with no class in the United States so anxious about the means of living as the farmers of New England." [22]

Quite as significant, moreover, as the changes we have noticed, is the fact of the Irish immigration. This constituted the beginning of a replacement of population, in New England, that continued through later years, until by 1910 nearly two-thirds of New England's population was either foreign-born or had one or both parents foreign-born. Even the small proportion of native New Englanders must be discounted by the fact that the statistics reckon the American-born children of the immigrants as natives.

The Irish had been coming to the United States from colonial days, and they had furnished distinguished men to the professions

---

[21] *Ibid.*, pp. 236, 246–47, 248, 249–50. See the references in the above-cited writings of Dr. Bidwell. He rightly points out that the community life of rural New England has been somewhat idealized, however, and gives interesting details. Files of agricultural newspapers, such as the *New England Farmer*, reports of agricultural societies, and Coleman's *Reports on the Agriculture of Massachusetts*, furnish illustrations of the sectional anxiety and the efforts (such as state bounties for raising wheat) to check the rural exodus.

[22] *Society in America* (London, 1837), II, 32.

and to the wars of the young nation. Natives of Ireland have been divided, however, into the Irish Presbyterians, or Scotch-Irish, of the north of the island, and the Irish proper.[23] Upon the Scots who had settled on the confiscated Irish lands early in the seventeenth century, the environment had worked a change, and intermarriage with the continuing Irish element, there, no doubt had its effect. But differences of religion and origin were in evidence in America as well as in Ireland.

In Ireland the Catholics, especially, had suffered from the confiscation of their lands, and the resultant tenancy. When potato culture grew to importance, the population increased to the margin of the food supply; rents advanced as improvements were made, and evictions were all too common. Irish grievances, political and economic, had pressed in vain upon the English government for many years. With the potato failure of 1845–47 came, for a time, a tragic solution of the problem of overpopulation, for hundreds of thousands starved, and a flood of emigration of the poverty-stricken survivors poured into America.[24] When, according to the census, there were nearly 307,000 tenants in Ireland holding less than five acres each, and when the crop on which they depended failed, it is not surprising that death and migration reduced the population of the island twenty per cent. Landlords encouraged emigration and helped defray the expense. American philanthropy was enlisted in the effort to feed the hungry population, and Boston was a center of such help.[25] It became the goal of Irish immigrants.

It was, therefore, a fact of importance that, with the trans-

[23] See: C. A. Hanna, *The Scotch-Irish* (New York, 1902); C. K. Bolton, *Scotch Irish Pioneers in Ulster and America* (Boston, 1910); and H. J. Ford, *The Scotch-Irish in America* (Princeton, N. J., 1915). Ina T. Firkins has a convenient bibliography, " Irish in the United States," in *Bulletin of Bibliography*, IX, 22–24 (Jan., 1916). The *Journal* of the Irish American Historical Society indicates, in various papers, the lack of historical recognition of the importance of the stock.

[24] Frances Morehouse, " The Irish Migration of the 'Forties," *American Historical Review*, XXXIII, 579–92, uses contemporary official sources, and offers excuses for the landlords' policies. See also: Marcus L. Hansen, " The Second Colonization of New England," *New England Quarterly*, II, 539–60; Stanley C. Johnson, *A History of Emigration from the United Kingdom to North America, 1763–1912* (London, 1913), *passim* (citing official documents on the movement); and *The Catholic Encyclopedia*, VIII, 136–37 (discussing the horrors of the famine conditions and of the ocean voyage).

[25] [R. B. Forbes] *The Voyage of the Jamestown on Her Errand of Mercy* [to Ireland] (Boston, 1847).

formation of New England to an industrial section and the migration of so large a portion of her people, the labor-population was recruited from foreign stock, differing in origin and religion from the old Puritan New England. A census of Boston in 1845 showed that the foreign element outnumbered the natives of Boston, itself, born of native parents.[26] Even in 1850 the population of Boston showed 35,287 natives of Ireland, as against 68,687 natives of all Massachusetts. In 1848 half the primary-school children of Boston were said to be of foreign parentage.[27] Theodore Parker commented on the Massachusetts census returns for 1855 : " Suffolk County is ' County Cork '; Boston is a young Dublin." [28] By 1850 the foreign-born population in New England numbered almost 300,000 (two-thirds of them Irish). At the time, there were 387,000 natives of New England living in New York and the North Central States — a significant exchange.

A writer of this period, T. C. Grattan, declared :

. . . All seem to agree, that New England, taken on the whole, is the hardest soil for an Irishman to take root and flourish in. The settled habits of the people, the untainted English descent of the great majority, discrepancies of religious faith and forms, and a jealousy of foreign intermixture of any kind, all operate against those who would seek to engraft themselves on the Yankee stem, in the hope of a joint stock of interest or happiness.[29]

There was much truth in this, for New England, unlike the newer sections of the country, was not a good mixing bowl. As early as 1837, Boston newspapers told of a riot at a military review, when five companies left the field, with the American flag flying, to the tune of " Yankee Doodle," because an Irish company took part in the parade. The mob beat up this company as it left the Common. A few months earlier, a riot had taken place between Irishmen and the fire department, which attracted some ten thousand people ; and several companies of light infantry and cavalry were required to break up the mob. Writing in 1842, Emerson says in his journal : [30]

[26] Lemuel Shattuck, *Census of Massachusetts, 1845*, p. 37.

[27] Jas. T. Adams, *New England in the Republic, 1776–1850* (Boston, 1926), p. 388, citing *Life and Works of Horace Mann* (Boston, 1891), IV, 331.

[28] John Weiss, *Life and Correspondence of Theodore Parker* (New York, 1864), I, 397.

[29] *Civilized America*, II, 28.

[30] *Journals of Ralph Waldo Emerson*, VI (Boston, 1911), 303.

Edmund Hosmer was willing to sell his farm five years ago for $3800 and go to the West. He found and still finds that the Irish, of which there are two hundred in this town [Concord], are underselling him in labor, and he does not see how he and his boys can do those things which only he is willing to do; for, go to market he will not, nor shall his boys with his consent do any of those things for which high wages are paid, as, for example, take any shop, or the office of foreman or agent in any corporation wherein there seems to be a premium paid for faculty, as if it were paid for the faculty of cheating. He does not see how he and his children are to prosper here, and the only way for them is to run, the Caucasian[!] before the Irishman.

The *Pilot* was established in 1829 as the organ of the Irish Catholic minority. It is significant of some lack of discernment in New England, however, that, at this time, Protestant ministers like Lyman Beecher fixed their attention upon the West as the region into which Puritan money, missionaries, and teachers should be poured to stem the apprehended tide of Catholicism.

Society formed in strata. For many years the older group retained the political control, but it is in the period of the thirties and forties that we must seek the beginnings of the movement which, by 1915, had reached proportions that emboldened the Irish mayor of Boston to boast that the " Irish had letters and learning, culture and civilization when the forbears of New England were the savage denizens of hyperborean forests "; that " the pestilent Irish " had " made Massachusetts a fit place to live in "; and that the " New England of the Puritan was as dead as Julius Caesar."

New England's capital was built up by commerce and shipping. The merchants, in colonial days, constituted an aristocracy that succeeded the former theocracy. Boston was the leading trading city of the section,[31] and New England as a whole was based on the seashore, with a tributary farming backcountry. By the close of the eighteenth century, a new world of adventure opened when Boston ships rounded Cape Horn into the Pacific, to reach the treasury of sea otter and seal on the Northwest coast. They learned that the Chinese mandarins were eager to clothe themselves in robes of these furs, and in turn had teas and cotton cloths and silks to give in exchange. Stopping at the Hawaiian Islands,

---

[31] A. M. Schlesinger, *The Colonial Merchants and the American Revolution, 1763–1776* (Columbia University *Studies in History, Economics and Public Law,* LXXVIII, Whole No. 182; New York, 1918), pp. 24–28, with bibliography.

as at an ocean road house, and adding sandalwood to their cargo, they passed on to their destination at Canton, and then sailed by Java Head and the East Indies around the Cape of Good Hope back to Boston [32] — a three or four years' venture in strange seas and among strange peoples.[33] Salem, a rival of Boston in the beginning of the oriental trade, discovered the wild pepper of Sumatra and thus revealed a route to wealth by way of the east, as Boston had by sailing to the west. But by 1825 Salem's trade had been largely absorbed by Boston, and some of her leading merchants took up their residence there, enlarging the group of dominant families.

Gradually, as the sea otter was exterminated and the sandalwood was exhausted, the problem of how to find an export cargo for the Pacific became serious. For a time, the hide trade with California and South America sustained Boston's interest in the Pacific.[34] The whaling industry was active in the middle forties, when Nantucket, New Bedford, and New London reaped a rich harvest until the diminished schools of whales scattered and coal oil and gas began to replace the whale-oil lamp. In its best days,

[32] On the history of New England commerce after the colonial period, S. E. Morison's scholarly and delightful *The Maritime History of Massachusetts, 1783–1860* (Boston, 1921), with its ample bibliography, is indispensable. The manuscript thesis on " American Foreign Commerce, 1825 to 1850," by Dr. Grace Lee Nute (done in my seminary in Radcliffe College), has been helpful on this aspect of American history in general. In the *New England Magazine*, N.S., IX, 545–63, there is an interesting illustrated article by H. A. Hill, on " Boston and Liverpool Packet Lines, Sail and Steam." Walter S. Tower, *A History of the American Whale Fishery* (University of Pennsylvania *Publications, Series in Political Economy and Public Law*, No. 20; Philadelphia, 1907), and Herman Melville's *Moby-Dick* (New York, 1851) [illustrative material of thrilling interest], make convenient accounts of this subject. On New England shipping, and especially Donald McKay and the clipper-ship era, see: John Robinson and G. F. Dow, *The Sailing Ships of New England*, Ser. 2 (Salem, Mass., 1924), illustrations; O. T. Howe and F. C. Matthews, *American Clipper Ships, 1833–1858* (Salem, Mass., 1926, 1927); and A. H. Clark, *Clipper Ship Era* (New York, 1910). New England's rush by sea to California is dealt with by O. T. Howe, *Argonauts of '49* (Cambridge, Mass., 1923). For biographies and local histories, see the excellent inventory by Professor Morison, noted above.

[33] There is an interesting glimpse of a returning Boston ship from Canton, and of the political attitude of two leading Boston merchants, G. W. Lyman and Wm. Gray, in Wm. Faux's journal, *Memorable Days in America* (London, 1823); see pp. 45–48 and 57–59 of R. G. Thwaites (ed.), *Early Western Travels, 1748–1846*, XI (Cleveland, 1905), which reprints the 1818–19 portions of the journal.

[34] R. H. Dana, *Two Years Before the Mast* (New York, 1840); and [Alfred Robinson] *Life in California* (New York, 1846).

the whaling industry was subordinate, in New England's economic interest, only to the cotton and shoe industries. Besides being a great adventure, it made the wealth of important families.

Thus, the interest of New England in the Pacific was on the decline at just the time when the problem of Oregon and California became acute in American diplomacy and politics. It was not New England, but the South and the Middle West, which demanded annexations, respectively, in the Southwest and on the Pacific Coast.[35] When the Oregon contest reached its height, New England capitalists sided with the South against pressing the British on the Northwest coast.

Gradually, Boston yielded the first place in oriental commerce, and in shipping, to New York, until by 1840 the latter city, which was the gateway for the commerce of the interior of the United States and had an advantage in banking facilities, became the center of foreign trade.[36] In 1850 the amount of Boston's exports was less than ten million dollars, while New York's was nearly five times that; Boston's imports amounted to a little over twenty-eight and one-half million dollars, and New York's, to four times as much.

With Yankee ingenuity, Boston sought compensation in out-of-the-way ports, and wove a fabric of indirect commerce with such remote places as the lands of the Mediterranean and the Baltic, Calcutta, the East Indian islands, California, Hawaii, and South America; but the old profits had gone. Boston merchants found that they could get a larger return by putting out their money at interest or investing in manufactures and, later, in railroads. The growing domestic market for cotton goods, and boots and shoes, fostered a large coastwise trade, and Yankee vessels still carried off a liberal portion of the surplus food products that came down the Mississippi from the interior to New Orleans. Between 1830 and 1850 the coasting vessels which arrived in Boston doubled in number. The historic cod and mackerel fisheries found a new market in the demand of the West; and trawling, the purse seine,

[35] I am indebted to the studies in my seminary by Frederick Merk, now a professor in Harvard, for evidence on the relations of New England's commerce to her political attitude at this time.

[36] Dr. Nute, as cited above. The British *Parliamentary Papers, Reports of Committees,* particularly 1830, 1840, and 1847, have important testimony regarding the India trade, including opium. On this trade, see also R. B. Forbes, *Personal Reminiscences* (Boston, 1892), pp. 143–47, 159–61.

and the seine boat increased the catch, at the same time that they concentrated the industry in fewer hands, with larger capital.

In 1839 the Cunard line made Boston the American terminus of its steamships. So proud were her citizens of this new victory over New York that, when the harbor froze over in the winter of 1844, they volunteered to cut a channel through the ice in order that they might not undergo the ridicule of the rival port. But by 1850 the American Collins line, subsidized by the federal government, was in full operation from the port of New York, and into that city the ocean steamships poured their immigrants and imports. The great trough of the Hudson and Mohawk valleys enabled New York's railroad system to engross the domestic trade from the interior. Thus, while New England grew as a highly industrialized section, she was forced to see the control over commerce pass out of her hands.

Nor can New England's commercial influence in these years be rightly understood without taking account of the fact that her sons migrated in large numbers to New York City, and that the metropolis also carried a considerable fraction of its shipping and commerce on Massachusetts' account. The influence of the New England stock was by no means limited to the field of commerce and finance, nor to the city of New York: no section was untouched by the activity and ideals of the migrated Yankee.

It was to manufactures that New England turned when the ocean trade proved unkind. The new West and South opened fresh markets, and the shrewd and farsighted merchants transferred their capital into these fields. Emerson recorded in his journal in 1837 [37] that he was " as gay as a canary bird " with the new knowledge that " the destiny of New England is to be the manufacturing country of America." " I no longer suffer," said he, " in the cold out of morbid sympathy with the farmer. The love of the farmer shall spoil no more days for me."

In 1810 two-thirds of the population of southern New England were living in towns of less than three thousand inhabitants (indeed, for the most part on farms), but in 1860 this fraction was only one-third. [38] The little industries, of household and of shops,

[37] *Journals*, IV (Boston, 1910), 207.

[38] Bidwell, in American Statistical Association *Publications*, XV, 816, and Grace P. Fuller, *An Introduction to the History of Connecticut as a Manufacturing State* (Smith College *Studies in History*, I, No. 1; Northampton, Mass., 1915), pp. 53-54.

which had made many a family in southern New England partly artisans and partly farmers, prepared the way for a fuller development of factories' use of water power. This had first become significant in the days of the embargo and the War of 1812. An intelligent and expert class of mechanics had been trained, and capital was available for its use in larger units. In the remoter rural districts, and especially in northern New England, the household industry of spinning and weaving persisted, but gradually gave way.

The factory system was applied to cotton manufacture in the twenties. Perhaps the first fully developed modern type was in Waltham, Massachusetts. With the opening of the Merrimac River manufactures, the system grew and spread throughout the Northeast. The three villages, with about 250 people, which occupied the site of Lowell in 1820, had become over 37,000 in 1855. As early as 1845, plans were under way for the construction, there, of the largest woolen factory in the world.

By the end of the period, the Irish immigrant began to furnish cheaper labor and to supplant the farmers' daughters, especially in southern New England. Sympathy between capital and labor was diminished as an alien labor supply entered. Problems of the wage system and the hours of labor appeared, a self-conscious labor class evolved, and there were strikes.[39] In 1845 the hours of labor in the Lowell mills, from May to September, were from five in the morning to seven in the evening, with a half hour out for breakfast at seven and another half hour for dinner, making a net working day of thirteen hours. The increased efficiency of labor and machinery brought no proportional increase in wages.[40] But these were far higher than those of Europe. Chevalier gives figures which contrast the average wages paid to women in 1834 in the Merrimac mills (around three dollars a week) with the dollar a week received by only a few women in Europe outside the great cities.[41]

All these developments were associated with the growing de-

---

[39] See John R. Commons [and others] (eds.), *A Documentary History of American Industrial Society*, V–VIII (Cleveland, 1910). The Introductions, V, 19–37, and VII, 19–44, are useful.

[40] See, for a fuller account, Norman Ware, *The Industrial Worker, 1840–1860* (Boston, 1924), and Adams, *New England in the Republic*, pp. 341–99.

[41] Chevalier, *Society, Manners and Politics in the United States*, pp. 137–38.

mand of the West and South for manufactured goods. The protective tariffs more and more centered the supply for these markets in the North Atlantic states. The Yankee vision which had been fixed upon the ocean road and the weaving of remote corners of the world into the net of New England's commerce, turned to the exploitation of these new American fields. Horace Greeley wrote: " A new state in the West implies new warehouses in and near lower Broadway, new streets and blocks up-town, new furnaces in Pennsylvania, new factories in New England. A new cabin on the prairies predicts and insures more work for the carmen and stevedores of New York." [42]

It was not only in the West that these new domestic markets appeared. By 1860 New England was reported to be selling sixty million dollars' worth of merchandise annually to the South, of which boots and shoes represented twenty to thirty millions, fish, about three millions, and furniture, something over a million. Most of it was transported by coasting vessels.[43]

The value of the annual production of New England in manufactures, mining, and mechanical arts is reported in the census of 1850 as $274,740,000, of which Massachusetts had over half. At the same time, New York is reported at over $237,500,000, and the Middle Atlantic States as a whole produced over $432,000,000. The North Atlantic production was well over two-thirds of the total in these fields for the United States. The value of the cotton goods manufactured in Massachusetts amounted to nearly one-third of the total for the United States. The value of New England's woolen manufactures was over three-fifths that of the country as a whole.

The characteristics of the Northeastern section, and its place in the Union for years to come, had been established; an industrialized and capitalistic region had been forming. According to the census of 1850, of each 1,000 of the population of the United States, only about 28 in New England were engaged in " commerce, manufactures, and mining," while the Middle Atlantic section (together with the states of Delaware and Maryland

[42] *New York Daily Tribune,* Aug. 25, 1860.

[43] Thos. P. Kettell, *Southern Wealth and Northern Profits* . . . (New York, 1860), p. 60, and Blanche E. Hazard, *The Organization of the Boot and Shoe Industry in Massachusetts before 1875 (Harvard Economic Studies,* XXIII; Cambridge, 1921), pp. 82–83.

and the District of Columbia) showed 67. But New England's industries were concentrated in its coastal and southern portions. In 1845 nearly a third of the townships in Massachusetts reported some textile manufacture. Mill villages, made up of company houses adjacent to the pond and dam, with " the proprietor's residence perched on the hillside," began to give a different look to the landscape of southern New England and to indicate a changing society.

Thereafter, the New England banker, railroad promoter, merchant, and manufacturer lifted his eyes to a remoter inland horizon and followed with his vision the extending frontier of New England's Western sons ; he felt the urge to build more largely, to see farther. Especially those young men who had moved to New York and to the West took advantage of these expanding opportunities. The very process of sifting, by which other sections called away the youthful, the less satisfied, the more optimistic and adventurous, tended, it is true, to leave in a stronger position the more conservative in those regions of New England which were the most affected. But, by the middle of the century, New England's domestic commerce and manufacture, and her political life in the nation, took a different form as the result of her new relations with other sections.

The economic position of the section was determined, at this period, as much by the development of the transportation system, which opened other markets and outlets, as by the rising manufactures which used the system. Prior to 1841, Boston became connected by railroads with Providence, New Bedford, Worcester, the Merrimac Valley, and Portsmouth. Thus, the manufacturing towns were attached to Boston, and localism within the section itself was diminished. By 1841 the Western Railroad was completed to the Hudson River. This brought New England into closer connection with the railroads which paralleled the Erie Canal. By 1842 there were railroad connections between Boston and the Great Lakes, at Buffalo. Although the Boston interests which promoted the connection were alive to the importance of diverting to that port a part of the internal commerce which sought New York, the railroad did not give Boston the control of Western trade. Rather, it hastened the rural decline of interior Massachusetts and northern New England, by increasing the competitive power of Western agricultural products and by facilitating the movement of migration of the country population to the cheap and fertile farm lands of the West.

During the second decade of the period, lines were opened southward to New York and northeast to the Maine lumber region tributary to Bangor. By the Central Vermont and other lines, Boston strengthened its hold upon the valleys of the Green Mountain State. Railroad connection was achieved in 1851 with the lower St. Lawrence, at Ogdensburg.

These changes had a marked effect upon New England's conception of her destiny. In 1837 Emerson, at his Concord home on the " Great Road " out of Boston, wrote in his journal:

> I listen by night, I gaze by day at the endless procession of wagons loaded with the wealth of all regions of England and China, of Turkey, of the Indies, which from Boston creep by my gate to all the towns of New Hampshire and Vermont. With creaking wheels at midsummer, and, crunching the snows, on huge sledges in January, the train goes forward at all hours, bearing this cargo of inexhaustible comfort and luxury to every cabin in the hills.[44]

But, five years later, he comments:

> The prosperity of Boston is an unexpected consequence of Steam-communication. The frightful expenses of steam make the greater neighborhood of Boston to Europe a circumstance of commanding importance, —and the ports of Havre and Liverpool are two days nearer to Boston than to New York. This superiority for the steam-post added to the contemporaneous opening of its great lines of railroad, like iron rivers, which already are making it the dépôt for flour from Western New York, Michigan, Illinois, promise a great prosperity to that city.[45]

The funds for this railroad construction came, in part, from Boston capitalists and, in part, from the small manufacturers and merchants of the interior towns, who felt the need of transportation for their raw material and for marketing their products. Although the Western connection was at first secondary to the desire to dominate the internal trade of the section, these undertakings were important even beyond New England. The bankers, whose capital was derived from ocean commerce and from the profits of the new manufactures, were becoming interested in the transportation net that formed in succeeding years across the West, and Yankee railroad promoters and railroad builders arose,

---

[44] *Journals*, IV, 203–4.
[45] *Ibid.*, VI, 269–70.

including some of the most farseeing and energetic railroad presidents of the national transportation systems of the fifties and sixties. The express business originated in Boston in 1839, when W. F. Harnden, a railroad contractor, carried parcels for customers, in his valise. Adams and Wells soon followed his lead, and the system spread to the other cities of the Union, and to Europe in the forties, reinforcing the railroad as a foe to localism.

More and more, the section's banking power centered in Boston,[46] where in the thirties the merchants were the controlling directors; and this was accompanied by strong opposition in the rural districts. Threatened with a flood of country-bank notes, Boston developed, especially in 1824–25, the Suffolk System. This provided for the redemption of the notes of those banks which made specified deposits with the Suffolk Bank, or were approved by that organization. Like a clearing-house system, it served as a regulator of New England banking, at the same time that it concentrated financial management in Boston. Although the section's banks rapidly increased in the expansive thirties (as did those of the nation), no other section was on a sounder banking basis or so independent of the Bank of the United States. A homogeneous economic section, New England had, also, conservative financial traditions. The capital stock of its local banks in 1834 was not much less than half of that of both North Atlantic sections, which, together, had nearly one-half of the nation's.

The dominant economic and social influences in New England were reflected in her politics and political leaders. As in other sections, the outcome was shaped by the varying influences of local and national issues; but beneath them all was the conviction that national interests were, or should be, the same as those of

[46] Davis R. Dewey, *State Banking before the Civil War* (in *Senate Document 581*, 61st Cong., 2d Sess. [National Monetary Commission; Washington, 1910]), pp. 83, 91, 94. See also: D. P. Bailey, " Banking in Massachusetts," *Bankers Magazine*, 1876; D. R. Whitney, *The Suffolk Bank* (Cambridge, Mass., 1878) ; Wm. M. Gouge, *A Short History of Paper-Money and Banking in the United States. . . . To Which Is Prefixed an Inquiry into the Principles of the System*, . . . (Philadelphia, 1833), pp. 153–60; *Hunt's Merchants' Magazine*, II, 134–53; Massachusetts *Senate Legislative Document 8*, 1838; Timothy Pitkin, *A Statistical View of the Commerce of the United States of America* (New Haven, 1835) ; and Samuel Hazard (ed.), *Hazard's United States Commercial and Statistical Register* (Philadelphia, 1840–42). *The American Almanac* (Boston), annually in the period, has banking statistics. The *Boston Times* is quoted in the *Emancipator,* 1837, as saying that the Irish owned " *five-eighths* of the nearly two million dollars in the Savings Bank."

New England. In the series of six Presidential elections from 1832 to 1852, inclusive, Massachusetts [47] remained consistently National Republican or Whig. Vermont, neighboring to New York, joined the Yankee element in that state as a stronghold of Anti-Masonry, and during most of the thirties, in its state elections, chose a governor who supported that party; but, in Presidential elections, its vote was cast like that of Massachusetts — except for 1832, when William Wirt, the Anti-Masonic candidate, received from Vermont his only votes in the electoral college. In all but two elections (1836 and 1852), Rhode Island and Connecticut went Whig. New Hampshire was consistently Democratic; and in Maine the Democrats lost only the election of 1840, in a campaign wherein issues were confused by the " log cabin " slogan which the Whigs adopted in emulation of the Jackson Democrats and which met an enthusiastic response among the rural population.

Although, judged by the voting in the electoral college, the section, as a whole, was decisively Whig, the popular vote was close. In fact, if the popular votes in all the New England states be added for all the Presidential elections named above, the totals show that the Whigs had but a slight lead, and in 1836 the Democratic candidate, Van Buren, won a majority of the popular votes of the section. In no Presidential election was the combined anti-Democratic vote of New England as much as sixty-four per cent of the total, and for half of those elections the Whigs had less than forty-four per cent of the total vote.

And yet New England's political attitude, as a whole, even in these changing years of her economic life, was notably united in its Congressional action. The trained leadership of a class long accustomed to rule, and the increase of the protectionist interest to which the industrial states of southern New England had committed themselves, were too strong for the rural democracy and the urban laborers.

In the various states of the section, the Whig power rested on the conservative well-to-do classes. Wherever the influence of accumulated property and interrelated wealthy families of bankers, merchants, and manufacturers was strong, there the " Whig

---

[47] On Massachusetts' state politics, I have found the history by my former graduate student, A. B. Darling, *Political Changes in Massachusetts*, very helpful.

aristocracy" controlled — " a commonwealth of property, of stocks, of machinery and of exclusive privileges," " an oligarchy of clubbists," in the eyes of its contemporary critics.[48] The Hartford (Connecticut) *Times* of April 8, 1833, reflects the class feeling in party voting, in its report of an exceptional election where the Democrats won: " Before them fled the ruffle shirt, and tights, the whole squad of Bank Presidents, Insurance Presidents, Bank Directors and Insurance Directors, loungers and money lenders, lawyers and lordlings. . . . The nobility in Prospect Street had to give way for a Farmer from ' up neck ' and a mechanic from ' South Side.' " [49]

In those country districts where farm values were relatively high and where what Charles Francis Adams aptly called " the squirearchy " — the country gentry — was strongest, the urban Whigs secured allies. On the other hand, the Democrats found their rural following among the less prosperous towns. The Democratic strongholds of Maine and New Hampshire were in the counties where farm lands had a relatively low value, and the same general trend appeared in southern New England. The Democratic towns of Massachusetts were in the Berkshire Hills, in the backward farm regions of the south of the state, and in the zone that crossed the " Old Colony " towns eastward to Plymouth. The poorer seafaring people reinforced these agricultural elements, and the urban labor classes (which became increasingly of Irish origin) were Democratic. Even the mill workers on the Merrimac tended, toward the end of the period, to support this party. The denominational alignments had much the same geographic distribution, the Congregationalists supporting the Whigs, while the Baptists and Methodists were usually of the Democratic political faith. Behind these divisions lies the history of the struggle of the sects that separated from the Congregational church establishment.[50]

[48] *Ibid., passim*, and W. G. Bean, " Party Transformation in Massachusetts, 1848–1860," manuscript thesis in Harvard University. Maps of party preponderance in elections, by towns, sustain the analysis.

[49] I am indebted to my former graduate student, Mr. W. F. Hall, for this quotation.

[50] Consult: A. E. Morse, *The Federalist Party in Massachusetts to the Year 1800* (Princeton, N. J., 1909); W. A. Robinson, *Jeffersonian Democracy in New England* (New Haven, 1916); R. J. Purcell, *Connecticut in Transition, 1775–1818* (Washington, 1918); Jacob C. Meyer, *Church and State in Massachusetts from 1740 to 1833* (Cleveland, 1930); and Isaac Backus, *Church History of New England, from 1620 to 1804*, . . . (Philadelphia, 1839).

There was also a clearly marked legislative contest between the upcountry rural population and the urban centers. As the cities and industrialism increased, this contest took the form of struggles over reapportionment of the legislature. The country population desired to retain its disproportionate representation by towns, in spite of the increasing population of the coast.

Attacks upon special privilege, common to the Democracy of the nation in these years, took the form in Massachusetts of a revolt against the dominance of the Boston élite. Harriet Martineau remarked in 1834 : [51] " A Massachusetts man has little chance of success in public life, unless he starts a federalist : and he has no chance of rising above a certain low point, unless, when he reaches that point, he makes a transition into democracy." There is some truth in this statement, and the career of George Bancroft is a case in point.[52] Deserting his social connections, he became a Jacksonian Democrat. The views of this " scholar in politics " of his day gained a wider hearing through the publication of his *History of the United States,* wherein the principles of the American Revolution and of democracy were extolled. In his opinion, " a hearty sympathy with popular liberty is the sole condition on which an American scholar can hope for enduring fame."

The real leadership of the Whigs lay among such masters of capital as the Appletons and the Lawrences, of the manufacturing and banking groups. Their representative — and, at times when he was in financial distress, the recipient of their bounty — was Daniel Webster, New England's greatest statesman. " Webster," said Emerson, " is very dear to the Yankees because he is a person of very commanding understanding with every talent for its adequate expression "; " the purest intellect that was ever applied to business." Few spoke of his person except in the most enthusiastic terms, whether in describing his " noble and majestic frame, his breadth and projection of brows, his coal-black hair, his great cinderous eyes," " the rich and well-modulated thunder of his voice," [53] or his intellectual ability.

[51] *Society in America,* III, 67.

[52] M. A. De Wolfe Howe, *The Life and Letters of George Bancroft* (New York, 1908), I, 185.

[53] Emerson, *Journals,* VI, 341, 345. Compare also such descriptions as Harriet Martineau, *Retrospect of Western Travel* (London and New York, 1838), I, 172–73, and Hamilton, *Men and Manners in America,* II, 78–80. In John Ware, *Memoir of the Life of Henry Ware, Jr.* (Boston, 1874), I, 142–45, there is an excellent contemporary analysis of Webster's different styles of speak-

Undoubtedly an orator of the first rank, Webster's strength was that of a great lawyer who brought his logic and his eloquence to the support of nationalism, of which he became the pre-eminent exponent among the people, even while he failed as a constructive statesman and political leader to win a nation-wide, or even a united sectional, support for his ambition for the Presidency.[54]

In fact, Webster's conception of nationalism was deeply saturated with the interests of his own section, after New England accepted the policy of the protective tariff and after the Southern type of sectionalism grew menacing. In New England he saw the ideals and policies which seemed to him proper for the nation as a whole, and he saw the need of nationalism if her policies were to succeed. He was the champion of vested rights, to be safeguarded against the excesses of the populace. In the days before well-organized campaign contributions, it is not entirely inexplicable that Webster's debts were paid, at times, by the manufacturing and banking interests which he had protected in the Senate. But it must be admitted that he had lax ideas in money matters generally, and especially in soliciting retainers from interests affected by pending legislation while he was still in the Senate. At a critical time, when the Bank of the United States was asking a renewal of its charter, he sought refreshment of his usual retainer from that institution; and he advised English financial interests, which had made loans to several of the states of the Union, to enlist the favor of leaders of public opinion, there, by paying them for their services.[55]

---

ing, by one who became an instructor in pulpit oratory. All lay stress upon the transformation he underwent when his natural indolence yielded to the passionate energy of his thought and speech as he rose to his argument. See the characterization in Henry W. Hilliard, *Politics and Pen Pictures at Home and Abroad* (New York, 1892), p. 2. The most recent biography is Claude M. Fuess, *Daniel Webster* (Boston, 1930).

[54] *The Autobiography of Martin Van Buren*, ed. John C. Fitzpatrick (American Historical Association *Annual Report*, 1918, II; Washington, 1920), p. 710. In this statesman's opinion, Webster had a New England passion for " the ceremonies and forms incident to public authority," " the enjoyment of official pomp and circumstance " — a feeling from which, Van Buren thought, the South was free and of which there was but little in the Middle Atlantic States. (*Ibid.*, pp. 258–59.) Whether well grounded or not, the significance of this opinion lies in its sectional diagnosis.

[55] On Webster's pecuniary relations, see: *Letters and Recollections of John Murray Forbes*, ed. Sarah F. Hughes (Boston, 1899), I, 118; *Memoirs of John Quincy Adams*, ed. C. F. Adams, X (Philadelphia, 1876), 43; *The Writings and*

The other great statesman of New England, John Quincy Adams,[56] like Webster failed to arouse the enthusiasm of the people of other sections. In his diary he was a bitter critic of his fellow Yankee statesman — as of most, if not all, of his contemporaries. He wrote in 1841 of " the gigantic intellect, the envious temper, the ravenous ambition, and the rotten heart of Daniel Webster." [57] His *Memoirs* must be read with full appreciation of his censorious attitude, which did not spare even himself. After the close of his term as President, Adams became, in large measure, a free lance in politics, though generally in connection with the Whig interests. He was the New England conscience incarnate and militant. Nor did the bitterly critical spirit, expressed with literary power and incisiveness, find a better exponent. Like Webster, he was solicitous about the rights of property and the strengthening of nationalism, but, unlike him, he was the true exemplar of the New England Puritan's antagonism to the slavery interests — an attitude made easier by the injury which the South had done to his political fortunes. As a Representative in Con-

---

Speeches of Daniel Webster ("National Edition"; Boston and New York, 1903), XVI, 232; *The Correspondence of Nicholas Biddle Dealing with National Affairs, 1807–1844*, ed. R. C. McGrane (Boston, 1919), p. 218; and *Van Buren Autobiography*, pp. 778–82.

T. W. Ward, Boston agent of the Barings (the well-known English bankers), wrote, September 15, 1843, to his principals, advising against giving Webster financial credit, saying: " With all Mr. Webster's greatness I do not give him my confidence. That he is desirous of sustaining his reputation as a great statesman and in all he does will have a view to that, I have no doubt; but he wants and must have money, and will in what he does or omits look very much to its results to himself." Ward also notes that Webster told him he had " urged his friends in Europe . . . to employ distinguished men on this side in the different states to aid in spreading right views [on the payment of state debts] and that such men could be found for a very moderate compensation who would do much good." (Baring MSS.) See also, on Webster's financial difficulties and his relations to English capitalists and a substitute for the assumption of state debts, Ward's letters of July 2, 1842, and November 1, 1843 (to Joshua Bates), and August 7, 1844 (to the Barings). (Baring MSS.) In the last-named, he suggested, as he had previously, that the firm return to Webster his acceptance for $500 and " charge it off, half to your account and half to the Pennsylvania Committee, as for services rendered." Ward added that, in case of Clay's election, he supposed Webster would be either Secretary of State or minister to London. (I am indebted to my colleague, Professor Frederick Merk, for the Baring items.)

[56] See W. C. Ford, in *Dictionary of American Biography*, I (New York, 1928), 84–93. J. T. Adams, *The Adams Family* (Boston, 1930), gives an interesting portrayal of J. Q. Adams as a member of this notable family.

[57] *Memoirs*, XI (Philadelphia, 1876), 20.

gress, this " Old Man Eloquent " gained his highest reputation as the courageous defender of the right of petition, which the South desired to deny when used against slavery. " He is no literary old gentleman," wrote Emerson, " but a bruiser, and loves the *mêlée*. . . . He is an old *roué* who cannot live on slops, but must have sulphuric acid in his tea." [58]

The power of literary expression possessed by New England statesmen, illustrated in Webster and Adams, was seen, also, in such leaders as Edward Everett, Wendell Phillips, William Lloyd Garrison, and Rufus Choate — representatives of different camps, but all of them characteristic voices of the section. Except for Bancroft and, to a limited extent, Caleb Cushing, the leaders of Democracy showed no such qualities.

The Democratic party of Massachusetts was under the guidance of Marcus Morton, relatively a moderate, whose strength lay in the rural areas. He had been a supporter of Calhoun (his fellow student in the Litchfield Law School) until the latter's break with Jackson, and the emergence of the slavery issue. He had been the party's candidate for the governorship at various elections in the thirties, winning the office in 1839 by a close vote, and again in 1842. A political organizer (often at odds with Morton) was David Henshaw, Boston tradesman, banker, newspaper owner, and party boss, who achieved the position of Secretary of the Navy under President Tyler. His rival was the historian George Bancroft, whose political strength rested in western Massachusetts, but who came to be newspaper editor, Collector of the Port of Boston, and then Secretary of the Navy in the cabinet of President Polk. Bancroft not only devoted his pen to the cause of the party but desired to be the biographer of Jackson.

The Massachusetts Democratic leaders, as a rule, however, came from the " middling class " and were graduates of Brown University, Rhode Island, rather than members of the leading families, with the Harvard imprint.[59] In New Hampshire, the rocky citadel of New England Democracy, the outstanding politician was Isaac Hill, newspaper editor and a member of Jackson's " kitchen cabinet." He became United States Senator and then governor of New Hampshire, and in 1840 an officer in the Subtreasury at Boston. He shepherded the New Hampshire Demo-

[58] *Journals*, VI, 349–50.
[59] Darling, *Political Changes in Massachusetts*, p. 28.

crats from the era of the War of 1812, and left a deep impress upon the thinking of his commonwealth. Levi Woodbury achieved a higher position in the nation's councils, as Senator, and Secretary of the Treasury under Jackson and Van Buren. In Connecticut, Senator John M. Niles, and the youthful Gideon Welles, later Secretary of the Navy under President Lincoln, were leaders. Caleb Cushing, of Massachusetts, ran the gamut of many parties. He was a Webster Whig and, as such, a defender of Tyler in the federal House of Representatives; became a Democrat after his return from his notable mission to China; was a general in the Mexican War; served as Attorney-General in Pierce's administration, when he stood with the Southern wing of the Democrats; was president of the Charleston and Baltimore Democratic convention in 1860; became an advocate of the proposal to allow peaceable secession, and then, when the War broke out, a supporter of the Union; and, as a Republican, was appointed counsel for the United States in the " Alabama " Claims case, by President Grant, who later nominated him as Chief Justice of the Supreme Court of the United States and, when confirmation was refused, sent him as minister to Spain. Few American political leaders have been so versatile.[60] Maine and Rhode Island furnished no such national figures among the Democrats.

In general, the Democrats of New England reflected the restraint of the section, in the relative moderation of their support of their party policies in this period. The attacks upon the banks and the whole credit system, which flourished among the Locofocos of New York and the Middle West,[61] were toned down among the states of this section,[62] and, on the whole, radical movements were moderated. The Workingmen's party, for example (which had a brief existence), was not a purely labor party, but

---

[60] See Claude M. Fuess, *The Life of Caleb Cushing* (New York, 1923), for a friendly view of his varied career.

[61] Consult the chapters on the Middle Atlantic States and the North Central States, *post*.

[62] See, for example, the " Declaration of Principles on Bunker Hill," July 4, 1837, printed in the *Boston Daily Advertiser*, July 6, 7, 1837. The meeting was largely made up of men from the country towns. Even so radical a leader of the Boston Democracy as David Henshaw attempted to procure a federal charter for a new national bank, on the downfall of the Bank of the United States. There was little extreme opposition to the credit system in New England, though there was much opposition to the concentration of that system in Whig hands.

one which included the middle class, generally, in its opposition to the control of the Boston " aristocracy." It was in the third parties — the Anti-Masons, the Native Americans, and the Free Soilers — that extreme political *isms* found their main support in this section.

Instead of relying upon the consultations of small groups of leading citizens (as had New England Federalists and their successors, the National Republicans and Whigs), the Democrats actively enrolled the rank and file in clubs and local organizations, and believed in the rule and ultimate triumph of the common people, even while they developed the system of the boss and the spoils of office. If they furnished fewer statesmen of distinction to the nation, they constituted an important factor in the political problems of the dominant Whigs. New England cannot be understood when conceived of — as has too often been the case — only in terms of the Whig leaders in politics and in society. These leaders were compelled to steer a course determined by the necessity of meeting a vigorous opposition — a course, therefore, different from that which they would have followed if unchecked.

No estimate of New England's political leadership would be adequate which did not take into consideration the fact that her migrated sons, scattered through many parts of the Union, had a political influence out of all proportion to their numbers in the population.

In the years we are considering, the domestic party-history of the different states of the section is too varied to be related in detail. But it reflected, in different ways in different regions, the underlying Puritan spirit, even when national campaigns drew the section into the general current of American politics. In most of the New England states, by the early thirties, the Congregational church had lost its traditional power in elections, and the former separating sects, with democratic tendencies, had gained. Congregationalism itself had been split by the Unitarian movement, and economic and humanitarian issues replaced theological discussions.

Despite — or perhaps because of — the conservatism of the dominant group in this intellectual, and often individualistic, section, New England was a fertile field for *isms* and third-party movements. It was in those portions of New York and Pennsylvania in which people of New England origin were numerous, that the Anti-Masonic party arose and flourished in the years between 1827 and 1840; and the state of Vermont, from which so large a portion of the westward migration proceeded, was, as we have seen, particularly devoted to that cause. As in other states, the Anti-Masonic movement was, however, only in part due to the spirit of Puritan opposition against secret organizations: it was also due to a demand for internal improvements and was evidence of a rural revolt against urban forces. Although, in Massachusetts, the movement received a qualified support from such leaders as John Quincy Adams (who was its unsuccessful candidate for governor in 1833), Edward Everett (who was nominated by the Whigs and accepted by the Anti-Masons in 1835), and Webster, none of these statesmen was devoted to the cause, and it did not produce a great leader from its own midst. By 1836 the party survived in many towns, but its membership was divided between Whigs and Democrats. Its significance in Massachusetts lay in its union with the forces antagonistic to the social and economic ruling class, within which Masonry flourished, and in the inherent weakness of the movement, shown by the choice of its candidates from the interests which its rank and file opposed.[63]

Contemporaneously with Anti-Masonry, in Massachusetts, the Workingmen's party had a brief existence. Not limited to wage-workers, it opened its doors to the " middling class " in general, and found followers on the farm as well as in the shop. From 1833–34, in a period of depression among the common people,[64] it had a considerable following, won some seats in the legislature,

---

[63] See: Chas. McCarthy, *The Antimasonic Party: A Study of Political Antimasonry in the United States, 1827–1840* (American Historical Association *Annual Report*, 1902, I [Washington, 1903], 365–574); Darling, *Political Changes in Massachusetts*, Chap. III; and manuscripts (HM 8253–8312), in the Huntington Library, on the Anti-Masonic party in Massachusetts.

[64] *Documentary History of American Industrial Society*, V, *passim*; H. F. Brownson, *Orestes A. Brownson's . . . Life*, I (Detroit, 1898), 113; and Darling, *op. cit.*, pp. 97–100, 102, 105, 113–17, 127. In the Bancroft manuscripts of the Massachusetts Historical Society, there is an interesting letter from Marcus Morton to George Bancroft (September 9, 1835), saying that the Democratic Workingmen and the Democratic Anti-Masons constituted a majority of the state, with identical feelings, principles, and interests. He hoped a union of these forces might be perfected in the election of 1836, unless Webster " sacrificed " himself as candidate. Morton asserted that he himself was altogether in sympathy with the workingmen and poorer classes and believed that the poor were in danger from the rich, rather than the reverse.

and, with the Anti-Masonic movement, endangered Whig ascendancy in Massachusetts to such an extent that Webster was induced to become a Presidential candidate for the election of 1836 in order to hold the section to the Whig party. In general, the movement had an affinity with the Locofoco agitation in New York (which will be considered in the next chapter), but it was more moderate and less urban in its quality.

Nowhere, perhaps, was the contest, between the conservative old order in New England and the new forces, more clearly illustrated than in " Dorr's Rebellion " in Rhode Island. This state's colonial charter, under which franchise was limited to freeholders, had been taken over as its Revolutionary constitution and had been retained. Large landholders and city owners of real estate constituted the conservative group in opposition to the landless workingmen. The revolution achieved by pioneer democracy, under the lead of Jackson and in the Harrison " log cabin " campaign of 1840, stimulated the workingmen to demand a broader suffrage. Their conservative opponents declared democracy the curse of a nation, and insisted that the " sound part of the community " was the " substantial freeholders of the state." Asserting the sovereignty of the people, Thomas W. Dorr began an agitation which lasted for years. After mass meetings and threats of the use of violence, the legislature finally called a convention chosen under the existing franchise. To this the agitators refused to assent, and, asserting the direct right of the people to form their own constitution, called a convention in 1841 and submitted a " People's Constitution " providing for white manhood suffrage. This constitution received nearly 14,000 votes, and the People's Convention declared it in effect. The General Assembly, however, stigmatized it as a violation of the rights of the existing government.

The concessions of the constitution submitted by the regular, or conservative, convention required a residence of two years in the state unless the individual was a freeholder; for foreign-born citizens, a year's residence was required after naturalization and the possession of a freehold estate. In place of the representation of towns on an arbitrary basis, the conservative constitution based representation on population. The Supreme Court of the state gave their opinion that the People's Convention was assembled without law and that an attempt to put it into effect by force would be treason. But the " Freemen's," or conservative, constitution was rejected by a close vote. The legislature then declared any attempt to vote under the People's Constitution treason, carrying with it the penalty of imprisonment for life. Nevertheless, an election was held, Dorr was chosen governor, and a General Assembly met in 1842. Dorr made an unsuccessful attempt to take the arsenal by military force and, failing to receive popular support, fled. Although regularity triumphed and the Freemen's Constitution went into effect in 1842, the movement had aroused popular feeling and embarrassment throughout the Northeastern states, had been brought before President Tyler, and had resulted in a new constitution more liberal than the colonial charter.[65]

Out of New England came the first state prohibition law, that of Maine in 1846 and 1851, under the leadership of Neal Dow — a movement which spread in the next decade to other Northern states and sections. The temperance agitation had gained in strength after the *Six Sermons* of Lyman Beecher, of Connecticut, had been widely printed; and the " Washingtonian " temperance movement had a large following in New England. Politically, the cause was confined to no single party; but when the Whig legislature of Massachusetts passed the " fifteen-gallon law " in 1838, designed to prevent the purchase of spirituous liquors in small quantities for drinking in the saloon, the poorer men resented it, so that the Democrats won a victory and repealed the law. Similar laws were passed and repealed in other states of the section at about the same time.

The slavery issue appealed strongly to all New England, for, as a whole, the section, in contrast with the North Central States, had no important Southern population in its midst, and was easily swayed by idealistic considerations under the Puritan doctrine of community responsibility for sin. Moreover, New England found in the slaveholding South a persistent opponent of the protective tariff. But New England's reputation as pre-eminently an antislavery section, needs modification in discussion of her politics in the years between 1830 and 1850. The relatively small group of radical abolitionists, headed by William Lloyd Garrison (who established the *Liberator* in 1831), and the larger group which

[65] For a contemporary view, see W. G. Goddard, *An Address to the People of Rhode-Island*, . . . (Providence, 1843).

formed the New England Antislavery Society the following year, led the way for the extremists; and, as the annexation of Texas, and the Mexican War, came on, public sentiment against Southern institutions and policy became more pronounced, and New England's poets gave the section the reputation of being in the van of the attack. Vermont was the state in which radical antislavery feeling was most general. Massachusetts divided her allegiance between her greatest leaders, John Quincy Adams (who on the floor of the federal House of Representatives roused the South to bitterness) and Daniel Webster. The latter found, not only in his own Presidential ambitions but also in his nationalism and in the economic interests behind him, inducements to that moderation which culminated in his seventh-of-March speech in the Senate debate over the Compromise of 1850. This event practically coincided with the break-up of the Whig party in Massachusetts. The break had been preparing for many years. When, in 1846, E. R. Hoar insisted that it was " as much the duty of Massachusetts to pass resolutions in favor of the rights of man as in the interests of cotton," the name " Cotton Whigs " gained currency, in distinction from the " Conscience Whigs." The intimate supporters of Webster and R. C. Winthrop were of the economic and social élite. Manufacturers and financiers like the Appletons and the Lawrences, influenced by the cotton interest, naturally at this stage of the contest were conservatives. Such radical antislavery men as Wendell Phillips and Charles Sumner found themselves unwelcome visitors to much of the " best Boston society," of which they were a part.

In the election of 1844, when the supporters of Polk, of Tennessee, for President, were pressing the issues of the acquisition of Oregon and Texas, Clay's Whig and James G. Birney's Liberty-party vote, combined, were only fifty-four per cent of the total popular vote of the section, and Maine and New Hampshire cast their votes decisively for Polk. But Massachusetts was strongly in the opposition, and soon a bitter contest was on between the Cotton Whigs, on the one side, and the Conscience Whigs (and the antislavery group in general), on the other. New political combinations were effected, in which such leaders as Charles Francis Adams, the son of John Quincy Adams, and Henry Wilson, " the Natick cobbler," found themselves allies. The Free Soil party drew from both Whigs and Democrats in 1848, when Zachary Taylor, the Whig candidate, polled only forty-three per cent of the section's popular vote. The Democrats and Free Soilers then formed a coalition, professing reform policies and antislavery views, and in the session of 1849–50 this alliance sent Charles Sumner to the United States Senate and enacted such Locofoco measures for Massachusetts as the general banking law, homestead exemption, a mechanic's-lien law, the secret ballot, and provision for a plurality instead of a majority as sufficient in state elections.

The nativistic and anti-Catholic movement had been foreshadowed by the burning of the Ursuline convent in a suburb of Boston in 1834 and the riots on the Common against the Irish in 1837. Although the anti-Catholic alarm took the form of contributions to Protestant churches and to missions and educational institutions in the West during the thirties, rather than of active political organization in New England itself, there was much concern over the growing power of the foreign element, which usually opposed the Whig candidates. By the middle forties, this resulted in the Native American movement. But it was after the period of this work that the extraordinary victory of the " Know Nothing " party (in the election of 1854) gave to this organization the almost complete possession of the legislature of Massachusetts and led to the extreme provisions in her law for prolonging the period of naturalization to twenty years.[66] This resulted in sympathetic attempts to enact such laws in all the Western states where the New England element was considerable, and gave to the founders of the Republican party one of its gravest problems — the choice between the nativistic and prohibition sympathies of its leaders of New England stock, and the vote of the German element in pivotal states of the Middle West.

Thus, the traits of New England colored its domestic party policies and affected the Union. But the New England spirit must also be considered in various other aspects.

A new tempo came into New England life as her population broke the crust of custom, moved to the cities and to the West, and shared more fully in the temper of the nation. New England was developing a spirit which resulted in generous institutions and movements for the amelioration of the lot of the common man and in a literature responsive to feeling and even to the love of beauty.

Yankee inventiveness [67] had long been proverbial, and in these years it was applied to the service of the housewife, by Elias Howe's invention of the sewing machine, patented in 1846; to the extension and acceleration of communication, by Samuel F. B. Morse, whose first electric telegraph line was in operation in 1844; to the innumerable uses of man, by Charles Goodyear's discovery, in 1839, of the process of the vulcanization of rubber; and to the relief of suffering and the development of surgery, by Dr. W. T. G. Morton, through his use of anesthesia under ether, in 1846. Private benevolence and public organization, alike, worked in humanitarian directions. The gift of the distinguished Boston merchant, Thomas Handasyd Perkins, made possible the opening of the Perkins Institute for the Blind, in 1832; and, in the same early years of the period, the lyceum system of public lectures was organized in Massachusetts, under county and state committees, and spread to other states. In these courses, lecturers like Emerson spoke to factory girls. [68]

An agitation in behalf of universal peace, in the years of this volume, also found support in New England, becoming, in its extreme form, the " non-resistance " doctrine of Garrison and his followers among the Abolitionists. [69] A former sea captain, William Ladd, of Maine, followed by Rev. G. C. Beckwith, organized the American Peace Society; Elihu Burritt, the " learned blacksmith," spread the doctrine abroad; and Rev. Samuel J. May, a follower of Garrison, was one of the prominent advocates. Charles Sumner gave the peace movement his aid, and James Russell Lowell's *Biglow Papers*, during the Mexican War, were so violently pacifistic that their language, if used during later wars, might have made trouble for the poet. To Emerson, in 1837, a company of soldiers was " an offensive spectacle "; but New England's poets later changed their attitude, when the slavery struggle threatened to result in the test of arms.

[67] For an account of inventions by Yankees in the West, see H. G. Underwood, " Wisconsin's Contribution to American Inventions," Wisconsin Historical Society *Proceedings*, 1901 (Madison, 1902), pp. 163–69.

[68] Lucy Larcom, *A New England Girlhood Outlined from Memory* (Boston, 1889).

[69] See M. E. Curti, *The American Peace Crusade, 1815–1860* (Durham, N.C., 1929).

Woman's rights also gained aggressive supporters in these years, and the champions of abolition were among the leaders of the feminist cause. Mary Lyon established her college for women at Mount Holyoke in 1837, and new opportunities were offered for a high-school education for girls. Catharine E. Beecher, the daughter of Lyman Beecher and the sister of Harriet Beecher Stowe and Henry Ward Beecher, was a voluminous writer on the promotion of the study of domestic economy, woman's education, and woman's duties. Among her activities was the organization of societies to send New England school mistresses to the West.[70]

The public lectures of the Lowell Institute in Boston, under the bequest of John Lowell, Jr., opened in 1839, bringing to the people of that city the scholarship of eminent men. About 1848 the Boston Public Library was authorized, and by this time the library of Harvard College, with 72,000 volumes, was the largest collection in America. Justice Joseph Story, of the federal Supreme Court, became professor in the Harvard Law School in 1829, and, by his teaching, textbooks, and decisions, carried forward the traditions of John Marshall.

In these years, also, the severe penalties for crime were mitigated.[71] The death penalty for treason, murder, rape, arson, burglary, and robbery, and statutes requiring imprisonment for debt, which were still in effect in Massachusetts as late as 1836, were moderated before the close of our period. Agitation for the abolition of capital punishment spread from New England to the Western states in which the New England element was strong. Connecticut abolished imprisonment for debt. Prison reform was a live issue and societies were formed to report upon conditions. In general, the prisons were in a deplorable condition;[72] but the same localism that made school improvement difficult was an ef-

[70] On feminism, see Susan B. Anthony [and others], *History of Woman Suffrage* (New York and Rochester, 1881-[1902]), and E. A. Hecker, *Short History of the Progress of Woman's Rights from the Days of Augustus to the Present Time* (New York, 1910). See also Frank Luther Mott, *A History of American Magazines, 1741-1850* (New York, 1930), *passim*, which gives an interesting account of the way in which American magazines, like *Graham's*, *Godey's Lady's Book*, and many others, found among woman subscribers much of their circulation. The character of the contents of these magazines was likewise shaped by their constituency.

[71] J. B. McMaster, *A History of the People of the United States, from the Revolution to the Civil War*, VII (New York, 1919), 145-47, 153.

[72] See the account and citations in Edward Channing, *A History of the United States*, V (New York, 1921), 184-94, 201-3.

fective obstacle to prison reform. Early in the forties, Dorothea L. Dix undertook valuable investigation and agitation for improvement in the treatment of the insane, then often chained and confined in cages, and she carried her work to other sections.[73] With the coming of the immigrant, the treatment of paupers also received more humane attention.[74]

Evidently the practical individualism of the Puritan was not inconsistent with a deep interest in the welfare of the community. A feeling of the brotherhood of man grew stronger with the growth of Unitarian and Universalist doctrines among the educated reformers. Thomas Hamilton, the English traveler,[75] looking forward a half century from 1830, predicted such pressure of population upon the means of subsistence, in the Atlantic states, that property would become insecure in the huge manufacturing cities whose rise he foresaw and where he expected the " Workies " to rule. But when he urged these ideas he found New England was unresponsive and disposed to let each generation look to itself. If, indeed, this indifference really existed in economic matters, it was not in evidence where New England ideals of religion and education were concerned.

In its preferences among religious denominations, New England showed sectional qualities of its own.[76] Although, by the census of 1850, here, as in the other sections, the sects which made the more emotional appeal — the Baptist and the Methodist — led in the number of churches (having over two-fifths of New England's total), the Congregationalists, unlike the proportions elsewhere, had the largest number of any single denomination; and Congregationalists, Universalists, and Unitarians, together, had about three hundred churches fewer than the Baptists and Methodists combined, but exceeded them in seating accommodations. The Presbyterians had but sixty-four churches out of the total of over forty-six hundred in New England — a smaller proportion than that of the Roman Catholics. The Episcopalians

[73] McMaster, *op. cit.*, pp. 151–53, with citations.

[74] Robt. W. Kelso, *History of Public Poor Relief in Massachusetts, 1620–1920* (Boston, 1922).

[75] *Men and Manners in America*, I, 161 ff.

[76] Data compiled from J. D. B. De Bow, *Statistical View of the United States . . . being a Compendium of the Seventh* [1850] *Census* (Washington, 1854), pp. 133, 136–37. Of course, these churches differed greatly in size of congregations, but the proportions of " church accommodations " are similar.

had church accommodations for somewhat fewer than the Unitarians or the Universalists. The Episcopalians found their greatest support in Connecticut. It was especially Massachusetts that gave the preponderance to the Congregational church. This historic Puritan organization continued to influence New England's thought, in spite of the rise and popularity of later sects, and of internal dissensions.

Congregationalism was particularly influential up the Connecticut Valley into Vermont, while Unitarianism had its stronghold in the Boston region, where it was a social as well as a religious factor. The Congregationalists took the leading part in promoting the Home Missionary Society,[77] though other sects followed them to those parts of the interior whither New Englanders had migrated. The desire to extend and perpetuate Puritan ideals in these newer states and territories, which by increasing population and economic resources promised to occupy a commanding position in the Union, and the alarm aroused by the activity of the Roman Catholic church in the West, stimulated the New Englanders to contribute funds for the conversion of the pioneer regions. Lyman Beecher's sermon entitled *A Plea for the West* (1832) was widely circulated in behalf of the cause, and this appeal was based upon the argument that the destiny of the nation was that of the West.

From its beginnings, New England had scrupulously provided for the schooling of its people, outranking other sections in this respect. By 1850 its illiterate white population (over twenty years of age and unable to read and write) [78] was but 1.89 per cent of the total white population of the section. New England's proportion of native white illiterates to all its native white population over twenty years of age, was less than one-half of one per cent — a record of almost no illiteracy in its *native* white population. The fact that white illiteracy as a whole had greatly increased in the section since 1840 was due to the immigrant element.

But, beyond the training in reading and writing, the common-school system was unsatisfactory to the reformers, who lamented the lack of public taxation for education and urged that the his-

[77] I have used with advantage the thorough study of Dr. Colin B. Goodykoontz on this topic — a manuscript thesis, prepared in my seminary in Harvard University, based upon the archives of the Congregational Society in New York City.

[78] See map of White Illiteracy, 1850 (at end of volume).

toric New England ideals should be applied to the changed conditions. In Massachusetts, in 1838, there was expended upon the one-sixth of the children who were enrolled in private schools a sum equal to nearly two-thirds of the amount expended upon the five-sixths who attended public schools.[79] Compulsory schooling was not well enforced, equipment was meager, and state administration and initiative were lacking. Under the leadership of such men as James G. Carter, Horace Mann, and William Ellery Channing, in Massachusetts, and Henry Barnard, in Connecticut, laws were enacted which, by the end of the forties, secured more-adequate local taxation for free schools, improved administration under superintendents, more-efficient grammar schools, free high schools in various cities of the section, normal schools and teachers' institutes for pedagogical training, prolongation of the school year, better instruction, and improved schoolhouses and equipment. The well-to-do taxpayer was influenced by the need of common education of the voters, as a protection to his property and as a bulwark against radicalism in this era of Jacksonian Democracy.

Although many of the pedagogical theories of these years were imported from Switzerland, and the administrative system was Prussian, these changes in the direction of educational improvement, in which Massachusetts led the way, bore the distinctive marks of American democratic and individualistic ideals. There was real contrast with the " blind acquiescence to arbitrary power . . . adapted to enslave, and not to enfranchise, the human mind," [80] which Horace Mann found in the Prussian system — from which he nevertheless borrowed such administrative features as seemed useful to American conditions.

When tested by the standards of the present time, higher education in New England during this period was not particularly strong. Whether judged by the number of students, the curriculum, the faculty, or activity in research, it was a time of relatively small things. Harvard and Yale were still prominent and, with the " little colleges," sent fertilizing rivulets both into this section and to the South and West. But Harvard, for example, early in the thirties had only 24 instructors and 236 undergraduates. Al-

---

[79] F. T. Carlton, *Economic Influences upon Educational Progress in the United States, 1820–1850* (University of Wisconsin *Bulletin*, No. 221; Madison, 1908), p. 89, citing *North American Review*, XLVII (1838), 304.

[80] *Life and Works of Horace Mann* (Boston, 1891), III, 240–41.

though the cost of student living, independent of personal expenses, was but $200 a year, even this sum was deemed prohibitive to sons of the "middling class." Harvard was criticized by the Democrats as a center of aristocracy, though its salaries to the instructional staff ranged only from $500 to $1,500, and Harriet Martineau "heard one merry lady advise that the professors should strike for higher wages." [81]

There were 20 colleges accredited to New England by the census of 1850, with 222 teachers and a little over 3,000 students — a ratio of one teacher to 14 students and one student to about 900 people. In the proportion of college students to population, if the census classification could be trusted, the Middle Atlantic States ranked with New England, and the South Atlantic Division was not far behind.

The newspaper and periodical statistics of 1850 show that readers were about in the same ratio to the population in New England as in the Middle Atlantic States, and these two sections each had about twice the ratio of circulation to white population that the South Atlantic States had.[82]

Boston was the "hub" of the New England press, as in other respects, although in all of the cities of the section there were important newspapers with able editors. But the influence of the editors of the section was little felt outside.[83] The conservative dailies of these years enlarged their size and their scope, and, under the pressure of competition and the new agencies of communication — the ocean steamship, the railroad, and the telegraph — they increased the rapidity and efficiency of their news service. Improved presses speeded-up the rate of printing twenty fold between 1830 and 1850.[84] Rivalry between the less conservative papers produced freak "blanket sheets," which in the extreme

---

[81] *Retrospect of Western Travel*, II, 95. For educational statistics, see: the annual *American Almanac; American Quarterly Register*, II, 228 (courses), III, 298 (student expenses); and *Compendium of the Seventh Census*, p. 141. Because of differences in classification, the statistics are unreliable for sectional comparisons.

[82] Compiled from the *Compendium of the Seventh Census*, p. 156.

[83] I have been much aided by the Radcliffe thesis (manuscript) done in my seminary by Dr. Priscilla Hawthorne Fowle, on the Boston newspapers of this period. See also Frederic Hudson, *Journalism in the United States, from 1690 to 1872* (New York, 1873), p. 378, and Jas. M. Lee, *History of American Journalism* (Boston, 1917), pp. 185–86, 190–92, 218.

[84] *Boston Evening Traveller*, June 16, 1849.

form printed some of Dickens' novels, as they appeared, on pages over five by seven feet in size. But the older papers maintained, in form and in spirit, the New England restraint, and catered to what Oliver Wendell Holmes called " the quality." Oldest of these, and stigmatized " the respectable paper " by upstart rivals, was the *Advertiser*, ably edited throughout these years by Nathan Hale as a business-man's paper with Whig politics. Other Whig organs were the *Atlas* (whose editor, Richard Haughton, had large political influence, and which numbered among its contributors Richard Hildreth, the Federalist historian) and the *Courier* (whose editor, J. T. Buckingham,[85] gave attention to reforms and to literature — Lowell's *Biglow Papers*, for instance, appeared in its columns). The *Morning Post*, conducted by the cheerful Charles Gordon Greene, was the leading Democratic organ; and the *Advocate,* under the aggressive editorship of Benjamin F. Hallett, supported the Anti-Masonic party. The *Transcript* was founded in 1830 by Lynde M. Walter. After his death in 1842, his sister Cornelia succeeded to the editorship, and lost social standing thereby, although she did her editorial writing at home.

These were, of course, only a few of the Boston dailies. There was a foreign-language press — French and German. The *Pilot* became an influential organ of the Irish Catholics. A multitude of weeklies were devoted to the interests of farmers, workingmen, physicians, reformers of all sorts, and religious sects, catering especially to the " family " readers. The taste of New England must be judged by the output of these weekly newspapers — much of it mawkish, sentimental, and commonplace — as well as by the work of the " New England school " of writers who were giving the section its distinction in literature.

One of these weeklies, at least, rose above the ruck to demand a place in history. William Lloyd Garrison's *Liberator*, beginning in a humble garret, stirred the nation with his war cry: " I shall strenuously contend for the immediate enfranchisement of our slave population. . . . I *will be* as harsh as truth, and as uncompromising as justice. On this subject, I do not wish to think, or speak, or write, with moderation. . . . I am in earnest — I will not equivocate — I will not excuse — I will not retreat a

[85] See his *Personal Memoirs and Recollections of Editorial Life* (Boston, 1852).

single inch — AND I WILL BE HEARD." [86] This was a voice from the early days of intolerant Puritanism, in the spirit of the martyrs refusing to enter into treaty with what was believed to be wickedness and convinced of the responsibility of the community for sin. This cutting declaration won but a small direct following, but wherever New England men went it probed the very nerve center of the New England conscience and stirred up hatred of slavery if it did not win adherents to the demand for immediate abolition.

Other forces were also operative in this period, and perhaps no more significant sign of the times appeared than the " penny press " — the little dailies produced by humble printers, the first of which seems to have issued from Boston,[87] followed by nearly twenty others in the period. They appealed to the masses, and were sold by newsboys. Their cheapness and brevity, their sensational reports of the police courts, their alertness in serving the news first, foreshadowed the methods of modern journalism and contravened the conventions of the conservatives. The populist was endangering the rule of the " élite."

Magazines for more scholarly readers developed at this time. The *North American Review*, which began in 1815, served, under such editors as Jared Sparks, Alexander H. Everett, J. G. Palfrey, and Francis Bowen, as an outlet for the scholarship and criticism of the section, as did the *Christian Examiner*, the *New-England Magazine*, and *Brownson's Quarterly Review*. *Littell's Living Age*, begun in 1844, brought to its readers republished articles from the foreign press. Well-known authors received one dollar a printed page from such important periodicals as the *North American Review*. The *Dial*, organ of the transcendentalist movement, left an impress upon New England thought and letters.[88] The mass of annuals, gift books, and schoolbooks [89] in these years help to furnish a picture of the times and to correct the impressions gained from exclusive attention to the greater names.

[86] Reprinted, from the *Liberator*, Jan. 1, 1831, in *William Lloyd Garrison, 1805–1879: The Story of His Life Told by His Children*, I (New York, 1885), 225.

[87] See Dr. Fowle's thesis, cited above.

[88] For a more detailed survey of New England periodicals, see Mott, *History of American Magazines, passim* (especially in Chaps. VI, VII).

[89] *The Cambridge History of American Literature*, II (New York, 1918), 160–75; Algernon Tassin, *The Magazine in America* (New York, 1916); and Channing, *United States*, V, 287–88, 294–97.

The popularization of education by better schoolbooks, the tales of Peter Parley (S. G. Goodrich), and Noah Webster's dictionary (published in 1828), indicate the increasing independence of the American spirit and the desire to reach the common people.

The literary output of New England between 1830 and 1850 was not only noteworthy because it constituted an epoch in the history of American letters, but it also reflected, in its varied aspects, the qualities of the section, the new contacts with European culture, and the spirit of Jacksonian Democracy with its exaltation of the individual and its break with the past.

New England's restraint, understatement, thrift, emphasis upon the strict construction of promise and performance, its quiet village life, and its interest in common things, found expression in poetry and fiction, infused with a satisfaction in the native scene and in the native material. Whittier and Longfellow, if not among " the grand old masters, the bards sublime," gave musical expression to the homely interests of life and became the household poets of America. Catherine Maria Sedgwick reflected countryside New England in her village tales, and D. P. Thompson's *Green Mountain Boys* remains a literary picture of the New England Revolutionary frontier.

Greatest of all her novelists, Nathaniel Hawthorne published his *Scarlet Letter* in 1850, presenting the problem of sin and salvation in the Puritan home of the seventeenth century, with a power of psychological analysis and a literary skill that have not since been equaled by any American writer. " The Puritan's parsimony in Hawthorne lies very close to the artist's passionate economy," [90] and his treatment of the operations of Fate in the Puritan environment almost rises to the severe dignity and beauty of the Greek dramatists. In his *Marble Faun*, Hawthorne exhibits the contact of the Puritan with the life of the Old World — a contact which was illustrated in other ways by various New England writers in the years when the fashionable habit of travel to Europe was followed by American scholars' discovery of German literature and philosophy and Spanish letters and history. Writers like F. H. Hedge promoted the study of German idealistic metaphysics; Bancroft, Edward Everett, George Tick-

---

[90] Carl Van Doren, " The Flower of Puritanism," *The Nation*, CXI, 649-50 (Dec. 8, 1920).

nor, and Longfellow sojourned in Germany or Spain, and brought
to American literature a transforming influence and a breadth of
interest from these Old World lands. New courses in European
literature entered the college curricula. Writers like W. H. Prescott, in his *Conquest of Mexico* and *Conquest of Peru*, and Tick-
nor, in his *History of Spanish Literature*, enriched the field of
history with new and broadening themes. Coleridge and Carlyle
became a fashion.

In American history, Jared Sparks, with the curiosity and
good housekeeping of the Yankee, made collections of the papers
of Washington and documents for the diplomatic history of the
Revolution. Bancroft and Francis Parkman, in their own way,
were indefatigable collectors of material, the former turning it
to the glorification of American democracy from the colonial era
to the Constitution. In 1846 Parkman had lived among the Indians of the Black Hills to acquire that intimate knowledge of
Indian life which he later used in his epic-like history of the
struggle between France and England in North America. J. G.
Palfrey was making the studies for his *History of New England*
in the colonial era, and Richard Hildreth, in dry but scholarly
fashion, furnished an antidote to Bancroft in his *History of the
United States* to 1821. An excellent picture of California in the
days before the coming of the gold seekers was made by Richard Henry Dana in his *Two Years Before the Mast*. Nor must
the contributions of other wandering descendants of New England be forgotten. The enduring portrait of the adventure of
Yankee whalers in the South Seas was made by Herman Melville
(grandson of the old gentleman depicted in Oliver Wendell
Holmes's " The Last Leaf ") in his *Moby Dick* and *Typee*.[91]
Albert Pike, a native of Massachusetts living in the Far Southwest, made a place for himself in the history of American literature, and Timothy Flint and other writers and editors exhibited
the New England quality, with a Middle Western flavor.

No literary tendency of these years proved more significant
than the work of the writers loosely — and sometimes incongru-
ously — grouped under the name of the " transcendentalists."
De Tocqueville had remarked early in the thirties: " I know of
no country in which there is so little independence of mind and

---

[91] Besides the various recent biographies of Melville, see the interesting
account of his Massachusetts home, in *Atlantic Monthly*, CXLIII, 136–38.

real freedom of discussion as in America." [92] It is difficult to accept this generalization in the field of politics, at any rate; but a similar comment was made at about the same time by Harriet Martineau, the English observer, and Emerson wrote in his journal in 1834: "We all lean on England; scarce a verse, a page, a newspaper, but is writ in imitation of English forms; our very manners and conversation are traditional." [93] It was the work of the transcendentalists to produce a literature of revolt and to usher in a new intellectual era. The Unitarian movement, as it grew less conservative, found in ministerial writers like Hedge, William Ellery Channing, Theodore Parker, George Ripley, and James Freeman Clarke a new life and a humanitarian impulse. The doctrines of Fourier, advocating the reorganization of society on a co-operative basis, caught the imagination of some of these and led to the Brook Farm experiment. Thoreau, the hermit of Walden Pond, turning from his making of lead pencils, wrote with quiet charm of the joys of the student of nature. A. Bronson Alcott, once clock maker and peddler, preached a mystic philosophy, so rarefied that it seemed to the unconverted to become a vacuum; but at the same time he put a new educational spirit into his school for children. Young writers destined to become famous in the field of journalism, like George William Curtis and Charles A. Dana, joined the Brook Farm community, and the *Dial* became the vehicle for the writers in the group.

No doubt Emerson was right when he called the transcendentalists' views, " not new, but the very oldest of thought cast into the mould of these new times." [94] The influence of the study of Plato, the pure speculative reason of Kant, with its intuitional philosophy (reaching its American public largely through Coleridge), and the mysticism of Swedenborg, all entered into the " new thought "; but its pre-eminent representative was Emerson himself, and there is in his poetry and essays a quality that made his work a native contribution. In this quality the " mould of these new times " was the important factor.

The descendant of a line of Massachusetts ministers, Emerson withdrew from the ministry in 1832 and took up the career of prophet, reaching his public from the lecture platform and

[92] Alexis de Tocqueville, *Democracy in America* (New York, 1898), I, 337.

[93] *Journals*, III (Boston, 1910), 308.

[94] *The Transcendentalist* (*The Complete Works of Ralph Waldo Emerson*, I [Cambridge, Mass., 1903], 329).

through his books. His position as an exponent of the new American spirit is now amply recognized. This serene philosopher was at one with his time, in his break with the past, his optimism and self-reliance, his use of the superlative, his love of speed. He wrote that he never saw a stagecoach which went fast enough for him; he rejoiced in the " dreamlike travelling on the railroad " when it came; but he thought that his era was " not quite yet fit for Flying Machines, and therefore there will be none." The practical interest of the Yankee mind in everyday things saturates his writings. " Machinery and Transcendentalism agree well," he says. " Stage-Coach and Railroad are bursting the old legislation like green withes." [95] " What would we really know the meaning of ? " he asks; and answers: " The meal in the firkin; the milk in the pan; the ballad in the street; the news of the boat; the glance of the eye; the form and the gait of the body; — show me the ultimate reason of these matters." [96] The same quality appears in a letter of Theodore Parker, written in Rome, to George Ripley, in which he admits that the fine arts do not interest him so much as " the coarse arts which feed, clothe, house, and comfort a people." " Mechanics' fairs, and ploughs and harrows, and saw-mills; sowing machines," etc., appealed to this Bostonian leader, who took " more interest in a cattle-show than in a picture-show," and would " rather be such a great man as Franklin than a Michael Angelo." [97] In all this, the spirit of Walt Whitman's poetry was anticipated.

Emerson's *American Scholar* (1837), his *Divinity Address* (1838), and his *Young American* (1844) shocked the conventional Boston, but they were, in truth, the spiritual descendants of the Boston Tea Party. Beyond any other New Englander, Emerson caught the spirit of the new West, America's youthful buoyancy, faith, and exaggeration, the belief in the perfectibility of the common man, the connection of wagon and star, the appeal to the imagination made by vast spaces, affording opportunity for a newer and finer society. His " declaration of independence " is in these words:

[95] *Journals*, VI, 339, 409, 397.

[96] *The American Scholar* (*Works*, I, 111).

[97] Quoted (from John Weiss, *Life and Correspondence of Theodore Parker*, . . . [New York, 1864], II, 377) by H. C. Goddard, in his *Studies in New England Transcendentalism* (Columbia University *Studies in English*, Ser. II, Vol. II, No. 3; New York, 1908), p. 165.

America is beginning to assert herself to the senses and to the imagination of her children, and Europe is receding in the same degree. . . . We cannot look on the freedom of this country, in connexion with its youth, without a presentiment that here shall laws and institutions exist on some scale of proportion to the majesty of nature. To men legislating for the area betwixt the two oceans, betwixt the snows and the tropics, somewhat of the gravity of nature will infuse itself into the code. A heterogeneous population crowding on all ships from all corners of the world to the great gates of North America, namely Boston, New York, and New Orleans, and thence proceeding inward to the prairie and the mountains, and quickly contributing their private thought to the public opinion, their toll to the treasury, and their vote to the election, it cannot be doubted that the legislation of this country should become more catholic and cosmopolitan than that of any other. It seems so easy for America to inspire and express the most expansive and humane spirit; new-born, free, healthful, strong, the land of the laborer, of the democrat, of the philanthropist, of the believer, of the saint, she should speak for the human race.[98]

Although Emerson was the prophet of a new intellectual dispensation and friendly to the Whig party, this entry in his journal in 1834 has a special significance:

Sometimes the life seems dying out of all literature, and this enormous paper currency of Words is accepted instead. I suppose the evil may be cured by this rank rabble party, the Jacksonism of the country, heedless of English and of all literature — a stone cut out of the ground without hands; — they may root out the hollow dilettantism of our cultivation in the coarsest way, and the new-born may begin again to frame their own world with greater advantage.[99]

The new world of thought and literature, to the promotion of which Emerson gave himself in these years, was made possible, partly by the release of the Puritan spirit through the development of the new religious liberalism embodied in the Unitarian movement; partly by the influence of European idealistic thought coming at a time when the material and social life of New England was being revolutionized; partly by the new opportunities afforded by the rise of a leisure class; but, not least, by the spirit of Jacksonian democracy in its largest sense. No idealistic philosophy was ever so compelled by its inner urge to show a pragmatic quality. "Metaphysics," said Emerson, "must be perpetually reinforced by life."[100] That these men of action

[98] *The Young American* (*Works*, I, 363, 370–71). See also the Emerson quotation, p. 378, *post*.
[99] *Journals*, III, 308.
[100] *Natural History of Intellect* (*Works*, XII [Cambridge, 1904], 13).

should become antislavery leaders, promoters of humanitarian reforms, defenders of democracy, and champions of liberty of thought, was inevitable.[101]

[101] In the survey of New England thought and literature, I have profited by the studies in the *Cambridge History of American Literature*, and especially by Goddard's *New England Transcendentalism*, the works and biographies of the various authors mentioned (particularly Emerson's works, including his *Journals* for the period), and various histories of Brook Farm and the transcendentalist movement, a convenient bibliography of which is in Goddard's essay. On the practical trend, see Emerson's *Works*, XII, 11; cf. VIII, 39, X, 289, XII, 6, 44.

CHAPTER IV

THE MIDDLE ATLANTIC STATES

Although the Middle Atlantic States (New York, New Jersey, and Pennsylvania) resembled New England in the importance of their industrial and capitalistic interests, and even had in their midst extensive areas settled by New Englanders, they were in many ways distinct from the Puritan region. Geographically, the section touched the Atlantic, the St. Lawrence, the Great Lakes, and the Ohio Valley, and was connected with the South by rivers, valleys, and mountain ranges. Its intermediate position between all other sections marked it out for a national destiny, while its combination of many geographic provinces symbolized the complexity of its population, economic interests, politics, and ideals.[1]

Northern New York is a part of the New England Plateau. Its eastern border is the Hudson Valley. There it is walled-off by the Berkshires and the mountains of northern New England on the east, and by the Adirondacks and the Catskills on the west. Across the state ran the trough of the Mohawk River, opening the way for the Erie Canal and, later, for the railroads that made up the New York Central system. This trough finally made New York City the metropolis of the Great Lakes Basin and of the adjacent prairie empire of the North Central States. While,

[1] On the geography, see: A. P. Brigham, *Geographic Influences in American History* (Boston, 1903), Chap. III; C. B. Trego, *A Geography of Pennsylvania* (Philadelphia, 1843); W. S. Tower, *Regional and Economic Geography of Pennsylvania;* and W. M. Davis, " The Rivers and Valleys of Pennsylvania," *National Geographic Magazine*, I, 183–253. The maps and monographs in the publications of the Geological Surveys of Pennsylvania, and in those of the United States Geological Survey, offer opportunity for more detailed study of the complexity of this region. The county boundaries of Pennsylvania bear a close relation to the topography of the state. Consult A. K. Lobeck's *Physiographic Diagram of the United States* (Madison, Wis., 1922) for the various provinces.

in New England, the narrow strip of the Connecticut Valley reached only the Vermont and New Hampshire hills and mountains, New York's extensive and fertile Mohawk Valley opened upon a wealth of fat agricultural lands, not only in the state itself, but in the Great Lakes Basin.

Even more composite was Pennsylvania. The Piedmont, the Blue Ridge, the Great Valley, and the Allegheny Mountains in the state, constituted a series of converging geographic provinces extending to the South. The Susquehanna Valley invited Baltimore to engage in rivalry with Philadelphia for economic dominance over the southeastern counties. Between the coastal lands about Philadelphia and the forks of the Ohio at Pittsburgh, successive mountain ridges placed serious barriers to commercial intercourse. In place of New England's little intervales, the broad and far reaching limestone valley of southeastern Pennsylvania, and the Lancaster plain, made a granary for the East.

Thus, in its magnitude, in its connections with West and South, in the persistence of its important agricultural interest, in the vital need of internal improvements to give unity to the eastern and western halves of its great states, this section had a place of its own. Moreover, in Pennsylvania the beds of anthracite and bituminous coal were just coming into decisive importance at the beginning of the period, and were to have a powerful effect upon the political course of the state as well as upon the destiny of the nation.

The Middle Atlantic was the most populous of all the Atlantic Coast sections, and its population was as complex as its geography. From somewhat over three and one-half million souls in 1830, these states had risen to nearly six millions in 1850. This gain is, in amount, over what it would have been if the entire population of New England in 1840 had moved to the Middle Atlantic States. About one-sixth of the section's people in 1850 were of foreign birth. As shown on the map of foreign-born,[2] the aliens were located in concentrated regions. Many remained, by reason of poverty or preference, in the large cities; others sought the mines; still others settled along the lines of canal and railroad construction, where cheap labor was in demand. To those whose means permitted, the farm lands of the West were accessible by canal and steamboat.

[2] At close of volume.

In addition to the large foreign-born population of the Middle Atlantic States, it must be remembered that it is estimated that, by the close of the colonial era, one-third of Pennsylvania's population was German and one-third Scotch-Irish. These stocks had been coming during the eighteenth century, and their large families continued to multiply. New York and New Jersey, also, had a considerable fraction of the descendants of foreign-born of various stocks. This Middle Atlantic section was, therefore, the stronghold of the non-English elements. New York City in 1850 reported more than forty-five per cent of its population foreign-born, the Irish outnumbering the Germans considerably more than two to one. In Philadelphia the foreign-born were about one in every four. The Pennsylvania Germans of the eighteenth-century migration had settled in the Great Valley and the Lancaster plain — an industrious and thrifty farming population, clinging to their language, religions, and customs, and resistant to assimilation.[3] They constituted a powerful political factor in the state. The Scotch-Irish had occupied the rougher lands of the interior, and, while more responsive to American influences, they had their own racial quality and affiliations, as the devotion to their kinsman, Andrew Jackson, showed.

In New York State the foreign-born element was relatively a recent addition, and amounted to about twenty per cent of the total white population, while that of Pennsylvania was thirteen per cent. As a whole, in the Middle Atlantic States the percentage was seventeen, while in New England and in the North Central Division it was about ten, and in the Southern sections, only three or four.

If, in fact, the American " melting pot " was composed of the ideals and institutions of the old English stock which had shaped the fundamental characteristics of the Union, it appears that the most difficult region for its operation was that of the Middle Atlantic States. In the South the problem of the negro took the place of that of the immigrant in the North; but in the slave-holding sections there was no question of assimilation.

New York City easily led as the gateway for the immigrants. In 1840, for example, in round numbers the total arrivals there

[3] On the Germans, see Albert B. Faust, *The German Element in the United States* (Boston, 1909), with maps showing areas. The Scotch-Irish locations are indicated in C. A. Hanna, *The Scotch-Irish* (New York, 1902).

were 60,000; in Baltimore, 7,000; in Philadelphia, 4,000; and in Boston, 5,000. The great number of immigrants landing in New York, as compared with Boston, did not result in such a disproportionate foreign element in the state of New York as might have been expected, because a noteworthy fraction of those who entered at this port passed to the interior. Moreover, a not inconsiderable portion went by railroad to Massachusetts. Nevertheless, the immigration greatly increased the number of paupers, created the city slums, and almost at once resulted in the introduction of politics, both in the management of immigration and in rivalry for the control of the naturalized foreigners.[4]

With the coming of the steamship, the cost of migrating to America fell. There was, at times, considerable pauper migration aided by foreign governments, and funds were sent to relatives by the earlier comers to enable them to join their kindred. The apprehension that the immigrants would become a public charge, together with humanitarian considerations, led various ports to regulate the conditions of immigration in the matter of space, food, cleanliness, etc., to impose a small head tax, and in some cases to exact a bond or a cash commutation from the ship master to insure against public loss occasioned by pauper immigrants. The federal Supreme Court in 1849 decided, in the case of *Smith* v. *Turner*,[5] that some of these regulations consti-

---

[4] On the subject of immigration in these years, I had the advantage of the studies in my Harvard seminary made by Marcus L. Hansen, in preparation for the doctor's degree. See his paper, " The History of American Immigration as a Field for Research," *American Historical Review*, XXXII, 500–518. The literature I have used is too voluminous for citation here, but mention should be made of the statistics in J. D. B. De Bow, *Statistical View of the United States . . . being a Compendium of the Seventh* [1850] *Census* (Washington, 1854), and in United States Bureau of Statistics *Report*, 1903; the state public documents listed in Adelaide R. Hasse, *Index of Economic Material in Documents of the States of the United States* (Carnegie Institution of Washington; 1907——) ; and federal public documents reached through the *Bibliography of Immigration* issued by the Library of Congress. The British *Parliamentary Papers* contain valuable reports of investigations, and Stanley C. Johnson, *A History of Emigration from the United Kingdom to North America, 1763–1912* (London, 1913), furnishes useful material and references. A list of " Books Relating to the American Irish " is in the *American Catholic Quarterly Review*, XXV, 528–30. On the German immigrants, there is a full bibliography in Faust, *German Element*. See the references, also, in Edward Channing, A. B. Hart, and F. J. Turner, *Guide to the Study and Reading of American History* (Boston, 1912), §§ 161 and 258.

[5] B. C. Howard, *Reports of Cases Argued and Adjudged in the Supreme Court of the United States, . . . ,* I (Philadelphia, 1843), 283.

tuted a violation of the control vested in the United States over interstate commerce.

The lot of the poor and ignorant immigrant was a hard one, for, in addition to the overcrowding and vile sanitary conditions of the voyage, frauds of all kinds were practiced upon him by sharpers (often his own countrymen) when he landed. To alleviate these conditions, private organizations were formed, both in New York and Boston. For example, in New York a society was organized by the Jews in 1831, the Erin Fraternal Benefit Society in 1840, and the Sons of Hermann, for the Germans, in the same year. Early in the forties, the Irish Immigrant Society of New York was founded.

The increase in numbers of the immigrants, the effect upon the larger cities (where they massed), the development of slums, the increase in defectives and paupers, the lowering of wages and the standard of living among day laborers, the religious animosities engendered — all caused apprehension among the native-born, and particularly alarmed the conservatives, who observed the trend of these new citizens toward the Democratic party. But the real significance of the movement lay in the fact that it was the clearly marked beginning of a process in American life that was to grow in importance and to test American idealism as to the capacity of free institutions and abundance of resources to mold into a new social type these varied recruits from the Old World. The effect upon the historic American type was to be determined.[6]

Men of New England origin played an important part among the leading merchants and statesmen of the Middle Atlantic States, as has been noted in the preceding chapter, and in large areas of the section New England settlers constituted the dominant element. The map of counties [7] in New York and Pennsylvania in which there was the largest representation of the Puritans in the forties, shows that it was in the group of counties

[6] See pp. 579-80, *post*, for General Walker's estimate of the changes in American society and in the fecundity of the old native stock coincident with the rising tide of immigration.

[7] Based upon the New York State census of 1845, in O. L. Holley (ed.), *New York State Register, . . .* (1845-46) (Albany); and data for Pennsylvania, from Trego, *Geography of Pennsylvania,* and county and regional histories. Compare with the maps in Lois K. Mathews, *The Expansion of New England* (Boston, 1909), reaching similar, but not identical, results by historical data.

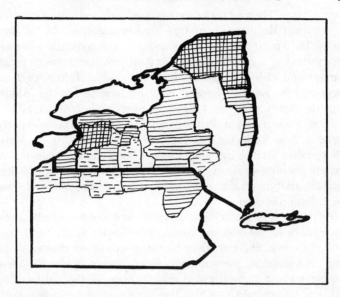

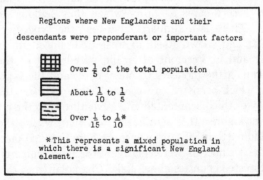

Regions where New Englanders and their descendants were preponderant or important factors

Over $\frac{1}{5}$ of the total population

About $\frac{1}{10}$ to $\frac{1}{5}$

Over $\frac{1}{15}$ to $\frac{1}{10}$*

*This represents a mixed population in which there is a significant New England element.

outside the zone of New England settlement that the Democratic party had its strongholds. The counties with a large New England native-born element had been receiving Yankee settlers, from the closing years of the Confederation. They lived on the northeastern border, in the Military Tract of central New York, and in the Genesee Valley and the Holland Purchase in the west (beyond the pre-emption line running through Seneca Lake), on lands that New York had yielded to Massachusetts. By 1845 the children of these first pioneers were reckoned as natives of

New York. Therefore, the figures based on nativity alone fail to represent the strength of this Yankee element. As the map shows, the " northern tier " of counties in Pennsylvania was likewise settled by a New England overflow, into the timbered rough country and valleys at the heads of the rivers. Taken together, these outlying parts of Greater New England within the Middle Atlantic States went far toward shaping fundamental qualities of New York if not of Pennsylvania. The Anti-Masonic party found its New York center in the " infected district " of the western counties settled by New Englanders, and the same region became the stronghold of the antislavery movement and the Republican party. It was the idealistic region, the home of *isms* and reform movements.[8]

But, when it came to labor agitation and Locofoco radicalism, the Yankee region was too conservative in its agricultural economic interests, and too unsympathetic with urban classes, to be won. Nevertheless, the wanderers from this region into the West became earnest supporters, in many cases, of the antibanking and land-reform policies which the labor philosophers advocated, and gave these dreams a reality which they seldom secured in the East. There is a similarity between the type of conservatism which had shown itself in western Connecticut and Massachusetts and in Vermont after the withdrawal of the earlier radicals among the pioneers to New York, and the type of conservatism which persisted in western New York after the exodus of so many of the discontented and adventurous to the prairies of the interior states. It is significant, too, that, within the regions of the Middle Atlantic States where the New England pioneers had settled, the Democrats were relatively the more numerous in the frontier forested counties about Lake Champlain and the Adirondacks and in the counties where the mountainous lands of Pennsylvania penetrated into southern New York.[9]

It must not be supposed, however, that New England in the Middle Atlantic section was the same as New England in the homeland. A change had come over the wanderers to these new regions, and a modified society and psychology had been de-

---

[8] See also Chapter III, *ante,* pp. 42–43, 72–73.

[9] See the maps of Physiographic Divisions (facing p. 2, *ante*), Distribution of Population (pp. 6, 7, 8, *ante*), and of Illiteracy and of Party Preponderance (at end of volume).

veloped in the " New York Yankee," which made him a distinct variety — less conservative, less Puritan, more adaptable, and more tolerant of other types than the Yankee who remained in the land of his birth.

Although the United States was still an overwhelmingly rural nation between 1830 and 1850, urban growth was in evidence. In this development the Middle Atlantic States led all the sections. In 1830 New York City numbered over 200,000 souls, and by 1850 it passed the half-million mark. Greater New York, which was made up of the city and its immediate neighbors, was an urban center of about three-quarters of a million. Philadelphia's population of over 160,000 in 1830 was more than doubled by 1850, and, counting the suburbs which it soon annexed, it reached a population of approximately 400,000.

The three largest cities of the Union lay on the middle coast of the Atlantic. Each was looking to the backcountry extending into the West as its sphere of influence in commercial rivalry, and each was in touch with Europe to a degree unshared by the interior. In the state of New York there were, in 1850, eight cities with a population of over twenty thousand each; in Pennsylvania, two; and in New Jersey, one.

Life in the cities took on characteristic form in these years. Within the period came waterworks (in 1842 the Croton aqueduct brought New York's water supply from a source forty miles distant), street cars, gas light, improved paving, better fire protection, and better-organized police. But, although the problem of the great city emerged, we are not to look upon the city of that time with the eyes of the present. No lofty buildings, rapid transit, electric lights, telephones, or radio existed to make the modern lure of the city. In the home of New York's mayor, Philip Hone, on Broadway near Park Place (which he sold for sixty thousand dollars in 1836), were neither toilets, bathrooms, nor furnace.[10] Country residences still occupied sites now business blocks, and the slums and roaring business centers of today are in areas then the home of the social élite. Union Square was rapidly becoming the center of New York City, and observers

[10] C. H. Haswell, *Reminiscences of an Octogenarian of the City of New York (1816–1860)* (New York, 1896), p. 323. *Putnam's Monthly*, I, II (in the years 1853–54), published illustrated articles portraying the city, under the title " New York Daguerreotyped."

remarked at the time that it would in a few years be " down town." By 1837 a contemporary writer found an attempt at crossing Broadway between omnibuses, coaches, etc., " almost as much as your life is worth." " Look up street and down street . . . and then run for your life." The same writer predicted for the city a population of six millions by the close of the century.

Thus, the expansion of peoples, the rapid changes, the new fortunes, which characterized the nation as a whole, were especially features of the city. After the great fire of 1835, brick and stone construction replaced the destroyed wooden houses, bringing a more substantial, if somewhat gloomy, aspect to New York streets; but before 1832 she had the reputation of being " the dirtiest city in the Union." At the opening of the period, James Fenimore Cooper related [11] that the best New York houses cost from thirty to forty thousand dollars, and a few even more. A typical residence row was made up of houses with a twenty-five-foot marble front and fifty-five feet deep, having three stories and a basement, on a lot two hundred feet in depth, selling at ten thousand dollars a residence.

In New York City, in the middle thirties, the Astor House charge for " bed and board " was $2.50 per day. The customary dining hour, of " people in genteel life," was, as in Boston, between two and six o'clock, and the *table d'hôte* at leading hotels, at three. There were vulgar exhibitions and rowdyism characteristic of the city " night life " of the period, but fashionable society, with luxury and improving taste, was already a marked feature.[12] The New York Opera Company erected the first structure for the production of Italian opera, early in the thirties; but it was not financially successful. Negro minstrelsy, which originated early in the succeeding decade, reached the height of its success in the era of the Mexican War, and reflected the popular taste.

[11] *Notions of the Americans* (Philadelphia, 1828), I, 129–31, 143–51. For what he calls " truth in burlesque," see Asa Greene's books: *A Glance at New York* (New York, 1837) ; *The Perils of Pearl Street* (New York, 1834) ; and *A Week in Wall Street* (New York, 1841).

[12] Haswell, as cited above, gives an amusing account of the resentment of New York society at the strictures of the English traveler and novelist, Mrs. Trollope, and of the salutary effect of her criticisms upon city manners, at the same time.

Although urban growth and influence clearly revealed the opening of a new era in the Middle Atlantic States, this section, unlike southern New England, also retained a highly important rural population, at the same time that it was exceeding New England in the number of pioneers sent to the prairies.[13] Some of the most important wheat-raising regions of the nation, in 1850, were still found in the Middle Atlantic States, especially in the Genesee country of New York, settled by New England farmers, and in the Great Valley of Pennsylvania,[14] where the thrifty Germans practiced intensive agriculture. In 1850 the Middle Atlantic States were producing an amount of wheat fully equal to the consumption of the population of the section, and by interstate trade were able to export a considerable quantity. In 1830 this section had led all others in the production of this crop, and even in 1840, when the North Central States were rapidly increasing their production, it fell only slightly behind them.

Its sheep industry, highly interested in the protective tariff on wool, exceeded that of any other section in 1840, and even in 1850 was not greatly exceeded by that of any other section. The sheep of the Middle Atlantic States were raised principally in the areas of New York occupied by men of New England origin and in the extreme western counties of Pennsylvania adjacent to the principal sheep-raising districts in northeastern Ohio.[15] New York and Pennsylvania were also among the largest cattle-producing states of the Union, and New York's dairy products were double those of Ohio, her nearest rival. The agriculture was more varied and intensive than that of other sections, and the farming class was to be reckoned with as an important factor in politics.

But the forces which were to dominate the growth of the Middle Atlantic States and to shape their influence in the nation were those of mining, manufacture, commerce, and the concentration of capital in the large cities. New York's and New Jersey's mining interest was unimportant; but Pennsylvania was

[13] See Chapters III, *ante*, and VII, *post*.

[14] Maps showing the concentration of wheat areas by decades are in the United States Department of Agriculture *Yearbook* for 1921 (Washington, 1922), pp. 90, 91, 94, 95.

[15] See Chester W. Wright, *Wool-Growing and the Tariff* (*Harvard Economic Studies*, V; Boston, 1910), and the maps in H. C. Taylor's article in University of Wisconsin Agricultural Experiment Station *Bulletin*, No. 16 (1911).

the leading state in this respect. Its manufactures of pig iron, as reported in the census of 1850, were valued at about half those of the Union. New York and Pennsylvania, together, produced nearly one-half the total value of the iron castings in the United States. In manufactures of wrought iron, Pennsylvania's product was valued at almost two and one-half times that of New York, and the section as a whole had over three-fifths of the value of this industry in the nation.

The changes in the methods of smelting iron ore, the general use of anthracite for smelting (about 1840), and the demand for iron created by the railroad-building after the middle forties, facilitated the rapid growth of the industry in Pennsylvania.[16] The age of steel had not yet arrived, but the proximity of the iron and coal fields in Pennsylvania, and their combination in the new methods of smelting, had given that state a comprehension of its destiny and had made the protective tariff a fundamental article of its economic creed. By the middle forties, there were corporations which combined investment in coal, limestone, coke, mining-railways, and ironworks, in all their processes. In New England, as we have seen, the textile industry had developed the modern factory type. In a similar way, in Pennsylvania in these years there was created the type of corporation uniting in itself the varied resources and processes of the iron industry — a type which was destined to play a large part in the economic and political history of the nation.

In general manufacturing, also, the Middle Atlantic States constituted the leading section. In 1850 over six per cent of their total population was employed in manufacturing establishments. In New England ten per cent was so employed. The importance of the manufacturing interests in these North Atlantic sections appears when it is noticed that, in the South Atlantic section, the percentage was but two; in the North Central, only two; and in the South Central, one. But, if New England's proportion of people engaged in manufacture to her total population was greater than that of the Middle Atlantic States, the value of the output

[16] The best general account of the development of manufactures is in Victor S. Clark, *History of Manufactures in the United States* (New York, 1929), I, with citations. Jas. M. Swank, *Progressive Pennsylvania* (Philadelphia, 1908), has data on the iron industry in that state; see also his *History of the Manufacture of Iron in all Ages*, . . . (Philadelphia, 1884; revised and enlarged ed., Philadelphia, 1892).

of the latter section greatly exceeded that of the former. Excluding home industries, the Middle Atlantic States reported in 1850 a manufacturing product valued at $432,000,000. New York's per capita production was somewhat greater than that of Pennsylvania, both in household industries and factory output. The combined value of cotton and woolen manufactures in the Middle Atlantic States was $23,500,000. Pennsylvania's share of the value of the section's cotton manufactures was over half, while the value of New York's woolen product was half that of the section.

Thus, the manufacturing interest of this section was varied and was concentrated in certain regions. The cotton mills were strongest in the Delaware Valley and along the Mohawk. In Pennsylvania the anthracite-coal mines lay along the Schuylkill district of the Susquehanna Valley; the bituminous coals were chiefly in the western counties; and iron mines existed in both eastern and western areas. Philadelphia had the lion's share of Pennsylvania's manufacturing. Allegheny County, containing Pittsburgh, came next, with less than one-fourth the value of Philadelphia's product. In general, the counties of Pennsylvania having the highest value of manufactures were in the southeastern corner of the state. In New York and New Jersey the overwhelming preponderance in the value of manufactured products lay in New York City and in the counties adjacent. Other strong centers were in the Albany region and about the head of the Mohawk. Buffalo and Rochester were the seats of an important flour-milling industry.

The influence of water power was, therefore, still effective in this section. The more densely settled coastal regions, with a laboring class, constituted one area of manufacturing concentration, while the cities at the gateways of the Great Lakes and the Ohio Valley found it profitable to manufacture the products needed in the new states of the North Central section, as well as to utilize their raw material. The distribution of manufactures in the different areas of the Middle Atlantic States was influential in shaping the action of members of Congress from that section, as the political maps will make clear.

Between 1830 and 1850 the Middle Atlantic States clearly led the rest of the country in foreign commerce. Early in the forties New York City passed Boston in ownership of tonnage, as well as in the number of vessels arriving from foreign ports, notwithstanding the fact that the figures for Boston were swelled by the many little craft which plied between that city and British-American ports. In 1835 the value of the exports of New York was three times as great as that of Boston, and of her imports, four times as great. Philadelphia ranked clearly behind New York City, but had half the value of Boston's exports and two-thirds the value of its imports.

In the hard times following the Panic of 1837, there was no marked development of commerce; but, toward the end of the forties, the surplus of the Great Lakes and the Mississippi Valley furnished exports, and the gold of California gave an impetus to trade at the very time when railroads were reaching out into the West and opening new channels for this flood of raw material to the Atlantic. By 1850 New York City had raised the value of her exports from $29,500,000, in 1835, to $47,500,000, while Boston's exports had hardly risen in value above the amount reached in 1835, although her imports had notably gained. New York exceeded her nearest rival, New Orleans, in the value of exports, by over $9,000,000.

Even more marked was New York's pre-eminence as the gate of entry, for her imports grew, in the period, from less than $88,000,000 to over $116,500,000 — twice those of the ports of Boston, Philadelphia, Baltimore, Charleston, and New Orleans, combined. Philadelphia and Charleston remained practically stationary from 1835 to 1850, both in imports and exports. New Orleans increased the value of her exports but slightly, and suffered a serious loss in her imports.[17]

The enrichment of New York City by her connection with the

[17] Samuel Hazard (ed.), *Hazard's United States Commercial and Statistical Register*, II (Philadelphia, 1840), 109–10, 148–50; MacGregor, in British *Parliamentary Papers*, 1846, XLIX, Pt. 1, 373; and, especially, *Report of Israel D. Andrews . . . on the Trade and Commerce of the British North American Colonies, and upon the Trade of the Great Lakes and Rivers* (*House Executive Document 136*, 32d Cong., 2d Sess.; Washington, 1853), pp. 758–59, 851–58. See also Dr. Grace Lee Nute's manuscript Radcliffe College thesis on "American Foreign Commerce, 1825 to 1850." E. R. Johnson [and others], *History of Domestic and Foreign Commerce of the United States* (Carnegie Institution of Washington, 1915), is useful on the general field, but does not make the analysis by sections. The federal statistics are defective, and in some respects deceptive, in this period, but probably are sufficiently reliable in the matter of sectional proportions.

" rising empire of the West," as Washington had called it, was unmistakable. The backcountry of early days, reaching to the Appalachians, had become too narrow to nourish the growth of great cities. In contrast with rival ports, New York and New Orleans both had found in the interior an accessible hinterland from which to draw raw material and to which to send the goods of their merchants and manufacturers. In the age when rail- road transportation was replacing waterways, New York City reaped the advantages of her superior position by sea and by land. These advantages compelled New Orleans to watch with concern the rush of New York to the position of commercial metropolis of the nation, and, as we shall see later, led to sec- tional rivalries and alarms. In the closing years of the era which we are considering, California furnished to New York City specu- lators the opportunity for new fortunes. The personnel of the merchant class in New York included a cosmopolitan as well as a national element.[18] While Boston merchants constituted a kind of family group of related natives of New England, New York recruited her merchants, not only from New England,[19] but also from the commercial centers of Europe, as well as from her own natives. The richest man in the city was John Jacob Astor, who emigrated from Germany. August Belmont and many other prominent importers and managers of foreign capital were agents of firms in England, France, or Holland. On the other hand, Philadelphia resembled Boston in having a native mercantile aristocracy.

To New York, and to a less extent to Philadelphia, came the

[18] Norcross, *Old New York Swamp; Hunt's Merchants' Magazine*, VIII, 57 ff.; Jos. A. Scoville [Walter Barrett, pseud.], *The Old Merchants of New York City* (New York, 1863); John Moody and G. K. Turner, " Masters of Capital in America," *McClure's Magazine*, XXXVI, 2–24, XXXVII, 73–87; Freeman Hunt, *Lives of American Merchants* (New York, 1858); Houghton, *Kings of Fortune* (Chicago, 1886); [M. Y. Beach] *The Wealth and Biography of the Wealthy Citizens of the City of New York* (New York, 1846); Geo. Wilson (compiler), *Portrait Gallery of the Chamber of Commerce of the State of New York* (New York, 1890); H. W. Lanier, *A Century of Banking in New York, 1822–1922* (New York, 1922); *Cincinnati Gazette*, Aug. 2, 1836, quoting *New York Journal of Commerce* (on relations of the merchants of the interior to New York City, Philadelphia, and Baltimore); *Wealthy Citizens of Philadel- phia* (Philadelphia, 1846); and G. W. Baker, *Review of the Relative Commercial Progress of the Cities of New York and Philadelphia*.

[19] See p. 48, *ante*.

country merchants of the interior, in order to make their annual purchases; they were entertained by the city merchants, and carried home metropolitan ideas and influences.

While, in Boston and New York, fortunes derived from commerce were turned increasingly to railroad investments, in Philadelphia investments in mines were more attractive. In the thirties and forties, in these larger cities of the North Atlantic (and especially in New York City), organized chambers of commerce and boards of trade rose or reached importance. Wall Street became a definite institution, the stock exchange took form, and, especially toward the close of the forties, mining speculation developed. At first the copper and iron mines of the Lake Superior region, and then the gold mines of California, cast their spell upon the city speculators.

The course of banking in New York and Pennsylvania in this period was of national significance. Capital and industry were sectionally concentrated in the Middle Atlantic States and New England. With twice the population of the latter section in 1834, New York and Pennsylvania, together, had only half as many state banks and not so large an amount of capital stock. But their circulation was twice that of New England and their specie was around five and one-half million dollars, as against New England's two millions.[20]

The real pre-eminence of the Middle Atlantic States in banking power lay, of course, in the fact that the Bank of the United States was located in Philadelphia. In a later chapter [21] discussing sectional contests in the thirties, the history of the war on the Bank will be considered, but in this study of the section itself it must be recalled that New York City was jealous of Philadelphia and that the personalities and policies of Martin Van Buren, as the supporter of President Jackson, and of Nicholas Biddle, the president of the Bank of the United States, exercised a determining influence upon the attitude of the section.

When Van Buren became governor of New York in 1829, the question of banking and currency at once engaged his attention. Against a strenuous opposition, which centered in New York City,

[20] Based on data in J. J. Knox, *History of Banking in the United States* (New York, 1903), I, and A. B. Hepburn, *A History of Currency in the United States*, . . . (New York, 1915), citing government sources.

[21] [Chapter IX.]

he used his influence to procure from the legislature of New York the enactment of the Safety Fund Bank law.[22] The law was based on the principle of common responsibility of all the banks of the state for the note issues of any one of them. By contribution from the various banks of a percentage of their capital, a fund was provided for the payment of the debts of an insolvent bank in excess of its assets. Bank examinations were required, and loans and discounts were not to exceed two and one-half times the capital. Until the constitution of 1846 made all stockholders personally responsible to an amount equal to their paid-in stock, they were free from personal liability. New York City had the lion's share of banking in the state. Its bank capital was nearly four times as great as that of the country banks, and its specie, about five times as great; but it had less than twice the amount of loans and discounts made by the country banks. Naturally, therefore, the bank interests in New York City were antagonistic to the Safety Fund act.[23]

When, in the fall of 1833, President Jackson, with Van Buren's reluctant acquiescence, ordered the removal of the deposits in the United States Bank, that institution, partly from considerations of its safety and partly from a desire to force recharter, entered upon a policy of restriction which resulted in great business distress that continued through most of 1834. Although intended to bring pressure upon Congress, this policy worked grave hardship in the industrial states, where the situation was aggravated by the obligations that these states had incurred with reference to internal improvements. Even Albert Gallatin, who was a friend of the Bank of the United States, accompanied a New York committee to protest against the severity of the policy of the Bank, and he found support in a similar committee from Boston, consisting of Nathan Appleton, Henry Lee, and P. T. Jackson — all of them important figures in banking and manufacturing in New England.[24]

[22] *The Autobiography of Martin Van Buren*, ed. John C. Fitzpatrick (American Historical Association *Annual Report*, 1918, II; Washington, 1920), pp. 221–22.

[23] Davis R. Dewey, *State Banking before the Civil War*, and Robt. E. Chaddock, *The Safety Fund Banking System in New York, 1829–1866* (both in *Senate Document 581*, 61st Cong., 2d Sess. [National Monetary Commission; Washington, 1910]).

[24] "Memoir of Hon. Nathan Appleton," Massachusetts Historical Society *Proceedings*, V, 287–88.

With the ending of the charter to the Bank of the United States in 1836, New York saw a great increase in the number of its banks.[25]   The orgy of chartering new banks by special action of the legislature, and the scandal which arose from the distribution of stock among the legislators, brought alarm to the Democratic politicians. On June 7, 1836, John A. Dix informed Van Buren that the legislature of New York had added nearly six million dollars to the bank capital. The legislature, he declared, had been a matter of " bargain and sale," " and if we cannot get a different class of men into the legislature, the sooner we go into a minority the better. . . . We must have less strength or more virtue if we would administer the affairs of the State either for our own honor or the public good." [26]

The New York Democrats became sharply divided on the question of banks. The Locofocos [27] stood for gold and silver as the only currency, and objected to the special privileges of chartered banks. Predecessors of modern radical parties, they aroused the apprehension of the conservative regular Democrats. When, following the Panic of 1837, President Van Buren gave aid and comfort to the Locofoco wing by advocating the Independent Treasury, whereby the government was to cease all connection with banks, the New York Conservative Democrats, under Senator N. P. Tallmadge, fought the administration policy, and even Governor William L. Marcy spoke bitterly of the " insolence of the Locofocos " and apprehensively of the destructive doctrines of the day.[28]

New York's general system of free banking was inaugurated in 1838, and thus one of the main grievances of the Locofocos was partly remedied. Under the terms of this law, securities to the amount and value of the notes issued were required to be deposited — an important precedent for a later national banking system.

[25] Chaddock, op. cit., pp. 281 ff.

[26] Van Buren MSS, Library of Congress. See also R. H. Gillet, The Life and Times of Silas Wright (Albany, 1874), I, 465–68 (letter of Apr. 8, 1836, speaking of " the false bubble of excessive credits " and stating that New York seems to be coming to Pennsylvania conditions; all Washington people, he thinks, are looking for severe pressure on the banks).

[27] See pp. 125–27, post.

[28] R. C. McGrane, The Panic of 1837 (Chicago, 1924), pp. 154–55, 165, quoting the papers of William L. Marcy.

Already, in these diverging views of Van Buren and Marcy, were to be seen the beginnings of the division between conservatives and radicals which resulted in the break-up of the party into " Hunkers " and " Barn Burners."

In Pennsylvania the story of banking, and of the resultant political questions, centers around the name of Nicholas Biddle. He became president of the Bank of the United States in 1823.[29] He was of an old and distinguished Philadelphia family, a graduate of Princeton, had been secretary to the ambassadors at Paris and London, and a man of letters (in his youth he was the compiler of the abridgment of the journals of Lewis and Clark and a writer in Joseph Dennie's *Port Folio*). The portraits [30] of him show the face of a poet, but behind the delicacy was power.

No American [wrote C. J. Ingersoll] had such European repute: Jackson's was the only one comparable, and that far inferior to it. Flattered, caressed, extolled, idolized in America, Biddle was praised and respected in Europe, as the most sagacious and successful banker in the world. Governors, senators, legislators, judges, clergymen, ladies, thronged his bank parlor, and by fulsome adulation entreated his favors. His town house and his country house were the seats of elegant hospitality, in which he shone with the blandishments of a polished gentleman, amiable, witty, liberal; never harsh or offensive to antagonists: but spoiled by sycophants of the highest rank. Chambers of commerce, boards of brokers, and other representatives of trading associations — cities, corporations, and sovereign States courted his support and solicited his favors.[31]

An able, energetic, self-confident, determined, and domineering personality, he was the predecessor of later kings of finance whose favor political leaders were glad to seek and whose influence over the moneyed interests of the country was profound. Once a Democrat, he attempted, when the war on the Bank of the United States began, to use all political parties, in turn, to the Bank's advantage, believing, nevertheless, that the institution should be nonpartisan. " In half an hour," he declared, " I can remove all the constitutional scruples in the District of Columbia. Half a dozen Presidencies — a dozen Cashierships — fifty Clerk-

---

[29] Ralph C. H. Catterall, *The Second Bank of the United States* (Chicago, 1903), p. 93, and *The Correspondence of Nicholas Biddle Dealing with National Affairs, 1807–1844*, ed. R. C. McGrane (Boston, 1919), Preface.

[30] E.g., see *ibid.*, frontispiece and pp. 12, 192.

[31] *Historical Sketch of the Second War between the United States of America and Great Britain*, [II] (Philadelphia, 1849), 285.

ships — one hundred Directorships — to worthy friends who have no character and no money." [32]

To him the war on the Bank seemed a contest " between Chestnut St and Wall St — between a Faro Bank and a National Bank." [33]   Jackson's veto of recharter of the Bank appeared to Biddle to be " a manifesto of anarchy — such as Marat or Robespierre might have issued to the mob of the faubourg St Antoine." [34] Labor leaders took careful note of Biddle's remarks in an address before the Alumni Association of Nassau Hall at Princeton, on the occasion of his receipt of an honorary degree:

From your own quiet elevation, watch calmly this servile route[*sic*] as its triumph sweeps before you. The avenging hour will at last come. It cannot be that our free nation will long endure the vulgar dominion of ignorance and profligacy. You will live to see the laws re-established. These banditti will be scourged back to their caverns.[35]

The contrast between this cultivated and wealthy man of the world and Andrew Jackson, trained on the frontier, was striking. Whereas the one was confident in his power over statesmen, editors, and Congressmen, and in the magic of money, and spoke thus contemptuously of the electorate, the other appealed from the representatives of the people to the people themselves. It was inevitable that there should be a fight between these two aggressive and dominating personalities. But it was more than a fight between personalities. Sectional strife and class war had their part in the struggle, and the Bank was located in a pivotal state. The contest came at a time when the power of the newly arrived self-conscious democracy was not realized by the leaders of finance and politics, whose conceptions belonged to an earlier generation.

At first Pennsylvania party leaders were almost a unit in supporting the Bank's application for recharter. But when the stringency caused by the Bank's policy of contracting its credits, after the removal of the deposits, brought the Democratic administration of Governor George Wolf financial embarrassment,

[32] Biddle to J. S. Barbour, Apr. 16, 1833 (*Biddle Correspondence*, p. 207).

[33] Biddle to Thos. Cooper, May 6, 1833 (*ibid.*, p. 209).

[34] Biddle to Henry Clay, Aug. 1, 1832 (*ibid.*, p. 196).

[35] Quoted in a speech by Ely Moore in the House, Apr. 28, 1836 (*Register of Debates in Congress*, XII, Pt. III, 3439).

he broke, though cautiously, with Biddle. This sealed the fate of the attempt to secure renewal of the Bank's national charter. But, when that expired in 1836, Biddle directed his attention to securing a state charter for the institution from Pennsylvania. Here Whigs, Anti-Masons, and Democrats had, at first, supported the Bank. At the beginning of 1836, Thaddeus Stevens, the leader of the Anti-Masonic allies of the Whigs, introduced a bill which resulted in a charter to the Bank of the United States in Pennsylvania. The title of the act indicates the way in which it was made acceptable to the legislature. It was called " An Act to repeal the State tax on real and personal properties, and to continue and extend the improvements of the State by railroads and canals and to charter a State Bank to be called the United States Bank."

In return for the grant of this charter for thirty years, together with exemption from taxation on its dividends, the Bank agreed to pay a bonus of two million dollars, besides half a million dollars in 1837 and one hundred thousand dollars annually thereafter, for twenty years, for public schools. It further promised to loan Pennsylvania up to six million dollars and to make the state a temporary loan up to a million dollars, in any one year, at low interest. The Bank also agreed to subscribe to the capital stock of certain designated railroad and turnpike companies.

Under this charter to the Bank, taxes on real estate and personal property were reduced from over two hundred thousand dollars in 1836 to less than three thousand dollars in 1840. Although this made possible the extension of public improvements in Pennsylvania without increasing the debt, it demoralized the voters; indeed, favorable action on the charter itself had not been secured without a liberal expenditure of money, though a legislative committee absolved the Bank from the charge of bribery. Biddle's later career in connection with the Bank of the United States as chartered by Pennsylvania, and particularly his use of the funds of the Bank in speculation in cotton, tend to justify the apprehension of Jackson and his friends with regard to the possibly dangerous power of that institution under federal control.[36] The Bank succumbed in 1841; but before its death it had succeeded in inducing the legislature to cancel the unfulfilled

[36] Leland H. Jenks, *The Migration of British Capital to 1875* (New York, 1927), pp. 95–97, and N. S. Buck, *The Development of the Organisation of Anglo-American Trade, 1800–1850* (New Haven, 1925), pp. 93–97.

portion of its pledges to make payments to the public-school fund.[37]

The details of the career of the Bank in Pennsylvania illustrate the power which industrial and financial groups were able to acquire in a state divided by antagonistic geographical regions and by differences in nationality. Pennsylvania was undergoing a transformation from the time when its rural democracy was powerful to a time when mining, manufacturing, and railroad interests acquired an influence similar to that which the Bank had wielded. The acquisition by the Pennsylvania Railroad of the state canals, though they were not in themselves a profitable possession, served as a means of securing control over the transportation system and over the legislature, at about the same time that Simon Cameron organized the large business interests of Pennsylvania into a political machine. The boss system, which he developed in that state, marked the culmination of a process to which Biddle had given earlier form.

In measuring the relative importance of the Middle Atlantic States, it should be noted that the census of 1850 gave the value of taxable personal estate in New York and Pennsylvania, combined, as less than that of New England by one hundred million dollars, although the population of those two states outnumbered that of New England two to one. The taxable real estate of New England was two-thirds that of New York and Pennsylvania, combined. The imperfect data on property, therefore, appear to show that New England's wealth, in proportion to its population, still outweighed that of the Middle Atlantic States. These two sections, however, seemed to the Western pioneers the center of the power of wealth; and the Southern planter found it hard to choose between the dangers of " mobocracy," after the Democratic party accepted some of the doctrines of the Locofocos, and the dominance of the " Northern money power " as embodied in the Whigs. As the slavery question emerged, new problems presented themselves to parties in all sections.

In party politics, the Middle Atlantic States constituted a fighting ground, a pivotal group. This might have been ex-

---

[37] *Biddle Correspondence*; J. A. Woodburn, *The Life of Thaddeus Stevens* (Indianapolis, 1913); and Henry R. Mueller, *The Whig Party in Pennsylvania* (Columbia University *Studies in History, Economics and Public Law*, CI, No. 2; New York, 1922), p. 70.

pected from the complexity of the section. The geographical factors, the variety of people and economic interests, and particularly the development of special types of the managing politician and boss to deal with this complex of interests, all worked to the same end. On the whole, the Middle Atlantic States were fairly closely divided between the two major parties. If we add together the popular votes of the Democrats, on the one side, and those of the Whigs and Anti-Masons, on the other, in New York, Pennsylvania, and New Jersey, in the six Presidential elections from 1832 to 1852, inclusive, the Democratic vote shows a plurality of only one-fourth of one per cent. New Jersey, following the historical tendency which had aligned her with the New England Federalists at the beginning of our national history, gave her vote to the Whigs in all these elections, with the exception of those of 1832 and 1852; but the vote was usually exceedingly close. In two of these Presidential elections (1840 and 1848), New York and Pennsylvania went Whig; but in 1840 William Henry Harrison drew largely from the rural democracy. In Pennsylvania the Whigs had a majority, in that election, however, of only six votes, and a plurality of less than 350. In New York the Whigs carried this election by a majority of a little over 10,000 in a total vote of over 441,000.[38] In 1848 New York Democracy was split by Van Buren's acceptance of the Free Soil nomination, and Pennsylvania was dissatisfied with the Democratic tariff reduction of 1846.

In all the elections from 1828 to 1836, inclusive, New York chose Democratic governors. They were notable men, indicative of the special type of successful politician which New York produced. Among them, Van Buren passed from the governorship to the Vice-Presidency and then to the Presidency; Marcy had three successive terms as governor, became the leader of the Conservative, or Hunker, faction in opposition to Van Buren, was made a member of the cabinet as Secretary of War in the administration of Polk, and had a distinguished career as President Pierce's Secretary of State. In the elections of 1838 and 1840, William H. Seward won the governorship as a Whig. In the years immediately preceding the Civil War, he became the most prominent leader of that party and the outstanding candidate for the

[38] Edward Stanwood, *A History of the Presidency* (Boston, 1906), was used for the returns which I have compiled.

Presidential nomination by the Republicans in 1860. As President Lincoln's Secretary of State, he gained his place in the history of American diplomacy. Silas Wright, who won the governorship in 1844 over the Whig candidate, Millard Fillmore (later Vice-President and President), held a high rank in the United States Senate for solid judgment and unselfish service. He refused the Democratic nomination for the Vice-Presidency in 1844. Of the other governors — all Whigs — only Hamilton Fish gained a national standing. He was Secretary of State during the two terms of President Grant.

This record bears testimony to the power of political leadership in New York. The national distinction of these men was in part due to the necessity of recognizing the Empire State in party appointments; but the distinction was personal as well. All of these governors showed special political ability in the handling of men and in the framing of issues. Leaders in New England showed no such power of affecting national public opinion and of acquiring the controlling position in the management of party. But most of these men of influence in New York were of New England birth or descent. Apparently, a transplantation from the original soil of southern New England was necessary to bring out the latent power of the Yankee stock in national politics.

In politics, Pennsylvania offers a sharp contrast to New York. It was Democratic, but it produced no comparably distinguished leaders. Albert Gallatin's advice was still listened to; but, though he lived until 1849, he was a survivor from Jeffersonian days.

Perhaps the only Pennsylvania Democratic politician who, in this period, achieved a national reputation, was James Buchanan. A native of the state, he had been a member of the lower house of Congress; was minister to Russia for two years under Jackson; returned to become United States Senator from 1834 to 1845; was Secretary of State under Polk; served as minister to Great Britain; and, finally, was President of the United States. Outstanding characteristics in Buchanan were extreme caution if not timidity, reliance upon the Democratic party and its faiths, and acquiescence in the wishes of the Southern leaders, who found in him a convenient instrument for managing the Northern Democracy in harmony with their policies. He was in favor of drawing the Missouri Compromise line, between freedom and slavery, through the territories to the Pacific. He was even anxious lest he should go further than the South required.[39] Tall, benevolent of aspect, correct in his habits, but devoid of anything like brilliancy, he stood firmly on Democratic Constitutional principles. In some respects he is not untypical of other Democratic leaders of the time; it is significant, however, that a rival, Martin Van Buren of New York, became the first candidate of the Free Soil party for the Presidency.[40]

Simon Cameron, banker and railroad promoter, exemplifies Pennsylvania's primary allegiance to her material interests. He began his career as a Jacksonian Democrat but became a United States Senator through a coalition of protectionist Democrats, Native Americans, and Whigs. On the origin of the Republican party, he easily passed into its ranks, and was Lincoln's unfortunate choice as Secretary of War.

Even less successful than the Democrats of Pennsylvania in producing names of national reputation, were the Whigs of the state. On the whole, their leaders were the party managers for large economic interests, skilful in making combinations on the political chessboard of a state deeply divided by regional and nationalistic groups.

While New England party leaders were influential in the spread of ideals, they lacked something of political skill, and warmth of personal connections; on the other hand, those of Pennsylvania, in this period, found the basis of their power in material interests rather than ideals; but New York's leaders were successful both as practical politicians and, within definite limits, as champions of ideals.

Although, as we have seen, the Presidential vote, when totaled for the period, was almost equally divided between the Democratic party and its rivals, this does not mean that there was a very close party division in all portions of the Middle Atlantic section. Here, as in other sections, there were regions, or groups of counties, which tended habitually to vote the same way. Often

---

[39] *The Works of James Buchanan*, ed. John Bassett Moore, VIII (Philadelphia, 1909), 369 (Buchanan to W. R. King, Mar. 6, 1850), and Roy F. Nichols, *The Democratic Machine, 1850–1854* (Columbia University *Studies in History, Economics and Public Law*, CXI, No. 1; New York, 1923), pp. 57–58.

[40] This followed the repudiation of Van Buren by the slaveholding states, in 1840 and 1844, while Buchanan grew steadily in their favor until he attained the goal of his ambition.

the majority was small, and consequently the maps of party preponderance sometimes conceal an important minority vote; but they do express the geographical distribution of party preferences and party habit within the section, and they bring into prominence the political connection with physiography, economic geography, and the social and racial composition of the people.

The Democratic counties were strongly marked in southeastern New York and northern and eastern Pennsylvania, and in the adjacent parts of New Jersey. In New York the Whig areas lay chiefly in the western counties; on the upper waters of the Susquehanna (where New Englanders had early settled); and in some of the northeastern counties (which likewise were colonized by Yankees).

In Pennsylvania, adjacent to the Whig areas of western New York, about the headwaters of the Ohio there were Whig counties. Another group was found in the south-central counties of Pennsylvania; and a peninsula of counties, pushing northwesterly toward the center of the state from Philadelphia, constituted another area of Whig power. Between these strongholds of the different parties were the unstable regions shown in the map.[41]

In general, in the Middle Atlantic States, the hilly and mountainous districts (including the " northern tier " of counties in Pennsylvania, and, at times, adjacent counties of New York) tended to be Democratic. Along the St. Lawrence, in the Empire State, there was a similar illustration of the Democracy of New England pioneers in rough country. On the whole, the better farm lands, the lines of communication, the areas settled by New Englanders, tended to vote the Whig ticket. It has been said that seven-eighths of the New Englanders who could afford to subscribe to the more expensive party papers were Whigs.[42]

But the danger of overgeneralizing on purely geographical and economic grounds is illustrated, not only by the Democracy of the Germans in the rich agricultural counties of the Great Valley of Pennsylvania, but also by the Whig affiliation of certain rough counties in the Adirondacks in New York. No doubt personal leadership accounted for some of this. Certain it is that stock

[41] See the composite map (at end of volume) of the elections from 1836 to 1848.

[42] D. R. Fox, " Economic Status of the New York Whigs," *Political Science Quarterly*, XXXIII, 512.

and personal leadership must be considered, as well as physical geography.

Similarly, it is unsafe to generalize as to the attitude of large cities in this section, for, while (with the single exception of 1848) New York City was consistently Democratic in its Presidential vote, Philadelphia was steadfastly Whig. One may say, however, that, as in New England, Democracy found its strength among the poorer people, while the capitalists, bankers, merchants, and manufacturers, and their following, were usually Whigs. This distribution is revealed, not only in social classes, but also in the political attitude of residential districts in the different city wards.

The era saw the birth and death of various parties peculiarly related to this section, and especially to the state of New York.[43] But the Democratic party continued. It found its power, in New York City, in Tammany Hall. Beginning as a philanthropic society, this organization had strengthened its hands by its influence over the newly arrived inhabitants, especially the Irish. Its membership included bankers and merchants, as well as workmen.

Although the power of the metropolis in politics was great even at this time, its influence was not so strong as in later years. In New York State at large, control was in the hands of the Albany Regency, a political " ring " of which Martin Van Buren was the leader. He had both the sagacity and the stubbornness of his Dutch ancestry. Few men in American life so united the ability to make practical political combinations and the power of critical analysis of underlying principles. Suave and conciliatory, Van Buren was perhaps the highest type of the New York politician. He rose to national greatness and achieved a reputation as a statesman, by his ability to think in national terms, to formulate Democratic party principles in a way that remained substantially

[43] New York politics have produced a wealth of historical and biographical material. Among the more important sources for this account are: Jabez D. Hammond, *The History of Political Parties in the State of New-York, from the Ratification of the Federal Constitution to* . . . [1847] (Syracuse, 1852), II and III; the autobiographies and works of Seward, Thurlow Weed, Horace Greeley, Fillmore, Van Buren, and Dix, and the lives of these leaders; D. S. Alexander, *Political History of the State of New York* (New York, 1906), I, 357–92, and II; D. R. Fox, *The Decline of Aristocracy in the Politics of New York* (Columbia University *Studies in History, Economics and Public Law*, LXXXVI; New York, 1919) ; and Nichols, *Democratic Machine.*

unchanged down to recent years, and at times to make courageous decisions hazardous to his career and to abide by them. He gathered around him a group of minor leaders, including William L. Marcy, Azariah C. Flagg, and John A. Dix — all natives of New England, and all from Democratic strongholds in eastern New York. But in national politics the wise and unselfish Silas Wright,[44] of St. Lawrence County, became his most effective lieutenant. He represented the moderate Democracy of Yankee pioneers in parts of northern New York. The strength of the Democratic party depended upon its ability to add to its normal following recruits from the regions which were responsive to idealistic programs; but such a union exposed it to the danger of losing the conservative wing.

The Whig party of New York was strong among the men of property in the urban districts (who possessed an influence beyond their numbers) and in the middle and western counties settled by New England farmers. Here a quick responsiveness to moral issues, coupled with respect for property and vested rights, was in evidence. The support of John Quincy Adams by western New York in the era of the National Republicans, and the later affiliation of the region with the Whig party, are largely explained by these qualities, together with the region's demand for improved transportation and banking facilities.

One connection of moral issues with material interests was brought about through the Anti-Masonic movement. Out of central New York and the Genesee Valley came Yankee ideas which stirred American life in the period between the War of 1812 and the Civil War. Here began such *isms* as Mormonism, Shakerism, spiritualism, and feminism. The expectation of new revelations, the urge to spread new gospels, had been a feature of the " come-outers " of New England from the earliest days. In the wilderness of western New York these tendencies had been accentuated and had gained an open field. The absence of the balance wheel of a ministerial ruling class, dominated by tradi-

[44] See Gillet, *Silas Wright*. Thomas Ritchie (editor of the Richmond *Enquirer*) wrote (Nov. 24, 1841): " The man who tries to think as little of himself as possible in these times (like Silas Wright) is in the best condition for serving his country, and ultimately of receiving the reward of his disinterestedness." (*Correspondence of John C. Calhoun*, ed. J. Franklin Jameson [American Historical Association *Annual Report*, 1899, II; Washington, 1900], p. 840.)

tion, in this region, freed the individualistic New England spirit from restraint.

This social and spiritual background must be borne in mind when considering the rise of Anti-Masonry. In 1826 the abduction of William Morgan, of Genesee County, followed his alleged exposure of the secrets of the Masonic order. Charged with attempts to control party politics and society by means of an oath-bound secret organization, as well as with the murder of Morgan, the Masons became the object of organized political attack, particularly in the vicinity of Rochester. The western Anti-Masonic counties became " the infected district," or, in their own words, " the area of the blessed spirit."

The excitement that swept this emotional western New York was manipulated by the friends of John Quincy Adams in the interests of his Presidential candidacy. It was also utilized by a group of Yankee politicians who added to the idealistic movement against the Masons practical demands for internal improvements in those western counties which the Erie Canal did not directly serve.[45]

Besides the fact that this agitation was strongest among the New England folk who rejected the Democratic party, that organization was also in disfavor because of its refusal to yield to the demand for lateral canals to connect the lakes of central New York with the upper Susquehanna and the tributaries of the Ohio. The banking interests of New York City, also (which, as we have seen, had been alienated by the Safety Fund System), found in the Anti-Masonic movement an opportunity to attack the Democratic party. The demand of the rural communities for a home market led the Anti-Masons to include the protective tariff in their creed. They also supported such humanitarian agitations as that for the abolition of imprisonment for debt.

Gradually the single-minded enthusiasts were deprived of leadership by such practical politicians as Thurlow Weed [46] and William H. Seward.[47] Weed had grown up among the pioneer

[45] Chas. McCarthy, *The Antimasonic Party: A Study of Political Anti-masonry in the United States, 1827–1840* (American Historical Association *Annual Report*, 1902, I [Washington, 1903], 365–574).

[46] See *Autobiography of Thurlow Weed*, ed. Harriet A. Weed (Boston, 1883), and Thurlow Weed Barnes, *Memoir of Thurlow Weed* (Boston, 1884).

[47] See: *The Works of William H. Seward*, ed. Geo. E. Baker (Boston, 1884); *Autobiography of William H. Seward, from 1801–1834. With a Memoir of*

conditions of western New York and had become a journeyman printer in Rochester. He now founded the *Albany Evening Journal* as the organ of political Anti-Masonry. He regarded politics as a fine art, to be practiced for the love of it rather than as the means of obtaining office for himself. Without scruples as to methods but with devotion to the purpose of building up a new party organization, this astute, conciliatory young leader, entirely devoid of illusions, turned a moral crusade into a political program. The other youthful leader, Seward, came from middle New York, which had been colonized by Puritan migrants and which was itself, at this time, colonizing the Middle West. Speaking at Madison, Wisconsin, in 1860, Seward said:

I speak to you because I feel that I am, and during all my mature life have been, one of you. Although of New York, I am still a citizen of the North-west. The North-west extends eastward to the base of the Alleghany mountains, and does not all of Western New York lie westward of the Alleghany mountains? [48]

Seward's personality was a compound of the emotional enthusiast, philosophic and responsive to ideals, with the man of affairs, ready to gain his political ends by some modification of principles. Henry Adams gives us a living portrait of him in 1860:

A slouching, slender figure; a head like a wise macaw; a beaked nose; shaggy eyebrows; unorderly hair and clothes; hoarse voice; off-hand manner; free talk, and perpetual cigar, offered a new type, — of western New York. . . . Underneath the surface he was conventional after the conventions of western New York and Albany. [49]

Anti-Masonry itself never succeeded in carrying the state of New York, and it became clear that, if Democracy was to be overthrown there, a new party was necessary. Accordingly, the *Albany Evening Journal,* as Weed remarked in his *Autobiography,* went " diligently and seriously to work, organizing the elements of opposition throughout the state into what soon became the Whig Party." [50]

His Life and Selections from His Letters from 1831 to 1846, by Frederick W. Seward (New York, 1877); and Frederic Bancroft, *The Life of William H. Seward* (New York, 1900).

[48] Frederick W. Seward, *Seward at Washington, . . . A Memoir of His Life, with Selections from His Letters, 1846–1861* (New York, 1891), p. 463.

[49] *The Education of Henry Adams* (Washington, 1907), p. 88. For Adams's impressions of Weed, see pp. 126–27.   [50] 1834.

To the political firm of " Weed and Seward " was now added Horace Greeley. An apostle of practical idealism, he emphasized those Whig doctrines which sought the uplifting of the common man. The protective tariff was to him not so much a means of promoting a home market and of assisting infant industries as of increasing the wages of labor. He supported land reform, temperance, Fourierism, scientific farming, antislavery, and other advanced movements, as well as such notions as phrenology.

When Greeley started the *New York Tribune* in 1841, after having edited various campaign newspapers (including the *Log Cabin*), he announced that its purpose would be to advance the interests of the people and to promote their moral, social, and political well-being. From the *Tribune* as a platform, Greeley's voice reached the colonists which New England and the Yankee stock of New York sent to the North Central States, and the paper came to have the greatest influence of any daily in America. Many of the men who became leaders of American journalism and of American letters were trained in its office.

In the Middle Atlantic States, therefore, the Whig party combined economic interests, skilful political organization, and an idealism represented in such different ways by Seward and Greeley. But, as was the case with the Democratic party, its continued existence was threatened by antagonisms between its economic interests and its idealistic elements.

These were not the only considerations affecting party divisions at this time. The Democratic party underwent a cleavage resulting from changing economic conditions. These conditions gave birth to the labor movement, and to a class contest which was also leavened with the idealistic yeast of the period. Early in the thirties, the railroad development had extended markets and created a group of merchant capitalists, and thus inaugurated a new era in the relations of labor and capital.[51] In place of household industries and local trade, came an organization shaped by the capitalists, who brought raw materials from a distance and undersold their rivals, the small manufacturers. These employers also produced for remote markets, and often were not residents of the towns in which their factories were located. They did not

[51] See John R. Commons [and others] (eds.), *A Documentary History of American Industrial Society*, V (Cleveland, 1910), 23.

have, therefore, the sympathetic local interests, in dealing with their workingmen, which employers formerly had.

At the same time that this break in the relations between master and workmen occurred, there was a rise in the cost of living. The increase in paper currency, that came with the downfall of the National Bank, was accompanied by high prices [52] that, together with the failure of wages to keep pace and the shortage of the wheat crop, resulted in bread riots, particularly in New York City, in 1836 and 1837.[53] Fitzwilliam Byrdsall, in his account of the Locofoco movement,[54] notes that, while the price of a bushel of wheat was formerly equal to a day's wages, by 1837 wheat had doubled in price while wages remained practically stationary. In the larger cities, especially in New York, there was also a serious rise in rents, following the increase in population and the congestion which was aggravated by the absence of urban transportation and by the lack of railroads to the North Central States, as well as by the cost of travel.

A Workingman's Party had been formed in 1828–29, the leadership of which rested at first in Thomas Skidmore, an agitator who favored the equal distribution of property, and then in Robert Dale Owen, who demanded that children should be under the guardianship of the state, in order that they might be educated together, apart from the family and under conditions productive of equal and free opportunity and development. With Owen was associated Frances Wright,[55] a Scot, who declared class war and professed extreme views regarding marriage, birth control, the position of woman in general, and the danger of evangelical religion in politics. " Fanny Wrightism " was a term of reproach hurled at this party. An Englishman, George H. Evans, began the publication of the *Working Man's Advocate* in 1829, in New York.

[52] See: *ibid.*, p. 18 (graph) ; Arthur H. Cole, " Wholesale Prices in the United States, 1825–45," *Review of Economic Statistics* (Harvard Economic Service), VIII, 69–84 (Apr., 1926) ; Alvin H. Hansen, in American Statistical Association *Publications*, XIV, 804–12 ; and J. B. McMaster, *A History of the People of the United States, from the Revolution to the Civil War*, VI (New York, 1920), 340, 390–91.

[53] On conditions in 1835, see *ibid.*, pp. 220–23 ; on bread riots in New York, consult Edward M. Shepard, *Martin Van Buren* (Boston, 1899 [in " American Statesmen " series]), p. 315.

[54] *The History of the Loco-Foco or Equal Rights Party* (New York, 1842).

[55] Wm. R. Waterman, *Frances Wright* (Columbia University *Studies in History, Economics and Public Law*, CXV, No. 1 ; New York, 1924).

As a remedy for the ills of the time, he advocated, through this organ, the use of the public lands as a free gift to settlers. He would place limitations on the power of selling the lands. His theory was that, when the laboring man was given the choice between working for low wages in the East or taking up a free farm of his own in the West, wages would, of necessity, rise to the level of the profit which the farmer might make in tilling his free land.

When Albert Brisbane brought the theories of Fourier to the attention of Americans, the land-reform movement enlisted the powerful support of Horace Greeley, in the forties, and the *New York Tribune* carried the gospel to the North Central States. But the later homestead legislation was inconsistent with the system of the philosophical land reformer, inasmuch as it did not prevent alienation of the lands to speculators and the building-up of large estates.[56] In fact, the Homestead Law of 1862 owes more to the concrete demands of the pioneer farmer than to the labor philosophers. It has also been rightly remarked that the humanitarianism of these philosophical reformers is " not . . . the authentic voice of the worker of the period." [57] But their utterances are important as a phase of American intellectual life and as evidence of the contemporary consciousness of class conflict.

The early thirties were also marked by strikes,[58] both in New York and Pennsylvania. In 1827 the Mechanics' Union of Trade Associations was formed at Philadelphia. Its members had a newspaper organ, and adopted the policy of giving their vote to whatever candidates would pledge themselves to support the working class. State-wide unions were formed in New York and

[56] B. H. Hibbard, *A History of the Public Land Policies* (New York, 1924), Chap. XVII.

[57] Norman Ware, *The Industrial Worker, 1840–1860* (Boston, 1924), p. 22, and Waterman, *op. cit.*, pp. 187–89.

[58] It is significant of the temper of the time, that rioting accompanied the demands of labor, of the tenant farmers, and of the Native Americans. In foreign relations, also, New York in the thirties became the scene of disorderly proceedings along the northern border. On the " Caroline " episode and " Hunters' Lodges," see: pp. 473–74, *post;* John Bassett Moore, *A Digest of International Law* . . . (Washington, 1906), II, 24–30, 409–14, VI, 261–62, 1014–15, VII, 919–20 (and citations in each case); Wm. L. Mackenzie, *The Life and Times of Martin Van Buren* (Boston, 1846), pp. 282 ff. (" On Canadian Annexation and Insurrection "); Chas. Lindsey, *The Life and Times of Wm. Lyon Mackenzie* (Toronto, 1863), II; O. E. Tiffany, *The Relations of the United States to the Canadian Rebellion of 1837–1838* (Buffalo Historical Society *Publications*, VIII [Buffalo, 1905], 1–118); and *Canadian Historical Review*, VII, 13–26.

Pennsylvania, and in 1834, following the strikes of the previous year, a national federation was organized. Ely Moore, a Tammany representative of labor in New York City, became the first president of this federation. So successful was this leader that he was elected to the lower house of Congress, where in 1836 a speech of his called out from John Quincy Adams the exclamation, " a thundering Jack Cade or Wat Tyler speech." " I overheard some gentlemen from the South say," wrote Adams in his diary, " that they thought they heard the high priest of revolution singing his war song." Moore's plea was for equal rights and for the abolition of exclusive privileges. To him the labor unions were the necessary " counterpoises against capital, whenever it shall attempt to exert an unlawful, or undue influence." [59]

This movement of the workmen, or " Workies " (as they were dubbed), resulted in attempts by the older parties to win them over by conceding some of their demands. In 1831 Democracy, then in power in New York, abolished debtors' prisons, and also reformed the old militia system. This system had been particularly onerous to the workmen, who were obliged to lose three days' wages every year inasmuch as they were not permitted to pay a fine in place of work. Tammany gave its support to a mechanic's-lien law, which was carried. The Whig supporters of the protective tariff came more and more to emphasize the argument that it raised the wages of labor. On the whole, however, it was the Democratic party which catered especially to the workmen.[60]

It has been pointed out, in the discussion of banking in the Middle Atlantic States, that the banking interests were divided between the advocates of the Bank of the United States and the rival advocates of the state banks. The scandals which followed the struggles of the bank men in the different parties to secure franchises for themselves and for their friends, strengthened the opposition to special privilege and, indeed, to the whole paper-money system. The Democratic radicals became organized in the

[59] *Register of Debates*, XII, Pt. III, 3428–39 (Apr. 28, 1836). The labor movement of this period is well presented in *Documentary History of American Industrial Society*, VI, VII; John R. Commons [and others], *History of Labour in the United States* (New York, 1918), I; Ware, *op. cit.*; F. T. Carlton, *Education and Industrial Evolution* (New York, 1908); and Selig Perlman, *A History of Trade Unionism in the United States* (New York, 1922).

[60] See, e.g., H. D. Gilpin to Van Buren, May 15, 22, 1837, and Wm. Foster and others to Van Buren, May, 1837 (Van Buren MSS, Library of Congress); see also Ware, *op. cit.*, Chap. VIII.

Locofocos.[61]   Although this party was not a direct outgrowth of
the workmen's movement, many of the prominent figures of the
latter were to be found in its ranks.   Among them were Ely
Moore, C. C. Cambreleng (who had come as a youth to New York
City from North Carolina and who served as a Democratic leader
in Congress from 1821 to 1839), and William Leggett (one of the
editors of the *Evening Post* — a man who loved to " trace principles to their remotest consequences, and who was ready to follow
them ").   The men of influence in the group included a chair
maker, a locksmith, and a carpenter.

The real significance of the Locofoco party is often obscured by
the story of the meeting at Tammany Hall, in 1835, when the
Conservative or " bank " Democrats turned off the lights, where-
upon the " Equal Rights " faction lit the newly introduced locofoco matches and took possession of the hall.   In reality, the movement was a landmark in the rise of organized demands of the
common people for the control of government in the interests of
their own economic and spiritual welfare.   It presaged a succession of later movements (strongest in the Western sections to
which New England and New York sent settlers) that included
the organization of Anti-Monopolists, Grangers, Populists, and the
whole group of later progressive parties.

The political philosophy which had been incorporated in the
American Declaration of Independence, but which had not, even
by the thirties, found logical and concrete expression in the realities of American life, was now made the basis of thoroughgoing
demands.   The Locofoco leaders, resting their case upon natural
rights and radical democracy, urged the menace of special privilege to equal rights.   The banking and credit system was denounced, not only because of the elements of monopoly and
privilege which the special charters to banks furnished, under
the system of party favoritism in the legislature, but also because
paper money bore with peculiar hardship upon the wageworkers.

[61] Byrdsall, *op. cit.*, is an important source.   The party origins and outcome were carefully studied by the late Professor William Trimble, whose investigation of the movement was begun in my seminary.   See his papers,
" Diverging Tendencies in New York Democracy in the Period of the Locofocos," *American Historical Review*, XXIV, 396–421, and " The Social Philosophy of the Loco-Foco Democracy," *American Journal of Sociology*, XXVI,
705–15.   William Leggett's editorials in the *New York Evening Post*, 1834 and
1835, and in the *Plain Dealer*, 1836, are significant.

The Locofocos demanded, therefore, hard money and the separation of government from all banking connection. Debts were to be merely debts of honor, not collectible at law. Judges were to be elected by the people and for short terms; the effects of legal precedents were to be very strictly limited and the composition of the Supreme Court was to be radically modified. Among the restrictions upon the lawmakers, the Locofocos proposed that no legislature could bind its successors, nor make loans without a referendum, nor create corporations. They also advocated nominations by the people, popular election of the President, abolition of capital punishment, free and equal education, and free grants of the public lands to the landless.

Pre-election pledges were required, and letters were written to the candidates of the various parties, demanding statements of their attitude towards the issues stressed by the Locofocos. This device, and the ability to cast a pivotal vote, gave them an influence in elections far beyond the actual votes cast by the party itself, and furnished weapons which later radical parties were quick to use.

Obviously, here was a new and significant political development, with a strikingly modern look to it. The *Democratic Review* saw in Leggett's editorials a tendency toward the separation of the Democrats into two camps: the timid friends of established order, partial to banks; and the young reformers. The movement left a deep impression upon the constitution-making of New York and of the Western states in the later forties and early fifties.[62]

Locofocoism belongs to the same period as the Reform Bill and the Chartist agitation in England; it is connected with the socialistic proposals of Fourier and Robert Owen, with the European revolutions of 1830, and with the triumph of Jacksonian Democracy in this country. The pioneer principles of equality and freedom, which developed out of actual experience in dealing with the unoccupied wilderness, now found companionship with the demands of city workers, whose philosophers, drawn chiefly from the Old World, furnished a theoretical setting for the concrete desires of the working classes and for a general reorganization of society.

Following Van Buren in his first Presidential message, the Democratic party, while it avoided the more extreme plans and philosophies of the radical members of the Locofocos, adopted so

[62] See pp. 127–29, 320–22, *post.*

many of the latter's specific proposals that it became stigmatized by its adversaries as " Locofoco." As we have seen, some of the force of the demands of the antibank group had already been weakened by the passage of the Safety Fund act in New York in 1829. The general banking law enacted in New York in 1838 assisted in diminishing the outcry for the abolition of all banks, at the same time that it did away with the old system of special charters to those banks whose friends won control of the legislature.

In his Presidential message in the fall of 1837, Van Buren declared in favor of the divorce of government from banking, and gained the approval of the Locofoco radicals by supporting the Independent Treasury plan. Bank Democrats became alarmed, however, at Van Buren's tendency to yield to the radicals, and Senator N. P. Tallmadge, of New York, joined Senator W. C. Rives, of Virginia, in organizing the " Conservative Democrats " [63] in 1837, with a newspaper of their own, at Washington, called the *Madisonian*. But these Conservative Democrats failed to influence the Presidential policy, and by 1840 many of the Conservative Democrats affiliated with the Whigs.

Locofoco ideas affected the state constitutional conventions which met at this period. The Pennsylvania Constitutional Convention, the delegates to which were chosen at the time of the Presidential election of 1836, was about evenly divided between Democrats, on one side, and Whigs and Anti-Masons, on the other. The conservatives expressed alarm over the possibility of radical innovations. " Once open a sluice in the constitution," cried the *National Gazette*, " and the very dregs of radicalism will flow through it and the embankment will be washed away." But the state constitution of 1838 hardly justified the alarm of the extreme conservatives. Owing to defections from the Democratic ranks, a compromise arrangement provided for appointment of judges by the governor, with the consent of the senate, for a definite term instead of during good behavior. Nor were the Democrats able to widen the suffrage: a tax-paying qualification was continued. But they did succeed in limiting the suffrage to whites.

In the New York Constitutional Convention of 1846, the contests were rather between reformers and conservatives than between the political parties. The opposition to the new constitu-

[63] See pp. 187, 460–64 (*passim*), *post*.

tion was strongest in the southeastern area — New York City and tributary counties. Among the subjects with which the convention had to deal were the finances of the state canals. Instead of general provisions, a precedent was now made for incorporating special legislation into state constitutions.[64]   Specified appropriations for branch canals were provided for in the constitution itself. Limitations were imposed on the discretion of the legislature. It was forbidden to dispose of any of the canals of the state, and was denied power to contract debts in excess of one million dollars except for military purposes. Indeed, no debt could be incurred unless authorized by a specific law providing for a direct annual tax sufficient to pay the interest and to extinguish the principal within eighteen years. It was further required that such a law must receive the approval of a majority of the voters at a general election. The judicial system was remodeled and the judges were made elective.

These indications of the people's distrust of their legislature and of their determination to check it by constitutional legislation, as well as of their desire to subject the judiciary to the will of the electorate, are features of Jacksonian Democracy and of later American history. They rapidly spread to other sections, and particularly to the North Central States. Moreover, the denial of economic power to the state legislature was a step towards subordinating the state to the corporation, on the one side, and to the general government, on the other — both of which were left unchecked in their power to borrow money and thus to acquire economic importance.[65]   The diminution of the economic power of the state also helped to strengthen the section in Congressional legislation.

The concern over the growing power of corporations was shown by the stipulation that all general laws and specific acts creating them might be altered or repealed. Stockholders in any corporation or association for banking purposes were to be held individu-

[64] F. N. Thorpe (compiler and ed.), *The Federal and State Constitutions, Colonial Charters, and Other Organic Laws of . . . the United States of America* (*House Document 357*, 59th Cong., 2d Sess.; Washington, 1909), V, 2666–70, and John H. Dougherty, *Constitutional History of the State of New York* (New York, 1915).

[65] Henry C. Adams, in his *Public Debts* (New York, 1887), brought this aspect of the subject into prominence; see also Horace Secrist, *An Economic Analysis of the Constitutional Restrictions upon Public Indebtedness in the United States* (University of Wisconsin *Bulletin*, No. 637; Madison, 1914).

ally responsible, to the amount of their respective shares, for the debts and liabilities. Ample security was to be required for redemption of all paper money in specie.

Important changes were made, also, with regard to land tenure. One of the reasons for calling the convention had been the " Antirent " agitation.[66] The tenants of the Van Rensselaer manorial land (consisting of the larger part of Albany and Rensselaer counties and a considerable portion of Columbia) held by lease, paying an annual rent of ten to fourteen bushels of wheat for each hundred acres. There were also feudal dues. Tenants who sold a perpetual lease were obliged to pay a quarter of the money to the owner of the manor, or if they did not hold in perpetuity they had to pay one year's extra rent. When, in 1839, the heirs of Stephen Van Rensselaer attempted to collect rents which were in arrears to the amount of some four hundred thousand dollars, and refused to sell lands to the tenants, riots occurred. Although troops were called out when the sheriffs were violently prevented from seizing the farms of these debtors, New York governors, whether Whig or Democratic, exhibited sympathy with the tenants.

Antirent associations urged that the state should take the lands by eminent domain and sell them to the occupants at a price to be fixed by a commission. After murders and riots, a report by Samuel J. Tilden [67] resulted in the passage of laws abolishing seizure for debt and so equalizing taxes that the landlord should pay a larger share. By the constitution of 1846, all lands within the state were declared alodial; the lease or grant of agricultural land, with reservation of rent or service, was forbidden, as were restraints on sale.

In contrast with the New York Constitutional Convention of 1846, that of Pennsylvania, of a decade earlier, had shown conservatism by retaining the appointive judiciary; it had also rejected the proposal of the Democrats that stockholders of a bank should be held individually responsible for its obligations, and had declared a charter to be a contract. Although the life of charters was limited to twenty years, with power of revocation and altera-

[66] E. P. Cheyney, *The Anti-Rent Agitation in the State of New York, 1839–1846* (University of Pennsylvania *Publications*, Political Economy and Public Law Ser., No. 2; Philadelphia, 1887), and McMaster, *United States*, VI, 519–23.

[67] The Democratic candidate for the Presidency in 1876.

tion vested in the legislature, there was a proviso " that no injustice be done thereby to the stockholders."

It is obvious that the demands of the Locofocos had compelled both the older parties to make important concessions to the voice of the lowly, and that an increase of popular political power had occurred.

While the Locofoco radicalism was gaining power and spreading to the North Central section with the pioneers, antislavery agitation was following the same path. Strongest in regions where New Englanders had settled in the Middle Atlantic section, and among the Pennsylvania Quakers, by 1840 the movement had become so influential that Thurlow Weed and his New York Whigs prevented the nomination, in that year, of Henry Clay, and the radical abolitionists, meeting in New York State, nominated James G. Birney for President. By their pivotal votes in the next national election, they may have defeated Clay. Again in 1848, the Free Soil convention told of the growing opposition to slavery. The moral fervor which had been exhibited in the Anti-Masonic movement and in the Locofoco agitation, was now embodied in this new crusade. Resentful Van Buren Democrats (stigmatized as " Barnburners " because of their supposed radicalism),[68] New England farmers in the western counties of New York (who had been the supporters of both the Anti-Masons and of the Whigs), and their relatives in the North Central States and in New England itself, made the strength of the movement.

The Free Soil party was composed of eastern and western wings, with New York as the bond of connection. It was appropriate that Buffalo was chosen for the meeting place of its convention. The whole zone stretching along the north and interior of New England to the Great Lakes and to the Mississippi, was the home of a society responsive to idealism and capable of political unity. New York showed its position as a complex region and a pivotal state. Many Whigs and Democrats of the Yankee stock, who were unwilling to leave their parties, had much sympathy with the program of the Free Soilers. With Greeley as their editorial prophet and Seward as their political spokesman, these New Yorkers became a storm center of the antislavery agitation. But

[68] Van Buren himself returned to the Democratic ranks in subsequent Presidential elections. See H. D. A. Donovan, *The Barnburners* (New York, 1925), p. 112.

New York City was, at the same time, a stronghold of those Northern Democrats who followed Marcy when he broke with Van Buren, and supported the Southern wing of the party.

Pennsylvania's politics,[69] in the years covered by this volume, were strongly affected by her geographical regions, her material interests, and by the moral outlook of the various elements in the composition of her population. At the beginning, the Anti-Masons were active here as in New York, and were strongest among the settlers of New England origin. Thaddeus Stevens, their ablest political leader, vainly attempted, for a time, to prevent them from merging with the Whigs. This native of Vermont, son of a shoemaker (he himself had learned that trade), lame and sickly from birth, had within him, nevertheless, a fiery spirit, will-power and an uncompromising nature, and the ability to present with clearness and force the ideals which he supported. The federal Congress — and, indeed, American history itself — were later to bear witness to the fierce determination of this legislator. Removing to Pennsylvania, he became a lawyer and was interested in the iron industry. In 1835 he made a successful fight in favor of free popular education, as against free education for the pauper classes only, which he characterized as " an act for branding and marking the poor." [70] The election in 1835 of Joseph Ritner, the Anti-Masonic candidate for governor of Pennsylvania, by a combination with the Whigs, marked the ending of the movement as an idealistic crusade.

The ferment of these years was evidenced by the coming of a political nativistic movement. Irishmen furnished the labor for digging the Erie Canal and the canals of Pennsylvania, and they tended to settle in the large cities. These vivacious newcomers, by their disregard for law and order, created apprehension in cities like New York and Philadelphia, as well as in Boston. To the native inhabitants, moreover, they were an object of special concern because of their religion. The Yankee, S. F. B. Morse, returned from Europe, in the early thirties, with the rumor of secret propaganda for overturning Protestantism and free government

---

[69] See: McMaster, *United States*, using indexes of volumes covering the period 1830–50; Mueller, *Whig Party in Pennsylvania;* Marguerite G. Bartlett, *The Chief Phases of Pennsylvania Politics in the Jacksonian Period* (Allentown, Pa., 1919) ; and McCarthy, *Antimasonic Party*.

[70] Woodburn, *Stevens*, Chap. IV.

in America by means of a Catholic organization which had its center in Austria.[71] As this was a period of reactionary alarm over the growth of democratic and revolutionary principles, and as Catholic Austria, especially, did not conceal its dislike of the American example, his *Foreign Conspiracy* found a receptive public. It fostered a movement of proscription, both in New England [72] and in the Middle Atlantic section.

The Irish immigrants — natural opponents of conservatism — had almost invariably joined the Democratic party. Therefore, like the Anti-Masons, the " Natives " merged with the newly formed Whig party. Nevertheless, Governor Seward, of New York, used his influence to bring about concessions to the Catholics in the matter of the division of funds, for schools, between them and the Protestant-controlled public schools.

In Pennsylvania a third-party movement, which rose to national importance, took form in 1842, beginning as a controversy over the demand of the Roman Catholic Bishop of Philadelphia that the use of the Protestant Bible should not be required in the public schools. Out of the agitation which followed this issue, came the Native American movement in Philadelphia. It was aimed both at the Catholics and the Irish. Riots resulted in the destruction of Catholic churches and in the loss of life. A Native American state convention was held, in 1845, which demanded that no foreigner should be naturalized until he had been in the country twenty-one years and which denounced a union of church and state. Naturally, this organization was drawn more from the Whigs than from the Democrats, because most of the Irish belonged to the latter party. By 1848 the Native Americans had suffered the fate of the Anti-Masons by becoming absorbed by the Whigs. Only after our period did nativism again come to life — in the " Know Nothing " movement.

When, after the interlude of fusion of Whigs and Anti-Masons, the Democrats regained power in Pennsylvania, it was a state Democratic party, with an individual flavor. It espoused the pro-

[71] *Samuel F. B. Morse: His Letters and Journals*, ed. E. L. Morse (Boston, 1914), II. The reports of the Leopold Foundation (a missionary organization which Morse thought particularly sinister) do not warrant the alarm. On the general movement, see Louis D. Scisco, *Political Nativism in New York State* (Columbia University *Studies in History, Economics and Public Law*, XIII, No. 2; New York, 1901).

[72] See Chapter III, *ante*.

tective tariff, which the national Democratic party opposed. The high tariff of 1842 was extremely popular in the state and received the support of Pennsylvania's Representatives and Senators, whether Democrats or Whigs, in Congress.

The history of the transportation system of the Middle Atlantic section had a determining influence on its regional politics and economics. Not only were both New York and Pennsylvania, at the beginning of our period, divided by their physical features into eastern and western halves, each of them influenced by their special interests, but there were also, within these two states, lesser regions whose inhabitants saw no advantage to themselves in the main lines of communication between east and west, but which in some cases found their natural outlets through other sections. South-central New York and northern Pennsylvania were regions that had much in common and raised special questions of transportation and politics.

On the completion of New York's canal system by 1827, the connection of the eastern and western parts of that state had been accomplished; but there remained, not only the problem of giving the counties adjacent to Lake Ontario access to the Erie Canal, but also that of furnishing transportation facilities to some of the southern counties of the state. For many of these counties, the natural trade outlet had been by boat down the headwaters of the Susquehanna River to Baltimore, thus giving to Maryland a portion of the commerce of the state. These southern counties were largely a rural region, with distinct affiliations with the contiguous " northern tier " of Pennsylvania counties, both in physical geography and in the New England sources of much of its population. The region had a grievance in the concentration of internal improvements upon main lines which were not serviceable to itself. In New York the Democrats had alienated the voters of the central counties by refusing to connect the Erie Canal with Pennsylvania's canal system by means of the Chenango Canal and Susquehanna River. " Whenever," said John A. Dix, in a letter to Van Buren, " a local project is started we are threatened with a dereliction of the region interested in it unless it is carried as a party measure." [73]

In the early forties, the development of railroad building by private corporations began to diminish the importance of canals.

[73] June 7, 1836 (Van Buren MSS, Library of Congress).

In 1842 the separate railroad corporations which were afterwards consolidated into the New York Central system had reached Buffalo, thus paralleling the Erie Canal and opening the Great Lakes Basin. A decade later, New York had all-rail connection with Buffalo. The construction of the Erie Railroad to Dunkirk on Lake Erie, by 1851, partly met the need of the southern counties, and in this enterprise the state of New York participated by a loan of over six million dollars and by other aids. Such legislation, it need hardly be said, was not secured without an effect upon the politics of New York. But it is to Pennsylvania that we must turn for the most striking indications of the relations between politics and internal improvements. It was clearly essential to the preservation of the economic unity of the state, to connect the cities of Philadelphia and Pittsburgh. By 1834 this led to the construction of a system of combined canals and railroads which opened transportation in the Keystone State between its eastern and western metropolises. The canal system, however, was supplemented by the Columbia Railroad, designed to divert trade to Philadelphia instead of allowing it to pass by water to Baltimore. There were also locks and railroads across the Alleghenies, from the basin of the Susquehanna to that of the Ohio. But the inclined planes and stationary engines on this portion of the route created so serious a handicap, as compared with the levels of the Mohawk Valley, that New York had a distinct advantage in reaching the West.

Even more than in the case of New York, transportation politics were complicated in Pennsylvania by the separate interests of diverse regions. These regions were not content to permit the construction of the east-and-west trunk line without concessions to the local interests which were not served by it.[74] The attempt to incorporate the Baltimore and Susquehanna Railroad Company, to connect Baltimore with a point in the Cumberland Valley, is an illustration. Violent and successful opposition to this was made in the Pennsylvania legislature, and one of the newspapers of the state dubbed it " An act to vest in the State of Maryland commercial jurisdiction over one-half the territory of Pennsylvania." [75]

[74] See the speech by David Wilmot, August 3, 1846, in the House of Representatives, quoted in C. B. Going, *David Wilmot, Free-Soiler* (New York, 1924), pp. 82–83.

[75] Quoted by McCarthy, *Antimasonic Party* (pp. 430–31), from the *Pennsylvania Reporter,* Jan. 30, 1829.

Mining counties in northeastern Pennsylvania presented demands on the legislature; southern counties asked turnpike appropriations; and western counties were divided as to whether the terminus of the main system should be at Lake Erie or tap the Ohio canal system. Here, as in New York, the Anti-Masons used these regional jealousies to embarrass the Democratic party. Ultimately, Pennsylvania undertook an overextended program, based upon the need of satisfying localities instead of pushing the trunk lines to completion. When this well-nigh sent the state into bankruptcy, private corporations took the place which the state had designed to occupy.

Railroad building in Pennsylvania started with the construction of roads to the coal fields by corporations interested in the mining districts. Private interests completed the Pennsylvania Railroad to Pittsburgh by 1852. So destructive was the competition of this corporation that, by 1854, the state's canals were sold to it.

Although the Middle Atlantic States, rich in political leaders, did not furnish such outstanding figures in educational reform as did New England, the movement for free public education was a marked feature of the section during this period. Labor organizations, stimulated by idealists who saw in the development of a free public-school system the hope of making actual the equality which American life had promised, pressed strongly, and with success, for educational changes.

By 1852 New York's expenditure for its public schools, exclusive of costs of construction, was nearly double that of 1835; but the percentage of enrollment increased slowly. In appropriations for libraries, New York led the way by its act of 1838, and it had the first state teachers' association (1845). In spite of the interest in the subject, Pennsylvania reported less than half the children of school age in attendance. Its first high school was not established until 1839. The Middle Atlantic States had a smaller proportion of white illiterates (native and foreign combined) [76] than the other sections, except New England. Pennsylvania had a better record than Massachusetts, and New York's illiteracy was but slightly greater than that of the latter.[77] The northwestern counties of New York ranked with the least illiterate states of New England.

[76] See map of White Illiteracy, 1850 (at end of volume).
[77] *Compendium of the Seventh Census*, p. 152.

In 1830 thirteen colleges were listed for the Middle Atlantic States, of which seven were in Pennsylvania, four in New York, and two in New Jersey. Eighty-one instructors cared for the nearly one thousand undergraduate students of the section. Union College, at Schenectady, New York, had the largest number of instructors, and of undergraduates, of any college in the section, and, counting volumes in student libraries as well as in the college library, had almost twice as many books available to the students as any other college of the Middle Atlantic States. It was fostered by the proceeds of a lottery in which its president had an interest, and it appealed to students by a liberal curriculum and by emphasis upon scientific instruction.

The opening of the University of the City of New York, in 1832, gave a stimulus to liberal education. Here S. F. B. Morse's telegraph was born, and John W. Draper's photography from life. Columbia, which had suffered a serious loss in attendance and was in a discouraging financial condition at the time, attempted to restore its position by introducing, in 1836, a " literary and scientific course " to afford training to architects, superintendents of manufacture, and those engaged in mercantile and nautical pursuits. This sounds ahead of the time and, perhaps for that reason, the course was dropped in 1843 for want of students. With only nine instructors in 1830 and but little over forty-five hundred volumes in her college and student libraries combined, and with only one hundred and forty undergraduates, Columbia gave but slight promise of the huge university of today, with over thirty thousand students in all its activities.

At Troy, New York, the Rensselaer Institute broke away from the old classical education and laid stress upon engineering studies. Here, also, Emma C. Willard, in the Troy Female Seminary, was opening a new era in education.

In New Jersey, Rutgers College and the College of New Jersey (Princeton) had about the same number of undergraduates in 1830. Mathematics and theology were stressed at Princeton, where Scotch-Irish Presbyterianism was intrenched; but in 1832 the coming of Joseph Henry, the physicist, at a salary of one thousand dollars, gave an impetus to scientific research. His work, there and at the Smithsonian Institution, was influential both in the later rise of the telegraph and the foreshadowing of the radio.

It is somewhat surprising to find that the greatest number of undergraduates (116) in Pennsylvania was at Jefferson College, in Canonsburg, and that Allegheny College, at Meadville, in the northwestern part of the state, had a large library (8,000 volumes), the quality of which had called forth the admiration of Jefferson. The University of Pennsylvania had only five instructors, and less than a hundred students in its undergraduate courses, in 1830, and, in 1850, only seven instructors and eighty-eight students; but there were more than five hundred students in its Medical Department, the largest in the country.

By 1850 there were, in all, some forty-four colleges in the Middle Atlantic States, with over three hundred and fifty teachers and in excess of sixty-five hundred students. This section was, therefore, proportionately equal, in number of students, to New England, though the number of teachers was relatively less.[78] Pennsylvania led in both number of colleges and enrollment of students, as well as in annual income.

Of course, comparisons are difficult when the statistics were furnished by institutions of such varying standards; and it must be remembered that, in many respects, the " colleges " of that day were little more than seminaries and high schools. On the other hand, in these little colleges professors of commanding natural ability and of high rank in the scholarship of the period were exerting a fruitful influence upon the young men who were about to become leaders in the nation.[79]

In the manner of dealing with the criminal, the Middle Atlantic States furnished rival prison systems that contended for adoption in other sections and were studied by European travelers like Alexis de Tocqueville. The Auburn system in New York provided for silent labor by the prisoners in association during the day and for solitary confinement at night. In contrast, the Pennsylvania system required solitary confinement both day and night, on the theory that repentance would follow the medi-

[78] See pp. 44, 83, 93, *ante*.

[79] Educational statistics for colleges of the Middle Atlantic States have been drawn from *The American Almanac* (Boston), 1832 and 1851; American Educational Society *Quarterly Register*, 1830 and 1850; and *Compendium of the Seventh Census*. The standard histories of the leading universities, and H. B. Adams (ed.), *Contributions to American Educational History* (U.S. Bureau of Education *Circulars of Information*), have been consulted.

tation of the isolated prisoner when his mind was concentrated on his sins.[80]

No other section was so noted for the ability and influence of its daily newspapers as the Middle Atlantic, and it was in this period that they took a new form. Increased attention was given to commercial and financial news; the money market and the rise and fall of stocks were reported in detail. The interest in the sensational news of the police courts contrasted with the older emphasis upon political and literary topics and marked the beginning of the modern newspaper era. A wider constituency was secured, in part by catering to the interests and emotions of the masses and in part by so cheapening the cost of the press that the common people could be reached. In New York City the first penny newspaper was the *Sun*, established in 1833. The *Herald*, founded by James Gordon Bennett in 1835, started, also, as a penny paper. In the following year three printers who had worked on the *Sun* brought out the first number of the *Public Ledger* in Philadelphia. This penny paper became a leader in the attack upon the United States Bank.

Perhaps at no time was the influence of the press on the politics and thought of the people greater in the United States than in the years we are considering. Every section had its noted editors; but in none was there such a distinguished group as in New York. Edwin Croswell was editor of the *Albany Argus*, the organ of the Albany ring. In 1834 Mordecai M. Noah, a Jew, associated with earlier newspaper enterprises in New York City, established the *New York Evening Star* as a Whig organ. In this and his other newspaper ventures, Noah exhibited intellectual edge and the quality of a free lance, which made him a prominent figure. The *Courier and Enquirer*, edited by James Watson Webb, came to support the Bank of the United States, and Webb borrowed such sums from it that the relationship was practically that of a subsidy. Horace Greeley (whose characteristics have been sketched in connection with New York politics) founded the *Tribune*, in 1841, in association with Henry J. Raymond, who ten years later

[80] For a detailed English survey of the penitentiaries and the criminal laws of the various states, see the *Report* (Aug. 1, 1834) of William Crawford to the Home Department, *Parliamentary Papers*. See also Edward Channing, *A History of the United States*, V (New York, 1921), 184–94, 201–3, with citations.

established the *New York Times*, the most influential Democratic organ of the city. Raymond was a pioneer in the emphasis upon the ideal of speedy presentation of the news. In 1843 he reported a speech of Webster in Boston, had it put into type on his way to New York City, aboard ship, and astonished the citizens by enabling them to read Webster's words at six o'clock the next morning.

A new note in American journalism was struck by Bennett when he said:

It is my passion, my delight, my thought by day and my dream by night to conduct the *Herald* and to show the world and posterity that the newspaper can be made the greatest, the most fascinating, the most powerful organ, of civilization that genius ever yet dreamed of. The dull, ignorant, miserable, barbarian papers around me are incapable of arousing the sensibilities or pointing out fresh paths for the intellectual career of an energetic generation.

At the outset, he had disclaimed all principles, all party, all politics, and asserted that his effort was to record facts, " stripped of verbiage and color, with comments when suitable, just, intelligent, fearless, and good tempered." He emphasized the value of brevity, variety, point, piquancy, and cheapness, and made his appeal to the great masses of the community. In the initial number of the *Herald* (1835), he made the interesting statement that only forty-two thousand daily sheets were printed to supply one hundred and fifty thousand people who read newspapers in New York City. He reported the proceedings of religious organizations and did not hesitate to attack the various denominations. He loved to shock his public with full reports of scandals, without respect for the privacy of life, and when he was assaulted he gave a full account of the incident under the caption, " Bennett Thrashed Again." At a time in which vituperation was a characteristic of the press, he more than held his own. " A peddler in thought and feelings," he called himself. He sent correspondents to the capitals of the world and, taking advantage of steam navigation, extended his foreign-news service. The " News Slips " which he sent to the country newspapers were precursors of the service rendered by the later Associated Press. They anticipated, also, the organizations which supply copy to .affect public opinion in the outlying districts of the Union.

In all this, Bennett represented the tendency of the era of Jacksonian Democracy. The speeding-up process, the vulgarization, the catering to the people by producing a newspaper at a price they could pay and distributing it upon the streets, the emphasis upon news rather than upon heavy leading editorials, the appeal to the ordinary man and to the love of " hustle," the use of the crisp paragraph straight to the point, the opening of doors, the substitution of direct information from the Old World for clippings from the English press — these were characteristic contributions of Bennett to American journalism, working in the spirit of the times and leading the way to the " yellow journalism " of a later period.[81]

Philadelphia, also, had its important editors, but none who could compare in influence with those of New York City. It was rather in Washington that the center of editorial influence for the neighboring states was found.

Writing at the close of the twenties, James Fenimore Cooper, the New York novelist, noted [82] that there was no one literary capital and that the habits of polite life, and even the pronunciation of the people, of Boston, New York, Baltimore, and Philadelphia, varied in many ways. He thought that a practiced ear could distinguish a native of any one of those places. He believed, however, that if there were to be a literary capital it would rest in New York City. In fact, at the beginning of our period the Middle Atlantic States were probably the leading section in literature. Philadelphia's prominence was based rather on periodical publication than on the production of authors of importance. In New York City Washington Irving had won his reputation early in the century and had produced some of his best writings in the twenties; but they were strongly influenced by the English style. After his sojourn as minister in Spain, his *Life of Columbus* (1828), *Granada* (1829), and *Alhambra* (1832) both reflected and produced an American interest in Spanish literature. Not until his return to New York, after an absence of seventeen years in Europe, did his pen find native material, in the history of the expeditions associated with the name of John Jacob Astor. His *Tour on the Prairies* (1835), his *Astoria* (1836),

[81] See Wm. A. Croffut, " Bennett and His Times," *Atlantic Monthly*, CXLVII, 196 ff.
[82] *Notions of the Americans*, II, 125.

and his *Bonneville* (1837) fed the interest of Americans in what was distinctive in their own country in contrast with Europe. In the decade following our period his *Life of Washington* appeared.

Cooper, who had lived as a boy under the pioneer conditions of the Otsego Lake region of New York, also turned to the frontier, and became the distinctive painter of its life in fiction. Out of his personal experience he had, prior to 1830, written a series of novels depicting life on the New York colonial frontier,[83] and on the ocean (on which he had sailed in his youth). Although he had grown up at the edge of the wilderness and had been stimulated by the opportunities offered for a new literary type, he was the son of a wealthy and aristocratic land speculator (William Cooper), who had been a gentleman promoter of backwoods settlement rather than a member of that kind of society.[84] Cooper's Indians and frontiersmen were idealized heroes, affected by the romanticism expressed in the novels of Walter Scott.

Like Irving, he spent his middle life in Europe, where he wrote a laudatory exposition of American society, under the title of *Notions of the Americans* (1828). But, when he returned to this country to be confronted with the changed America of Jacksonian Democracy, his critical *Letters to His Countrymen*, *Homeward Bound*, and *Home as Found* expressed disappointment over the actual conditions. Although this sojourn in Europe had made him a man of the world, on whom the new America grated, nevertheless, in the forties, he returned to his theme of the forest, in his novels *The Pathfinder* and *The Deerslayer*. Visiting southern Michigan in 1847, he portrayed in his *Oak Openings* the pioneer life of that portion of the Middle West, into which he brought some of the characters who had figured in his earlier novels. His death in 1851 coincided with the end of a notable period in New York literature. Along with the poetry of William Cullen Bryant, his works illustrate the transition from a dominant interest in European literature to an interest in what was distinctively American.

As in other regions, the Revolution and its heroes became a

---

[83] Including the famous *The Last of the Mohicans* (1826).

[84] See William Cooper, *A Guide in the Wilderness* (Dublin, 1810), and his speeches in the federal House of Representatives. James Fenimore Cooper's reactions in this period are illustrated by his *Correspondence,* edited by his grandson, James Fenimore Cooper (New Haven, 1922).

favorite theme for New York authors. James K. Paulding's *The Dutchman's Fireside* (1831) was one of the best novels based upon this subject.[85]

The deep interest of the Middle Atlantic section in business and politics, during these years, and its position as a center of influence, were shown by the publication of such periodicals as *Hunt's Merchants' Magazine* (1839–70), the *American Whig Review* (1845–52), and the *Democratic Review* (1838–59). In New York were published some of the most influential of the agricultural newspapers and periodicals of the time. Advocating more-scientific farming, they had a wide circulation not only in their own state but in the West.

The *American Quarterly Review* (1827–37) had a following among those fond of ponderous articles, while such family magazines as *Godey's Lady's Book* (1830–98), with its colored fashion plates and its poetry and fiction chiefly of the sentimental type, had a wide circulation. This periodical and *Graham's Magazine* (1841–58) were advertised by booksellers in frontier towns of the West of that day, and letters from country homes in those regions often contained orders for them. In New York the *Knickerbocker* (1833–65) had a high reputation.[86] In general, the magazines of the Middle Atlantic States paid better rates to authors than did those of New England, and for that reason, perhaps, sometimes obtained contributions of scholars and litterateurs of the latter section.[87]

In all of the states of the Middle Atlantic group, the Methodists had, by 1850, the largest number of churches. Except for New York, the Presbyterians stood second in strength, due in large measure to the many Scotch-Irish. In New York the Baptists ranked second but the Presbyterians had almost as many churches and about three times the number of those of the Congregationalists. This was due to the fact that, even in the areas of the state which had been settled by New Englanders, Pres-

[85] *The Cambridge History of American Literature* (New York), I (1917) and II (1918), furnishes excellent accounts and interpretations of American literature during this period, as well as exhaustive bibliographies.

[86] The *New York Mirror* also had a long and influential career.

[87] For a more detailed survey of the periodicals, see Frank Luther Mott, *A History of American Magazines, 1741–1850* (New York, 1930), Chaps. VI, VII (which deal particularly with New England and Middle Atlantic publications).

byterianism had proved better suited to Western conditions. Under agreements for united action between the Presbyterians and the Congregationalists, the former had gradually superseded the distinctive New England sect. In this fact lies one of the means of measuring the differences between the migrated Yankee stock in New York and the New England people at home. The Dutch Reformed denomination exceeded in numbers both the Episcopalians and the Congregationalists in the state of New York. It was in this state, also (particularly in the region settled by New Englanders), that politics, as we have seen, reflected the emotionalism of new sects and new " revelations." [88]

Thus, the Middle Atlantic group — a varied storehouse of natural wealth in soil, mines, and ports, and abounding in easy routes to all the other parts of the nation — held within itself so many of the elements which were characteristic features of other sections that it became typical of the deep-seated tendencies of America in general. It was based solidly on things; but a process of cross-fertilization of differing societies reflecting differing nationalities and native stocks, of institutions and ideas, went on, and was carried into other states by migration. To the section's representative position in the life of the Union, the important exception is, of course, the absence in the Middle Atlantic States of the institution of slavery. But, even in the slaveholding sections, there were vestiges of early Pennsylvania influence, due to the large portion of the backcountrymen in the south who, as Scotch-Irish, Irish, Welsh, or German colonists, had come from Pennsylvania and whose descendants still had relatives, correspondents, and church connections there.

[88] See pp. 118–19, *ante*.

CHAPTER V

THE SOUTH ATLANTIC STATES

So pre-eminently has the South stood as the exponent of sectionalism in American history that writers have found difficulty in thinking of it except as the " solid South." Its later devotion to the doctrines of state sovereignty and secession, and above all the presence of the negro, and the system of slavery which extended, although unevenly and disconnectedly, throughout its whole area, give plausibility to this conception. But it was not the unchanging and uniform section which has often been assumed. Variety, regional differences, and transformations in the internal life of the South, were at least as marked in these years as in any other part of the United States.

Geographically viewed, the " South," in present usage, is composed of the larger portion of the Atlantic Plains, the Piedmont Plateau, the Blue Grass basins, the Mississippi alluvial land (embayment), the portion of the Appalachian Valley and of the Appalachian Plateau south of Pennsylvania, and the Gulf Plains or southern half of the Central Lowlands. These facts of physical geography in themselves indicate a land far from uniform, and certain to reflect the differences based on natural conditions.[1]

In the factor of climate, also, " the South " includes the various zones between the latitude of Philadelphia and the southern extremity of Florida — zones that range from a characteristically

[1] On the physiography of this section, see A. K. Lobeck, *Physiographic Diagram of the United States* (Madison, Wis., 1922), and Hugh H. Bennett, *The Soils and Agriculture of the Southern States* (New York, 1921). The latter author supplied an excellent map of the soil regions of the Cotton Belt, in the *Atlas of American Agriculture,* Pt. v, Sec. A, " Cotton " (U.S. Dept. of Agriculture; Washington, 1918), p. 8. See also A. E. Parkins, " The Antebellum South: A Geographer's Interpretation," Association of American Geographers *Annals,* XXI, 1–33 (this paper refers to both the South Atlantic and South Central sections). On Virginia, there is a thesis (with map) by G. T. Surface, *Studies on the Geography of Virginia* ([Philadelphia] 1907).

northern climate to a semitropical one. The Appalachians constitute a wedge that carries conditions of climate and life similar to those in Pennsylvania, down to the northern boundary of the Lower South, and — what is equally important — interposes a mountainous wall between the eastern and western divisions. Both military history and the development of manufacture and capitalism were profoundly influenced by this mountain lancehead of industrial society pushing into the South. Both in the period of this survey [2] and more recently, this has had important influence on party geography.

A tier of border states parallels the southern boundary of Pennsylvania and the Ohio River, and includes Delaware, Maryland, the western counties of Virginia, Kentucky, and parts of Tennessee, together with Missouri, beyond the Mississippi. This unstable northern frontier of the South found kindred conditions and people in the Appalachian extension already mentioned. The states around the Delaware and Chesapeake bays were a transitional zone, in themselves intimately connected by river systems and commercial ties with Pennsylvania and the Ohio Valley. Between the Chesapeake and the port of Charleston, the Atlantic coast and its backcountry lacked effective harbor facilities. The Cotton Belt, extending from South Carolina across the Mississippi, in the zone now ordinarily called the " Lower South," came to have, both in the proportion of slaves and in the importance of the great staple, a unity of its own.

Early in the thirties, there was a marked antagonism between the interior and the seaboard South. Even within the South Atlantic States, which fronted the coast, the group of interior counties, or upland South, situated west of the fall line, was in many respects an extension from Pennsylvania, with strong Scotch-Irish and German elements — a land controlled (particularly on its western borders) by a relatively nonslaveholding, pioneer society; while the lowland, tidewater South was made up of slaveholding planters, descendants of seventeenth-century English stock, reinforced in South Carolina by a French Huguenot element. In origins, in economic and social conditions, even in religious affiliations, lowland and upland constituted two contrasting peoples; and in the upland areas there was, around 1830, much hostility to the continuation of the slavery system.

[2] See maps at the close of the volume.

Between 1830 and 1850 the lowland came to dominate the up-country counties, and also gave birth to new slaveholding societies in the Gulf Basin, whose interest reached out toward the promising cotton lands of Texas. The spread of the cotton plant and slaveholding planters into the new Southwest was as natural as was the extension of the upland stock into the less fertile counties north of the Ohio and into the less favored portions of the Gulf Basin. The creation of a Greater South gradually went on in these decades, contemporaneously with the creation of a Greater New England.

By the end of the period, there were clear indications of the formation of Southern unity in spite of these differences and of the particularism based on the doctrine of state sovereignty. This result is one of the evidences in history of the power of migration, and of leadership when exerted in behalf of a dominant domestic interest. Slaveholding proved to be more effective in drawing the South together than were the physical and party factors in keeping it apart. Through practically all the years treated in this volume, political parties reflected the regional differences, and their Southern wings kept in touch with the Northern; but by 1850 the ties of party, and even of churches which had national organizations, were snapping, and the South was becoming a single separatist section.

In our own time, the Census Bureau divides the Southern States into South Atlantic and South Central divisions, bounded, roughly, by the line of the Alleghenies. As I have shown in Chapter II, on the United States in 1830, the distinction is historically fundamental. I shall accordingly consider these sections in separate chapters. Naturally, the common institution of slavery, the extension of cotton planting, and the migration of people, made a community of interest between the two; but it was only as time went on that this bond became close.

Each of the commonwealths in all of the vast region now called " the South " had its own traits, compounded of the origins of its people and of their experiences in the different environments. Each was so varied in detail that we must often hesitate in characterization and must recall that what is distinctive and peculiar — the flavor — in a state is often dwelt on, not so much because it represents the general traits of the commonwealth as a whole, as because it is the uncommon feature which differentiates the state from its sisters.

Turning to consider the South Atlantic Division, we may recall the society of historic Virginia as the American version of the English country gentry, and South Carolina as the offspring of a West Indian planting society, reinforced by the incisive intellects of French Huguenots and Scotch-Irishmen — self-centered, haughty, and fiery-tempered, the Hotspur of the states. " Between these two mountain peaks of pride," as an after-dinner speaker put it, lay the " valley of humiliation," the then democratic and backward North Carolina. Georgia was deeply influenced by its history as a frontier outpost, based solidly on things, Western in its practical action, less responsive to ideals, a commonwealth with an Indian question and a frontier — as much Western as Southern. During most of the period, Florida was still a frontier, the scene of Indian wars and of survivals of the Spanish régime.[3]

In 1830 the South Atlantic States had not much over three and a half million souls. By 1850 they had over four and a half million; but this was not greatly in excess of the population of the young South Central States, which were the offspring of these older states of the South Atlantic. A movement of people was obviously under way which was likely to transfer the power of population and politics to the interior.

When this survey begins, the South Atlantic States were in a period of depression. Not only were they contributing great numbers of their people to a migration which passed both to the Northwest and to the Southwest, across or around the mountains, seeking more-fertile soils, cheaper lands, and better transportation facilities, but in many cases they were also retreating before the advance of slavery and were suffering from economic pressure. Tobacco cultivation and wheat growing were feeling the competition of the interior, soils were becoming exhausted, and the price of lands was falling.

Between 1830 and 1840, there was in the South Atlantic States

[3] In the Huntington Library is a manuscript journal, with an accompanying scrapbook of letters home, by Lt. H. W. Merrill, U.S.A., with accounts and drawings of army life among the Florida Indians, 1838–40. See also Caroline M. Brevard, *A History of Florida from the Treaty of 1763 to Our Own Times*, I (Deland, Fla., 1924), Chaps. I-XVI.

an increase of only somewhat more than 200,000 whites and 68,000 negroes, while in the South Central States the white increase was well over 500,000 and the negro increase not far behind that number.

This tells its own story. The seaboard states were losing their population to the Mississippi Valley and the Gulf Basin, and the loss of slaves was numerically greater than the loss of whites. In other words, the strength of slavery was being transferred to the interior. An outlet had been found for the slaves, who had become unprofitable in large portions of the older South. Between 1830 and 1850 the South Atlantic States increased their population by only a million, while the South Central States added two and one-quarter millions to theirs.

The relative loss of population rank was more noteworthy between 1830 and 1840 than between 1840 and 1850. In the former period, Virginia (including West Virginia) increased its white population less than 7 per cent; North Carolina, 2.5 per cent; and South Carolina, .5 per cent. In Georgia, on the other hand, where there were newly opening Indian lands, the increase was nearly 37.5 per cent. For the other states of the section, the percentages represent substantially a stationary condition. By 1850 about a third of the white and free colored natives of Virginia and of North Carolina were living in other states, and of South Carolina, about 40 per cent.[4] J. D. B. De Bow concluded that, according to the census of 1850, " more than one quarter of the free persons born in the Southern States [in which term he includes only Virginia, North Carolina, South Carolina, Georgia, and Florida] have left those States for other sections."

This migration on a large scale, to other sections, started earlier than in New England, and the lure of the wilderness peculiarly appealed to the Southern backwoodsman of the hunter type. When a surplus began to appear in the farming country of the Piedmont, the inability to ship to a market because of obstructions in the rivers, and the restricted demand, made added inducements to cross the mountains to the " Western Waters," where the produce could float down the Mississippi to New Orleans.

The South Atlantic States had contributed in this manner to Kentucky and Tennessee and also to the pioneer population of

---

[4] J. D. B. De Bow, *Statistical View of the United States . . . being a Compendium of the Seventh* [1850] *Census* (Washington, 1854), pp. 114, 115.

most of the southern counties of the states north of the Ohio. Following the War of 1812, South Atlantic settlers had reinforced the migration from Kentucky and Tennessee into the newly opened states adjacent to the Gulf.[5]

The Greater South occupied a more extensive area than Greater New England.[6] Numerically, the nonslaveholding white population vastly exceeded the planters in this exodus. But, by the thirties, the exhaustion of the soil in the South Atlantic States had gone so far that many of the planter class, with their slaves, likewise moved in great numbers to the cheap and fertile lands beyond the mountains.

There was a marked tendency for small plantations to become smaller and for the larger plantations to absorb them and to spread to new regions.[7] Whereas the wealthy Northerner turned his capital into commerce, transportation, manufacturing, and banking, or into speculative purchases of lands or stocks, the Southern capitalist, as a rule, used his to expand his plantation and to buy more slaves. As the lands of the pioneer farmers were sought for cotton cultivation in some of the counties of interior North Carolina and through the whole Piedmont of South Carolina and Georgia, these farmers, as a rule, felt it more profitable and more congenial to repeat on a new frontier the type of life to which they were accustomed. Lacking capital, moreover, the pioneer was usually unable to become a cotton planter, even had he so inclined.

It was this process which, in the course of the twenties and thirties, extended the Black Belt, where the negro was in a majority, into the Piedmont and at the same time accentuated the movement of migration. The old state of Virginia, whose people in 1840 numbered more than twice those of Alabama, was unable, in the following decade, to surpass the gain in population achieved by the latter in that period. The South Carolinian, J. H. Hammond, estimated that, between 1830 and 1850, an annual average

[5] F. J. Turner, *Rise of the New West, 1819–1829* (*The American Nation: A History*, XIV; New York, 1906), Chaps. v, vi.

[6] See map of Interstate Migration (at end of volume).

[7] I am much indebted to Professor U. B. Phillips' *American Negro Slavery* (New York, 1918) and to his paper on " The Origin and Growth of the Southern Black Belts," *American Historical Review*, XI, 798–816. This chapter was written, however, before the appearance of his illuminating book, *Life and Labor in the Old South* (Boston, 1929). That work is useful for both the South Atlantic and South Central sections.

of $500,000 capital and 83,000 slaves left South Carolina under the temptations of the more productive soils of the West.[8]

Lowland Virginia had been in distress ever since the War of 1812. " In a few years more," wrote John Randolph in 1813, " those of us who are alive will have to move off to *Kaintuck*, or the *Mississippi*, where corn can be had for sixpence a bushel, and pork for a penny a pound. I do not wonder at this rage for emigration. What do the bulk of the people get here, that they cannot have for one-fifth of the labor in the western country? "[9] Similarly, there came lamentations from North Carolina over the loss of her citizens by migration. In the upland counties of both states, an agitation began for internal improvements, better transportation conditions, extension of the suffrage, and a more adequate representation in the legislature — even for the gradual abolition of slavery.

Senator Robert Y. Hayne, of South Carolina, drew a gloomy picture of his state, in a speech in the Senate at the beginning of 1832:

. . . the condition of the South is not merely one of unexampled depression, but of great and all-pervading distress. . . . If we look at the present condition of our cities, (and I will take Charleston by way of example,) we find every where the mournful evidence of premature decay. . . . Sir, it is within my own experience, that, in the devoted city in which my lot has been cast, a thriving foreign commerce was, within a few years past, carried on direct to Europe. We had native merchants, with large capitals, engaged in the foreign trade. We had thirty or forty ships, many of them built, and all owned, in Charleston, and giving employment to a numerous and valuable body of mechanics and tradesmen. Look at the state of things now! Our merchants bankrupt or driven away — their capital sunk or transferred to other pursuits — our shipyards broken up — our ships all sold! . . . our mechanics in despair; the very grass growing in our streets, and houses falling into ruins; real estate reduced to one-third part of its value, and rents almost to nothing. . . . If we fly from the city to the country, what do we there behold? Fields abandoned; the hospitable mansions of our fathers deserted; agriculture drooping; our slaves, like their masters, working harder, and faring worse. . . . It has often been my lot, sir, to see the once thriving planter reduced to despair, cursing his hard fate, gathering up the small remnants of his broken for-

[8] Chauncey S. Boucher, " The Ante-bellum Attitude of South Carolina towards Manufacturing and Agriculture " (Washington University *Studies*, III, Pt. II, No. 2, pp. 243-70; St. Louis, Apr., 1916).

[9] Hugh A. Garland, *Life of John Randolph* (New York [copyright, 1850]), II, 15.

tune, and, with his wife and his little ones, tearing himself from the scenes of his childhood, and the bones of his ancestors, to seek, in the wilderness, that reward for his industry, of which your fatal policy has deprived him.[10]

Hayne's explanation of this decay was the protective tariff, but E. S. Thomas, of Charleston, a newspaper editor, attributed it to the introduction of steam navigation, whereby the produce of the interior was no longer brought to Charleston by wagon but found an outlet on the Savannah in the region of Augusta. When hauled to Charleston it was carried off by traders from other states.[11] Changes in the routes of ocean commerce, effected by new navigation devices, had for a generation been at work to divert shipping from Charleston, as "a half-way house," to the port of New York.[12]

More fundamental, however, was the competition of the abundant and cheaper cotton soils in the newly settled states. In Georgia the decline was postponed by the possession of a backcountry of its own, but by 1850 many of the richer counties, there, were "worn out, leaving a desolate picture for the traveler to behold. Decaying tenements, red old hills stripped of their native growth and virgin soil, and washed into deep gullies, with here and there patches of Bermuda grass, and stunted pine shrubs, struggling for a scanty subsistence on what was once one of the richest soils in America." [13]

To the critics who attributed a part of this decline to slavery itself, the Virginia economist, Professor Thomas R. Dew, replied by the argument that slavery was an essential condition of Southern agriculture, and that the planter who was forced to sell his slaves, nevertheless received a higher price because of the Western demand; the real hardship came, he pointed out, in the loss of the white population, and particularly the young adults whose rearing had been a charge upon the community and who, when they left, took with them this capital accumulated in their own persons.

[10] *Register of Debates in Congress*, VIII, Pt. 1, 80–81.

[11] E. S. Thomas, *Reminiscences of the Last Sixty-five Years, Commencing with the Battle of Lexington. Also, Sketches of His Own Life and Times* (Hartford, Conn., 1840), II, 226 ff.

[12] Lt. M. F. Maury, in J. D. B. De Bow, *The Industrial Resources, etc., of the Southern and Western States*, III (New Orleans, 1853), 2–3.

[13] De Bow, *op. cit.*, I (New Orleans, 1852), 363, and R. P. Brooks, *The Agrarian Revolution in Georgia, 1865–1912* (University of Wisconsin *Bulletin*, No. 639; Madison, 1914), pp. 84–85.

In all this, there are striking similarities, as well as contrasts, to the loss which we have described for New England. There were objections to migration from South Carolina, as from Connecticut. A Southern periodical warned that

The West is without doubt the place for wealth, but prosperity is a trial to character. In the West money is everything. Its pursuit, accompanied as it is by baneful speculation, lawlessness, gambling, sabbath-breaking, brawls and violence, prevents moral attainment and mental cultivation. Substantial people should stay in South Carolina to preserve their pristine purity, hospitality, freedom of thought, fearlessness and nobility.[14]

But New England believed that, in immigration and in the development of industrialism (especially manufacture), she had found compensation for the decline of her rural population. Both of these offsets were largely absent in the South. Agriculture was the main industry of the section. The institution of slavery and the raising of staples for export were the controlling factors in its economic life and politics. The slave interest was concentrated geographically, as we shall see, and also in the proportion of slave owners who were large planters.

In 1850, in the South Atlantic States, the Black Belt (where negroes exceeded the whites in number) embraced the following regions: the counties along the lower Potomac in Maryland; the eastern half of Virginia, including parts of the Shenandoah Valley; the adjacent counties of North Carolina in its northeastern corner, about Albemarle and Pamlico sounds; the entire state of South Carolina, except for the mountainous counties in the northwest and the infertile ones along the northeastern border; and the conterminous counties of central Georgia, which crossed the state in a wedge-like formation, together with her tidewater counties.[15]

The historian, James Ford Rhodes, declared [16] that slavery

[14] *Southern Literary Journal*, II, 259–62 (June, 1836), quoted in Phillips, *American Negro Slavery*, p. 184. Cf. pp. 52–53, *ante*.

[15] See map of Interstate Migration (at end of volume). Also see Phillips, in *American Historical Review*, XI, 810. Outlying isolated counties, shown in the map but not enumerated above, have geographical and political importance. *Compendium of the Seventh Census* and *Negroes in the United States* (Bulletin 8, Bureau of the Census, Dept. of Commerce and Labor; Washington, 1904) have been used as the sources of my tabulations.

[16] *History of the United States from the Compromise of 1850*, I (New York, 1893), 346.

existed for the small portion of the people of the slaveholding states which consisted of the eight thousand planters who owned over fifty slaves apiece, and the professional classes associated with it. Logically, this would lead to the conclusion that the institution of private property in the United States rests on the interest of only the most prosperous, who control the larger portion of the property but constitute only a very small percentage of the population.[17] The great slaveholders of the South represented the concentration of wealth in slaves on a scale comparable with the present concentration of holdings of private property, generally, in the United States. " The negro-slave plantation system created and maintained a huge special vested interest." [18] But the small slaveholders, and even the nonslaveholding poor whites in the slaveholding regions, were often more aggressive champions of the institution than were the wealthier and more timid holders of this kind of property. In the regions where slavery flourished, there was a society which depended upon the institution, and this society was dominant throughout the South.

There were in 1830, in the South Atlantic States, about 2,100,000 whites and 1,500,000 negroes. By 1850 there were about 2,800,000 whites and less than 1,900,000 negroes. This indicates the migration of slaves to the Southwestern states. The surplus of Virginia slaves, for example, was sent into the Cotton Belt, and the Old Dominion found this a resource in her declining prosperity.[19]

The ratio of whites and blacks, during the period, underwent few changes in this section. In Virginia and North Carolina, both in 1830 and 1850, not far from two-thirds of the population were whites. Georgia remained well over half white in each census year, while in South Carolina the negroes outnumbered the whites both in 1830 and 1850. In Maryland, a border state, the whites constituted two-thirds of the population in 1830 and almost three-

[17] It has been estimated that the wealthiest two per cent of the total population, in 1910, possessed three-fifths of the property in the United States. Even on the basis of income, the most prosperous one-fifth had nearly half of the national income in 1920. See the discussions in W. I. King, *The Wealth and Income of the People of the United States* (New York, 1915), p. 82, and W. C. Mitchell [and others (staff of National Bureau of Economic Research)], *Income in the United States* (New York), I (1921), 147, II (1922), 334.

[18] U. B. Phillips, in *Essays in American History Dedicated to Frederick Jackson Turner* (New York, 1910), p. 204.

[19] Frederic Bancroft, *Slave-trading in the Old South* (Baltimore, 1931), pp. 88–91, 117–19, 384–86, *et passim*.

fourths in 1850. Nearly one-third of the white families of Virginia in 1850 were slaveholders, and one-tenth of these were " large planters " (holding twenty or more slaves apiece). In North Carolina one-fourth were slaveholders and about the same proportion of the slaveholders as in Virginia were large planters. In South Carolina nearly one-half of the white families were slaveholders, and about half the planters of the Union who owned two hundred or more slaves each were in this single state. Two of them owned a thousand or more each. In Georgia over one-third of the families held slaves, and of these slightly under one-sixth were large planters. In Maryland the slaveholding interest was comparatively slight in numbers but not without large influence.[20]

Thus, it is clear that slavery had a geographical distribution and that it affected social stratification. These facts were significant in the political history of the period of this book. Editors and statesmen were aware of this complexity and of the transformations within the Old South. They, at least, realized that there was not a " solid South," nor an unchanging section.

The South Atlantic States contained no large cities south of the border city of Baltimore, which by 1850 had approximately 170,000 people. Washington, in the District of Columbia, had risen to 40,000; Charleston, South Carolina, with less than 43,000, was the most populous of the cities of the section, below the border zone; and Richmond, Virginia, had less than 28,000. For the rest, the census of 1850 gave Wilmington, in Delaware, Petersburg and Norfolk, in Virginia, and Savannah and Augusta, in Georgia, between twelve and fifteen thousand each, while Raleigh, North Carolina, and Columbia, South Carolina, had but five or six thousand. In several of these cities the negroes were almost as numerous as the whites.

The South Atlantic States were noteworthy in the small number of foreign-born. Maryland had the most considerable alien element — over 50,000 in 1850, or about eleven per cent of foreign-born to total white and free colored in that state. Virginia had nearly 23,000, but this was only about two and one-half per cent of her white and free colored population. Roughly speaking, there were about 106,000 foreign-born in the South Atlantic Di-

[20] Based on *Compendium of the Seventh Census* and *Negroes in the United States.*

vision in 1850 — less than those in the individual states of Illinois or Wisconsin and far less than those in Massachusetts.

Out of some half million white families in the South Atlantic States in 1850, only one-third owned slaves, and of these slaveholders about one-sixth held but one slave each. Of those who possessed between ten and twenty slaves, constituting nearly one-sixth of the slave owners of the section, nine-tenths lived south of Maryland. It is plain, therefore, that, in any consideration of the Southern population, this overwhelming preponderance of nonslaveholding whites must be fully recognized.

At the bottom of the scale were the " poor white " dwellers on the sandy pine flats and in similar inferior regions. These victims of malaria and the hookworm [21] — the indolent, shiftless, anemic, sallow-faced " crackers " and " clay eaters " of the south-central counties of Georgia, and the " hill billies " of the Carolinas — extended into like areas of the South Central States. While even the colored population looked down with scorn upon this " pore white trash," the latter nevertheless found in racial superiority a reason for opposing emancipation without removal of the blacks. To them, even as to the great planter, " menial labor " was obnoxious. While game and fish abounded in the wilderness about them, and corn and potatoes could be raised with slight labor, they were content to live in their rude cabins set in little clearings. Whiskey was easily made and freely used. The " poor whites " were too ambitionless to have joined the westward-moving tide of pioneers, and constituted the illiterate slums of the South, the prey of political demagogues who flattered them and catered to their prejudices, or the hangers-on and dependent followers of their planter neighbors.[22]

[21] See the *Publications* (Washington, 1910–15) of the Rockefeller Sanitary Commission for the Eradication of Hookworm Disease, and C. W. Stiles, *Report upon the Prevalence and Geographic Distribution of Hookworm Disease . . . in the United States* (Bulletin 10, Hygienic Laboratory, U.S. Public Health Service, Treasury Dept.; Washington, 1903).

[22] On the people of this type, see: Paul H. Buck, " The Poor Whites of the Ante-bellum South," *American Historical Review*, XXXI, 41–54 (with references to sources) ; A. B. Hart, *The Southern South* (New York, 1910), Chap. III; U. B. Phillips (ed.), *Plantation and Frontier Documents: 1649–1863 (A Documentary History of American Industrial Society*, ed. John R. Commons [and others], I–II; Cleveland, 1909), II, 165–68; and W. E. Dodd, *The Cotton Kingdom (The Chronicles of America*, XXVII; New Haven, 1919), pp. 31, 34, 94–95. Although F. L. Olmsted's various books belong to the decade following our period, much of his description is applicable to the thirties and forties, as

Another class of nonslaveholding whites, but of a different type, were the mountain whites.[23] Descendants, generally, of good Scotch-Irish and English families that had crossed the southern Alleghenies, they lived in the counties of the South Atlantic States, for the most part, above the thousand-foot contour. In " coves " and little valleys, these families had settled down in isolated communities, ignorant of the world about them; inbreeding, and overpopulation of their narrow homes, had pushed them farther and farther up the mountain sides. They constituted a " retarded frontier," a survival of backcountry eighteenth-century colonial types. Elizabethan words and pronunciations, folk lore, superstitions, and balladry made them fossil remains of an earlier age. The blood feud flourished between rival clans. Moonshine whiskey was often the only product they could raise from their surplus corn for a cash return. Illiterate, narrowly provincial, their emotional life found vent in the religious excesses of camp meeting and revival; they took their religion straight; their amusements and their social life centered around the husking bee, the quilting bee, the house raising, the wedding celebration. Household economy, with homespun clothing, the cabin loom on which with native artistry they wove their " kivers," wooden utensils for the kitchen — in short, the life, in the log house, that had characterized their ancestors and which was rapidly dying out in the northern New England and New York mountain districts — here remained unchanged. Their self-sufficing agriculture had no place for staple crops, for the use of slaves or even servants. But the stock was good and vigorous, capable of producing results when progress should reach them by schools, communications, and the opportunity for employment. It was an intensely democratic, as well as a conservative, society, ready to fight for its ideals.

Between the area of the mountain whites and the region of the slaveholding planters lay a transitional zone of farmers, with few or no slaves, often antagonistic to the historic tidewater society and sympathetic with the mountaineers. Akin to these were the

---

is D. R. Hundley, *Social Relations in Our Southern States* (New York, 1860). See also H. R. Helper, *The Impending Crisis of the South* (New York, 1857).

[23] John C. Campbell, *The Southern Highlander and His Homeland* (New York, 1921); Horace Kephart, *Our Southern Highlanders* (New York, 1913 and [enlarged ed.] 1922); and Hart, *op. cit.*, Chap. III.

yeomen of the low country, who might possess a slave or two, often plowing and hoeing side by side with their negroes in the field. These men were sturdy and independent, and, while they often followed the lead of their neighboring great planters, they were men whose vote must be won by persuasion, not by compulsion. Where the map shows high illiteracy in tidewater belts, it indicates, as a rule, a dependent class. The yeomen constituted a large population of real importance — too often lost sight of by the writers of history and of fiction, who have dealt with planter and slave as contrasting types and have ignored this middle class.[24]

The free negroes constituted a class by themselves. Of approximately 320,000 in the United States in 1830, the South Atlantic Division had nearly one-half, and the slaveholding states as a whole had nearly fifty-seven per cent, leaving about two-fifths to the free North, particularly in the states of the Middle Atlantic Division. By 1850 the number of free negroes in the nation had become almost 435,000, more than half of whom belonged to the slave states. These Southern free negroes were most numerous in Maryland and Virginia, and less than one-eleventh of them lived in the South Central group.[25]

This class of the colored people underwent interesting vicissitudes during these twenty years. In general, the slaveholding states adhered firmly to the idea that emancipation and removal should go together. But, by the process of emancipation by the

[24] See Julia A. Flisch, " The Common People of the Old South," American Historical Association *Annual Report*, 1908, I (Washington, 1909), 133–42. J. S. Bassett, *Slavery in the State of North Carolina* (Johns Hopkins University *Studies in Historical and Political Science*, Ser. XVII, Nos. 7–8; Baltimore, 1899), p. 47, does not exaggerate, for that state at least, in calling the yeomen " the backbone " of Southern society.

[25] Based on admittedly imperfect statistics in the *Compendium of the Seventh Census*, p. 63. See also: Carter G. Woodson, *Free Negro Heads of Families in the United States in 1830* (Washington, 1925); *idem, The Negro in Our History* (Washington, 1922), Chap. VIII; and Phillips, *American Negro Slavery*, pp. 436–53. Among the monographs useful on free negroes are: J. C. Ballagh, *A History of Slavery in Virginia* (Johns Hopkins University *Studies in Historical and Political Science*, Extra Vol. XXIV; Baltimore, 1902); Bassett, *op. cit.;* J. H. Russell, *The Free Negro in Virginia, 1619–1865* (Johns Hopkins University *Studies in Historical and Political Science*, Ser. XXXI, No. 3; Baltimore, 1913); and Jas. M. Wright, *The Free Negro in Maryland* (Columbia University *Studies in History, Economics and Public Law*, XCVII, No. 3; New York, 1921). On the free negro in the North, see Edward R. Turner, *The Negro in Pennsylvania* (Washington, 1911).

master, by purchase by the slave of his freedom, by escape to the North (it was reckoned that, in the years 1849–50, over one thousand had absconded and had not been heard from), and by natural increase, their numbers were recruited. Investigators have found interesting occasional instances where they became wealthy, and plantation owners themselves, and where they rose to eminence as preachers, even to white and colored congregations in the South. There are numerous cases of the purchase, by free negroes, of slaves (usually members of the family), for philanthropic reasons and to avoid the legal restraints on emancipation and residence.[26]

But, for the most part, the free negro was an unwelcome and disturbing element, not only in the South but in the North as well. The presence of free negroes was a menace to the restraints on slave society. Race antagonism; the problem of adjustment to free competitive industrial society by negroes so recently slaves; the protests of white mechanics against the competition of cheap negro labor,[27] coupled with objections to working alongside the colored man — resulted in enactments preventing the advancement of this class, and to laws, in various states, requiring a bond, on emancipation, for their removal within a given time and to insure their not becoming a burden on the community. Northern cities also often required guarantees before admitting them. Riots against their colonization in free states were far from unknown.

With the Southampton, Virginia, uprising known as Nat Turner's rebellion, in 1831, when the negro foreman of a plantation, a religious fanatic, led a massacre of white families, and when similar attacks were reported as preparing in neighboring parts of North Carolina, a wave of fear of servile insurrection swept the South Atlantic States.[28]

26 " Free Negro Owners of Slaves in the United States in 1830," *Journal of Negro History*, IX, 41–85.

27 See Chas. H. Wesley, *Negro Labor in the United States, 1850–1925* (New York, 1927).

28 Phillips (ed.), *Plantation and Frontier*, II, 101 ff.; *idem, American Negro Slavery*, pp. 480–87; J. W. Cromwell, " The Aftermath of Nat Turner's Insurrection," *Journal of Negro History*, V, 208–34; Woodson, *Free Negro Heads of Families*, pp. xxvii ff.; Chas. H. Ambler, *The Life and Diary of John Floyd* (Richmond, Va., 1918), pp. 88–92, 155–62, 164–67, 170; and Theodore M. Whitfield, *Slavery Agitation in Virginia, 1829–1832* (Johns Hopkins University *Studies in Historical and Political Science*, Extra Vol., N.S., No. 10; Baltimore, 1930).

Synchronizing with the advent of William Lloyd Garrison's crusade and with the activities of the antislavery societies of the North, conservative sentiment of the South demanded stricter repressive measures. The activity of negro preachers and the education of the slave were curtailed, freedom of movement of the slaves was restrained, the patrol system was stiffened. The principle of governing by fear gained supporters in some states. In all, there was a tendency to render increasingly difficult the lot of the free negro.

On the other hand, there were men, even in the lowland of Virginia and North Carolina, but especially in the upland counties, who used the alarm to reinforce the sentiment for gradual abolition and deportation.[29] Even Governor John Floyd, of Virginia, who was so prominent in his sympathy with nullification that he became South Carolina's choice for President in 1832, was alarmed lest western counties should separate from tidewater Virginia. " Before I leave this Government," he wrote in his diary, " I will have contrived to have a law passed gradually abolishing slavery in this State, or at all events to begin the work by prohibiting slavery on the West side of the Blue Ridge Mountains." [30] The violent debates in the Virginia legislature of these years, and in the constitutional convention and legislature of North Carolina in the early thirties, reinforce these views of Floyd. George Tucker, professor of political economy in the University of Virginia, and once a Representative in Congress, writing in the early forties, concluded on Malthusian principles that abolition was inevitable in time, because, as density of population in the South increased, the price of free labor would fall until negro slavery became unprofitable. This process he expected to begin in Maryland, Virginia, and North Carolina, and finally to prevail throughout the slaveholding states.[31] But such views were not general. On the other hand, Calhoun's efforts in Congress against " incendiary literature " show the depth of alarm and the political reactions in the cotton states.

In spite of the fact that the yeomen and nonslaveholders con-

[29] J. S. Bassett, *Anti-slavery Leaders of North Carolina* (*ibid.*, Ser. XVI, No. 6; Baltimore, 1898), and *Slavery in North Carolina.*

[30] Nov. 21, 1831. (Ambler, *op. cit.*, p. 170.)

[31] *Progress of the United States in Population and Wealth in Fifty Years,* . . . (New York and Boston, 1843), Chap. XIII. Cf. L. G. Tyler, *The Letters and Times of the Tylers*, II (Richmond, Va., 1885), 254–55.

stituted the mass of Southern whites, the plantation was the controlling economic, political, and social institution of the South. It existed in varied and intermingled types, not only as to size but also as to crops raised. Shading from the farm type of northern and interior Maryland and Virginia, where wheat and corn were replacing the older tobacco culture, there were the tobacco-plantation areas of south-central Virginia and the adjacent counties of the northern zone of North Carolina, the cotton plantations of interior South Carolina and across Georgia, and the rice plantations of the coastal plain of these two states.

The Virginia tidewater colonial regions had suffered loss of prestige as settlement and wealth had passed away from them and as their soils had become exhausted and their land values had fallen with the opening up of Western lands. Here was a region of exceptional white illiteracy, showing dependent and unprosperous whites alongside the mansions of the historic Virginia families — a region where the Whig party became preponderant. But, by the time with which this survey begins, Maryland and Virginia had started an agricultural revival, reflected in the growth of shipments of flour and grain from the back counties to Baltimore and Richmond, in internal improvements for transportation, and particularly in the development of new methods of replenishment of the soil, through improved rotation of crops, better forms of tillage, and the use of fertilizers.

Edmund Ruffin became famous by his advocacy of the application of calcareous marl and manure to reduce the acidity of outworn soils. Cottonseed and guano came into use as fertilizers. Interest in scientific agriculture grew, accompanied by agricultural conventions (which not seldom became vehicles for political denunciation of the protective tariffs). Ruffin himself edited an influential agricultural periodical, and was called to South Carolina to make a soil survey of that state. Among the intelligent leaders of the tidewater region, such applications of chemical science to restoration of their lands found a response which resulted in doubling the value of lands in eastern Maryland. Between 1838 and 1850 the Virginia tidewater lands, alone, appreciated by over seventeen million dollars — a large sum for those days.[32] Varied agriculture replaced the single crops, and this

[32] I am indebted for information on this topic to Avery O. Craven, *Soil Exhaustion as a Factor in the Agricultural History of Virginia and Maryland,*

diversification brought much of Virginia and Maryland into resemblance to the neighboring free states at the same time that large slaveholding planters found their negro property enhanced by demands from the Lower South. In the area of diversified farming, corn production was general, but especially strong in the region of large live-stock production, east of the fall line, in Virginia and North Carolina.

The important region of the South Atlantic characterized by the tobacco plantation lay in lower Maryland and especially in a compact group of counties of the Piedmont south of the James, in Virginia, with a highly important overflow into adjacent counties of North Carolina.[33]   Interestingly, this tobacco region divided its party preferences by an irregular line through the center, east of which the counties tended toward Democratic majorities and west of which they almost always went Whig in the Presidential elections of these twenty years. The Whig counties had higher land values — a condition accompanied by a higher white illiteracy that indicated a dependent group of less prosperous whites. The North Carolina tobacco counties, with the exception of Granville, were almost invariably Democratic. The greatest tobacco planter of this region had some sixteen hundred negroes on his plantation. Near Richmond, Virginia, "Belmead,"[34] owned by Philip St. George Cocke and devoted to tobacco and wheat, had in 1854 one hundred and twenty-five slaves, including a dozen house servants, a field corps of thirty-eight, and slave carpenters, stonemasons, a miller, blacksmiths, shoemakers, spinners, and weavers — a small town's industrial force in itself, apparently self-sufficing, but under the control of one man, the planter.

In eastern North Carolina the extraction of turpentine and tar and the making of barrels, staves, and naval stores, constituted an important forest industry employing poor whites and slaves.

In the coastal counties running from the southeastern corner of South Carolina to the southern boundary of Georgia, lay the

---

1606–1860 (University of Illinois *Studies in the Social Sciences*, XIII, No. 1; Urbana, 1925).

[33] See map of Crops, 1850 (at end of volume).

[34] Described, from original material, in Phillips, *American Negro Slavery*, pp. 230–32, and *idem* (ed.), *Plantation and Frontier*, I, 208–14.

region of rice and sea-island-cotton plantations. At the close of our period, the greatest rice planter owned over four thousand acres in cultivation (divided into fourteen plantations) and possessed two thousand slaves. In general, the rice planters had large holdings of diked and drained tide lands, in plantations averaging one hundred and forty-five acres but running in some cases to over a thousand. Here the slaves constituted a special class, often more newly African, less assimilated, than their fellows in the interior. They were worked by the " task " system, which exacted a specified " piece " cultivation each day, after which they were at leisure. Absentee ownership was complicated by the necessity for the planter to summer in the interior, away from the malarial coast. These large estates made use of machinery and of more-highly-paid overseers,[35] but the character of the managers, the task system, and the absence of the planter sometimes led to harsh treatment of the slaves.

Contrary to some of the conventional impressions (derived largely from the picture presented by novelists), plantations varied, naturally, as size, regions, and character of masters varied.[36]

The large plantation, with its colonnaded mansion (a Southern version of colonial architecture), approached by drives lined with trees and hedges, and presided over by a cultured master and the efficient " mistress of the plantation," his wife, was the highest type, and was in evidence, though by no means so common as descriptions of the antebellum South would indicate. An abundance of negro house servants, the pride of lineage, the sense of mastery, a sensitiveness to honor, and a quick reaction to an affront, characterized such homes. As in the case of the English

[35] Basil Hall, *Travels in North America, in the Years 1827 and 1828* (Philadelphia, 1829), II, 229–39, gives a favorable description of a Georgia sea-island-cotton plantation at the beginning of the period; F. L. Olmsted, *A Journey in the Seaboard Slave States*, . . . (New York, 1856), Chap. VII, and Phillips, *American Negro Slavery*, pp. 247–59 (using contemporary manuscripts), give details for rice regions.

[36] Jay B. Hubbell, *Virginia Life in Fiction* [Dallas, Tex., 1922]. Francis P. Gaines, *The Southern Plantation* (New York, 1925), also examines the plantation as it actually existed, in contrast with its idealization in fiction, reaching the conclusion that, while examples of the general type there portrayed were to be found, it was not of common occurrence and rarely attained all the excellences ascribed to it. For a contemporaneous account, in fiction, see Geo. Tucker, *The Valley of Shenandoah* (New York, 1824).

country gentry, there was a feeling of responsibility for a large number of dependents. The slaves and poor-white clients of the Southern planter, and the yeoman neighbors who followed his lead, gave him position, executive experience, and a training in politics which made it hard for him to brook opposition from Northern opponents.

A generous hospitality characterized these homes. Their owners intermarried, exchanged long visits with each other, and formed a related group — the aristocracy of the South. It was an aristocracy with traditions, scornful of manual labor, which was regarded as menial.[37]

Estates were often divided into separate plantation units. The size of the farm, and the number of slaves possessed by the planter, increased as one passed from north to south. In 1850, in Maryland, the average farm embraced 212 acres; in Virginia, 340; in South Carolina, 541. In contrast with this, the contemporary average farm in Massachusetts contained less than 100 acres, and the farm in the North Central States tended to approach the 160-acre pre-emption tract. Planters like Wade Hampton, of South Carolina, who cultivated 1,600 acres of cotton and half as many of corn, and George McDuffie, with 5,000 acres, of which 750 were in cotton, were unusual. "Virtually half of the total cotton crop each year was made by farmers whose slaves were on the average hardly more numerous than the white members of their own families," and about six full hands producing thirty bales of cotton would constitute the average.[38] But in the long run the larger part of the cotton crop was made by the relatively few great planters. The small planter in his log cabin was even more affected by a fall in cotton prices than was the great slave-owner, who had the economic advantage of large-scale operation.

The overseer,[39] agent, or manager (operating under a steward in the case of large estates with separate plantations) was an

[37] Besides the references, on the plantation, already cited, see a typical account by Thos. C. Johnson, in *The Life and Letters of Robert Lewis Dabney* (Richmond, Va., 1903), pp. 14–24. See also E. M. Coulter, " A Century of a Georgia Plantation," *Mississippi Valley Historical Review*, XVI, 334–46.

[38] Phillips, *American Negro Slavery*, p. 226.

[39] Ellis W. Putney's Plantation Book, with the printed manual, *Plantation and Farm Instruction . . . By a Southern Planter* (Richmond, Va., 1852) [in Huntington Library]; J. S. Bassett, *The Southern Plantation Overseer as Re-*

important element in the slave system. This white manager was
not of the social class of the planter, but was a hired intermediary
to execute his orders when present and to represent him in his
absence. The instructions, often incorporated in formal con-
tracts between planter and agent, placed on the latter the
obligation to see that the slave was well cared for; the food
ration and clothing allowance usually were specified; directions
to avoid cruelty in work and punishment were explicit, but necessarily left much to the discretion of the overseer. Although
warned to combine humanity with firmness, he was responsible for
profitable returns and therefore was not free from the temptation
to look after this result rather than the careful treatment of the
slave property. Overseers were chiefly uneducated, and were
paid, usually, from $250 to $600 a year, with the addition of a
house, service, and food, their wages seldom rising to $1,000 in
money. Planters' letters abound in complaints of the inefficiency
of overseers, who were frequently changed. That they were
sometimes deficient in character may be gathered from such
letters and from an essay by the Baptist minister, C. F. Sturgis,[40]
who, in the discussion of duties of masters to servants, urges that
the overseer be encouraged to marry, adding that " the reasons
for this are of a nature too delicate to comment upon." Thus
the overseer became, as J. S. Bassett puts it, " the buffer " between the slave and his master, without the loyalty and affection which the slaves gave to the planter himself but serving to
make the plantation profitable if possible.

Below the overseer was the negro slave-driver, armed with the
whip as a badge of authority, whose duty was to see that his
gang was kept at work.

The weekly food rations for a " full hand " usually consisted
of a peck to two pecks of corn meal, two and one-half to four
pounds of meat, usually bacon, and salt and molasses. Fresh
beef, mutton, or pork, and tobacco, were dealt out at times. In
addition, there were vegetables from the garden in season. Chil-

---

vealed in His Letters (Northampton, Mass., 1925); Phillips (ed.), *Plantation
and Frontier*, I, 112–29; *idem, American Negro Slavery*, pp. 261–83; *idem* and
J. D. Glunt (eds.), *Florida Plantation Records from the Papers of George Noble
Jones* (St. Louis, 1927 [in Missouri Historical Society *Publications*]), with useful Introduction; and H. N. McTyeire, C. F. Sturgis, and A. T. Holmes, *Duties
of Masters to Servants* (Charleston, S.C., 1851).
    [40] *Ibid.*, p. 87.

dren were rationed in proportion. Food cost less than twenty dollars a year for an adult slave. Clothing, blankets, and shoes, varying according to the winter and summer months, might cost from eight to ten dollars per annum. In all, perhaps forty or fifty dollars was roughly reckoned as the yearly cost of a slave in the items of food, clothing, housing, medical attention, etc.[41]

So widely, however, did the cost vary according to periods, types of plantation, and individual masters, and so difficult are many of the factors (such as supplies from slave gardens, etc.) to reckon, that definite conclusions as to the relative profitability of free and slave labor are hard to reach, and estimates can be made only in the most general terms. To the yearly maintenance cost of forty or fifty dollars, for an adult slave, must be added an item to cover interest on invested capital, wages of the overseer, depreciation, death or escape of slaves, etc. This would raise the planter's annual maintenance cost per slave to, say, one hundred dollars. How much of this was offset by the slaves' progeny is a question, affected by the large infant-mortality rate, the cost of raising a child to the maturity needed for work in the field, etc.

There was an appreciation of slave value, due to the exclusion of further negro importation and to the demand for slaves in new cotton regions. But the relative ineffectiveness of slave labor was acknowledged.[42] Planters like Governor J. H. Hammond, of South Carolina, a strong proslavery man, Thomas Cooper, an

---

[41] The weekly food ration for a sailor in the free states was not notably more generous, but cost much more. (See *Hunt's Merchants' Magazine*, II, 126.) According to Olmsted (*op. cit.*, p. 46), a white farm-laborer could be obtained in New York for $105 a year, with board, the laborer clothing himself at a cost of about $20 a year. Slaves were hired-out by the year at from $100 to $120, and food, housing, and clothing. On slave maintenance, see: the form book, *Plantation and Farm Instruction*, cited above; William Galt's Plantation Book, 1845–49 [in Huntington Library]; Governor J. H. Hammond, of South Carolina, quoted in Geo. M. Weston, *The Progress of Slavery in the United States* (Washington, 1857), p. 228; Thos. Cooper, *Lectures on the Elements of Political Economy* (Columbia, S.C., 1826), pp. 94–95; De Bow, *Industrial Resources*, I, 150, II (New Orleans, 1852), 331; quoted manuscripts in Phillips, *American Negro Slavery*, pp. 265, 277, 348; *idem* (ed.), *Plantation and Frontier*, I, 126; *idem* and Glunt (eds.), *Florida Plantation Records;* R. Q. Mallard, *Plantation Life before Emancipation* (Richmond, Va., 1892), pp. 30–31; and Bassett, *op. cit.*, p. 25.

[42] See, however, the paper by L. C. Gray, " Economic Efficiency and Competitive Advantages of Slavery under the Plantation System," *Agricultural History*, IV, 31–47, for criticisms of this view.

economist of South Carolina, and Nehemiah Adams, a defender of slavery, for example, admitted its unprofitability as compared with free labor. To most planters, at any rate, the problem was compounded of the realities involved in the presence of the negro, the practical impossibility of colonization, the safeguarding of property in slaves ("Were ever any people, civilized or savage, persuaded by any argument, human or divine, to surrender voluntarily two thousand million dollars?" asked Governor Hammond [43]), and the planter's social and political horror at the prospect of a society made up of freed negroes and the white race.

As a rule, the owner aimed to produce sufficient corn and swine to furnish the food for his plantation, but, in the case of some estates and regions, food supplies were purchased outside, and droves of mules and swine from the Ohio Valley passed to the Cotton Belt. Ordinarily, the amount of fallow and untilled land constituted at least half the plantation.

On the cotton plantation, about half the slaves were the full field hands, and the others were either on the domestic staff as house servants, mechanics, and stablemen, or were children and those who could not work. Near the planter's house was an office building, and to the rear were the kitchen, smokehouse, and abodes of the house servants. More remote, were quarters of the slaves engaged in field work, with the overseer's house nearby. These quarters seldom seemed satisfactory to Northern travelers, and there were criticisms from Southern writers; but the negro slave's demands were not those of the Northern white laborer, and the milder climate made a difference. However, for sanitary reasons it was to the planter's interest to see that the conditions were not too unsatisfactory, and there were requirements, in planters' instructions, for house cleaning in spring and fall and for annual whitewashing of the premises inside and out.

Called by the overseer's horn at dawn, the slave began work at sunrise; breakfast followed after work till nine in the morning, and another meal at one or two, usually brought to the field unless the cabins were near. Sunset ended field work, and by half-past nine the slave was expected to be in his cabin for the night. Inspection and patrol were supposed to enforce these regulations, and visits away from the plantation required a written permit.[44]

---

[43] Weston, *op. cit.*, p. 185.

[44] For slave statutes and discussion thereof, see: Helen T. Catterall (ed.),

Whipping for bad conduct was restricted in the usual plantation regulations, both as to the number of lashes and as to allowing a certain period (sometimes a day) to intervene between the offense and the whipping, in order to prevent the anger of overseer or driver from inflicting undue punishment. But unfulfilled threats were discouraged lest they produce uncertainty of penalty, or result in running away. That there was cruelty on the part of some cannot be doubted, but the testimony seems to indicate that it was the exception rather than the rule.

In the older regions, although marriage outside the slaves of the plantation was discouraged, the better planters hesitated to break families by sale to the South and Southwest, except where a slave was incorrigible. But the marriage tie was far from rigid. The evil of white intercourse with attractive female slaves was one of the darker sides of family life in the South — made much of, and probably exaggerated in its extent, by antislavery writers.

Religious instruction of the blacks, except during the short period of hysteria after Nat Turner's insurrection, was encouraged. Often, white and colored worshipped in separate parts of the same church. Sometimes the planter arranged for religious services by approved colored preachers under his supervision, or even conducted them himself. It was realized that a common denominational faith on the part of master and slave was an advantageous bond. Educational instruction seldom went beyond teaching the slave to read and write, and, in general, this was discouraged lest it might be followed by servile revolt.

It would seem that Northern men, in their conclusion that the slave was unhappy, tended to attribute to him their own feelings and reactions to the conditions under which he lived. In general, he was sufficiently fed, with a coarse diet, adequately clothed, but poorly housed (though not to such a degree as to produce discontent in the slave's mind), and allowed opportunity for expressing the natural joyousness of the African temperament; and hardship was felt rather by individuals than by the mass of slaves.[45] It was the system's failure to allow the black man to

---

Judicial Cases concerning American Slavery and the Negro, I (Carnegie Institution of Washington, 1926) ; Phillips, *American Negro Slavery*, p. 501 ; and J. M. Mecklin, in *Journal of Negro History*, II, 229–51.

[45] In reaching this conclusion, I have used the opinions of contemporary Northerners as well as of the Southern defenders of the system. See, e.g., *Prose*

develop new wants, to rise to his full possibilities under freedom, its economic disadvantage, its effect upon the psychology of the master himself, and its inconsistency in a nation and a world tending toward a free, competitive, democratic society in an age of humanitarianism and idealism, that constituted its fundamental weaknesses.

Some planters made five bales (of four hundred pounds each) of cotton to the hand, using one hand to about six acres of cotton, but often three bales or less to the hand was the normal product. When cotton was down to five cents, even the great planter, with his economy and efficiency of administration, hardly made a profit. In most of the forties the export price of cotton fell below ten cents (to less than six cents in 1844), while in the thirties it ranged from nearly nine cents to nearly seventeen, averaging fourteen cents.[46]

In 1840 a little over one-third of the nation's cotton came from the states of the South Atlantic group. Georgia and the Carolinas produced almost all of this and were thus becoming more closely tied in interest with the cotton-raising regions of the South Central States, to which the bulk of the cotton industry had migrated. By 1850 South Carolina had nearly doubled its production, and, in spite of the fact that Virginia and North Carolina had greatly declined in theirs, the section as a whole produced a somewhat larger fraction of the total than in 1830.

The exported cotton of the nation rose from somewhat over a half-million bales (of five hundred pounds each) in 1830 to nearly two million by the end of the twenty years. Measured in terms of money, the export of raw cotton rose from less than thirty million dollars in 1830 to over seventy million in 1850,

Writings of William Cullen Bryant, ed. Parke Godwin (New York, 1884), II, 34, on treatment in South Carolina, 1843.

[46] *Atlas of American Agriculture*, " Cotton," pp. 8 (soil map), 16, 18 (statistics on cotton trade), 19; United States Department of Agriculture *Yearbook* for 1921 (Washington, 1922), p. 339 (soil map). See also: Thos. Ellison, *Cotton Trade of Great Britain* (1886) and *Centennial Sketch of the Cotton Trade of the United States* (1893); *Parliamentary Papers, Committee Report on Manufactures*, 1833, VI, and 1847–48, IX, 52; Geo. K. Holmes, *Cotton Crop of the United States, 1790–1911* (Circular No. 32, Bureau of Statistics, U.S. Dept. of Agriculture; Washington, 1912); *Niles' Register*, LVI, 249–50, 349–51, LVII, 184–87; and *Hansard's Parliamentary Debates*, 3d Ser., LXXXIV, *passim*.

or more than half of the total value of the exports of the United States,[47] and far in excess of any other item in our exports.

As cotton cultivation spread into the South Central States, including Texas, it brought with it dynamic influences upon parties, political and social philosophy, and ideals. A new section was created between 1830 and 1850, and the result was profoundly important in the history of the nation.

Here, therefore, was an American interest of the greatest importance. The lion's share of the export went to England, thereby constituting an important factor in our diplomatic relations. Cotton also brought foreign imports, in return, which paid heavy revenues under the protective tariff.

As later history made plain, water power, the potential poor-white labor,[48] and the proximity of cotton, iron, and coal, made possible the development of manufactures in the Southern sections. This should have reproduced, there, the process by which New England found compensation for her losses in agriculture and shipping and for the westward migration. A self-sufficing South might have arisen.

Indeed, strong efforts were made by leaders, in such states as Virginia and South Carolina, traditionally hostile both to a manufacturing society and to the protective tariff, to imitate the North. Men like William Gregg, of Charleston, reasoned that, even in the case of disunion, it was to the interest of the section to diversify its agricultural pursuits sufficiently to become independent, and, with foresight, argued that there were abundant water power and thousands of unemployed whites for whom manufacturing towns would mean better education and more comfort. Even the blacks, in Gregg's opinion, could be used as a labor supply when properly taught. The Charleston *Mercury*, in 1845, admitted that manufacturing would have a good general effect. Charles Lyell, in his *Second Visit to the United States*,[49] comments upon the cotton mills established at Columbus, Georgia, and upon the existence of an anti-free-trade party. In Virginia,

---

[47] *Statistical Abstract of the United States, 1924* (U.S. Dept. of Commerce; Washington, 1925), pp. 649, 426, 446.

[48] The term is, of course, indefinite. Just before 1850, Hammond estimated those in South Carolina at 50,000, but William Gregg reckoned them at 125,000. ([J. D. B.] *De Bow's Review*, VIII, 518, XI, 133.)

[49] *A Second Visit to the United States of North America* (London, 1849), II, 34.

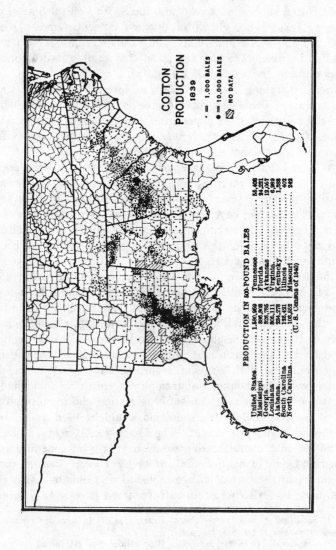

COTTON
PRODUCTION
1839

· = 1,000 BALES
● = 10,000 BALES
▨ = NO DATA

PRODUCTION IN 500-POUND BALES

United States	1,680,969
Mississippi	886,948
Georgia	326,785
Louisiana	365,968
Alabama	294,278
South Carolina	132,421
North Carolina	108,853
Tennessee	55,408
Florida	34,221
Arkansas	12,057
Virginia	6,949
Kentucky	1,838
Illinois	402
Missouri	243

(U. S. Census of 1840)

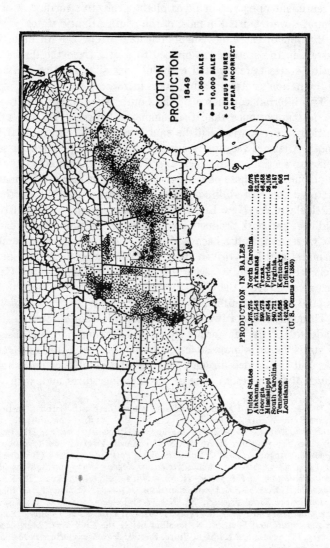

COTTON
PRODUCTION
1849

- 1,000 BALES
- 10,000 BALES
* CENSUS FIGURES
  APPEAR INCORRECT

PRODUCTION IN BALES

United States 1,976,275	North Carolina 59,078
Alabama 461,643	Arkansas 52,276
Georgia 899,278	Texas 46,468
Mississippi 387,464	Florida 58,106
South Carolina 240,721	Virginia 3,157
Tennessee 156,696	Kentucky 605
Louisiana 162,990	Indiana 11

(U. S. Census of 1850)

near Richmond and at points in the Shenandoah Valley and in the northwestern counties, iron manufacture was developing, and a sentiment appeared in favor of the protective tariff.[50]   Cotton factories were started in most of the South Atlantic states.

But few of these movements had real strength.   An industrial system in the section was obliged to wait.   Even the distinctive cotton states were credited with only one sixty-fifth of the value of the nation's cotton manufactures in 1840.

The internal commerce of the South Atlantic section was of far less importance than the commerce between this and other sections.   From what will be said later, it will appear that the South Atlantic was, in its agriculture, to a large extent a self-sufficing section, whose corn and live stock compared favorably in amount with those of other sections; but its demand for manufactured goods of all kinds furnished a market for other sections, particularly for New England.[51]   A large volume of breadstuffs and beef and pork products from the upper Mississippi descended the river, and, as has been said, there was a considerable number of mules and hogs driven from the Ohio Valley into the Cotton Belt.   In the twenties, according to Senator Hayne, South Carolina received from the West, through Saluda Gap, live stock to the amount of over a million dollars a year.

Throughout these two decades, there was a large internal slave trade to supply the forming Cotton Kingdom.   In the absence of statistics, it is impossible to say how extensive the movement was, but it afforded an outlet for the unprofitable or undesirable slaves of the northern zone of slaveholding states and, with ille-

[50] See: Governor Hammond's address before the South Carolina Institute, reprinted in *Western Journal* (St. Louis), IV, 182 ff. (June, 1850), from *De Bow's Review;* Boucher, in Washington University *Studies*, III, Pt. II, No. 2, pp. 243–70; Chas. H. Ambler, *Sectionalism in Virginia from 1776 to 1861* (Chicago, 1910), p. 116; A. C. Cole, *The Whig Party in the South* (Washington, 1913), pp. 94–95, 206–11; Phillips, *American Negro Slavery*, pp. 378–79; *idem* (ed.), *Plantation and Frontier*, II, 302–3, 312–13, 332–41; Robt. R. Russel, *Economic Aspects of Southern Sectionalism, 1840–1861* (University of Illinois *Studies in the Social Sciences*, XI, Nos. 1–2; Urbana, 1924), p. 52; Edward Ingle, *Southern Sidelights* (New York, 1896), Chap. III; E. M. Coulter, " Southern Agriculture and Southern Nationalism before the Civil War," *Agricultural History*, IV, 77–91; and Kathleen Bruce, *Virginia Iron Manufacture in the Slave Era* (New York, 1931).

[51] Thos. P. Kettell, *Southern Wealth and Northern Profits . . .* (New York, 1860), p. 60; and *United States Magazine, and Democratic Review* (New York), N.S., XXVI, 10 ff. (Jan., 1850).

gal importations, enabled the Cotton Belt to find its labor supply. The auction block and the coffles of slaves carried south and west were not agreeable features even to the Virginia slave-holders, and furnished to Northern abolitionists some of their most effective arguments against the institution.[52]

Transportation development [53] in the South Atlantic and South Central sections was closely related to the needs of the basins of agricultural surplus. By the thirties, the Piedmont had become the " Eastern Cotton Belt." Shut off from water transportation by the mountain barriers toward the Mississippi Valley, and by the falls of the rivers and the infertile pine barrens toward the east, this cotton belt had, from the earliest days of the settlement of the Piedmont, been in urgent need of internal improvements to connect it with the rest of the world. At the southern extremity of the Appalachian system lay Atlanta, a center through which the outflanking roads to the northwest could pass to Chattanooga and the Tennessee Valley. Minor outlets through the mountains were to be found at such openings as Saluda Gap, whereby the Piedmont of South Carolina was brought into touch with the Tennessee Valley. Asheville, in North Carolina, by the waters of the French Broad, gave exit to the same valley.

The extension of the cultivation of cotton into the interior of Georgia and of the Lower South had at first worked to the advantage of Savannah by opening a river route from the cotton-raising Piedmont directly to the coast at that harbor. Charleston, without such river connection, saw ruin facing her as her shipping declined and her commercial prosperity vanished. Under the pressure of the demand of the interior, there was heated presentation, both in the Virginia Constitutional Convention of 1829-30 and in the North Carolina Convention of 1835, of the grievance of the upcountry against the lowland slaveholding

---

[52] Bancroft, *Slave-trading*, pp. 89–91, 109–16, 118–19, 283–84, 290, and W. H. Collins, *The Domestic Slave Trade of the Southern States* (New York, 1904).

[53] See U. B. Phillips, *A History of Transportation in the Eastern Cotton Belt to 1860* (New York, 1908), Introduction (reprinted from *Quarterly Journal of Economics*, May, 1905). For the discussion that follows, I have made use of this valuable work. See also T. D. Jervey, *Robert Y. Hayne and His Times* (New York, 1909). I have, however, based my conclusions also upon the study of source materials and monographs.

region because of the failure of the latter to support the demands
for internal improvements, which would require additional revenue from the taxation of slave property.

By 1851 the Baltimore and Ohio had connected Maryland with
the Ohio Valley, and the fall-line cities of Virginia had been
partly joined with the seaboard, at Wilmington, North Carolina.
Slowly the South Atlantic section constructed a system of combined river-and-railroad transportation. Traveling in 1843, William Cullen Bryant found that, in going from Richmond, Virginia,
to Charleston, South Carolina, he had to change cars at Petersburg, and again at the Roanoke had to leave his train, at two
in the morning, and walk " in long procession for about a quarter
of a mile down to the river." " A negro walked before us," he
adds, " to light our way, bearing a blazing pine torch, which
scattered sparks like a steam-engine, and a crowd of negroes
followed us, bearing our baggage." Taking a steamboat for
an hour, he ascended the two and a half miles to Weldon, where
he again boarded a train, for the journey to Wilmington, North
Carolina, whence he went by steamer to Charleston.[54]

South of Baltimore (which was quite as much a North Atlantic
as a South Atlantic port), the states of the Southern seaboard
remained unconnected with the Mississippi Valley, by continuous
railroad routes, at the end of our period. While the North
Atlantic and the North Central states were being joined by
rail, the eastern and western halves of the so-called " solid
South " remained separated, so far as a railroad system was
concerned.

The first compelling interest in railroad building in the South
arose from the rivalry of Charleston and Savannah as markets
for the Eastern Cotton Belt. South Carolina chartered a railroad, in 1828, to run between Charleston and Hamburg, opposite
the city of Augusta, Georgia, on the Savannah River; and, by
the fall of 1833, the road was in full operation, extending over
one hundred and thirty-three miles. At the time, it was the longest railroad in the world. But Augusta, partly, perhaps, from
state feeling against the diversion of traffic to Charleston, and
also because of the local interests of her draymen, forbade the
continuation of the railway across the river and thus compelled
the breaking of cargo.

[54] *Prose Writings of Bryant*, II, 23 ff.

As the road approached completion, cities of the cotton belt in central Georgia secured the construction of the Georgia Railroad from Augusta. This would have left Savannah quite to one side of the movement of cotton. By 1845 the road had been extended to Atlanta. The Central Road of Georgia was chartered in 1836, to run from Savannah to Macon. Checked by the hard times after the Crisis of 1837, it did not reach Macon until the fall of 1843. In the meantime, Georgia had undertaken to build a state-owned railroad to connect with Memphis, to prevent the diversion of trade from that point into Charleston by way of proposed railroads through northern Alabama. This railroad, the Western and Atlantic, reached Chattanooga by the spring of 1851.

When the subject of the split in the commerce of the Mississippi Valley is considered,[55] we shall have to note the bearing of the various westward railroad extensions upon the problem of intersectional rivalry; but for the present it may suffice to point out that, as early as 1835, the design of connecting the South Atlantic ports and the West by rail had aroused the interest of Calhoun and Hayne, of South Carolina. It was Hayne's desire to construct a railroad, by way of the French Broad, from Charleston, through Knoxville in the Tennessee Valley, to Cincinnati and Louisville on the Ohio. In the interests of this undertaking, a railroad convention of four hundred delegates, from nine states,[56] met in Knoxville on the Fourth of July, 1836. It was believed that the road would compete favorably with the Mississippi River as an outlet and that it would give a southeastern exit to the products of the Ohio Valley instead of allowing them to pass by canals and railroads to the seaports of the Northeast. There were also political considerations. A toast was given by Hayne which ran: " The South and the West. We have published the banns — If anyone know aught why these two should not be joined together let him speak now, or forever after hold his peace."

Differences, however, appeared. Even in the convention, Georgia delegates emphasized the advantages of their state as a terminus, while Charleston laid stress upon her claims. At the

---

[55] [This portion of the book was never written.]

[56] Ohio, Indiana, Kentucky, Tennessee, Virginia, North Carolina, South Carolina, Georgia, and Alabama.

close of November, 1835, Calhoun had already proposed that Georgia and South Carolina combine in an effort to obtain the distribution of the surplus revenue in the federal treasury, to secure funds for railroad building toward the west. " I do sincerely believe," he said, " that a judicious system of rail roads would make Georgia and Carolina the Commercial centre of the Union and the two most prosperous and influential members of the Confederacy." To another correspondent he wrote that by proper exertions Georgia and South Carolina might " turn half of the commerce of the Union through their limits." This was interesting in view of Calhoun's former hostility to distribution, on the ground of unconstitutionality, when suggested by President Jackson.

But Calhoun differed with Hayne, both as to route and northern terminus of such railroads. Writing in 1838, he reiterates his belief that a connection with the West was important to the South, " politically and commercially "; " I do verily believe," he said, " that Charleston has more advantages in her position for the Western trade, than any city on the Atlantic." But he thought that South Carolina should " look to the Tennessee instead of the Ohio, and much farther to the West than Cincinnati or Lexington." It was his opinion that the South should " turn the Alleghany to the South West, as New York had to the North East " and, for the time at least, make Memphis the terminus. He therefore resigned as a director of the Charleston and Cincinnati company.

Although nowhere in his letters does Calhoun indicate a political purpose in the creation of a purely Southern system free from Northern connection, it must be remembered that in just these years he was becoming increasingly doubtful of the continuance of the Union and increasingly urgent in his demands on behalf of slavery. That his desire for a more southern route to the Mississippi Valley was affected by political considerations is probable,[57] especially in view of the fact that, in his letter of resignation as a director, he urges the importance of a Southern

[57] On this subject, see: Jervey and Phillips, as cited in n. 53; *Correspondence of John C. Calhoun*, ed. J. Franklin Jameson (American Historical Association *Annual Report*, 1899, II; Washington, 1900), pp. 346–47, 349–53, 411–16; *National Intelligencer*, Sept. 7, 1836, quoting Augusta *Constitutionalist*, Aug. 23; and E. D. Mansfield, *Memoirs of the Life and Services of Daniel Drake*, . . . (Cincinnati, 1855), p. 258.

convention and asserts, " I look only to ourselves for permanent security." The quicker the issue and the bolder the measures, the better for all parties, he thought.

There was also an instinctive apprehension, in his mind, regarding the effect of the union of banking and railroads upon political purity. Various of these railroad companies had secured banking privileges by their charters, and such an arrangement was favored by Hayne for his company. Calhoun feared the effect of capitalism, or the " money power," upon the independence of the agricultural South.

No important result followed from the effort to join the Southeast with the Ohio Valley. In the Lower South, the continued influence of water transportation, the brevity of the period during which the railroad could rely upon the cotton crop as freight, and the absence of other inducements for railroad building, together with the lack of cheap white immigrant labor, account for the delay in developing the railroad net in the Southern sections as compared with the North.

Banking in the South Atlantic States took a special form. They conducted their plantation economy, to a large extent, by securing financial credit, in advance, for the production of their crops, and turned their profits into lands and slaves. The National Bank found, here, one of the important fields of its operations. One-fourth of its circulation, and in 1832 the ownership of well toward half of the shares of its stock (aside from the holdings of the government and of foreigners), were located in South Atlantic states. Next to Pennsylvania, South Carolina held the largest number of such shares.[58] State-rights leaders, like Calhoun and George McDuffie from that state, were among the Bank's major advocates. Maryland and South Carolina, together, possessed over one-third of the total of these shares in the United States, and they account for over three-fourths of the section's total.

Virginia, on the other hand, like Massachusetts, had a strong system of state banks, and a relatively small holding of National Bank stock. In 1834 Georgia had more state banks than Virginia, and more specie, but much smaller loans and discounts, circulation, and deposits. By the end of our twenty years, Virginia had

[58] Ralph C. H. Catterall, *The Second Bank of the United States* (Chicago, 1903), pp. 168, 508.

almost twice as many banks as Georgia, more specie, and larger deposits, but a smaller circulation.

In the South Atlantic Division, between 1834 and about 1850, state-bank loans and discounts nearly doubled, specie and circulation more than doubled, and deposits rose from about $10,000,000 to over $16,000,000. But both in New England and in the Middle Atlantic Division, by 1850, loans and discounts had mounted to over $100,000,000, while those in the South Atlantic Division were but $70,000,000. The latter section's deposits were only one-half those in New York banks. But the South Atlantic banks held more specie than those of New York and Pennsylvania, combined.

Banking credit and financial power, however, lay strongly in the Northeast. The profits reaped by the North Atlantic Division from Southern need of its banking services, shipping and commerce, and manufactures, were observed with increasing jealousy and resentment by the slaveholding states.

By 1842 the public indebtedness of the South Atlantic States amounted to around $33,000,000, of which nearly $25,000,000 was borrowed for public and internal improvements — over half by Maryland. In contrast, the South Central States did most of their borrowing to establish state banks, for which their public indebtedness amounted, in 1842, to over $47,000,000.[59] The territory of Florida repudiated her debt, and Maryland defaulted interest in 1842 [60] but resumed by 1848.

As the Cotton Kingdom extended its domain from the South Atlantic to the Lower South, including the Gulf Basin of the South Central States, and as the distinction between the two sections grew faint in the period when slavery and cotton culture seemed menaced by the North, a Southern self-consciousness emerged. Conventions were held which included representatives of both slaveholding sections, and which aimed to draw the whole Mississippi Valley, or, at least, in the language of the time, " the South and Southwest," into dependence upon the Lower South.

At first, these conventions laid stress upon the need of creating a Southeastern outlet for the trade of the Ohio and Missis-

---

[59] Henry C. Adams, *Public Debts* (New York, 1887), p. 301.

[60] J. B. McMaster, *A History of the People of the United States, from the Revolution to the Civil War*, VII (New York, 1919), 34, 36-40; and W. A. Scott, *The Repudiation of State Debts* (New York, 1893), pp. 43-54.

sippi valleys, as did the Knoxville Convention of 1836 already mentioned, and upon the creation of commercial independence and direct foreign trade for the South Atlantic. State and local agricultural conventions, which seldom limited themselves to problems of the soil and of varied crops, gave attention to the tariff and to the perils menacing the slaveholding states. In the second half of the forties, the Southern conventions were usually held west of the Alleghenies, and they combined consideration of the improvement of the Mississippi with projects for railroads and isthmian canals to open the trade to the Pacific, the exploitation of the Amazon Valley by Southern trade, the need of imported slaves, and proposals for expansion, with threatenings of revolt from a nation steadily increasing in its Northern majority — and in radical Northern policies. The culmination, in the period of this book, was in the Nashville Convention, held while the Compromise of 1850 was being considered. Leaving the discussion of the conventions of the forties to another chapter, and considering only those held in South Atlantic cities, we find that they included meetings, between 1836 and 1840, in Augusta, Georgia, Richmond and Norfolk, Virginia, and Charleston, South Carolina. From 1845 to 1850, the idea grew of a South organizing itself by conventions and under the lead of South Carolina's statesman, Calhoun.

The conventions of the later thirties [61] may be illustrated by that which met in Charleston in 1839, with a large attendance from South Carolina and Georgia and some representatives from North Carolina and Florida, of the South Atlantic, and from Alabama and Tennessee, of the South Central, states. Robert Y. Hayne and McDuffie made the more important reports. They argued that Southern and Southwestern states produced three-fourths of the domestic exports of the Union and imported scarcely one-tenth of the merchandise received in return; that the profits of shipping and banking accrued to the North, and especially to New York City. In 1836 her imports were around $118,000,000, said McDuffie, while all the Atlantic states south of the Potomac, together with the Gulf states, were credited with but $20,000,000, and the cotton states of South Carolina and Georgia, with less than $3,500,000. But, of the domestic exports of the United States in 1836, amounting to $107,000,000, New York furnished

[61] See, for 1837, *Baltimore Merchant*, Sept. 7–Oct. 27, 1837.

less than $20,000,000, while the states south and southwest of the Potomac furnished $78,000,000, as contrasted with the $20,000,000 of their imports. Thus, he argued, the profit of Northern cities " upon the exchange of our staples for foreign merchandise, is as effectually abstracted from the wealth of the staple-growing states, as if those cities belonged to a foreign jurisdiction." Considering that " every political community should endeavor to unite within itself, and have under its own control, as far as circumstances will permit, all the elements of national wealth," he protested that, since Southern agricultural products were marketed abroad, the agency of transfer should not be entrusted to citizens of other and distant states, prejudiced against the institutions of the South. He is obviously thinking of a section, not of individual states, and he urges the South to provide for the contingency of dismemberment of the Union.

The remedy for Southern ills, the Convention found in securing credit from abroad, and in the use of surplus income from cotton production, not to buy more land and slaves to make more cotton, but to accumulate capital to be used in financing direct commerce with Europe on a large scale, by packet ships sailing to and from Southern ports, and in building railroads to connect the South Atlantic States and the navigable waters of the West. This, it was hoped, would give the South the command of the whole valley of the Mississippi. " Whether," said McDuffie, " we *scale* the interposing mountain barriers, like Hannibal, or *turn* them like . . . [Napoleon], . . . we shall . . . conquer and bless, by the peaceful weapons of industry and enterprise, plains incomparably more rich and extensive than those which they overran." Commercial education was also urged, to create a body of Southern merchants.[62]

The fact that Southern agricultural staples, and particularly cotton, constituted by far the largest part of American exports

[62] De Bow, *Industrial Resources*, III, 92 ff. On these conventions in general, see: Russel, *Economic Aspects of Southern Sectionalism*, with citations; Wm. W. Davis, in State Historical Society of Alabama *Proceedings*, V (1906), 153; St. Geo. L. Sioussat, " Memphis as a Gateway to the West," *Tennessee Historical Magazine*, III, 1–27, 77–114 (Mar., June, 1917); *idem*, " Tennessee, the Compromise of 1850, and the Nashville Convention." *Mississippi Valley Historical Review*, II, 313–47; and H. V. Ames, " John C. Calhoun and the Secession Movement of 1850," American Antiquarian Society *Proceedings*, N.S., XXVIII, 19–50.

and that, on the other hand, the South was forced to pay the protective tariff on the imported goods she used, or a resultant higher price for domestic goods she did not produce, sank deeply into Southern consciousness. The expenditure of federal revenue disproportionately upon Northern internal improvements still further aroused indignation at what seemed to be a sectional injustice. Even in 1828 Calhoun urged that over two-thirds of the total domestic exports were attributable to the planting states, and raised the ominous question of what would result if these states had separate customs houses.

At the very time, moreover, when the pride of the Cotton Kingdom was at its height, the slaveholders found themselves attacked by abolitionists and Free Soilers. Social revolution, economic ruin, and the political encirclement of the South, shutting it off from participation in the historic movement of expansion into new territories, seemed to the section to be the inevitable consequence of the tendencies of the Northern majority. The slaveholding states did not lack statesmen whose vision was wide and whose policies were founded on careful reasoning, but few of them gave adequate weight to the effects of slavery itself. The planter was apt to think of the accumulation of capital, by saving, as unworthy avariciousness characteristic of the Yankee, and to seek the cause of his difficulties only in the legislation of Congress under a Northern majority.

In the fields of legislation and politics, the section's leaders found full expression of their quality. From the earlier days, when Virginia was the Mother of Presidents, through the years when Tennessee took Virginia's place, to the close of the period, when the Lower South, led by South Carolina, became the power behind the throne, the South Atlantic statesmen showed determination and capacity that were of deep influence upon American history.

By custom and by the long continuance of freehold qualifications, the planter controlled the legislatures of his states. In many of them, the governor, the state officers, and important members of the judiciary were chosen by the legislature. The county courts likewise were, in practice, under planter control — close corporations; [63] and these courts selected the county clerk

[63] Judge W. R. Staples, "The County Courts," an address before the Virginia Bar Association, 1894, used by Johnson in his *Dabney*, cited above;

and the sheriff, and handled county taxation and expenditures. Although a boisterous attendance of Virginia freeholders gathered on court days, in that state, and listened to stump speeches by rival candidates, the government was in fact dominated by the leading slaveholders. A South Carolinian wrote, " A stranger might live among us for years and see no traces of a government." [64]

As in the case of other sections, the vote between the principal parties was close. If we add all the Presidential votes cast in the South Atlantic States from 1832 to 1852, inclusive, the Democrats had a majority of only about sixty-seven thousand out of a total of nearly a million and three-quarters — not quite four per cent. These figures, however, exclude South Carolina, where the electors were chosen by the legislature, which in several of the elections followed a course of its own. Less than a thousand Free Soil votes were cast in the two elections of 1848 and 1852, in all this section. In 1836 and 1840 special conditions existed. In the campaign of the former year, William Henry Harrison, of Ohio, and Hugh L. White, of Tennessee — both of them of Southern ancestry — ran in opposition to Van Buren, the Democratic candidate; but they professed to be better representatives of real Jacksonian Democracy than was Van Buren himself, and they made their appeals to the pioneers and pioneer ideals. Up to that time, White, a fellow-Tennesseean of Jackson, had supported the measures of his administration. Again in the " log cabin " campaign of 1840, the same appeal was made by Harrison to Western Democratic farmers and the rural classes suffering under the hard times following the Crisis of 1837. Omitting these two elections, the Democratic majority rises to ninety thousand, and the percentage is nearly doubled.

As the maps show,[65] the counties which gave Whig majorities occupied tidewater areas of the Chesapeake, in Maryland and Virginia, and of Albemarle and Pamlico sounds, in North Carolina, and the regions in South Carolina and Georgia best suited

and Herbert A. Kellar, " Rockbridge County Virginia, in 1835," in *The Crusades and Other Historical Essays Presented to Dana C. Munro by His Former Students*, ed. L. J. Paetow (New York, 1928), pp. 321–65.

[64] *De Bow's Review*, XVIII, 127.

[65] See maps, pp. 413, 443, 485, and 529, and the maps of the elections of 1848 and 1852, at the end of the volume.

to cotton culture. As if to prove, however, that physical geography was not absolutely controlling, there were extensive strong Whig regions even in western North Carolina, up to the crest of the mountains. Here a deep-seated antagonism had been aroused by the economic, political, and social contrasts between that region and the counties of the coastal plain. This illustrates the fact that long-continued grievances of one region against another do result in a definite geography of politics, although this geography may not influence party action in the same way in all regions.

In the general trend of politics in the South Atlantic States between 1830 and 1850, what is striking is the gradual assimilation of Whigs into the Democratic party, and the decline of the Jacksonian element in that Democracy. There was also a change from the time when the upcountry alarmed the seaboard by discussing emancipation of the slaves and demanding re-apportionment of political power according to the number of white citizens rather than according to property, to the time when the alarm over the fate of slavery and the power of the section in the Union brought upland farmer and seaboard planter into united action. At the end of the period as at the beginning, the section was predominantly Democratic in its party affiliations, but these were with the Calhoun Democracy, which found its center of gravity in the Lower South (composing the " Cotton Kingdom " which stretched across the South Atlantic and South Central sections), supported by the tractable portions of the party in the North, instead of a Democracy that found its leadership in the Tennessee Valley.

At the opening of the thirties, there were sharp differences between the tidewater and the upcountry. In the Virginia Constitutional Convention of 1829–30, the tidewater representatives strongly urged that the man with property has the greater stake in society and is entitled to the protection which flows from possession of power. The Jeffersonian ideas, as voiced in the Declaration of Independence, were repudiated by tidewater speakers. This reasoning followed from the consideration that the interests of the several parts of the commonwealth were not identical and, therefore, rule by a mere majority of persons was not admissible as a form of government.

At that time, the Virginia house of delegates was so apportioned that the transmontane country had a much smaller representation in the legislature, proportionate to white population, than had the eastern counties. As one of the upcountry members put it,

Their principle is, that the owners of slave property, must possess all the powers of Government, however small their own numbers may be, to secure that property from the rapacity of an overgrown majority of white men.   This principle admits of no relaxation, because the weaker the minority becomes, the greater will their need for power be, according to their own doctrines.[66]

A representative from the tidewater declared that " in every civilized country under the sun, some there must be who labour for their daily bread, either by contract with, or subjection to others, or for themselves." [67]   Asking whether those who are obliged to depend on their daily labor for daily subsistence can or ever do enter into political affairs, he pointed out that the proposal was that the men of property in the west should have a representation for all of their day laborers, without their contributing an additional cent of revenue, and that the men of property in the east should contribute in proportion to all the slave labor they employed, without any additional representation. He lamented that

if any evil, physical or moral, arise in any of the States south of us, it never takes a northerly direction, or taints the southern breeze; whereas if any plague originate in the North, it is sure to spread to the South and to invade us sooner or later: the influenza — the smallpox — the varioloid — the Hessian fly — the Circuit Court system — Universal Suffrage — all come from the North — and they always cross above the falls of the great rivers: below, it seems, the broad expanse of waters interposing, effectually arrests their progress.[68]

It is not without significance that speakers grouped the western counties of Virginia with Pennsylvania and the Ohio Valley. The attitude of these mountain regions had long been a matter of alarm to state-rights politicians, who lamented the " overweening passion for Internal Improvement " in the West and charged that the object was

to overturn the doctrine of State Rights, of which Virginia has been the very pillar, and to remove the barrier she has opposed to the interference

---

[66] *Proceedings and Debates of the Virginia State Convention, of 1829–30* (Richmond, 1830), p. 87. For an interesting elaboration of the different classes of society and their claims to political power, see pp. 121–22.
[67] *Ibid.*, p. 158.   [68] *Ibid.*, p. 407.

of the Federal Government in that same work of Internal Improvement, by so re-organizing the Legislature, that Virginia too may be hitched to the Federal car.[69]

To some Virginians, in later years, the extension of the suffrage marked the time of the state's decline in the councils of the nation.

The constitution framed by Virginia in 1830, and that by North Carolina in 1835, proved to be compromises between the tidewater and the western counties of both states in the matter of franchise and apportionment of representatives. But those interior counties in which slaveholding was growing gained the balance of power in those states. Violent legislative debates marked the early thirties in both states, in which these questions and that of abolition and colonization were raised, but from then on the proslavery element was in control.[70]

When we consider the political leaders in the South Atlantic section, we find that those of Maryland, with Baltimore as its metropolis, reflected the connections of parts of that state with Northern economic life. Even Roger B. Taney had begun his career as a young Federalist lawyer. He had freed his inherited slaves and, later, others which he had acquired. In 1819 he had successfully defended a Methodist presiding elder who had declared slavery a sin and who had been arrested on the charge of instigating slaves to mutiny. In the course of this defense, Taney had spoken of " the galling chain of slavery." As a Federalist, he resented the action of John Quincy Adams in leaving the Jeffersonian party, and he voted for Jackson. As one-time counsel and director of a Baltimore bank, he had gained knowledge of banking institutions, and became an opponent of the United States Bank. His later rise to the positions of Attorney-General of the United States, Secretary of the Treasury, and Chief Justice in succession to John Marshall, and his decision in the celebrated case of Dred Scott, need not be here rehearsed.[71]

---

[69] *Ibid.*, p. 154.

[70] On these debates, see: Thos. R. Dew, *An Essay on Slavery* (2d ed.; Richmond, Va., 1849) ; Weston, *Progress of Slavery*, Chap. XIII; Ambler, *Sectionalism in Virginia*, Chap. VI; Henry H. Simms, *The Rise of the Whigs in Virginia, 1824–1840* (Richmond, Va., 1929), pp. 36–39; and W. H. Sparks, *The Memories of Fifty Years* (Philadelphia, 1872), p. 23.

[71] On Taney see the citations on p. 423 (n. 136), *post*.

On the other hand, John Pendleton Kennedy [72] married the daughter of a wealthy Baltimore mill owner and developed into a protectionist and, in general, a follower of Clay. His *Quodlibet* (1840) was a clever satire on Jacksonian Democracy. Under President Fillmore he served as Secretary of the Navy.

By 1830 Virginia had passed the apogee of her political power. In the Constitutional Convention of 1829–30, Madison, Monroe, Marshall, and John Randolph of Roanoke were in attendance, but they were old men making their last appearance on the stage. The newer leaders were but political lieutenants of men in other states. In the group that became Whigs, young men like R. M. T. Hunter and Henry A. Wise were later to be the spokesmen of Calhoun. John Tyler, likewise (although he became President by succession at the death of Harrison),[73] belonged to the Virginia group of state-rights Whigs who combined in the motley opposition to the Democrats in the election of 1840. But he had been at one time a Democrat and was to return to that party in 1844. Nevertheless, Tyler was a characteristic Virginia type, too little understood by the historians who have criticized him. Possessed of a mind that loved to emphasize delicate distinctions, and unable to understand the failure of others to grasp them, he had a definite policy with regard to the leading issues, such as banking and the tariff, and was devoted to strict construction and the Virginia idea of the rights of the states.[74] William Wirt, the noted author of *Sketches of the Life and Character of Patrick Henry* and a prominent attorney, although he was a Whig accepted the nomination for the Presidency on the Anti-Masonic ticket and was defeated in 1832.

Another Virginia group, in the beginning, supported the fortunes of Jackson, and afterwards of Van Buren. The Richmond " Junto," consisting of banker-planters and Thomas Ritchie, greatest of Southern editors, who voiced their policy, followed Jackson in his war on the National Bank. The removal of the deposits brought temporary ascendancy to the President's foes in the state. Governor Littleton W. Tazewell (at first a strict-constructionist Democrat) condemned Jackson's course. As a

[72] His literary work, particularly his *Swallow Barn*, is later referred to.

[73] See Chapter XI, *post*, on the Presidency of Tyler.

[74] In the critical period of the nullification struggle, he urged delay, and compromise between the ideas of Virginia and those of South Carolina.

result of the reaction that followed, Benjamin W. Leigh was made Senator. By his leadership, in the debates of the Constitutional Convention of 1829-30,[75] of the aristocratic planting interests of the eastern part of the state, as against demands of the west, he had antagonized the latter, and Virginia sectionalism was accented by his candidacy. When Van Buren, whose ideas had been influenced by Dr. John Brockenbrough, of Richmond, advocated the withdrawal of the government from all banking operations, the Virginia leaders split, Editor Ritchie and Senator William C. Rives opposing the idea and favoring the use of deposit banks. The consequence was that a group of Conservative Democrats, led by Rives, came into existence, still adhering for some time to Van Buren but refusing to accept his independent-treasury proposals.[76] Many other Virginia leaders, like Andrew Stevenson, Senator James Barbour, Representative John S. Barbour (a nullifier), and P. P. Barbour (later the Democratic candidate in Virginia for the Vice-Presidency), were important factors in the politics of the state.[77]

No statesman in North Carolina exercised dominant control.[78] Those who were most distinguished were leaders rather of the nullification minority than of public sentiment in general. Of these, perhaps the greatest was Willie P. Mangum, whom Calhoun picked in 1836 to receive South Carolina's electoral vote for the Presidency.

The tobacco-planting aristocracy yielded to the claims of the cotton planter. Political power followed the southward movement of economic power.

By far the greatest of Southern statesmen was Calhoun. As a descendant of a Scotch-Irish pioneer who passed down the

[75] See pp. 183–85, ante.

[76] On the Conservative Democrats, see: Chapter x, post, on the Presidency of Van Buren; Cole, Whig Party in the South, pp. 46–55; and Ambler, Sectionalism in Virginia, pp. 228–31. The Richmond Enquirer, September 28, 1838, has an interesting discussion of whether Rives would follow Tallmadge and the Madisonian into the Whig party. See also Calvin Colton, The Life, Correspondence, and Speeches of Henry Clay (New York, 1857), IV, 432–33; and Tyler, Letters and Times of the Tylers, I (Richmond, Va., 1884), 591.

[77] See the indexes in: Ambler, op. cit., and Thomas Ritchie (Richmond, Va., 1913); Cole, op. cit.; and Simms, op. cit.

[78] The North Carolina superior type is illustrated in The Correspondence of Jonathan Worth, ed. J. G. de R. Hamilton (North Carolina Historical Commission Publications; Raleigh, 1909), and The Papers of Thomas Ruffin, ed. idem (ibid.; 1918, 1920).

long road from Pennsylvania to the Piedmont of the South, he had a following, not only from his principles and personal qualifications, but as the representative of that zone of Scotch-Presbyterian people which stretched from Pennsylvania to Georgia, along the foothills of the Alleghenies — a fact which helps explain his reliance upon Pennsylvania at various crises in his political career. Fate might have made him a national statesman, and, indeed, at the outset of his political life that seemed to be his destiny. But the hot blood of South Carolina, so exclusively devoted to slavery and the cotton interest that she occupied the exposed position in the contest, compelled Calhoun, as the price of his continued career, to represent, first, the interests of South Carolina, and then those of the South as a whole, in opposition to the rest of the country.

As a statesman, Calhoun deeply influenced the course of American history, and his philosophy of the political rights of minority interests, geographically distributed, has an enduring significance. Personally, he is one of the striking figures in the group of Scotch-Irishmen who have helped to shape the nation's course. With a face which might have been carved from the gray granites of his ancestral home, hair whitening as the years of these decades went on, a " mind-quelling eye," a look of " conscious power," as sentence after sentence of terse argument fell impetuously in silvery tones from his firm lips he made a deep impression on the Senate.[79] His speeches were as free from superfluous oratory as were the bodies of his lithe and muscular frontier ancestors from superfluous flesh. With a Scotch-Presbyterian gift for logic, he bound his hearers in a net of reasoning which (if the premises were granted) was hard to break. Nor was Calhoun, as some biographers have made him seem, a cold, machine-like logician. Intensely ambitious, he coveted the Presidency, and shaped his course to finding accommodation between sectional interests until events and the need of holding his constituency of South Carolina and the slave states changed him from one of the most nationalistic of statesmen to the high priest of state sovereignty and sectional separation.[80] He was one of the most sagacious and win-

[79] See the characterization of Calhoun in Turner, *Rise of the New West*, pp. 182–85, 246, 324–30. See also Henry W. Hilliard, *Politics and Pen Pictures at Home and Abroad* (New York, 1892), pp. 3–4.

[80] For Calhoun's earlier career, see W. M. Meigs, *The Life of John Caldwell*

ning of politicians, captivating to aspiring young Congressmen and with an uncanny perception of the implications of political events. But Senator Dixon H. Lewis, of Alabama, intimate with Calhoun, writing in the spring of 1840, called him " too intellectual, too industrious, too intent in the struggle of politics to suit me except as an occasional companion. There is no *relaxation* with him." [81] But Lewis weighed around four hundred pounds!

Calhoun's contribution to Southern politics, between 1830 and 1850, lay chiefly in the way he set forth the claims of a minority section, dominated by the slaveholding interest, and formulated a theory for its defense under the doctrine of state sovereignty. He did not take the lead in this position. To a large extent, his hand was forced by impetuous South Carolina leaders. Between 1825 and 1828, while he watched events from the Vice-Presidential chair in the Senate, he had ample opportunity to revise his earlier support of nationalism. But it was as an interested spectator, for, not only was his own part of South Carolina changing to a distinctively slaveholding and cotton-raising region, but the protective tariff was arousing violent resentment among his constituents, and Chief Justice John Marshall's decisions in the federal Supreme Court had produced a reaction against the growing power at Washington. President Cooper, of South Carolina College, was arguing for the sovereignty of the state, denying the constitutionality of the protective tariff, and leading his students to question the value of the Union.[82] R. J. Turnbull, under the pseudonym of " Brutus," was inflaming the public and demanding direct action. He approved the decision of the United States Supreme Court that the federal government was " supreme within its sphere of action, and the States equally sovereign as to their

---

Calhoun (New York, 1917), I, and Turner, *op. cit.*, pp. 182–85. Contemporaneous impressions of him are abundant; for example, see: the journal of a Virginian, in the middle thirties, printed in the *Atlantic Monthly*, XXVI, 337–38; John Wentworth, *Congressional Reminiscences. Adams, Benton, Calhoun, Clay, and Webster* (*Fergus Historical Series*, No. 24; Chicago, 1882), pp. 20, 21; Harriet Martineau, *Retrospect of Western Travel* (London and New York, 1838), I, 179, 181–82; and Richmond *Enquirer*, Feb. 13, 1838 (Ritchie's estimate).

[81] Southern History Association *Publications*, VII, 355 (Sept., 1903).

[82] Dumas Malone, *The Public Life of Thomas Cooper, 1783–1839* (New Haven, 1926), Chaps. IX, X; D. F. Houston, *A Critical Study of Nullification in South Carolina* (*Harvard Historical Studies*, III; Cambridge, 1896); Gaillard Hunt, *John C. Calhoun* (Philadelphia, 1908); and Meigs, *op. cit.*, I, Chap. XIII.

reserved powers "; but he believed the Court, by allowing to
Congress the use of implied powers, had destroyed the safeguards
of the Constitution. In the case of a disputed power, he held
that, if the assent of three-fourths of the state legislatures could
not be gained for an amendment to grant it, this " would prove
that the power ought not to be exercised." The objection of one-
fourth of the states to a law resting on Congressional and judicial
interpretation, he thought, would be prima facie evidence that
the law was unconstitutional.[83] Calhoun's rival, William Smith,
was denouncing him for his failure to stand for the extreme state-
rights doctrines. James Hamilton, J. H. Hammond, Hayne,[84]
and even McDuffie [85] (who not long before had gone farther than
Calhoun in repudiating radical assertions of state sovereignty)
— all leaders of the planter class — precipitated the crisis which
Calhoun, ambitious to win the Presidency by retaining a nation-
wide following, would avoid.

His Exposition of 1828 was an attempt to find a solution short
of war.[86] Fundamentally, his reasoning was affected by the
Virginia and Kentucky Resolutions of 1798 and 1799 and the
writings of John Taylor of Carolina, Judge Spencer Roane, and
Turnbull. It also grew out of South Carolina's own experience.
The contest between upland and lowland South Carolina had
resulted in a revision of the legislative apportionment, under
amendments to the constitution in 1808, whereby the senate
passed under the control of the property-owning slaveholders of
the tidewater and the house became representative of the upcountry farmers, so recently pioneers. Thus, a mutual veto by
the respective geographical interests was apparently provided;
but this was fallacious, for in fact slavery was even then rapidly
extending into the Piedmont.[87] For the time, however, in Calhoun's impressionable youth, the solution seemed a real one.[88]

When a commonwealth was constituted of diverse regional

---

[83] See his *The Crisis* (Charleston, S.C., 1827), p. 111, and *Observations on
State Sovereignty* (New York, 1850), p. 107. Cf. *The Works of John C.
Calhoun*, ed. R. K. Crallé, VI (New York, 1855), 177–78, 189.

[84] See Jervey, *Hayne and His Times*.

[85] On McDuffie's traits, see Sparks, *Memories*, pp. 87–92.

[86] See Turner, *op. cit.*, Chap. XIX.

[87] W. A. Schaper, *Sectionalism and Representation in South Carolina*
(American Historical Association *Annual Report*, 1900, I [Washington, 1901],
237–463), p. 436.

[88] *Calhoun Works*, I (New York, 1853), 402–6.

interests, it seemed to Calhoun that the minority should have a veto power to prevent exploitation by a mere majority. This principle he would apply to the relations between such a state as South Carolina and the Union as a whole. The antagonism which had once existed between South Carolina's seaboard counties and the state as a unit, he now found repeated in the relations between her and the majority of the nation. His defense of the minority, he formulated in his doctrine of the " concurrent majority." Instead of considering a given society, made up of conflicting interests, as a unit, he would require the concurrence of separate majorities of these several interests, rather than permit government by an absolute majority of the whole.[89]

This doctrine he combined with the extreme conception of state sovereignty. Viewing the Constitution as a compact between sovereign states, he conceived of the Union as a league in which the central government was merely the agent of the respective states and limited, in the terms of its agency, by the Constitution strictly construed. The Supreme Court, being a part of the central government, had, in his opinion, no right to decide finally between a state and that government. In the last resort, the individual state had the right to interpose its veto — in other words, to nullify an act deemed unconstitutional. It was his belief that the undivided sovereignty of the state rested, in the last resort, in a constitutional convention, and that this convention was, in effect, the state itself exercising its power, and not a body of delegates.[90] Following action by such a convention of the sovereign state, the disputed power or law would become inoperative unless three-fourths of the states (that is, the number required to amend the Constitution) declared in its favor. The device was presented as a peaceful remedy, operating through delays and adjustment of grievances.

Calhoun did not avow authorship of the South Carolina Exposition of 1828 until after his break with Jackson. His course was precipitated by his friends. He was compelled to choose between a career as a national statesman and the leadership of his state

[89] *Ibid.*, pp. 24–29, and Calhoun's speech in the Senate, Feb. 15, 1833 (*Register of Debates*, IX, Pt. 1, 547).

[90] On the repudiation by South Carolina, in the Civil War period, of Calhoun's theory of a constitutional convention as the embodiment of sovereignty, see Laura A. White, " The Fate of Calhoun's Sovereign Convention in South Carolina," *American Historical Review*, XXXIV, 757–71.

and section with possible loss of national preferment. In successive documents, he worked out, with increasing rigidity and definiteness, his theory of nullification,[91] and finally South Carolina attempted to put it into effect by the Ordinance passed by her state convention, November 24, 1832, declaring the tariff act of that year null and void within her limits.

The attitude of President Jackson and of Congress toward this Ordinance, as expressed in the President's Proclamation, the Force Bill, and Clay's compromise tariff of 1833, will be discussed in Chapter IX, on the interplay of the sections during Jackson's Presidency. It was clear that civil war would result unless South Carolina retreated; the compromise tariff afforded her a way of escape.

The response to South Carolina's doctrine by other states [92] had left her alone in defense of Calhoun's nullification principles, and, even within her own boundaries, war was threatened between the Union and state-rights parties. Delaware and Maryland insisted that the Supreme Court of the United States was the tribunal for final settlement of constitutional disputes beween the federal government and the states. Virginia contended that nullification was not sanctioned by her resolutions of 1798, but she also denied the correctness of the doctrines of Jackson's Proclamation, and voted to send a commissioner to South Carolina to mediate.[93] North Carolina declared nullification revolutionary, leading to disunion. Georgia abhorred the doctrine as neither a peaceful nor a constitutional remedy; but she considered calling a convention (interestingly, to include only Virginia, North Carolina, South Carolina, Georgia, Alabama, Mississippi, and Tennessee) to devise modes of relief from the tariff system.[94]   But

[91] For these documents, and details of the movement, see: *Calhoun Works*, VI; Houston, *Nullification in South Carolina;* Chauncey S. Boucher, *The Nullification Controversy in South Carolina* (Chicago, 1916); H. D. Capers, *The Life and Times of C. G. Memminger* (Richmond, Va., 1893); E. J. Harden, *The Life of George M. Troup*, . . . (Savannah, 1859); and Chas. J. Stillé, *Life and Services of Joel R. Poinsett* (Philadelphia, 1888).

[92] *State Papers on Nullification* (Massachusetts General Court *Miscellaneous Documents;* Boston, 1834), and H. V. Ames (ed.), *State Documents on Federal Relations*, No. IV (Philadelphia, 1902).

[93] Tyler, *Letters and Times of the Tylers*, I, Chap. XIV (especially pp. 440 ff.), and Henry A. Wise, *Seven Decades of the Union* (Philadelphia, 1881), Chap. VI (especially pp. 121 ff.), differentiate the Virginia doctrine of state rights from Calhoun's South Carolina doctrine of nullification.

[94] E. M. Coulter, " The Nullification Movement in Georgia," *Georgia His-*

there was a vigorous minority in Georgia ready to support nullification if force were attempted by the federal government.

The attitude of the South Central States, where Jackson was still the Western " hero," but where, toward the close of the forties, Calhoun and South Carolina became ascendant in the Gulf Basin, was equally decisive. Alabama rejected nullification as essentially revolutionary, but would approve a federal constitutional convention to pass on the constitutionality of the tariff act; Mississippi denounced Calhoun and opposed the " heresy " of nullification as fatal to the Union and as meaning civil war; Kentucky, in 1830, asserted the right of the majority to govern, and refused to accept nullification as conforming to her resolutions of 1798 and 1799, which, the legislature held, merely expressed disapprobation of unconstitutional laws. " There it stopped, and that is the limit which no state should pass, until it has formed the deliberate resolution of lighting up the torch of civil war." [95] Louisiana affirmed the constitutionality of the tariff of 1828.[96] Missouri, the only slaveholding state of the North Central Division, denied the principle of nullification.[97]

Although the rejections of the nullification doctrine were naturally affected by the contemporary party conflicts between the followers of Jackson and of Calhoun, and in Georgia by survivals of the W. H. Crawford-Jackson feud and by state rivalry and reluctance to follow South Carolina's leadership, yet the decisive majorities by which these rejections were carried make it clear that the Southern sections had not reached Calhoun's position and that co-operation of both South Atlantic and South Central states was the only mode of real resistance to the federal government. It was the *section*, not the *state*, that was in reality significant. The whole South must be won.

To the accomplishment of that end Calhoun turned his attention. It had taken more than fifteen years of public life to transfer him from the ranks of the nationalists to those of the state-

torical Quarterly, V, 3–39 (Mar., 1921); R. H. Shryock, Georgia and the Union in 1850 (Durham, N.C., 1926); and U. B. Phillips, Georgia and State Rights (American Historical Association Annual Report, 1901, II [Washington, 1902], 3–224), Chap. v.

[95] Acts of Kentucky, 1829–30, pp. 287–300, quoted in Ames, op. cit., pp. 26–29.

[96] Acts of Louisiana, 1830, pp. 70–72, quoted ibid., pp. 29–30.

[97] National Intelligencer, Mar. 15, 1833.

sovereignty particularists; but an even longer interval separated
his nullification phase from his deliberate conclusion that the
South must demand sectional assurances, under a revised constitution, or withdraw from the Union. From around 1826 to
1846, he still looked to placing the Southern sections in such
a balance of power between parties as would enable them to dic-
tate action of Congress.

Georgia had lifted her voice with no uncertainty for state
rights when her control of Indian lands within her bounds, and
the right of extending her jurisdiction and laws over the entire
state, had been threatened in the period of the administration
of John Quincy Adams.[98] But Jackson had supported Georgia's
claims, and thus had won friends there. Crawford, his one-time
rival for the Presidency, was now a paralytic, and died in 1834.
Courtly John Forsyth, Senator from Georgia, experienced in diplomacy, a tactful and captivating debater, supported Jackson
against the nullifiers and became his Secretary of State. J. M.
Berrien, on the other hand, after the " voluntary " resignations
from the President's cabinet,[99] asserted the state-rights doctrine,
and finally transferred his allegiance from the Democrats to the
Whigs. But the extreme supporter of nullification in this state
was Judge A. S. Clayton, one of her Representatives in Congress.

In Georgia the feeling for co-operation of the section as a whole
in a Southern convention was a strong and growing one. A body
of younger men (from the heart of her cotton belt), less impatient than those of South Carolina but forceful and determined,
took the reins.[100] The greatest Whigs of Georgia were Alexander
H. Stephens, crippled in body but brilliant in intellect,[101] and
Robert Toombs. Burly, sometimes crude, but compelling in his
influence, Toombs came to hold a position, embodied in the Georgia platform of 1850, which advocated postponement of secession
in order to try out the possibility of a settlement by compromise
under Whig leadership. It was not many years, however, before
even these conservatives, with Howell Cobb, the Democratic

[98] Phillips, *Georgia and State Rights*, Chaps. II–V.

[99] See p. 392, *post*.

[100] See *The Correspondence of Robert Toombs, Alexander H. Stephens, and
Howell Cobb*, ed. U. B. Phillips (American Historical Association *Annual Report*,
1911, II; Washington, 1913); and U. B. Phillips, *The Life of Robert Toombs*
(New York, 1913).

[101] See the characterization in Hilliard, *Politics and Pen Pictures*, p. 118.

leader (who was the third of the triumvirate of Georgia politicians), passed over to the ultra wing. In the end, Georgia, which had refused to follow South Carolina in its nullification episode, became almost as ardent, both in its threats and its program.

As Calhoun conceded, the tariff was " the occasion, rather than the real cause," [102] of the grievance of the slaveholding states. Underneath all, lay the conditions of soil and climate and the existence of slavery. When the compromise tariff of 1833 brought temporary relief to these states, Calhoun, after having led his state-rights wing of the Democrats into an alliance with the Whigs against Jackson, led them back to an alliance with Van Buren. He felt that the danger of a powerful personality in the Presidential chair had passed, and when, in 1837 (following the panic of that year), Van Buren proposed to divorce the government from all banks by the use of the Independent Treasury, Calhoun saw an opportunity to break with his former unnatural associates — the friends of what he called the " money power," the tariff, and internal improvements — led by Henry Clay.

From that time, the slavery question came more clearly into the open. Seizing every opportunity to use the balance of power of his followers, he pressed the defense of slavery against Northern critics. He would permit Southern postmasters to deny the use of the mails to " incendiary " (that is, abolition) literature. With most of the Southern Congressmen from the slaveholding states, he would refuse the right of petition when intended to prevent debate upon the morality of slavery. He sharply challenged attempts to prevent the annexation of new territory when slavery was to be permitted therein. He urged the right of the slaveholding states to the " equilibrium " in political power which they had originally held in the Senate. Again and again, he offered resolutions asserting the theory of state equality, which, he argued, would be violated by the prevention of entrance of slaves into new territories. He aimed at a concert of interests between the South Atlantic and the South Central states — an alliance to which he would add, if possible, the entire Mississippi Valley. With the aid of those Northern Democrats who would accept the leadership of the Southern sections, he hoped to secure safety in the Union and the dominance of the slaveholding states. This, he thought, was a matter of self-defense against the grow-

[102] J. S. Bassett, *The Life of Andrew Jackson* (New York, 1925), II, 547.

ing power of the industrial North, which tended continually to resist the expansion, and even the continuance, of slavery.[103]

It was far from a stationary section to which such South Atlantic leaders looked. The development of Southern railroads, and of commerce independent of the North, appears by the reports of the various conventions to have been a matter of deep concern. In fact, some of the principal participants in the conventions were men prominent in the promotion of railroad construction, both in the slaveholding sections themselves and in the wider sphere of influence which they hoped to establish between the Lower Mississippi Valley and the Pacific Coast.[104]

The political and social philosophy of the South had, by 1850, come to be that of a distinct section, but of a section still discordant and varied on all subjects but one.

The average planter, no doubt, did not think deeply on the subject of his political philosophy. Here, as in all sections, many leaders who reasoned about the tendencies, considered programs, and even formulated a philosophy were hardly representative.[105]

The most noticeable item in an inventory of Southern political ideas is the change in the attitude toward slavery. Whereas, in the period of the Missouri Compromise, it was common (with the exception, perhaps, of Georgia and of South Carolina) to apologize for slavery, to look with leniency, at least, upon the idea of emancipation and colonization, or to advocate slavery extension as a means for mitigating its evils, before long it was defended as the basis for all orderly and cultivated society. Professor Dew, who had spent some years as a student in Germany, came for-

---

[103] The political developments in the South Atlantic section, in the forties, are so connected with those in the South Central States and in Congress that they will be considered in subsequent chapters (XI, XII).

[104] See, for example, Sioussat, in *Tennessee Historical Magazine*, III, 1–27, 77–114 (Mar., June, 1917), and in *Mississippi Valley Historical Review*, II, 313–47; and the other citations on p. 180, *ante*.

[105] See: W. E. Dodd, in *American Journal of Sociology*, XXIII, 735–46; *idem*, *Cotton Kingdom*, p. 118; U. B. Phillips, in *The South in the Building of the Nation* (Richmond, Va., 1909), IV, 401–4, 422; *idem*, " The Literary Movement for Secession," in *Studies in Southern History and Politics* (New York, 1914), pp. 33–60; C. E. Merriam, " The Political Philosophy of John C. Calhoun," *ibid.*, pp. 319–38; and A. C. Cole, in *Mississippi Valley Historical Review*, I, 376–99.

The great mass of material stating the proslavery argument, may be reached through the citations in these essays and in A. B. Hart, *Slavery and Abolition, 1831–1841* (*The American Nation: A History*, XVI; New York, 1906), pp. 337–38.

ward as a champion of the idea that slavery was historically the normal condition, leading to the accumulation of property, which, in turn, was the basis of civilization. He believed that leisure, and its accompaniments of art and literature, depended upon a system of forced labor. He argued the economic advantages, and even the necessity, of slavery to the South, and proved that, in view of the birth rate, the project of colonization of the slaves was impracticable.[106]

The South had always been responsive to orthodoxy in religion, and its ministers used the Bible to prove both the existence of slavery among the "chosen people" and the sanction of the Scriptures for the institution. Writers like Chancellor William Harper, of South Carolina, urging that all owners of property were virtually rulers and that the first care of society was the production of leaders, denied the Jeffersonian doctrine that all men are created free and equal. Among most of the large planters, the Declaration of Independence ceased to have validity. J. H. Hammond, writing to Calhoun at the end of our period, said:

I trust that you have taken the ground that the fundamental object of Government is to *secure* the fruits of labor and skill — that is to say *property*, and that its forms must be moulded upon the social organization. . . . "*Free Government*" and all that sort of thing has been I think a fatal delusion and humbug from the time of Moses. Freedom does not spring from Government but from the same soil which produces Government itself; and all we want from that is a guarantee for property fairly acquired.[107]

But nowhere was the matter stated with more directness and force than by Calhoun himself. Declaring slavery "a good — a positive good," he said:

I hold then, that there never has yet existed a wealthy and civilized society in which one portion of the community did not, in point of fact, live on the labor of the other. . . . There is and always has been in an advanced stage of wealth and civilization, a conflict between labor and capital. The condition of society in the South exempts us from the disorders and dangers resulting from this conflict.[108]

This emphasis upon property as the end of government and the basis for civilized society was given especial direction in the South

---

[106] Dew, *Essay on Slavery.*   [107] *Calhoun Correspondence*, p. 1212.
[108] *Works*, II (New York, 1853), 631–32.

by the contemporaneous Locofoco movement in the North and the socialistic discussions in England. A Virginian, George Fitzhugh, wrote a book, entitled *Sociology for the South*,[109] in which he used the reports of English Parliamentary committees and the writings of English social reformers to show the hard lot of the common laborer in free society. He argued that the system of slavery was far better. Comparing that system with the English army, he likened the position of the slave to that of the English soldier who enlisted for life, received his food, clothing, and shelter, and was guaranteed against the suffering of old age. The organization and the discipline of the army were, likewise, compared with those of the slave system, which assigned to every man his duty and provided for the distribution and exercise of due authority to promote the interests of society as a whole. These ideas were not limited to Fitzhugh; many others looked upon the development of the labor question in the North, with its radical criticism of special privileges and the rights of property, in much the same way. There was a close connection between the defense of the slave system and the philosophy of aristocratic government. Slavery was pitted against democracy and was defended as the only sound basis for that liberty which safeguarded property and insured civilization against the ignorant and turbulent mob of the poorer classes. Calhoun believed that a

social experiment was going on both at the North and the South — in the one with almost a pure and unlimited democracy, and in the other with a mixed race. . . . Southern society had been far less agitated . . . In fact, the defence of human liberty against the aggressions of despotic power had been always the most efficient in States where domestic slavery was found to prevail.[110]

To these writers, a white-yeoman agricultural class was acceptable, but the wageworker was not. Slavery, it was argued, eliminated the real problem of democracy by eliminating the free workingmen, who even threatened to form a dangerous " mobocracy," or a suffering political army controlled by corrupt and artful contrivances of a master class. The direct control over the laboring element, under the system of slavery, seemed to them vastly preferable to the indirect control of the " money power."

[109] Richmond, Va., 1854.
[110] *Register of Debates*, XIII, Pt. I, 718–19.

The problem of party affiliation among the thinking men of the South was a complicated one. J. A. Campbell, later a justice of the federal Supreme Court, wrote to Calhoun from Mobile, in 1847: ". . . the Whig party is *governed* by its leading and reflecting men. The tone of the party is derived from men of property and character and they are in a measure held to respect property guaranteed by the constitution and laws of the country." [111]   This attitude was reinforced by apprehension of the tendency of Jacksonian Democracy. Speaking of the legislators of the Western states, Campbell added: " Their notions are freer their impulses stronger their wills less restrained. I do not wish to increase the number till the New States already admitted to the Union become civilized."

On the other hand, the areas of the Northern Whigs were not only those in which property rights were most emphasized, where banking and the protective tariff, and franchises and donations for internal improvements, were popular, but they were also the very regions in which the New York-New England stream of population had settled and where opposition to slavery, and particularly to the expansion of slavery, was strong. As the political history developed, this became clear to the South, and the instinctive apprehension of the readiness of the Northern Whigs to turn to the national government for support of the system of protective tariffs, under loose construction of the Constitution, alarmed the Southern wing of the party. It is true that there was, among the Southern Whigs, a pronounced softening of their opposition to protection, [112] but there was, at the same time, increasing alarm over the antislavery tendency of the Northern Whigs. All of this aided the Democratic leaders, who insisted that the Northern wing of their party was a safer reliance for those who depended upon a strict construction of the Constitution, state rights, and opposition to " New England fanaticism." It also brought accessions to those who followed Calhoun in his insistence that the South must hold the balance of power in the Union by organizing an independent state-rights party, to maintain what were held to be the older conceptions of the Constitution and to resist the tendencies which menaced that section.

Although the Southern Whigs tended to repudiate the Calhoun

[111] *Calhoun Correspondence*, p. 1141.
[112] Cole, *Whig Party in the South*, pp. 101–2.

interpretation of the Virginia and Kentucky resolutions of the early years of the Republic, and to reject nullification as a Constitutional remedy, they were ready to accept sectional secession under the right of revolution, unless the fundamental rights of the South, as understood by them, were conceded. By the closing years of the era, the conservative Whig leaders were in doubt whether the Union could be preserved. The attitude of a Democratic planter is expressed in a letter of 1838:

> "The Bank & the metallic basis " — & the " paper currency " are all debatable questions — but the *Black* Currency is *not*. How am I to be benefited by either "Bank" or "Sub. Treasury" without my land on Cooper River & the *Negroes* that work there? What signifies to *me* all the jargon *about* Whigs & Conservatives etc. etc. if the abolitionists stand between me & the White Gate at Longwood? [113]

Obviously, the slaveholding society of the South was threatened by the liberal tendency of the age. The section saw Northern power growing with its expansion into new Western states, reinforced by the tide of foreign immigration, which avoided the South. At the same time, it saw the established order of society threatened by the agitation of both the pioneer and the city laborer for the logical extension of democracy on the principles of the Declaration of Independence; for universal education; for an elective judiciary; for woman suffrage; for the adjustment of the Constitution, under loose construction, to all of the changes involved in the extension of the settlement of the public lands; for development of transportation through federal aid.

The favored books of the South Atlantic section were still those of the eighteenth century, though it found in Scott's novels the type of aristocratic chivalry which it was fond of regarding as the picture of its own society. It has been said that slavery was an antiseptic for the bacteria of innovation. In New England, the ruling classes had shown alarm over radical tendencies, but that alarm was increased many-fold in the Southern sections by the fact that not only their property but their whole social system was threatened. Their aggressiveness was therefore the aggressiveness of a minority which found itself threatened both by

[113] *The Correspondence of Nicholas Biddle Dealing with National Affairs, 1807–1844*, ed. R. C. McGrane (Boston, 1919), p. 306, n. The editor gives the planter's name as " Alfred Hager(?)." I conjecture that it may have been Alfred Huger, a leading South Carolina supporter of Jackson and Unionism.

the spirit of the times and the increasing power of rival sections. When the South Atlantic and the South Central sections came into unison as the " South," it would save itself by bold challenge to the opposing forces.

The cultural aspects of the South Atlantic States have a special interest in a comparison of those free and slave sections whose history runs back to the colonial period. In such a comparison, the illiteracy of the common people at once arrests the attention. Not only was the great body of negroes almost totally illiterate, but, in adult-white illiteracy in proportion to white population, the section's record was most unfavorable. Although New England, which had a white population about equal to that of the South Atlantic States, had nearly trebled its own ratio of illiteracy between 1840 and 1850 (due, no doubt, to immigration), this was still less than a fourth of that of the South Atlantic Division. Reckoning only the part of the division below Maryland, these distinctively slaveholding states were five times as illiterate as New England.[114]

This illiteracy was, as the map [115] shows, regionally distributed. The worst white illiteracy lay, in 1850, in North Carolina,[116] in the pine barrens of Georgia, and in the mountain counties generally; but there were also markedly illiterate areas in tidewater Virginia. On the other hand, the best white records were made by counties in the Cotton Belt, where the negroes constituted a majority. These facts have, of course, a significance in politics as well as in culture. The rural life of the South, in contrast with the town system and Puritan emphasis upon schools in New England, helps explain this difference.[117] Though some of the states of the section made provision for education of the indigent, it was not until after the Civil War that free public schools became general. Interestingly, some of the best seed for future development of the educational system was sowed in the reports of A. D. Murphey, a North Carolina legislator, whose activity began soon after the War of 1812.

The family tutor (often from New England) and the local

[114] *Compendium of the Seventh Census*, pp. 145, 152.
[115] At end of volume.
[116] But see Chas. L. Coon (ed.), *North Carolina Schools and Academies, 1790–1840* (North Carolina Historical Commission *Publications;* Raleigh, 1915) and *The Beginnings of Public Education in North Carolina* (*ibid.;* 1908).
[117] Tucker, *Progress of the United States*, p. 146.

academy, however, cared for the families of the planter class, and in the field of higher education the South was probably abreast of other sections in number of colleges, size of faculties, and membership of the student body in proportion to white population. If the census report could be trusted to set a uniform standard of what constituted a higher educational institution (which is not the case), the South Atlantic Division had double the number of New England's colleges, not far from twice as many professors, and seven hundred more students, not reckoning the considerable number who went to Northern institutions. Princeton, Yale, and even Harvard, received not a few of such students. Calhoun had attended the celebrated academy of Dr. Moses Waddell, in Georgia, where many of the eminent men of that state and South Carolina were trained [118] in a classical education. Graduating from Yale with other men who became leaders in South Carolina, he went for his law training to the Litchfield Law School, in Connecticut. Also, from colonial days, sons of well-to-do planters had gone to England for their college work, and scholars like Dew had been in German universities.

In the section itself, there were old colleges with distinguished men in their faculties. William and Mary, Washington,[119] and Hampden-Sidney, in Virginia, began in colonial and Revolutionary days. In North Carolina a charter was given by the general assembly to " the Trustees of the University of North Carolina," in 1789, with power to receive donations, and the institution opened in 1795. South Carolina College was begun early in the nineteenth century. The University of Virginia, founded by Jefferson on a broader and more cosmopolitan plan than any other American institution of higher learning, opened in 1825. Its influence upon higher education in other sections, North and West, was important.[120] Many lesser colleges sprang up, in the thirties, throughout the South. In the faculties of all these institutions were men of intellectual acumen and scholarship.

South Carolina College, in the nullification period, was an interesting center of politics and scholarship. Its president was

---

[118] Meigs, *Calhoun*, I, 64–65.

[119] Now Washington and Lee.

[120] W. P. Trent, *English Culture in Virginia* (Baltimore, 1889), and H. B. Adams, *Thomas Jefferson and the University of Virginia* (Washington, 1888), pp. 123–34.

the philosopher and economist, Thomas Cooper, an emigrant from England. During his residence in Pennsylvania, he had been an advocate of the protective tariff, on the theory of fostering infant industries for defense; in South Carolina, however, he became an ardent opponent of the tariff and an extreme champion of state sovereignty, and his teaching influenced the men who became leaders in that state. In England an antislavery man, he was, in South Carolina, not only a defender of slavery but the predecessor of the most eminent of the men who formulated the pro-slavery philosophy.[121] Originally an idealistic Jeffersonian Democrat, assailed as a " Jacobin," fined and imprisoned under the Alien and Sedition Act for criticism of President John Adams, he became, in South Carolina, a critic of democracy and of the social assumptions of the Declaration of Independence. Originally an antagonist of the National Bank, he became its supporter, and even urged Nicholas Biddle to allow the use of his name as a candidate for nomination for the Presidency of the United States. Perhaps these conformations to the thought of South Carolina explain why, in one of the most conservative of communities, he was able violently to attack the clergy and ecclesiasticism and to expound in his classes a materialistic and utilitarian philosophy for years before he was forced to retire.

Francis Lieber, an exile from Germany because of his liberal politics, came to the same college in 1835. At that time, he disavowed being an abolitionist, and, in answer to those who feared his attitude on nullification, he declared that " concentration of power leads always to absolutism," of which the democratic form was the most dangerous. He urged his critics to test him by his career while at the college.[122] He spent twenty years in South Carolina before joining the faculty of Columbia University, New York, where he was a correspondent of Lincoln and a supporter of the Union.[123] There is a modern note in his letters to Calhoun, whom he informs that he is giving " Newspaper Lectures " explaining " leading events and transactions as they occur around

[121] Malone, *Thomas Cooper*, p. 288.

[122] *Columbia Telescope*, Aug. 1, 1835. This item was called to my attention by Dr. C. B. Robson, of the University of North Carolina, while a Research Fellow at the Huntington Library (1930–31).

[123] Lieber MSS are in the Huntington Library. [See Robson, " Papers of Francis Lieber," *The Huntington Library Bulletin*, No. 3 (Feb., 1933), pp. 135–55.]

us, and to teach the students how to read the papers of the day with profit . . . reminding them . . . that what happens to-day is history to-morrow." [124]   He had an international reputation as a political scientist.

The College of William and Mary had suffered by the founding of the University of Virginia, but it still remained a strong force, among the tidewater planters, under its president, the economist and historical teacher Thomas R. Dew,[125] and it had been the *alma mater* of some of the most distinguished leaders in the South.[126]   Nathaniel Beverley Tucker, professor of law there and an influential writer,[127] was a stout defender of state sovereignty and, so early as 1820, an advocate of secession.[128]   " What are our democracies," he asked, " but mobs? "   He was a correspondent and adviser of Henry A. Wise and President Tyler.   In the forties, his brother, Henry St. George Tucker, lectured on constitutional law at the University of Virginia, where George Tucker, friend and biographer of Jefferson and author of works on economic subjects,[129] held the chair of ethics and political economy for the two decades preceding 1845.

While it was in the field of government that the planters of the South made their especial contributions, the importance of that section in letters cannot be overlooked.

Its newspapers were proportionately more numerous in the field of politics than those of New England or the Middle Atlantic States.   The agricultural renaissance in the section, however, brought into existence a number of agricultural newspapers, of which the most important was edited by Ruffin.[130]   In all the South Atlantic Division, in 1850, there were thirty-three dailies, while New England had forty.   Delaware, North Carolina, and Florida had none.[131]

[124] Dec. 29, 1847 (*Calhoun Correspondence*, p. 1156).

[125] H. B. Adams, *The College of William and Mary* (Washington, 1887), p. 55, ranked Dew's historical lectures as among the best in the United States at the time.

[126] *Ibid.*, pp. 48–54.

[127] See p. 206, *post*.

[128] W. P. Trent, *William Gilmore Simms* (Boston, 1892), pp. 183 ff.

[129] Later the writer of *The History of the United States, from Their Colonization to the End of the Twenty-sixth Congress, in 1841* (4 vols.; Philadelphia, 1856–57).

[130] Avery O. Craven, " The Agricultural Reformers of the Ante-bellum South," *American Historical Review*, XXXIII, 309.

[131] *Compendium of the Seventh Census*, pp. 155–58.

The ablest editor of the section was Thomas Ritchie, of the Richmond *Enquirer*, whose ability and independence of thought compelled Northern Democrats to weigh his opinions and seek his aid. R. B. Rhett, of the *Charleston Mercury*, exhibited the " fire-eating " quality of the Southern editor, and led the way in extreme proposals. Gales and Seaton, the publishers of the *National Intelligencer* in Washington, as the spokesmen for the Whig party occupied a national rather than a sectional position. Duff Green (whose daughter had married Calhoun's son) was a sometimes injudicious supporter of Calhoun. He edited newspapers in Washington and Baltimore and persistently pushed the fortunes of his chief. In all the states, there were newspapers which served as mouthpieces for the political leaders. Francis P. Blair, a native of Virginia who had become a bank president in Kentucky, came to Washington to edit the administration's organ, the *Globe*, in which were sounded the keynotes of Jackson's policies. Ritchie and Blair were at times a hard team to drive in the same party harness, as Jackson and Van Buren learned. The selection of public printer became, in these years, a test of party affiliation and a matter of bitter rivalry.

The literary periodicals of the South Atlantic give evidence that, in spite of conservatism and the extensive subscription to Northern magazines, there was a Southern expression of itself in this medium. The *Southern Literary Messenger*, founded in Richmond in 1834, was, part of the time, under the editorship of Edgar A. Poe (who contributed to its columns), and was a vehicle for Northern as well as Southern writers. Its contributors give evidence of literary taste, as well as of zeal in the defense of slavery.[132]

Charleston was the home of the *Southern Quarterly Review*,[133] established in 1842. In 1849 it passed under the editorship of another man of letters, William Gilmore Simms.[134] The circulation of both these magazines, however, was small.

In Baltimore *Niles' Weekly Register* was a nationally important weekly (which ran from 1811 to 1849), more Northern than

---

[132] B. B. Minor, its editor in the forties, summarized the contents, and characterized the contributors, in his *The Southern Literary Messenger, 1834–1864* (New York and Washington, 1905). See also Frank Luther Mott, *A History of American Magazines, 1741–1850* (New York, 1930), pp. 629–57.

[133] *Ibid.*, pp. 721–27.

[134] *Ibid.*, Index, under " Simms."

Southern, with a distinct protectionist attitude. Its value lies, to a large extent, in the republication of extracts from contemporary newspapers in various parts of the Union.[135]

As I have said, the literary genius of the South expressed itself in politics. In part, this was caused by the fight for existence which the slave society had to make — a fight which naturally took the form of the defense of slavery and the critical examination of the principles of liberty and government. Men like John Randolph of Roanoke, Jefferson, Taylor, Justice Roane of the Supreme Court of Virginia, Cooper, Dew, and the Tuckers, had led the way in the application of literature to the defense of state rights and to the criticism of national tendencies. But they were surrounded by a multitude of lesser planter-statesmen who, through the newspapers, pamphlets, and correspondence, revealed the ability of the South Atlantic States in political polemics.

As a class, the large planters were cultivated people, with leisure and with an ardor which might have reflected a feeling for literature. But the safety of slavery depended upon conformity to the settled ideas of the section. Radicalism and innovation were, therefore, viewed with apprehension and even with alarm. To the slave owners, moreover, the life of a man of letters seemed inferior and not entirely worthy. Quite as important factors were the isolation of the plantation and the lack of large cities. Literature flourished best in an urban environment, although the writers may have come from the country to the city. The absence of large libraries and of an educated people in touch with each other was an obstacle to the formation of the type of society that fosters literature. No doubt, the outdoor life of the South, and the relatively shorter winter evenings, also had an effect upon the general tendency to read.

Nevertheless, there was an interesting combination of writers on public affairs and men of letters. Two of the Tuckers — George (*The Valley of Shenandoah* [1824]) and Nathaniel Beverley (*The Partisan Leader*) [136] — essayed fiction as well as economics and law. William Gilmore Simms, in his *Guy Rivers* (1834) and *The Yemassee* (1835), dealt with the Georgia and South Carolina frontiers, and, in his *The Partisan* (1835) and

[135] For a more detailed survey of South Atlantic periodicals, see *ibid.*, *passim* and, especially, pp. 380–84.

[136] A novel (1836) popularizing secession and the Calhoun doctrine.

other novels, depicted Revolutionary life in the section. Plantation portrayals in the fiction of the time were affected, both North and South, by the abolition controversy,[137] and Simms was one of the outstanding controversial writers in defense of the South. His fiction reflects the mode of Scott and Cooper, while *Swallow Barn* (1832), by Kennedy of Maryland, is of the Irving type. William A. Caruthers, in his *Kentuckian in New York* (1834), showed the attitude of a liberal of interior Virginia and presented an interesting intersectional picture in the correspondence of the Kentucky characters, illustrating life in New York and the Carolinas. Although he was a Southerner, his pages give a sympathetic view of New York and a critical view of slavery and social conditions in South Carolina as compared with those in Virginia.

The old Southwest, passing from frontier conditions, at the beginning of the period gave rise to a type of humorous writings that became, in later authors like Mark Twain, one of the most characteristic and distinctive American contributions to literature. Georgia, where South and West met in a crude and racy frontier, was the natural soil for this growth in letters, and A. B. Longstreet (at one time president of Emory College) led with his *Georgia Scenes* (1835). William T. Thompson, author of *Major Jones' Courtship* (1840), was another Georgian whose pen portraits of this society preserve its traits much in the way that cartoons are recording characteristics of our own time.

In poetry the South produced nothing noteworthy in these years, except for Poe. The child of strolling players, he was connected by his father's ancestry with Virginia, and there he spent some of his most productive years in publishing criticism, weird short stories, and verses whose strange melody made him a world figure. Parts of his tragic life were spent in New England and the Middle Atlantic States, as well as in the South. The content of his writings reflects less of the South than of himself; but America has been distinguished by his fame as the contributor of new literary forms.

In art, also, the South itself made no distinct contributions, though, in later times, the negro melodies affected American musical forms. But, even thus early, negro minstrelsy became popular in Northern cities.

There is a very modern scientific outlook in the address of

---

[137] P. 162, *ante*.

Joel R. Poinsett,[138] of South Carolina, at the first anniversary of the [Smithsonian] National Institution for the Promotion of Science, in Washington. He emphasized the need of bringing the various arts and sciences together in order to afford mutual assistance, and proposed governmental aid to literature and the fine arts as well as for the promotion of the application of science to the useful arts. Many of the organizations which have arisen in Washington in these fields in recent years are foreshadowed in his projects.

Lieutenant Matthew Fontaine Maury, a native of Virginia, became one of the outstanding scientists of the world, in this period. His studies of oceanography began a new science. Among other contributions he made were influential articles, in Southern magazines, designed to encourage direct trade between Southern ports and Europe and commerce with the Amazon. The founding of the Naval Academy was promoted by his writings, and he was also active in the beginnings of the Hydrographic Office and became superintendent of the National Observatory at Washington. Studies of the flow of the Mississippi, made under his direction, influenced later scientific development, and his articles on naval affairs, especially concerning protection of the commerce in the Gulf of Mexico, helped to shape both national policy and later naval writings.

Charities and corrections, which in the North were conducted by institutions, public and private, were to a large extent left to the plantation in this section.[139]

There were eight medical schools, with about six hundred students in all, in 1850, in the South Atlantic Division, though some of the best of the physicians received their training in the North. The priority of the discovery and use of anesthetics is still disputed between New England and this section.[140]

In the churches, the common people of the section, white as well as colored, and even some of the planting class, adhered to the emotional denominations. The most numerous sect, judging

[138] Published in Washington, 1841.

[139] In the prisons of the section were some four hundred white inmates, in 1850, and around half as many colored, most of the latter in Maryland, Delaware, and the District of Columbia. At the same time, in New England, with about an equal white population, there were eight hundred white prisoners in state prisons and penitentiaries.

[140] See, for example, Dr. J. Marion Sims, "History of the Discovery of Anaesthesia," *Virginia Medical Monthly*, May, 1877.

from the statistics of church accommodations in 1850, was the Methodist, followed by the Baptist and the Presbyterian. The Episcopalian came next. Catholics were located chiefly in Maryland, with scattered groups farther south. Northern and Southern wings of several denominations split apart on the slavery issue. The churches, however, were foremost in investigating the condition of the slave, in recommending reforms, and in demanding religious services for the negro. However, the texts from which sermons were preached were naturally those most suited to cultivate obedience to the master.

Considering the two decades as a whole, it becomes increasingly clear that the presence of the negro was the most important single factor in shaping the history of the section itself and its relations with the rest of the country. In all the fields of human activity — economic, political, and social — the thinking of the slave states was determined by the existence of slavery as the mode of dealing with the negro. The forms of industry, and profits and losses, were dependent upon this institution. South Atlantic political parties, however much they differed on the question of general policies and underlying principles, were committed to the defense of slavery. Whig and Democrat might hold opposing views on state sovereignty and the Constitutional right of secession, but they were one in the determination to preserve the basis of the section's whole life. This fixed the boundaries of their thinking, their literature, even their religion. Although there were minority regions which supported emancipation, in general poor white, mountaineer, and great planter came to agree in opposing Northern attacks upon slavery. The attitude of the South Atlantic States, when questions like the tariff, internal improvements, banking, the disposition of the public lands, and foreign relations were involved, was an outcome of this foundational element in the make-up of the section.

Since the southern half of the Mississippi Valley — the South Central section — had come, in the later years of the forties, to merge its interests with those of the seaboard South on this great issue, and since the western wing was expansionist and quick-tempered and still preserved the Jacksonian fondness for direct action, it is obvious that an *entente cordiale* between these two sections was to have important results in the Congressional struggle of sections.

CHAPTER VI

THE SOUTH CENTRAL STATES

The South Central States (Kentucky, Tennessee, Alabama, Mississippi, Louisiana, Texas, and Arkansas) were an emanation from the South Atlantic. In the days of Daniel Boone, there had come the exodus of the Southern-upland folk — the pioneers who explored beyond the Alleghenies, fought the Indians, and won and occupied Kentucky and Tennessee. In the generation before 1830, the backwoodsmen had extended this wedge of settlement to the southern counties of the states beyond the Ohio River, on the north, and had followed Jackson into the lands of the Gulf Basin.

Much of the South Central section [1] is a hilly land, and the rough, or less fertile, country was the home of the forest pioneer, the strength of Jacksonian Democracy. The Coastal Plain included sandy belts like those of Georgia.[2] Within this division, however, there were certain favored regions which became the home of prosperous and slaveholding planters — islands, as it were, of an aristocracy comparable to the tidewater planters who ruled the South Atlantic States. In the heart of Kentucky, surrounded by the Highland Rim, was the limestone basin known as the blue-grass country, the center of which was the Lexington Plain, a land of rich soil, originally the paradise of game hunters and later the home of the Kentucky thoroughbreds. After the Revolution, there had come into this fertile region Virginia planters (with their slaves), who took advantage of the defective land titles of the pioneers to amass the estates which made this region, in its social type, an outlying fragment of the Old Dominion.

[1] See Hugh H. Bennett, *The Soils and Agriculture of the Southern States* (New York, 1921), map (frontispiece).

[2] W. H. Sparks, *The Memories of Fifty Years* (Philadelphia, 1872), pp. 331 ff., describes southern-Mississippi poor whites.

Within it were concentrated not only much of the slaveholding population but also the hemp and tobacco industry. With the Ohio lands adjacent to it in the Miami Valley, it constituted a basin in which surplus crops and live stock found an outlet in the rising cities of Louisville and Cincinnati and flowed out to the planting districts by the roads that led through Cumberland Gap and Saluda Gap into the cotton belt of the Carolinas and Georgia. The Ohio and Mississippi rivers, however, were the great avenues for its products, which, at the beginning of the period, still passed down by flatboats and steamers to New Orleans.

South of Kentucky, also walled-in by the Highland Rim, lay the kindred Nashville Basin of central Tennessee, attractive by reason of its limestone soils. Farther to the south was a minor limestone strip, the Huntsville region, along the boundary of Tennessee and Alabama.

To the east, between the mountain ridges, were the fertile river valleys of eastern Tennessee, and, to the west, the cotton lands of the counties of Tennessee bordering on the Mississippi.

The curving line which bounds the southern end of the Appalachians incloses northern Alabama, which was destined, because of its wealth of coal and iron, to become the seat of manufacturing, but in these years was the home of the backwoodsmen. The Black Belt of central Alabama was a long strip of calcareous prairie (running across the state into the neighboring counties of Mississippi), some fifteen to twenty-five miles wide and over three hundred miles in its maximum length. It embraced an area about as great as Connecticut and Rhode Island, combined.[3] Known also as the " Black Prairie," it was, when the pioneers first saw it, a wide, extended meadow with intervening strips of oak and pine, with sunlit vistas expanding into the wide horizon of extensive rolling prairies.[4] Prior to 1830, the scarcity of good water, the difficulties of the sticky soil, the poor roads and means of transportation, and the original unhealthfulness of much of

[3] R. M. Harper, " Geographical Report," Geological Survey of Alabama Monographs, No. 8; idem, in South Atlantic Quarterly, XIX, 201, and in Georgia Historical Quarterly, 1922; and H. F. Cleland, " The Black Belt of Alabama," Geographical Review, X, 375–87, VIII, 274.

[4] Thos. P. Abernethy, The Formative Period in Alabama, 1815–1828 (Alabama State Department of Archives and History Historical and Patriotic Series, No. 6; Montgomery, 1922), p. 22, quoting Cahawba Press, June 2, 1821.

this area, had led the pioneers to prefer the river lands. But the rush of the cotton planter, in the thirties, to these rich soils, not only resulted in their occupation but also brought about a segregation of social types. Such pioneers as had occupied the region found themselves elbowed into the rougher and less fertile lands. The coffles of slaves came in so rapidly that, in counties along this belt, the negroes soon outnumbered the whites and it became a Black Belt in a double sense. By 1840 it appears on the census map as a clearly-marked zone of greater density of population. South of it were the less fertile Red Hills. Together, the Black Belt and the Red Hills formed the home of the planter aristocracy. Up the Coosa River into the southern end of the Appalachian Valley was a more slender line of good soils, and here, also, was a region of large planters.

On both sides of the Mississippi, south of the Ohio, were the Mississippi alluvial lands, bordered by bluffs. The Yazoo River valley embraced two tiers of counties. In this embayment, with Memphis, Vicksburg, and the old settlement of Natchez as their market towns, there grew up the planter aristocracy of Mississippi.[5] The region includes counties in southeastern Louisiana as well, where cotton and sugar were the rival products of the wealthy planters of that state. New Orleans, settled by the French early in the eighteenth century, rose from a population of less than fifty thousand, in 1830, to over one hundred and sixteen thousand, in 1850, and was the queen of the Mississippi Valley commerce during most of the period. Pittsburgh, at the forks of the Ohio; Cincinnati, controlling the trade of the Miami country; Louisville, at the falls of the Ohio; St. Louis, the mistress of the upper Mississippi and the Missouri; and the cities of the lower reaches of the " Father of Waters " — all poured their contributions into New Orleans and made it warder of the gates of exit from the interior of the nation, just as New York was the guardian of the gates of entrance.

The valleys of the Arkansas and Red rivers constituted other fertile zones in contrast with the surrounding lands, and espe-

[5] See: Sparks, *Memories*, pp. 245–49, 253, 321–29 (for an admirer's account of the physical appearance and society of western Mississippi) ; *A Memoir of S. S. Prentiss*, ed. by his brother [Geo. L. Prentiss] (New York, 1855) (letters) ; and Jos. Hodgson, *The Cradle of the Confederacy; or, The Times of Troup, Quitman, and Yancey* (Mobile, 1876), Chap. 1 and p. 204.

cially with the hilly Ozarks. Texas will be dealt with in the chapter on the Far West.

Here, then, was obviously a complex section, full of different physical regions. Two things stand out prominently, however: the favored fertile regions, isolated from each other, on the one hand, and the surrounding mountainous, or rough and less fertile, lands, on the other. This section, in these formative years, was to be deeply affected, in its economic, political, and social developments and divisions, by the pattern of its geography.

If the South Central section was complex in its regions, it was likewise heterogeneous in its states, due in part to geographic factors, in part to economic conditions, and still more, perhaps, to the sources of population.

Kentucky, the child of Virginia, was classified by the Census Office, in this period, as a part of the Northwestern States. By its relations to the Ohio Valley, and by its attitude on the tariff, internal improvements, and similar issues, this classification was justified. Tennessee, daughter of North Carolina, also was a transitional zone between the Ohio Valley and the Gulf States. Louisiana, by reason of its French origins, its considerable Northern population, and, especially, its interest in commerce, navigation, and sugar production, occupied a place of its own. The states which, by 1850, were the heart of the Cotton Belt — Alabama and Mississippi — became more closely tied to their Southeastern kin as these twenty years went on, but in the beginning they were a part of the Jacksonian West.[6]

The South Central States grew rapidly in population in the years of this volume. While the older section, the South Atlantic, gained less than 300,000 in the decade between 1830 and 1840, the South Central gained over three times that number. Between 1840 and 1850, the gain of the South Atlantic was 753,000, but that of the South Central was 1,278,000. By 1850 the South Central States had a population of about 4,300,000, while the older and parent section had 4,600,000.

Together, these two divisions, in 1850, slightly exceeded in numbers the Middle Atlantic States and New England, combined. When the counties north of the Ohio settled by Southern stock are included in the reckoning, the Southern sections are seen to have occupied, not only by far the larger area in the

[6] See Chapter II, *ante.*

Union, but also to have furnished the majority of the native population.

While, in the thirties, Virginia increased its whites by less than 7 per cent and its negroes by only 3.5 per cent, and while North Carolina and South Carolina were practically stationary, Alabama had increased its whites 76 per cent and its negroes 114 per cent, and Mississippi, its whites 154 per cent and its negroes 197 per cent. The actual gain in population of Alabama, between 1830 and 1840, was ten fold that of Virginia — the Old Dominion with which English colonization began — and twenty fold that of South Carolina. Of the total number of natives of South Carolina alive in 1850, over 40 per cent were residents of other states. About one-third of the natives of North Carolina had left the state of their birth, and about one-fourth of those of Georgia. In general, nearly one-half of the people of the cotton states of Alabama, Mississippi, and Louisiana, together, were born outside the state in which they resided. The foreign-born element was only 80,000, of which 85 per cent were in Louisiana.

These South Central States were settled by the extension of the people of the nearer states. In 1850, in Kentucky, the natives of Virginia outnumbered those of any other contributing state. In Tennessee the natives of North Carolina greatly exceeded those of Virginia. In Alabama the Georgian element was largest, with South Carolina following. Taking into account the sources of Georgia's population, the two Carolinas furnished the bulk of Alabama's people. The large number of her natives of Tennessee were principally of the same derivation. To Mississippi's population, Alabama was the chief contributor, but South Carolina and Tennessee each gave birth to nearly 18 per cent of her white and free colored, born outside her own confines, and North Carolina furnished over 13 per cent. Louisiana had been so long settled that its own natives, originally French, constituted over half of the population; but, even by the beginning of the nineteenth century, the American element had entered the state in large numbers. By 1850 its people included more natives of Ireland, of Germany, and of France, respectively, than any one of the other South Central states. New York natives furnished to Louisiana were almost as numerous as those of Georgia; but the largest American contribution to Louisiana was that of Mississippi.

Throughout the whole region south of Tennessee, there was a mingling of people from all the South Atlantic states, and from all the regions of these states. But the migration of the South Carolinians has a special significance, in that the settlers were often men of means and political leadership, who carried South Carolina's ideas of nullification into the regions where they moved, at a time when formative influences were strong.

Even the Yankees were not absent from this movement of population. In most of the commercial cities, especially Mobile and New Orleans, many of the leading merchants were transplanted Yankees,[7] and very commonly the newspaper editors and the tutors in the planters' families came from New England.

A correspondent of the *Portland Advertiser*, writing from Huntsville, Alabama, in the spring of 1833, remarks: " It would seem as if North and South Carolina were pouring forth their population by swarms. Perhaps I have gone by in the Creek nation, over 3,000 persons, all emigrating, including negroes, of course. The fires of their encampments made the woods blaze in all directions." The rapidity with which the lands later ceded by the Indians were brought into cultivation astonished the travelers. In lands which, less than two years before, were wilderness, were fields of over a hundred acres in corn and cotton; and the Alabama pioneer could subsist on half the quantity of land required for the family supply of corn from the outworn fields of Virginia.

So rapidly did slavery enter the South Central section, which in 1830 was still a part of the pioneer West, that, twenty years later, over half the slaveholders of the Union were living in the trans-Allegheny states. Some seventeen hundred great planters (those holding from one hundred to over one thousand slaves) lived in the South as a whole, and, of these, over half were in the South Central section — four-fifths of them in Louisiana, Alabama, and Mississippi (almost all of whom lived in the Black Belt). In Mississippi and Louisiana the negroes were more numerous than the whites. The section held only one-fifth as

---

[7] Later this caused alarm to Calhoun's friends. See *Correspondence of John C. Calhoun*, ed. J. Franklin Jameson (American Historical Association *Annual Report*, 1899, II; Washington, 1900), e.g., pp. 1134, 1189, 1193, for expressions of fear of Northern influence in such cities as Mobile, New Orleans, and Augusta.

many free colored as did the South Atlantic, and the mass of this small fraction lived in Louisiana, Kentucky, and Tennessee.

At the beginning of the period, the latter two states were the scene of efforts for gradual abolition. The way had been prepared by the agitation for gradual emancipation and removal. Henry Clay, of Kentucky, president of the American Colonization Society, called slavery a " foul blot " [8] and spoke for gradual emancipation in Kentucky. Cassius M. Clay, his nephew, educated in Yale College, carried the " fire-eating " spirit into his campaigns in opposition to slavery.

The act of 1833 to prevent the importation of slaves into Kentucky decreased the percentage of slaves to the total population. Other slaveholding states looked with concern upon the antislavery agitation in Kentucky, fearing its effect in the border states. But demands for a constitutional convention to provide for gradual abolition continued, to the embarrassment of Henry Clay, whose position as a candidate for the Presidency led him at times to try to check a movement to which Garrisonian abolition gave the color of outside pressure. So far did the reaction go, that Kentucky's act of 1849 repealed her nonimportation law, and, when the constitutional convention met that year, although Henry Clay favored a provision for gradual emancipation and removal,[9] the convention failed to accept this and even made emancipation more difficult.

While Virginia, North Carolina, and Kentucky were debating the question of gradual emancipation, early in the thirties, Tennessee also discussed the subject, in its constitutional convention of 1834. In 1843 the nonslaveholding mountaineers of east Tennessee were reported as proposing separate statehood. But, as in these other states, the outcome was a proslavery reaction.

The mountain whites of this section were like those of the South Atlantic States, and, when reinforced by the dwellers in the Ozark and Ouachita plateaus and the hilly country surrounding the favored regions already mentioned, they made a

---

[8] Quoted from American Colonization Society *Annual Report*, 1827, by Asa E. Martin, *The Anti-slavery Movement in Kentucky Prior to 1850* (*Filson Club Publications*, No. 29; Louisville, 1918), p. 55. Cf. pp. 126, 132, 144, 145.

[9] Thos. Hart Clay, *Henry Clay* (Philadelphia, 1910), p. 340. Cf.: Martin, *op. cit.*, pp. 55, 126, 132, 144–46; [anon.] *The Views and Sentiments of Henry Clay and Abraham Lincoln on the Slavery Question;* and *Congressional Globe*, 31st Cong., 1st Sess., Pt. 1, 404 (Clay in Senate, Feb. 20, 1850).

mass of farmers owning few or no slaves but responsive to the influences which have been considered in the previous chapter. Taking the section as a whole, only approximately one-third of the white families were slaveholders.

The agriculture of the South Central section was, as would be expected, a varied one, ranging from the raising of horses, mules, and swine, and the production of tobacco and hemp, in the Kentucky blue-grass lands about the Lexington Basin, to the concentration upon cotton-growing in the Gulf States.[10] The mixed-farming lands constituted the basis of the great mass of the agriculture. Even in the Cotton Belt, however, the planters aimed to produce a large part of the food products for their slaves, although they also drew upon the down-river trade for this supply.

The plantations in the South Central states differed, in important respects, from those of their eastern sisters, although most of what has been already said with reference to this institution applies generally. The Kentucky blue-grass region, in particular, carried on the patriarchal type of stock-raising and tobacco-planting life that characterized its Virginia predecessor. What is distinctive in the plantations of the South Central section derives from two facts: (1) the sugar plantation of Louisiana differed from the cotton plantation; and (2), more important, the section's cotton plantations were the result of the rush into the vacant lands of the West. It is true that the Natchez region had an agricultural history running back to the Revolution, but, in the rest of the cotton-raising portions of the section, the plantations were rapidly established in the course of the migration that had hurried to the Gulf on the heels of Andrew Jackson's victories in the War of 1812, followed by his removal of the Indians, in the beginning of the thirties.[11] This exploitation of virgin soils attracted the more adventurous and forceful type of cotton planter.

A considerable portion of the slaves were drawn from various states by domestic trade, and by some illegal smuggling from abroad, as well as by transfer of inherited property. It has already been noted that the tendency was to sell the undesirable slaves to the Southwest. Such considerations combined to make

[10] See map of crop areas, 1850 (at end of volume).

[11] See maps (pp. 6, 7, *ante*) of Distribution of Population in 1830 and 1840.

the plantation in this section less patriarchal, more affected by purely commercial interests, and under more stringent regulation, than the plantation of the East.

The plantation's beginnings in the log house raised on lands so recently Indian; the rapid development of the mansions of the newly rich in the greater plantations of the Black Belt; [12] the process of adjustment of backwoodsman and planter; the establishment of plantations expanding over the fertile black prairie to form single extensive units; the large-scale production, with consequent economies — these are some of the things that made the cotton plantation of the South Central States a special type.[13]

A plantation of over thirteen hundred acres, near Natchez, is described by F. L. Olmsted.[14] A Louisiana planter, quoted in J. D. B. De Bow's *The Industrial Resources, etc., of the Southern and Western States*,[15] gave a detailed estimate of the annual net profits of a cotton plantation, with one hundred slaves, on rich bottom land, where $100,000 was invested in capital, at only $1,750, not counting interest on the investment, nor support of the planter's family, nor depreciation. This was based on cotton at five cents per pound and on a production of seven bales, of four hundred pounds, to each full hand. Food for one hundred slaves and the overseer's family was put at $750 a year. Obviously, only in exceptional years could five-cent cotton be profitable, even on a large plantation. Nevertheless, five-cent cotton was only a temporary phenomenon.

De Bow, who should be a fair reporter of conditions in the Cotton Belt, declared, in 1860, that " the large slaveholders and proprietors of the South begin life in great part as non-slaveholders " — overseers, city clerks, traders, and merchants; and that " the sons of the non-slaveholder are and have always been among the

[12] See references, pp. 162–63, *ante*; and, especially, pictures in *Geographical Review*, VIII, 274 (cf. X, 375).

[13] On the plantation of this section, see the references in the previous chapter, and: A. de Puy Van Buren, *Jottings of a Year's Sojourn in the South;* Basil Hall, *Travels in North America* (Philadelphia, 1829); Anne Royall, *Southern Tour* (Washington, 1830); and Abernethy, *Formative Period in Alabama*, Chap. VII, and pp. 149–52 (bibliography of contemporary sources). J. M. Peck, *A New Guide for Emigrants to the West* (Cincinnati, 1848), Chap. IV, gives the impressions of a resident of the Upper Mississippi Valley.

[14] *A Journey in the Back Country* (New York, 1860), p. 46.

[15] I (New Orleans, 1852), 150–51.

leading and ruling spirits of the South; in industry as well as in politics." [16]

The rice plantation in Louisiana was not much unlike that in South Carolina, but the sugar plantation of the former state stood by itself. By 1850 nine planters in Louisiana annually produced over one thousand hogsheads of cane sugar each. One-half the whole crop of the state was made by about one hundred and sixty planters along the Mississippi, from over fifty miles below New Orleans to nearly one hundred and ninety miles above, and on Red River. Steam power in the sugarhouses was adopted early in the twenties; the researches of French and American chemists were studied, and improved processes, with costly machinery, were introduced. The importance of drainage was recognized, and Irish ditchers were often used in this unhealthful work, to spare the slaves. The sugar industry [17] thus came to be a highly capitalized and technical one, conducted by men of intelligence and large means,[18] on great estates. By 1850 some 250,000 hogsheads of sugar were produced. A large portion of the sugar planters were French Creoles. With the highly developed commercial and social life of New Orleans near by, the sugar producers became an exceptional class of planters, ready to join with the hemp raisers of Kentucky and the manufacturers of the Northeast in supporting the protective tariff.

The persons employed in manufacture in the South Central Division, in 1850, did not greatly exceed fifty thousand — not much over half the number in the South Atlantic States, less than

[16] *The Interest in Slavery of the Southern Non-slaveholder* (in 1860 Association Tracts, No. 5; Charleston, 1860), pp. 9, 10.

[17] See: crop map, 1850 (at end of volume); De Bow, *Industrial Resources*, III (New Orleans, 1853), 277–78, 285–87; *Statistical Abstract of the United States, 1924* (U.S. Dept. of Commerce; Washington, 1925), p. 608; and De Bow, *Statistical View of the United States . . . being a Compendium of the Seventh* [1850] *Census* (Washington, 1854).

[18] By the outbreak of the Civil War, one of them, a native of Ireland, once a grocer's clerk, who had made a fortune in New Orleans, had purchased from former owners 6,000 acres of sugar cane in one field, with an additional 16,000 acres in corn, and 18,000 acres of wild land, besides. (W. H. Russell, *My Diary, North and South* [New York, 1863], pp. 368 ff., and *Appletons' Cyclopaedia of American Biography, s.v.* John Burnside.) Early in the fifties, the Aime plantation, of 15,000 acres, required over 200 slaves. Even in far-away Brazoria County, Texas, prior to 1853, one of the sugar plantations had a sugarhouse costing $50,000, and negroes valued at $60,000. The 29 sugarhouses in the county represented a total outlay of $1,134,000, estimating the average value of the land at $20 an acre. (De Bow, *Industrial Resources*, III, 284–85.)

half of those in the North Central, less than one-fifth of those in
New England, and less than one-seventh of those in the Middle
Atlantic States. Inasmuch as more than three-fourths of the
manufacturing element of the section belonged to Kentucky and
Tennessee,[19] the lower half of the Mississippi Valley had here an
occasion for sharp sectional difference. In spite of the fact that the
Cotton Belt lay in the two Southern sections, in 1840 the value of
their manufactures of cotton was less than $4,000,000, out of over
$46,000,000 for the nation.[20] This was at the same time that the
slaves of the South, engaged in cotton cultivation, numbered
1,200,000, according to the estimate of De Bow, and the capital
invested in that production was put at $800,000,000.[21]

At the beginning of the thirties, New Orleans, by the river
trade, received the mass of the products of the Mississippi Valley, amounting to some $26,000,000,[22] chiefly in cereals, animal
food, and the many raw products of these Western states. By
1851–52 the surplus thus reaching New Orleans had grown to a
value of over $108,000,000,[23] of which cotton furnished over $48,-
500,000; sugar and molasses, nearly $16,000,000; pork and its
products, about the same amount; tobacco, over $7,000,000; and
corn, flour, and wheat, over $5,500,000.

The larger share of this down-river trade, however, went to
supply the food and the factory needs of New England and the
Middle Atlantic States, or was exported to foreign countries.
The exports of New Orleans, which in 1825, before the great development of the Mississippi Valley surplus, had merely equaled
those of Charleston, surpassed those of New York in 1835. But,

[19] The files of [J. D. B.] *De Bow's Review*, and of the *Western Journal*
(St. Louis), contain interesting data on manufacture in the Mississippi Valley in
the closing years of the period. Peck, *op. cit.*, Chap. IV, gives information on
the manufacture of cotton bagging, rope, etc., in Newport and Covington,
Kentucky.

[20] Based on *Report* made Nov. 16, 1855 (*Executive Document 10*, 34th Cong.,
1st Sess., pp. 86 ff.). On attempts at cotton manufacture in the South Central
States, and especially on Daniel Pratt's cotton mill in Autauga County, Alabama,
see *Western Journal*, I, 154–56 (Mar., 1848). Pratt was from Lowell, Massachusetts. He paid average wages of $8 a month, and did not employ slaves.

[21] De Bow, *Industrial Resources*, I, 175.

[22] F. J. Turner, *Rise of the New West, 1819–1829* (*The American Nation:
A History*, XIV; New York, 1906), p. 105, and citations.

[23] *Report of Israel D. Andrews . . . on the Trade and Commerce of the
British North American Colonies, and upon the Trade of the Great Lakes and
Rivers* (*House Executive Document 136*, 32d Cong., 2d Sess.; Washington, 1853),
pp. 756–57.

by 1845, the rise of the surplus from the Great Lakes Basin and from that part of the Ohio Valley which found its outlet at New York, put New Orleans in second place.

In spite of the emphasis upon cotton-raising, the South Central, as well as the South Atlantic, states were substantially self-sustaining in the food consumed by their labor population. The South Central Division (exclusive of Kentucky) produced, in 1850, about as many swine and sheep per capita as did the North Central States (together with Kentucky), and the production of corn was not much below the ratio for the latter.[24] Even the states of the Cotton Belt were far more able to supply their own food than is usually supposed. Alabama, for example, had a per capita production of swine (her meat staple) higher than that of Illinois or Indiana. Nevertheless, the Piedmont plantations still received droves of hogs, mules, and horses from the Ohio Valley, by way of Cumberland Gap and Saluda Gap. Over a million and a half dollars' worth of stock was reported to have passed through Cumberland Gap in 1835. By the beginning of the forties, nearly fifty-five thousand hogs annually went through this gap.[25] The Wilderness Road and its southeastern branches, because of this movement of drovers and the wagon trade, became a line of intercourse, influential, as we shall see, in political-party grouping, as well as in banking and economic life in general. Responding to the rising production, the tonnage of the vessels of the Mississippi, and its tributaries, grew from 76,000 in 1834 to 275,000 in 1850.[26]

Within the Mississippi Valley, there were important local exchanges of products.[27] Kentucky hemp was manufactured into cotton bagging, rope, etc., at Louisville, Lexington, and Cincinnati, for the plantations south; Louisville and St. Louis were tobacco markets; lead from Missouri, Illinois, Iowa, and Wisconsin passed to Cincinnati, Louisville, and New Orleans, as well as to Pittsburgh; Cincinnati pork-packing gradually replaced droving, and sent its products south.

[24] *Compendium of the Seventh Census,* p. 175.

[25] E. L. Parr, "Kentucky Overland Trade with the Ante-bellum South," *History Quarterly,* II, 77.

[26] Isaac Lippincott, *Internal Trade of the United States, 1700–1860* (Washington University *Studies,* IV, Pt. II, No. 1, pp. 63–150; St. Louis, Oct., 1916), pp. 148–49, with citations; cf. *The Works of John C. Calhoun,* ed. R. K. Crallé, V (New York, 1855), 248–50, and *Andrews Report,* p. 733.

[27] Lippincott, *op. cit.,* pp. 94 ff.

In fact, the great river became, for a time, the all-important artery of commerce for the whole Valley. The flatboats and keel boats of the earlier days [28] survived into the steamboat era. They were the recourse of neighboring pioneer farmers for carrying the surplus of their little farms down the Mississippi. The contemporaneous descriptions of them, their picturesque crews, and the gathering of the boats into floating villages on some stretches, exchanging news and bartering goods, make a chapter in the history of transportation on the Mississippi River, and its tributaries, that is a revealing one in pioneer life. Even so late as the middle forties, it was estimated that four thousand flatboats navigated this river, manned by some twenty thousand persons and having half the tonnage of the river's steamboats.[29]

Steamboat transportation by river, beginning after the War of 1812, grew steadily, not only in numbers of boats but in their size and tonnage. By 1829 two hundred plied the " Western Waters "; over twice that number in 1842; and in 1848 twelve hundred. By that time many of them had become luxurious passenger craft, whereon frontiersmen, pioneers and planters, gamblers, negroes, and immigrants found an abundance of drink and an elegance of equipment out of keeping with the simplicity of Western life.[30] The best time of steamboat travel from New

[28] On these craft, see interesting data in: Timothy Flint, *Recollections of the Last Ten Years* (Boston, 1826), pp. 101–10; Jas. Hall, *Statistics of the West* (Cincinnati, 1836), p. 236; E. S. Thomas, *Reminiscences of the Last Sixty-five Years, Commencing with the Battle of Lexington; also Sketches of His Own Life and Times* (Hartford, Conn., 1840), I, 290–93; Peck, *New Guide*, Chap. iv; *Indiana Magazine of History*, IX, 272–75; and A. B. Hulbert, *Waterways of Westward Expansion: The Ohio and Its Tributaries* (*Historic Highways of America*, IX; Cleveland, 1903), Chap. iv.

[29] The same estimates, however, appear in a report of 1832 (by C. A. Wickliffe, of Kentucky, in the House of Representatives; *Register of Debates in Congress*, VIII, Pt. II, 2714), in 1843 (*Milwaukee Courier*, May 17, 1843), and in 1848 (Thos. Allen, in *Western Monthly Magazine*, I, 412).

[30] [Robt. Baird] *View of the Valley of the Mississippi, or The Emigrant's and Traveller's Guide to the West* (published by H. S. Tanner; Philadelphia, 1834); W. V. Pooley, *The Settlement of Illinois from 1830 to 1850* (University of Wisconsin *Bulletin*, No. 220; Madison, 1908), pp. 364–68; Hulbert, *op. cit.*; [J. T.] *Lloyd's Steamboat Directory, and Disasters on the Western Waters*, . . . (Cincinnati, 1856); E. W. Gould, *History of Navigation on the Mississippi* (St. Louis, 1889); *Tenth* [1880] *Census of the United States*, IV; G. B. Merrick, *Old Times on the Upper Mississippi* (Cleveland, 1909, and in Wisconsin Historical Society *Proceedings*, 1911 [Madison, 1912]); Hulbert, *The Ohio River: A Course of Empire* (New York, 1906); H. M. Chittenden, *Early Steamboat Navigation on the Missouri River* (New York, 1903); and Herbert and Edward Quick, *Mis-*

Orleans to Louisville, in the thirties, was between six and seven days.[31]

The Mississippi trade met with obstacles. The snags which had resulted in so many disasters were being removed by the newly invented snag boats; but the sand bars and the rapids compelling transfers from steamer to flatboat, the periods of low water (sometimes increasing the cost of transportation one hundred and fifty per cent), frequent explosions and accidents, the ice which occasionally put part of the upper-river boats out of commission for five months of the year, the leakage and spoiling of the bags and barrels of grain, the bars at the Mississippi mouth (which allowed only light-draft vessels to pass to and from New Orleans), the lack of efficient facilities and business methods, credit, and free capital (compared with Northern and Eastern cities), the absence of finished products to exchange with the upper Mississippi — all combined to put the river trade at a disadvantage when the Erie Canal, and its successors in Ohio, opened routes to New York City.[32]

The railroads of the Northern zone were rapidly pushing their way toward the rich prize of the commerce of the great valley, and the rivalry of seaboard cities was intense. It is not surprising, therefore, that the South Atlantic ports engaged in efforts to furnish Southeastern outlets for the Mississippi Valley surplus, and to bind this region politically, as well as economically, to the Old South. These two objects, and the desire for direct trade with Europe — in short, the ambition to create Southern industrial independence in the event of Northern pressure upon its political, economic, and social sectional interests — went hand in hand in these years of increasing divergence between North and South. The natural American spirit of expansion, as well as the instinct for preservation of its peculiar institutions, led the South Central Division to desire to shape its own destiny.

But this desire encountered the ambition of the various states of the section to prevent their different regions from being drawn into commercial dependence upon other states. In Alabama, for

sissippi Steamboatin' (New York, 1926). A résumé, with references, is in Edward Channing, A History of the United States, V (New York, 1921), 20 ff.

[31] G. H. Preble, History of Steam Navigation, p. 71.

[32] Geo. W. Stephens, in Washington University Studies, X, 285–90.

example, the Mobile area was unwilling to see northern Alabama send its cotton to New Orleans or to Charleston instead of to Mobile. Alabama, therefore, found difficulty in chartering or giving financial aid to railroads which would result in drawing part of her surplus to other states.

In the early thirties, various South Central cities were planning railroad construction to the Cotton Belt, to intercept the commerce to New Orleans; and by 1834 a horse railway around the Muscle Shoals at the great bend of the Tennessee River, in northern Alabama, gave a tangible suggestion of an incomplete east-and-west line, as well as of a combination of rail and river. Mobile saw the opportunity, by building a railroad to this river, to furnish a shorter route to the sea, and thereby to drain the trade of eastern Tennessee, as well as of the cotton region of northern Alabama, to that port. Georgia and South Carolina interests saw the possibility of uniting the various minor roads projected by Memphis, Vicksburg, Natchez, and Nashville, into a trunk line that should draw the surplus, not only of the Cotton Belt but of the Mississippi Valley, to Charleston or Savannah. Memphis and Charleston were most active in these large visions. New Orleans, as yet, was hardly awake to the danger that threatened her. The divergent regional interests within the states delayed action until the Panic of 1837 put a temporary stop to these projects.[33]

After the panic, in years of agricultural depression, there was a lull in actual railroad undertakings and in conventions to promote them. But, in Memphis, General E. P. Gaines, a frontier officer with visions of the future, was circulating his sketch map of a railroad system for the United States, in which the proposed lines had a north-and-south trend between the Great Lakes and the Gulf of Mexico and in which Memphis appeared as the Southern nucleus. Urging on his department and on Congress the importance of defense, he proposed the extension of a military road from Memphis into Arkansas, on the way to a remoter West.

Lieutenant M. F. Maury, writing in the *Southern Literary Messenger* on the importance of improving Mississippi River

---

[33] R. S. Cotterill, " The Beginnings of Railroads in the Southwest," *Mississippi Valley Historical Review*, VIII, 318-26, citing contemporary newspapers and mapping the situation in 1840.

navigation, on uniting the Great Lakes with this river, and on a connection with the Pacific, found his letters republished in Illinois and Missouri newspapers and periodicals. In Charleston such leading men as Colonel James Gadsden, the railroad promoter, and F. H. Elmore, the banker, were active in pushing the larger trunk-line projects to connect the Mississippi Valley with the Southeastern seaboard. But, so late as 1852, these were still only visions.

With all the roads projected and those partly completed, the South Central section still lacked a connected system to bind it to South Atlantic and North Central states. While the North Central section, by this time, was in full connection, by canal, lake, and rail, with the Northeast, the two Southern sections were but slowly feeling their way toward unity by rail.[34]

Meantime, however, there had come the two sessions of the Memphis Convention of 1845, which constituted an important landmark in the economic and political history not only of this section but of the whole slaveholding area and of its Northern rivals. Its object was to combine the Southern sections and the North Central States in an economic — and, indirectly, a political — alliance. The attitude of the Northern Democrat, E. A. Hannegan, of Indiana, was significant. On the eve of the convention, he was reported to have said that " the West will be united and will demand funds for the improvements of their harbours, rivers and the Cumberland road, and the graduation of the price of the public land, and that if the South will give these to the West the West will go with the South on the tariff." [35]

The West was becoming self-conscious and was ready to make demands upon the nation for full recognition of its special interests; and South Carolina and Georgia leaders were anxious to meet its wishes, so far as the Constitutional scruples of their states permitted. Gadsden appealed to Calhoun to attend the convention.[36] " Now is the time," he wrote, " to meet our Western friends at Memphis — to set the ball in motion which must

---

[34] On South Central railroads, see: St. Geo. L. Sioussat, " Memphis as a Gateway to the West," *Tennessee Historical Magazine*, III, 1–27, 77–114 (Mar., June, 1917); *Andrews Report*, pp. 335–53; and Cotterill, in *Mississippi Valley Historical Review*, VIII, 318–26 (cf. III, 427–41).

[35] Duff Green to Calhoun, Sept. 24, 1845. (*Calhoun Correspondence*, p. 1055.)

[36] *Ibid.*, p. 1062.

bring the Valley to the South: and make them feel as allies of the Great Commercial and Agricultural interests — instead of the Tax gathering and Monopolizing interests of the North."

Calhoun accepted, and was made president of the convention, which included delegates from all the South Central States and from Virginia, North and South Carolina, Florida, Pennsylvania, Ohio, Indiana, Illinois, Iowa Territory, and Missouri. Georgia had no representative.[37] Over five hundred delegates were in attendance. Considering the object of the convention to be the development of the resources of the Western and Southwestern states, Calhoun argued that the Florida peninsula made a serious obstacle to commerce by way of the Gulf and that the completion of railroads converging upon Atlanta would meet the needs. The improvement of the navigation of the Mississippi was, he urged, also necessary, as well as its connection with the Great Lakes by canal.

Proceeding to the Constitutional question, he placed himself in harmony with Western interests by asserting that developments had now made the Mississippi as legitimate an object for financial assistance from the federal government as the Gulf, the Lakes, and the Atlantic Coast. For general purposes, he supported the right of grants of the public lands for roads and canals. He favored, as he had before, the graduation of price of the public lands and cession of unsold lands to the states in which they lay. Within a generation, he predicted, deliberations would be held to extend communication to the Pacific, as then to the Atlantic.

Calhoun expected, at the time, to re-enter the race for the Presidency in 1848, and his enemies criticized his liberal attitude toward the improvement of the Mississippi as a bid for Western support. But it is noticeable that he did not commit himself to the constitutionality of a canal in Illinois to connect the Great Lakes and the Mississippi.

The memorial of the convention embraced many objects, but, when the committee reported in the Senate, it laid stress upon: the demands of the convention for improvement of the Mississippi and its tributaries; a ship canal to the Lakes; security and

[37] *Calhoun Works*, V, 246, and *Niles' Register*, LXIX, 212-14. Florida is not included in the latter's list of states represented. The best discussion of the Convention is in the paper by Sioussat cited above.

defense of commerce between the Gulf and the Atlantic Coast; reclamation of inundated lands by embankments; and the connection of the Valley and the South Atlantic States by rail.

But President Polk vetoed the river-and-harbor bill; and the bitterness between North and South, in the period of the Mexican War and the Wilmot Proviso, turned Calhoun to other plans. His withdrawal as a candidate for the Presidency marked a turning point in the negotiations for an economic and political alliance between the South Atlantic States and the Mississippi Valley as a whole. The Valley had already divided into North and South.

Like the states of the South Atlantic Division, those of the South Central felt the lack of the capital required for their large designs. Northern and foreign investors furnished the greater part of the funds used in the section's banking. The Bank of the United States, through its branches, supplied the machinery of exchange. Early in the thirties, about one-half of that institution's loans were attributable to domestic exchange in the Mississippi Valley. State banks also operated in the same field.

The South Central section purchased most of its manufactured supplies from North Atlantic cities. In general, the planters sold their surplus crops and live stock to local commission merchants, who went to the bank and drew upon their correspondents in New Orleans bills of exchange to the amount of about half the price of the shipment; these bills were discounted by the bank (often at a total charge of over ten per cent), and the net proceeds were received by the planter in cash. When the shipment was sold in New Orleans, the remainder of the net proceeds belonged to the planter. The funds due on his account were transmitted from New Orleans to Northeastern ports, in the form of bills of exchange on London. These bills resulted from exports of cotton from New Orleans, and were at a premium in the North Atlantic cities, where they were used to pay for manufactures imported from England. The interior planter purchased his manufactured supplies in the same cities, and thus completed the round of exchange.[38] The process was similar when the planter borrowed, on his note, from a local bank.

[38] Henry Clay's speech in the Senate, July 12, 1832, describes the process; Biddle outlines it in much the same way. See also Thos. P. Abernethy, " The Early Development of Commerce and Banking in Tennessee," *Mississippi Valley Historical Review*, XIV, 317.

The sanguine temperament of the Southwest made it impatient with restraints on credit. Not only did the planter find it inconvenient to build up a supply of capital by saving: he confused capital and the currency. When, therefore, the Bank of the United States showed signs of curbing the borrowing of the section, it became an object of attack. Even before Jackson went from Tennessee to the Presidency, his friends were denouncing the Nashville branch.[39]

Fifty-three banks were listed for the section in 1834, with loans and discounts of over $52,000,000, circulation over $10,000,000, deposits of nearly $9,000,000, and specie of over $3,500,000.

Toward the close of 1833, the decision of President Jackson to make selected " pet " state banks the depositories of federal funds instead of continuing to place them in the Bank of the United States, followed by the distribution of the Treasury surplus among the states, increased the rage for state banks. Even railroad promoters were eager to procure banking privileges in the charters for their roads. The banking capital of Mississippi in 1839, for example, was twenty fold what it was in 1830, but only about forty per cent of this was paid in.[40] In the South as a whole, over eighty banks existed in 1837, whereas some fifty were reported in 1830.

In some cases, only the credit of the state lay back of the state banks and their currency. The character of state banking is indicated by the laws of some states, typical of the section in the previous years, permitting loans proportionate to the population of the respective counties, to relieve agricultural distress.[41]

The boom years saw land values, both urban and rural, rise to absurd heights. The rush to the new cotton lands had attracted speculators and combinations among buyers, which usually forced the small squatter to abandon his claim on the good cotton soils of vacant lands, or to sell and remove to rougher and poorer soils. This process of segregation fostered antagonistic regional divisions characteristic of Alabama and Mississippi even to the present day.

[39] St. Geo. L. Sioussat, " Some Phases of Tennessee Politics in the Jackson Period," *American Historical Review*, XIV, 64–67; and Abernethy, *op. cit.*, p. 321.

[40] R. C. McGrane, *The Panic of 1837* (Chicago, 1924), p. 25.

[41] Davis R. Dewey, *State Banking before the Civil War* (in *Senate Document 581*, 61st Cong., 2d Sess. [National Monetary Commission; Washington, 1910]).

Borrowing was natural to the optimistic Western sections. Not only was this characteristic of the planter, but of the states as well. By 1842 the South Central group had borrowed over $52,-000,000. Directly or indirectly, the mass of these loans was furnished by English investors. Of the section's borrowings, only about $5,500,000 was for internal improvements, chiefly by Kentucky, Tennessee, and Louisiana. Kentucky's share, alone, was over $3,000,000. The significant fact was that the cotton-raising states of the section invested over $47,000,000 of their borrowings in establishing banks.[42] The demand of the planters, who raised their crops on the credit system, was for banking facilities rather than for internal improvements. For the time, river transportation was sufficiently abundant to furnish the necessary outlet for the cotton crop.

A division between the political parties existed in the matter of banking institutions throughout the whole period. Inasmuch as the Whigs were strongest among the larger planting and business interests, they were especially anxious to increase bank capital. The Democratic small farmers, on the other hand, became violently opposed to all banks.

When hard times came, in the early forties, the borrowing states were in distress. Apparently, Eastern investors, and the English financial corporations with whom they dealt, had not exercised the caution with respect to the legality of bonds, and the procedure of the agents for their disposal, that in later years became usual. When Mississippi repudiated part of her bonds in 1841, she asserted that the debt had been incurred in violation of her constitution and laws, as well as against public sentiment. Arkansas, also, argued that the sale of her bonds had been illegal, and defaulted interest for some years, as did Alabama. Tennessee, Kentucky, and Louisiana (although for a time she defaulted interest) resolved that their obligations were sacred.

The result was to alarm and anger the British investors and

42 See: Henry C. Adams, *Public Debts* (New York, 1887), p. 301; *Tenth Census: Valuation, Taxation and Public Indebtedness*, p. 523; Samuel Hazard (ed.), *Hazard's United States Commercial and Statistical Register*, I, 36–40; *United States Almanac for 1843* (Philadelphia, 1842); Leland H. Jenks, *The Migration of British Capital to 1875* (New York, 1927), Chaps. III, IV; A. C. Cole, *The Whig Party in the South* (Washington, 1913), pp. 76–78; Abernethy, *op. cit.*, pp. 319–25; and Sioussat, *op. cit.*, pp. 59–69.

to check the flow of their capital to American enterprises. Fortunately, the era of prosperity which began at the close of the forties made a new situation.[43]

In 1850 the state banks in the South Central section numbered seventy-eight; loans and discounts were less than in 1834; circulation had risen to over $16,500,000; deposits, to around $12,500,000; and specie, to over $16,500,000. With a free population about that of New England, the section had nearly three times New England's specie in state banks. But over two-thirds of this was in Louisiana.[44]

After the decline of the Old Dominion, following Monroe's Presidency, political energy and leadership passed across the mountains to the South Central States. It is true that South Carolina's voice was powerful and her initiative of great importance. Her leader, Calhoun, came, by 1850 (as we have seen), to exercise influence upon the thought of the Lower South, but, in the interval, political energy and leadership for the nation rested, first, in Kentucky and Tennessee. Mississippi Valley ideals and traits colored both political parties. As population and industry moved across the Alleghenies, the Valley seemed destined to rule the nation. These were the zenith years of rural political power.

The influence of Kentucky and Tennessee finds explanation, in part, in the way in which they had spread their population into the neighboring states. No other states of the South Central Division — and perhaps no other states of the Union — sent such important contributions of their people to West and South. Tennesseeans had moved up the Missouri Valley, had settled Arkansas, had followed Jackson to the Lower South (in Alabama and Mississippi), and, finally, had colonized and defended Texas. The whole Lower Mississippi Valley was to them a single neighborhood.[45] It should also be remembered that, as the child of

[43] On repudiation, see W. A. Scott, *The Repudiation of State Debts* (New York, 1893), and J. B. McMaster, *A History of the People of the United States, from the Revolution to the Civil War* (New York), VI (1920), 624-28, VII (1919), 19-22.

[44] The figures for 1834, and around 1850, are tabulated from J. J. Knox, *History of Banking in the United States* (New York, 1903), I.

[45] Justice John Catron wrote to Jackson (Jan. 4, 1838): " Tene is the old hive from which Ala Misspi Arka Misso & Ills have swarmed; her influence on these states is great." (Jackson MSS, Library of Congress.) Also see p. 22, *ante*.

North Carolina, Tennessee had a sympathetic and influential tie with that state.

In the years to which this volume is devoted, the South Central States furnished three (Jackson, Polk, and Taylor) of the five elected Presidents and two of the unsuccessful candidates (Clay, of Kentucky, and Hugh Lawson White, of Tennessee). In the following decade, John Bell, of Tennessee, and J. C. Breckinridge, of Kentucky, were defeated leaders of their parties for the same office. Andrew Johnson, born in North Carolina, was a poor, illiterate tailor-lad who had migrated to Tennessee. He learned from his wife how to write, rose to leadership of the Democratic land reformers, reached Congress, and, as a Unionist, was chosen Vice-President and succeeded Lincoln. In the years between 1830 and 1850, Kentucky furnished two Vice-Presidents, and Alabama one. The President of the Confederate States was afterwards chosen from the same section. Of the nine Speakers of the House, in these years, all but two came from the slave-holding states. The South Central section furnished three of these — Bell and Polk, of Tennessee, and John White, of Kentucky.

It was a section of pioneers, and its leaders — pioneers or sons of pioneers — possessed the buoyancy, the confidence, and the " mixing " ability that the times demanded.

In politics the section was closely divided. Taking the total of all the votes in the South Central States for President, in the elections from 1832 to 1852, inclusive, the Democrats had a majority of less than ten thousand.[46]

Kentucky voted against the Democratic candidate in all these elections, and Tennessee in all but 1832. The invariably Democratic states were Arkansas and Alabama; Mississippi went Whig in 1840 only. Louisiana went Whig in 1840 and 1848, and her Congressional delegation usually supported the tariff legislation of the Whigs.

Within each of the states, there were groups of counties which were normally Whig, and others normally Democratic.[47] The

[46] But this omits the vote of Alabama in 1832, when Jackson met with little or no opposition in a total vote of around 20,000. Not counting this vote, the Democratic majority was less than one-half of 1%; including it, the Democratic majority was 1.6% of the aggregate vote.

[47] See: map of Party Preponderance, 1836–48 (at end of volume); Jas. R. Robertson, " Sectionalism in Kentucky from 1855 to 1865," *Mississippi Valley*

more favored areas and those tributary to cities, interested in banks and internal improvements, gave Whig majorities, while isolated rural counties, the more illiterate, less fertile regions which contained a backwoods population living in the rougher country, were the strongholds of Democracy. To this, there are the notable exceptions of northern parts of the Kentucky blue-grass basin, the southern part of the blue-grass lands of Tennessee, and the counties of northern Alabama in the limestone belt along the Tennessee River — all of which were normally Democratic. Whig counties in unfavorable regions were chiefly along routes of commercial connection leading from Kentucky and Tennessee to the Cotton Belt.

But here, as elsewhere, it must be remembered that party regions were by no means exclusively Democratic and Whig, respectively. On the contrary, the vote was often very close. They represent preponderance, not unanimity, in political action. Nevertheless, the nucleal portions of these areas — those portions that carried the characteristics of the region to the highest point — tended to be overwhelmingly Whig or Democratic, according to the quality of the region. This quality includes several factors: not only soil and illiteracy, but also communication, inheritance, personal leadership, etc., must be considered. But, as the map shows, the combination of several of these factors — resulting, as a whole, in adverse or in favorable conditions, respectively — tended to shape the pattern of party geography.

Charles Lyell, in his *Second Visit to the United States*,[48] writes of the " aristocratic democracy " of the newly settled slave states. The " ostracism of wealth " found expression in the lately cleared country, where the gentleman settler's fences were pulled down, his cattle left to stray, and other depredations committed by neighbors with " a vulgar jealousy of his riches." In politics, then as later, the candidate often found it necessary to solicit votes on foot rather than on horseback, and the finer garments of his family were a handicap to political success.

Nevertheless, the important leaders of both parties lived, as a rule, in the fertile, more literate regions, and in or near towns.

Historical Review, IV, 49–63 (with maps); and C. O. Sauer, " Geography and the Gerrymander," *American Political Science Review*, XII, 403–26 (with maps).

[48] *A Second Visit to the United States of North America* (London, 1849), II, 69–70.

As, in the South Atlantic States, Howell Cobb, Robert Toombs, and A. H. Stephens resided in adjacent districts in the eastern part of the Cotton Belt (which extended through central Georgia), so, in the South Central Division, the Black Belt and the Coosa Valley connecting with it were the home regions of Alabama men of especial ability,[49] and, in Mississippi, Jefferson Davis, John A. Quitman, and Robert J. Walker lived on the rich alluvials of the Mississippi. The fertile part of the eastern Tennessee Valley was the home of Hugh Lawson White; the middle Nashville Basin, that of Jackson, Polk, Felix Grundy, and Bell; while David Crockett represented the district of western Tennessee bordering on the Mississippi. Henry Clay's home was in the heart of the Lexington Basin of Kentucky, and John J. Crittenden and R. M. Johnson (who became a Democratic Vice-President) came from the same region.

The leaders of this South Central section occupied the center of the national stage in the years of Jacksonian Democracy. Besides Jackson himself, whose traits are portrayed in an earlier chapter, Tennessee furnished a notable group.[50]

Among Jackson's supporters, James Knox Polk stands out pre-eminently. He was born in North Carolina, of Scotch-Irish ancestors who followed the long trail toward North Carolina down which had gone the Boones, the Calhouns, and the forbears of Abraham Lincoln, Jefferson Davis, and Sam Houston.[51] It was an expansionist background for the President whose treaties carried the United States to the Pacific. Taken by his father in his youth to middle Tennessee, he was brought up as a Jeffersonian Democrat, gained his college degree at the University of North Carolina, studied law, and was sent to Congress in 1825. He made the journey to Baltimore on horseback, and was, at first, of the same boarding house, or " mess," in Washington, as Calhoun and Hugh Lawson White, his later political foes.

Polk was by no means the commonplace person that Whig historians, and his political enemies in his own party, have made him out. In Congress he was one of Jackson's most effective supporters, particularly on the bank issue. He became Speaker for

[49] W. L. Fleming, *Civil War and Reconstruction in Alabama* (New York, 1905), p. 6 (map).

[50] See n. 45, p. 230, *ante*.

[51] Turner, *Rise of the New West*, p. 51.

two terms; won the governorship in Tennessee when Jackson himself was losing control of the state; and, finally, attained the Presidency when Van Buren, whom he had supported, lost renomination, in 1844, by reason of his opposition to the annexation of Texas.

This serious-minded, hard-headed Scotchman — formal, punctilious, devoted to the details of his office — did not possess the magnetic, spectacular personality of Jackson or Clay, but, with all his urbanity, he lacked nothing in decision and in achievement. His *Diary* reveals his conscientious hard work and compels a revision of the historical estimate of the man. Although stigmatized by his enemies as a mediocrity and the " first dark horse," he was the master of his able cabinet.[52]

Polk had studied law under Felix Grundy, one of the " War Hawks " of 1812. Grundy was a native of Virginia, who removed to Kentucky and became its Chief Justice, before he settled in Nashville, Tennessee, in 1807. Stout of heart as he was of body, Grundy, as United States Senator, championed the policies of Jackson, both in Congress and in Tennessee. Van Buren made him Attorney-General in 1838, but toward the close of 1839 he resigned, and died the next year.

Of the courtly John H. Eaton, Senator, Secretary of War under Jackson, pivot of the cabinet dissensions, minister to Spain, more will appear in a later chapter.[53]

The career of Hugh Lawson White,[54] the leader of eastern Tennessee, illustrates the strength of the demand, in that state, that one of its sons should succeed Jackson, and at the same time

[52] E. I. McCormac, *James K. Polk: A Political Biography* (Berkeley, Calif., 1922), pp. 324, 330, quoting from letters of Gideon Welles and Geo. Bancroft.

[53] Chapter IX. For a discussion of minor Jacksonian Tennessee leaders, and indications of the quality of their correspondence, see: Sioussat, in *American Historical Review*, XIV, 51–69, and (ed.) in *Tennessee Historical Magazine*, I, 209–56 (Sept., 1915) [" Letters of James K. Polk to Cave Johnson, 1833–1848 "], II, 43 ff. (Mar., 1916) [" Diaries of S. H. Laughlin, of Tennessee, 1840, 1843 "], and III, 51–73 (Mar., 1917) [" Letters of James K. Polk to Andrew J. Donelson, 1843–1848 "], *et passim;* Abernethy, " Andrew Jackson and the Rise of Southwestern Democracy," *American Historical Review*, XXXIII, 64–77, and " The Origin of the Whig Party in Tennessee," *Mississippi Valley Historical Review*, XII, 504–22; J. S. Bassett, *The Life of Andrew Jackson* (New York, 1925); and McCormac, *op. cit.* Tennessee politics were complicated and fateful, and the warring factional leaders were able politicians.

[54] Nancy N. Scott (ed.), *A Memoir of Hugh Lawson White, . . . with Selections from His Speeches and Correspondence* (Philadelphia, 1856).

it shows the complicated political problems which that President had to face. Born in North Carolina, White had gone with his pioneer father to Tennessee in 1786, served against the Indians under John Sevier, studied in Pennsylvania, and risen to the position of a justice in the Supreme Court of Tennessee. His career as president of the State Bank of Tennessee prepared him for some of the problems that met him when he served as a Senator of the United States between 1825 and 1839; and Samuel Jaudon, the cashier of the Bank of the United States at Philadelphia, the confidant of Nicholas Biddle, was White's son-in-law.[55] At the outset, White was a supporter of Jackson. He voted for the Force Bill to crush nullification, and against recharter of the Bank of the United States in 1832. But he was independent in his support, for he favored Clay's land bill, and refused to accept Jackson's decision to make Van Buren his successor.

Meantime, John Bell,[56] of Tennessee, who had surprised the old-time leaders in that state by defeating Felix Grundy, backed by Jackson, for the House of Representatives in 1827, had won the speakership of the House over Polk, the spokesman for the President, in 1834. He had achieved this success, not only by his ability as a debater but by a combination of some of the Jackson men with a group of opponents of the President. In the succeeding Congress, Polk had defeated Bell, and, in the preliminary campaign, the latter had criticized as demagogic the administration's policy of an exclusively metallic currency.

Tennessee, with its important banking and business interests, as well as its fear of the North, its " clannishness," and its influence through the widespread colonization of its people, was ripe for a revolt against the selection of Van Buren for the succession.

Even in 1833, White had declined the support of his friends in Tennessee as a candidate for the Presidency. And now, with Bell, he found himself at odds with the administration on important measures and policies. The outcome was that a meeting of the Tennessee Congressional delegation (excepting Grundy, Polk, and Cave Johnson) was held, in December, 1834, and White consented to their request to become a Presidential candidate.

Already, David Crockett, the frontier celebrity from western

Tennessee (later a hero of the Alamo in the Texan revolution), had broken with Jackson in Congress. Now White, the " Nestor of the Senate " — Jackson's friend, to whom he had offered a cabinet post and a room with him in the White House — went into the opposition. History seldom recounts a more striking upturn than the victory in Tennessee politics of this mild, serious-minded embodiment of Senatorial dignity and conventions, over the fiery Jackson. At first, White refused to admit that he was a Whig. It was Jackson, he insisted, and not he, who had changed principles.[57] But, when Jackson threatened to make him " odious," he accepted the support of Clay men, even though his candidacy seemed likely to throw the election into the House, to the advantage of the Whigs.[58]

Jackson, in his correspondence and through the *Globe*, his official organ, denounced White as the tool of nullifiers and National Bank men.[59] Bell insisted that White would not veto a bill to establish the Bank; [60] he favored *a* bank himself, and declaimed against party as " that eternal foe to the repose and stability of all free states! " [61] White himself, however, insisted that he still believed it was unconstitutional to charter a national bank, with corporate powers within the states, and that he should act on that opinion until satisfied that he was in error. He was also against a national bank based on the public funds.[62]

But more important than the personal utterances of Bell and of White was the fact that, in Presidential elections, Tennessee now ceased to follow her frontier hero, " Old Hickory." Even in 1844, when Polk was the Democratic candidate, Tennessee gave its vote to Clay. In 1856 James Buchanan won, but in 1860 Bell, as the Constitutional Union candidate for President, carried his state. Bell's strength as a candidate was in the old Whig regions [63] and his principles were those of the Southern Whigs. White's break with the Democratic administration resulted in victory, in 1836, only in Tennessee and Georgia. He died in 1840.

[57] *National Intelligencer*, Sept. 17, 1836.

[58] Clay thought White might carry the undivided " South " and Southwest. (Calvin Colton, *The Life, Correspondence, and Speeches of Henry Clay* [New York, 1857], IV, 394.)

[59] *National Intelligencer*, Sept. 17, 1836.

[60] *Niles' Register*, XLVIII, 330–36; cf. 263, 312.

[61] *Ibid.*, and McCormac, *op. cit.*, p. 84.

[62] *Niles' Register*, LI, 44, 178.

[63] See map of Party Preponderance, 1836–48 (at end of volume).

Henry Clay,[64] the spokesman of the National Republicans and Whigs of the Ohio Valley, was the first of the Westerners to win a national position in politics. He drew a following from all sections, but was strongest in the prosperous regions where wealth and the interests of bankers, manufacturers, and promoters of internal improvements prevailed. The aristocracy of the Cotton Belt found it possible to ally with these Northern forces, with Clay as the compromising leader, in common alarm over the tendencies of Jacksonian Democracy. Men of frontier training, also — such as the youthful Abraham Lincoln — followed him with devotion.

A native of Virginia, Clay had gone to Lexington, Kentucky, where he had built up a successful law practice and his plantation of " Ashland." Tall and spare, with " long limbs . . . loosely put together," with gray eyes, large nose, lips that wandered engagingly across his fair, mobile face, Clay captivated his followers by his mere presence. His ardent spirit, hopeful and buoyant, found expression in impetuous eloquence. Clay's silvery voice — " one of the sweetest imaginable " — bore his large and liberal views of public affairs, not only to his companions in House and Senate but to the masses.[65] Kentucky had placed its seal upon the man. To Puritans like John Quincy Adams, Clay's love of gaming and of drink, his profanity, seemed inconsistent with the qualities that made a New England gentleman, but to the gentlemen of South and West he appeared as a delightful companion.

He spoke for the right of the West to recognition in national legislation. He demanded a more liberal construction of the Constitution, its adjustment to the needs of a nation whose expansion into the Mississippi Valley had created conditions inconsistent with an interpretation suited only to the states of the Atlantic seaboard.

Clay had made the speakership of the House of Representatives his instrument for political leadership,[66] and it was natural that, in the formulation of policies (except during the years of John Quincy Adams's administration, when he was a member of the cabinet), he aimed to subordinate the Executive to Congress.

[64] The standard biography is Carl Schurz, *Henry Clay* (Boston, 1899 [in " American Statesmen " series]).

[65] See the characterization of Clay in Henry W. Hilliard, *Politics and Pen Pictures at Home and Abroad* (New York, 1892), p. 3.

[66] Turner, *Rise of the New West*, p. 187.

He attacked Monroe for his South American policy and for his veto of internal improvements; Jackson, for his bank policy and for "executive usurpation"; Van Buren, for his fiscal system; and Tyler, for refusal to follow the policies which Clay dictated to the Whigs after an election that had been won by them without a platform.

But Clay had to meet two men who were the most difficult of all on whom to try the system of Congressional control. Jackson, with his awful will, had small respect for Constitutional restraints, while Tyler, at the other extreme, had such state-rights scruples in Constitutional interpretation as to find Clay's program for Congressional legislation impossible. The ax of Jackson and the rapier of Tyler afforded ample protection to executive power through the use of the veto.

John J. Crittenden, of Kentucky, served in the Senate during nearly half of his life on the national political stage, extending from 1817 to 1863. Attorney-General under both Harrison and Fillmore, he is best known for his support of the Union and for his attempts to find a compromise when the Civil War came. He carried on the spirit of Henry Clay. Another distinguished Kentuckian was R. M. Johnson, a supporter of Jackson; he gained fame in the War of 1812 as the reputed killer of Tecumseh, served long in the House and Senate, and became Vice-President under Van Buren. Harriet Martineau, however, was chiefly impressed by the absence of his cravat,[67] and Southern correspondents of Jackson objected to Johnson's peculiar domestic relations as odious in a slaveholding society.[68]

Louisiana's contribution of public men illustrated the varied sources of her population. Not only were many of her Senators and Representatives in Congress of the old French stock, but she drew on all quarters of the Union for her leaders. Most distinguished of them in these years was Edward Livingston. Born in New York, a member of the distinguished Livingston family, he became a Jeffersonian Congressman. Accused of default while

---

[67] *Retrospect of Western Travel* (London and New York, 1838), I, 155.

[68] Catron to Jackson, Mar. 21, 1835 (*Correspondence of Andrew Jackson*, ed. J. S. Bassett, V [Carnegie Institution of Washington, 1931], 331), and Alfred Balch to Jackson, Apr. 4, 1835 (Jackson MSS, Library of Congress). See also: *Baltimore Patriot*, Oct. 31, 1836; *Cincinnati Gazette*, July 9, 1835; and Herbert A. Kellar, "Rockbridge County Virginia, in 1835," in L. J. Paetow (ed.), *The Crusades and Other Historical Essays Presented to Dana C. Munro by His Former Students* (New York, 1928), p. 349.

United States District Attorney in New York City, he removed to New Orleans. Although it seems that a dishonest clerk was the cause of his trouble, he later paid the debt with interest. In New Orleans he gained distinction at once by his codes of law, and he entered the Senate of the United States at the beginning of Jackson's Presidency. Called to the cabinet as Secretary of State in succession to Van Buren, he served the President wisely in the various domestic issues and later as minister to France in a critical period.

John Slidell, likewise of New York birth, and a graduate of Columbia, went to New Orleans, became a Congressman, and was named by Polk as minister to Mexico, but his extreme expansionist views led that country to refuse to receive him. His later career in the Senate, and his capture while on his way to Europe to secure recognition of the Southern Confederacy, gave him his position in history.

But an even more striking contribution to the varied population of New Orleans was the stormy petrel, Pierre Soulé, a native of France. Because of a conspiracy against the Bourbons, he was compelled to flee. A shepherd in the Pyrenees, a refugee in Haiti, a wanderer to Baltimore and to Tennessee, a gardener in Kentucky, he became a brilliant jury lawyer in New Orleans and, in 1847, a Senator of the United States. His hot-headed ultimatum to Spain in 1854, while he was serving as President Pierce's minister to that nation, was disavowed; but his determination to secure Cuba for the United States brought him notoriety, again, in the Ostend Manifesto.

Zachary Taylor was a resident of Louisiana when he was elected President; but his career illustrates the South Central mobility of population. Born in Virginia, he grew to manhood in Kentucky, served as Indian fighter before and during the War of 1812, was stationed in Wisconsin in the Black Hawk War, then in Florida, and not until 1840, when his headquarters were in Baton Rouge and he engaged in cotton planting, did he, for a few years, find himself settled in Louisiana. As a general and hero of the Mexican War, he won a national prominence and was elected President in 1848 by the Whigs, only to die in 1850. There was little in his brief occupancy of the Presidency to indicate a South Central connection, for his frontier military service gave him a national attitude and he relied even more upon the Northern than the Southern wing of his party for advice.

From western Mississippi came the most famous of her leaders, for here were both the important enemies and friends of Jackson.

George Poindexter, Virginian by birth, removed to Natchez early in the nineteenth century and became a leading lawyer, famous for his Mississippi code. He was a territorial delegate to Congress, participated in the War of 1812, and became Senator in 1830, as a follower of Jackson. But he quarreled with his chief over the appointment of a Tennesseean to a federal land office in Mississippi. So bitter was the enmity between them that the President believed that Poindexter was connected with an attempt on his life. Poindexter thereafter denounced Jackson fiercely. He finally closed his career a victim to drink.

Robert J. Walker, born in Pennsylvania, became, as husband of a descendant of Benjamin Franklin, the brother-in-law of George M. Dallas. With the Bache and Dallas connections in Pennsylvania, his future there seemed promising, but he migrated to Natchez in 1826, in the boom days of the taking-up of Indian lands. Here he developed an extensive law practice and was active in the formation of associations to prevent the bidding-up of public lands. This led to an investigation, pushed by Senator Poindexter (but to the latter's political loss). Moving to central Mississippi, Walker gained the support of the pioneer element by his land policy, endeared himself to Jackson by opposing nullification, and won the Mississippi Senatorship from Poindexter.

He was an ardent advocate of the annexation of Texas, and, by pamphlets combining this issue with the acquisition of Oregon, he was influential in effecting the alliance of Western and Southern Democrats by which Polk won the Presidency in 1844. As Polk's Secretary of the Treasury, he not only fixed his name in tariff history by his lowered tariff of 1846, but also used every effort to persuade Polk to acquire all of Mexico by the war with that country, and urged upon him imperial expansion to the Pacific Coast.

His career as Mississippi repudiationist, governor of Kansas at a critical stage, lobbyist, railroad promoter, and agent in England at the time of the Civil War (to promote the interests of the federal government), need not be detailed here. He was a striking example of the Pennsylvania politician working in the new environment of Mississippi.[69]

Jefferson Davis, of Kentucky birth, had been taken as an infant to Mississippi. Graduating from West Point, he became an officer on the Wisconsin frontier, serving in the Black Hawk War. Having married the daughter of Colonel Zachary Taylor, he settled as a cotton planter near Vicksburg in 1835, and until 1843, when he entered politics, devoted his leisure to reading and study. In 1844, partly by Walker's assistance, he was elected to Congress. Resigning in 1846, he became one of the heroes of the Mexican War. He was made Senator by appointment in 1847 and was re-elected; but, believing that the Compromise of 1850 had not adequately secured the interests of the South, he resigned in order to run for governor, on that issue, against his colleague in the Senate, the Unionist Henry S. Foote, who defeated him. Davis' later career, as a great Secretary of War and as secessionist Senator and President of the Confederacy, requires no rehearsal.[70]

Another of this group was John A. Quitman, a New Yorker by birth, son of a German pastor and a Dutch mother whose father had been governor of Curaçao in the West Indies. He had studied law in Ohio and at the age of twenty-two migrated to Natchez, where as planter he became even more Southern than those who were native to the slave states. He fought for the independence of Texas and was given a sword by Congress for his brilliant services in the Mexican War. He held the governorship of Mississippi in 1850, and his later career as Congressman and supporter of a Cuban filibuster is well known. A friend relates a conversation with him to the effect that, in his opinion, General Winfield Scott missed a great opportunity in not making himself dictator of Mexico and awarding titles of nobility to American officers in an independent empire to be established there.[71]

---

[69] See W. E. Dodd, *Robert J. Walker, Imperialist* (Chicago Literary Club, 1914).

[70] On the nationalistic and opportunistic aspects of his policy as Southern President, and their relation to his frontier, roving, military experience, see N. W. Stephenson, " A Theory of Jefferson Davis," *American Historical Review*, XXI, 73–90. See also Dunbar Rowland (ed.), *Jefferson Davis, Constitutionalist: His Letters, Papers and Speeches* (Jackson, Miss., 1923).

[71] Sparks, *Memories*, p. 347. See also J. F. H. Claiborne, *Life and Corre-*

S. S. Prentiss, a native of Maine, coming to Natchez as a youthful tutor just graduated from Bowdoin, achieved a remarkable hold upon the Whigs of Mississippi, as lawyer, orator, and political leader. His speeches are credited with having much to do with overturning the Jackson power, in that state, after the Crisis of 1837. Although a lame and lisping youth, he quickly won recognition by his animated and glowing speech and by his gift of wit and ridicule, coupled with a copious eloquence which not only suited the Southwest but won the admiration of New England Whigs like Webster and Edward Everett. In one of his political campaigns, for ten weeks he averaged upwards of thirty miles a day on horseback, speaking two hours each week day. His contested-election case in Congress, in which Speaker Polk gave the deciding vote against the Whigs, was a notable example of the influence of politics upon legal questions. Drink and illness brought his brilliant career to a close in 1850. His letters to his family in Maine, running through the whole of his life in Mississippi, reveal his strong New England quality in spite of his success in Mississippi. Opposed to nullification, he was also discontented with slavery, though he saw no escape from the system.[72]

The Black Belt furnished the leaders of Alabama. William R. King, a native of North Carolina, had represented that state in Congress in the period of the War of 1812, had been secretary of legation in Russia, and, on his return in 1818, became a planter in the rich cotton area of Alabama. He was a delegate to the convention that framed the state's first constitution, and from 1819 to 1844 was United States Senator. After serving as minister to France, he was returned to the Senate and continued there until his election as Vice-President with President Pierce.

Dixon H. Lewis, of Virginia birth, educated at South Carolina College, moved to the Alabama Black Belt as a youth and, following the doctrines of John Taylor, of Virginia, espoused the cause of state sovereignty and of Andrew Jackson on the Indian question. As Representative in Congress and after 1845 as Sena-

spondence of John A. Quitman, Major-General, U.S.A., and Governor of the State of Mississippi (New York, 1860).

[72] Prentiss' letters are an interesting source for this period of Mississippi life as seen by a transplanted and assimilated Yankee. See: Memoir of S. S. Prentiss; Sparks, op. cit., pp. 349–72; and American Whig Review, XIV, 236 (portrait).

tor, he fell under the spell of Calhoun, and remained one of the most radical supporters of state sovereignty.[73]

William Lowndes Yancey's father had been in South Carolina in the law office of Calhoun. With this background, it is not unnatural that he, a native of Georgia (1814), should have passed unscathed from his Northern education in New York and at Williams College, Massachusetts. In 1836 he became a planter and editor in the Alabama Black Belt, and succeeded Lewis in the House when the latter became Senator. His real career did not begin until the close of the period, when he became the " fire-eating," uncompromising champion of state sovereignty, the right of the South to carry slavery into the territories without hindrance by Congress. His unsuccessful attempt to compel the Democratic convention in 1848 to incorporate into its platform a plank protective of slavery in the territories, led him to withdraw for a time from public life, only to emerge as the extremist orator for the Southern cause in later years. His oratory was remarkable for the quiet flow of its beginning, until it plunged into a cataract of emotional eloquence which a contemporary called " sublime ravings." He was one of the politicians to whom the reputation of the Lower South for aggressive impetuosity was due.

Although, as shown by the map,[74] the Black Belt of Alabama was Whig and was the home of the educated and prosperous planters, it was from this region that the leaders of the Democratic masses came, in this normally Democratic state. Nor was the region without distinguished Whig leaders.

Henry W. Hilliard was born in North Carolina and educated at South Carolina College. In 1831 he became Professor of Law in the University of Alabama, and, on the issue of the Subtreasury, was elected to the legislature, in 1838, as a Whig. Chargé d'affaires in Belgium under Tyler, on his return he became a Representative in Congress, where he supported the party op-

---

[73] T. M. Williams, " Dixon H. Lewis," Alabama Polytechnic Institute *Historical Studies*, 1912. See also F. W. Moore (ed.), " Calhoun as Seen by His Political Friends: Letters of Duff Green, Dixon H. Lewis, Richard K. Cralle during the Period from 1831 to 1848 " (Southern History Association *Publications*, VII, 159–69, 269–91, 353–61, 419–26), *passim*.

[74] Party Preponderance, 1836–48 (at end of volume). See Theodore H. Jack, *Sectionalism and Party Politics in Alabama, 1819–1842* (Kenosha, Wis., 1919).

position to extreme state rights and favored the Compromise of 1850. He favored Bell for President in 1860, but went with his state when she seceded.[75] He was typical of the moderation of the Whigs of the Black Belt.

A. F. Hopkins, a Virginian by birth, began the practice of law in Huntsville, Alabama, in 1816. He became a justice of the Supreme Court of his state, and was three times the candidate of his party for the United States Senate. He was an ardent Whig, serving on the Harrison electoral ticket in 1840 and acting as the temporary chairman of the national convention in 1844. Mobile was his later residence, and, as president of the Mobile and Ohio Railroad in 1857, he represented the interest of Whig leaders in economic fields.

This incomplete, though considerable, list of important men in the politics of the South Central States suggests concretely the power that the section exerted in the Union, in the thirties, through Kentucky and Tennessee leaders, and in the later ante-bellum period by those of the Cotton Belt.[76] The section's Western quality is illustrated by the varied origin and aggressive temper of its public men. The youth of the section; its bold, ardent, adventurous, imperialistic qualities; its will-power, sometimes domineering and usually exhibiting the demand for direct action; the common feeling in the Lower South against any restraints upon the right of the slaveholder to participate on equal terms in the opening of new territories, and the insistence that attempts to forbid such expansion were an insult to Southern honor [77] — marked, especially, the dominant figures of the Cotton Belt in the later years of our period. For, in the two decades after 1830, the Gulf Basin changed from a region ruled by pioneer ideals to a region in which the slaveholding aristocracy won control, but which still responded to the earlier urge to action and expansion. On the border, Kentucky and much of Tennessee continued to constitute a transition zone between the Lower South and the North Central States.

[75] Henry W. Hilliard, *Speeches and Addresses* (New York, 1855) and *Politics and Pen Pictures*.

[76] See Wm. G. Brown, *The Lower South in American History* (New York, 1902).

[77] Not a few of them were duelists, and some of the most prominent had killed their opponents.

Youthfulness and wide difference in nativity appear in this list. Not a fourth of these leaders were born in the South Central States; over a fourth came from the North and from foreign countries; half of them were from the South Atlantic.[78] The soul of the section found expression in such imperious, temperamental leaders as Jackson, Clay, Poindexter, Quitman, Soulé, Yancey, and Houston (who carried Tennessee characteristics into Texas). Emerging from frontier conditions, its climate reflected in the hot blood of its sons, sensitive to insult or restraint, eager for expansion, it was a section of direct and passionate action. The spirit of the master of slaves in a new country, where the restraints of a historic, patriarchal society were less in evidence, is exhibited in many of these leaders.

The spirit of the western half of the Southern people was that of the eastern half, but infused with the greater recklessness, initiative, energy, and will-power of the West, and more suffused with feeling. As the material interests of slavery passed to the southern half of the Mississippi Valley, these qualities were obvious in its defense.

It was the planters of the Gulf Basin whose eyes opened to the vision of tropical colonization and tropical empire. The shining waters of the Gulf invited these descendants of a migrating people to extend their empire to Texas, Cuba, Mexico, Central America, and the Isthmus. In this conception of " Young America " and " manifest destiny," the tendencies which had brought the Southern-upland folk into Kentucky and Tennessee, into Louisiana and Florida, were given a new form as new conditions and new lands opened before them. The expansion of the pioneer became involved in the creation of new slave states. It was in the Gulf States of the South Central Division that this first clearly appeared, and it was here that the imperiousness and heated feeling attained sufficient power to force the issue. The older portions of the section, especially Kentucky, remained a region of moderation and of compromise.

The cultural life of the South Central States had a quality of its own. As might be expected from the urban influence and

---

[78] Since this chapter was written, I have seen the illuminating paper by N. W. Stephenson, " An Illustration of the Frontier as Seed Bed," *Proceedings* of Pacific Coast Branch of American Historical Association, 1928, pp. 56–66.

from the old French and Spanish factors, New Orleans and its tributary area had a distinctive character. The gay life of the city, its quadroon balls, the exclusive and charming character of Creole society, have made their place in American literature.

In the South Central section, white illiteracy was alarming. The best educational record was made in the black prairie lands, on the alluvials adjacent to the lower Mississippi, and in the limestone basins of central Kentucky and Tennessee. The worst illiteracy was in the hilly or infertile counties which surrounded these areas.[79] In spite of the newness of the South Central States, by 1850 the illiteracy of the section as a whole was no greater than that of the South Atlantic, if the census figures can be trusted. But it was nearly twice that of the North Central States, in the upper half of the Mississippi Valley, nearly three times that of the Middle Atlantic States, and over fourfold that of New England.[80]

Nor was the common-school education on a par with that of the South Atlantic. Although private tutors trained the children of the richer planters, the poor whites remained almost uncared for. Even in the older state of Kentucky, not more than one-third of the children between the ages of four and fifteen attended school. Lyell, the English traveler, reported, in the middle forties, that there were still seven counties in Mississippi without a single schoolhouse.[81] Whereas, in the South Central States, there was but one pupil to ten white people, in the North Central there was one to five. There were nearly twice the number of college students, in proportion to the white population, in New England that there were in the South Central Division, and the latter section had but three-fifths the proportion of whites in college that the North Central States reported. Adding the huge negro illiteracy, it is clear that, as a whole, the section's position in mass culture was low. But this did not prevent the existence, in special areas, of a cultivated aristocracy. For it must be remembered that fairly sharp boundaries separated the prosperous and favored regions from the mass of the section. What was true of the geography of political leadership was true, also, of the

[79] See map of White Illiteracy, 1850 (at end of volume).
[80] The sectional cultural statistics were compiled from the figures, by states, in the *Compendium of the Seventh Census.*
[81] *Second Visit to the United States,* II, 213.

centers of culture.[82] Over the section as a whole, however, the influence of pioneering and slavery was still felt as a limitation to the development of refinement.

Colleges were, nevertheless, developing at the beginning of these years.[83] In Kentucky the University of Transylvania, at Lexington, chartered in 1798, had long been a center of culture. Cumberland College, in Tennessee, became the University of Nashville. The University of Alabama, on a Congressional land grant, opened its doors in 1831 and drew its first president, a New Englander in origin, from Transylvania. In Mississippi a seminary near Natchez was incorporated. In Louisiana various institutions, hardly worthy of the name of colleges, reflected French and English antagonisms. New Orleans had a flourishing Catholic college and an academy, the " University of Louisiana," where law and medicine were taught. New England teachers furnished a disproportionate number of educational leaders in the section; [84] but they sometimes had difficulties because of their Northern origin, and student rioting was characteristic of the section.

The newspaper editors of the South Central States included some who came to rank among the most distinguished and influential in the nation, for, if this Southwest welcomed a scurrilous journalism, with very personal encounters between rival editors, and if pistols lay beside the inkstand in the sanctum, this type of journalist knew how to appeal to the people with a style in which vituperation, humor, and pungency, as well as forceful directness, had a telling effect upon the men of the section.

Some of the Kentucky editors, like many of the schoolmasters and leaders in higher education, were transplanted Yankees, notably George D. Prentice and Amos Kendall.

Prentice, of Connecticut birth, an alumnus of Brown, had been a literary editor in his native state, but, when he visited Kentucky in 1830 to secure material for a campaign " life " of Clay, he accepted the editorship of the Whig *Louisville Journal*, and, for some forty years, his pungent paragraphs (forerunners of

[82] As a type of this, see Fleming, *Civil War and Reconstruction in Alabama*, p. 6 (map).
[83] *American Quarterly Register*, III, 127 (Nov., 1830) *et passim*.
[84] *The South in the Building of the Nation* (Richmond, Va., 1909), VII, 298–313.

present-day modes), editorials, and poems made his name a familiar one.[85] He had the gift for personal attack, and rather coarse humor, that pleased his Kentucky readers and made his paper a power among its Whig supporters. Although an opponent of the duel,[86] finding it necessary to defend himself he was frequently engaged in encounters resultant from his witty and bitter personalities; and Kentucky whiskey had its effect upon his career. But no editor in the section had a wider circle of admirers among the Unionist Whigs.

Kendall was born in Massachusetts and graduated from Dartmouth. He went in his youth to Kentucky, to be a tutor in the family of Henry Clay. Soon becoming the editor of the Frankfort *Argus*, he supported the Democratic party so vigorously that Jackson, on his election to the Presidency, made him an auditor in the Treasury, and he became one of the intimate group of advisers known as the " kitchen cabinet." To this mysterious and retiring editor were attributed keynote editorials furnished to the *Globe* and to the country press, and even the state papers of Jackson.[87]

Kendall had not shown, in his newspaper work, the eagerness to turn to personal abuse which characterized his rivals. With a New England delicacy of distinction, when he felt it necessary to give blow for blow he issued a separate broadside! But he could wield a very sharp pen and was involved in various physical encounters.

After his services in the war on the Bank, which he had waged even during his editorial career in Kentucky, he was appointed Postmaster-General by Jackson. In this position, he showed administrative skill, economies, and a reforming spirit, even going to jail for refusal to pay certain claims against the government, which he deemed unwarranted. But he incurred the enmity of his native section by his instructions to postmasters regarding the confiscation of the " incendiary publications " of the abolitionists. On the triumph of the Whigs, his paper,

[85] His *Poems* (ed. J. J. Piatt) were published in Cincinnati in 1880; paragraphs (from his paper), under the name of *Prenticeana*, appeared in New York in 1860. See also *Harper's Magazine*, L, 193.

[86] The frequence of duels in which one of the participants was an editor, is remarkable. For examples see Frederic Hudson, *Journalism in the United States, from 1690 to 1872* (New York, 1873), pp. 762–64.

[87] Martineau, *Retrospect of Western Travel*, I, 155–57.

Kendall's Expositor, and later the *Union Democrat,* carried on his political influence. In the end, he became associated with S. F. B. Morse's telegraph enterprise, made a fortune, and became the benefactor of various religious and charitable institutions.[88]

In short, one finds, throughout the career of this secretive and silent politician, a quality which reveals his Yankee origins.

Prentice and Kendall, with Francis P. Blair, made up a trio of famous Kentucky journalists. Blair,[89] whose ancestors had included presidents of William and Mary and of Princeton, had gone from his native Virginia to study at Transylvania College, Kentucky. He was a supporter of the relief party in that state and, as president of the Bank of Kentucky, was an enemy of the Bank of the United States. He contributed articles to Kendall's *Argus,* and, when the breach between Calhoun and Jackson made the advisers of the President desirous of replacing the *Telegraph,* under the editorship of Duff Green, with a friendly organ, the *Globe* was established, in 1830, with Blair as its editor. He became the champion, and the uncompromising spokesman, of the administration. Political propaganda has seldom been more skilfully used. Few editors have had a wider national influence, not only upon the intelligent but also upon the masses; and the tone of the paper reflected the directness, the fighting qualities, and the will-power of the South Central section and its hero. After Polk's election, Blair retired to his Maryland farm. This Jacksonian editor joined the Republican party at its birth.

Tennessee editors did not achieve the national reputation of those of Kentucky, but a notable group were active in these years. Out of Massachusetts, in 1838, came Jeremiah George Harris (a confidant of George Bancroft and editor of his *Bay State Democrat*),[90] to become, at Polk's desire, for four years the editor of the newly established Nashville *Union.* It became Polk's organ — the promoter of his political fortunes. Harris met the most vigorous of his rivals in scurrilous invective, and, as a result, his body bore the marks of the pistol. His support of Polk and of

[88] *Autobiography of Amos Kendall,* ed. Wm. Stickney (Boston, 1872).

[89] For an enthusiastic impression of him, see *Colonel Alexander K. McClure's Recollections of Half a Century* (Salem, Mass., 1902), p. 43.

[90] See A. B. Darling, *Political Changes in Massachusetts, 1824–1848* (New Haven, 1925), pp. 176 (n. 6), 219–21, and McCormac, *Polk,* pp. 124, 140–41.

Bancroft had not a little to do with their success and with the latter's inclusion in Polk's cabinet.

S. H. Laughlin,[91] a Virginian by birth, who preceded and followed Harris as editor of the *Union*, was an adroit politician and intimate of Polk; but his intemperate habits seriously interfered with his editorial efficiency. However, upon Polk's election, he became Recorder of the General Land Office.

Quite as picturesque a representative of the section was " Parson " William G. Brownlow, whose career began in Virginia as a carpenter. He lived as an itinerant Methodist in South Carolina, where he fought nullification, and in eastern Tennessee, where in 1838 he became editor of the Knoxville *Whig* — a fiery opponent of secession, though not antagonistic to slavery itself. Reckless in his bravery, his editorials and speeches were abusive and defiant — in the " sword-thrust " style, as he called it. His opponents were " God-forsaken and hell-deserving "; but if (as he claimed) his paper had the largest circulation of any in the state, the eastern-Tennessee Unionists approved of him, even in the days of secession.[92]

New Orleans, as the metropolis of the section, had its own editorial group, characteristic of the region. So late as the close of the period, the leading papers were published in French and English editions, or with separate sheets for the two languages. The *Courier*, the *Bee*, and the *Picayune* were notable in the field of politics; the *Price Current*, a weekly, remains a mine of information on the commerce of the Mississippi Valley; while *De Bow's Review* was a magazine full of ably edited material on the economic life of both the slaveholding sections.[93]

Peter Wagner, the fighting editor of the *Courier*, was famous for his aggressiveness and his duels. George W. Kendall, who, with Francis A. Lumsden (a North Carolinian), edited the Whig *Picayune*, was of New Hampshire birth, and had had experience on the *National Intelligencer* and the *Telegraph*, in Washington,

[91] *Ibid.* (consult Index); and *Tennessee Historical Magazine*, II, 43 ff. (Laughlin's " Diaries," 1840, 1843).

[92] His *Sketches of the Rise, Progress and Decline of Secession* (Philadelphia, 1862) includes a brief autobiography. *Parson Brownlow* (New York: Beadle & Co., 1862) gives some examples of his slashing style.

[93] On South Central periodicals, see Frank Luther Mott, *A History of American Magazines, 1741–1850* (New York, 1930), *passim*.

as well as on the New York *Tribune*. Fleeing from yellow fever in New York, in the middle thirties, he came, strangely enough, to New Orleans, where he founded the *Picayune*. Its clever and witty character showed Kendall as a humorist, and he soon added the distinction of war correspondent, by his participation in the Santa Fe expedition and the Mexican War, and later became a historian of these events. He closed his career as a large sheep rancher in Texas.

Mississippi, where the great planters along the river were undoubtedly supplied with news by New Orleans, possessed no noteworthy paper. In Alabama, Mobile, like New Orleans, was an urban center, with a large Northern element. Here Charles C. Langdon, of New England origin, was a Whig leader and editor.[94] Yancey, who for a time had been the editor of an antinullification paper in South Carolina, combined planting with rural journalism, when he came to Alabama, and, as we have seen, became the outstanding Democratic figure in that state in the years preceding the Civil War.

This sketch of South Central editors, in our era, brings out, as no generalization could, the mixed and changing character of the population, the sources of influence upon its thought, and some of its essential traits. Combined with the sketch of political leaders, it should make clear the way in which this relatively new section adjusted itself to the frontier and to its regional geography, and how, in this process, even the Yankee migrants came to conform to the manners, customs, feelings, and modes of thinking of their new South Central homes.

In the field of letters, no such representative of either fiction, essays, or poetry appeared as in the South Atlantic Division. The most characteristic contributions were made by a group of writers whose rather broad humor portrayed the foibles of the people. Some of them have already been mentioned in discussing the editors. Perhaps the best representative of the type was Joseph B. Baldwin, whose *Flush Times in Alabama and Mississippi* became a classic of the frontier period.[95]

[94] Wm. Garrett, *Reminiscences of Public Men in Alabama, for Thirty Years* (Atlanta, 1872), pp. 184–85, 119.

[95] See also: J. J. Hooper, *Some Adventures of Captain Simon Suggs, Late of the Tallapoosa Volunteers* (Philadelphia, 1846); *A Narrative of the Life of David Crockett . . . Written by Himself* (Philadelphia, 1834); Geo. W. Harris, *Sut Lovengood's Yarns* (New York, 1867); and Prentice, *Prenticeana*.

John J. Audubon's *Birds of America* was the work of a son of New Orleans, distinguished both as artist and ornithologist.

In religion the South Central States showed an even stronger tendency to orthodoxy than the South Atlantic. Methodists and Baptists were preponderant in the section, although Tennessee's and Kentucky's Scotch-Irish element carried with it a large proportion of Presbyterians. The emotional element, expressed in the camp meeting and the revival, was a marked feature of the religious quality of the section. When one appreciates this responsiveness to waves of religious enthusiasm, he can understand the campaigns that brought Andrew Jackson and Harrison, as representatives of the pioneer, to the Presidency. Indeed, these campaigns were the political side of the same type of mind that produced the camp meeting and the revival. Partly because of the isolation of the rural communities and the lack of outlet in the way of nervous excitement — the absence of normal amusements — the great gatherings in religion and politics served as a means of liberating surplus energy. They took the place of opera and theater and athletic contests.

Surveying the economic, political, social, and cultural life of the South Central section in this period, we see a common quality, in spite of the diversity of regions, classes, and origins — a blend of a disappearing frontier and rising slaveholding society in the lower half of the Mississippi Valley, not to be understood, in these changing years, as either purely Western or Southern. Even after this section became a part of the " South," it retained an important heritage of its frontier spirit.

CHAPTER VII

THE NORTH CENTRAL STATES [1]

Like the southern half of the Mississippi Valley, the northern section of its people was a projection into new geographic provinces from the older sections of the Union; but it was more complex in its origins, for, not only was there a mingling of the northern and the southern streams of native migration, but Europe, also, sent to the North Central States an influential tide of emigrants.

Included in this division are the states of the Old Northwest — Ohio, Indiana, Illinois, Michigan, and Wisconsin — and of the West North Central, made up of Missouri, Iowa, Minnesota, and what was, at the time of this history, an Indian country composed of the present states of Kansas, Nebraska, and the two Dakotas.

The section was a vast geographic mold, so located in the nation, as constituted in later years, that it was able, not only to react upon the parent eastern sections and to influence the newer ones which it colonized, but also to rival and profoundly to affect the history of the southern half of the Mississippi Valley. The formation of its people and its society, in these years, has, therefore, much significance.

Vast, but relatively simple in their geographical form, those of its states and territories which were undergoing settlement prior to 1850 equaled in area pre-War Germany and Austria-Hungary, combined, or all of the old thirteen states of the Atlantic seaboard. From merely that portion of the section that was being

[1] [Professor Turner thought of dividing "The North Central States" into two chapters, and for that purpose provided the following introductory paragraph: "Because this section was one of rapid transformations in the thirties and forties, the area of a forming society that was deeply to affect the nation in all ways, and even Europe, and because it exercised an important influence upon sectional conflicts and adjustments in Congress, it requires the fuller treatment of two chapters."]

occupied in 1850, every family in the Union could have been equipped with a fifty-acre farm.

The larger regions of the area are: that bordering the Ohio River; the Great Lakes Basin; the upper Mississippi; and the Prairie Plains. Vast pine forests stretched along the shores of Lake Superior and the adjacent parts of Lakes Michigan and Huron; mingled conifers and hardwoods made a zone south of these; a belt of oak groves and prairies came next; and, farther to the south, were the prairies, which crossed northern Indiana and Illinois and widened into the far horizons of Iowa, Minnesota, and the Indian country of the Dakotas, Kansas, and Nebraska. Along the Ohio and in the Ozark region of Missouri lay rougher lands, covered with hardwood forests.

As influential upon the course of history, in the section, as these areas of forest and prairie, were the two divisions of the section produced by the work of successive glaciers.[2] The first glaciation even reached parts of the Ohio River; but, in the ages that followed, erosion had modified its topographical engraving and its soils. The later (Wisconsin) ice sheet left borders that reflected, broadly, the lobe-like contours of the Great Lakes. Roughly, these borders crossed the state of Ohio diagonally from northeast to southwest, curved fan-like below the central region of Indiana, and swept northerly in a great arc through Illinois and Wisconsin, about midway between their eastern and western limits.[3]

From the point of view of glacial geography, the later ice sheet included within its boundary the larger part of the East North Central States, together with New York, the northern corners of eastern and western Pennsylvania, and New England — a fact eventually related to the spread of population, to economic, political, and social life, and to sectional combination.

This ice sheet not only shaped the landscape but brought with

[2] See the map (facing p. 2, *ante*) of Physiographic Divisions, showing the " Wisconsin Drift Boundary."

[3] See: map facing p. 2, *ante;* Ernst Antevs, *The Last Glaciation* (American Geographical Society, Research Series No. 17; New York, 1928); the maps in United States Geological Survey *Monographs*, Nos. 38, 41, 53; bibliography in Lawrence Martin, *The Physical Geography of Wisconsin* (Wisconsin Geological and Natural History Survey, Bulletin No. 36; Madison, 1916), pp. 89–92; *Geological Survey of Ohio*, V, 755; and H. H. Barrows, *Geography of the Middle Illinois Valley* (Illinois State Geological Survey, Bulletin No. 15; Urbana, 1910), Chap. III (maps, pp. 27, 31).

it deposits of soil which, with the formation of the prairies, made the lands that it covered one of the richest corn and wheat belts of the world. Even after all the exploitive farming of the pioneers, the agricultural counties that lay within its boundary exceeded in land value and in wealth those (in the North Central section) outside the area of glaciation.[4]

The regions, to the south, not covered by the glacial sheets, are known as the " driftless areas," including counties of southeastern Ohio and the extreme southern portions of Indiana and Illinois. Like a great island in the glaciated lands, also lay the driftless area of southwestern Wisconsin, northwestern Illinois, and the adjacent part of Iowa — an area that, in its deeply dissected landscape, resembled parts of the rough country of Kentucky. It included lead mines that attracted settlers from that state.

Along the Great Lakes were iron and copper deposits, which, by the close of our period, began to have an influence upon speculation. But the coal, oil, and gas fields of the North Central States played no part, in these years. The economic resources of the section furnish a progressive revelation of the relations between industrial demands and the various gifts of nature.

On the whole, it was agricultural; and its suitability to the raising of corn and live stock at first, and then wheat, constituted its attraction for the migrating Eastern farmers, and, as we have seen, brought ruin, through competition, to many a farm in the agricultural areas of New England.[5]

The forest and the prairie regions of the section had important effects upon population and upon agriculture. Not until the end of the forties did the northern forests begin to yield to the axes of lumbermen and to the German farmers. The timbered southern counties, and the tree-clad river valleys, early attracted the Southern pioneers, trained in the frontiersman's agriculture.

Beneath the shade of these primeval forests, which furnished fuel and food, the Southern pioneer, sallow and lean, made the kind of home to which generations of woodsmen had accustomed him. The prairie was something new and different. It lacked,

[4] *Thirteenth* [1910] *Census of the United States,* volumes on *Agriculture: Reports by States* (Washington, 1913): VI, 411, 461, 505, 767, 807, 891; VII, 305, 899. See my map of Land Values, 1850 (at end of volume), and G. D. Hubbard, " A Case of Geographic Influence upon Human Affairs," American Geographical Society *Journal*, XXXVI, 145.   [5] See Chapter III, *ante.*

to his mind, both fuel and sufficient water, shelter from the winter's cold, and fertility. Accustomed to gauging the richness of the soil by the kind of trees it produced, he could not appreciate the significance of these open prairies, where rank grasses and flowers took the place of forest. Kentucky had taught him to regard as " barrens " even those areas where trees and prairies interlocked. And so, for the most part, the prairies remained for occupation by the Northern pioneers.

The prairies themselves were of various types.[6] The open prairies (of which the " Grand Prairie " of Illinois, and the trans-Mississippi lands, are examples) were not a homogeneous flat expanse. Wet prairie and dry prairie (sometimes with sloughs between the crests of the undulating surface), rich soils and poor soils, were to be found in this great stretch of vacant plowlands.

James Hall,[7] writing especially of Illinois, describes how prairie and woodland alternate,[8] by suggesting that his reader draw

a colored line of irregular breadth, along the edges of all the water courses laid down in the map. The border thus shaded, which would represent the woodland, would vary in width from one to five or six miles, and would sometimes extend to twelve. As the streams approach each other, these borders would approximate, or come into contact; and all the intermediate spaces, not thus colored would be prairie.[9]

Where the country was predominantly prairies, these communicated with each other, like a chain of lakes, by numerous avenues or vistas — still, however, surrounded by timber, never out of sight of the deep green outline.

The open prairie, on the other hand, gave to travelers the impression of the green rolling ocean, as its grasses bent in the breeze; occasional groves resembled strange sails on the distant horizon. But, in season, the wild flowers gave to the prairie an intense beauty — " dotted and slashed with gold and azure, vermilion and orange, white and violet." [10] Grasses on the prairie

[6] A contemporary description is in J. M. Peck, *Gazetteer of Illinois* (Philadelphia, 1837).

[7] *The West: Its Soil, Surface, and Productions* (Cincinnati, 1848), pp. 69 ff.

[8] Cf.: Fred. Gerhard, *Illinois as It Is* (Chicago [1857]), pp. 271, 276; J. P. Goode, *Geography of Illinois* (Chicago); *The Voters and Tax Payers of Bureau County, Illinois* (Chicago, 1877), map; Barrows, *op. cit.*, pp. 69, 79 (maps); B. H. Hibbard, *The History of Agriculture in Dane County, Wisconsin* (University of Wisconsin *Bulletin*, No. 101; Madison, 1904), maps; and T. C. Chamberlin, *Report on the Geology of Wisconsin* (1873).

[9] *Op. cit.*, pp. 76–77.

[10] A. D. Jones, *Illinois and the West* (Boston, 1838), p. 92.

grew two or three feet high and, on the bottom prairies, even rose above the head of a man on horseback.[11]

Horace Greeley, writing in the later forties from Kane County, in northern Illinois, says:

> Before and beside you rolls an " inland sea " of verdure and luxuriance —hundreds of acres of Wheat, Corn, Oats, darkly waving in the emerald glory of early summer, while behind them stretch the immeasurable meadows, coëval with Eden, their untold wealth of herbage and flowers undulating in the fresh breezes like a gently troubled ocean; and still behind these, at points not very far distant, and again far as the eye can reach, or farther, swells the graceful outline of the nearest woods, marking the winding way of some sluggish water-course, or, more commonly, crowning some scanty elevation with the glossy foliage of the scattered Oaks . . . The New and the Old do not palpably wrestle here as in the forest clearings, where the narrow field of Man's victory stands out in scathed and blackened contrast with the verdure and stateliness surrounding it, but all seems peaceful, genial and bounteous. The Prairies are the Capua of Nature.[12]

Projecting southwestward from the lower end of Lake Michigan, the Grand Prairie of Illinois was typical of the open prairies.[13] Settlement hesitated on the verge of this expanse, or penetrated only in single file up the wooded streams, until the railroad, and the higher price of wheat in the time of the Crimean War, brought a tide of farmers, after the middle fifties.

The prairies which attracted the earlier settlers, chiefly as range for their stock, were those adjacent to river courses — where long strips of timber extended into prairie; where prairie aisles reached into timber; or where groves of one hundred to two thousand acres lay, island-like, in the prairie, in the northern half of Illinois and in other parts of the section.

Farther to the north, the prairie groves gave way to the " oak openings," where, like lakes, small prairies lay surrounded by the trees. Southern Michigan and southern Wisconsin named their prairies, while northern Illinois named its groves and chose them for the earlier settlement.[14] These oak openings had a special charm for the travelers who emerged from the forest into

11 *Ibid.*, p. 93; and *Prose Writings of William Cullen Bryant*, ed. Parke Godwin (New York, 1884), II, 13, describing his visit to Illinois in 1832.

12 *New York Daily Tribune*, July 20, 1847.

13 Gerhard, *op. cit.*, pp. 271 ff.

14 See the data in *Voters and Tax Payers of Bureau County, Illinois*, comparing dates of settlement with the map of prairie and woodland in the county.

their park-like spaces. Freed from underbrush by frequent
burnings, their spreading oaks, " with the order of a well-set
orchard," promised warmth and shelter, while the greensward
demanded little or no clearing, or cutting of resistant sod as in
the case of the open prairie. But the humus of these openings
was shallow and their advantage for the wheat farmer proved
temporary.[15]

On the peripheries of the section were navigable waters, including the Ohio, the Mississippi, and the Great Lakes, which,
with their harbors and tributaries, afforded connections with the
East, the South, and the Far West.

Into this province came tides of settlement that, in rapidity of
flow and in variety of sources, brought a new American society
into existence. Between 1830 and 1850, a new section was born
in the lands between the Ohio, the Great Lakes, and the Mississippi, and came to power in the Union.

At the beginning of these two decades, the North Central
States had a population of not much over a million and a half,
which was less than that of New England at the time and was
about one-eighth of the nation's total. By 1840 the section's
population was three and one-third millions — over a million
more than New England's; and in 1850 it was well over five and
one-third millions — nearly one-fourth that of the whole country,
and approaching that of the Middle Atlantic States. Numerically, the gain in population, in the twenty years, was about
three and four-fifths millions, which far exceeded the gain of
the old North Atlantic Division (New England and the Middle
Atlantic States) and even surpassed the gain of the South Atlantic and South Central states, combined. The actual population of this new section, in 1850, was twice that of historic New
England, and was about equal to that of the old South Atlantic
Division.

It was an extraordinarily quick growth. Between 1836 and

---

[15] D. S. Curtiss, *Western Portraiture, and Emigrant's Guide* (New York,
1852), p. 339; C. F. Hoffman, *A Winter in the West* (New York, 1835), I,
142–43; R. Russell, " Agricultural Notes in Ohio and Michigan," *Journal of
Agriculture*, Oct., 1856, p. 10; Frank Leverett, *Surface Geology and Agricultural
Conditions of Michigan* (Michigan Geological and Biological Survey *Publications*, No. 25 [Geological Ser., No. 21]; Lansing, 1917); and James Fenimore
Cooper, *The Oak Openings* (1848; fiction, with descriptions based on his Michigan visit in 1847).

1840 the population of Iowa approximately doubled every two years.[16] Counties in the newer states rose from a few hundred settlers to ten or fifteen thousand, in less than five years. A new society, made up of varied peoples, institutions, and ideals, drawn from all quarters of the Union and from Europe, was being extemporized with astonishing rapidity.

In the years from 1830 to 1850, the frontier of settlement [17] was extended from northwestern Ohio, central Indiana and Illinois, and the vicinity of Detroit, to include the broad zone of southern Michigan, southern Wisconsin, and eastern and southern Iowa. In Missouri the strips of settlement up its great river widened to cover most of the state and to bank-up against the Indian country at its western border. The lead-mining driftless area of Illinois, Wisconsin, and Iowa, like an island in the wilderness sea in 1830, was conterminous in 1850 with the agricultural settlements; and, up the Mississippi in Minnesota, lumber towns made a new nucleus of advancing population.

In 1830 over half of the section's population lived in Ohio, and in 1850 this state still held over one-third of the people of the North Central States, although it had become a hive from which swarms of pioneers sought new homes. In addition to those who were only transient residents of the state, Ohio, by 1850, had sent around a quarter of a million of its natives to the other states of the Middle West, nearly half of this number to Indiana. Almost one-sixth of the people of the frontier state of Iowa were of Ohio birth.

In Ohio itself, frontier conditions were disappearing. Clearings were touching elbows, the log cabin was giving way to the frame house, and, even in such smaller towns as Dayton, waterworks and gaslighting revealed a new era.[18] But as late as the fifties, in country districts of the Western Reserve, the primeval forest spread over half the land, and stumps " as thick as harvest stubble " dotted the pastures; deer were abundant and bear still to be seen.[19] Charles Lyell,[20] the English geologist, traveling from Cincinnati to Cleveland in the early forties, saw in the mid-

---

[16] Cardinal Goodwin, " The American Occupation of Iowa, 1833 to 1860," *Iowa Journal of History and Politics*, XVII, 89.

[17] See maps, pp. 6, 7, 8, *ante*.

[18] W. D. Howells, *Years of My Youth* (New York, 1916), p. 41.

[19] *Ibid.*, pp. 82, 114.

[20] *Travels in North America* (London, 1845), II, 74.

dle of the state a succession of new clearings where the felling, girdling, and burning of trees was going on, and " lost sight for many leagues of all human habitations," save where empty movers' houses enabled the pioneers to pass the night.

But men who lived in Wisconsin, at this time, spoke of the Wabash Valley, in Indiana, as " finished." The older and the newer parts of the section were in sharp contrast. In the early forties the Illinois prairies were in parts a lawless frontier, sometimes infested by desperadoes who burned courthouses, defied the constituted authorities, and in places even elected the constables and justices, as in the later frontier of Montana. In some of the counties of this region, there were " two nearly balanced parties, one stealing, swindling, burning, and murdering, from the blackest motives, — and the other mobbing, lynching, and murdering in the protection of their life and property." [21]

In the pineries, by the middle of the century, was still a different type of frontier, out of which red-shirted Irishmen, harddrinking, profane, and virile, were floating their rafts of lumber down the shores of the Great Lakes and the tributaries of the Mississippi, stirring up the peaceful towns on the way, much in the fashion of the later cowboys on the Far Western frontier.

By the middle of the nineteenth century, the prairies of the Great Lakes Basin and the Upper Mississippi Valley had received the pioneer farmer. Even the hardwoods of the border of Lake Michigan were yielding to the axes of German immigrants.

Within the Middle West before 1850, there were few large cities. Cincinnati (the queen of the Ohio Valley), with about 25,000 people in 1830 and over 115,000 in 1850, easily led. St. Louis, the metropolis of the upper Mississippi, grew from 6,000 to nearly 78,000. On the Great Lakes, city development was slower. Cleveland had less than 2,000 in 1830 and only 17,000 in 1850 — somewhat less than the population of Columbus, in the central part of Ohio. Detroit rose from a little over 2,000 to 21,000. Hardly more than a frontier trading post in 1830, unrecorded in the census, Chicago had by 1850 a population of 30,000; and Milwaukee, its rival, grew from almost nothing to 20,000. Toledo had less than 4,000 in 1850; St. Paul, on the upper Mississippi, a little over 1,000. Indicative of belief in the permanency of the Union was the fact that, at the western end of Lake Superior, Congressional speculators, including Stephen A. Douglas and a group of his Southern friends, had already invested in lands on which, later, were to grow the cities of Duluth and Superior.

Aside from the older settlements in Ohio, like the regions of Marietta and Cleveland, the first pioneering was mainly [22] an inundation of men of the Southern-upland stock that spread to the frontier line of 1830; but Yankees and Pennsylvania Germans had also helped to settle the counties north of the Ohio River. After 1830 the tide from the South ebbed, and the North Atlantic pioneers (joined, especially in the later forties, by immigrant peoples) laid the foundations of a new society in the prairies of the Great Lakes Basin. Roughly, the line between these people of the Southern and the Northern stocks ran along the head of navigation of the tributaries of the Ohio; but important exceptions occurred.[23]

The men who traced their ancestry to the upland South were, as we have seen,[24] different from the tidewater Southerners. Scotch-Irish, German, and English pioneers had commingled west of the fall line and had learned the use of ax and rifle in the winning of the colonial woods. This upland South found it hard to adjust its democratic, self-sufficing farm life to the advance of cotton culture and slavery into its lands. The same urge for new countries — the impetus that had resulted in the settlement, by these pioneers, of Kentucky and Tennessee and, later, of parts of the Gulf Basin in the Lower South — carried the stock into the southern counties of the states and territories across the Ohio and the Mississippi. Here they mingled with similar folk from the Pennsylvania their ancestors had left.

Nearly seven hundred thousand North Central white and free colored people, in 1850, were natives of the South Central and South Atlantic states.[25] Including the descendants of Southern

---

[22] But not by any means exclusively. See F. J. Turner, *Rise of the New West, 1819–1829 (The American Nation: A History*, XIV; New York, 1906), pp. 76, 77, and S. J. Buck, " The New England Element in Illinois Politics before 1833," Mississippi Valley Historical Association *Proceedings*, VI, 49–61. Ohio, especially, was settled by various stocks, including Pennsylvania Scotch-Irish and Pennsylvania Germans. See map of Interstate Migration (at end of volume).

[23] See map of Interstate Migration.

[24] Chapter v, *ante*.

[25] Native Kentuckians in the North Central States, in 1850, were over 212,-

and Southwestern parents, in the North Central States, who had
begun to settle there at the close of the eighteenth century, the
number of people of this stock, by 1850, was probably not far
from the number of those of North Atlantic birth or ancestry in
the section. This is of importance in understanding the history
of the North Central Division in the following decade.

A considerable portion of the settlers from the upland South
were of the hunter-farmer type of backwoodsmen.[26] The great
bulk of them were poor. They migrated in large numbers, during the first third of the nineteenth century, from the Carolinas,
Maryland, Virginia, and Kentucky especially, by flatboat and by
heavy canvas-covered wagon (later called the " prairie schooner "
— the Conestoga wagon, which the Pennsylvania Germans had
brought from the Rhenish Palatinate).[27] Around some spring,
there would collect little centers of settlement, with perhaps a
Baptist or Methodist meetinghouse; but, for the most part, they
came as individuals or family groups, lived apart, and came together only for the neighborhood occasions when there was a
logrolling, a house raising, a husking bee, a wedding, or a camp
meeting. They were a self-sufficing people, spinning and weaving like their colonial ancestors.[28]

The traits of the society thus formed have been portrayed by
the biographers of Lincoln, whose father was a type of these frontier folk and who himself spent his youth among them — one of
them and yet recognized even by his fellows as different.[29] In

---

ooo — equal to nearly 22 per cent of the population resident in Kentucky at
the time. Of Virginia birth, there were 204,000, which equals over 14 per cent
of her population in 1850.

[26] J. M. Peck, *A New Guide for Emigrants to the West* (Cincinnati, 1848),
Chap. IV, gives a good description of them.

[27] On the contrasting modes of travel to the Mississippi Valley, by the
Northern and the Southern stocks, see Timothy Flint, *The History and Geography of the Mississippi Valley* (Cincinnati, 1833), I, 188–91.

[28] Peck, *op. cit.*, Chap. IV, gives a contemporaneous account of the pioneer
home. See also Flint, *op. cit.*, I, 194–97.

[29] For this type, see the earlier chapters of the biographies of Lincoln, particularly those by A. J. Beveridge, J. G. Nicolay and John Hay, Ida M. Tar-
bell, Carl Sandburg, and W. E. Barton, and their citations. These writers are
prone, as a background to his later career, either to exaggerate the rudeness, or
to idealize the qualities, of this society. Judge John E. Iglehart, and his associates of the Southwestern Indiana Historical Society, have pointed out that
southern Indiana contained cultivated families, including able men whose
libraries were considerable, even in the days when Lincoln lived near by. See
C. G. Vannest, *Lincoln the Hoosier* (St. Louis and Chicago, 1928), with bibliog-

this Ohio Valley society were families, and even communities, whose members, seeking opportunities for advancement in a new country, brought with them the social amenities, the cultivation, and the intellectual interests of the older centers from which they migrated. These men and women came from the South, the East, and various European countries, and their influence upon the raw frontier was fruitful.

The lead mines of Wisconsin, Iowa, Illinois, and Missouri, especially in the thirties, exhibited the frontier conditions of a mining region. Drinking and gambling were common, even among the leading citizens. The pistol and the bowie knife were articles of dress, and former Governor Henry Dodge, of Wisconsin, who came from this region, furnished campaign material to his political enemies among the Northerners when he left his bowie knife under his pillow on departing from his hotel. Writing of Iowa at the close of the forties, Sidney Smith, the author of an emigrants' guide,[30] said:

This territory . . . is the frontier territory of the west, and the *ultima thule* of civilization. . . . its population are rude, brutal, and lawless, and possessing no settled institutions or legislature, it is obvious that it will be avoided by all persons of character and orderly habits. Its miners, like those of Galena, are worse than savages.

---

raphies. See also: Logan Esarey, *A History of Indiana* (Fort Wayne, Ind., 1924), I, 283, 474; Meredith Nicholson, *The Hoosiers* (New York, 1900), Chap. 1; Baynard R. Hall [Robt. Carlton, pseud.], *The New Purchase* (New York, 1843; reprinted, Princeton, N.J., 1916); J. A. Woodburn, "Indiana and Her History," *Indiana Magazine of History*, XXVII, 10–22; S. S. Visher, "Distribution of the Birthplaces of Indianians in 1870," *ibid.*, XXVI, 126–42; and Woodburn, *The Scotch-Irish Presbyterians in Monroe County, Indiana* (Indiana Historical Society *Publications*, IV, 435–522). A. C. Boggess, *The Settlement of Illinois, 1778–1830* (Chicago, 1908), and W. V. Pooley, *The Settlement of Illinois from 1830 to 1850* (University of Wisconsin *Bulletin*, No. 220; Madison, 1908), are theses that were begun, and partly completed, in my seminary in American history at the University of Wisconsin; their bibliographies indicate the wide range of sources, including a mass of pioneer reminiscences (too numerous to cite) in the publications of the historical societies of the region. Interesting accounts of Ohio, in this period, are in: Wm. C. Howells, *Recollections of Life in Ohio, from 1813 to 1840* (Cincinnati, 1895); and W. D. Howells, *Years of My Youth,* and *A Boy's Town,* . . . (New York, 1890).

[30] *The Settler's New Home: or The Emigrant's Location* (London, 1849), p. 93. I have found the manuscript Cyrus Woodman Papers and Moses M. Strong Papers, in the Wisconsin State Historical Society, useful on the manners and customs of the lead region, at the time, and on the relations thereto of their writers, who were graduates of New England colleges. The early messages of the territorial governors of Iowa are interesting evidence of unrest over the conditions.

But this was gross exaggeration of a temporary condition. Iowa was a state before his book appeared, and its society was rapidly improving. Outside of the more settled regions of the Missouri Valley, frontier conditions were to be seen in parts of Missouri.[31]

Thus, in this section as in the South Central States, characteristic features of the edge of the Southern-upland advance were revealed — a rough frontier shading into the Indian country, but steadily rising in population, in economic life, and in civilization.

In 1830 the southern half of Ohio, Indiana, and Illinois contained the great bulk of the population of the North Central Division: it was an Ohio Valley society.[32] Writing in 1838, a Cincinnati author [33] asked the question, Where will be the future great city of the West? He predicted that it would be Cincinnati, Louisville, St. Louis, or Alton — all of them within the sphere of influence of the Ohio Valley. But, five years later, the same writer (in an article in *Hunt's Merchants' Magazine*[34]), again raising the question, decided that Cincinnati would continue until 1890 to be the dominating city; but he concluded that such had been

the influx of settlers within the last few years to the lake region, and so decided has become the tendency of the productions of the upper and middle regions of the great valley to seek a market at and through the lakes, that we can no longer withstand the conviction that, even within the short period of forty-seven years, a town will grow up on the lake border greater than Cincinnati.

For this future metropolis, the author picked out Maumee (near Toledo) as likely to outstrip Chicago.[35]

Light is thrown upon the lack of success of the men of the

[31] S. B. Harding, in his *Life of George R. Smith, Founder of Sedalia, Mo.* (Sedalia, 1904), gives an interesting picture of this frontier. See also the references in F. J. Turner and Frederick Merk, *List of References on the History of the West* (Cambridge, Mass., 1922), pp. 61-63.

[32] F. J. Turner, *The Frontier in American History* (New York, 1921), Chap. v.

[33] J. W. Scott, in Chas. Cist, *Cincinnati in 1841: Its Early Annals and Future Prospects* (Cincinnati, 1841), App., p. 283.   [34] IX, 35-46.

[35] The rapidity of the rise of the Middle Western towns into cities is illustrated by the case of Chicago. In 1823 Calhoun wrote (see *Correspondence of John C. Calhoun*, ed. J. Franklin Jameson [American Historical Association *Annual Report*, 1899, II; Washington, 1900], pp. 208-9):

" Tho' Chicago may be important in War, I cannot consider it, in a general view, as connected with the peace arrangement, near as important as Green Bay. . . . Nor do I consider it, as connected in any essential degree, with the extension of settlement in that quarter, as our population must approach that point early forties in forecasting the tendency of the time, by their emphasis upon the importance of canals and their failure properly to estimate the importance of the railroads, which had already reached Buffalo and were soon to connect the Great Lakes with New York. As a matter of fact, in 1890 Chicago ranked next to New York and had over a million inhabitants, while Toledo had about eighty-one thousand.

Though an imperfect prophet, the author recognized that the statistics of growth between 1830 and 1840, in the states of Ohio, Indiana, and Illinois, showed that the northern counties, adjacent to the Great Lakes, increased their population over eight hundred thousand, while the counties tributary to the Ohio River gained hardly more than half this number. Between 1840 and 1850 southern Michigan and Wisconsin also received a tide of settlers that increased the population of these two states by nearly half a million over that at the beginning of the decade.

An interesting earlier recognition of the change is to be found in a letter from John Law, of Vincennes, Indiana, to Van Buren,[36] July 6, 1835, after a tour to eastern Illinois and western Indiana. He wrote:

Who are now filling up Ohio Indiana Illinois and Michigan? Who will fill up the New States of the North West? New York and New England. Out of the hundreds emigrating to the West along the Lake Shore whom I met and with most of whom I conversed, I found no one either on foot, on horseback, or in carriages, who was emigrating from the South of New York. They were all from that state or New England. It requires no "prophet or son of a prophet" to predict what their influence is to be, or what their political feelings and attachments are now, and what they will forever remain.

Thus, we have to consider the volume and character of the population that entered the regions of prairie and Great Lakes borders subsequent to the movement from the upland South to the Ohio Valley forests. The interactions of these two zones of population were to have a profound effect upon the economic life, the politics, and the culture of the section, and to write significant chapters in the history of the nation.

---

by the gradually increasing of the settlements on the frontier of Illinois and Indiana."

In the summer of 1834, Chicago had a population of 800; by fall this had doubled; in 1835 the population was 3,000; and by 1850 it was 30,000.

[36] In Library of Congress.

In the discussions of New England and the Middle Atlantic States, the causes and results of this flow of the northern stream of migration into the North Central States have been considered. In a way, it was a continuation of the old movement of pioneering, out of the harbors and intervales of southern New England, to found towns in the interior parts of Connecticut and Massachusetts, in Maine, New Hampshire, and Vermont, and in portions of New York and Pennsylvania. But, in the decades between 1830 and 1850, the pressure of population, the call of new wildernesses to the adventurous and the unsuccessful, the facilities for transportation afforded by the Erie Canal and subsequently the railroads, the opening of steamboat navigation on the Great Lakes, the hard times of the later thirties and early forties, the competition of the crops of the fertile virgin soils of the West with those of the stony fields of northern New England, swelled the exodus.[37]

In spite of rural New England's large families, Vermont, and counties of western Massachusetts and Connecticut having kindred conditions, became practically stationary. Slight increases in the forties were partly due to incoming Irish and French Canadians. The " sheep craze " aggravated the difficulty. In 1842 Vermont's governor called wool " the staple industry " of the state. But the sale of their lands by small farmers to their more prosperous neighbors, who combined them in large estates for sheep raising, produced a foot-free population and diminished the need of a farm-labor supply. When, on the other hand, changes in the protective tariff, in the forties, and the advantages of the cheaper lands in the West, hit the profits of sheep raising and transferred the area of concentration of that industry from western New England and New York to western Pennsylvania and to Ohio and Michigan,[38] there was an additional blow to the prosperity of rural New England.

Vermont found no opportunity to develop large-scale manufac-

[37] The injury to the wheat crop of northern New England by insects was a contributing cause (see *Albany Cultivator*, cited by *Vermont Watchman*, Aug. 14, 1845). I am indebted to Professor L. D. Stilwell, of Dartmouth College (a former member of my seminary in Harvard University), for the opportunity to use his manuscript thesis on " Migration from Vermont, 1776–1860," in which the conditions are interestingly described, with scholarly use of sources.

[38] Chester W. Wright, *Wool-Growing and the Tariff* (*Harvard Economic Studies.* V; Boston, 1910) ; and H. C. Taylor, in University of Wisconsin Agricultural Experiment Station *Bulletin*, No. 16 (1911), maps.

tures by way of compensation, for, until the close of our period, adequate transportation facilities by canal and railroad were lacking. Many a youth whose labor and wages until the age of twenty-one belonged to his father, " bought his time " and went West; and some escaped imprisonment for debt, in the period of hard times, by joining the procession to new frontiers. Youth was attracted, also, by the opportunity for advancement in the professions and in business, to the new section where age and vested interests were not in possession. Letters from contented settlers to their homefolk, land speculation, and advertisements in local newspapers, heightened the fever of migration.[39] Gaining volume during the War of 1812 and the cold summer of 1816,[40] New England and New York migration to the prairie states grew to a flood in the decade preceding the Civil War. The early movement West, from the North Atlantic sections, was by the " covered wagon " and on foot, along the poor roads, to Ohio, Indiana, and Illinois. Then the Erie Canal, and steam navigation on the Mississippi and the Great Lakes, swelled the current to the zones adjacent to the river ports and lake harbors. When, by the middle fifties, the railroad lines reached the open prairies, the full significance of the advance was revealed in increasing tides of migration.

The normal New England and New York colonization was that of individual families, as had been that from the South; but there was a special element in the settlement from the Northeast. Just as individualism and rural separatism, in the main, characterized the Southern-upland settlers, so the historic tendency to community life prevailed among the Yankees. There were very many cases, even before they moved West, of the organization of communities. The formation of land companies to settle the new country was even more common. The history of various college towns, such as Oberlin in the Western Reserve (whose founders hailed from Vermont and subscribed to a covenant that brings to mind the Pilgrim compact), and Beloit in Wisconsin, furnishes examples of the type.

Vermontville, in southern Michigan, is an illuminating type.

---

[39] Pooley, *Illinois from 1830 to 1850*, Chap. III, is a useful résumé of the forces inducing migration.

[40] S. G. Goodrich, *Recollections of a Lifetime, or Men and Things I Have Seen* (New York, 1856), II, 78.

It was an organized colony of Vermonters, promoted by a minister and provided with a written constitution made in 1836 (before the colony left New England). This constitution furnished a plan for a " pious migration," and the members of the community were to enjoy the same social, literary, and religious privileges as those they had left behind. All of the characteristic features of the migrating New England towns, in the colonial era, were reproduced here. The association provided for careful inquiry into the character of prospective members and required the consent of a committee representing the community before they could be admitted. Lands were assigned among the settlers according to a plan agreed to by the community. No individual was to have more than one farm lot of one hundred and sixty acres and one village lot of ten acres, within the limits of the settlement. As in the old New England town, there was also a reservation for the parsonage;[41] and, like so many New England villages, the town was laid out with a public square in the center. It took three weeks for these settlers to go from Vermont to Michigan. In some ways, the colony was an epitome of migrating New England.[42]

All along the upper waters of the Rock and Fox rivers, and elsewhere in Illinois and Wisconsin, can be traced similar community migrations. They were not typical of the mass of Yankee migration; but the frequency of the procedure, by its contrast with that of other sections, is significant.[43]

Vermont and Connecticut, in proportion to their populations, furnished to the North Central States the largest numbers of natives of New England. Vermont had been mainly settled by Connecticut stock, and a large proportion of the migrating natives of New York were of Vermont or Connecticut ancestry.[44]

[41] See Jos. Schafer, *The Origin of the System of Land Grants for Education* (University of Wisconsin *Bulletin*, No. 63; Madison, 1902), Chaps. IV, V.

[42] E. W. Barber, in *Michigan Pioneer and Historical Collections*, XXVIII, 197–287, and G. N. Fuller, *Economic and Social Beginnings of Michigan* (Lansing, 1916), pp. 412, 445–51.

[43] Lois K. Mathews, *The Expansion of New England* (Boston, 1909), *passim*, and her " The Mayflower Compact and Its Descendants," in Mississippi Valley Historical Association *Proceedings*, VI, 79–106, and Pooley, *op. cit.*, pp. 377–78, 387, 565, *et passim*, furnish other examples of this by no means unusual New England device.

[44] Vermont natives in the North Central States, in 1850, numbered over 52,500, which equals almost 17 per cent of the population of that state at the time; Connecticut natives, nearly 45,000, or 12 per cent. J. D. B. De Bow,

Ohio rose from much less than a million inhabitants in 1830 to a million and a half in 1840, and toward two millions in 1850. Of its population at the latter date, its own natives amounted to over three-fifths of the total. Some light is cast upon the ancestry of those born in Ohio, by the nativities of the Ohio legislature in 1822,[45] when members born in the Middle Atlantic States were around 38 per cent, born in the South Atlantic, 31 per cent, and born in New England, 25 per cent. Pennsylvania led with 27 members, Virginia furnished 18, Maryland, 11, and Connecticut, 13; the only foreigners (6) were of Irish birth. These figures present a composite picture of the stock at that time.

By 1850 the Middle Atlantic States — led by Pennsylvania, with two-thirds of the total — had contributed around 300,000 of their natives to the population of Ohio. The Southern sections had sent over 150,000 (nearly 90 per cent of these from the South Atlantic group), while New England had furnished only 66,000. Foreigners in the state numbered well over 200,000. More than half of these were Germans; and the natives of Pennsylvania also included a large contingent of descendants of Germans. Ohio was, therefore, definitely of Northern stock, but with an important Southern element — strongest along the Ohio River, the economic interests of which also tended toward the South.

Indiana, in comparison with other states of the section, had received few New Englanders and foreigners. Cut off from direct access, by the bad roads of the Black Swamp in northwestern Ohio and by the lack of Indiana harbors and the presence of sand dunes south of Lake Michigan, the Northern migration seeking the Great Lakes Basin found the line of least resistance into

---

Statistical View of the United States . . . being a Compendium of the Seventh [1850] *Census* (Washington, 1854), pp. 116–17, furnishes the basis for my computation. I have used approximate rather than exact figures. See also the map of nativities in New York and Pennsylvania (in which I have been able to use the New York State Census of 1845), p. 97, and the general map of distribution of stocks (Interstate Migration), at end of volume. The latter map takes account of the historical evidence that a large share of the natives of the Middle Atlantic States were of New England ancestry. I have used a mass of local histories, reminiscences, obituary notices, church histories, newspapers, and the biographical data regarding the nativities of members of legislatures and of state constitutional conventions, as well as Lois K. Mathews' important *Expansion of New England*, whose maps are based rather upon the presence of considerable numbers of New Englanders than upon the preponderance of the stock in the regions so marked.

[45] *Niles' Register*, XXI, 368.

Michigan, northern Illinois, and southern Wisconsin to be by lake steamers, and then by railroads, to Detroit, Chicago, and to the latter's rival, Milwaukee.

But, to the southeastern counties of Indiana, Carolina Quakers, some of New England descent, had come early in the nineteenth century, and, along with these Hoosiers of South Atlantic origin, there had gone a small New England element. The Hoosier stock had advanced in a column of pioneers well up the central counties of the state toward the north.[46] An increase of over 300,000 was shown in Indiana's population in 1840, and again in 1850. Of the total population of Indiana in the latter year (less than a million), about 11,000 were natives of New England, and about 76,000 of the Middle Atlantic States (much over half of them Pennsylvanians) — all together, only 87,000 born in these two sections — while the South Atlantic had furnished 93,000, and the South Central over 82,000. In Indiana, in addition to these 175,-000 natives of slaveholding states, the larger fraction of her own half-million natives, and of the nearly 130,000 natives of other North Central States resident in Indiana, were from Southern stock. Therefore, a sympathetic connection with the slaveholding states was certain to show itself in the years that followed. Less than 55,000 foreigners lived in the state, over half of them of German birth.[47]

Illinois prairies, and especially a northern zone of counties, equal in area to Connecticut, received tides of settlers from the North Atlantic states. Chicago and St. Louis were centers of dispersion of these pioneers. The Fox River Valley and the Rock River Valley, with limestone soils and woodland adjacent to prairie, were favorite Illinois destinations, and southern Wisconsin received the same kind of people on the upper courses of these rivers. The boundary line cut across a society essentially one.

By 1850 Illinois held 344,000 of its own natives, 85,000 from the South Central States (all but 3,000 of them from Kentucky and Tennessee), 53,000 from the South Atlantic (nearly half of

---

[46] With relation to later effects, see S. S. Visher, *Geography of American Notables* (Indiana University *Studies*, No. 79; Bloomington, 1928), and Robt. La Follette, " Interstate Migration and Indiana Culture," *Mississippi Valley Historical Review*, XVI, 347–58.

[47] Foreign communities, important in their cultural influence, had an effect, however, on the state. New Harmony, home of the Rappites and, later, of the followers of Robert Owen, was the most notable.

them Virginians), 112,000 from the Middle Atlantic (over half from New York), and 37,000 from New England. From natives of the neighboring states of the North Central section, Illinois derived nearly 110,000, over half of them from Ohio. Its foreign element numbered about 110,000, of which the Germans constituted over one-third, the rest being chiefly of Irish and English nativity.

In Illinois the Northern stock had, therefore, outnumbered that from the Southern sections, unless the natives of earlier Illinois, as is probable, preserved the Southern preponderance. But it is likely that the balance of power by 1850 rested, for the most part, in the hands of the foreign immigrants, German and Irish.

Michigan's colonization, delayed by the War of 1812 and by unfavorable reports of surveyors upon her lands,[48] gained in volume after more accurate information appeared in the middle twenties. The opening of the Erie Canal, the development of steam navigation on the Great Lakes, the speculative activity of the middle thirties, the completion of the Indian cessions by the treaties of 1821 and 1836, and the coming of the railroads in the later thirties and the forties, placed Michigan in proximity to the flood of settlers that was advancing from New York and across the border from Canada. As a result, the oak openings of the state, and, before the close of the forties, even the forests adjacent to Saginaw Bay and the iron and copper mines of the Upper Peninsula, were receiving settlers or becoming a new factor in speculation.[49] The old French settlement of Detroit was a center of dispersion for the pioneers. In 1830 Michigan's population was less than 32,000; by 1840 it became over 200,000; and by 1850 the state numbered toward 400,000. The earlier pioneers were from a great variety of sections and regions of the Union,[50] but New York preponderated. By 1850 the natives of the Middle Atlantic States in Michigan were nearly 150,000 (of whom all but 15,000 were born in New York); New England natives were about 31,000 (over a third of them from Vermont); less than 3,000 were born in the South Atlantic States (more than half of

48 A. C. McLaughlin, *Lewis Cass* (Boston, 1899 [in " American Statesmen " series]), and in American Historical Association *Papers*, III, 311–27; and Fuller, *Economic and Social Beginnings of Michigan*, pp. 49 ff.

49 See maps, pp. 6, 7, 8, *ante*.

50 Fuller, *op. cit.*, Chap. IX. Hoffman, *Winter in the West*, has picturesque examples.

these in Virginia); the South Central contributed less than 1,000; and the North Central, outside of Michigan itself (140,000), gave approximately 18,000 (most of them from Ohio). Of nearly 55,000 foreign-born, 14,000 came from British America, some 13,000 from Ireland, over 10,000 from England, 10,000 from German countries, 2,500 from Holland, somewhat fewer from Scotland. The slight immigration from Scandinavian lands in contrast with Holland, the large proportion of British stocks, and the negligible numbers from South Central states, put Michigan apart from other North Central states in the sources of population.

Wisconsin was the mecca of many different peoples. The lead mines in the southwestern counties, even in the twenties, attracted miners from south of the Ohio; the Green Bay and the Prairie du Chien regions had been French fur-trading settlements from pre-Revolutionary days; and, in the period of this survey (especially after the Black Hawk War and the opening of land offices early in the thirties), the New York–New England stream sought the oak openings and the edges of the prairies in southern Wisconsin, while, toward the end of the forties, German pioneers attacked the wooded lands adjacent to Lake Michigan. By 1850 the new settlements were united with the older ones by contiguous farming lands and little hamlets. In the Lake ports and on the canal route of the Fox and Wisconsin rivers, long the highway of fur traders, Irish workmen were remaining to do the rough work and to take up farms. The state grew from a population of around 30,000, in 1840, to over 300,000 in 1850. Of the native Americans at the latter date, the Middle Atlantic States furnished nearly 80,000 (of whom over 68,000 were born in New York); New England, 27,000 (10,000 of them Vermonters); the South Atlantic, a little over 3,000; the South Central, around 2,000; and the North Central (besides Wisconsin's 63,000), 23,-000. There were 38,000 of German nativity (located chiefly in the forested lands along the shore of Lake Michigan).[51] English, Irish, Norwegians, Welsh, Scotch, and Swiss added to the mixed population. All together, 198,000 Americans were commingled with nearly 107,000 foreigners.

Thus, in this young state, there was brought together, sud-

---

[51] Jos. Schafer, "The Yankee and the Teuton in Wisconsin," *Wisconsin Magazine of History*, VI, 125–45, 261–79, 386–402, VII, 3–19, 148–71, has interesting comment on the relations of these stocks.

denly and from various stocks, a population which had to learn how to live together — how to give-and-take in a new country.[52] The Northern stream and the German migration swelled in the fifties.

Political leadership passed definitely to the northern-New England settlers and their New York and Ohio descendants. For example, in the forty-second Congress, both Senators and all but two Representatives from Wisconsin were of northern-New England birth. Vermont furnished one-half of the whole delegation. Even so early as Wisconsin's Constitutional Convention of 1846, there were forty-two members of New England birth (half of them from Vermont) and fifty-five born in Middle Atlantic states. New York's share was forty-six, and, as the biographies show, most of them came from counties where the northern-New England ancestry was strong. Ten, in all, were born in the South Atlantic and South Central sections. For the most part they were young men. On an average they had lived in three different states; at least four had moved eight times, and fifteen, five times or more.[53]

A typical Yankee community was Southport (now Kenosha). With only 300 people in 1840, it doubled in two years, and at the close of 1843 numbered about 1,800. Of its population in that year, there were approximately 300 under five years of age and 200 between five and ten — in all, about 500 young children. Nearly a third of the population were between twenty and thirty years of age; nine-tenths were under forty. It was a community of the youthful. Males outnumbered females by 128. Of this little city 756 were natives of New York, 141 of Vermont, 77 of Connecticut, 76 of Massachusetts, 52 of Ohio, 34 of Illinois, 34 of New Hampshire, and 32 of Pennsylvania; the rest of those of American birth were of scattered origins. There were 386 foreign-born, of whom 170 were Irish, 129 English, and 15 German. Of the 1,434 native Americans, the Middle Atlantic States supplied 802 and New England 352. Thus, the North Atlantic sections

[52] On the difficulty of assimilation in the case of immigrants who did not speak English, see Percy H. Boynton, *The Rediscovery of the Frontier* (Chicago, 1931), pp. 127–28.

[53] Biographical data in M. M. Quaife (ed.), *The Convention of 1846* (*Wisconsin Historical Collections*, XXVII). Professor Stilwell's investigation of Vermont migration leads him to conclude that three-fourths of the pioneers who migrated from that state were under thirty.

furnished, all together, four-fifths of the native stock and nearly three-fourths of the total population of this community. But the foreigners included, besides those mentioned, Scots, Canadians, Norwegians, Swedes, French, and Welsh.[54]

Although Southern and Northern nativities were not far from equal in Iowa by 1850, the portion of the population born in the state itself approached that supplied by all the sections outside of the North Central. Ohio-born Iowans constituted about half of the number drawn from other states of the North Central group. It is impossible to apportion statistically Iowa's Southern and Northern stock in 1850, because we do not know the ancestry of those born in the North Central States; but that there was a large preponderance of Southern origins is probable, in view of the known historical facts of Iowa settlement and the attraction of Iowa's lands for the restless pioneers who had moved on from the infertile soils of the southern counties of Ohio, Indiana, and Illinois (which the later glacial sheet had not reached), and of the nativities of the settlers from Missouri and of the descendants of the first Iowa pioneers. But Pennsylvania was also a notable contributor to Iowa, as well as to Ohio, taking, in both, the leading place, among the Middle Atlantic states, which New York held elsewhere in the section.

In the thirties, the statistics of nativities of members of the Iowa legislature show a very distinct preponderance of settlers born in the Southern sections. But, by the early forties, the tide began to turn.[55] The regions of settlement were naturally, at first, the lead mines and the counties adjacent to the Mississippi River. The northeast and the prairie received the Northern settlers.

Fur traders, missionaries to the Indians, and straggling Swiss settlers from Lord Selkirk's colony at Winnipeg, led the way to Minnesota.[56] By 1837 treaties with the Indians opened new

[54] *Southport American*, Nov. 18, 1843. See also Jos. Schafer, *Four Wisconsin Counties: Prairie and Forest* (*Wisconsin Domesday Book, General Studies*, II; Madison, 1927), p. 198, n. 4.

[55] Chiefly after Indian cessions of this period. See: I. Galland, *Iowa Emigrant* (Chillicothe, O., 1840); B. F. Shambaugh (compiler and ed.), *Fragments of the Debates of the Iowa Constitutional Conventions of 1844 and 1846* (Iowa City, 1900), Apps. A and B; F. I. Herriott, "Whence Came the Pioneers of Iowa?", *Annals of Iowa*, 3d Ser., VII, 367–79, 446–65; John B. Newhall, *Sketches of Iowa* (New York, 1841) and *A Glimpse of Iowa in 1846* (Burlington, Ia., 1846); and *Western Journal* (St. Louis), II, 385.

[56] Wm. W. Folwell, *A History of Minnesota*, I (St. Paul, 1921), Chaps. VI–X.

areas, but it was not until 1848 that land sales gave the squatters, on the ground, the chance to bid-in their claims. Red River carts and steamboats brought food and supplies. By the close of the thirties and the beginning of the forties, sawmills, and the faint beginnings of agriculture, initiated a new era around St. Paul and neighboring sites of water power. The opening prairies were demanding lumber, but wheat farming did not make its transit to the Red River Valley until long after our period.

Although it was an early center of French settlement, Missouri did not receive its tide of American pioneers until about the time that southern Indiana and Illinois were sought by the same stock. Many of these migrating colonists from Kentucky, Tennessee, and the older slave states, crossed free Illinois to occupy the Missouri Valley, where slavery was permitted. Therefore, along with the backwoodsmen, the planter class took possession of these fertile lands, soon to be shared with German immigrants.

Missouri is a state hard to classify, for, although by slavery it belonged to the South and found the outlet for its products in New Orleans, it was also the metropolis of the upper Mississippi. The fur trade of the Great Plains and the Rocky Mountains, together with the caravans to Santa Fe, gave it a Far Western flavor.[57] In the census reports, however, it is listed with the North Central States, and is so reckoned here. In fact, it was the fighting ground for different sections; and the rivalry of St. Louis and Chicago was an important factor in the economic, political, and cultural life of the forties and fifties. Into the Ozarks drifted the descendants of Southern uplanders, kin of pioneers like the Lincolns,[58] who had followed the colonial trail from Pennsylvania into the interior of Virginia and the Carolinas and on to the Kentucky and Tennessee mountains.

Missouri's population had increased fivefold between 1830 and 1850. Her negroes had risen from 26,000 at the former date to 90,000 at the latter. Nearly 280,000 natives of Missouri, largely descendants of Southern stock and of a small population of French origin, lived within its borders in 1850. The 17,000 of

[57] See: the files of the *Missouri Historical Review;* Flint, *Mississippi Valley,* and *Recollections of the Last Ten Years, . . . in the Valley of the Mississippi,* . . . (Boston, 1826); references in Chapter VIII, under fur trade and Santa Fe Trail; *Western Journal,* VI, 71 ff.; and *Missouri Republican,* Jan. 10, 1854 ("Annual Review, History of St. Louis").

[58] See an interview with Lincoln kin by A. E. Morgan, in *Atlantic Monthly,* CXXV, 208–18.

North Atlantic birth were overwhelmed by nearly 190,000 natives of the South Atlantic and South Central states. Of those born in the latter section, Kentucky furnished well over half and Tennessee all but about 6,000 of the remainder. Missouri was a state dominated by this element in population and economic connections. But, already, over 72,000 foreigners had come, much over half of them of German birth and residing in the regions adjacent to St. Louis — a fact of later significance.

The cost of moving to the West varied in different periods and in different regions, according to the distance of the frontier of free or cheap lands from the settled area that furnished the migration, according to class of accommodation, and according to the changing modes of transportation, by road, canal, steamer, and railroad. The significant fact is that, in the years before the construction of railroads reaching from the Atlantic Coast to the prairies, the opportunity of direct access to cheap Western lands was not open to the poorer people of the Northeastern states and of Europe.

Around 1830, if the settler went by horseback, the cost was reckoned at 75 cents to $1.50 a day; if by stage, at six cents a mile.[59] The Southern stock, of course, could move cheaply by land in their wagons and on the waters of the Ohio by flatboat or raft.[60] Some of the early movers from the Northeast used the lumber rafts from the upper waters of the Allegheny, in New York and Pennsylvania.[61] Some of them also moved by their own wagons, or even came afoot, but the wretched roads of the time made the use of water routes attractive. The expense of traveling by stage and steamboat from Philadelphia to St. Louis, about 1830, was reckoned around $55, " including every thing." [62] This was the most expensive mode of travel at the time. Deck passage, where the traveler furnished bedding and provisions, could be obtained from Beaver, Pennsylvania, to St. Louis for $7, or from New Orleans to St. Louis for $8. By the summer of 1848, the latter cost had fallen to from $2 to $2.50. About 1830 it cost nearly $10, first-class, by canal boat from New York to Buffalo,[63] and $6 by steamer from Buffalo to Cleve-

[59] Peck, *Gazetteer of Illinois*, p. 326.

[60] Jones, *Illinois and the West*, pp. 35 ff.

[61] W. C. Howells, *Life in Ohio*, pp. 84–85.

[62] Details are given in the *Illinois Monthly Magazine*, II, 53.

[63] [Robt. Baird] *View of the Valley of the Mississippi, or The Emigrant's*

land.[64] From New York to St. Louis, first-class, in 1837, required $40 to $45. The cost of travel from Boston to St. Louis, "without extra baggage," was put at $50, everything included.[65] In the *New York Tribune*, Horace Greeley reported cabin passage, in 1847, by steamer from Buffalo to Chicago, at $8, in a period of competitive rates. An agent for an Eastern land company [66] paid $40 for his week's journey from Boston to the lead mines of southwestern Wisconsin, in 1846. Of this amount, $16 was for railroad fare from Boston to Buffalo, and $12 for steamer from Buffalo to Milwaukee.

Thus, in the forties, something like $50 would cover the cost of travel for one adult from the Atlantic Coast to the Mississippi Valley, first-class.[67] Second-class, without lodging and food, might be half that.

In the same years, the usual price of passage, and necessary provisions, to the interior of the United States from European ports, by steerage, was not far from $40 or $50 for an adult, or around $100 for a family of four.[68]

---

and *Traveller's Guide to the West* (published by H. S. Tanner; Philadelphia, 1834).

[64] *Illinois Monthly Magazine*, as cited.

[65] Jones, *op. cit.*, p. 254.

[66] Woodman MSS, Wisconsin Historical Society.

[67] *Michigan History Magazine*, V, 429, gives a letter of 1846 confirming this estimate.

[68] This conclusion is reached from a study of guides, gazetteers, travelers' accounts, letters, etc. See bibliographies in my *Rise of the New West* and in A. B. Hart, *Slavery and Abolition, 1831–1841* (*The American Nation: A History*, XVI; New York, 1906). There were varying rates in different seasons and years, and they depended on whether the rate, under various competitive conditions, was for a company of emigrants, by contract, or for an individual. Moritz Beyer and Louis Koch (*Amerikanische Reisen* [1834–] [Leipzig, 1839]) put adult pasage from Bremerhafen at $40 in gold for middle deck, or from $80 to $100 in the cabin. In 1833 a German immigrant from Bremen to Baltimore (quoted in the *Missouri Historical Review*, XIV, 33) gives the usual rate as $30, including poor and insufficient food, cooked by the immigrants themselves. The consul of the United States at Hesse-Cassel reported that steerage passage could be had for $16, resulting in pauper immigration. (J. B. McMaster, *A History of the People of the United States, from the Revolution to the Civil War*, VI [New York, 1920], 424–25.) Edward Waylen (*Ecclesiastical Reminiscences of the United States* [New York, 1846]) paid £20 for a passage, by sailing ship, from Bristol to New York, in 1834. Baron Straten-Ponthoz (*Recherches sur la situation des émigrants aux États-Unis* [Brussels, 1846]) relates that 1,000 Prussians were carried in four ships, in 1839, for about $42 per capita, including transportation to their destination in the interior. By bargaining, an emigrant from Bremen to Philadelphia, in 1844, secured passage for $19 gold. (Conrad

In addition to travel cost, there was the sum needed for the purchase of lands and, even in the case of a squatter, for the erection of a cabin, the furnishing of implements and stock, and the supplies to tide over the pioneer during the year or so between his arrival and the harvesting of his crop. These aspects of the farmer's budget will be taken up shortly. For the present, it suffices to point out that the westward-moving pioneer with a family must either be in possession of considerable cash or credit, or, if an immigrant, must first go to work in an Eastern city to secure funds for farther travel or else move westward by successive stages, working in the interim, or find labor in a Western town or on a farm until he accumulated the money necessary for owning and operating his land. In the course of the forties, in most of these states, the squatter period, when men occupied government land without paying for it, gradually came to an end.

The Atlantic Coast, by reason of the distance and cost of migration to the interior, as well as of the industrial preferences of her inhabitants, was able to hold a labor class. The conservatism born of habit, and affection for home, reinforced these in-

---

Collip, in [C. W. Butterfield, ed.] *History of Columbia County, Wisconsin, . . .* [Chicago, 1880], p. 886.) A study of the governmental reports leads to the conclusion that the ordinary fare from British ports was approximately £4 or £5, for most of the years here dealt with. (Stanley C. Johnson, *A History of Emigration from the United Kingdom to North America, 1763–1912* [London, 1913], p. 127.) Frances Morehouse (" The Irish Migration of the 'Forties," *American Historical Review*, XXXIII, 586) notes that, in 1841, 19 families, numbering 63 persons, were given passage, by contract, for £126 5*s*., or around $33 per family; and the next year the charge for 5 families, numbering 23 persons, was £67 5*s*. The inferior boats from Irish ports would partly account for these low rates for assisted emigration. See Helen I. Cowan, *British Emigration to British North America, 1783–1837* (University of Toronto *Studies in History and Economics*, IV, No. 2; Toronto, 1928), pp. 107, 113–14, 131.

The ordinary sailing voyage lasted over six weeks, and food had to be provided for twice that time. Sanitary conditions on shipboard were so bad that governments intervened. The advent of the Cunard steamship line, in 1840, improved the time and lowered the cost of crossing. If the traveler went by cabin, and food was provided, the fare was $75, with children at half price. (Dr. C. Büchele, *Land und Volk der Vereinigten Staaten von Nord-Amerika* [Stuttgart, 1855].) In the middle forties, the emigrant fare from New York to Chicago, deck passage, second-class, without meals, was $10 or $12; or by way of New Orleans to St. Louis, $8 for an adult. The costs of travel from the emigrant's home to the port of departure are not, of course, included in the figures given above. The trying experiences and the expenses of an emigrant from Glarus, Switzerland, to Wisconsin, in 1845, are given in *Wisconsin Historical Collections*, XV, 292–337.

fluences. But, at the same time, the prairies were saved from occupation by masses of the very poor and by those with slight initiative and courage. Not only some means and the spirit of adventure and discontent, but also faith, determination, and the creative urge, were factors in the movement of the prairie pioneers.

Perhaps Friedrich Kapp's estimate [69] of an average of $150 as the cash and personal property brought by each immigrant to the United States is not far from the truth. The indigent Irish immigrants of the famine period tended to remain, for some years at least, in the East.

The tide of immigration from Europe, which had resulted by 1850 in the location in the North Central States of people of foreign birth to the number of over 640,000, or not far from one-eighth of the section's population, furnished new problems in the composition and the future of these states.[70] Dr. Eduard Brückner [71] calls attention to the fact that the section's rainfall, from 1845 to 1855, was above normal, which, in this part of the United States, insured good cereal yields, while the contemporaneous wet years in western Europe's moist climate meant poor crops. In the United States, these were years, also, of accelerated canal and railroad building, of the opening of new areas of the West to occupation, and of increased demand for labor. By this time, too, the letters of emigrants to their friends in the Old World, the books of travel, emigrant guides and even European magazines and newspapers devoted to the subject,[72] and the agents of transportation companies, had spread far and wide in western Europe the news of the opportunities in the United States.

While more than two-thirds of the foreign-born, in 1850, were

[69] See his " European Emigration to the United States " (New York, 1869; reprinted from American Social Science Association *Journal*, II), pp. 11 ff. See also August Rauschenbusch, *Einige Anweisungen für Auswanderer nach den westlichen Staaten von Nordamerika, und Reisebilder* (Elberfeld, 1848).

[70] Dr. Marcus L. Hansen, in an article on " The History of American Immigration as a Field for Research," *American Historical Review*, XXXII, 500–518, exhibits the breadth and importance of the subject. To his earlier reports, made when a student in my seminary in Harvard University, I am also indebted.

[71] " The Settlement of the United States as Controlled by Climate and Climatic Oscillations," in *Memorial Volume of the Transcontinental Excursion of 1912 of the American Geographical Society* (New York, 1915), pp. 125–39.

[72] Hansen, *op. cit.*, pp. 516–17, n. 11.

located in other sections, chiefly in New England and the Middle
Atlantic States, the immigration to the North Central section had
a special significance. In the Atlantic states, from colonial days,
the rule of the older stock was well established, and institutions,
manners, and customs—the cultural life of the sections—had been
largely fixed by tradition. But in the new West society was plastic and democratic. All elements were suddenly coming in, together, to form the section. It would be a mistake to think that
social classes and distinctions were obliterated, but, in general,
no such stratification existed as was to be found, especially, in
New England. Moreover, in the latter section almost two-thirds,
and in the Middle Atlantic States over half, of the foreign-born
were Irish. In the South, the foreign-born were an unimportant
fraction. But, in the North Central States, approximately 44
per cent were Germans, only 23 per cent Irish, 14 per cent English, 7 per cent British American, about 3 per cent Scotch, less
than 3 per cent French, around 2 per cent Scandinavian, and
under 2 per cent Welsh. Numerous Dutch and Swiss added to
the variety, and over 130,000 negroes (two-thirds of them in
Missouri) still further complicated the problem of the native
white settlers plunged into a mixing bowl with foreigners in the
occupation of a new country.

As the map [73] shows, the shores of the Great Lakes, the banks
of the upper Mississippi and the Missouri, and the routes of
canals and of railroads, revealed the influence of transportation,
and the demand for labor, upon the distribution of the immigrants. The Irish, especially, were the common laborers and
tended to remain along the routes when their work was done, or
to seek the cities.

The Germans took the cheaper Congressional lands in the hardwood forests bordering the western shore of Lake Michigan above
Milwaukee, and the adjacent lands; and spread from St. Louis
up the Missouri, and across the Mississippi into Illinois. The
older Pennsylvania-German stock had extended into Ohio through
the counties south of the Western Reserve and into the Miami
Valley. The speculators' early grabbing of the best available
lands and town sites in the prairie regions, and the fondness of
the German immigrants for wooded and watered lands, yielding
fuel and timber for building and being nearer market centers, help

[73] Foreign-born, 1850 (at end of volume).

to explain the Germans' occupation of these counties in spite of the rough work involved in clearing the hardwood forests.[74]

There were over 280,000 people of German birth in the North Central States in 1850, besides the considerable number of native American children born of German immigrants, and the Pennsylvania-German stock. Numerically, Ohio led the states of the section in its German-born, but they constituted only about 6 per cent of its total population; Missouri had around 7 per cent; Illinois, but 5 per cent; Indiana, only 3 per cent; and Michigan, less than 3 per cent; while in Wisconsin they rose to over 12 per cent.

The great mass of these Germans [75] had left their native land for economic reasons. The destruction of hand industries by the factory system, and, toward the close of the forties, the failure of crops and the damage to the vineyards of southern Germany, made the appeal of the cheap lands of the North Central section most effective. Less important, but still of some significance, was the exodus of sects like the Old Lutherans, of northern Germany, who sought relief in the New World from attempts to unite them with the Reformed churches.

But, to this mass of thrifty and laborious German peasants and

---

[74] Schafer, " Yankee and Teuton," *passim*, and *Four Wisconsin Counties*, Chaps. v–vii. For a similar explanation of Norwegian selection of land, see Gunnar J. Malmin (translator and ed.), *America in the Forties: The Letters of Ole Munch Raeder* (Minneapolis, 1929), pp. 73–76.

[75] Albert B. Faust, *The German Element in the United States* (Boston, 1909), is the standard treatise, with a good bibliography. See also Ernest Bruncken, " German Political Refugees in the United States during the Period from 1815–1860," *Deutsch-Amerikanische Geschichtsblätter*, III, 33 ff. (July, 1903). Various numbers of the *Americana Germanica*, and its continuation as *German-American Annals* . . . , have useful articles. Types of many special sources used are: Schafer, " Yankee and Teuton," *passim;* Kate A. Everest [Levi], " How Wisconsin Came by Its Large German Element," *Wisconsin Historical Collections*, XII, 299–334; *idem*, " Geographical Origin of German Immigration to Wisconsin," *ibid.*, XIV, 341–93; Wilhelm Hense-Jensen, *Wisconsin's Deutsch-Amerikaner*, . . . (Milwaukee, 1900); *The Reminiscences of Carl Schurz*, I–II (New York, 1907); L. F. Frank [ed.], *Pionierjahre der Deutsch-Amerikanischen Familien Frank-Kerler in Wisconsin und Michigan, 1849–1864* [Milwaukee? 1911]; the articles by Wm. G. Bek on Gottfried Duden and his followers, in *Missouri Historical Review*, XII–XIX, *passim* (for Missouri); Gustav P. Körner, *Das deutsche Element in den Vereinigten Staaten von Nordamerika, 1818–1848* (Cincinnati, 1880); Anton Eickhoff, *In der neuen Heimath;* . . . (New York, 1884); Franz [von] Löher, *Geschichte und Zustände der Deutschen in Amerika* (Cincinnati and Leipzig, 1847); and German travelers' books, emigrants' guides, etc., too numerous for citation.

artisans, there came the leaven of the political refugees from the revolutions of 1830 and 1848. Men with the training of universities, with the love of art, with a passionate idealism in behalf of liberty and democracy, fleeing from the failure of their efforts to institute republican government in their own country, now furnished a leadership and a new direction to Germanism in America. In numbers they were not important, but in politics and culture they deeply influenced the life of Germans in this country.

Affected by the philosophical idealism of the time, as well as by the quest for liberty, they looked to the West as a land of opportunity for the reorganization of society. The German of this era was not characterized by the scientific efficiency and disciplined action that came later. Large — and even fanatical — visions of complete freedom under a republican form of government, wherein the German spirit might develop, animated this migration of the " Latin farmer " to the American West. To not a few of these idealists, this seemed a land in which they might realize their dream of a German republic with personal freedom as its cornerstone. Texas, Missouri, and Wisconsin became the goals of the larger number of them. Societies — one led by nobles — were formed, and newspapers established, to promote the concentration of settlement in some Western territory or state until, through voting power, a republican form of government, under the control of natives of Germany but within the federal organization of the United States, could be evolved.[76] The vigorous assertion of the doctrine of state sovereignty, in this period, made such a course seem not altogether impossible.[77]

But German leaders like Carl Schurz and Friedrich Kapp showed wiser insight. Said the latter:

A German nation within the American they [the Germans] cannot be, but they can throw the rich treasures of their life and thought into the

[76] Professor Marcus L. Hansen calls attention to the idea of Duden (*Bericht über eine Reise* . . . , p. 235) that the Germans might form a *Stadt* (city) as the cultural center of the surrounding region, as contrasted with that of the Giessener Gesellschaft, which would allow the entrance of a German *Staat* (state) into the Union.

[77] In the J. C. Bluntschli-Karl Brater *Deutsches Staats-Wörterbuch* (Stuttgart and Leipzig, 1856–70), Dr. Brater pointed out that the legislative power of the American government is too limited to make it lawfully possible for the Anglo-Americans successfully to oppose this danger to the sovereign authority, though it might hasten a catastrophe feared by many observers of American affairs — namely, the breaking-up of the Union into two or more groups of states, in part under Anglo-American, in part under German, rule.

struggle for political and human interests, and their influence will penetrate the more deeply and create for them a wider field of activity, the less
peculiar they make it.[78]

Later, to Carl Schurz the movement of the Germans into the
West was an inspiring spectacle — the movement, not of

a barbarous multitude pouncing upon old and decrepit empires; . . . but
. . . the vigorous elements of all nations, . . . peaceably congregating
and mingling together on virgin soil, . . . undertaking to commence a new
era in the history of the world, without first destroying the results of the
progress of past periods; undertaking to found a new cosmopolitan nation
without marching over the dead bodies of slain millions.

In this process in the West, he saw the foundations of

the *great colony of free humanity*, which has not old England alone, but
the *world*, for its mother-country. . . . the dream of the truest friends of
man from the beginning.[79]

German societies, however, now developed, both in the East
and West, which sought the union of the Germans in the United
States, the promotion of German customs and culture, the support of the principles of pure democracy, and the nourishing of
love and attachment for the Old Country and the improvement
of its conditions. They promoted the insistence upon the teaching of German in the public schools, the printing of the laws in
German as well as in English, and, in general, the perpetuation
of Germanism in their new home. Radicals among them urged
that the United States had only started on the pathway of true
democracy, and demanded the modification of the American Constitution, including revision to make the choice of the President
by primary election. But, for the most part, the German population, in this era, was intent upon making a living in its new
home, and asked only the right of manhood suffrage without regard to nativity.

The most noted German political refugees, exiled because of
their love of liberty, settled in the West, and especially in those
portions of Missouri and Illinois adjacent to St. Louis.[80] This

[78] Quoted (in translation) by Everest [Levi] (*Wisconsin Historical Collections*, XII, 309–10) from Kapp, *Die Deutschen im Staate New York während
des achtzehnten Jahrhunderts* (*Geschichtsblätter, Bilder und Mittheilungen aus
dem Leben der Deutschen in Amerika*, ed. Carl Schurz, I [New York, 1884],
228).

[79] *Speeches, Correspondence and Political Papers of Carl Schurz*, ed. Frederic
Bancroft (New York, 1913), I, 55–57.

[80] Belleville, Illinois, was an important center.

region was a center of German culture, and from it came some
of the distinguished scientists, scholars, and men of affairs of
the nation. By 1850 the Germans were a marked element of the
Western population, strong in the older cities like Cincinnati and
(to a less degree) Cleveland, but powerful, also, in St. Louis and
Milwaukee. In these regions of concentration, they formed
something like German provinces, with characteristic German
architecture and with general use of the German language. In
various states of the section, before long, they held the balance
of political power. In all the little communities that sprang up
like mushrooms in the West in these years, Germans became the
retail merchants and artisans, but their characteristic occupation
was farming. They brought to this new land the same experience
in thrift that the German farmers had brought to the Great Valley of Pennsylvania a century before, and their intensive agriculture and their economies enabled them or their sons to add field
after field to their possessions and thus gradually to acquire the
farms begun by the Yankee pioneers.

Next, numerically, to the contribution of the Germans to the
North Central States, in this period, was that of the Irish. According to the census of 1850, less than 150,000 Irish-born were
located in the section, out of nearly a million in the nation. The
cities of the Atlantic Coast still held the mass of this unfortunate
folk. In the West, also, it was the cities they sought in largest
numbers. Chicago's population of 30,000 in 1850, for example,
included more Irishmen than Germans. In Cincinnati and Milwaukee, on the other hand, the Germans outnumbered the Irish
by more than two to one.

The population of English, Scotch, Welsh, and British-American
birth, in the North Central section in 1850, amounted, in all, to
164,000, of which nearly 89,000 were English, 19,000 Scotch,
12,000 Welsh, and 45,000 British-American. Some of the latter
were Canadian French.

These elements contributed less distinctive features to the section than did the German and Irish. Most of them lost themselves in the Protestant English-speaking population already
there. But, in many a locality, they formed little communities
and left a special impress. The twenties had seen a considerable
beginning of such group migrations. Some of them were of discontented farmers aiming to carry to the New World their su-

perior methods of agriculture, only to learn that, with cheap virgin land, these methods were better suited to the conservation of the soil than to immediate profits in competition with the exploitive practices of their neighbors.[81]   The hard times also brought artisans, such as those sent out by the Potters' Union to various localities in the section.[82]   Cornish miners migrated to the lead region of Wisconsin.[83]

The Scandinavian immigration at this time is of interest rather as the beginning of a movement destined to be important in the composition of some of the states of the section than as numerically significant. It became considerable in the thirties and forties, stimulated by the hard times and by the reports of returned travelers regarding the attractions of the Illinois prairies. By 1850 nearly 14,000 Scandinavians (by birth) were credited to the section, but, as they had long been coming, the figures by no means represent the importance of the element.[84]   It is interesting that Minnesota, which became almost dominated by this stock, had at that time only a dozen inhabitants of Scandinavian birth.   Norway sent most of the Scandinavian element to the section, and, in 1850, nearly two-thirds of it was in Wisconsin. So much like the Yankees were these people that assimilation was rapid, in spite of the difference in language and the counteractive efforts of the ministers in various sects.

[81] Types are noted in Geo. Flower, *History of the English Settlement in Edwards County, Illinois, . . .* (Chicago Historical Society *Collection,* I; Chicago, 1882). See also Pooley, *Illinois from 1830 to 1850,* pp. 501–4.

[82] See Johnson, *Emigration from the United Kingdom.* The experiences of a patternmaker (in an English woolen mill), who emigrated to Wisconsin, are given in the letters of Edwin Bottomley, 1842–50, published in the *Wisconsin Historical Collections,* XXV.

[83] L. A. Copeland, " The Cornish in Southwest Wisconsin," *ibid.,* XIV, 301–34.

[84] Theodore C. Blegen, *Norwegian Migration to America, 1825–1860* (Northfield, Minn., 1931), and Kendric C. Babcock, *The Scandinavian Element in the United States* (University of Illinois *Studies in the Social Sciences,* III, No. 3; Urbana, 1914). Consult the publications of the Norwegian-American Historical Association (two series: Minneapolis and Northfield, Minn.), among which are the interesting *Letters of Raeder* (ed. Malmin) ; Swedish Historical Society of America *Year-Book* (Chicago) ; and Geo. M. Stephenson, *A History of American Immigration, 1820–1924* (Boston, 1926). In the *Wisconsin Magazine of History,* I, 149–67, R. B. Anderson gives an account of the unique book of Ole Nattestad, describing his journey to North America in 1837, and a translation of the pamphlet follows (pp. 167 ff.). Nattestad paid $50 for passage on a vessel carrying Swedish iron from Gothenburg to Fall River, Mass. Babcock estimates the usual fare at $60, including board.

The mingling of people from different sections, and from different nations of the Old World, coming suddenly into an undeveloped land, produced a situation hardly paralleled in American history (at least since the days of colonial Pennsylvania), and it raised the problem of assimilation and of the future of a section composed of such diverse elements. The reaction of these various stocks, with their different habits, moral and religious doctrines, and ideals, upon one another, led to cross-fertilization and the evolution of a profoundly modified society. A new contribution to American life was making in the West.

It was evident that the North Central States were not to be a melting pot, with fusion of the manifold ingredients, but rather a mixing bowl, with a process of adjustment, of giving-and-taking, at work; and the section's physical features themselves demanded new ways of dealing with the problems of economic, political, and social development — new uses for old tools, new adaptations of old institutions. But the past, and Europe, were entering the Great Lakes Basin.

A traveler to Michigan in the early thirties writes:

The effects of the Yankee were generally limited to a Dearborn wagon, a feather-bed, a saddle and bridle, and some knickknack in the way of a machine for shelling corn, hatchelling flax, or, for aught I know, manufacturing wooden nutmegs for family use. . . .

But still further do the Swiss and Germans carry their love of family relics. Mark that quaint-looking wagon which lumbers up a dozen square feet of the deck. You may see a portrait of it among the illuminated letters of a vellum-bound edition of Virgil's Bucolics. It was taken from an Helvetian ancestor that transported Cæsar's baggage into winter-quarters. It might be worth something in a museum, but it has cost five times its value in freight to transport it over the Atlantic. What an indignity it is to overwhelm the triumphal chariot with the beds and ploughs, shovels, saddles, and sideboards, chairs, clocks, and carpets that fill its interior, and to hang those rusty pots and kettles, bakepans, fryingpans, and saucepans, iron candlesticks, old horse-shoes, and broken tobacco-pipes, like trophies of conquest over Time, along its racked and wheezing sides.[85]

In this plastic society, all the various stocks intermingled, but they did not lose their separate individualities. " Bowie-knife Southerners," " beer-drinking Germans," " wild Irishmen," were phrases bandied among them. To the Yankee Puritan, the customs, and very appearance, of the Southerner seemed uncouth —

[85] Hoffman, *Winter in the West*, I, 106-7.

and often ungodly. To him the Catholicism of so many of the immigrants of varied nationalities, and the Germans' mode of spending the Sabbath, their beer gardens, and their radicalism, threatened American institutions. But the Germans, with their love of music and art, brought a leavening cultural element to the pioneering stock of the native Americans. Gradually, differences of race and religion gave way to toleration and mutual acceptance. Nativism and prohibition, spreading from the East, were to bring disharmony in the fifties, but, when the Republican party saw the need of conciliating the immigrant vote, these issues were abandoned in the North Central States.

The folk from the older sections of the Union, and from across the sea, who mingled in this evolving new society of the West were all American pioneers — not mere outlying fragments of New England, the South, Germany, Ireland, Scandinavia. Says Timothy Flint, a contemporaneous observer, of the people from various parts of the country who had here come together:

They meet half way, and embrace; and the society thus newly organized and constituted, is more liberal, enlarged, unprejudiced, and, of course, more affectionate and pleasant, than a society of people of *unique* birth and character, who bring all their early prejudices, as a common stock, to be transmitted as an inheritance in perpetuity.[86]

One of the travelers of the fifties [87] warned the newcomers that they must abandon their racial animosities. " Such quarrels provoke merely the laughter of the Americans," he said. Particularly in the mixed zone shown on the map [88] was there this intermingling. The same township or little hamlet might contain representatives of all the stocks that entered the West — sometimes tilling their farms in small groups, but uniting in town and county meetings for the conduct of common affairs, the construction of roads and schoolhouses, the apportionment of taxes. Often the local political conventions gave careful attention, in party nominations, to representation of the various groups; and not infrequently it was a New York politician who managed the arrangements and shepherded the people.

The influences that were to fashion these varied pioneers into a common society were not apparent on first view. New England-

[86] *Mississippi Valley*, I, 140.
[87] Thos. Mooney, *Nine Years in America* (Dublin, 1850), p. 50.
[88] Foreign-born, 1850 (at end of volume).

ers, leaving a steamboat with their Yankee notions and traveling by wagon to the edge of the prairie, made a different picture from Germans in their peasant garb and wooden shoes, raising their voices in choral song as they entered the harbors of the Great Lakes. Unlike either of these were North Carolinians crossing the fords and making their way in the long-bodied Southern wagons. They spoke a dialect of their own and carried a store of special experiences to the West. But all were entering a promised land, enthusiastic over its future and pledged to promote its interests. All were neighbors. The house raising was a symbol of their society and of their ideals. It represented the act of forming a new section by the joint labors of the whole community, a readiness to abandon differences in the advancement of the common cause.

C. F. Hoffman describes a German immigrant, on a steamboat in the thirties, with crooked pipe and blue cotton frock. " Ten years hence . . . you will find him . . . at home among his neighbours . . . while that clean-looking Englishman next to him will still be a stranger in the land." [89] A Wisconsin editor, writing of his boyhood, tells of sitting before the fireplace, " lulled to sleep by the soft thunder of my mother's spinning wheel," and of his first alarm over visits of the Indians who still wandered along the Rock River Valley. He adds: " I soon learned to have no fear of the tribesmen, . . . but the first Germans who came to our parts nearly scared the life out of me. Their heavy beards, long coats, broad-visored caps, and arm-long pipes " made them seem to him like denizens of another world.[90] W. D. Howells, on the other hand, found pleasure in meeting with the Germans in their beer saloons in Ohio, enjoyed their rendition of Schiller's plays, worked in a German printing office, and long remembered the " kindly German printer-folk, and the merry times we had with them, in the smoke of their pipes and the warmth of their stove heated red against the autumnal cold." But he adds that, though he knew a few German families, he never afterwards met them at American homes; the cleavage between the two peoples, in everything but politics, was absolute.[91]

[89] *Winter in the West*, I, 108.
[90] E. D. Coe, " Reminiscences of a Pioneer in the Rock River Country," Wisconsin Historical Society *Proceedings*, 1907 (Madison, 1908), pp. 193, 195.
[91] *Years of My Youth*, pp. 43, 135-36.

The West was the land of opportunity for young men, on whom the weight of tradition and the rule of their elders pressed heavily in the seaboard sections. The statistics of the constitutional conventions in the North Central States, in these years, show that they were made up of young men. When one finds expressions of deference to the judgment of a " Nestor " of a convention and discovers that he had not reached middle age, one begins to see how dominant was youth in this new and composite society, and how important in making easy the mixing process.

The disposition of the public domain was of great interest to Congress and to the settlers, in these years. Inasmuch as by far the larger part of the federal public lands lay in the North Central States, the problem was acute in this division. The various solutions offered in Congress gave rise to sectional and political rivalries, which will be treated in later chapters. To the settler, some of the aspects of the matter were of pressing importance.

When our survey begins, the lands were disposed of under the law of 1820, which, after cession of the Indian titles and the running of surveys, permitted the purchase from the federal government of a minimum of eighty acres, under the auction system, at not less than $1.25 per acre. Thus, $100 would enable the settler to secure an eighty-acre farm. By an act in 1832, the minimum tract was reduced to forty acres, thus making it possible to buy a farm for $50.

But, from colonial days, many of the pioneers had not waited for extinction of Indian title, for surveys, or for sale in the land offices. Into the wilderness they had gone, in advance of government, and, " squatting " on land that seemed good to them, made their improvements and raised their crops without title but with the intention of acquiring the lands from the government at the minimum price, when offered for sale. So common was the practice, that it raised important issues between the squatters and the government, between them and the actual settlers who had conformed to the law, and between the squatters and the speculators.[92]

---

[92] In a speech by A. G. Harrison, of Missouri, in the House of Representatives (*Congressional Globe*, VI, App., 392–96), there is an interesting characterization of squatters. See also the speech of A. W. Snyder, of Illinois (*ibid.*, pp. 398–99), and compare the speeches of Archibald Yell, of Arkansas (*ibid.*, pp. 501–3), and Reuben Chapman, of Alabama (*ibid.*, pp. 389–92), contrasting the rights of the speculator with those of the squatter.

The act of 1807 to prevent settlement prior to authorization by law, on lands ceded to the United States, had become a dead letter. Congress itself, by numerous local and temporary acts, had allowed the squatter the right of pre-emption (the privilege to purchase before others, and at the minimum price), instead of compelling him to bid at the auction sales. The settler came to feel that both natural right and customary law warranted him in freely taking up land on the public domain. His clearing and improvement, and, earlier, his defense against the Indian, had given the real value to his own lands and to those of the government and of the later comers. All neighboring lands were raised in price by his having carried society into the wilderness. Backwoodsmen of the outer fringe of the frontier even made a business of squatting, clearing the land, erecting a log cabin, and then selling out their improvements to the thriftier farmers, with cash, who followed them.

The proportion of squatters to actual settlers by purchase cannot, of course, be accurately stated, but it was very large. In some counties of Illinois, at the close of 1828, there were from five to ten times as many voters as freeholders, and a contemporary writer estimated that two-thirds of Illinois voters owned no land, though in fact the great majority were actually engaged in farming.[93] Senator John Tipton, of Indiana, declared in 1838 that four entire counties of northwestern Indiana were occupied by squatters.[94] Senator James Buchanan, of Pennsylvania, asserted that there were more than thirty thousand squatters on public lands of Iowa that had been formed into counties and given federal judges, and asked, " Could you now expel such an entire community from their homes? "[95] Senator Webster, also, felt that Congressional action had led to a legitimate expectation on the part of the squatters that their right to pre-emption would be respected.[96] But to Clay they were " a lawless rabble," who " might as well seize upon our forts, our arsenals, or on the public treasure, as to rush out and seize on the public lands."[97]

[93] *Senate Document 9*, 20th Cong., 1st Sess., and Jas. Hall, *Statistics of the West, at the Close of the Year 1836* (Cincinnati, 1836), pp. 172–86. Hall's figures, however, need correction.

[94] *Congressional Globe*, VI, App., p. 134.

[95] *Ibid.*, p. 132.

[96] *Ibid.*, p. 135.

[97] *Ibid.*, p. 134.

Calhoun, expecting the system to operate for the " benefit of the rich, the strong, and the violent," joined Clay in calling the squatters lawless.[98]

The squatters, in order to meet the situation produced by the fact that Eastern speculators, or their agents, and newly arrived seekers after land, could outbid them in the auction sales, and to insure their purchase of their farms at the minimum price, banded together into " Claim Associations," settled their own disputes by referring them to a committee of their members, appointed one of their number to buy their claims, and, by threat of violence, prevented rivals from acquiring their land through higher bids. Various were the sanctions for enforcing the will of these extralegal organizations. Sometimes they resolved that, if any person should deprive claimants of their just expectations, " we will not fail to rebuke his conduct with such severity as has been common in the settlement of this western country."[99] This might mean anything from a social and economic boycott, to tar and feathers, ducking through the ice, or persuasion by rifle or shotgun. One of the associations denounced intruders as " dishonest & no Gentlemen " and resolved " that if any member of this club finds his or any of his friends Clames has been Jumpt that they inform this Club of the fact and that this Club forthwith put them off said clame without trobling the sivel law." Not seldom these associations had formal rules and regulations, or constitutions, and records.[100]

Acting under such organizations, " The *Settlers*, when thus abiding by their own equitable laws, and acting in good faith towards each other," congratulated themselves that they " need not the benevolent aid of our law-givers at Washington to secure themselves in the undisputed possession of their rights and privileges."[101] Plainly, here was a case of custom growing into law,

[98] *Ibid.*, p. 137.

[99] B. H. Hibbard, *A History of the Public Land Policies* (New York, 1924), p. 206. See also his Chap. XI.

[100] The best-known is the Johnson County (Iowa) Claim Association, whose *Constitution and Records* have been edited, with an Introduction, by B. F. Shambaugh (Iowa City, 1894). See also his " Frontier Land Clubs or Claim Associations," American Historical Association *Annual Report*, 1900, I (Washington, 1901), 69–84, and Prof. Jesse Macy's *Institutional Beginnings in a Western State* (Johns Hopkins University *Studies in Historical and Political Science*, Ser. II, No. 7; Baltimore, 1884).

[101] *Milwaukee Sentinel*, Mar. 5, 1839.

and here was a frame of mind that gave the later doctrine of "squatter sovereignty" strength among the followers of Lewis Cass and of Douglas.

An act was passed, in 1841,[102] granting permanent and general pre-emption, thus putting the well established practice of the pioneers into the form of law. This act, however, did not satisfy the Western pioneers, who urged upon Congress the free grant of a homestead. Meantime, additional opportunities to secure lands were open to settler and to speculator, by the purchase of state lands or of the scrip for bounty lands offered to veterans, and by other means. To nine states in the Mississippi Valley, 500,000 acres, each, had been given by the act of 1841.[103] Other grants were made for internal improvements, and (by the close of our period) there were grants of swamp lands. Not infrequently the needs of the state and the desire to attract settlers resulted in a low price, and (toward the end of the forties) the scrip disposed of by soldiers to speculators furnished still cheaper lands. In 1841 it was reported that, when lands in one of the counties of southern Michigan were offered at auction in Boston, most of them sold for from $37\frac{1}{2}$ to 60 cents per acre.[104]

Speculators or their agents often sought out and entered the best lands and most desirable town or mill sites, in advance of the coming of the pioneer. In a sense, the settler himself was a speculator, for he bought more land than he could farm, hoping for the increase in value that would benefit his children if not himself. But the culling of the lands was a serious evil, for it spread and dispersed population, and often left to the poorer settler only the rejects. Eminent Senators engaged in these land speculations, and Eastern companies kept offices in the regions to which settlement was moving. Increasing facilities of transportation, and increasing security of the squatter rights through pre-emption, made the speculators' profits more than doubtful in many cases. But by various devices, sometimes in concert with fraudulent land officers, they withheld large tracts, awaiting a rise in values. Senator R. J. Walker, of Mississippi, who had himself been charged with organizing speculative combinations to prevent the government from receiving more than the mini-

[102] See R. M. Robbins, "Preëmption — A Frontier Triumph," *Mississippi Valley Historical Review*, XVIII, 331–49.

[103] But note limitations due to previous grants; see Hibbard, *op. cit.*, p. 232.

[104] *Milwaukee Sentinel*, Nov. 27, 1841.

mum price and to control the lands best for cotton, reported in
1836 that " the [nation's] sales within the last year have amounted
to nearly thirteen millions of acres, being almost three times the
amount sold in any preceding year," and he believed that eight
million acres of these sales were made for speculation.[105]   In the
year 1836, about twenty-five million dollars was received from
the public-land sales, and over seventy per cent of the amount
came from lands of the North Central section.[106]

When the speculative capitalist found the lands less immediately remunerative, he turned to the loaning of money at exorbitant rates to the needy newcomer, who must go into debt for
supplies and stock and who might even lose his claim if he failed
to make payment when his lands were brought on the market.
Sometimes this interest ran to one hundred per cent.[107] Even the
legal rate was $12\frac{1}{2}$ per cent in Wisconsin.

Such were the conditions of geography, peoples, and land, in
the section to which the Northern pioneer farmers were rushing
in these years.   Two factors were fundamental in shaping the
activity of these settlers: the land was divided into forest and
prairie, and the terminal moraine of the later glacier made a
boundary line between the richer and the poorer soils.   These
factors were influential upon the location of the different elements of the population, upon the kind of agriculture, and upon
the economic, political, and social life that emerged from the
occupation of the section by this rural people.

The settler who cleared his farm in the forest was usually of
Southern stock long accustomed to that kind of work, or the German whose life in his native land had taught the value of wood,
springs, and access to water transportation, and who found the
prairie land too expensive.   Not the flood plain, but higher lands,
attracted the men who occupied the woods, and they estimated

---

[105] *American State Papers, Public Lands,* VIII, 878. On the subject in
general, see Hibbard, *op. cit.,* pp. 214–22. In the *New York Tribune,* Mar. 21,
Apr. 18, 1845, Horace Greeley scathingly denounces the land speculators.
Schafer, *Four Wisconsin Counties,* pp. 59–64, 69, 72–79, 123–25, gives details for
one region.

[106] Arthur H. Cole [with the assistance of the authorities of the Public Land
Office in Washington], " Cyclical and Sectional Variations in the Sale of Public
Lands, 1816–60," *Review of Economic Statistics* (Harvard Economic Service),
IX, 51–52 (Jan., 1927).

[107] Geo. M. Stephenson, *The Political History of the Public Lands from
1840 to 1862* (Boston, 1917), p. 99, n. 5, cites examples.

the value of the soil by the kind of hardwoods upon it. Felling the trees outward with his ax, the pioneer made room for the log house. This was rapidly erected, usually with the unpaid aid of neighbors gathered for the " log raising." Around the cabin the larger trees were girdled and left to die, while the smaller ones were cut out. Some years later the dead and decayed trees were burned and the stumps removed. The typical backwoods clearing was some dozen acres, gradually enlarged according to the family's labor power and diligence. A " worm fence " of split logs laid zigzag inclosed the clearing, to keep the cattle out. The farmer raised corn and had a small truck garden. A few cows, and hogs that roved the forest to feed on the acorns, constituted the live stock. The abundant game furnished meat. As another wave of forest pioneers came on, such a frontier farmer often sold his " improvements " and moved to new lands. The later comer added horses, oxen, and plow, but one man and horse could hardly cultivate as much as twenty acres in a season. Wheat could not be raised on the virgin soil to advantage until several years of corn planting had fitted it to produce a crop in which the stalk did not thrive at the expense of the kernel. At first the grain was threshed by flail as in the days of Egypt, or trodden out by oxen and winnowed by a sheet, for fan, and a coarse sieve. The corn husking was done commonly in a husking bee, in early years, but later the farmer stripped the ears on the stalk.

The Ohio and Missouri river valleys in the section, settled by pioneers of Southern origin, produced large numbers of oxen, mules, and hogs, which, in the mild climate of these regions, received little attention in housing and feeding.

When a surplus of corn was raised, it was fed to the live stock or turned into whiskey. Since animals could walk to a market, they became an early export. Hogs and cattle could also be turned into bacon or salt beef and floated down the Mississippi. Something like three years sufficed the better pioneer farmers of the forest areas to produce a shipment, but there was a large proportion of these men to whom a market was a matter of indifference. They " lived on their own," or bartered in neighboring towns.

Thus was established the exploitive forest farming. The trees were enemies to be chopped and burned; the wilderness seemed to the frontiersmen, not a resource for governmental treasuries, nor for the East, nor for posterity, but a free area to be held by conquest. Even the original richness of the humus must be robbed before small grains could be raised. Not a surplus, but economic self-sufficiency, characterized this agriculture in its distinctively pioneer period.[108]

As the pioneer farmer of the forest regions pushed out to where prairie and woods mingled, the type of farming changed. With wood and water at command, the temptations of the prairie for grazing land grew. At first merely an open range for cattle, which all might share, the prairie lands were gradually encroached upon by cultivation. As the clearings extended in the smaller prairie areas, farms joined each other, and the pioneer learned how to handle the prairie. Already, this process had gone on in Ohio, and it was the Eastern rather than the Southern settler who ventured most boldly into the open fields.

The valley of the Rock and Fox rivers, where prairies were broken by groves, with denser woodland along the rivers and their tributaries,[109] afforded such opportunities in northern Illinois and southern Wisconsin. In Michigan, also, the broad zone of oak openings across the south of the state was attractive to wheat raisers.

The great open prairies, remote from wood and water and exposed to the winds of winter, did not become the goal of the pioneer until the fifties. But, even in the forties, Northern settlers were advancing beyond the wooded lands, and, as the map of crops in 1850 [110] shows, both corn- and wheat-concentration areas were clearly outlined by that time. The steel plow dates back at

[108] I have used manuscript notes by my former graduate student, Nils A. Olsen, now of the federal Department of Agriculture, and have also found Josiah T. Marshall, *Farmer's and Emigrant's Hand-book* (Utica, N. Y., 1852; copyright, 1849), useful for the later forties, and S. C. Cox, *Recollections of the Early Settlement of the Wabash Valley* (Lafayette, Ind., 1860), helpful. Earlier accounts by authors of travels, guides, and gazetteers, cited in my *Rise of the New West*, have been used, particularly writings of James Hall, J. M. Peck, and Timothy Flint.

[109] See: Pooley, *Illinois from 1830 to 1850*, Chaps. v, vii; Schafer, " Yankee and Teuton," *Wisconsin Magazine of History*, VI, 125–45, 261–79; *idem*, *A History of Agriculture in Wisconsin* (*Wisconsin Domesday Book, General Studies*, I; Madison, 1922); *idem*, *Four Wisconsin Counties; Wisconsin Domesday Book, Town Studies*, I [Madison, 1924]; and Fuller, *Economic and Social Beginnings of Michigan*, pp. 42–43 (also consulting Index, under " Oak Openings ").

[110] At end of volume.

least to 1837, and the McCormick reaper, in its experimental
form, to 1831. In 1851 Mr. McCormick (whose factory was
moved to Chicago in 1847) estimated that he had sold a thousand machines in the past eleven years.[111] Yankee inventors were
at work on many devices for promoting prairie farming and
diminishing the need of man-power.[112]

In the selection of land, the federal rectangular surveys by section lines had important effects upon the convenience and character of the settlers' locations. But an experience in Iowa illustrates that these surveys were not always effective. Pioneers,
who had previously located their lands, agreed that those first
on the claims after the legal opening of the New Purchase on
May 1, 1843, should hold them. On that date thousands rushed
by torchlight into these new counties.[113] The claims having been
laid out irrespective of the points of the compass, the settlers inter-
changed deeds after the land sales, so that each might hold within
the lines of his own claim.[114]

The oak openings of Michigan, already described, were early
centers of attraction. Prairie Ronde, for instance, as clearly defined as the bed of an ancient lake five miles in diameter,[115] soon
became a waving wheat field of thousands of acres. The settlers
on the small " prairies " of southern Wisconsin and around the
" groves " of northern Illinois gradually pushed their fences into
the open prairie range. Between the cattle raisers and the wheat
farmers dissension arose over the question of whether the law
should require the stockman or the farmer to make the fence.

Over a large portion of the zone of oak openings, and mixed
prairie and groves, wheat was as much a " single crop " as was
cotton in the South. In the regions of new settlement, labor and
capital were scarce, and good land abundant and cheap. As a

[111] R. G. Thwaites, " Cyrus Hall McCormick and the Reaper," Wisconsin
Historical Society *Proceedings*, 1908 (Madison, 1909), p. 245.

[112] See: Hadley W. Quaintance, *The Influence of Farm Machinery on Production and Labor* (American Economic Association *Publications*, 3d Ser.,
V, No. 4, pp. 1–106) ; Geo. K. Holmes, " Progress of Agriculture in the United
States," United States Department of Agriculture *Yearbook*, 1899 (Washington,
1900), pp. 307–34; and Wm. H. Brewer, " History of American Agriculture,"
Tenth [1880] *Census*, III, *Agriculture* (Washington, 1883), pp. 513–21 [" Report on the Cereal Production of the United States," pp. 133–41].

[113] Named after noted Indian chiefs.

[114] *Home Missionary*, XVI, 172 (Dec., 1843).

[115] Russell, in *Journal of Agriculture*, Oct., 1856, p. 10; and Cooper, *Oak
Openings*, Chap. xxx.

cash crop [116] wheat was suited to the frontier settled by Northern folk, who sought a market for their surplus rather than the self-sufficing economic life of the backwoodsman.

To pioneers in general, scientific farming, the use of manures and other fertilizers, or even much attention to the rotation of crops, seemed to indicate a lack of appreciation of Nature's bounty. The fertile virgin soils needed no enrichment, and ever new stores of these free or cheap lands opened for single-crop exploitation. Whatever the effect upon remote posterity, for the time being the pioneer found it more profitable to draw upon the soil's fertility than to practice conservation.[117]

The rush to the wheat lands was speeded-up by tales of men who had paid for their land, its clearing and fencing, and the construction of the farmhouse, with the profits of the first year's crop.

If a pioneer from western New York bought from the government a 160-acre tract, under his pre-emption right, and improved half of it, something over a thousand dollars would be needed to cover the cost of purchase of the land, moving his family, building a log cabin (at fifty dollars), breaking, fencing, supplying farm implements, a team of horses, two cows, a well, and the supplies to sustain his family until the harvesting of his first crop. But, since squatting or the exercise of pre-emption rights was common, and because costs varied in different regions and times, and the statistics are defective and the meaning of the word "improvement" uncertain, it would be unsafe to generalize.

Some impression of the cost of pioneer farms may be obtained by a consideration of the statistics for 1850. In the North Central States, farm values per acre shaded off from the vicinity of cities toward the frontier. The outlying counties of Wisconsin, for instance, where strictly pioneer conditions prevailed, returned their farm valuation at six or eight dollars per acre, while in agricultural counties, in the southeast of the state, adjoining the shore of Lake Michigan the value per acre ran to twelve or fifteen

[116] John G. Thompson, *The Rise and Decline of the Wheat Growing Industry in Wisconsin* (University of Wisconsin *Bulletin*, No. 292; Madison, 1909).

[117] See the comments of Jos. C. G. Kennedy (Superintendent of the Census), in *Agriculture of the United States in 1860; Compiled from the Original Returns of the Eighth Census* (Washington, 1864), p. viii; and Percy W. Bidwell and John I. Falconer, *History of Agriculture in the Northern United States, 1620–1860* (Carnegie Institution of Washington, 1925), pp. 272–73.

dollars. With government land at $1.25 per acre, this would give for the interior counties something like five to seven dollars per acre for the " improvements " of the pioneer, or, say, five hundred dollars on eighty acres at the edge of cultivation. For the more settled counties the increase over the cost of that acreage of government land would be somewhere around one thousand dollars, part of which, however, was due to the increment secured by the land speculator. The ordinary pioneer could farm about forty acres without hiring additional help, leaving the remainder of his 160-acre pre-emption tract, at the minimum price of $1.25 per acre, for later development or sale.

The following table gives the data in the census of 1850 regarding the size of farms and the portion improved, in the North Central States: [118]

	Average acres per farm	Improved acres per farm
Ohio	125.0	68.5
Indiana	136.2	53.7
Illinois	158.0	66.1
Michigan	128.6	56.6
Wisconsin	147.5	51.8
Missouri	178.7	54.0
Iowa	184.8	55.7
Minnesota	183.9	32.1

Part of the pioneer's compensation for what Eastern critics thought of as the hardships of making a farm in the wilderness was that he himself was, in a sense, a land speculator. If, in fact, his work for a year or two brought-in a return for his wheat sufficient to repay the entire expenses of making his farm (as actually might be the case in good years),[119] it is easy to see how attractive the future would seem and how he would incur temporary privations for the sake of his family.

But, when the pioneer came without the ready cash, he often

[118] *Thirteenth Census*, V (Washington, 1913), *Agriculture*, p. 75.

[119] *Milwaukee Sentinel*, May 1, 1838; Thompson, *op. cit.*, p. 35, n.; Norris and Gardiner, *Illinois Annual Register*, 1847 (Chicago, 1847); [C. W. Butterfield, ed.] *Illustrated History of Rock County, Wisconsin* (Chicago, 1879), p. 337; and Gerhard, *Illinois as It Is*, pp. 293 ff. Budgets are also given in: [Baird] *View of the Valley of the Mississippi*, p. 232; in the files of the *Prairie Farmer* (e.g., Jan., 1843); Marshall, *Farmer's and Emigrant's Hand-book*, pp. 21–25; and Bidwell and Falconer, *op. cit.*, pp. 270 ff. See also *Letters of Raeder* (ed. Malmin), p. 64, citing [anon.] *Sketches of the West or the Home of the Badgers* (Milwaukee, 1847).

found himself obliged to borrow at exorbitant interest in order to pay for his land and improvements, and, as Greeley in his zeal for " land reform " put it, " live like a toad under a harrow " for years. Many such farmers lost their squatter rights or pre-emption to later comers.[120]

It was not until the forties that seed drills commenced to replace the sowing of wheat broadcast by hand, in Ohio; the cradle was still employed in harvesting the grain; but, with the removal of Cyrus H. McCormick to Chicago in 1847, the reaper came into wider use. In frontier counties the crop was still threshed by the primitive method of tramping out the grain, but by 1840 the threshing machine was making progress. The farmer was learning to use new tools and to multiply man-power by machine-power many fold, just at the time when the railroads were opening the prairies and connecting the pioneer farms with the markets of old England and New England.[121] The rising importance of the agricultural interest in the nation was evidenced by an appropriation for an agricultural report in 1839 and the attention to statistics of agriculture in the contemporary census.[122] By the closing years of the period, the repeal of the English corn laws further incited the prairie farmer to produce a surplus.

As wheat farming extended into the North Central Division, revolutionary changes occurred in the nation's production and disposition of the crop. The later thirties were years of wheat scarcity. Grain was imported from various European countries to supply the deficit, and New York prices ranged from $1.10 to $2.12 per bushel. In part this was due to the slowness of railroads in reaching the lands of western New York and the Great Lakes Basin suited to wheat cultivation, in part to the local demands of the incoming pioneers for food supplies and seed before their farms became productive, in part to deficient harvests, and in part to the fact that the forest farmer, with the soils unsuitable

[120] Hibbard, *Agriculture in Dane County, Wisconsin*, p. 196.

[121] On the significance of the development of agricultural machinery, see Bidwell and Falconer, *op. cit.*, pp. 337–38, and citations in Everett E. Edwards, *A Bibliography of the History of Agriculture in the United States* (U.S. Dept. of Agriculture *Miscellaneous Publication 84;* Washington, 1930), pp. 199–204, and Wm. Trimble, *Introductory Manual for the Study and Reading of Agrarian History* (N.D. Agricultural College; Fargo, 1917), pp. 34–36.

[122] *Ibid.*, p. 46.

for rapid wheat raising and his primitive methods, was not the producer of a considerable export surplus. Whereas in earlier times the day's pay of the common laborer was equal to the price of a bushel of wheat, by 1836 his wages lagged below this ratio.

In the forties, the prairies were opening; land pre-emption had been made permanent; railroads were in touch with the Great Lakes and the Ohio; and wheat raising had become the "rage." A great surplus was accumulating from the new wheat states and territories, and the price fell. The problem became one of finding a market for this surplus.

In 1840 the leading wheat-producing states, in order of yield, were Ohio, Pennsylvania, and New York; by 1850 they were

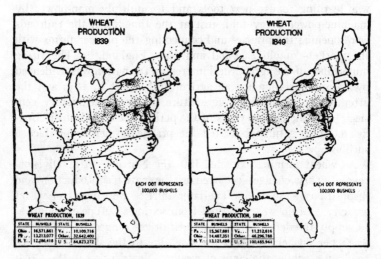

Pennsylvania, Ohio, and New York, with Virginia, Illinois, and Indiana following. But the effect of the trend to the prairies was evident in 1860, when the order was Illinois, Indiana, Wisconsin, and Ohio. Even by 1840 the North Central States produced nearly a third of the nation's wheat, and a decade later over two-fifths, while in 1860 the results of the occupation of the prairies were made evident by the fact that more than half the supply came from this section — almost three-fifths of this furnished by Illinois, Indiana, and Wisconsin.

As the maps show, there was a definite concentration of wheat regions within the section; and these areas moved year by year toward the frontier, recording, so to speak, the discovery and occupation of the oak openings and the valleys of the Fox and Rock rivers. Within these valleys, though crossed by the boundary line between Illinois and Wisconsin, lived the pioneers, largely of New England stock, who were forming the wheat kingdom.

How slight was England's realization of the significance of this movement is shown by the testimony of J. R. McCulloch, the British economist, in 1841, when he declared: " It is needless to take up the reader's time by entering into any lengthened details with respect to the corn [grain] trade of the United States. It is abundantly certain that we need not look to that quarter for any considerable supplies." [123] By 1850 the surplus wheat of the North Central States, alone, could have supplied three-fourths of England's importation, or the whole deficit of New England; and this was but the earlier phase of the movement.[124] The shipments of wheat from Chicago in 1838 were but seventy-eight bushels. In 1848, after the English famine and the abolition of the corn laws made an exceptional market abroad, and when the Illinois and Michigan Canal was completed and the railroads had partly bridged the gap between the wheat regions and the Atlantic Coast, over two million bushels were shipped from Chicago.[125]

Newspaper files, and debates in Congress, in the forties, reveal the apprehension of the wheat-raising section over the question of a foreign market for the surplus that was already evident in the wheat regions.[126] Tariff politics and foreign relations, as we shall see, reflected this apprehension.

As has been indicated in previous chapters and on the map of products, corn cultivation was widely spread in the nation. In 1840, when the first agricultural returns became available, Tennessee, Kentucky, Virginia, and Ohio (in that order) were the leading producing states; but in the census of 1850 Ohio led, followed by Kentucky, Illinois, and Indiana. In the former census year the North Central States furnished less than three-tenths of

[123] *Statements Illustrative of the Policy and Probable Consequences of the Proposed Repeal of the Existing Corn Laws* (London, 1841), p. 14.

[124] I have profited by the researches, in my Harvard seminary, by Mr. O. C. Stine, of the United States Department of Agriculture; but any errors in generalization should be attributed to me.

[125] Kennedy (compiler), *Agriculture of the United States in 1860*, p. cxlix.

[126] *Western Journal*, I, 579 ff.

the nation's corn crop; but in 1850 the proportion had approached two-fifths. The Corn Belt, south of the wheat zone, was evolving and extending westward.

Unlike wheat, corn was marketed chiefly in the form of cattle and hogs fed on this crop and sent, at first by droving and then by packing, to the South, the Northeast, and abroad. The transit of feeding grounds to which cattle were driven preparatory to finding an Eastern market, had followed the movement of population to the West. The Potomac Valley had been the resort in Revolutionary years, followed by the Scioto Valley in Ohio, where the corn-bearing levels of the Virginia Bounty Land region received cattle, for feeding, from the open ranges or small prairies of Ohio and Illinois. This locality was at the height of its operation in the middle forties. From here and from the neighboring Kentucky lands, cattle in droves of around a hundred head, making some eight or ten miles a day, were taken by a " boss " and two hands per drove over the thousand miles or so to New York City. The cattle worked havoc with the wet clay roads, which dried into " cattle billows." In New York the Bull's Head Tavern of Daniel Drew was the rendezvous.[127] By the later forties droving declined. Grass-fed cattle could soon be shipped by rail to Eastern markets in so short a time that they held their weight.

The packing industry, at first conducted in part by the pioneer farmers and raftsmen, who took their products to New Orleans, gradually concentrated in Cincinnati in the early thirties, but in the next decade Louisville and St. Louis also became important. By the close of the forties Chicago rose as a new Western center; but not until the Civil War did her packing industry pass that of Cincinnati.[128]

Hogs played an important part in the Western surplus, though the production did not increase in the North Central States with the same rapidity as did cereals. By the middle forties over a million were annually slaughtered in the section, more than two-thirds of them from the Ohio Valley. Western editors proudly

[127] On cattle droving, see: I. F. King, in *Ohio Archaeological and Historical Quarterly*, XVII, 247–53; Illinois State Historical Society *Transactions*, 1923, pp. 75–79, giving the experience of B. F. Harris, a pioneer of Illinois; Kennedy (compiler), *op. cit.*, pp. cxxx–cxxxii; and Bidwell and Falconer, *op. cit.*, pp. 177–79, 391–93.

[128] Howard C. Hill, in *Mississippi Valley Historical Review*, X, 253–73.

asserted that eight Western states, with six million people, had as many swine as Great Britain, France, Prussia, and Bavaria, with seventy-five million.[129] A large proportion of the hogs had, in the twenties, been driven through Saluda Gap to the cotton plantations. Early in the thirties this trade fell off, but the routes taken by the hog drivers tended to fall within the regions of the Whigs, who were supporters of banks. Drovers traveled through the producing regions and brought the hogs to the Ohio, whence they were driven to the plantations or butchered in cold weather and shipped down the Mississippi. This created a demand for capital and credit. The buyer of live stock generally depended on Eastern capital to pay the farmers in advance, and his employees cultivated friendship for banks and capital along the routes of their operations.[130]

The live-stock areas lay along the Ohio and Missouri valleys. The state of Ohio, with its larger population, remained first in 1850, but the neighboring states of that zone were rapidly diminishing this leadership. By that date the value of the section's live stock exceeded that of the Middle Atlantic States. In the counties near the Ohio River, oxen were the main work animals. Missouri, the starting point for the " covered-wagon " migration to the Far West, led with about as many of these animals as Michigan, Wisconsin, and Iowa, together, reported, and with not far from twice as many as Ohio (which had three times the population). Mules for the Southern market were raised in Missouri and parts of the Ohio Valley.

Nowhere did the westward march of agriculture appear more strikingly than in the transit of sheep raising from the East to this new section.[131] Between 1840 and 1850 the sheep in New England and the Middle Atlantic States, combined, fell from nearly eleven millions to well under eight millions, while those of the North Central States rose from about three and one-half millions to as many as grazed in the former two sections at the end

---

[129] [J. D. B.] *De Bow's Review*, I (1846), 476, quoting *Cincinnati Price Current*. See also Hall, *Statistics*, pp. 145–47.

[130] Compare the maps of votes with the lines of intercourse. On the demand for bank credit, see Logan Esarey, *State Banking in Indiana, 1814–1873* (Indiana University *Studies*, No. 15; Bloomington, 1912) ; and *Prairie Farmer*, IX, 305 (Oct., 1849).

[131] See the maps by Taylor, in University of Wisconsin Agricultural Experiment Station *Bulletin*, No. 16. Valuable data are in Bidwell and Falconer, *op. cit.*, pp. 406–7, 412–17, and Wright, *Wool-Growing and the Tariff*.

of the decade.   Half of the North Central sheep belonged to Ohio.
Not only was sheep raising passing to these western lands in the
period when the hard times and low prices for cereals prevailed
(in the early forties), but the interest of parts of the section in
the protective tariff on wool became an important factor in tariff
discussions during the forties.   Woolen factories increased, and
even the southern half of the section changed from the household
industries of the forest pioneer to the use of factory products.
Ready-made clothing became a feature of advertisements in
Western newspapers.

Although the section found its exportable surplus chiefly in the
products we have been considering, lumber, minerals, and furs
also demand attention.

When the prairies began to be occupied, the splendid forests of
white pine that stretched through northern Michigan, Wisconsin,
and Minnesota were hardly touched.   Indeed, the *Western Journal*, in October, 1852, published an article, sent by Chancellor
J. H. Lathrop, of the University of Wisconsin, which said:

> Scarcely ten years have elapsed, since the Alleghany pine of Western
> New York and Pennsylvania, had undisputed possession of the market,
> not only of the Ohio valley but of the Mississippi and its tributaries, above
> New Orleans; at which point it competed with the lumber of Maine
> and New Brunswick.[132]

The census of 1840 reported the value of New York's lumber
product as nearly four million dollars, while that of Michigan and
Wisconsin, together, amounted to not much over half a million.

But even in 1830 there were scattered sawmills in southern
Michigan for local supply, and in 1848 Saginaw Valley began to
ship lumber to Chicago.   In Wisconsin, mills at Green Bay and
on the upper waters of the Wisconsin River began, by the later
thirties, to raft their products to St. Louis.   The demand of the
prairie pioneers for building material grew in the forties, and,
toward the close of our period, when the Chicago and Illinois
Canal opened, Chicago was a center of supply.   The value of the
northern forests became realized, and popular sentiment tolerated
or even praised the lumbermen who took timber from the public
lands without buying them.   Officials drew a distinction between

[132] IX, 23.   See also: Hoffman, *Winter in the West*, I, 77; G. W. Hotch-
kiss, *Lumber and Forest Industry of the Northwest;* and Barrows, *Geography
of the Middle Illinois Valley*, p. 94 (with citations).

trespass on these lands before and after survey. The pioneer farmer's conception of his rights in the public lands passed over to the lumberman.

The mineral resources of the section added to its surplus. The Fever River lead region of northwestern Illinois, southwestern Wisconsin, and the adjacent area of Iowa, together with the Missouri fields south of St. Louis, had long been used by Indians and French traders,[133] and by 1830 the Galena district had become an outlying island of settlement of the South Central stock. At first the lead was shipped to St. Louis and New Orleans. The receipts at the latter point grew from 295,000 pigs (of seventy pounds) in 1836 to 785,000 in 1846. The census of 1840 attributed to the section about a million dollars invested in the production of lead, of which the largest part was in Wisconsin. The Galena district, in 1843, shipped around a million dollars' worth of the product.

The obstructions to navigation on the Mississippi led to demands for canals and railroads from this lead region to the Great Lakes and an Eastern market. Toward the end of the forties, overland trade to Milwaukee had developed, and the trade down the Mississippi fell by even a greater percentage than the decline due to the miners' rush to the California gold fields, the exhaustion of the shallow lead diggings, and the loss of the protective tariff in 1846.

The projects for railroads, in these years, were strongly affected by the magnet of the lead trade. The Upper Mississippi Valley, as well as the Great Lakes Basin, was turning to the North Atlantic outlet. The federal government, which had used the leasing system in the lead lands, decided, by acts passed in 1847 and in 1850, to sell its mineral lands outright, and thus abandoned its public-ownership policy in relation to these lands, just before the opening of the California gold fields[134] and when the treas-

---

[133] See R. G. Thwaites, in *Wisconsin Historical Collections*, XIII, 271–92. There is a detailed map of the various lead mines east of the Mississippi River in 1829, in the same series, XI, facing p. 400. Later developments in this region (in the forties) are discussed by: O. G. Libby, *ibid.*, XIII, 293–334; John MacGregor, *The Progress of America, from the Discovery by Columbus to . . . 1846* (London, 1847), II, 817; Walter R. Ingalls, *Lead and Zinc in the United States* (New York, 1908); and Isaac Lippincott, " Industrial Influence of Lead in Missouri," *Journal of Political Economy*, XX, 695–715.

[134] See also the act of 1829 for selling the reserved Missouri lead lands, and President Polk's message, December 2, 1845 (Jas. D. Richardson [compiler],

ury of iron deposits in the North Central States was becoming known.

By 1850 the census reported the value of pig-iron production for the North Central States at about a million and three-quarters dollars, the greater part of which came from Ohio, whose rank in the nation was next to that of Pennsylvania in this product. Her mines lay east of the Scioto. The ores of Missouri were also coming into use,[135] and even in northern Michigan, by 1850, iron mines were attracting notice.[136]

But it was the copper country of Michigan in which adventurers and speculators were feverishly interested.[137] By 1843 a company of speculators (some of them Boston capitalists) brought Cornish miners from the lead district to Eagle Harbor to exploit the copper fields. Traveling in 1845, William W. Greenough, of Boston, tells in his journal[138] how, in Pontiac, Michigan, he found the neighborhood excited by the copper fever. The Boston company, with fifty dollars per share paid in, was believed to be about to declare a dividend of at least a thousand dollars; but he was presented with shares of a mining company out of pity for his ignorance. Horace Greeley, in the *Tribune*,[139] described a trip to Eagle Harbor, where he visited ten mining companies. The *Lake Superior News*, the organ of the copper district, reported that, up to the fall of 1847, over ten million pounds of ores and metals had been raised there and 1,693,000 pounds had been shipped.[140]

Thus, not only the pioneer farmer was drawn to the new opportunities opening in the North Central section, but also speculative Eastern capital for investment in its mines, its banks, and its railroads.

Messages and Papers of the Presidents, 1789–1897, IV [Washington, 1897], 410), pointing out that the cost of administering the leasing system greatly exceeded the actual rent received. On the loss to the Treasury from the failure to retain royalties on the mining of iron ore, see Chas. R. Van Hise, *The Conservation of Natural Resources in the United States* (New York, 1910), p. 98.

[135] *Western Journal*, I, 36–39.

[136] *Report of Israel D. Andrews . . . on the Trade and Commerce of the British North American Colonies, and upon the Trade of the Great Lakes and Rivers (House Executive Document 136, 32d Cong., 2d Sess.*; Washington, 1853), p. 237, and Peter White, *Mining Industry of Northern Michigan*.

[137] L. L. Barbour, " Peter White as Man and as Citizen, 1830–1908," *Michigan Pioneer and Historical Collections*, XXXVII, 620–39, and MacGregor, *op. cit.*, II, 793. [138] Massachusetts Historical Society *Proceedings*, XLIV, 352.

[139] July 10, 1847. [140] *Western Journal,* I, 101.

In the thirties the coal fields of the section were also beginning to be mined, chiefly in eastern Ohio, but also in Indiana and Illinois. The old-time fur trade continued to add to the section's surplus. By 1840 nearly a million dollars' worth of this item came to these states.

Responding to the natural resources we have been describing, the development of basins of surplus in the section became important in shaping the regional economic interests, in determining the lines of transportation routes, and in affecting the distribution of political-party preponderance. The Pittsburgh, Wheeling, and Buffalo gateways to the section developed manufactures; the Western Reserve, of Ohio, tributary to Cleveland, became a region of mixed farming; eastern Ohio combined mining and agriculture; the Scioto Valley, abounding in live stock, was in some ways an outlying peninsula of the Kentucky blue-grass basin about Lexington; the Miami country, finding its metropolis in Cincinnati, was a center of swine raising, and that city shared manufacturing development with those about the upper waters of the Ohio River; Indianapolis was the nucleus for the growing agricultural interests of central Indiana; the Wabash Valley was an agricultural region where pioneer conditions were passing; southern Illinois (" Egypt," in common parlance) and parts of southern Indiana, together with the driftless southeastern counties of Ohio, had common characteristics based on the occupation of the hardwood lands by Southern folk; the northern tributaries of the Illinois River, particularly the Fox, together with the Rock River, made the lines of attack into the prairie lands for Illinois and Wisconsin pioneers of Northeastern origin, as has been mentioned. These prairie lands, together with the oak openings of Michigan, made the wheat zone. Chicago and Milwaukee were, in the forties, rivals for the outlet of the prairie surplus. The Fever River lead region, with Galena as its chief town, was another center of attraction for capital and transportation. St. Louis, across the Mississippi, drew its resources from the Missouri Valley, from the mining counties, from the Rocky Mountain fur trade, and from the Santa Fe trade, bringing back the Mexican dollars that furnished so considerable a part of the nation's specie. It was an economic dependency of New Orleans while the Mississippi River commerce remained ascendant. When the Mississippi yielded to the east-and-west rail and canal routes,

St. Louis lost much of its sectional importance to Chicago, but at the same time found new interests in the projected railroads to the Far West. As we have seen, the pine forests of the northern zone of the section were becoming important as the region of lumber supplies for the prairies, the furs from the forested areas continued to be a regional interest, and the copper and iron mines of northern Michigan opened another potential industrial district.

The interdependence of these various surplus basins demanded transportation connections, which shaped the location of canals and the railroad net.

Meantime, the section had passed through an era of hard times. The Crisis of 1837 did not immediately affect the North Central States so disastrously as it did the East. But in the early forties and, indeed, down to about 1847–48, the prices of agricultural products fell until they hardly paid for production. In Warren County, Illinois, in 1843, for example, wheat brought only 27 cents a bushel in cash or 33 cents in trade; corn, 8 cents a bushel.[141] Marketing by road one hundred miles cut the return for wheat one-half. In Illinois, horses which brought $100 each in 1836 fell in price to $60 in 1843; beef dropped from $6 to $3 per hundredweight; pork, from $22 a barrel to $8; and flour, from $11 a barrel to $3.50.[142] In 1836 the price of hogs at Cincinnati was around $6 per hundredweight; by 1842–43 it had fallen to less than $2, and, except in 1846, it did not reach half the figure for 1836 until a decade later.[143]

The ending of the local market furnished by newcomers, the lag in providing transportation facilities, and, for most of the period, the operation of English tariff laws, aggravated the depression. But by 1850 the new gold of California, the opening of the English market, and the coming of railroads, and of steamers on the Great Lakes, wrought a change and helped to bring this era of low prices to a close.

---

[141] *Prairie Farmer*, Feb., 1843. The *Southport American*, July 6, 1843, reported Iowa wheat as selling " last fall " as low as 25 cents. See also the table of prices in McLean County, Illinois, in Illinois State Historical Library *Publications*, No. 9, p. 537. The *Manchester* [England] *Guardian* (Dec. 21, 1842) reports a statement from Vermilion County, Illinois, that wheat would not bring 25 cents, cash, per bushel.

[142] J. W. Putnam, " An Economic History of the Illinois and Michigan Canal," *Journal of Political Economy*, XVII, 292, n. 85, citing Davis and Swift's *Report of the Illinois and Michigan Canal*, 1844; and *Home Missionary*, XVII, 55 (July, 1844).   [143] *Western Journal*, I, 279.

Meanwhile, the depression exhibited its influence, in part, in the rush to Texas from the cotton states of the Southwest and to Oregon from the prairies of the North Central Division. Discouragement, as well as the spirit of adventurous youth and the instinct for pioneering, was at work in these years. The discontent of the suffering farmers of the West over the corn laws of England (while they remained in effect) made the section less amenable to compromise with that nation when the Oregon question arose, and more ready to support the Mexican War.[144] The depression increased the demand for transportation facilities, and helps to explain the spread of Locofoco doctrines, and especially antibank legislation, in the period.[145]

The rise of a great surplus in the North Central States had important results in interstate and intersectional, as well as in foreign, commerce. It furnished arguments, also, for a more liberal Eastern policy in the matter of opening the public lands to settlers. Walker put the case thus in the Senate in 1836:

The current of emigration from one part of the Union to the other, from the old to the new States, rolls back a golden tide of trade and business. The old States now supply nearly all the wants of the farmers of the valley of the West, and hence its prosperity wonderfully promotes the welfare of the older States of the Union. The poor emigrant from the old States, who establishes a farm in the West, soon contributes more to the wealth and commerce of the State he left than if he had remained there in dependent poverty.[146]

The value of the surplus products of the West reaching New Orleans in 1830 is estimated at $26,000,000, and two decades later at over $108,000,000. But by 1846 Buffalo was receiving more grain and flour from the interior than New Orleans. Of course, these estimates do not cover an extensive regional interchange within the interior itself. In his report as Secretary of the Treasury, Walker estimated the total interstate commerce of the United States in 1846 at $500,000,000 at least, and foreign commerce, both exports and imports, at only $305,000,000.[147]

---

[144] E.g., see Edward Everett, " Narrative of Military Experiences " (Illinois State Historical Library *Publications*, X, 181 ff.), p. 194. Cf. Nashville broadside, 1836, in Jackson MSS, Library of Congress.

[145] See pp. 124–27, *ante*.

[146] *American State Papers, Public Lands*, VIII, 881–82. Cf. *Hunt's Merchants' Magazine*, III, 295. See Greeley's comments, p. 61, *ante*.

[147] *Finance Report*, 1847–48, and *Andrews Report*, pp. 687–88. See also

By 1850 the tonnage of the Mississippi and its tributaries had reached 275,000, and the estimated value of the cargoes was over $100,000,000. Colonel J. J. Abert estimated the value of this river trade in 1846 at over $183,000,000, net, after eliminating duplications arising from the fact that the imports of one place were the exports of another.

Transportation at the beginning of the years of this survey of the North Central section included a large use of highways. Although the turnpike era was coming to an end in the thirties, construction and improvement of the roads that led to the principal routes of travel still received legislative appropriations; " plank road " corporations [148] were chartered, with tollgate privileges; and stagecoaches [149] and wagon freight companies continued to operate. By 1844 Ohio possessed over eight hundred miles of macadamized roads.[150] The Old National Road, or Cumberland Road, designed to connect the Potomac with St. Louis, was still under construction through Columbus, Ohio, Indianapolis, Indiana, and Vandalia, Illinois, when other transportation agencies replaced it in importance.[151]

Canals and railroads were coming to constitute the main arteries of transportation for the section and thus to give cheaper and more efficient connections between the basins of surplus production and between the section and the East. But it was not until toward the close of the forties that the Mississippi surrendered its pre-eminence as an outlet for the surplus produce of the North Central States.[152]

Steamboats had reached the site of St. Paul before 1830. Al-

Isaac Lippincott, *Internal Trade of the United States, 1700–1860* (Washington University *Studies*, IV, Pt. II, No. 1, pp. 63–150; St. Louis, Oct., 1916), and his citations. *Hunt's Merchants' Magazine, Niles' Register, De Bow's Review*, and the *Western Monthly Magazine* (Cincinnati), have a wealth of material, and the debates in Congress at various periods are helpful. The early estimates vary.

[148] *Western Journal*, IV, 71–76, 91–98.

[149] Dickens' *American Notes* gives a graphic description of stagecoach travel in Ohio in 1842. According to L. B. Swan, *Journal of a Trip to Michigan in 1841* (Rochester, N.Y., 1904), the stagecoach driver picked his own route through Michigan woods.

[150] *Hunt's Merchants' Magazine*, XI, 226.

[151] The last appropriation was in 1838. See: A. B. Hulbert, *The Cumberland Road* (*Historic Highways of America*, X; Cleveland, 1904), Chap. II, and map, p. 79; J. S. Young, *A Political and Constitutional Study of the Cumberland Road* (Chicago, 1902); and J. B. Searight, *The Old Pike* (Uniontown, Pa., 1894).

[152] See pp. 222–23, *ante,* for the river trade.

though the traffic increased by the middle forties, only about one hundred steamers arrived there in the year 1850. By the early thirties steamboats up the Missouri had reached the mouth of the Yellowstone, and commerce on the Missouri became important. Here, as on the Great Lakes, it was the American Fur Company that developed navigation.

The basins of surplus production, which have already been described, not only resulted in the development of commerce by river, but led to the increase of shipping on the Great Lakes, the digging of canals, and the building of railroads.

Even around a century before the beginning of our period, vessels had been built on Lake Superior to transport the furs and copper of that region. Apparently, the first steamer on Lake Superior arrived at Copper Harbor in 1845. On Lake Michigan the first steamer was run in the late twenties, and by 1832 Chicago was visited by steamer. After the Black Hawk War the use of steam on Lake Michigan, to transport the newly arriving pioneers, increased. Meantime, the shipping and steamboat traffic on Lake Erie had steadily increased, with the result of pressure for the deepening of harbors and the erection of lighthouses. By 1833 a Steamboat Association, or "pool," of eleven boats had been formed, and by 1840 numbered nearly fifty steamers. This combination, which met with the opposition and rivalry of the railroads, was also violently objected to by the pioneers. It is an interesting example of how early the apprehension of the West was aroused toward combination.

It was estimated that, by 1829, the tonnage on the Great Lakes amounted to less than 6,000; by 1850, to over 184,000. In 1841 the value of the lake trade by way of the Erie Canal was put at $65,000,000; in 1851, at $300,000,000. Thus was reflected the increasing influence of settlement and the grain trade.[153]

153 On the lake trade see: Jas. L. Barton, *Lake Commerce: Letter to the Hon. Robert M'Clelland . . . in Relation to the Value and Importance of the Commerce of the Great Western Lakes* (Buffalo, 1846); S. G. Brock, *The Commerce of the Great Lakes,* . . . (in *House Executive Document 6*, Pt. II, 52d Cong., 1st Sess.; Washington, 1892); *Andrews Report;* J. D. B. De Bow, *The Industrial Resources, etc., of the Southern and Western States,* I (New Orleans, 1852), 447 ff.; G. R. Turnell, *Statistics of Lake Commerce* (Washington, 1898); E. R. Johnson [and others], *History of Domestic and Foreign Commerce of the United States* (Carnegie Institution of Washington, 1915), I, 233; Burton, *Early Navigation of the Great Lakes;* Wm. Hodge, *Papers concerning Early Navigation on the Great Lakes: I. Recollections of Capt. David Wilkeson;*

A new inland sea had been created, with an outlet by way of the Erie Canal to the Atlantic Coast. The furs, minerals, and farm products of the northern half of the Great Lakes Basin were reaching the East by that route.

Even more noticeable was the effect of the new canal building, which must now engage our attention. Naturally, the desire was to connect the Great Lakes with the Ohio and with the Mississippi.

Ohio canals had been discussed even before the Erie Canal was completed,[154] but the success of that enterprise by the state of New York gave a great impetus to the movement. Not until the rivalry of the railroad checked canal building did the emphasis upon water transportation decline. Aided by appropriations of land from the federal government, Ohio undertook a canal system under the act of 1825, and by 1832 the Ohio and Erie was opened from Portsmouth to Cleveland, while the canal connecting Cincinnati with the Miami country, Maumee, and Toledo was completed to Defiance by 1840 and was brought into touch with the Wabash and Erie by 1845. Canada had opened the Welland Canal by 1833, and connections had been made by canal with the Pennsylvania system by 1840. The result was quickly felt in increasing urban development and wheat raising in Ohio, and — of quite as much importance — in the gradual transfer of the larger share of the internal commerce from New Orleans, by way of the Ohio and the Mississippi, to the Eastern outlet. Even by the middle forties, something like twelve times as much wheat went to Cleveland as to Portsmouth on the Ohio.[155] In Ohio, as in other states, the rivalry between the various minor canals and roads interfered with the rational development of the canal system, and the Panic of 1837 also checked progress.[156]

II. The Pioneer Lake Erie Steamboats, Walk-in-the-Water and Superior (Buffalo, 1883); Jas. D. Butler, " Early Shipping on Lake Superior," Wisconsin Historical Society *Proceedings*, 1894 (Madison, 1895), pp. 85–96; Geo. Ware Stephens, in Washington University *Studies*, X, Humanistic Ser., No. 2, pp. 285–90; and the contemporaneous files of *Hunt's Merchants' Magazine*, especially Vol. VI. See the résumé in Edward Channing, *A History of the United States*, V (New York, 1921), 23.

[154] G. W. Dial, in *Ohio Archaeological and Historical Publications*, XIII, 460–82.

[155] Johnson [and others], *op. cit.*, I, 230–31; Kennedy (compiler), *Agriculture of the United States in 1860*, pp. cxlviii, clvi; *Andrews Report;* and De Bow, *op. cit.*, III (New Orleans, 1853), 506.

[156] On canals see: Michel Chevalier, *Histoire et description des voies de communication aux États-Unis, . . .* (Paris, 1840–41); S. A. Mitchell, *Compendium*

In Indiana the Wabash and Erie Canal,[157] long under discussion, opened another important route to the Great Lakes. Indeed, in a letter of 1818, Governor De Witt Clinton, the promoter of the Erie Canal, had declared: " I have found the way to get into Lake Erie and you have shown me how to get out of it. . . . You have extended my project six hundred miles." Inasmuch as the Wabash and Maumee area was then regarded as the grain belt of the Northwest, this canal was peculiarly important and led to the cheapening of commodities and to the rapid increase of settlement along the canal. Although Ohio's part of the Wabash and Erie Canal was not completed until nearly the middle of the forties, Indiana's portion had been opened in 1835. Just before the Crisis of 1837, the state of Indiana had undertaken a comprehensive system of internal improvements designed to satisfy the rival localities, but the Wabash route was the most important.

The Illinois and Michigan Canal, connecting the waters of the Mississippi and Lake Michigan, collapsed following the Panic of 1837, immediately after the frenzy of expenditures for internal improvements by the state in 1836. Eastern investors, like Abbott Lawrence, sent representatives, including John Davis, of Massachusetts (twice governor of his state, and United States Senator for two periods, in the course of the years between 1834 and 1853), whose report led to refinancing of the company in 1845. The construction of the canal resulted in an increase of population and products, as elsewhere, and the growth of Chicago to the disadvantage of St. Louis.[158]

After the Crisis of 1837, the railroads of the section [159] began to overtake, and before the end of the fifties practically to supplant, the canal system.

of the Internal Improvements of the United States (Philadelphia, 1835); H. S. Tanner, Description of the Canals and Railroads of the United States, . . . (New York, 1840); Andrews Report; " Report on the Canals of the United States," Tenth Census, IV, Transportation (Washington, 1883), pp. 725–64; Dial, op. cit.; A. B. Hulbert, The Great American Canals (Cleveland, 1904), II (Historic Highways of America, XIV); Johnson [and others], op. cit., I, 227–28; and various volumes of Hunt's Merchants' Magazine, passim.

[157] E. J. Benton, The Wabash Trade Route in the Development of the Old Northwest (Johns Hopkins University Studies in Historical and Political Science, Ser. XXI, Nos. 1–2; Baltimore, 1903).

[158] Putnam, in Journal of Political Economy, XVII, 281–93, 413–23.

[159] E.g., see Hunt's Merchants' Magazine, X, 542, 549, 552, and American State Papers, Public Lands, VIII, 593.

Capital accumulated from the oriental operations of Eastern merchants now began to be applied to the building of railroads in this new West.[160] By the end of 1850, railroads extended from Cincinnati to Sandusky, connecting the Ohio and Lake Erie, and from Detroit to Michigan City, near the southern extremity of Lake Michigan. At the end of the period, railroads were pushing to the west from Milwaukee and Chicago. Central Indiana had been reached from the Ohio, and Springfield and Meredosia, in Illinois, had been joined by an isolated line. It was not until 1852 that Chicago was brought into railroad contact with the Michigan lines, and not until the middle of the next decade that the Mississippi River was connected, at various points, with the lines that were extending from the Great Lakes.[161]

As has been seen in previous chapters, the existence of these railroads brought the North Atlantic sections into contact with the North Central. The financing of the intersectional roads is illustrated by a statement, in 1842, that an Iowa man had

expressed entire confidence, (based upon letters from some of the leading Boston Capitalists,) that if a liberal charter should be granted by the Legislature, a large proportion of the capital necessary to construct the road, would be at once subscribed in Boston.[162]

The effect of these roads in tying together the North Atlantic and the North Central sections can hardly be overestimated, in view of the facts that trade was diverted toward the Northeast from the Ohio and the Mississippi and that Eastern capital was not only available in the North Central States but that it was even seeking those new opportunities for investment.

The convention (with well over two thousand delegates in attendance) that met in Chicago in 1847, partly for the purpose of counteracting the influence of the Memphis convention of 1845, was a Northern indication of rivalry for the control of the section.[163] While Chicago and Milwaukee were competitors with each other and with St. Louis for ascendancy over the western

[160] See, e.g., *Letters and Recollections of John Murray Forbes*, ed. Sarah F. Hughes (Boston, 1899), and H. G. Pearson, *An American Railroad Builder: John Murray Forbes* (New York, 1911).

[161] See Frederic L. Paxson, "The Railroads of the 'Old Northwest' before the Civil War," Wisconsin Academy of Sciences, Arts, and Letters *Transactions*, XVII, 243–74; and map in *Western Journal*, II, facing p. 1.

[162] *Milwaukee Sentinel*, Jan. 22, 1842.

[163] On this convention, see *Wisconsin Historical Collections*, XIII, 301 (Libby), and XIV, 246 (B. H. Meyer). Also see, on the Pacific Railway Con-

parts of the area, the section as a whole began to realize its possibilities in the field of communication. Already, the agitation for a railroad to the Pacific Ocean had brought the new Northwest into that rivalry with the new Southwest which became so important in the fifties.[164]

It is possible, however, to overstress the railroad as the colonizer of the North Central section. When one compares the increases in population in the trans-Allegheny states and territories with those of the East, it is seen that the gains of the West almost equaled those of the East in the decade before the coming of railroads in the East; and by 1840, before the railroads reached the Great Lakes or the Ohio River, the increase of the West was nearly twice that of the East. The railroads were attracted toward the West by the natural resources and the rapid settlement of the section; and, in turn, the railroad net when established increased the rapidity of gain in population of the North Central States.[165]

By the middle forties the receipts of flour and wheat at Buffalo exceeded those at New Orleans; and a few years later the larger part of the groceries for the use of the interior came by river to Cincinnati, and thence to the Great Lakes Basin. Livestock products still tended down the Mississippi. The grain trade was drawing bankers, merchants, and the builders of lake fleets and railroads, to the new opportunities furnished by the Upper Mississippi Valley.[166]

---

vention at St. Louis (Oct. 15, 1849), *Western Journal*, III, 71–75 (consulting Vol. II as well).

[164] L. H. Haney, *A Congressional History of Railways in the United States to 1850* (University of Wisconsin *Bulletin*, Economics and Political Science Ser., III, No. 2; Madison, 1908), pp. 256–58; *idem*, *A Congressional History of Railways in the United States, 1850–1887 (ibid.*, VI, No. 1; Madison, 1910), Chap. VI; M. F. Maury, " A Rail Road from the Atlantic to the Pacific," *Western Journal*, I, 353–63; St. Geo. L. Sioussat, " Memphis as a Gateway to the West," *Tennessee Historical Magazine*, III, 1–27, 77–114 (Mar., June, 1917); and R. S. Cotterill, " Southern Railroads and Western Trade, 1840–1850," *Mississippi Valley Historical Review*, III, 427–41. The Huntington Library contains one of the few known copies of [Geo. Wilkes] *Memorial for a National Rail-Road, from the Missouri River to the Pacific Ocean* [n.p., n.d. (1846?)].

[165] Cf. Channing, *United States*, V, 40, for a different view.

On the development of the railroad net, see, besides the references cited in the discussion of canals: B. H. Meyer [ed.], *History of Transportation in the United States before 1860* (Carnegie Institution of Washington, 1917); Johnson [and others], *Domestic and Foreign Commerce; Poor's Manual of Railroads of the United States*, 1881; and the histories of the various railroad systems.

[166] On details of the internal commerce and the division between North

Around forty million dollars in exports from the Great Lakes Basin, and something over thirty million from Cincinnati, seem to have left that part of the section east of the Mississippi River by 1851. The future of the grain trade, which soon became one of the " marvels of modern commercial history," belonged to the North Central States. Following the pioneer farmer came the merchant, lake and ocean fleets, canals, railroads, and a commercial system. A new factor had been introduced not only in our domestic but in our foreign relations.[167]

The development of the canal and railroad system of course diminished freight rates. It has been estimated that, prior to these transportation agencies, to move a ton of corn 170 miles by ordinary road extinguished its value, and, likewise, to move a ton of wheat 330 miles; the price of wheat was so reduced by the cost of transportation that it hardly paid to market it more than 150 miles by road. The coming of the railroad, however, soon lowered these charges and increased the interest in agricultural production.[168]

The wages of labor in this new country were affected by the fact that, in spite of family industry, the supply was dependent to some extent on the men who were temporarily engaged as common laborers or mechanics but who looked forward to the ownership of a farm. A St. Louis magazine [169] estimated, in 1848, that the money price of mechanical labor was less in the healthful and settled sections of the West than in New England. Ordinary labor was not far from fifty cents a day and keep, which was usually reckoned at around two dollars a week. Of course skilled labor brought a somewhat higher wage, especially in the rising cities. It was a common belief that the laborer could save

and South of the Mississippi Valley trade, see: *Andrews Report*, p. 56; Jas. L. Barton, *Commerce of the Lakes* (Buffalo, 1847); Hall, *Statistics;* De Bow, *Industrial Resources;* J. W. Monette, " The Progress of Navigation and Commerce on the Waters of the Mississippi River and the Great Lakes, A.D. 1700 to 1846," Mississippi Historical Society *Publications*, VII, 479–523; *Hunt's Merchants' Magazine; Niles' Register;* and Isaac Lippincott, *Economic Development of the United States* (New York, 1921), and *Internal Trade.*

[167] Kennedy (compiler), *Agriculture of the United States in 1860*, pp. cxxxv ff.

[168] John Gregory, *Industrial Resources of Wisconsin* (Chicago, 1853), p. 236; *Hunt's Merchants' Magazine*, VIII, 447–58; *Western Journal*, II, 59 (quoting freight rates in 1849); and *New York Tribune*, Mar. 25, 1847 (for the relative cost of transportation by different routes).

[169] *Western Journal*, I, 177.

in one or two years a sum sufficient to buy a farm. The price of labor seems to have been regulated largely by custom, but varied in different localities and years. The existence of free lands in the West had an effect upon the wages of labor in the East.[170]

The manufactures of the section were rising, particularly as there was an element of protection in the distance of the newly arriving pioneers from the Eastern industrial areas. Moreover, the tendency of manufacture to seek the source of raw materials was clearly in evidence. In this new section, even more rapidly than in the outlying regions of the Northeast, household industries declined, and the farmer found it possible to purchase more profitably by the use of his crop.[171] Of course Cincinnati and St. Louis were prominent centers of industry, and on the edge of the new West, at Pittsburgh and Buffalo, manufactured supplies reached the new states. Ship- and steamboat-building were important at Cincinnati and Pittsburgh. As these centers of industry developed, the prices of adjacent lands advanced and the demand for a home market and protection by tariff was strengthened.

Turning to consider the banking and currency of the North Central States, we find that the section depended largely on the Bank of the United States until its fall.[172] In 1828 no local bank operated in Indiana, Illinois, or Missouri.[173] It is not surprising, therefore, that, even in a section chiefly devoted to Andrew Jackson, the Senators voted generally in favor of the recharter of the National Bank. When, following the refusal to recharter, the state banks increased, they soon came under the control of the

[170] *Ibid.;* Mathew Carey, *Essays on the Public Charities of Philadelphia,* . . . (Philadelphia, 1829), as quoted by Gustavus Myers, *History of the Great American Fortunes,* I (Chicago, 1909), 93–94; Archibald Prentice, *A Tour in the United States* (London, 1848), p. 50; Mooney, *Nine Years in America,* p. 22; *Report* of the Commissioner of Patents [Agricultural Commissioner], 1848; Peck, *New Guide,* Chap. IV; [Baird] *View of the Valley of the Mississippi,* p. 232; and *Aldrich Report* (*Senate Document 3074,* 52d Cong., 2d Sess.).

[171] See Victor S. Clark, *History of Manufactures in the United States* (New York, 1929), III, 398, and Isaac Lippincott, *A History of Manufactures in the Ohio Valley to the Year 1860* (New York, 1914).

[172] Ralph C. H. Catterall, *The Second Bank of the United States* (Chicago, 1903), Chap. VII, *passim.*

[173] Wm. M. Gouge, *A Short History of Paper-Money and Banking in the United States. . . . To Which Is Prefixed an Inquiry into the Principles of the System,* . . . (Philadelphia, 1833), p. 36.

Whigs, followed by opposition in the North Central States to banks of all sorts.

There are two distinct phases in the bank history of the section in our period: first, the years between the fall of the United States Bank and the Crisis of 1837 were a time of " wildcat " banking (for which Michigan was notorious), marked by a great increase of state banks, with enlarged circulation but inadequate specie facilities; second, an antibanking movement followed in most of the states.[174]

Of all the banks in the section, the state bank of Indiana has a peculiar interest, both because of its relative soundness and because it furnished precedents for the national banking system and for the regional feature of the present system of Federal Reserve banks. The state favored the United States Bank and its own banking institution, as well as a high tariff and internal improvements, at the same time that it supported Jackson. By 1837 Indiana had the largest amount of circulation and of specie, proportionate to its capital, of any state in the Union. Dealing with the Ohio- and Mississippi-river commerce and with the overland droving, its management was of special interest to the men of means in the state.

In the years between the extension of state banks, following

---

[174] For details see: C. C. Huntington, *A History of Banking and Currency in Ohio before the Civil War* (*Ohio Archaeological and Historical Publications*, XXIV, 235–539); A. B. Coover, " Ohio Banking Institutions, 1803 to 1866," *ibid.*, XXI, 296–320; Esarey, *State Banking in Indiana;* Hugh McCulloch, *Men and Measures of Half a Century: Sketches and Comments* (New York, 1888), pp. 56–60, 113–22; letter (in Woodman MSS, Wisconsin Historical Society) written from northern Illinois, Oct. 5, 1841; G. W. Dowrie, *The Development of Banking in Illinois, 1817–1863* (University of Illinois *Studies in the Social Sciences*, II, No. 4; Urbana, 1913); C. M. Thompson, *A Study of the Administration of Thomas Ford, Governor of Illinois, 1842–46* (*Illinois Historical Collections*, VIII, 29–118); Breckinridge Jones, " One Hundred Years of Banking in Missouri, 1820–1920," *Missouri Historical Review*, XV, 345–92; the articles on Missouri banking in *Western Journal*, XV; T. M. Cooley, *State Banks of Issue in Michigan* (Michigan Political Science Association *Publications*, I, 4); Alpheus Felch, " Early Banks and Banking in Michigan," *Michigan Pioneer Collections*, II, 111–24 (reprinted in *Senate Executive Document 38*, Pt. I [pp. 72–83], 52d Cong., 2d Sess.); W. W. Wight, " Early Legislation concerning Wisconsin Banks," Wisconsin Historical Society *Proceedings*, 1895 (Madison, 1896), pp. 145–61; F. D. Merritt, *The Early History of Banking in Iowa* (State University of Iowa *Bulletin*, N.S., No. 15; Iowa City, 1900); and S. A. Patchin, " The Development of Banking in Minnesota," *Minnesota History Bulletin*, II, 111–68. On state banking in general in this period, see the references in previous chapters (pp. 64, 106–8, 227–30).

the refusal to recharter the United States Bank, and the close of our period, there had occurred a distrust of all banks, at the same time that the need of banking facilities was continuing.

State borrowing in this section, as compared with the South Central States, was rather for internal improvements than for state banks. The success of the English canals and of the Erie Canal, followed by the optimism with regard to the profits of railroads as state enterprises, led several of the states of the section to extensive indebtedness to the East and, indirectly, to English capitalists. It has been estimated that nearly $300,-000,000 of foreign capital was lent to the United States as a whole between 1815 and 1840.[175] The indebtedness of Ohio, beginning at an earlier time, and that of Indiana and Illinois, had risen to absurd heights in the period of expansion prior to the Crisis of 1837. By 1842 Ohio had $10,924,000 of indebtedness for public and internal improvements; by the same date, Indiana had $11,751,000, Illinois $10,371,000, and Michigan $5,420,000.[176]

Illustrative of the rage for internal improvements, at this time, is the act of Illinois, February 27, 1837, for an expenditure of about $10,250,000 on a state system of turnpikes, railroads, and canals gridironing the state, and for the distribution of money to counties where no internal improvements were provided. In a state sparsely settled by pioneers, this was obvious evidence of overconfidence. Some of the Eastern banking companies which contracted to lend money to these new Western states failed even before the bonds were received.[177]

The Crisis of 1837 temporarily put a stop to canal and railroad development in the North Central States and made their financial problems serious. The large interest of English capitalists in this matter of indebtedness led to proposals of federal assumption of state debts or the use of the public lands as a fund for guaranteeing them. The correspondence of Webster and the Baring Brothers casts light upon the close interest, in these Western states, of the American statesman and the European capitalist.[178]

[175] G. S. Callender, " The Early Transportation and Banking Enterprises of the States in Relation to the Growth of Corporations," *Quarterly Journal of Economics*, XVII, 38.

[176] Henry C. Adams, *Public Debts* (New York, 1887), p. 301.

[177] E.g., see McMaster, *United States*, VII (New York, 1919), 24–25.

[178] See p. 68, *ante*, and pp. 476–77, *post*.

As a result of these financial difficulties, a movement in North Central states for repudiation of state debts met with much support. Michigan defaulted its interest in 1842, and Indiana and Illinois were in arrears in their payments. In Ohio, Indiana, and Illinois, the southern counties favored repudiation, and the areas of descendants of New England stock led the opposition.[179]

The failure of local banks in the years immediately following the Crisis of 1837, together with the antagonism to Eastern and English capitalists, made the North Central States a friendly field for the Locofoco movement against all banks and the credit system.[180] Perhaps the most enduring effect of Locofocoism is to be found rather in this section settled from the North Atlantic states than in the parent sections. The inflow of Democratic settlers from New England and the Middle Atlantic States, together with the historic attitude of the Jacksonian Democrats who had entered the section from the South, strengthened the hard-money and antibanking movement represented by Jackson and Van Buren. The importance of this was emphasized by the later attitude of the section toward what it called " special privilege," corporations in general, and banks in particular. Antimonopoly parties, Grangers, Populists, and Progressives were easily grown in this historical soil. Between 1842 and 1848, there were practically no banks in Illinois, and likewise between 1843 and 1852 in Wisconsin, and between 1846 and 1857 in Iowa. In 1843 Missouri forbade banks, except the state bank, to make or use paper money. In the constitutional conventions that were held in several of these states toward the close of our period, this subject of antibanking was one of the most violently debated.

For instance, in the Constitutional Convention of 1850–51 in Ohio, limitations were imposed on the power of taxation, the contracting of debts for internal improvements was forbidden, and, with certain stipulated exceptions, the incurring of state indebtedness was prohibited. While the formation of corporations under general laws was permitted, the power to alter or appeal such laws was conferred on the legislature; and the incorporation of banks was to be subject to a popular referendum.[181]

---

[179] On the general subject, see W. A. Scott, *The Repudiation of State Debts* (New York, 1893), and McMaster, *op. cit.*, pp. 22–25, 28–34.

[180] See Chapter iv, *ante,* pp. 124–26.

[181] I. F. Patterson (compiler), *The Constitutions of Ohio, . . .* (Cleveland, 1912), and F. N. Thorpe (compiler and ed.), *The Federal and State Constitu-*

The Indiana constitution of 1851, which was adopted following a convention controlled by Jacksonism, permitted the incorporation of banks of issue, only, under a general banking law and set a twenty-year limit to bank franchises. The establishment of corporations was allowed solely under general laws, and restrictions were placed upon state debts.[182] Illinois, by its convention of 1847, forbade the creation of corporations except under general laws, unless in the judgment of the legislature the objects of the corporation could not be attained thereunder.[183] In the convention of 1846 in Wisconsin, Locofocoism was ascendant and banks were outlawed, but the constitution there drafted was defeated, and that resulting from the convention of 1847–48, and ratified by the people, authorized the legislature to submit the question of banks to popular vote.[184]

The North Central conventions of this era [185] were important as exhibiting the Locofoco attitude toward general economic, political, and social reorganization. Nowhere, unless in the debates in the Virginia convention of 1829–30, is there clearer evidence of the trend of public opinion upon governmental and social matters than in these constitutional discussions in the North Central section. Michigan's first constitution was adopted in 1835; Iowa's constitution of 1844 was rejected and she entered the Union under that of 1846; Missouri's convention of 1845 produced an instrument, but it was not accepted by the people; Wisconsin rejected a constitution made in 1846, as we have seen,

---

tions, *Colonial Charters, and Other Organic Laws of . . . the United States of America* (*House Document 357*, 59th Cong., 2d Sess.; Washington, 1909), V, 2925–26, 2930–31, 2932.

[182] Chas. Kettleborough, *Constitution Making in Indiana* (*Indiana Historical Collections*, I, Pt. IV), and Thorpe (compiler and ed.), *op. cit.*, II, 1087, 1088, 1089.

[183] *Ibid.*, p. 1005.

[184] M. M. Quaife (ed.): *Convention of 1846; The Struggle over Ratification, 1846–1847* (*Wisconsin Historical Collections*, XXVIII); and *The Attainment of Statehood* (*ibid.*, XXIX). See also Frederic L. Paxson, in *Mississippi Valley Historical Review*, II, 3–24.

[185] See the works already cited on this page. The spirit of some of these North Central conventions is illustrated in: Shambaugh (compiler and ed.), *Iowa Constitutional Conventions of 1844 and 1846; idem, History of the Constitutions of Iowa* (Des Moines, 1902); J. A. James, *Constitution and Admission of Iowa into the Union* (Johns Hopkins University *Studies in Historical and Political Science*, Ser. XVIII, No. 7; Baltimore, 1900); and T. C. Pease, *The Frontier State* [Illinois], *1818–1848* (Springfield, Ill., 1918).

but became a state under that ratified in 1848; the revised Illinois constitution drafted by the convention of 1847 was adopted the following year; and new constitutions found acceptance in Michigan (in 1850) and in Ohio and Indiana (in 1851). The influence of New York's constitution of 1846 was prominent in these conventions. In most of them the majority of the members were Democrats and fairly young men. Lawyers were less numerous, and there were more farmers, than in later conventions. In all appear strong indications of new popular demands.

There was a distrust of the legislature and a tendency to refer important subjects to popular vote. Another distinctly democratic movement was that for an elective judiciary.[186] By 1853 the entire Mississippi Valley had constitutional provisions for an elective higher judiciary, although only partially in Iowa, Arkansas, and Alabama. A map showing the distribution of the states in which the judiciary was elective by popular vote, and those in which it was not, reveals that all the Atlantic coastal states, with the exception of New York, Pennsylvania, and Maryland, were in sharp contrast with the central states. In the constitutional conventions of the North Central section, the reforming urge was still further shown by the importance given to discussions of the property rights of married women, naturalization, land limitation, and prohibition. Indeed, before the influence of the coming of the foreign element in such numbers to the section, constitutional provisions or laws favorable to prohibition were, or were about to be, enacted by most of the states; but the significance of this belongs rather to the next decade.

Local government in the North Central States reflected the combination of Southern and Northern stocks. In place of the town system of New England or the county system of the South, the example of the Middle Atlantic States was followed, in a mixed town-and-county system with a division of functions. In Illinois the law provided for an option by the people of every county between the two systems; and a mapping of the resultant choices shows close conformity to the areas of Northern and Southern settlement. Similarly, in Indiana and Illinois, elections on the question of support of common schools by taxation found the counties arrayed, in general, according to Northern or South-

---

[186] For a lawyer's adverse comment on the provisions for an elective judiciary, see Roscoe Pound, *The Spirit of the Common Law* (Boston, 1921).

ern origins of the population, except that urban regions as a rule were strongly favorable.

In this period several of the North Central states voted on the subject of negro suffrage, and here again there was a close relationship between the results and the distribution of Northern and Southern settlers. In Wisconsin, in 1847, the counties whose opposition defeated negro suffrage by a nearly two-to-one vote were those dominated by Southern settlers, in the lead-mining area of the southwest, and those along the shore of Lake Michigan settled by the Germans. Also, the strength of the Free Soil party, in all of the states of the section, was greatest in the counties in which the New England element was most numerous — particularly in the Western Reserve of Ohio and in the prairie regions of southern Wisconsin and northern Illinois. In other words, political sentiment on this question was shaped by the transmitted sectional prepossessions of the settlers themselves.

The political complexion of the North Central States has a special importance in these years, because the section was rapidly rising in relative power in the Union, already possessed a balance of power, and was expected in no short time to become the dominant political influence in the nation. Before the War of 1812, New England and the Middle Atlantic section each had a much larger representation in the House than had the entire West; and the combined votes of these two Northeastern sections was double, that of the West in the Senate. By 1845 the North Central section alone had a representation of ten in the Senate and forty-six in the House. It thus became of greater political weight than New England, equaled the power of the South Atlantic States in the House, and was not far behind them in the Senate. The section's representation exceeded that of the Middle Atlantic States in the Senate, but was still behind in the House. It had greater political power in the House than the South Central States. By a combination of the two North Atlantic sections with the North Central, the power of the Union would definitely rest in the Northern zone; on the other hand, a combination with the South Atlantic and South Central states would transfer the power to the South.

Not only this position of the North Central States, but their population, composite in sectional origin, made them a section to be fought for.

The aggregate of the popular vote of all the Presidential elections of the two decades from 1832 to 1852, inclusive, showed that the North Central States (of course omitting territories) gave a Democratic vote of 1,779,537 and a Whig vote of 1,642,487 — an excess of Democratic votes over Whig votes for the whole period, in the section, of 137,050. In party politics, therefore, the North Central States constituted a Democratic section. But it must be remembered that, during these years, the Liberty and Free Soil parties cast 166,124 votes. In the election of 1848 a considerable fraction of the Free Soil votes represented the votes of disgruntled Van Buren Democratic followers. It must be borne in mind, moreover, that both the Whig candidate in 1840, William Henry Harrison, and the Democratic candidate in 1848, Lewis Cass of Michigan, were favorite sons of the section and derived a considerable following from that fact. Furthermore, account must be taken of the very considerable element, in both parties, that was opposed to slavery expansion.[187] Therefore, both Whigs and Democrats of this section differed from their fellows in the North Atlantic states and in the two Southern sections. Party upheavals on the slavery issue impended.

It is interesting to see how the changing population of the section modified its political attitude during the period of our survey. The rapid settlement of the northern portion by the New York-New England stock, and by the Germans, was later to carry the section into definite opposition to Democracy, to unite it in close alliance with the colonizing states of the North Atlantic sections, and ultimately to make it one of the strongholds of the Republican party. By the election of 1856, there is a close resemblance between the Republican area of the section and the area once covered by the later glacial sheet.[188] This became clearer in the election of 1860, when the full effects of the migration from the Northeast were revealed. The tendencies so marked in the business world were also showing themselves in the political alignment: the valley of the Ohio River, both on its northern and southern sides, was coming to take a middle ground between the

[187] T. C. Smith, *The Liberty and Free Soil Parties in the Northwest* (*Harvard Historical Studies*, VI; New York, 1897).

[188] See map of Physiographic Divisions (facing p. 2, *ante*), and map of Election of 1856 (at end of volume).

extremists of the Wheat Kingdom, controlled by the New York-New England influence, and the Cotton Kingdom, ruled by the political ideas of South Carolina. About the same time that New Orleans lost its dominance over the commerce of the section, by 1846, the majority of the representatives of the North Central States abandoned the protective system and voted in favor of the so-called " free trade " tariff in that year. But, in the same year, the attitude of the section on slavery was exhibited in the vote of its Representatives in Congress for the Wilmot Proviso. In that vote the northern and the southern counties, representing the different streams of settlement, were the approximate line of division. On the other hand, about the same time occurred the change from the section's demand for banks to the intense antibanking movement already described. In the election of 1844 the North Central States had cast a majority of their popular vote for James K. Polk, on the general program of the annexation of Texas and the occupation of Oregon; but the reluctance of the South to support the Oregon side of the bargain produced a Democratic split that checked the tendency of the section toward a union with the South.

The entrance of the German and Irish immigrants, toward the later part of the period, gave an impetus to Democracy. Even as early as 1842 the English geologist, Charles Lyell, notes, in his *Travels in North America*,[189] that Ohio lawyers were expressing fears of the increased numbers in the Democratic party, in that state, due to the influx of the foreign voters, who had turned the election. It would seem that, by the close of our period, the German element (including the native-born) had nearly a balance of power in Ohio.[190]

The comments on the differences between Whig and Democratic principles in the other sections serve, in a measure, to characterize the two parties in this section. In general, the Whigs supported the industrial interests, such as banks, internal improvements, and the tariff, and the Democrats opposed them, although, in the height of the internal-improvements fever and the rage for banking, these distinctions were not clear. Nevertheless, the economic contrast between the two parties was contempo-

[189] II, 79.
[190] See the " Votes by Counties — German Voters, 1848–51," in the S. P. Chase MSS, Library of Congress.

raneously recognized. A speaker in the Whig state convention of Wisconsin in 1851 said:

> Remove the Whig party, and you would take from the State two-thirds of its intelligence, its respectability and its enterprise. — Go into any city or village of the State and enquire for its leading men, the educated, the refined and the enterprising, and you will find them, with scarcely an exception, the whigs of the place.[191]

The Democrats also recognized these distinctions. A Democratic editor wrote in 1850: [192]

> The whig looks to government for almost everything. The democrat looks to government for nothing which he can otherwise obtain. The whig looks to government as the dispenser of favors from some vast reservoir, ever full, and filled from some hidden source. The democrat looks upon the dispensation of favors by government as necessarily involving humbug or robbery.

He urged that "great aggregate national wealth may co-exist with great national misery and degradation." In the opinion of the average Democrat, "The majority of the people always do right." [193] But a Michigan Whig pointed out,[194] in the constitutional convention of that state, that "The mass is as likely to do wrong as are the individuals composing it"; and he called attention to the fact that each member of the convention was a representative of a special interest in addition to the general interests he represented in common with his fellows.[195]

The Western Whigs had a distinctly different quality from those of the Northeast or of the South. The whole party, in the North Central States, was essentially more democratic than were the Whigs in the nation at large. In this section there had not

[191] *River Times* (Fort Winnebago, Wis.), Oct. 6, 1851, quoting *Wisconsin Democrat*.

[192] *River Times*, Aug. 19, 1850.

[193] Paxson (in *Mississippi Valley Historical Review*, II, 4), quoting an Indiana Democrat in 1833.

[194] *River Times*, Aug. 12, 1850 (article by W. N. McLeod, on "Constitutional Convention").

[195] Thus, he said, Detroit might represent a commercial interest, Oakland an agricultural interest, Jackson a mechanical interest, St. Clair a saw-log and shingle interest, Mackinac a whitefish and trout interest. "Now," he observed, "as in a community of prairie dogs, each individual must raise himself above the level of the surrounding plain. In order to do this, he must scrape together the grains of sand — the small interests of his district — and thus construct his little hillock from the summit of which he may bark and whisk at pleasure."

been developed an aristocracy like that of the planting class in the South and Southwest and like that of the mercantile and banking classes in the Northeast, with their social distinctions and the intermarriage of families of the leaders.

In the territorial period there was a strong tendency to avoid party division on lines of national issues, but, as the prospect of statehood arose, territorial issues became mingled with national politics.

Boundary disputes had occurred in most of the North Central states and territories. There had been a controversy between the territory of Michigan and the state of Ohio, based upon the Ordinance of 1787, which involved the possession of Toledo, where the Wabash Canal delivered the surplus of that valley to Lake Erie. This discussion turned on the right of a territory to form its state constitution with the boundary determined by the Ordinance. It is not unlikely that the contest had large influence in shaping the popular-sovereignty views of Cass at a later time. But in the end Michigan's admission to statehood was on the basis of a boundary conformable with the claim of Ohio, while its northern area was made to extend west of the line of the Ordinance. Thus the state gained a region including iron and copper mines important at a later period though not properly appreciated at the time.[196]

When Illinois was admitted in 1818, its northern boundary, in violation of the provisions of the Ordinance, was moved to the north in order that the state might have harbors on the Great Lakes as well as a southern outlet by the Mississippi. It was thought that this would minimize the danger of the adhesion of Illinois to either a Southern or Western confederacy. The added area was about equal to that of Connecticut; it included the site of Chicago, the region of the Galena mines, and the prairie counties later occupied by settlers from New York and New England. There can be little doubt that the addition of this area made possible the success of Abraham Lincoln in Illinois in 1860. But, when Wisconsin began to consider statehood, she remembered the

[196] Annah M. Soule, " The Southern and Western Boundaries of Michigan " (in *Michigan Pioneer and Historical Collections*, XXVII, 346–90, and in Michigan Political Science Association *Publications*, II, 29–81); C. E. Sherman (compiler), *The Ohio-Michigan Boundary* (*Final Report*, Ohio Co-operative Topographic Survey, I [1916]), with the bibliography, therein, compiled by Prof. A. M. Schlesinger; and J. C. Parish, *Robert Lucas* (Iowa City, 1907).

provisions of the Ordinance of 1787 and asserted a right to these fourteen lost counties of northern Illinois. The disputed zone, suffering from the weight of heavy debt and taxation incurred by Illinois in the legislation of 1836, and bound by ties of sectional kinship to the similar region of southern Wisconsin, showed in public meetings and elections an overwhelming desire to join Wisconsin. This was reinforced by the ambition of leading politicians of Chicago to achieve a career, which the preponderance of the Southern stock in Illinois made difficult. The economic and social unity of the Fox- and Rock-river wheat valleys crossing the boundary between the two states was clearly exhibited in politics. Asserting the continued validity of the Ordinance, the Wisconsin agitators held that Wisconsin could become a state, by the action of its own people, with the boundary contemplated by the Ordinance, and if not admitted by Congress they would by force of fact be a " State out of the Union." [197] Here, as in the Michigan controversy, there was a precedent for the assertion of the doctrine of squatter sovereignty, in the reasoning of the more radical supporters of Wisconsin's claim, who believed that

It is *the people* of a State who determine for themselves *when* they are a State; they are the judges of their own rights and interests. Congress may admit new States into the Union, but the people form them.[198]

However, the constitution of 1848 for Wisconsin accepted her present boundary lines. Just before this final settlement, a futile attempt was made to organize the northern peninsula of Michigan and a portion of Wisconsin south of Lake Superior into the state of " Superior," thus recognizing the economic unity of the zone of white-pine forests and the northern mines.[199] Missouri and the territory of Iowa also had a boundary conflict.[200]

[197] A. H. Sanford, " State Sovereignty in Wisconsin," American Historical Association *Annual Report*, 1891 (Washington, 1892), pp. 177–95; and A. Church, *History of Rockford and Winnebago County, Illinois* (Rockford, 1900). I have also used contemporary correspondence and newspapers of Wisconsin in the State Historical Society of Wisconsin, particularly, e.g., *Milwaukee Sentinel*, Feb. 18, 25, Mar. 10, 31, June 2; 9, 1840, Jan. 22, 1842.

[198] *Milwaukee Sentinel*, Mar. 31, 1840.

[199] R. G. Thwaites, " The Boundaries of Wisconsin," *Wisconsin Historical Collections*, XI, 451–501; " Papers of James Duane Doty," *ibid.*, XIII, 220–46; and James Doty MSS in the Huntington Library.

[200] Parish, *op. cit.*, pp. 312 ff., and Shambaugh, *Constitutions of Iowa*. See also *idem* (ed.), *Messages and Proclamations of the Governors of Iowa* (Iowa City, 1903–5), and *Executive Journal of Iowa, 1838–1841: Governor Robert*

Perhaps the most impressive fact in connection with the political leaders of the North Central States is the preponderance of Democrats who gained a national reputation, as compared with Whigs. So dominant was the influence of Henry Clay over the Ohio Valley and the industrial communities in the zone of the Great Lakes, both of which found the American System in their interest, that there was hardly a Whig leader in the section who could be regarded as more than a lieutenant of Clay.

Of those whose prominence belongs especially to this period, perhaps the best-known was Thomas Ewing, of Ohio, a Virginian by birth, who had migrated in 1792, while still a child, to an Ohio farm. He became Secretary of the Treasury under President Harrison and Secretary of the Interior under Taylor. He left no enduring evidence of political initiative, having been for the most part active in promoting the wishes of greater statesmen.

Thomas Corwin, another Whig, who achieved a reputation for his political oratory, was a Kentuckian, and became Secretary of the Treasury under Fillmore and minister to Mexico in the Presidency of Lincoln.

The most distinguished son of the Western Reserve in these years was the Whig, Joshua R. Giddings, born in Pennsylvania in 1795, who won his position by his ardent opposition to slavery.

Although Abraham Lincoln ranks as the supreme example of the political leadership which the pioneer North Central section produced, and the outstanding opponent of the Democratic party in the decade before the Civil War, he was, in the period of this history, hardly more than a local Illinois Whig politician, an advocate of appropriations for internal improvements and of protective tariffs, a friend of banks, and an opponent of the Mexican War. His marriage brought him into connection with powerful Illinois families and threatened his popularity among the masses.[201] Although once denounced by Wendell Phillips, for his opposition to the abolition of slavery in the District of Columbia, as " that slave hound from Illinois," his career revealed him as the pre-eminent opponent of the expansion of slavery and ulti-

---

Lucas (Iowa City, 1906) ; *idem*, in *Iowa Journal of History and Politics*, II, 369–80 (with maps) ; and W. B. Stevens, in *Missouri Historical Review*, XV, 3–35.

[201] On this phase of his career, see Albert J. Beveridge, *Abraham Lincoln, 1809–1858* (Boston, 1928), I, Chaps. III–IX, *passim*.

mately as the "Great Emancipator"; but, reflective perhaps of his origins in the society of the Ohio Valley, he was no "abolitionist."

Harder to classify is William Henry Harrison,[202] born and schooled in Virginia and a descendant of the well-known Harrison family of the Old Dominion. The Northwest Territory had chosen him its delegate to Congress; he had been territorial governor of Indiana for over a decade following the turn of the century; and had won such renown in the War of 1812 that he had become a hero of the Old Northwest comparable to Jackson as the idol of the Old Southwest. In 1814, after having resigned his military commission, he retired to his farm at North Bend, Ohio. Commencing in 1816, he sat, successively, in the House of Representatives at Washington as a member from Ohio, in the senate of that state, and later in the federal Senate. His years in Congress were marked by activity in land legislation in the interest of his adopted section. He resigned his Senatorship in the spring of 1828 to become minister to Colombia, continuing at that post until the autumn of the succeeding year. When the time came for the selection of candidates from the North to oppose Van Buren, Harrison was one of those chosen. Defeated in 1836,[203] he was successful in the campaign of 1840, in which pioneer ideals and emotionalism were used by the Whigs as a substitute for a platform of principles.[204] But his incumbency was cut short by death a month after he took office.

Of the Democrats of the period, one of the most notable was Lewis Cass, of Michigan. He was of New Hampshire birth, and his father was an officer under General Anthony Wayne in the Indian fighting of Washington's administration. In 1799 Cass walked from Delaware to the Ohio Valley and settled in Marietta, where he helped clear land and pound corn in a hollow stump. After the War of 1812 he became governor of Michigan Territory. Here he showed energy in dealing with the Indians, traversing the shores of Lake Superior and Lake Michigan and living the life of a backwoodsman. Rising rapidly in the confidence of his party, he became governor of Michigan on its admission, Secre-

[202] See *Messages and Letters of William Henry Harrison*, ed. Logan Esarey (*Indiana Historical Collections*, VII, IX), and Mrs. Dorothy B. Goebel, *William Henry Harrison* (*ibid.*, XVI).

[203] See pp. 430, 438, 441–43, *post*.

[204] See pp. 478–80, 481–86, *post*.

tary of War in Jackson's second cabinet, minister to France in 1836, and the nominee of his party for the Presidency in 1848. It was a long, suggestive journey from the time when he held Indian councils in the wilderness to the days when he trod the courts of Versailles. Like the other Democrats of his section, he was a strong expansionist. Finding in the doctrine of popular sovereignty a campaign platform in 1848, he aimed to avoid the issue regarding the control of slavery in the territories by the general government. His position as a member of the cabinet under Buchanan, at a later time, is well known.

No statesman from the North Central States had a greater influence upon Congress and the executive policy, during most of the years between 1830 and 1850, than Thomas Hart Benton, of Missouri. He can hardly be called a typical representative of the section, however, for he was too ponderously read and he lived on the Western frontier — as deeply interested in the Far West as in the Middle West. Texas, Oregon, the fur trade, and the Santa Fe trade bulked large in his mind. But he was the pre-eminent spokesman of the elements in the North Central States that demanded hard money and professed the Locofoco doctrines with regard to banks. He was the champion of the rights of the squatter on the public lands and supported the demands of the pioneer for graduation of the price of those lands and for pre-emption. In the proposal to give the refuse lands to the needy actual settler, he was in a sense a prophet of the later homestead agitation. In his youth in Tennessee he had quarreled with Andrew Jackson; indeed, that hero bore in the War of 1812 the wound resulting from a tavern brawl between himself and the Benton brothers. But, in the contest against the National Bank, Benton became Jackson's efficient supporter. As the result of his upholding the President in the Nullification struggle, he became the implacable enemy of Calhoun — a fact that had a deep influence upon his later career. He saw in Calhoun's proslavery activity nothing less than a plot to disrupt the Union and to form an independent Cotton Kingdom. Although he was a firm champion of the St. Louis idea that the Mississippi Valley found its natural metropolis in New Orleans, and in spite of his early opposition to the attempts to restrain the expansion of slavery, he became one of the Western leaders who made difficult the path of this expansion. He was against the annexation of

Texas, fearing the probability of a war with Mexico, and fought
the friends of Calhoun in Missouri on the issue of opening the
Western lands to slavery. He had glowing visions of the future
of the West as it should build up commonwealth after commonwealth to the Pacific Ocean and engage in free intercourse with
the Orient. Although he never achieved Presidential nomination,
this was always a possibility in his career and no doubt sharpened
his criticisms of rivals like Calhoun and Buchanan.

Destined to rise to a high place in American political history
was Stephen A. Douglas, of Illinois. A native of Vermont, he
was obliged by a severe illness to abandon his apprenticeship
there as a cabinetmaker. Attending school in western New York,
he followed the westward movement in 1833 to Cincinnati, Louisville, St. Louis, and finally Jacksonville, in Illinois, where he
arrived with a dollar and a quarter in his pocket, taught school,
was admitted to the bar, and became a district attorney. In
1843 he went to Washington as a Representative and served in
the Lower House until he entered the Senate in 1847. He shared
with Benton championship of the elevation of the Mississippi
Valley to an independent position in the life of the nation. To
Douglas the great valley was not a bone of contention between
the Northeast and the South, its destiny dependent on the outcome of the conflict between other sections, but an important part
of the Union, with the right to shape its own course and with the
obligation to foster its deep-seated love for local government, development of its natural resources, and its expansion, territory
by territory and state by state, until it reached the Pacific Ocean.
As chairman of the Committee on Territories, he had a deep influence upon the conditions under which the lands west of the
Mississippi were organized. Short of stature, with a great head
set on a diminutive body, the " Little Giant," shaking his masses
of black hair and fiercely gesticulating, forced home his arguments for a Western point of view. Eager to promote the development of Chicago in railroad connections, he found himself
obliged to come to terms with its rival, St. Louis, and to make
concessions to the proslavery leaders in Missouri with reference
to the adjoining territory. Never profoundly moved by ethical
considerations, Douglas found it easier to make this adjustment
because he was himself, by marriage to a Southern woman, the
owner of slaves in the South and because his political strength

rested largely in the southern portion of his own state. Like Cass, he found in the doctrine of squatter sovereignty a solution of his problem.

It is interesting that, in spite of his Vermont birth and early training, Douglas became completely westernized.

> True [he said], I was not born out west here. I was born away down in Yankee land, I was born in a valley in Vermont, with the high mountains around me. . . . Vermont is the most glorious spot on the face of this globe for a man to be born in, *provided* he emigrates when he is very young. . . . I came out here when I was a boy, and I found my mind liberalized, and my opinions enlarged, when I got on these broad prairies, with only the heavens to bound my vision, instead of having them circumscribed by the little narrow ridges that surrounded the valley where I was born.[205]

In this reaction to his new environment, Douglas was typical of many if not most of the migrated New Englanders; but it was a strange piece of juggling by destiny that made him the leader of the Southern-upland stock of this section, against Abraham Lincoln his adversary, who, born in Kentucky, became the idol of the antislavery men of the Northern prairies.[206]

Still another type of North Central Democrat was Henry Dodge, a descendant of one of the first settlers of Block Island, Rhode Island. His uncle and his father had migrated to the Illinois country. Born at Vincennes, Indiana, in 1782, at an old trading post, he took part in the War of 1812 and in the Black Hawk War, and became the leader of the mounted rangers or dragoons who in the thirties policed the Santa Fe trail. He was chosen governor of the Territory of Wisconsin in 1836, delegate to Congress in 1841, and United States Senator upon the state's admission. Like his associates, he was an expansionist, but his record in Congress and his influence were such as to lead the New York Free Soilers in the Utica convention of 1848 to nominate him as the running mate of Van Buren. He declined, however.

John McLean, of New Jersey birth, went, at the beginning of our Constitutional period, to Virginia, Kentucky, and finally Ohio.

---

205 Sept. 15, 1858.

206 Frank E. Stevens [ed.], "Autobiography of Stephen A. Douglas," *Illinois State Historical Society Journal*, V, 323–42; Allen Johnson, *Stephen A. Douglas* (New York, 1908); Beveridge, *Lincoln* (consult Index, under "Douglas"); and Stevens, *Life of Stephen Arnold Douglas* (Illinois State Historical Society *Journal*, XVI, 247–673).

Elected in 1812 to the federal House of Representatives as a Democrat, he was made Postmaster-General in 1823 and, perhaps because of a desire on the part of Jackson to transfer a more than doubtful follower, was appointed an Associate Justice of the Supreme Court in 1829. In our period, he was active as a candidate for the Presidential nomination by various parties, but is best known for his objection to the Dred Scott decision.[207]

An almost forgotten Democrat was William Allen, of Ohio, who in his day was the trusted friend of the leaders of his party and had a reputation as one of the most effective of its speakers.[208]

Salmon P. Chase was a Western man whose distinction came later than the years of this volume but who had won a position of importance in the section before 1850. Coming from the Scotch-Irish stock of New Hampshire, he had followed his uncle, the Bishop of Ohio, to the West, and finally settled as a lawyer in Cincinnati. He became an active antislavery man, but in 1847 declined the nomination of the Liberty party for the Vice-Presidency and hoped to convert the Democratic party to the cause of antislavery under the banner of " Free Democracy." In 1848 he supported the Free Soil movement.

While the Whig leaders reflected the ideas of other sections, and particularly the views of Henry Clay, the Democrats, as a rule, were evangelists of the conception of " Young America " as a protagonist of free government, democracy, and expansion. Their belief that it was the mission of the republic, and especially of their own section, to spread the principles of individualistic democracy throughout the world, had a deep influence upon them. Cass, Douglas, and Hannegan of Indiana, were prominent in the propagation of this gospel. Jingoes by conviction, the Democrats thought they had found, in the growth of the section and in the opportunities it afforded for development of the individual, the type of a better order in the world. They conceived of this, however, as a program for the white race. Many of them did not sympathize with the view of the Southern states. Resting firmly on a doctrine of state rights and of squatter sovereignty, they looked to the West itself for a solution of the slavery problem, con-

[207] On his character, see Francis P. Weisenburger, " John McLean, Postmaster-General," *Mississippi Valley Historical Review*, XVIII, 23–33.

[208] See the Wm. Allen MSS in the Library of Congress.

fident that Western growth would shape the nation and that the slavery question was subordinate to that of union and democracy.

By 1850, society in the North Central States had revealed many of its essential features. Although a section in which, as a whole, almost three-fifths of the population engaged in gainful occupations were in agriculture, the proportions varied in the different states. In Ohio, Missouri, and Wisconsin, where mining and shipping activities were prominent, only about one-half the population was in agriculture, while in Michigan more than three-fifths, and in states like Illinois, Indiana, and Iowa, over sixty-five per cent, were so engaged.

The importance of the country lawyer in these new communities was great, and, with their rapid growth in population and in complexity, the opportunity of the lawyer to enter politics may have helped to recruit the ranks of the legal profession. It would often take ten years to get a business of fifteen hundred dollars a year in a large city.[209] For the most part, these Western lawyers were educated in the office of some older friend, and the examinations for the bar were not very serious.

An interesting type of the country town in the wheat belt was the community that became Kenosha, Wisconsin.[210] With a population of 1,800 in 1843, it had six resident ministers (but only three churches), ten lawyers, six physicians, and a dentist. There were an academy, three select schools, and an Irish Catholic parochial school. Nineteen dry-goods stores, four hotels, a bookstore, two weekly newspapers, two literary associations, and a Mechanics' Institute were reported. The community also boasted a brass band, a daguerreotyper, a portrait painter, two engravers, two watchmakers, and three barbers. Indicative, perhaps, of German influence, was a brewery; and over half a dozen shops made products from wood. The early adjustment of industry to natural resources is indicated in the observation of Harriet Martineau [211] that, in Tecumseh, Michigan, every other house seemed a chair manufactory.

---

[209] [The author struck out a sentence emphasizing the difficulty even the successful lawyer had in acquiring a practice sufficiently large to support him.]

[210] See pp. 273–74, *ante.*

[211] *Society in America* (London, 1837), I, 320. On pp. 312 ff. she describes Detroit in that period. In the Woodman Papers, in the Wisconsin Historical Society, are the impressions of a Yankee traveler, in 1839, of the Cincinnati of the time. See also the various histories of Cincinnati, for further illustrations.

Ohio reported, in the census of 1850, one domestic servant to every 1,700 people. Iowa, with a population of nearly 200,000, reported only ten domestic servants.[212] The Western dislike of the word *servant* no doubt conceals the fact that in other states the " hired help " were so reported, but this in itself evidences a sectional antipathy toward class distinctions. In short, the correspondence and recollections of the pioneers of this period show clearly that society was already varied, but in flux. Many of the men employed in industrial occupations were on their way to the ownership of a farm, and all of them were impressed with the fact that conventional views in older sections concerning the working class must be modified to meet the new conditions.

As would be expected, illiteracy [213] in the section reflected both geography and the sources of the population. Ohio, with a little over 3 per cent of white illiterates (white people over twenty years of age unable to read and write), reported its worst record in the driftless area in the southeast portion of the state (along the Ohio River) and in the northwest counties in the region of the Black Swamp, while the most favorable returns were from the Yankee-settled Western Reserve. White illiteracy reached its highest proportion in the section (except for the frontier territory of Minnesota) in the state of Indiana, where it exceeded 7 per cent and was most conspicuous in columns of counties running northward from the rough country of the driftless area, along the lines of Southern backwoods migration of the Hoosier type. In Missouri, also influenced strongly by the Southern stock, there was over 6 per cent of white illiteracy, with the most marked prevalence in the rugged country of the Ozark plateau and in the tier of frontier counties on the north, and the least in the Missouri Valley, where land values were highest, slaves most numerous, and prosperity greatest. The lowest percentages of illiteracy in the section were in Michigan and Wisconsin, in each case about 2 per cent, and in these states the outstanding areas were those settled by the descendants of New Englanders. Of the native-born, Wisconsin reported only .8 per cent illiterate, which may be compared with the .2 per cent in Massachusetts and the 1.25 per cent in New York. In both Michigan and Wisconsin the least satisfactory record was on the frontier, in the

[212] *Compendium of the Seventh Census*, pp. 40, 128.
[213] See map of White Illiteracy, 1850 (at end of volume).

regions of sawmills and lead mines. The counties of German settlement in Wisconsin reported a very good record in literacy among foreigners, contrasting with Massachusetts and New York, where the Irish element was strong. In Illinois, also, the relation between the driftless area and Southern settlement was indicated; and both that state and Iowa had over twice the percentage of white illiteracy shown by Michigan and Wisconsin.[214]

Taken as a whole, therefore, the section's record was more promising than Eastern critics would have expected.[215] Leaders from the Atlantic seaboard were already apprehensive that the North Central States might be a menace to an educated democracy. Writing in 1832, Lyman Beecher, in his *Plea for the West*, declared that " the religious and political destiny of our nation is to be decided in the West." Here he saw a composite population rushing suddenly into power, and was alarmed lest " those great institutions linger which are necessary to form the mind, and the conscience, and the heart of that vast world." [216] In his inaugural address at Antioch College, Ohio, Horace Mann, the well-known New England reformer, expressed the same ideas.[217] In a public speech as early as 1832, Abraham Lincoln declared that he viewed education as " the most important subject which we as a people can be engaged in." [218]

But, far too frequently, the new Western commonwealths paid only lip tribute to the relations between liberty, democracy, and the public schools. For example, the legislature of Iowa enacted a very liberal and advanced school law, which, however, was intended rather to attract immigration than to be enforced.[219] Too often the federal grants of lands were sacrificed in order to furnish cheap lands to immigrants rather than saved as an endowment for common schools. In general, the Southern stock showed a reluctance to favor taxation for common schools.[220] Ohio adopted

[214] *Compendium of the Seventh Census*, p. 152.

[215] F. J. Turner, " The Children of the Pioneers," *Yale Review*, XV, 645–70 [reprinted (as Chap. x) in Turner, *The Significance of Sections in American History* (New York, 1932)].

[216] *Idem, Frontier in American History*, pp. 35–36.

[217] *Life and Works of Horace Mann* (Boston, 1891), V, 314–18. See also Edward Everett, *Orations and Speeches on Various Occasions* (3d ed.; Boston, 1853), I, 344 ff.

[218] *The Writings of Abraham Lincoln*, ed. A. B. Lapsley, I (New York, 1905), 127.   [219] Macy, *Institutional Beginnings in a Western State*.

[220] Esarey, *Indiana*, I, 251, 282, 328 ff.

a mandatory school law in 1825, and in 1837 sent Calvin E. Stowe (the husband of Harriet Beecher Stowe) to Europe to study school systems. His report to the state assembly led to the establishment of a new system of schools supported by public funds, but it was not until 1853 that Ohio made her schools entirely free. Circumstances did not permit the realization in Indiana of the liberal ideas in its constitution of 1816, but in 1850 the constitutional convention of the state, under the leadership of Professor Caleb Mills, of Wabash College (a Yankee graduate of Dartmouth), provided for funds for common schools. This was declared unconstitutional, however, and in fact it was not until 1867 that a tax for public schools in Indiana was enacted into law. Illinois had passed a liberal general school law in 1825, but soon repealed its provision for free schools, and the charge for pupils in the common schools was not abolished until after our period. In general, the establishment of high schools, and public taxation for free common schools, did not come before the fifties. In this movement the example of New England and the influence of her leaders were strong factors.[221]

In most of the North Central states, correspondence was carried on between leaders and their former instructors in New England colleges. These letters reveal a desire to examine the school laws and similar material in the older section as a basis for action in the new. The interest of New England people in education in the West was due in part to the alarm created by the growth of Catholic schools and churches, and in part to rivalry between the denominations strongest in New England and those that were entering the North Central States from other sections. Attention has already been called to the activity of Lyman Beecher in this field; but the work of his daughter, Catharine E. Beecher, is important, both in her efforts in promoting feminism, particularly in the direction of teaching and household economics, and in spreading the influence of the " Yankee schoolma'am " in the new states.[222] It was the purpose of the " Ladies'

---

[221] On common education in the section, see: E. G. Dexter, *History of Education in the United States* (New York, 1904), Chap. x; A. D. Mayo, in *Report* of the United States Commissioner of Education for 1898–99, I (Washington, 1900), 357–450; and Channing, *United States*, V, 246–48, 255.

[222] See her: *Suggestions respecting Improvements in Education*, . . . (Hartford, Conn., 1829); *A Treatise on Domestic Economy* . . . (Boston, 1842); *The Evils Suffered by American Women and American Children* (New York

Society for the Promotion of Education at the West," formed in 1846, to send woman teachers there. This organization invited Governor William Slade, of Vermont (who was prominent in anti-slavery and Anti-Masonic politics and had served as a Representative at Washington during a half dozen successive Congresses in the thirties and early forties), to become its agent, and for some years he traveled in its behalf.[223]

In the development of common-school education, Ohio naturally led the way. In 1831 the " Western Literary Institute and College of Professional Teachers " was formed at Cincinnati to promote better teaching, and for a decade held annual meetings attended by teachers from various states. Among the subjects considered by this organization were the rapidity of immigration into the section, demanding " Americanization "; the need of state-supported and -controlled systems of education; the content of the curriculum; and the importance of initiative and cooperation.[224] In its discussions are to be found many of the ideas that were later to characterize the peculiarities of the section's educational aims. For example, emphasis was already laid on practical education, especially in agriculture.

In higher education, the North Central States came to make important contributions. Even before the section's special contribution in the shape of state universities, sectarian influence had established colleges and seminaries. This activity was by no means limited to the New England stock, for some of the earliest of these institutions were founded by the Southern element; but it was men and women of New England descent who were most ardent and effective in the fostering of education of this type. The apprehension of New England that her ideals and her society would be lost by those of her children who went into the wilder-

---

[1846]); and *Letters to the People on Health and Happiness* (New York, 1855). See also: reports of the Board of National Education (I–XI), Ladies' Society for the Promotion of Education at the West (I–VII), and American Woman's Education Society (I–IV); and *Barnard's American Journal of Education*, XXVIII (1828), 65–96.

[223] There is a portrait of Slade in A. M. Hemenway (ed.), *The Vermont Historical Gazetteer*, I (Burlington, Vt., 1867), frontispiece.

[224] See Allen O. Hansen, *Early Educational Leadership in the Ohio Valley* (*Journal of Educational Research Monographs*, No. 5; Bloomington, Ill., 1923). The Transactions of the " Institute and College " are to be found in the city library in Cincinnati.

ness, her concern lest this prospective center of American civilization [225] should turn against Puritan conceptions, led her to be
active in subscribing funds for the support of schools and colleges
in the North Central States and in sending missionaries of education to that section.[226]

Between 1830 and 1850, over thirty new colleges were added
in the North Central States.[227] At times, certain of these colleges,
representing different sects, combined in a single agency their
efforts to secure funds in the East; but, on the whole, denominational rivalry was in evidence. By 1850 the section had about
the same proportion of colleges to population that New England
had. Of course the term " college " was used for institutions in
the North Central States that would not have been so dignified
in New England, and the faculties of the colleges of the West
were not comparable. Moreover, while in the North Central
States (omitting Iowa and Minnesota, for which there are no
reports in the census) there was one college student for about
every twenty-eight hundred people, the proportion in New England was one to only eleven hundred, approximately.[228] The
West sent a considerable number of college students to Eastern
institutions, but toward the end of the period was developing its
own system.

Early in the thirties, Oberlin had opened its doors to women,
and a year or two after that, to colored students. In its emphasis
upon " an acquaintance with common things " and in the requirement of four hours' daily manual labor, it was indicating traits
that became sectional characteristics.[229] Most of the denominational colleges were, in their origin, conceived of as primarily for
the purpose of giving a college training to men preparing to enter

[225] C. F. Thwing, *A History of Higher Education in America* (New York,
1906), p. 295, quoting Horace Mann (*Life and Works*, V, 315) as saying: " This
youthful Western world is gigantic youth, and therefore its education must be
such as befits a giant. . . . Wherever the capital of the United States may be,
this valley will be its seat of empire."

[226] [Baird] *View of the Valley of the Mississippi*, Chap. xxv.

[227] See the table in Dexter, *op. cit.*

[228] See C. D. Wright, *The History and Growth of the United States Census*
(*Senate Document 194*, 56th Cong., 1st Sess.; Washington, 1900), p. 37, quoting contemporary criticism of the gross errors in the Census of 1840 on the
numbers of colleges and of students.

[229] G. W. Knight and J. R. Commons, *The History of Higher Education in
Ohio* (Bureau of Education Circular of Information, No. 5, 1891; Washington,
1891), pp. 58–60.

the ministry. Devout bands of educational missionaries went to the section and left a deep impression upon it.[230]

Salaries and student living expenses at the denominational colleges, at the beginning of the thirties, may perhaps be fairly illustrated by conditions at Kenyon, an Episcopal institution, supported to a considerable extent by the benefactions of Englishmen. There, the president received $800 annually, and the professors $500 and foodstuffs. Board, tuition, room, light, and fuel, together, cost the student between $50 and $70 a year.[231]

It was in the North Central States that the state university achieved its most characteristic form. The provision in the land grant to the Ohio Company, made by Congress in 1787, setting aside two townships of land for the support of higher education, applied to this new section the precedent that had been made in New England in the practice of town grants for education.[232] While, in the East, the tendency was for the state universities to gain independence both of state control and of state funds, in the West the reverse was the case. To some extent this was due to the federal land grants made to various states on their admission,[233] but the important influence of the Prussian system was manifested, and more significant still were the tendencies of the section itself. In the 1816 constitution of Indiana, it was directed that provision should be made " for a general system of education, ascending in a regular gradation from township schools to a State University, wherein tuition shall be gratis, and equally open to all." [234] But this proved to be, rather, a pious hope than an actuality in our period; nor did the grant of lands to Ohio for

[230] See the various histories of the " Yale Band " and the " Iowa Band," and the histories of typical colleges, particularly C. H. Rammelkamp, *Illinois College: A Centennial History, 1829–1929* ([New Haven] 1928). See also C. B. Goodykoontz, " The Home Missionary Movement and the West, 1798–1861 " (MS thesis in Harvard University, with bibliography), and Lois K. Mathews, " Some Activities of the Congregational Church West of the Mississippi," in *Essays in American History Dedicated to Frederick Jackson Turner* (New York, 1910); and consult Turner and Merk, *References on the History of the West*, pp. 93–94.

[231] See B. C. Steiner, *Life of Henry Winter Davis* (Baltimore, 1916). The *American Quarterly Register*, III, 127, 296, gives a view of literary institutions in the Mississippi Valley, about 1830, and statistical data on the colleges.

[232] Schafer, *Origin of the System of Land Grants for Education.*

[233] F. W. Blackmar, *The History of Federal and State Aid to Higher Education in the United States* (Washington, 1890).

[234] Thorpe (compiler and ed.), *Federal and State Constitutions*, II, 1069.

a university, which resulted in the " Ohio University " at Athens, result in a real type of state university. In Michigan the " Catholepistemiad or University of Michigania " was proposed in 1817, with an elaborately organized faculty; but it was not until 1837 that the state university was founded. To Isaac E. Crary, a son of Connecticut who had recently come to Michigan, was due the report, in the constitutional convention, in favor of a better system of public education and a state university. He had studied Victor Cousin's report on the Prussian system of education. While the pretentious plan of professorships was too far in advance of the time to be adopted, it was indicative of what later developed in the section.

We see, therefore, that, already, there had been shown the readiness of the West to consider new ideas in education, to turn to the state for aid and control, and to emphasize the relations of democracy and education.

The intellectual life of the North Central States, in these decades, is impossible to sketch with accuracy, not only because of the wide variety of the regions and people involved, but also because of the rapidly changing characteristics of the section. Two things stand out in the impressions an investigator receives. First, even with the purely pioneer conditions, under which emphasis upon culture would not be expected, there was always a center from which streams of influence were flowing. Whether among such older groups as that in Cincinnati, where there was an advanced type of New England culture as well as of the German artistic life, or even in Indiana, where there was a focus of Southern social and intellectual distinction, centers uncharacteristic of a frontier were observable.[235] Moreover, the sudden rush, to this new country, of ambitious individuals representative of journalism, the teaching profession, law, medicine, and religion, brought to the section influences that, even thus early, began to make themselves felt.

---

[235] Aside from works relating to the better-known centers of New England settlement, and to the foundation of colleges such as Oberlin and Xenia (Ohio), Jacksonville (Illinois), Beloit (Wisconsin), and Grinnell (Iowa), see: Frank, *Pionierjahre der Deutsch-Amerikanischen Familien Frank-Kerler;* Anna Howard Shaw, *Story of a Pioneer* (New York, 1915); and Mrs. Elizabeth F. Ellet, *Pioneer Women of the West* (New York, 1852). See also Mary S. Watts, *The Legacy* (New York, 1911) and *The Tenants* (New York, 1908), for a recognition in fiction of this aristocracy.

But, second, among the ordinary people who were flocking into the northern zone of colonization, there was an interest in intellectual things, not always recognized by the historian. Indeed, it is doubtful whether at any time there was a higher type of intellectual interest and ability among the rural classes of the section. This may be illustrated by the fact that, according to the Census of 1850, there were well over 500 weekly newspapers and periodicals in the North Central States. Ohio had more than 200 of these, with a ratio of number of papers to population, of 1 to 9,900. Iowa, with 1 to 7,700, Michigan, 1 to 8,400, and Wisconsin, 1 to 8,700, showed the newspaper and periodical interests of the Northern stream, and may be compared with the fact that Massachusetts, at the same time, had a ratio of 1 weekly paper to 7,900 people, and New York of 1 to 10,000. States more affected by the Southern element were Indiana, with 1 to 10,400, Illinois, 1 to 10,100, and Missouri, 1 to 15,200. As might have been expected, dailies were not so clearly in evidence; but even at that time Ohio had more of these than had Massachusetts. In the ratio of circulation of all newspapers and periodicals to population, however, the North Atlantic sections showed about three times the proportion in the North Central States. But it must be remembered that Middle Atlantic papers circulated widely in the West and had a deep influence. It is interesting to find that such a young state as Wisconsin had a per capita circulation, of its own papers, approximately equal to that of Vermont or of New Hampshire. Indeed, in some of the new communities, the editor, with his little printing outfit, was on the scene as early as was the settler.

The overoptimistic attitude of the Western editor is exhibited in these words, from the *Milwaukee Sentinel* in 1837: [236]

Others have *feared* that the people in this new country, are so entirely absorbed in their business and their labors — so occupied in providing homes, subsistence, and comforts for their families — that they can have no leisure time to devote to books and newspapers, and must consequently in a measure lose their taste for reading. But such is not the fact: the Settlers of Wisconsin are mostly emigrants from the Eastern and Middle States, [(]where almost every householder enjoys the luxury of having a Newspaper, weekly or daily, dropped at his door) and the members of his family would almost as soon go without their dinner, as to deny themselves that " feast of reason and flow of soul " which *the news*, fresh from

[236] June 27.

the Press, is so well calculated to afford. — These habits and taste, so far from being weakened, are rendered more acute, and become more deeply seated, on a removal to the " far west."

Three years later, however, this flattering analysis was seen not to apply to this paper, at least, as the following quotation shows: [237]

> *We have been trying to collect money!* Some *can't* pay, others *won't*. Out of near a thousand dollars due us in this town, after " *shinning it,*" (to use a common and not very classical phrase) for two weeks, we have obtained a *loan of ten dollars!* which enables us to print our paper this week.

Comparing the files of newspapers of this section and period with those of the South Central States, the relative absence of bitter vituperation is noticeable, although there were instances of it. The editor was a man of influence in the community, and his writings assumed a large amount of intelligence on the part of his readers. During this period, purely local news was subordinated, but one cannot fail to see that rural local opinion was more independently expressed and read at that time than in our own. It was before the days of " patent insides " and syndicated articles, and the editors kept their readers informed of state and national news and commented upon events in a spirited and keen fashion. The literary matter was in the stilted style of the time, and the columns abound with advertisements of Western periodicals as well as those of the East. Particularly in such agricultural papers as the *Prairie Farmer*, intelligent pioneers carried on agricultural discussions on a high plane.

In the earlier portion of the period, the first page of the average North Central newspaper was occupied by literary extracts, stories, etc., usually florid and sentimental. The proceedings of the House and Senate of the United States were reported more in detail than at present. As time went on in the period, there was an increasing tendency to substitute political data for the literary material on the first page.

On the other hand, the city press furnished no such editors as those of the larger Eastern centers, nor did the city have the influence upon thought that it came later to exert. For the most part, both dailies and weeklies were aggressively partisan, and seem to have derived a considerable part of their funds from po-

[237] May 19, 1840.

litical support or perquisites of an official nature. While quick
to catch the keynotes furnished by leading Northeastern and
Washington editors, they were by no means servile in their
following.

Periodicals bloomed and perished like prairie flowers.[238] W. D.
Howells seems to have found an early impulse to his realism in
the attempt to give authentic expression to the Western quality.
He describes how he followed his father to drive the cow through
the autumnal woods, talking " of the books and authors so dear
to the boy who limped barefooted by his father's side, with his
eye on the cow and his mind on Cervantes and Shakespeare."
His father warned him against translating his impression of the
beauty of fields and woods into terms of poets of England, where
larks and nightingales, daisies and cowslips were the favorite
themes.[239]

Some of the periodicals of the Ohio Valley, such as the *Western
Messenger* (1835–41), were in reality the organs of New England
thought. This magazine was edited, at different times, by
Ephraim Peabody, James Freeman Clarke, W. H. Channing,
Unitarian pastor in Cincinnati, and the Reverend James H. Per-
kins, a descendant of one of the important mercantile families
of Boston. To it contributed Eastern men like Oliver Wendell
Holmes and Jones Very. Such early poems of Emerson's as
" Each and All," " The Humble-bee," " Good-bye," and " The
Rhodora," appeared in it. Of New England origin, also, was the
Reverend Timothy Flint, editor of the *Western Magazine and
Review*, of Cincinnati. James Hall edited the *Illinois Monthly
Magazine* and the *Western Monthly Magazine* in the beginning
of the period. W. D. Gallagher's *Hesperian* appeared in 1838.
One of the longest-lived of these magazines was the *Ladies'
Repository and Gatherings of the West*, published in Cincinnati
(1841–76).[240]

In a St. Louis magazine, the *Western Journal* (1848–56),[241]
M. Tarver, one of the leading magazine editors, complains:

---

[238] See, e.g., W. C. Howells, *Life in Ohio*, pp. 166 ff.

[239] W. D. Howells, *Years of My Youth*, pp. 17, 46–47, 75, 89, 95.

[240] See W. H. Venable, *Beginnings of Literary Culture in the Ohio Valley*
(Cincinnati, 1891).

[241] For a more detailed survey of North Central periodicals, see Frank
Luther Mott, *A History of American Magazines, 1741–1850* (New York, 1930),
passim.

. . . if we except party politics, newspaper notices of legal and moral of-
fences, paragraphs of personal abuse, and kindred subjects, a writer in the
west would meet with little less patronage among the Camanches of the
plains, than among his own countrymen.[242]

This, of course, is the observation of an editor closely associated
with the South Central section. However, a friend writing from
the North Central States to a young graduate of Bowdoin College, in 1835, says to him:

If you are disposed Cyrus to give up your literary pursuits and embark
in the business of farming, raising stock, etc. and lead the hardy life of a
backwoodsman — come out here and you will do well but bear in mind,
after you are once out here you will pay no more attention to your
books.[243]

In fact, however, Woodman's papers show that he did make
purchases of books, including works on the French explorers,
novels, periodicals, and the like, and even tried to buy first editions of the *Jesuit Relations*. He became one of the founders
of the State Historical Society of Wisconsin and was influential
in the early development of the state's educational system. However, toward the close of the forties, he writes:

I am still fond of my books and long to devote myself to them, but the
busy life which I have led since coming to the West has prevented me
almost entirely from gratifying my inclinations in this respect.[244]

Ultimately, he returned to live in Cambridge, Massachusetts.

The older centers of culture had already made considerable
collections in their public libraries, and there are indications of
the beginnings of private libraries. On the whole, the section
was revealing its relation to the New England influence in this
respect.

The quality of the literary leaders of the section, such as
Coates Kinney, Sarah Bolton, Stephen C. Foster, the Cary sisters,
and, later, William Dean Howells, shows the interest of the
section in the common things of life. The Western emphasis
upon humor as a phase of American literature may have been
predicted in the influence of the Ohio Valley upon Josh Billings

[242] *Western Journal*, II, 214.
[243] T. I. S. Flint to Cyrus Woodman, Nov. 24, Dec. 15, 1835 (Woodman
MSS, Wisconsin Historical Society).
[244] Woodman to A. T. Nickerson, July 26, 1846 (*ibid.*).

during his temporary sojourn there and of the North Central States upon Mark Twain, as shown by such later writings as *Huckleberry Finn, Tom Sawyer,* and *Life on the Mississippi.*

On the whole, however, the section was too busily engaged in making clearings and developing society in this new land, to attract men and women immediately to literature. But the predictions of New England leaders that the West was to grow up in rudeness and barbarity were falsified. From among the children of the pioneers came a large number of the important figures, not only in literature and the humanities, but in the fields of art, science, and education and in all directions of eminence, whose names are later distinguished in Eastern states. After all allowance is made for the fact that so many who became scholars and writers went East in their young manhood for higher education, there was in them a Western quality — the initiative, the exploring instinct, born of pioneer customs and ideals. In all their work, their emphasis upon interest in the common man, and his rise to new levels, is prominent.[245]

As has been seen in other connections, the North Central States were a field for the competition of a multitude of rival religious sects, emphasized by the coming of foreign immigrants. As in the South Atlantic and Middle Atlantic sections, the most numerous were the Methodists. They outnumbered the Presbyterians and the Baptists, together. The Congregational sect, in spite of its activity and influence, was far exceeded by the Catholics.[246] It is not surprising, therefore, to find a serious apprehension on the part of the newcomers from the Northeast that earnest efforts must be made to foster their type of religion. The withdrawal of the incoming families from the established institutions and fixed moral code of their older homes, as well as the sparser settlement in the West, threw the pioneer upon his internal resources.[247] In

[245] Turner, " Children of the Pioneers."

[246] In these estimates of the proportionate strength of sects, I have been obliged to use the figures in the *Compendium of the Seventh Census,* with reference to the respective seating accommodations of the churches of the several sects. While this is far from satisfactory, the basis of church membership was so different among the various sects that, in a comparative view, the figures, as representative of the relative numbers, are probably not untrustworthy.

[247] The relation of the Methodist circuit rider to this fact has frequently been dwelt upon. See, e.g., Wm. W. Sweet, " The Coming of the Circuit Rider across the Mountains," *Mississippi Valley Historical Review,* Extra Number, Oct., 1918, pp. 271–82; and also *idem, Circuit-Rider Days in Indiana* (In-

general, it may be said that the Protestant churches of the West tended to draw away from the ritualism and formality of those in the parent sections and to lay greater emphasis upon such emotional aspects of religion as are illustrated in the camp meeting and the revival. Particularly was this the case among the people of Southern stock. Lacking the balance wheel of a considerable body of trained ministers, backwoods zealots carried creed and theology into unusual paths and threw into their disputations the energy of Western life.

There is a striking relation between the geography of the section [248] and the location of the various sects. For example, the Disciples of Christ were proportionately strongest in the areas of rough country settled by the Southern-upland pioneers, and especially in the driftless area of southern Ohio and Indiana. A map of the regions where the Congregationalists were in the lead might also serve as a map of the migration of the New England stock, for the strongest membership of this sect was found in the old Puritan settlement of the Ohio Valley tract about Marietta, in the Western Reserve, and in the oak openings of Michigan and Wisconsin, together with the portions of northern Illinois and of Iowa adjacent to the latter. The strength of the Quakers was most marked along the eastern border of Indiana, with Richmond as their center. Into this zone had come a migration of antislavery Quakers from the Piedmont region of the Carolinas, to which they had originally gone from New England.[249]

One of the striking features of the time was the spread of rival missionary societies. The American Home Missionary Society, formed in 1826 and supported by Eastern subscriptions, sent out its various bands. Organized the next year, in Austria, the Leopold Association, financed by members of the Austrian royal family and missionary groups, created unjustified alarm with respect to

---

dianapolis, 1916) and (ed.) *Circuit-Rider Days along the Ohio* (New York, 1923).

[248] See maps of Physiographic Divisions (facing p. 2, *ante*) and Interstate Migration (at end of volume).

[249] Stephen B. Weeks, *The Religious Development in the Province of North Carolina* (Johns Hopkins University *Studies in Historical and Political Science*, Ser. X, Nos. 5–6; Baltimore, 1892); Mathews, "Congregational Church West of the Mississippi," in *Essays Dedicated to F. J. Turner;* and Harlow Lindley, "The Quakers in the Old Northwest," *Mississippi Valley Historical Association Proceedings*, V, 60–72.

its predicted attack upon American democracy. The West was especially a field for its activity. The French Society for the Propagation of the Faith, formed in 1822 as a world organization, seems to have spent more money.[250]

In estimating the value of reports of missionaries and preachers in this new section, it must be taken into account that the often unfavorable comments bear a certain relation to the prejudices of the reporter, unable to discriminate between his own conceptions of morality and religion and those of the settlers from other regions and sects.

While the Middle West was the scene of the competition of sects for dominance in that new and vast area in which society was developing, there was also a marked interest in moral reforms, as has already been suggested in connection with the constitutional conventions at the close of the period.

In fact, it would be a fundamental mistake to think of this forming society as purely materialistic. The Western man was responsive to ideals, and, if he dealt in the superlative and saw his destiny with altogether too optimistic eyes, it is not surprising. Magnitude played upon the Western imagination and tempted the pioneer to brag. Behind him were the great spaces already won, the hamlets transformed into cities; before him stretched a world of opportunities; and he mingled the reality and the dream. Of course, it must not be thought that the ordinary pioneer was consciously influenced by these dreams; but leaders were, and often carried them to amusing extremes. Of " The Western Man," an editor wrote in 1851:

He steps longer and higher, and thinks faster than the people of other countries. His spirit is free like the wild wind which sweeps his magnificent woods and prairies and his thoughts are grand, as of one who looks on glorious landscapes, careering rivers, waving forests, limpid lakes, and gorgeous sunsets.[251]

---

[250] Goodykoontz, manuscript thesis cited above; *Catholic Historical Review*, I, 51–63, 175–91; and article by A. I. Rezek, in *The Catholic Encyclopedia*, XVI, 52. The literature of these various organizations is too extensive for citation in detail; see Turner and Merk, *References on the History of the West*, pp. 93–94. The files of the *Home Missionary* are important sources, but it must be recalled that they were published in a form, after editing in the East, to promote the Society's activities. An interesting report on the Catholic centers at this time is in Jos. Salzbacher, *Meine Reise nach Nord-Amerika im Jahre 1842* (Wien, 1845).

[251] *River Times*, Oct. 20, 1851.

Editors were constantly commenting on the short time in which the older regions of the section had been changed from the wilderness to new homes. All was motion and change; restlessness was universal. A pioneer from Virginia, who is thoroughly typical, moved in 1819 to Ohio, six years later to Indiana, a decade afterwards to Wisconsin, and in 1849, he reports,

. . . I reached the Pacific, and yet the sun sets west of me, and my wife positively refuses to go to the Sandwich Islands, and the bark is starting off my rails, and that is longer than I ever allowed myself to remain on one farm.[252]

It was natural that the Western man should emphasize the break with the past. B. Gratz Brown, in a Fourth-of-July oration in 1850 in Missouri, declared:

With the Past we have literally nothing to do, save to dream of it. Its lessons are lost, and its tongue is silent. We are ourselves at the head and front of all political experience. — Precedents have lost their virtue, and all their authority is gone. . . . Experience . . . can profit *us* only to guard from antiquated delusions.[253]

This idea occurs with frequency. F. J. Grund declared:

The West — not the East continually troubled with European visions — is ultimately destined to sway the country. The sea does not separate America from Europe; but behind the Alleghanies is springing up a new life, and a people more nearly allied to the soil that nourishes them, than the more refined and polished population of the seaboard.[254]

It must not be forgotten that the frontier had distinct conventions and prejudices of its own; but the new conditions were continual incentives to toleration and to modification of the older views.[255] The West demanded that ideals should be tested by their direct contributions to the betterment of the average man rather than by the production of men of exceptional genius.

Our people [said a writer in 1857] are eminently practical, but too stupid or too gain-loving to appreciate very highly the refinements of the

[252] Henry F. Janes, in *Wisconsin Historical Collections*, VI, 426, 434. Illustrations could be multiplied indefinitely. E.g., see: Howells, *Years of My Youth*, p. 33; *Milwaukee Sentinel*, June 27, 1837; *Wisconsin Courier*, Aug. 31, 1842; and H. C. Whitman to Wm. Allen (the Ohio Senator), Jan. 4, 1844 (in Allen MSS, Library of Congress).

[253] *River Times*, Aug. 19, 1850.

[254] *Aristocracy in America* (London, 1839), II, 328.

[255] See, e.g., Boynton, *Rediscovery of the Frontier, passim.*

mere scholar . . . If the scholar will in any way bring his knowledge to bear upon the practical interests of society, he may do well enough.[256]

In his inaugural address at the University of Missouri in 1850, President James Shannon, learnedly construing the word " education " to have been derived, not from *educere*, " to lead out," but from *educare*, meaning " to feed," stresses the practical aspects of instruction.[257]

Besides their emphasis upon equality and democracy, therefore, the North Central States were developing certain ideals that were later to be of significance in the characteristics of the section. Even equality was thought of as resulting from the action of free competition in the midst of illimitable opportunities. This section believed it was to shape the nation's ideals and society into a new world in all ways.

[256] Gerhard, *Illinois as It Is*, p. 450, quoting Edson Harkness, " Volunteer Advice to Immigrants."

[257] *Western Journal*, V, 162 ff. (Dec., 1850).

CHAPTER VIII

TEXAS AND THE FAR WEST

Heretofore, our surveys of sections in these years have dealt with those that were already well established in the East or with those in the West that were rapidly being settled by Americans and becoming in themselves important factors in shaping the nation's activity. The formation of society in the Far West, however, did not become characteristically American and influential until well toward the end of the forties, although before the close of that decade, and especially in its last years, the section played a part that deeply concerned the nation.[1]

Under the head of the Far West will be considered both the Western Division, consisting of the Rocky Mountain States and the Pacific Coast States, and, for the purposes of this chapter, Texas. All the emphasis that has been previously laid upon the transformations wrought by vast spaces and new provinces in the path of American expansion is strengthened by the story of the section we are here to consider. Indeed, it was more than a section: it was a series of extensive belts that stretched between the prairies and the Pacific and between Mexico and British America. The arid Great Plains,[2] some five hundred miles in breadth (within the limits of the Central States); the Rocky Mountains, lofty and massive obstacles, roughly another five hundred miles; the Great Basin, a desert empire, again five hundred miles across; the high Sierras and the peaks and precipices of the Cascades, walling-off the sun-bathed interior valleys of California and the valleys of the lower Columbia and the Willamette; and, finally, the Coast Ranges along the Pacific — all these were included. Unlike the Atlantic Coast, with its many harbors, the Pacific was broken at but few points, except for

[1] See Chapters xi, xii, in this work, on sectional influence in Congress.
[2] See Walter P. Webb, *The Great Plains* (Boston, 1931).

Puget Sound, the mouth of the Columbia with its concealing bar, the Golden Gate at San Francisco, and the harbor of San Diego. From St. Louis to San Francisco was farther than from London to Constantinople. Eastern standards of measurement were entirely inadequate for this new land. Along its borders, already ran that cordon of frontier forts that, in 1830, marked the edge of the advancing American settlement.[3]

The conquest and occupation of this extensive empire, and especially Texas, has too often been dealt with by historians who were under the spell of the slavery issue or swayed by the divisions between Whigs and Democrats. In fact, in our period, the movement was at first primarily the continuation of an old process of western advance. By 1830, probably hardly more than 16,000 Americans and 3,000 or 4,000 Mexicans lived in Texas; scarcely an American and only a few British subjects, in Oregon; and in California, but a few hundred Americans in a total white population of about 4,000, mostly Mexicans. Some 40,000 Mexicans lived in New Mexico, and around 2,000 in Arizona. Altogether, it is probable there were not over 20,000 Americans in all the Far West beyond the borders of Missouri, Arkansas, and Louisiana — a land half as large as Europe. Within this area were the intruded Indians removed from east of the Mississippi, as well as the wilder savages who roamed over these vast spaces.[4]

---

[3] Compare the stages of advance of similar frontiers in the seventeenth and early eighteenth centuries, described in F. J. Turner, *The Frontier in American History* (New York, 1921), Chaps. II, III. On the frontier forts in the middle thirties, see: *American State Papers, Military Affairs*, VII, 598, and map facing p. 781; *House Report 401* (Mar. 3, 1836), Serial No. 294, 24th Cong., 1st Sess.; and *Senate Document 104* (Jan. 22, 1841), Serial No. 377, 26th Cong., 2d Sess. Of local studies of particular forts, see, e.g., A. J. Turner, "The History of Fort Winnebago," *Wisconsin Historical Collections*, XIV, 65–102, and Marcus L. Hansen, *Old Fort Snelling, 1819–1858* (Iowa City, 1918). The episode of the Black Hawk War (1832), which was followed by an increase of settlement in southern Wisconsin and northern Illinois, has been treated in R. G. Thwaites, "The Story of the Black Hawk War," *Wisconsin Historical Collections*, XII, 217–65, and Frank E. Stevens, *The Black Hawk War* (Chicago, 1903). See also: Benton's speech in the Senate, Mar. 23, 1830 (*Register of Debates in Congress*, VI, Pt. I, 272–74); speech by Grundy (*ibid.*, p. 218); and Louis Pelzer, *Henry Dodge* (Iowa City, 1911) and *Marches of the Dragoons in the Mississippi Valley* (Iowa City, 1917).

[4] Livingston Farrand, *Basis of American History, 1500–1900* (*The American Nation: A History*, II; New York, 1904). See also: Frederic L. Paxson, *The Last American Frontier* (New York, 1910), Chaps. II, III; K. W. Colgrove, "The Attitude of Congress toward the Pioneers of the West, 1820–1850," *Iowa Journal of History and Politics*, IX, 196–302; Josiah Gregg, *Commerce*

Sparsely occupied as was the Far West when the American advance became significant, every part of the land was claimed by one or more nations. In the settlement of these claims, the future of the Pacific Ocean was involved and the relations with Asia. The determination of these diplomatic questions also precipitated sharp differences between the various sections of the nation, particularly with reference to the spread of slavery. It was clear, as well, that the formation of this later West was bringing into the Union a more pronounced spirit of individual adventure, self-reliance, and the idea of sudden riches for the new occupants.

The movement of settlement out to this Far West may be briefly sketched, but no attempt will be made to deal in detail with the fascinating and romantic story, because the real significance of the section in the nation comes only at the end of our period.[5]

The occupation of Texas had fairly begun by 1830. Geographically, this region is a portion of the coast and back country of the Gulf of Mexico and consequently, in common with Florida, it holds a commanding position with respect to the outlet of the Mississippi Valley. The curving shore of the Gulf, like the jeweled scimitar of Kipling's *Naulahka*, seemed to have a fatal influence upon its possessors. Along its warm waters, revolution seemed to breed spontaneously; and a special form of society developed from the meeting of the Spanish and American frontiers and the different habits, institutions, and purposes of the two peoples.

Fundamentally, the colonization of Texas resulted from the same advance of the Southern stock, particularly from the South Central States, of which we have already taken notice; but all

---

of the Prairies (New York, 1844), II, Chaps. xiv, xv (reprinted, from 2d ed., New York, 1845, in R. G. Thwaites [ed.], *Early Western Travels, 1748–1846*, XX [Cleveland, 1905], Chaps. xxx, xxxi); T. J. Farnham, *Travels in the Great Western Prairies* . . . (Poughkeepsie, N.Y., 1841), Chap. iii (reprinted, from London ed., 1843, *ibid.*, XXVIII [Cleveland, 1906], Chap. iii); and Annie H. Abel, *The History of Events Resulting in Indian Consolidation West of the Mississippi* (American Historical Association *Annual Report*, 1906, I [Washington, 1908], 233–450). There are maps of the emigrant Indians, for this period, in Col. Henry Dodge's *Report of the Expedition . . . to the Rocky Mountains, during the Summer of 1835* (*House Document 181* [in Vol. IV], 24th Cong., 1st Sess.), and Smithsonian Institution *Report*, 1885, Pt. ii (Geo. Catlin's map). On cessions to make room for the removed Indians, see Bureau of Ethnology, 18th *Annual Report*.

[5] A useful brief view, with citations, is in Edward Channing, *A History of the United States*, V (New York, 1921), Chap. xvi.

sections shared in the movement. It was as inevitable as any part of the Western advance, but, because it involved the spread of cotton culture along the Gulf Basin, carrying with it some of the slavery that existed in the South Central States, and because at the beginning the movement was into territory outside the limits of the United States, it came to have, as we shall see later, a special bearing upon the sectional antagonisms of the period. Particularly to the North, it has been too often interpreted as merely an attempt of the so-called " slavocracy " to extend their power and political influence into new areas.

Even before the revolutionary movements of the period of the War of 1812, Texas had been a field for American intrigue, and attempts had been made to establish independent American settlements there; and, throughout the two decades here considered, the American advance was complicated by a kaleidoscopic series of revolutions, first of Mexico against Spain and then within Mexico itself. The situation, therefore, changed almost year by year with reference to the new conditions that were thereby brought about.

The real founder of American colonization in Texas was Stephen F. Austin, whose father was a native of New England and whose wanderings illustrate the migration to the West. From Connecticut, the father had passed to Pennsylvania, to western Virginia, and to Missouri; and the son had won official position in Arkansas. Succeeding to his father's grant for colonization in Texas, Stephen F. Austin [6] had procured, in the midst of revolutionary changes, the ratification of that grant. Its lines followed the old *empresario* system under which large land grants were made by the Mexican government to promoters.[7] Before many years Austin's grant was augmented by those to others, with the hope that a body of settlers professing the Catholic religion and loyal to Mexico could be induced to fill up the vacant spaces of that great area. The American market was soon flooded with Texan scrip of these companies and others professing title to Mexican land, so that interest in Texas spread throughout the nation. While the Mexican grants varied in area at different

[6] For details, see the scholarly work of Eugene C. Barker, *The Life of Stephen F. Austin, Founder of Texas, 1793–1836* (Nashville and Dallas, 1925).

[7] Besides Barker, see, e.g., Ethel Z. Rather, *De Witt's Colony* (University of Texas *Bulletin*, No. 51; Austin, Jan. 15, 1905).

times and in different regions, as a rule they gave a *sitio*, or about 4,428 acres, of grazing land to each family brought in by an *empresario*; and to each family engaged in farming agricultural land, a *labor*, or about 177 acres; or if both activities were followed, a *sitio* and a *labor*. But the distinction between grazing land and agricultural land was laxly made. At a time when the Western land system of the United States limited the size of land grants, these opportunities to acquire extensive ranches were especially attractive to American settlers.

Austin himself was opposed to slavery, but, inasmuch as his colonists and those of the other *empresarios* depended upon the South Central States for their immigration, the system had to be accepted by the American promoters; but at the beginning there was only a handful of slaves, and it would be an entire mistake to regard the movement as merely a deliberate attempt of Southern leaders to extend their type of culture to these new lands.

By 1830, however, Mexico had become alarmed over the influx of slaveholding Americans and fearful of the possible independence of the area. As a result, by the colonization law of April 6, 1830,[8] an attempt was made to exclude Americans from the colonization of Texas. But, in consequence of the protests of Austin and his friends that the property rights that had led to the formation of these colonies were violated, Texas seems to have been excepted from the operation of the law.

As revolution after revolution went on in Mexico and the constitution was changed from the more liberal form of 1824 to centralized control, and Antonio López de Santa Anna, the Mexican leader, enforced the newer views against the American demands for a federal system allowing greater self-government to the separate states of Mexico, the Americans began to consider more seriously the necessity of independence and of military opposition to Mexican authority.

By 1832 there had arrived upon the scene a leader from the South Central section — quite unlike the moderate and compromising Austin — the picturesque, adventurous, intemperate Sam Houston, of Tennessee. His career in that state and as a dweller among the Indians adjacent need not detain us here.[9] He

[8] Barker, *op. cit.*, Chap. x.
[9] The most recent biography of Houston, *The Raven*, by Marquis James (Indianapolis, 1929), contains a bibliography.

was a close friend of Andrew Jackson, and it has been stated by Northern historians, but without sufficient evidence, that Jackson himself was involved in Houston's desire to bring about revolt and independence. At any rate, a considerable party of Americans had already reached the conviction that direct action and annexation to the United States were the remedies for Texan ills. Although Austin, the founder, with his conservative desire to work with Mexico, had gone to the capital of that nation to intercede in behalf of constitutionalism, he had been imprisoned, and on his return, hopeless of favorable results, joined the ranks of those who favored independence. The story of the fighting at the Alamo and Goliad, where American settlers were overwhelmed by superior numbers of Mexicans, was borne rapidly through all parts of the United States and led the South, particularly, to sympathy and reinforcements. This was a natural result of the differences between the two peoples and, therefore, is not to be explained, as Northern antislavery men explained it, as purely an attempt to bring about annexation and the increase of Southern political power. Finally, in the battle of San Jacinto, Houston defeated the Mexicans. The capture of Santa Anna resulted in his forced treaty of peace and Texan independence of Mexico, in 1836; but Mexico refused to accept their validity.

The situation now becomes complicated with the diplomatic efforts of European countries to make of Texas an independent buffer state, of the Southern group to force annexation, and of the Northern resistance to that movement as an attempt to increase the power of the South.[10]

Even so early as 1834, the Mexican commissioner, J. N. Almonte, estimated the total population of Texas (exclusive of over 15,000 Indians) at about 21,000.[11] By 1850 Texas had a total population of over 212,000, including 58,000 slaves. Of the 154,000 white and free colored people in 1850, nearly a third were natives of the state itself (many, of course, children of South Central settlers), a third were born in South Central states (Tennessee, which supplied almost 18,000, being by far the section's largest contributor), and approximately 22,000 were credited to the South Atlantic States — well toward half of these from the Carolinas

---

[10] See Chapters XI, XII, *post*.

[11] Wm. Kennedy, *Texas: The Rise, Progress, and Prospects of the Republic of Texas* (London, 1841), II, 69–81.

(though it is probable that a large share of the natives of North Carolina actually migrated from Tennessee). It is worth noting that the natives of Kentucky, Tennessee, and Missouri, where slavery was less extensive in proportion to population, surpassed those of distinctly slaveholding states. Attempts to bring foreigners into Texas had resulted in a foreign-born population (other than those of Mexican birth) of over 12,000, of which more than 8,000 were natives of Germany.

Over a quarter of the total population of Texas, in 1850, were slaves — a higher proportion than in Tennessee, Kentucky, or Arkansas — and, of the state's white and free colored people, there were less than 8,000 slaveholders, well over half of whom owned less than five slaves apiece.

It is seen, therefore, that, even so late as 1850, after the large migrations that followed independence and the Crisis of 1837, when so many Southern slaveholders went to the virgin cotton lands of Texas to retrieve their fortunes, the state was practically the child of the South Central States, but comparable to the northern half of that section in the proportion of free people to slaves.

Meantime, a movement had been in progress connecting the frontiers of settlement in the United States itself with Santa Fe. An examination of the map of density of settlement in 1830 [12] shows that there were two peninsulas of American advance up to the borders of the country reserved for the Indians: one of them ran from St. Louis up the Missouri to the extreme limits of that state, and the other up the Arkansas to the boundary of that state. From each of them economic penetration had been going on toward the old Spanish settlements in New Mexico. The Santa Fe traders, who were outfitted even as far east as Pittsburgh and New York, had long been pushing from the Missouri frontier toward the Southwest. [13] At the well-known Council Grove, [14] the straggling bands of independent traders gathered into caravans for safety against the Indians. Here some hundred canvas-covered wagons would meet and the traders choose a captain, with subordinate officers, for the caravan. Provision was made for

[12] P. 6, *ante.*

[13] F. J. Turner, *Rise of the New West, 1819–1829* (*The American Nation: A History*, XIV; New York, 1906), Chap. VIII.

[14] Morris County, Kan.

guard duty at night, and on reaching the vicinity of the hostile Indians a camp was made by forming the wagons into a great square, with wheels interlocked to make a barricade — a kind of nomadic fort. This arrangement was later followed, both by caravans of emigrants to the Pacific Coast and by the Mormons in their exodus to Great Salt Lake.

The Santa Fe trade [15] was significant, not only from the fact that American goods were exchanged for the silver bullion so important to the circulating medium of the United States, but also for live stock and hides. This wagon trade had become of importance early in the twenties, and had been one of the factors that gave to Benton his name of " Old Bullion " and that led him to urge the exclusive use of specie in retail trade. Owing to the onerous customs duties of the Mexicans, to imprisonment for smuggling, and to the inevitable clashes between American frontiersmen and Mexican officials, trouble arose.

But the Santa Fe caravan trade was not the only American movement that was penetrating the new lands of the Southwest. The Bent brothers [16] had established themselves at Fort Bent, not far from La Junta, Colorado ; and in 1826 Ceran St. Vrain went from Missouri to trap on the Gila River.[17] This visit, besides those of the Patties,[18] William Wolfskill, and others, brought new areas of the Southwest to the knowledge of Americans, and even, in some cases, extended to California.[19]

From the frontier of Arkansas, also, particularly from Fort Smith and from Shreveport, Louisiana, expeditions had gone out to Santa Fe and Chihuahua in Mexico, especially after the blockade of the Mexican ports by the French, in 1838–39, as a means of securing payment of the indebtedness of that country to French citizens, had shut off the exports of bullion from Chihuahua by

[15] See Gregg, *Commerce of the Prairies.* The volumes of the *Missouri Historical Review* contain journals of the early traders. See also H. M. Chittenden, *The American Fur Trade of the Far West* (New York, 1902), and Jas. J. Webb, *Adventures in the Santa Fé Trade, 1844–1847* (Glendale, Calif., 1931).

[16] A. H. Bent, *The Bent Family in America* (Boston, 1900).

[17] T. M. Marshall, " St. Vrain's Expedition to the Gila in 1826," *Southwestern Historical Quarterly,* XIX, 251–60.

[18] *The Personal Narrative of James O. Pattie* . . . [1824–30], ed. Timothy Flint (Cincinnati, 1831) (reprinted in Thwaites [ed.], *Early Western Travels,* XVIII [Cleveland, 1905]).

[19] Jos. J. Hill, " The Old Spanish Trail," *Hispanic American Historical Review,* IV, 444–73.

sea and had given impetus to the overland trade by way of El Paso.[20]

Even thus early, therefore, Texas had become interested in the Santa Fe area. Indeed, at the end of 1837 the Texan Secretary of State, whether from a desire to forward the movement for annexation by the United States or from a genuine policy of expansion, had written to the representative of his government in Washington that the " small Republic," if she had " *to exist separately,*" would pursue the " destiny " suggested by her emblem, " the evening star," until she would " embrace the shores of the Pacific as well as those of the Gulf of Mexico "; and had added that she would become an immense cotton- and sugar-growing nation, in intimate contact with England and other commercial and manufacturing countries of Europe.[21] In fact, in 1841 President M. B. Lamar of Texas organized an unsuccessful expedition against Santa Fe; [22] and in 1844 Houston himself, shaping his policy to the outcome either of independence or annexation, wrote that his country could gain European support for permanent independence and that California and other portions of Mexico would be glad to join it.[23]

Thus, the United States was faced with the possibility of an independent nation, protected by European powers, controlling the entire Southwest and the Pacific Coast.

At the same time that the American penetration was proceeding toward the Southwest and the old frontier of Spanish people, a comparable maritime advance was being made toward the West and Northwest. Beginning with Washington's period, New England, as has already been noted, had been deeply interested in the exploitation of these new fields. Already, through the activity of Yankee missionaries, Hawaii had become " a suburb of Boston "; but here the supply of sandalwood and other native products had declined, while the trade for the sea otter of the American Northwest coast was no longer profitable. Also, the whaling

[20] T. M. Marshall, " Commercial Aspects of the Texan Santa Fé Expedition," *Southwestern Historical Quarterly*, XX, 242–59.

[21] *Diplomatic Correspondence of the Republic of Texas*, ed. G. P. Garrison, Pt. I (American Historical Association *Annual Report*, 1907, II; Washington, 1908), p. 277.

[22] Marshall, " Texan Santa Fé Expedition."

[23] Houston to Gen. W. S. Murphy (American representative in Texas), May 6, 1844 (printed in Wm. C. Crane, *Life and Select Literary Remains of Sam Houston, of Texas* [Dallas, 1884], pp. 366–70).

industry, which reached its zenith in the middle thirties, had, in the northern Pacific, moved farther toward Japan and was ceasing to engage New England as an American interest. Meantime, the oriental trade, particularly in Chinese tea, had passed from Boston to New York, though it still made considerable use of New England capital and boats.[24] A revival of New England's maritime activity on the Pacific Coast was brought about by the trade in hides and tallows, stimulated by the secularization of the missions in 1833, when the fathers slaughtered great numbers of their cattle.[25]

While, then, New England had a declining stake in the Northwest, the North Central States, in consequence partly of the agricultural depression that came in connection with the depreciation that followed the Panic of 1837, partly of their inability directly to market their surplus crops in England while the Corn Laws were unrepealed, and partly of the interest aroused by missionary activity, had begun to replace the Northeast in the demand for American advance toward the Oregon coast.

Meantime, from Missouri as a center, lines of economic penetration were extending westward. The Rocky Mountain fur traders had already revealed the passes through the mountains, both to the Northwest and to California. Jedediah Smith [26] had reached California in his operations as a fur trader and had passed northward to the center of British fur activity in the Oregon country. Thus, the English frontier and the American frontier were meeting in a region disputed between the two nations. The Snake River Brigade had enabled the British fur traders, under the leadership of Dr. John McLoughlin, to widen their field, and P. S. Ogden, one of their agents, had reached the area of Great Salt Lake.[27] In 1832 the silk hat had begun to replace that made of

[24] See Chapter III, *ante*. I am indebted to my colleague, Professor Frederick Merk, for his researches on these and other points in connection with the Northwest. For information on the foreign trade connected with this subject, I have also used with profit the researches with me of Dr. Grace Lee Nute, at Radcliffe College; and S. E. Morison, *The Maritime History of Massachusetts, 1783–1860* (Boston, 1921).

[25] [A portion of this paragraph, deleted by Professor Turner in an uncompleted revision, has been restored by the editors.]

[26] See H. C. Dale (ed.), *The Ashley-Smith Explorations* . . . (Cleveland, 1918).

[27] The classical work on the subject as a whole is Chittenden, *American Fur Trade;* the monographs used are too numerous for individual mention.

beaver, so that the price of the fur of this animal, as well as the supply, had steadily declined. The era of the fur trade had passed its height; but the problem of occupation of the contested territory became serious at the very time that the vanguard of American fur traders was approaching the Columbia Valley; and hard on their heels came an active movement of American settlement of the lands in controversy, stimulated in part by the missionaries and in part by New Englanders like Hall J. Kelley and the more practical Nathaniel J. Wyeth.[28]

Hoping to engage in a profitable trade in the Far Northwest, Wyeth had organized a company of New Englanders, who left Missouri in 1832 with a trapping party. Repeating the journey in 1834, he allowed a Methodist missionary, the Reverend Jason Lee, and others, to go with him, and established Fort Hall, in Idaho. Here he met the opposition of the Hudson's Bay Company, under the control of McLoughlin, whose generosity toward American explorers and settlers was noteworthy, though he was loyal to his company and, in accordance with its policy, had discouraged settlement north of the Columbia. Moreover, the Hud-

---

By the kindness of Professor C. J. Brosnan, a member of my seminary at Harvard, I have consulted unpublished Ermatinger material on the Snake River Brigade. See also A. B. Hulbert, "Historical Reprints, 1830–1930: The Oregon Trail Centennial," with documents, published by State University of Montana, Missoula, in *Sources of Northwest History*, No. 9, and reprinted for Stewart Commission on Western History from "Historical Section" of *The Frontier* (a magazine, likewise published by State University of Montana), X, No. 2 (Jan., 1930); and *The Journal of John Work*, ed. W. S. Lewis and P. C. Phillips (Cleveland, 1923). Since this chapter was written, there has been published *Fur Trade and Empire: George Simpson's Journal*, ed. Frederick Merk (*Harvard Historical Studies*, XXXI; Cambridge, Mass., 1931).

[28] See *The Correspondence and Journals of Captain Nathaniel J. Wyeth, 1831–6*, ed. F. G. Young (*Sources of the History of Oregon*, I, Pts. 3–6; Eugene, 1899). On the history of Wyeth's Boston supply ship, the brig "Sultana," see Oregon Historical Society *Quarterly*, II, 36–54. On the occupation of the Oregon country in general, I have found Dr. Jos. Schafer, *A History of the Pacific Northwest* (New York, 1918), helpful, and the other histories of Oregon (and particularly the numerous monographs, the Oregon Historical Society *Quarterly*, and the *Washington Historical Quarterly*). See also the interesting monograph by J. C. Bell, Jr., *Opening a Highway to the Pacific, 1838–1846* (Columbia University *Studies in History, Economics and Public Law*, XCVI, No. 1; New York, 1921), and the recent popular account by W. J. Ghent, *The Road to Oregon* (New York, 1929), with bibliography. In this brief survey, it has not seemed advisable to cite the mass of material used. Useful bibliographies are: C. W. Smith (compiler), *Pacific Northwest Americana* (New York, 1921), and H. R. Wagner, *The Plains and the Rockies* (San Francisco, 1921).

son's Bay Company now built Fort Boisé in order to intercept the Indian trade from Fort Hall, and, shortly after, Wyeth was obliged to sell that station to his British rivals.

By this time, therefore, the traders had outlined the course of the Oregon Trail, which ran from Independence, Missouri, along the old Santa Fe Trail into Kansas, where it crossed the Kansas River to the Platte and followed the latter to its forks, and then, by way of the North Platte, proceeded to Fort Laramie (begun in 1834), in Wyoming. Reaching the Sweetwater River, the trail led to South Pass, and thence, by several routes, to Soda Springs, and, by way of Fort Hall, to the Snake River. From there it continued to Fort Boisé and Walla Walla, and down the Columbia, by boat, until later migrations, when a wagon road was established.[29]

In the westward movement from the beginning, the missionary had closely followed the fur trader, who served as his guide. As has been seen, Wyeth had taken with him representatives of the Methodist Missionary Society, to work among the Flathead Indians. This party, however, went on to the Willamette Valley, where they transferred their activity to agricultural settlement and were soon recruited by other missionaries of the sect. Next in the field were the Presbyterians, and particularly Dr. Marcus Whitman, about whose influence in the diplomatic contest for the Oregon country has raged a storm of controversy. In his first expedition (with the missionary, Samuel Parker), however, he did not remain. Returning in 1836, Whitman and a colleague, H. H. Spalding, with their wives, overtook a fur-trading expedition and proceeded by wagons, parts of one of which reached Fort Boisé. Whitman finally located his mission in the Walla Walla country, while the Spaldings founded a home near Lapwai. Catholic missionaries labored around Vancouver and in western Washington, and, in 1841, Father de Smet began activities among the Flatheads in Montana and Idaho.[30] Meantime, Whitman, be-

---

[29] The Oregon Trail changed in detail from time to time and varied in different localities. The route has been followed most carefully by Professor Archer B. Hulbert, in the volumes of *The Crown Collection of Photographs of American Maps.* See also his "Oregon Trail Centennial," fully cited on p. 362, *ante.* By 1830 traders had already taken a caravan of wagons from St. Louis to the head of Wind River, involving nearly three months of travel. This was an important change that later proved a precedent for the farming colonists. (See Hulbert's "Oregon Trail Centennial," just referred to.)

[30] Pierre Jean de Smet, *Letters and Sketches* [1841–42] (Philadelphia, 1843) (reprinted in Thwaites [ed.], *Early Western Travels,* XXVII [Cleveland, 1906],

coming concerned over the possibility of the abandonment of his
mission and desirous of promoting the movement of Americans
into this new land, had made his celebrated and perilous ride, in
the winter of 1842–43, back to the East. His visit to New York
was reported by Horace Greeley, editor of the *Tribune*, and he
went on to Washington, in March, to interest the government.[31]

The movement of the fur trader and the missionary now gives
way to the advance of the farmer as the colonist of the Oregon
country.[32] The hard times and low prices in the North Central
States in the early forties,[33] following the Crisis of 1837, promoted
migration to these distant lands. In view of the route by sea as
compared with that of the Mississippi, and even taking account
of the absence of railroads, the difficulty of disposing of a future
agricultural surplus seemed not insuperable to the farmers who
forsook that section for the Pacific Northwest. In fact, however,
had it not been for the purchases of the Hudson's Bay Company
and of Alaska, these Far Western pioneers would have suffered.[34]

Although the bill introduced in 1842 by Senator L. F. Linn, of
Missouri, making a grant of 640 acres in Oregon to adult white

---

123–411); *idem, Oregon Missions and Travels over the Rocky Mountains, in
1845–46* (New York, 1847) (reprinted, *ibid.*, XXIX [Cleveland, 1906], 103–424).

[31] J. Q. Adams notes, in his *Memoirs* (ed. C. F. Adams, XI [Philadelphia,
1876], 347), under date of March 27, 1843, that Webster had assurances from
Lord Ashburton that England would accept the Columbia boundary. In private letters from Edward Everett and Ashburton, he is told that England would
allow the United States, in return, to extend into California at the expense of
Mexico. Therefore, the real question regarding the influence of Whitman belongs to the period after the Ashburton Treaty. (See pp. 501–3, *post.*)
Hence, it is not pertinent that Whitman's visit occurred after the ratification
of the treaty negotiated by Ashburton and his return to England, as Channing
(*United States*, V, 549) thinks. Besides the mass of conflicting literature per-
taining to Whitman, I have had the advantage of seeing some of the researches,
in the Huntington Library and elsewhere, by Professor A. B. Hulbert. See his
paper, " Undeveloped Factors in the Life of Marcus Whitman," in J. F. Willard
and C. B. Goodykoontz (eds.), *The Trans-Mississippi West* (Boulder, Colo.,
1930), pp. 87–102. On the diplomatic aspects, see also Chapters XI, XII, *post.*

[32] In his *Great Plains* (p. 149), Webb makes the excellent point that the
plains were not only an obstacle, but also a highway, for the Oregon pioneers.
Had they been heavily timbered, they would have daunted the migrants, and,
if desirable soils had prevailed, expansion would have been by the slow settlement characteristic of other frontiers. The Oregon pioneers did not undertake
to live on the Great Plains.

[33] See pp. 308–9, *ante.*

[34] See J. H. Gilbert, *Trade and Currency in Early Oregon* (Columbia University *Studies in History, Economics and Public Law*, XXVI, No. 1; New
York, 1907).

males who would cultivate the land for five years or more, failed early in the succeeding year to pass the House, it was still expected that the government would adopt a liberal land policy. Returning missionaries and their supporters had spread, throughout the nation, an interest in the Oregon country; but perhaps a fundamental explanation of this new movement of migration was the ancestral fever for opening new lands — the advance into the West that had been going on since colonial days.

The early movement of settlers was facilitated by the herds of buffaloes that still roamed over the Great Plains and helped to furnish the food, and, by buffalo chips, the fuel, for these colonists. Not infrequently, plundering Indians — and sometimes more actively hostile ones — impeded the advance; [35] but, on the whole, this aspect of the migration of the Western farmer, in our period, has been somewhat exaggerated. The employment of experienced mountain men as guides and the use of the caravan and the wagon corral (already described in connection with the Santa Fe trade) helped to diminish the danger of Indian attack. Nevertheless, the American agricultural expansion was passing across — without occupying — a vast area that not until a generation later was to be settled, by the extension of the agricultural frontier and by the eastward movement of mining prospectors from the Pacific Coast.[36]

The migration of 1841 included both the John Bidwell party of settlers bound for California and a small group that went to Oregon. In the following year, a more noteworthy migration occurred, led by Dr. Elijah White, who had already been with the missionaries in the Willamette Valley and had been appointed Indian subagent for Oregon.[37] Leaving Independence by the middle of May, the party met John C. Frémont (Senator Benton's son-in-law) at Fort Laramie, on his first governmental exploration.[38] Thence, with Thomas Fitzpatrick, a

[35] For a vivid picture of the hardships of this travel to Oregon, and of the migrations to California, see A. B. Hulbert, *Frontiers* (Boston, 1929), pp. 170–77.

[36] See Paxson, *Last American Frontier*.

[37] On this expedition, see "Journal of Medorem Crawford," ed. F. G. Young (*Sources of the History of Oregon*, I, No. 1; Eugene, 1897).

[38] The "Pathfinder's" explorations have recently been sympathetically dealt with by Allan Nevins, *Frémont, the West's Greatest Adventurer* (New York, 1928), and critically by Cardinal Goodwin, *John Charles Frémont* (Stanford University, 1930). See also the brief résumé in the *Century Magazine*, XLI,

fur trader, as guide, they went by way of South Pass to Fort Hall, where they abandoned wagons. Before the middle of September they had reached Whitman's mission, and in the first week of October Crawford, the journalist of the expedition, had arrived in the Willamette Valley. Thus, approximately five months had been consumed in the toilsome and hazardous journey between western Missouri and the Willamette Valley. While this expedition was important as the beginning of secular colonization on a considerable scale, that of the following year was far more important. As we have seen, Whitman had made his ride back to the East at the time when the interest, of the North Central States especially, in the Oregon country had become a fever. In many little centers, companies were being organized to go to the region.[39] It was the ambition of Whitman to lead a numerous band there, and by the time of the gathering of this large migration of 1843 he became its animating spirit. Something like a thousand people, together with about a hundred and twenty wagons and nearly fifteen hundred oxen and other cattle, made up this great dust-covered caravan from Missouri. Thus, it was a real colonization, chiefly from the Middle West.[40]

A writer in the New Orleans *Picayune* [41] gives a pen picture of the adventurers just after crossing the Kansas River. He describes the

large body of men wheeling and marching about the prairie, . . . On arriving among them, however [he relates], we found they were only go-

759 ff., and John C. Frémont, *Memoirs of My Life* (Chicago, 1887). Frémont's governmental report of his first expedition was published in 1843 (*Senate Document 4*, 27th Cong., 3d Sess.). This and the reports of his later expeditions (*Senate Executive Document 174* [in Vol. XI], 28th Cong., 2d Sess.; and *Senate Miscellaneous Documents, No. 148*, 30th Cong., 1st Sess.) were widely circulated, and furnished subsequent emigrants with valuable details regarding routes, water supplies, etc. As a " pathfinder," however, Frémont had been preceded, for the most part, by the fur traders, and it was from these mountain men that he obtained his guides.

[39] See H. C. Dale, " The Organization of the Oregon Emigrating Companies," *Oregon Historical Society Quarterly*, XVI (in No. 3). I have also profited by the newspaper researches, regarding such organizations, made by Dr. Jos. Schafer. A good account of the formation of an emigrant group is quoted, from the *Bloomington* (Iowa) *Herald,* in the *Ohio Statesman*, April 26, 1843.

[40] Jesse Applegate, " A Day with the Cow Column in 1843," republished in *Oregon Historical Society Quarterly*, I, 371–83, is the classic and moving description of the experiences of these pioneers.

[41] Nov. 21, 1843 (reprinted, *ibid.*, I, 398 ff.).

ing on with their elections in a manner perhaps old enough, but very new and quizzical to us. The candidates stood up in a row behind the constituents, and at a given signal they wheeled about and marched off, while the general mass broke after them "lick-a-ty-split", each man forming in behind his favorite so that every candidate flourished a sort of a tail of his own, and the man with the longest tail was elected! These proceedings were continued until a captain and a council of ten were elected; . . . These men were running about the prairie, in long strings; the leaders, — in sport and for the purpose of puzzling the judges, doubling and winding in the drollest fashion; so that, the all-important business of forming a government seemed very much like the merry schoolboy game of "snapping the whip." It was really very funny to see the candidates for the solemn council of ten, run several hundred yards away, to show off the length of their tails, and then cut a half circle, so as to turn and admire their longitudinal popularity *in extenso* themselves.

Doubtless this was the first indication of the later Oregon primary election!

In 1844 a somewhat smaller migration, and the next year one numbering nearly three thousand, passed over the Oregon Trail. Around 1,350 accomplished the journey in 1846, and, following the treaty of annexation in that year, probably some four or five thousand sought the far-away new country in 1847.

The fur trade of the Northwest had ceased to be profitable, and English authorities recognized that the American farmer was taking possession south of the Columbia and, in slight numbers, had even advanced to the north of it. At this time, an optimistic belief that the colonization was also the forerunner of trade with China and the rest of the Orient was prevalent; and both English and American interests changed from a desire to hold to the Columbia as a boundary, to the determination to secure an adequate harbor on the Pacific. There was also a fear on the part of the Hudson's Bay Company that the American migrations not only constituted a possible threat to English control but might result in the pillaging of the company's stores on the Columbia.[42] The attempt at joint occupation by England and America was evidently foredoomed to failure; and, after a futile movement in 1841 to gain support, of both Canadian and American settlers, for a new government, the swelling American population facilitated the formation of what may be called a constitution, in the spring

[42] See the discussion of diplomatic relations, in Chapters XI, XII, *post.*

of 1843.[43]   As will later be seen,[44] by the treaty of 1846 England
and the United States compromised their differences by the creation of a boundary line along the forty-ninth parallel.

The census of 1850 showed that Oregon had a population of
over 13,000, of which natives of the North Central States aggre-
gated slightly more than 5,000 (including 2,200 furnished by Missouri alone). The number born in the South Central States was
about 1,200; in the South Atlantic, somewhat in excess of 800;
in the Middle Atlantic, around 1,000; and in New England, less
than 600. Taking into consideration the origins of the Missouri
element and of that in the zone to the north of the Ohio, the people
of Southern stock in Oregon far outnumbered those of Northern
birth; but the preponderance of natives of the North Central
section was unmistakable. The territory itself had given birth to
more than 3,000; and the foreign-born (largely former British
subjects) numbered 1,150. The oxcart migrations bore a natural relation to Missouri's leadership in the raising of oxen;
and the caravans organized on the Oregon Trail resembled
interestingly those that had formed long ago on the Santa Fe
trail.

As has been seen, the movement into the Far West had deeply
interested the Mississippi Valley by the middle forties. The next
great migration was to lodge a center of expansion in the vast
arid country that extended from Great Salt Lake as a nucleus. A
new and characteristic phase of the religious emotionalism of the
period; [45] the creation of a church hierarchy capable of dealing
with the problem of irrigation in this great region; the spread of
the New England type of community, modified by the conditions
of the desert; and the inhospitable reception of this religion, and
its Yankee followers, in the parts of the North Central States that
had been occupied by the Southern stock, with its conservatism
and religious prejudices — these were involved in this migration.
Suddenly, there were opened, in the Far West, conditions differing radically from those in the areas to which other colonization

[43] See the papers by R. C. Clark (formerly a student in my seminary in
Wisconsin): "How British and American Subjects Unite in a Common Government for Oregon Territory in 1844," Oregon Historical Society *Quarterly*,
XIII, 140–59; and "The Last Step in the Formation of a Provisional Government for Oregon in 1845," *ibid.*, XVI, 313–29.

[44] See Chapter XII, *post*.

[45] See pp. 42–43, *ante*.

had gone, as well as a society entirely unlike that of the settlers on the Pacific Coast. In its leadership, Utah was the offspring of New England, as were western New York and the Western Reserve of Ohio.

As we have seen,[46] the Puritans had a strain of mysticism; they listened to the voice of God; their souls were his direct concern; and they found in the Old Testament a rich repository of examples of God's revelations through his angels and the prophets. Even down to the beginning of our period, the clergy and " the elect " were still powerful; but, as men passed into the Western wilderness, the control exerted by the former, acting in accordance with tradition, was lost, and in the ferment of the twenties opportunities were furnished for different applications of the older religious ideas. The balance wheel of the closely settled town, with its conventions, was gone. Some of the migrated New Englanders became freethinkers and skeptics; others joined emotional sects; and still others, versed in the literature of the Old Testament, listened for new revelations and had visions of their own. It was an era of sectarian controversies and of prophetic inspirations.

Of this type were Joseph Smith [47] and the other founders of the Church of Latter-day Saints, subsequently called Mormons. They combined the conception of an anthropomorphic God with the American union of materialism and ideals. Without repeating the story of the belief of the later Mormons that angels and the patriarchs mentioned in the Old Testament as leaders of the " chosen people " revealed this new religion to Smith, it is sufficient for our purpose to notice that, in 1831, the center of the church was transferred from western New York, where the movement originated, to Kirtland, a suburb of Cleveland, in Ohio. Here a temple was begun, but the Panic of 1837 caused a new removal, to the vicinity of Independence, in Missouri. Early in the decade, a " New Zion " had been started there by a few hundred Saints, and in 1836 they had moved to Caldwell County, where they had laid out the town of Far West; but the intolerance of the Southern stock toward both the religious ideas and the sectional origin and abolitionism of these settlers, forced an exodus from Missouri

[46] Pp. 118–19.

[47] A psychological study by a gentile is I. W. Riley, *Founder of Mormonism* (New York, 1902).

to Illinois, where in 1839 they founded the town of Nauvoo, on the Mississippi River, and extended their settlements from that center.[48] Some five thousand Mormon colonists located in Illinois around that time, and by the end of 1844 it is possible that as many as thirty thousand adherents of the sect lived in the region.[49] They acquired a pivotal political position and were granted a charter, for the city of Nauvoo, that authorized a military organization under its control, a university, and manufacturing. This charter, though not unlike those of other cities of the state, was so used by the Mormon-church authorities that they exercised an almost autonomous government. In 1841 the cornerstone of a temple was laid. Missionaries were sent to European nations, particularly England, as well as to American states, and the number of colonists was increased by immigrants.[50]

By this time, however, the Mormons had become obnoxious to their neighbors, partly for political reasons, partly because of their church and charter, and partly because of the tales that were spread regarding Joseph Smith's "revelation," unpublished as yet, in favor of polygamy.[51] Smith and some of his followers were jailed, and he and his brother were murdered by a mob that included Illinois militiamen.

There now seized the mantle of the Prophet a man who was the sword of the flesh, as Smith had been the sword of the spirit. Brigham Young [52] is one of the great colonizing and organizing personalities of American history. Under him it was decided to migrate to the Far West. No migration up to that time had been so extensive or so well organized as that which, in 1845, under the leadership of this native of Vermont, started westward. The destination is a matter of dispute. One party, under Samuel Brannan, went around Cape Horn and reached California; but the main body passed overland — probably influenced by Fré-

[48] See Illinois Historical Society *Publications*, No. 11, p. 88; cf. *ibid.*, No. 10, p. 183.

[49] W. V. Pooley, *The Settlement of Illinois from 1830 to 1850* (University of Wisconsin *Bulletin*, No. 220; Madison, 1908), citations on pp. 513, 517.

[50] *Ibid.*, citations on p. 514.

[51] See, however, the favorable view of Smith and the future of Mormonism, by the well-known New Englander, Josiah Quincy, in his *Figures of the Past from the Leaves of Old Journals* (Boston, 1883), pp. 376–400.

[52] See M. R. Werner, *Brigham Young* (New York [1925]), a biography by a gentile; and Susa Young Gates and Leah D. Widtsoe, *The Life Story of Brigham Young* (New York, 1930), a Mormon interpretation.

mont's Reports [53] — to the region (not as yet acquired by the United States) around Great Salt Lake. By the fall of 1846, over twelve thousand Mormons, with some three thousand wagons and thirty thousand cattle and sheep, moved across Iowa to the vicinity of Council Bluffs, where crops were planted for the support of the colonists; and there were Mormon detachments located along the route.[54] In the spring of 1847, Brigham Young led an advance party that, in general, followed the Oregon Trail to Fort Bridger, on Green River. Here they left the trail and made their way through the mountain gorges until they reached Great Salt Lake, and almost immediately began to irrigate and plow. Other companies, systematically organized by the church in accordance with Young's " revelations," followed. By the spring of 1849, a convention was called to form the " State of Deseret." Although dissenting branches had been left behind in various parts of the North Central States,[55] particularly in Iowa, and other " prophets " [56] had arisen to contest the field with Young, Utah was now peculiarly the home of the Latter-day Saints.[57]

[53] See p. 365 (ante), n. 38.

[54] On the Mormons in Iowa, see Jacob Van der Zee, " The Mormon Trails in Iowa," Iowa Journal of History and Politics, XII, 3–16. Besides the general works, some of which are cited later, special treatments of the Mormon migration into and out of the Middle West are: D. L. Leonard, " Mormon Sojourn in Ohio," Ohio Church Historical Society Papers, I (1890), 43; Pooley, op. cit. (for Illinois); and J. S. Morton, Illustrated History of Nebraska (Lincoln, 1907–13), II, Chap. IV. See also the citations in F. J. Turner and Frederick Merk, List of References on the History of the West (Cambridge, Mass., 1922), p. 117.

[55] Jos. Smith and H. C. Smith, History of the Church of Jesus Christ of Latter Day Saints, 1805–1835 (Lamoni, Ia., 1897).

[56] See, e.g., M. M. Quaife, The Kingdom of Saint James: A Narrative of the Mormons (New Haven, 1930), and H. E. Legler, " A Moses of the Mormons " [James J. Strang, in Michigan and Wisconsin], Michigan Pioneer and Historical Collections, XXXII, 180–224. The author of the former had access to a hitherto unused mass of Strangite material, showing the dissensions within the Mormon church over the succession of Brigham Young to the leadership, some of which he seems to accept as evidence of the validity of the most serious of the allegations that have been brought against Young's followers. It may be doubted whether such material is to be regarded as trustworthy. See also W. E. La Rue, The Foundations of Mormonism (New York [etc.], 1919).

[57] There are bibliographies of the formation of Utah in some of the works previously cited. I have examined the important " Peirce Collection " of the Harvard Commission on Western History, described in Harvard Alumni Bulletin, XVI, 544. The standard Mormon version is B. H. Roberts, A Comprehensive History of the Church of Jesus Christ of Latter-day Saints (Salt Lake City, 1930). Consult also H. H. Bancroft, History of Utah (San Francisco, 1890).

By 1850 Utah had a population of over 11,000, of whom more than half lived at Salt Lake City; but "stakes" were beginning to be established in adjoining arid regions. Of the total population of Utah, some 2,000 were natives of foreign countries (most of them British). Of those born in the United States, nearly 3,700 were natives of the North Central States. Illinois, much the largest contributing state of the section, furnished almost 1,300, while Iowa and Ohio supplied in the neighborhood of 700 apiece and Missouri was responsible for about 500. Around 2,000 of the territory's people were born in the Middle Atlantic States, and approximately half that number in New England, which was the total likewise for the two Southern sections combined. Almost 1,400 were of Utah birth.

The same inexorable advance, of the Americans, that percolated into Texas and Oregon was, as we have partly seen, at work in California.[58] Also, as in Texas, the situation was complicated by the succession of revolutions taking place in the Mexican government. Into the old lands sparsely occupied by the missions and pueblos of the Spaniards, in earlier days,[59] came Americans (many of them connected with the trade from Boston that has been mentioned) to settle in California in the later twenties and the thirties,[60] and some of them to accept the Catholic faith and to

---

[58] See Robt. G. Cleland, "The Early Sentiment for the Annexation of California: An Account of the Growth of American Interest in California, 1835–1846," *Southwestern Historical Quarterly*, XVIII, 1–40, 121–61, 231–60.

[59] A scholarly Catholic history of the missions is Fr. Zephyrin Engelhardt, *The Missions and Missionaries of California* (4 vols.; San Francisco, 1908–15). See also H. E. Bolton, "The Mission as a Frontier Institution in the Spanish-American Colonies," *American Historical Review*, XXIII, 42–61. Besides the general works on the Spanish and Mexican periods, I have made use of special collections in the Huntington Library: for example, the tabulation in that library giving, by separate jurisdictions and their subdivisions, the statistics of population and products in 1828; and the copy of the "Narrative of W. D. Wilson," who, after living in Arizona, came in 1841 to California, where he bought a ranch.

[60] Among the general histories of California that I have used are: H. H. Bancroft, *History of California* (7 vols.; San Francisco, 1884–90), in the biographical appendices to which is an interesting realization of the numbers and character of these early settlers (See also: his volume, *Literary Industries* [San Francisco, 1890], especially Chaps. x, xi, xxiv, in which he explains the unusual way in which he worked with the co-operation of assistants; C. V. Langlois and Chas. Seignobos, *Introduction aux études historiques* . . . [Paris, 1898], p. 4; and, on the authorship, Oregon Historical Society *Quarterly*, IV, 287–364. Bancroft's library, now in the possession of the University of California, contains indispensable sources.); T. H. Hittell, *History of California* (4 vols.; San

marry Mexican wives. One wandering graduate of Harvard, " Dr." John Marsh (class of 1823), had passed overland from Michigan, Wisconsin, Minnesota, Missouri, New Mexico, and Sonora to California, where his ranch, established at the beginning of 1836 at the foot of Mount Diablo, served as an objective for some of the later American expeditions.

Several of the New Englanders, such as Abel Stearns, were leaders in the revolutions in which authorities of Mexico were engaged at a time when that country was undergoing its series of uprisings. Already, according to the testimony of many contemporary authorities, Mexican as well as others, California was a derelict almost certain to change its *de facto* independence of the mother country into a formal declaration. Reports of conditions were being made by English, French, and American observers. Moreover, it was not until 1841 that the Russian company actually sold its fur-trading stations in California. Thus, the problem of future occupation of that region was under serious consideration by several nations when the stream of American emigrants began to trickle into California.

The first of the noteworthy overland migrations for coloniza-

Francisco, 1885–97); Robt. G. Cleland, *A History of California: The American Period* (New York, 1922); and R. D. Hunt (ed.), *California and Californians* (Chicago, 1926), I, II. Wagner's bibliography, *Plains and Rockies* (cited on p. 362, *ante*), will be found useful.

Among the mass of contemporary works relating to the pre-American period may be mentioned: *Pattie's Narrative;* Alexander Forbes, *California* (London, 1839); R. H. Dana, *Two Years Before the Mast* (New York, 1840); Eugène Duflot de Mofras, *Exploration du territoire de l'Orégon, des Californies . . .* [1840–42] (Paris, 1844) (Duflot de Mofras is dealt with in: A. P. Nasatir, "French Activities in California before Statehood," *Proceedings* of Pacific Coast Branch of American Historical Association, 1928, pp. 76–88; and G. V. Blue, " Unpublished Portions of the Memoires of Duflot de Mofras," *ibid.*, pp. 89–102.); [Alfred Robinson] *Life in California* (New York, 1846); Walter Colton, *Three Years in California* [1846–49] (New York and Cincinnati, 1850); Bayard Taylor, *Eldorado* (New York, 1850); and Edwin Bryant, *What I Saw in California: . . .* (New York and Philadelphia, 1848). See also such secondary accounts as: H. E. Bolton, *The Spanish Borderlands* (*The Chronicles of America*, XXIII; New Haven, 1921), Chaps. VII, X; I. B. Richman, *California under Spain and Mexico, 1535–1847* (Boston, 1911); and T. J. Schoonover, *The Life and Times of Gen'l John A. Sutter* (Sacramento, 1895 and [revised and enlarged ed.] 1907). There is a survey of Mexican conditions in California, in Justin H. Smith, *The War with Mexico* (New York, 1919), I, Chap. XVI. In addition to the foregoing, consult Jos. Ellison, *California and the Nation, 1850–1869* (University of California *Publications in History*, XVI; Berkeley, 1927), earlier chapters.

tion was that fostered by Bidwell (later known for his candidacy for President on the Prohibition ticket). He had gone West (to Iowa), as a young man, and had become interested in California through the stories of trappers there. In 1841 his party of sixty-nine proceeded from Missouri along the Oregon Trail to Fort Laramie. Here they parted company with Father de Smet, the Catholic missionary, and others, whose expedition they had overtaken and who, joined by some of the members of their own group, now went on to Oregon, while Bidwell and his remaining companions turned toward California, going by way of the Humboldt and Walker rivers and along the Stanislaus, ultimately reaching the ranch of Marsh, of whom they had heard before starting.[61]

The Bidwell party was only one of several in the years prior to the discovery of gold. The largest of these was in 1846, by which time it had become not unusual for westward-bound groups to divide into those destined for Oregon and those whose objective was California. The tragic story of the snow-blocked Donner party, that went from Illinois by way of the Truckee in the Sierras, is well known.

The migration seeking California as agricultural colonists was accelerated after the acquisition of Oregon. Just at the close of the Mexican War, following the treaty of 1848,[62] the Americans had taken possession of the land that had been in dispute by various nations. On his second expedition, in the winter of 1843–44 (on his homeward trip), Frémont [63] had traversed parts of Oregon, and California to Sutter's Fort (near Sacramento), and thence, by way of San Francisco and the region of Los Angeles, had returned to the East, and thus increased the knowledge of California. In his third expedition — the last under governmental auspices — he found himself again in California, and engaged in the Bear Flag insurrection (1846),[64] in which Americans set up a revolutionary government and asserted independence.

[61] See Bidwell's recollections of " The First Emigrant Train to California," *Century Magazine*, XLI, 106–30, and Geo. D. Lyman, *John Marsh, Pioneer* (New York, 1930).

[62] On the diplomacy of the forties, see Chapters XI and XII, *post*.

[63] Goodwin, *Frémont*; Nevins, *Frémont*; and Frémont, *Memoirs*.

[64] See p. 566, *post*, and the material in Frémont's Reports, previously cited; *Century Magazine*, XLI, 518–25, 780–83, 917–28; [Simeon Ide] *Biographical Sketch of the Life of William B. Ide* (Claremont, N.H., 1880); and

Writing of Frémont's entry into Monterey, Lieutenant Frederick Walpole, of the English admiral's flagship present in that harbor, said:

A vast cloud of dust appeared at first, and thence in long file emerged this wildest wild party. Frémont rode ahead, a spare, active-looking man, with such an eye! He was dressed in a blouse and leggings, and wore a felt hat. After him came five Delaware Indians, who were his body guard; they had charge of two baggage horses. The rest, many of them blacker than the Indians, rode two and two, the rifle held by one hand across the pommel of the saddle. . . . The dress of these men was principally a long, loose coat of deer-skin, tied with thongs, in front; trousers of the same. The saddles were of various fashions, though these and a large drove of horses and a brass field-gun were things they had picked up in California. . . . They are allowed no liquor . . . and the discipline is very strict. . . . One man, a doctor, was six feet six high, and an odd-looking fellow. May I never come under his hands.[65]

A new American frontier had appeared across the continent.

It was the discovery of gold in California that revolutionized the movement to that region. Even in 1843, Bryant and Sturgis, the Boston traders to the Coast, had forwarded some thirty ounces of rough gold to be minted in Philadelphia. This gold came from a mine discovered the previous year, in the area tributary to Los Angeles. But it seems to have aroused no particular attention.[66] On January 24, 1848, however, the Mormon, J. W. Marshall, working at Coloma on a mill in the foothills neighboring Sutter's Fort, discovered gold. The news was carried, by September of that year, to the Atlantic states, and in January of 1849 began the gold rush to California. The yield in 1848 was estimated at around five million dollars, in the next year twenty-three million, and by 1850 fifty million. While no considerable profit was made by the average participant in this rush, stories of exceptionally lucky individuals continued the excitement. Profits in trade as well as mining soon became increasingly important. A cartoon of 1849 pictures a Yankee, mounted on a steam flying machine, with the

---

Josiah Royce, *California, from the Conquest in 1846 to the Second Vigilance Committee in San Francisco* [1856] (Boston, 1886 [in " American Commonwealths " series]).

[65] Quoted in Richman, *California*, p. 318.

[66] Bryant and Sturgis Papers, Harvard University Library (MS letter). Cf. J. M. Guinn, " Early Gold Discoveries in Southern California," Historical Society of Southern California *Publications*, III (Los Angeles, 1893), 10–16, and Duflot de Mofras, *Exploration*, I, 357.

legend, " When I get to CaliforNy I'll let others do the diggins
while I do the swappins ! " From all quarters men rushed by sea
and land to this new El Dorado; by the old overland routes [67]
and by sea around Cape Horn and via the Panama isthmus, they
swarmed.

It is estimated that, in the spring of 1849, some twenty thousand
were waiting for the grass to start on the frontier of Missouri; and,
in spite of cholera, the movement grew. The volume of overland migration cannot be stated. The Society of California Pioneers shows a membership of those who arrived thus, before 1850,
of only 208; those who came by way of Cape Horn, 518; by Panama, 213; and by other routes, 77 — a total of 1,016; but, of
course, this falls far short of including all those who were eligible,
and the proportions are doubtful. From Australia, Chile, Mexico,
the South Sea Islands, Peru, and China, gold seekers reached
California. The arrivals in 1850, via Cape Horn, are estimated at
over 11,000 males and 560 females; those who took the Panama
route, at about 13,500 males and upwards of 300 females; while
from Pacific ports there came not far from 10,000 males and in
excess of 1,500 females — in all somewhat beyond 34,500 males
and around 2,400 females.[68]

Viewing California as a conquered territory and acting under
squatter convictions, this influx of Americans little understood
the distinction between taking the country and taking private
land titles. Sometimes emigrants would seize the horses of the
Californians, and, in general, their proceedings left an aftermath
of ill-feeling.[69]

In 1850 California had a population of 92,600, including 6,600
of its own natives. In all, there were not far from 70,000 born
in the United States and somewhat more than 22,000 foreign-
born. Of the natives of the United States (not counting those of
California birth), nearly 27,500 came from the North Atlantic
states and almost 7,500 from the South Atlantic States, or slightly
less than 35,000, altogether, from the Atlantic Coast, leaving approximately 28,000 from the interior.

In older settlements like Monterey, at first so many rushed to

[67] See A. B. Hulbert, *Forty-niners* (Boston, 1931), for an attempt at a composite diary, with a considerable bibliography.

[68] *Century Magazine*, XLII, 593.

[69] See, e.g., Royce, *California*, pp. 203–12 and Chaps. IV, VI.

the " diggings " that it was hard to find servants and food.[70] The gold seekers spread along the foothills of the Sierras. The abandonment of the government's leasing system for its mineral-bearing lands and the triumph of the pre-emption system just before this gold rush, facilitated the unregulated descent of the newcomers upon the gold area. The old institution of Regulators and the extemporizing of government by squatter gatherings [71] were applied to the mining camps. Mining-camp law made by associations formed in this manner preceded the coming of formal law and governmental order. In contrast with later English practice, the American was improvising regulations of his own.[72] Society had gone in advance of government. Aside from the rules of these rough-and-ready organizations, individualism ran riot. Along with the sober and industrious, there had come, in the rush, a scum borne by the advancing flood; gamblers, adventurers, and desperadoes joined the movement. The pictures drawn by Bret Harte in his novels have been criticized by men who lived in the region and the period, as not representing the realities of mining-camp law.[73] Yet the conventions of the older sections suffered great modifications. No longer restrained by customary morals, men were placed " on their own." Many of those who came to California were led by the speculative spirit of " make your pile " and " get rich quick," and expected to return to their former homes after accumulating wealth. But gradually the charm of California asserted itself, agriculture and varied business interests developed, and this mobile population began to settle down in a new home and to create a different type of sectional ideals in America.

Before the coming of the transcontinental railroad, California, in spite of its maritime connection, was measurably isolated; and in those years characteristics that were peculiar to the region had time to become fixed. The result has been manifest even to our own day.

The influence of the new gold rapidly spread throughout the country. The era of hard times gradually came to an end with

[70] See, e.g., Colton, *Three Years in California.*

[71] See pp. 291–92, *ante.*

[72] See C. H. Shinn, *Mining-Camps: A Study in American Frontier Government* (New York, 1885), and W. J. Trimble, *The Mining Advance into the Inland Empire* (University of Wisconsin *Bulletin*, No. 638; Madison, 1914).

[73] See, e.g., Royce, *op. cit.*

the augmented supply of precious metals, commerce increased, an impetus was given to banking, the development of the railway system was greatly facilitated, and a speculative movement was in progress.

The idea of " manifest destiny," which for some years had been agitating the American democrat, found fresh stimulus in the advance to the Pacific Coast. Even the New England Emerson, writing in 1844, before Oregon was acquired or California annexed, had declared:

The bountiful continent is ours, state on state, and territory on territory, to the waves of the Pacific sea;

> " Our garden is the immeasurable earth,
> The heaven's blue pillars are Medea's house."

The task of surveying, planting, and building upon this immense tract requires an education and a sentiment commensurate thereto. . . . We in the Atlantic states, by position, have been commercial, and have . . . imbibed easily an European culture. Luckily for us, now that steam has narrowed the Atlantic to a strait, the nervous, rocky West is intruding a new and continental element into the national mind, and we shall yet have an American genius. . . . It is the country of the Future. . . . a country of beginnings, of projects, of designs, of expectations.[74]

[74] *The Young American* (*The Complete Works of Ralph Waldo Emerson*, I [Cambridge, Mass., 1903], 364–65, 369–71). See, further, his observations as quoted on p. 90, *ante*. See also the favorable impression made, later, upon Horace Bushnell, the well-known New England divine, who had gone to California (*California: Its Characteristics and Prospects* [San Francisco, 1858]). This is interesting in connection with his utterances cited on pp. 52–53, *ante*.

CHAPTER IX

SECTIONS AND NATION: JACKSON
ADMINISTRATIONS

We have now seen the broader lines of development in the various sections from 1830 to 1850.

The Northeast had become the seat of a new industrialism and of a society modified by the immigration of the period. Its relative power on the sea and on the farm had diminished.

The South Atlantic had accepted the plantation-and-slave system as its cornerstone, and, growing doubtful of the validity of a democratic society, had become a minority section, more united within itself but increasingly disunited from the nation as a whole.

The South Central, largely an emanation from the South Atlantic, had in the first stages of its development, under the influence of pioneer Jacksonian Democracy, diverged from the older section, but, by 1850, through a gradual process had assimilated to it (particularly in the Lower South) — though there persisted a strong Western quality, not only in economic relations but in a tendency toward a frontier, " fire-eating " character.

Meanwhile, the North Central States had become a home for the wheat-raising pioneers in contrast with the cotton planters of the Southern sections. These Middle Western farmers had left the Northeast and had mingled their lives with those of the migrated Southern uplanders and the foreign-born, who were evolving a new democracy and gaining an ever increasing share of political power in the Union. Developments were under way by which this North Central section was contended for, on the one hand, by the slaveholding sections, which hoped to control its destiny through the importance of the Mississippi River trade, and, on the other, by the North Atlantic sections, which sought to attract it by ties of social and economic interest, facilitated by the extension of the railroad net that was connecting the two.

By the close of the period, therefore, a distinct split had occurred between the northern and southern halves of the Mississippi Valley; but, at the same time, the North Central section had shown its ambition to stand as a distinct and pivotal factor in the fortunes of the nation.

In the midst of the hard times of the forties, the frontier had projected into the Far West a predominantly Southern-upland population. The Texan lands along the Gulf had been settled; beyond the plains and mountains a new American society had been founded in the Oregon country; in the arid region about Great Salt Lake a Mormon theocracy, begun by New England stock, had been established; and, finally, a national impulsion had poured people from the East and West into the gold fields of California.

By 1850, then, not only had the country been greatly enlarged, but problems had been created by the occupation of the Pacific coast and by the question of the relation of slavery to the newly acquired territory.

Turning to the consideration of the way in which these changing sections acted upon one another, it will be the next purpose of the survey to relate the history of the United States, between 1830 and 1850, with reference to the development of the political parties and major issues, primarily from the point of view of the influence of sectional rivalries upon the nation as a whole.

It will be seen from the text and maps that an interesting interplay was in progress between various factors. Each section had its own interest, and worked to make it effective in the entire United States. Within each *section* there were the varied *regions* that have been described. These regions limited sectional unanimity, especially in Presidential elections. At the same time, the existence of political parties extending into all sections, particularly after the formation of the Whigs in 1834, created nationalizing influences that usually worked like elastic bands, holding the sections together, but in years of special stress yielded to the sections' individual fundamental demands.

The American statesmen of the years between 1830 and 1850, at least, were, on the whole, representative of the sections from which they came, authentic exponents of these sections' fundamental traits and ideals; but they were more than this, for they had, also, to deal with the nation. The condition of their rise from mere sectional ascendancy was that they should be able to combine other sections with theirs in a common policy; to find bases on which to build up a country-wide following while still maintaining a hold upon their own people. They must be able to find adjustments between sections, much in the same way that a skilful European diplomat would form alliances, offensive and defensive — or at least ententes — between different countries.

In Congress, both Whig and Democratic parties, as well as minor ones, found the centers of their strength, North and South and East and West, in those regions, within the various sections, that had common economic and social interests.

Even in the election of 1824, the regions of the Lower Mississippi Valley most under the influence of the planting aristocracy and particularly of those living in the areas where slavery was preponderant, furnished their largest minority vote to Adams.[1] A prefiguring of the later Whig party was even then in progress in such regions.

But, when measures of importance arose, party lines usually gave way to *sectional* divisions. Even at such times, party served as a moderating influence, forcing the adjustment and compromise between the sections in the policies of the leaders. Sectional divisions were clearly evident in the action of committees in the shaping of bills, and were manifest in their third reading. In the final votes, however, party, as expressive of similar regional interests in the nation, not seldom triumphed; but (as has been noted and as the maps show), where major sectional interests were involved, these parties, based on regions, yielded to sectional voting. This was a phenomenon by no means peculiar to the period.[2]

[1] Professor Franklin L. Riley kindly furnished me the election returns from Mississippi, as given in the *Woodville Republican*, November 23, 1824. In that state, the counties that gave the largest Adams minority votes were Warren, Claiborne, Adams, Jefferson, and Wilkinson — all of them important centers of the slaveholding aristocracy. For an analysis of the Alabama vote, see Thos. P. Abernethy, *The Formative Period in Alabama, 1815–1828* (Alabama State Department of Archives and History *Historical and Patriotic Series*, No. 6; Montgomery, 1922), p. 109.

[2] F. J. Turner, "Sections and Nation," *Yale Review*, XII, 1–21; *idem*, "The Significance of the Section in American History," *Wisconsin Magazine of History*, VIII, 255–80; and *idem*, "Geographic Sectionalism in American His-

Undoubtedly, initiative and important influence arose from personal leadership; but history is prone to attribute to such leadership an effect that is exaggerated. The names of the principal men are used as symbols in a way that conceals the part played by the lesser leaders who worked with them and who sometimes shaped their action. The larger tendencies, in section and state, that determined much of the course of the outstanding statesmen are too little considered.

The influence of the section upon the leader has already been stressed in characterizing the Democracy that took the name " Jacksonian." While Calhoun made his own contribution and gave to state sovereignty and the right of secession a logical formula beyond that reached by the minor leaders of his section, it is clear, also, that his hand was sometimes forced by them and by the conditions that controlled his action as a representative of the South. Webster's nationalism was deeply shaped by New England's sectional interests. His conception of the nation was adjusted to the economic needs of his New England supporters. Nevertheless, his orations gave classic expression to a growing national feeling that had results transcending even the personal and sectional aspects of his oratory. Clay's compromises and espousal of important issues owed their special form not only to his personal genius and his influence upon his party in various sections, but bore an impress from the social and economic ideas of the Ohio Valley. Thomas H. Benton had a vision of the Far West as a new factor in American life, but behind him were many men with a similar vision. Like comments might be made upon other leaders, such as J. Q. Adams, W. H. Seward, Stephen A. Douglas, James Buchanan, and James K. Polk.

Attention has been called to the fact that the Middle Atlantic section — New York and Pennsylvania particularly — turned the scale in the election of 1828. The political followers of Jackson were a varied and incongruous group, in which the main unifying factor was his personal popularity. South Atlantic leaders expected that, after a single term, he would be succeeded by one of

---

tory," Association of American Geographers *Annals,* XVI, 85–93. [These three essays are reprinted, as Chaps. XII, II, and VII, respectively, in Turner, *The Significance of Sections in American History* (New York, 1932).] See also D. E. Clark, " Sectional Antagonisms in the United States," University of Oregon *Commonwealth Review,* XI, 108 (Oct., 1929).

them, probably Calhoun; and, on the other hand, the New York friends of Van Buren hoped to see him the heir of Jackson. It was inevitable, therefore, that the administration should show a division between these differing groups, or, as Clay put it, so early as July 18, 1829:

> Whatever the President may say or recommend in his message to Congress, his friends in the body must divide on certain leading measures of policy. Each section of it will claim him as belonging to it, if he should be silent, and a quarrel between them is inevitable. . . . If, for example, he comes out for the Tariff, the South leaves him, and will try another change, if it can effect it, of the office of chief magistrate. If he comes out in opposition to the Tariff, there will be such an opposition to him in the Tariff States, as must prevent his re-election.[3]

But not alone the tariff was involved in this test of policies: the disposition of the public lands, and the issues of internal improvements, the National Bank, state sovereignty, and slavery were to be vital forces in the alignment of sections and regions.

Shortly before his inauguration, Jackson had advised with the South Carolina delegation over the composition of his cabinet, but had definitely turned down their demands. He reports, concerning the choices made, that Major John H. Eaton, of Tennessee, whom he made Secretary of War, had recommended John M. Berrien, of Georgia, as Attorney-General, and John Branch, of North Carolina, as Secretary of the Navy;[4] and Martin Van Buren, of New York, who was chosen as Secretary of State, asserts that, with the exception of Samuel D. Ingham, of Pennsylvania (Secretary of the Treasury), he had not learned of the men to be included in Jackon's cabinet, until he received the news of their selection. He adds that the best-known and most powerful politicians of Virginia and South Carolina, who had been prominent in the support of Jackson, were dissatisfied, and that they had been his own zealous friends.[5]

Although at least Ingham, and John McLean, of Ohio (who had been Postmaster-General), were friendly to Calhoun, the South Carolinians were unhappy. There was no representative of

---

[3] Calvin Colton, *The Life, Correspondence, and Speeches of Henry Clay* (New York, 1857), IV, 239.

[4] *Correspondence of Andrew Jackson*, ed. J. S. Bassett, IV (Carnegie Institution of Washington, 1929), 235.

[5] *The Autobiography of Martin Van Buren*, ed. John C. Fitzpatrick (American Historical Association *Annual Report*, 1918, II; Washington, 1920), p. 231.

either Virginia or South Carolina, which had lent such important support to Jackson during the campaign. The group from these states had been denied the particular positions desired. In short, " A new combination was formed in which the West and Southwest were the controlling force." [6] The reorganization of the cabinet in the spring of 1831 [7] still further emphasized the dominance of the Mississippi Valley in that body.

Even during the first years of his Presidency, Jackson found his more intimate counselors in the so-called " kitchen cabinet," composed chiefly of subordinates in office and editorial friends.[8] In this reliance upon a group of advisers outside the cabinet, Jackson is by no means exceptional in the history of American Presidents; and, as differences among the members of the cabinet increased, he came more and more to depend upon this inner circle.

None of the more important questions, however, first came to the fore. A moral issue, involving the attitude of Washington society toward the wife of Secretary of War Eaton, threatened the unity of the cabinet in the beginning and brought about a collision between the followers of Calhoun and of Van Buren. Early in 1829, with Jackson's approval, his warm personal friend, Major Eaton, had married Mrs. John B. Timberlake (formerly Peggy O'Neal), whose chastity was doubted by the social leaders of the city. When, therefore, Eaton was included in Jackson's cabinet, the wife of Calhoun (the Vice-President), the women members of the families of Ingham, Branch, and Berrien, and even Mrs. A. J. Donelson, the wife of Jackson's nephew and private secretary and the hostess of the White House, refused to call upon Mrs. Eaton or attend receptions to which she was invited. It is not necessary to enter into the merits of this controversy, except to point out that Jackson's own sympathies were deeply enlisted.

While Mrs. Calhoun was one of the leaders in the refusal to give social recognition to Mrs. Eaton, on the other hand the Vice-President's rival, Van Buren, the Secretary of State, a widower without the restraint of wife or daughters, warmly espoused her

[6] J. S. Bassett, *The Life of Andrew Jackson* (New York, 1925), II, 420.

[7] Pp. 392–93, *post*.

[8] For a friendly and interesting characterization of the members of the " kitchen cabinet," see Claude G. Bowers, *The Party Battles of the Jackson Period* (Boston, 1922), Chap. VI.

cause and not only called upon her but made every effort to have her received. The pages of Jackson's correspondence [9] give abundant evidence of the fact that this subject engrossed much of his attention and aroused his anger.

Many of the supporters of the President were alienated by his spoils policy in the use of the patronage. This employment of appointments to office, however, was not unnatural, in view of the fact that so many of the incumbents held over from previous administrations and had opposed his election. Both in Pennsylvania and New York State the spoils system was already an established institution.[10]

While Jackson came into office with an overwhelming majority in both houses, we have next to consider the steps by which that majority was diminished, both by personal rivalries and by the rise of dividing economic issues.

Even in 1827 and before that, the question of the distribution of the public lands in connection with the problem of state sovereignty had arisen. Governor Ninian Edwards, of Illinois, had presented to his legislature, in his message of December 2, 1828,[11] the claim that the public lands within a state were the property of that state rather than of the general government, and that they should, therefore, be ceded to the state. He was a friend of Calhoun; and Duff Green, who was at the time fostering Calhoun's candidacy for the Presidency, wrote commending him for his attitude.[12] Here, therefore, was an opportunity for the Calhoun group to conciliate the West and ally parts, at least, of that section with the South Atlantic.[13]

[9] Edited by Bassett; particularly Vol. IV.

[10] See C. R. Fish, *The Civil Service and the Patronage* (*Harvard Historical Studies*, XI; New York, 1905), and Lucy M. Salmon, *History of the Appointing Power of the President* (American Historical Association *Papers*, I [New York, 1886], 291–419).

[11] See the comments in R. G. Wellington, *The Political and Sectional Influence of the Public Lands, 1828–1842* (Cambridge, Mass., 1914), pp. 7 (n. 4), 13 (n. 2), 15–19, 23.

[12] "*Your* position," wrote Green, "in relation to the public lands brings you into company with the South and West and in direct conflict with the East." (Quoted *ibid.*, p. 21.) Green's newspaper, the *United States Telegraph*, asserted: "If our fellow-citizens of the West will place themselves upon their high constitutional rights instead of presenting themselves to Congress in the attitude of mendicants, they will soon hold the balance of political power." (Quoted *ibid.*, p. 22.)

[13] *Ibid.*, pp. 9–10.

The North Central States wished to obtain their lands at a low price (and, if possible, for nothing) and were interested in internal improvements and a high tariff; the South Central States also desired low-priced public lands, and internal improvements, but preferred a lower tariff; the seaboard South was interested in a low tariff, no federal internal improvements, and high-priced public lands — points on which, however, they might be induced to trade with rival sections for considerations favoring their other demands; while the North Atlantic states sought a high tariff and high-priced public lands and were divided on internal improvements.[14]

Richard Rush, the Secretary of the Treasury under John Quincy Adams, had pointed out, in his report of December 8, 1827, the intimate relation between the disposition of the public lands and the encouragement of manufacture, and had advocated a higher tariff as an offset to the high wages that were imposed in the East by the temptation to workmen to migrate to the cheap or free lands of the West.[15] On the question of the graduation of the public lands, and on pre-emption, solutions interesting to the West had been brought forward, particularly by Benton. In view of the large amount of public lands already in the market and not yet sold, coupled with the concern of New England lest her laboring population should be withdrawn, Senator S. A. Foot, of Connecticut, on December 29, 1829, introduced his resolution to inquire into the expediency of limiting the disposition of public lands to those then remaining for sale, of suspending the service, and of abolishing the office of Surveyor-General. The debate that followed in January, 1830, and was prolonged into the spring, was bitter. John Quincy Adams, of Massachusetts, characterized it as the " Tape-worm debate." In the course of that discussion, it was brought out that so much of the public lands in the new states and the territories was occupied by squatters, but not purchased, that the unsold lands were not a fair indication of the needs of Western settlers. Benton's idea of graduation of the price of the public lands, and the whole subject of the numbers and

[14] Clay spoke with John Quincy Adams (December 31, 1828) " with great concern of the prospects of the country — the threats of disunion from the South, and the graspings after all the public lands, which are disclosing themselves in the Western States." (*Memoirs of John Quincy Adams*, ed. C. F. Adams, VIII [Philadelphia, 1876], 87–88.)

[15] *Register of Debates in Congress*, IV, Pt. II, 2831–32.

rights of squatters in respect to extending the pre-emption law, received much attention. Indeed, Robert Y. Hayne, of South Carolina, remarked [16] that over half the time of Congress had been taken up with a discussion of propositions connected with the public lands and that more than half of the Congressional acts embraced provisions growing out of this fruitful source. Supported by Hayne, Benton charged that New England had always been unfriendly to the growth of the West; and amplified this charge with much detail. The merits of the public-lands controversy were merged, therefore, with sectional recriminations. John Quincy Adams declared that the object was to " break down the union of the Eastern and Western sections " and to restore " the old joint operation of the West and the South against New England." [17]

In the course of the debate, Webster took advantage of Hayne's support of the doctrine of state sovereignty, as he understood it to have been expressed in the South Carolina Exposition of 1828, to change the issue from the public lands to the right of nullification; and the interchange of blows, over the question of nationalism or state sovereignty, between these two orators has led to calling the controversy the " Hayne-Webster Debate."

Nevertheless, it must be borne in mind that the dispute arose over the important part that the public lands played in the policies of the different sections and that it was participated in on that basis by many speakers and for many weeks. As yet, Calhoun had not avowed his authorship of the South Carolina Exposition, and, while desiring to keep himself in touch with his own section, he still hoped to procure such a following from other sections as would maintain his position as a national statesman.

At the very time that this controversy was in progress, the whole subject of Jacksonian Democracy was being agitated in Vir-

[16] *Ibid.*, VI, Pt. I, 31–32.

[17] *Memoirs*, VIII, 190–91. Adams's view receives support in the remarks of Charles Hammond, quoted in the *Cincinnati Advertiser,* of June 5, 1830: " The south have made up their minds to barter the western lands for western votes. They propose to bribe the west with these lands to the abandonment of the protection of American industry and of the system of internal improvements." (Adams's ideas of the failure of the alliance are in his *Memoirs*, IX [Philadelphia, 1876], 235.) Suggestions came to Calhoun that attacks which his friends were making on New England were being used by Van Buren's supporters to transfer the Calhoun following, there, to him.

ginia, in the constitutional debates of 1829–30.[18] The discussion, there, over the basis of apportionment of the legislature had resulted in a conflict of views between the interior counties and those of the tidewater. Issues were made with regard to the gradual abolition of slavery, the development of internal improvements, etc.; and the tidewater planters represented in the convention repudiated the ideas of Jeffersonian Democracy as voiced in the Declaration of Independence, and urged the rights of property holders as against majority rule.[19]

While, then, Calhoun and his friends, who had supported Jackson, were seeking an alliance with the West on the question of the disposition of the public lands, they were basing their demands upon the principle of state sovereignty and were antagonizing fundamental conceptions of Jackson's supporters with reference to the common people and the right of majority rule. Although no decision resulted from the debate over the public domain, its sectional importance is evident, and the coming break between Calhoun and the President might have been foreseen.

Even so early as the close of 1829, Jackson had picked Van Buren as his successor.[20] No doubt the different attitudes of Calhoun and Van Buren in the Eaton scandal influenced him toward this conclusion. But the nullification issue strengthened his decision.

On the thirteenth of April, 1830, at the dinner in memory of Jefferson (at which it was probably intended by the South Atlantic extremists to reinforce their state-sovereignty cause through the use of his name), Jackson's celebrated toast, " Our Federal Union: it must be preserved," clashed with Calhoun's " The Union — next to Liberty most dear."

Calhoun, still believing that Jackson would not become a candidate in 1832 and expecting to defeat Van Buren for the suc-

[18] See pp. 183–85, *ante.*

[19] Besides in the debates themselves, as already discussed, the Virginia differences are dealt with in Chas. H. Ambler, *Sectionalism in Virginia from 1776 to 1861* (Chicago, 1910), Chap. v, and Henry H. Simms, *The Rise of the Whigs in Virginia, 1824–1840* (Richmond, Va., 1929), pp. 36–39.

[20] See New York Public Library *Bulletin*, III, 298, and *Jackson Correspondence*, IV, 108–9. Major W. B. Lewis, quoted by Bassett (the editor of the *Correspondence*) in a footnote, takes credit for this letter, and states that it was called out by the serious debility of the President, leading to alarm, and to his desire to express his confidence in Van Buren. The letter was to be used, in case of his death, to promote the latter's candidacy.

cession, was desirous of conciliating the administration. When an opposition group was objecting to the approval of some of the President's important nominations, Calhoun denied that his friends were delaying this approval.[21] Confirmation of the nomination of Isaac Hill, of New Hampshire, had been refused on April 5, 1830, and in that refusal some of Calhoun's influential friends had joined. When, however, on May 10, the appointment of Amos Kendall, one of the "kitchen cabinet," was acted on, Calhoun, as Vice-President, gave the casting vote in his favor, as he did, also, in the case of the reconsideration of the vote against Editor M. M. Noah.

But there was evidently forming in the Senate a group of the Jackson party that was not ready to follow the President in all of his measures. Two days after his casting votes sustaining Jackson's appointments, Calhoun wrote to a friend:

The times are perilous beyond any that I have ever witnessed. All of the great interests of the country are coming into conflict, and I must say, and with deep regret I speak it, that those to whom the vessel of state is entrusted seem either ignorant, or indifferent about the danger.[22]

And he added that he considered it perfectly uncertain whether Jackson would run again or not.

The final break with Calhoun was not made until the revelations regarding the latter's opposition to Jackson's action in the Seminole campaign (1818) came to the attention of the President. Some of his friends had been aware of this from an early period ;[23] but it was only when he learned from Major W. B. Lewis of Calhoun's opposition, in the Seminole discussions in the Monroe cabinet, to his Florida invasion, that his suspicion became so aroused that he secured from Senator John Forsyth the correspondence in which William H. Crawford [24] revealed the secrets

[21] *Correspondence of John C. Calhoun*, ed. J. Franklin Jameson (American Historical Association *Annual Report*, 1899, II; Washington, 1900), pp. 271, 272.

[22] *Ibid.*, p. 273.

[23] *Jackson Correspondence*, IV, 229, n. 2; *Van Buren Autobiography*, pp. 367–73; and Bassett, *Jackson*, II, 506–8.

[24] The manuscript Papers of Martin Van Buren, in the Library of Congress, contain letters from Wm. H. Crawford, under date of December 21, 1827, and October 21, 1828, remonstrating against Van Buren's supposed willingness to have Calhoun continue in the Vice-Presidency, and threatening (in the second letter) that, in case Jackson thought of calling him (Calhoun) to his cabinet: " I will myself cause representations to be made to Genl Jackson that will prevent his

of the cabinet meeting and made it clear that not he, but Calhoun, had proposed to try Jackson. Having received the letters making this charge against Calhoun, Jackson sent them, on May 13, 1830, to Calhoun, whose reply intensified the wrath of the President. The correspondence between Calhoun and Jackson [25] was not published until the middle of February, 1831. Even after this revelation, Calhoun hoped (in vain) that the breach could be healed, and he sought to convince the country that the intrigue was attributable to Van Buren and his friends.[26]

It was probably at about the time that Jackson received Calhoun's answer to his Seminole inquiry that he definitely decided to become a candidate in 1832, although the *Globe* of March 30, 1830, had already made the announcement that he would run again, Pennsylvania Democratic legislators had placed him in nomination the day following,[27] and, some two weeks later, Democratic members of the New York legislature had gone on record as strongly desirous of his re-election.[28]

A bill for a federal appropriation for the Maysville (Kentucky) Road passed the House of Representatives on April 29, 1930. A map of that vote shows that support of the measure was largely in the old Federalist regions of New England, New Jersey, and Delaware, together with northern and western New York and the districts along much of the Potomac and Ohio rivers, including the tributaries north and south. Opposition came from southeastern Maine, the state of New Hampshire, the Democratic parts of New York, portions of southeastern Pennsylvania, a small area in southern Kentucky, and zones in eastern and central Tennessee, but was chiefly centered in the South Atlantic and South Central states, with the exception of Louisiana and northwestern Alabama. It is clear, therefore, that there was party voting, and that the Jackson strength was principally in the two

---

being taken into the Cabinet of Genl Jackson." Although Crawford did not further explain, it would seem that he referred to his intended use of the Seminole incident.

[25] *The Works of John C. Calhoun*, ed. R. K. Crallé, VI (New York, 1855), Appendix.

[26] Van Buren's denial is in his *Autobiography*, pp. 376, 386–87.

[27] W. M. Meigs, *The Life of John Caldwell Calhoun* (New York, 1917), I, 395; *Niles' Register*, XXXVIII, 169–70; and J. B. McMaster, *A History of the People of the United States, from the Revolution to the Civil War*, VI (New York, 1920), 116.

[28] *Ibid.*, citing *Albany Argus*, Apr., 1830.

Southern sections, in alliance with those parts of New York, and all of New Hampshire, under the influence of Van Buren. The measure passed the Senate on May 15, and a mapping of this vote shows the same general pattern.

Jackson's veto of the bill (a bill dear to the heart of Henry Clay, inasmuch as it concerned his immediate region) was presented on May 27.[29] The President refused his assent on the ground that such an appropriation for internal improvements was not warranted by the Constitution, because the project was local rather than national. There is reason for believing that Van Buren drafted this veto,[30] and it corresponded with his doctrines regarding national internal improvements. In view of the interest of the Mississippi Valley in internal improvements, the veto, of course, hurt Jackson in regions of commercial intercourse which looked to federal rather than state aid; but these were naturally friendly to Clay. Jackson himself was convinced that it had defined parties sharply; [31] and it led Webster, in a letter to Clay, to designate the Kentuckian as necessarily the leader of the opposition.[32] Van Buren informed the President of the approval of the veto in the Middle Atlantic section, which had already initiated state internal improvements.[33]

Clay's idea that issues would finally come to the front was being justified. The spring and summer of 1830, therefore, marked a definite step in the development of political parties. To John Quincy Adams, it seemed (even so late as April of that year) that Jackson's popularity was such that, while it lasted, his majorities in both houses would " stand by him for good or evil." [34] At the same time, the divisions in the cabinet were becoming serious. Not only the difficulty arising from the Eaton affair continued to make enemies, but the rivalry of Calhoun and Van Buren for the successorship was being used to split the cabinet. Fearing that the Democratic newspaper organ edited by Duff Green was

[29] Jas. D. Richardson (compiler), *Messages and Papers of the Presidents, 1789–1897*, II (Washington, 1896), 483.

[30] *Jackson Correspondence*, IV, 137. See *Van Buren Autobiography*, Chap. xxv, for his account of the veto and its effects.

[31] New York Public Library *Bulletin*, IV (1900), 298, and *Jackson Correspondence*, IV, 157.

[32] *The Writings and Speeches of Daniel Webster* ("National Edition"; Boston and New York, 1903), XVI, 197–99.

[33] *Jackson Correspondence*, IV, 166.

[34] *Memoirs*, VIII, 215. See also Colton, *Clay*, IV, 257.

employed by Calhoun, the President decided that he must get another mouthpiece,[35] and he therefore called Francis P. Blair from Tennessee to Washington; and the first number of the *Globe* under his editorship appeared on December 7, 1830. Thus, the organ of Presidential policy was transferred from Southern to Western editorship.

Finally, Van Buren reached the conclusion that only a reconstruction of the cabinet would solve the President's difficulties, and he broached to him the proposal that this should be brought about by his own resignation, to be followed by others'.[36] While Jackson was more than reluctant to see Van Buren retire, he had already determined to " purge " his cabinet,[37] if necessary; and this conclusion was strengthened by the information that came to him of the activity of some of the members to force his hand with reference to the successorship of Calhoun and of the attitude of Pennsylvania in the next campaign.[38] Accordingly, between the seventh and nineteenth of April, 1831, he received and accepted the resignations of all of the cabinet save Berrien and Barry; and the resignation of Berrien was sent and accepted on the fifteenth of June.[39] While, in their final form, these resignations appeared to be voluntary, it is clear that the Calhoun group were reluctant and felt that the retirements were forced.[40] A contemporary cartoon represented the cabinet break as of " rats leaving a falling house." [41]

In the selection of his new cabinet, the President replaced Van Buren by Edward Livingston, of Louisiana; Ingham, by Louis McLane, of Delaware; Branch, by Levi Woodbury, of New Hampshire; Berrien, by Roger B. Taney, of Maryland; and, after trying in vain to persuade his old friend, Hugh Lawson White, of Tennessee, to succeed Eaton and to take up his residence at the White House,[42] finally chose Lewis Cass, of Michigan.

[35] New York Public Library *Bulletin*, IV, 298.

[36] See Van Buren's account in his *Autobiography*, Chap. XXIX. John Quincy Adams believed (*Memoirs*, VIII, 184) that Jackson had determined, as early as February 6, 1830, to remove Branch, but was deterred by the warnings of his friends that North Carolina would join the opposition in that case.

[37] *Jackson Correspondence*, IV, 252.   [38] *Ibid.*, pp. 249–51.

[39] *Ibid.*, pp. 257–58, 260–63, 264–65, 266, 268, 279–80, 295.

[40] *Ibid.*, pp. 263–65, 266, 268. On Jackson's view of Calhoun's influence in this reluctance, see pp. 286, 318–21, 341–42, *et passim*.

[41] See also *Adams Memoirs*, VIII, 359–60.

[42] *Jackson Correspondence*, IV, 258–59, 267–68.

It is clear, therefore, that the reconstructed cabinet represented a definite break between the President and the Calhoun group, to the advantage of Van Buren and the diminution of South Atlantic influence. In fact, it was distinctly a move toward a combination of the North and the West of that time.[43] Thus, the apprehensions that were expressed when Jackson selected his first cabinet were shown to have been well founded.[44]

We may next consider the earlier progress of the issue of nullification. On coming to the Presidency, Jackson was confronted by the South Carolina Exposition of 1828 and by the contest that had arisen between the administration of John Quincy Adams and Georgia over the Indians within the borders of that state.[45] With the attitude characteristic of a Western man and an Indian fighter, Jackson was in hearty sympathy with Georgia, although, in defiance of John Quincy Adams's administration, she had announced advanced ideas on the subject of " state sovereignty." This phrase, however, was used at the time without accurate consideration of its implications, and, when the Cherokees adopted a national constitution, on July 26, 1827, asserting that they were a sovereign and independent nation, with complete jurisdiction over their territory, Georgia countered by an act (December 20, 1828) extending her laws over the entire state, to be fully effective after June 1, 1830. The rush of gold miners into the Cherokee region raised the question to a critical position, and Jackson withdrew the federal troops,[46] which had been ordered there by the previous administration.

When the subject came before the Supreme Court of the United States, Georgia announced her determination not to appear, nor to allow the Cherokees to exercise authority, but to defend her own sovereignty. The court declined to take jurisdiction, and denied the desired injunction against Georgia.[47] Not until 1832

[43] Cf. Bassett, *Jackson*, II, 538. See Calhoun's strictures upon the sectional line-up of this cabinet, as quoted on p. 32, *ante*.

[44] See pp. 33–34, 383–84, *ante*.

[45] Annie H. Abel, *The History of Events Resulting in Indian Consolidation West of the Mississippi* (American Historical Association *Annual Report*, 1906, I [Washington, 1908], 233–450) ; and U. B. Phillips, *Georgia and State Rights* (*ibid.*, 1901, II [Washington, 1902], 3–224), Chaps. II, III.

[46] His ideas respecting Georgia's rights over the Indians are stated in a memorandum printed in *Jackson Correspondence*, IV, 219–20.

[47] Richard Peters, *Reports of Cases Argued and Adjudged in the Supreme Court of the United States*, V, 1.

was the opinion of the court finally expressed, in the case of Worcester *v.* Georgia.[48]   In the decision of the case, Chief Justice John Marshall reached the conclusion that the Cherokees were under the protection of the United States, which had the sole right of managing their affairs, but that they should be recognized as a distinct national state, within the territory of which Georgia's laws could have no force.

On January 3, 1832, however, the House of Representatives of the United States had tabled a resolution to facilitate the enforcement of the decisions of the Supreme Court by federal action.   In the Congressional representation of South Carolina, Georgia, Alabama, Mississippi, and Tennessee, only one vote was cast for enforcement of the decisions.   Even Kentucky gave as many votes in favor of tabling as against.   On the other hand, in Vermont and all of southern New England there was but a single vote (from Connecticut) for tabling.   The Middle Atlantic section was divided, the majority, in New York, favoring tabling, but overwhelmingly opposing the motion, in Pennsylvania, where the Quaker and missionary friends of the Indians were influential. In all, ninety-nine votes were cast for tabling and eighty-nine against.   Jackson's alleged refusal, therefore, to use the power of the federal government against Georgia to enforce the decision of the court was not unwarranted by this action of the House of Representatives.   Nevertheless, it was undoubtedly a satisfaction to him to withhold the use of federal troops to carry out " John Marshall's decision."   He finally avoided the difficulty by procuring the cession of the disputed lands and the removal of the Indians to the west of the Mississippi.

But the attitude of Jackson in this Georgia controversy gave to the advocates of state sovereignty the impression that he would support their claims; and the President's action not only won friends for him in Georgia but at the same time strengthened the belief of the nullificationists that he might not oppose their policy. Even at the time of the Jefferson dinner, at which Jackson gave his celebrated Union toast, the Calhoun group attempted at first to explain his words as indicating the preservation of a Union of the type that admitted the contentions of the nullificationists. They were soon undeceived.   In the hope for possible ascendancy of the South Atlantic in the next administration and for revision

48 *Ibid.,* VI, 515.

of the tariff in accordance with the demands of South Carolina and her sister states in the South, decisive action was postponed.

Even within the state of South Carolina, marked divergence of sentiment existed.[49] At the Charleston dinner of July 4, 1830, one of the leaders, William Drayton, refused to accept the doctrine of nullification.[50] On the same occasion, Langdon Cheves declared in favor of a program of co-operation of Southern states rather than of individual action; and on the fifteenth of September he wrote [51] elaborating his objections to extreme measures by a single state; but he felt that the opposition should be on the " consecrated ground " of revolution, and deprecated " all action by one State," going on to say, " I have no confidence in any resistance, peaceable or forcible, which shall not embrace a majority of the suffering States." He recognized that the states were divided into " western, eastern, middle and southern sections," and that " the south has thus a separate identity and a common public sentiment among themselves." If the section united and left the Union, it would be " called back by such an impatient wooing, as neither romance nor poetry hath typified."

Here, therefore, was a clear indication that behind South Carolina's action would necessarily rest that of the section, if an outcome satisfactory to the South were to be expected. It would seem, therefore, that state sovereignty, as expressed in the doctrine of nullification, was in reality only the shield to be used for sectionalism.

Even Calhoun recognized that, not the tariff, but slavery, was the ultimate source of difference.[52] He felt, however, that it was essential that some one state (South Carolina) should take the lead in opposition.[53] Yet, on the eighteenth of March, 1831, a

---

[49] Chauncey S. Boucher, *The Nullification Controversy in South Carolina* (Chicago, 1916); D. F. Houston, *A Critical Study of Nullification in South Carolina* (*Harvard Historical Studies*, III; Cambridge, 1896); H. D. Capers, *The Life and Times of C. G. Memminger* (Richmond, Va., 1893); Chas. J. Stillé, *Life and Services of Joel R. Poinsett* (Philadelphia, 1888); and W. A. Schaper, *Sectionalism and Representation in South Carolina* (American Historical Association *Annual Report*, 1900, I [Washington, 1901], 237–463).

[50] He even voted for the Force Bill of 1833, and finally left South Carolina; see Meigs, *Calhoun*, I, 416.

[51] E. S. Thomas, *Reminiscences of the Last Sixty-five Years, Commencing with the Battle of Lexington. Also, Sketches of His Own Life and Times* (Hartford, Conn., 1840), II, 232 ff.

[52] Meigs, *op. cit.*, I, 417–19.

[53] *Calhoun Correspondence*, pp. 281, 306.

conversation between him and J. H. Hammond, of South Carolina, shows that he still hesitated and had his ideas of a series of sectional compromises that would avoid the issue and perhaps make his Presidential aspirations possible of realization.[54] To the West (he suggested) he would give internal improvements by the use of the public lands, seeking a Constitutional amendment for that purpose; to New England, a moderate protective tariff; and to the South, such changes in protection as would satisfy her needs.

Calhoun's course, however, was brought to a decisive issue at the dinner given George McDuffie at Charleston, on May 19, 1831, where extreme state-rights toasts and the attitude of Calhoun's friends (which he characterized as " imprudent " [55]) forced him to come out in the open on nullification. His Fort Hill address [56] expounding nullification followed on the twenty-sixth of July of that year. In this he sharpened and elaborated the doctrines that he had worked out in the Exposition of 1828.[57] At about this time, the state-rights faction in South Carolina dropped the name of Jackson from its party designation. In November Calhoun still further explained his nullification doctrine, in a report and an address prepared for the South Carolina legislature.[58]

But discussion of the later developments of nullification may be deferred for a few pages in order to consider what had been occurring in the meantime with reference to the issues of public lands, the tariff, and the Bank, for they were all connected.

We may first turn to a consideration of the subjects of the public lands and the tariff in these years, and then see how, contemporaneously, the issue of the Bank complicated these problems.

As has already been noted, the public domain was of great practical importance to the North Central States, while, at the same time, the older states were unwilling to yield their rights in that field. From the beginning of Jackson's administration, it was evident that the approaching extinction of the public debt and a consequent surplus arising from the combined influx into

[54] *American Historical Review*, VI, 744.

[55] *Calhoun Correspondence*, p. 294.

[56] *Calhoun Works*, VI, 59–94. See also *Calhoun Correspondence*, pp. 296–97, 300.

[57] Van Buren notes, in his *Autobiography* (p. 541), that, when he left for England (in August), Calhoun had just committed himself to the doctrine of nullification.

[58] *Calhoun Works*, VI, 94–123, 124–44.

the treasury of funds derived from the public lands and the tariff, raised the question of what should be done with this surplus. The retention of both the high protection provided by the tariff of 1828 and of the revenues from the sale of public lands brought concern to the advocates of a protective tariff (which would be endangered by the surplus) ; and, on the other hand, accumulation of the revenue from these two sources would arouse the enmity of the South, whose grievances in respect to the tariff of 1828 had led to the South Carolina Exposition of that year.

Clay's American System rested upon an alliance between the manufacturing states of the North Atlantic sections (and particularly of New England) with those parts of the North Central Division that had accepted his doctrine of the home market. Indeed, for some years the almost unanimous vote of those Western states had been cast in favor of the protective tariff and had been pivotal in the determination of the contests.

But, at the beginning of Jackson's administration, the combination of tariff and lands had been clearly manifested.[59]

In the debates over the Foot resolution,[60] an attempt was made at the beginning of 1830 to effect an alliance of the South with the West in favor of a land policy satisfactory to the latter sections, and a reduction of the tariff.

Although no decision was reached in these debates, Benton's graduation bill won in the Senate on its third reading, May 7, 1830, with the support of all the Senators of the North Central Division except one from Ohio, and of all those save two from the states below the Potomac in the Southern sections, while, on the other hand, all of the Eastern Senators north of the Potomac, except one from New Hampshire, voted against the bill.[61]   In the House, however, the larger representation of the North Atlantic states succeeded in tabling the measure.

Jackson's earlier record and sympathies were not adverse to a protective tariff, and his reliance upon the vote of Pennsylvania made it important to retain that strong manufacturing state.   In his message of December 8, 1829, he had therefore tried to hold his supporters together by a policy of reduction of duties that

---

[59] Wellington, *Influence of the Public Lands*, pp. 23–26.

[60] See pp. 386–88, *ante*.

[61] Wellington (*op. cit.*, pp. 33–34), who attributes this vote to the passage of the bill.

would, at the same time, safeguard the interests of those manufactures in which there was European competition; and he had urged that a Constitutional amendment should be passed that would permit the distribution of the surplus revenue among the states.

In his message of December 6, 1831, Jackson recurred to the question of the tariff, and proposed a reduction by a process of conciliation that should do justice to all interests. His language was not free from ambiguity, and the reappearance of Clay as the leader of the opposition party sharpened the issue. On the ninth of January, 1832, Clay's resolutions provided for the lowering of duties on noncompetitive items and against the general distribution of the surplus revenue.[62] But neither his plan nor that of the administration would have been sufficient to solve the problem of this surplus.

The speech of Clay in favor of his resolutions caused great excitement among Senators from the South, and the radicals even spoke of the dividing of the Union by the Potomac. John Quincy Adams was at this time willing to compromise, in view of Southern opposition to the tariff, but declared that he would not sacrifice the manufacturing interests.[63] His report was favorable to protection, but apparently in part reflected views of the Secretary of the Treasury. His frank charge that a conflict between the planting and manufacturing states would result in the dissolution of the Union and would mean war, and his raising of the question of the effect of that war upon slavery, was a prophetic utterance, which naturally aroused the wrath of the South.

Clay believed that portions of the two Southern sections were ready to purchase Western antitariff support by sacrificing the public lands to the states within which they lay.[64] His letter to this effect was called out by the fact that, on the twenty-second of March, 1832, a combination of Southern and Western men had referred to his Committee on Manufactures the rival proposals regarding the tariff, together with the question of the reduction of the price of public lands and the cession to the states of the unsold lands. The joining of tariff and lands in these references was not purely a matter of politics designed to place Clay in an

---

[62] Edward Stanwood, *American Tariff Controversies in the Nineteenth Century* (Boston, 1903), I, 370.

[63] *Memoirs*, VIII, 451-63 (*passim*), 470.   [64] Colton, *Clay*, IV, 330-31.

awkward position with regard to his Western support: it was reasonable, in view of the close relation between the two issues, and of the prospective existence of a surplus that must affect tariff bills.

The report of Clay, on the sixteenth of April, 1832, was skilfully contrived to retain his following among the Eastern men favorable to a general distribution of the receipts from the public lands, and, at the same time, to separate the older from the newer states of the West on that question. He opposed the reduction of the price of public lands or the cession of them to the states within which they lay, and argued that the lowering of the price would both diminish the value of privately held lands and increase the emigration from Ohio, Kentucky, and Tennessee — already under way in large numbers — to regions farther to the west. He argued, moreover, that the population of the younger Western states was increasing with sufficient rapidity. A dangerous situation was predicted in the antagonism of states and in the debtor relation that would be involved in the arrangements arising from the proposal to exact payment from the states in return for cession of the public lands. He therefore favored a bill for the distribution of the proceeds of the sales of public lands. By this he hoped to keep his following in the older and more populous Western states, and to satisfy Eastern friends of a protective tariff by making import duties the main reliance of the government for its revenues.

It is clear, therefore, that the public lands had become an important factor, both in the question of the tariff and in the matter of candidacies for the Presidential election in 1832.

On July 3, 1832, Clay's bill for the distribution of the net proceeds of the public lands passed in the Senate (26 to 18) by a party vote, with the assistance of a few administration Senators from the East. In this vote the North Atlantic sections cast all but two of their votes in favor.[65] But postponement won in the House of Representatives. The North Central States, balked in their expectation of Southern assistance in their land policy, were in a mood to break away from the South on the tariff.

On the twenty-eighth of June, 1832, the protective-tariff bill

[65] See also the analysis of Wellington, in his *Influence of the Public Lands*, on page 39 (where he follows the older practice of including Delaware in the North Atlantic group of states).

sponsored by John Quincy Adams passed the House of Representatives by a vote of 162 to 65. On the whole, it was designed as a compromise measure. Adams, as shown in his diary, was apprehensive of the menace of Southern opposition, while Clay exhibited a willingness to defy the South.[66] Clay's plan provided for the retention of the protective principle and the reduction of revenue by remission of the duties on tea, coffee, wine, and certain noncompetitive manufactures. The question of woolens was uppermost in Massachusetts, and that of iron, in Pennsylvania; and on these issues the latter state and New England were in disagreement. A majority of the Southern members voted in favor of the bill, in view of its reductions from the tariff of 1828.

The Senate amended the bill, in various schedules, to restore greater protection, and passed it, on July 9, 1832, by a vote (32 to 16) that clearly revealed the subordination of party to sectionalism. The following table discloses the Senate situation:

	National Republican		Democratic		Unclassified	
	Yeas	Nays	Yeas	Nays	Yeas	Nays
New England	6	0	4	0	2	0
Middle Atlantic	3	0	3	0	0	0
South Atlantic	1	1	2	6	1	1
South Central	2	0	1	4	0	3
North Central	1	0	4	1	2	0
	13	1	14	11	5	4

In the conference between the two houses, the Senate was finally obliged to abandon its changes, much to the unhappiness of Clay and Webster, who realized that the outcome was unsatisfactory to the New England woolen industry. The following table shows the sectional grouping on the final passage in the House of Representatives, June 28, 1832, by a vote of 132 to 65:

	National Republican		Democratic		Unclassified		Totals	
	Yeas	Nays	Yeas	Nays	Yeas	Nays	Yeas	Nays
New England	5	12	7	2	5	3	17	17
Middle Atlantic	1	4	31	6	12	7	44	17
South Atlantic	6	5	19	17	6	3	31	25
South Central	4	2	13	4	5	0	22	6
North Central	5	0	11	0	2	0	18	0
	21	23	81	29	30	13	132	65

[66] *Adams Memoirs*, VIII, 444-49.

Here, as in the Senate, party ties yielded to sectional interests. New England's dissatisfaction with the Senate amendments was shown in her vote of 17 yeas against 17 nays, with 5 not voting.

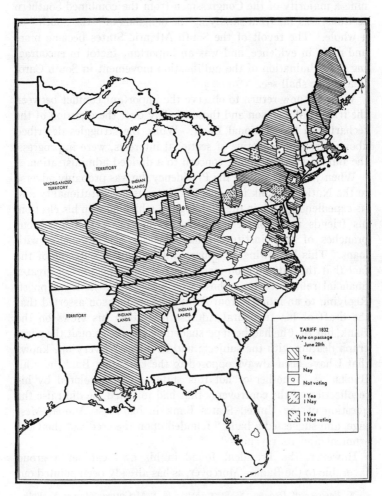

The alliance of the North Central States with the South had not resulted in the fulfilment of the former's hopes of a more liberal land policy, and her favorable attitude upon the tariff was doubtless influenced thereby. In the South Atlantic and South Central sections, the votes in favor were due to the desire to find relief from the high tariff of 1828. Jackson signed the measure on the fourteenth of July.

But it soon became apparent that this tariff act, although winning a majority of the Congressmen from the combined Southern sections, was far from satisfying the demands of " the South " as a whole. The revolt of the South Atlantic States became more and more in evidence, and was an important factor in encouraging the culmination of the nullification movement in South Carolina, as we shall see.

We must now return to observe the important conflict between the friends of Jackson and those of Clay over the question of the recharter of the National Bank. While the struggles described above, strongly reflective of sectional interests, were in progress, the Bank issue was giving concern to a divided administration.

When Jackson came to the Presidency, he was probably adverse to the National Bank in respect both to its constitutionality and its expediency; and, in the campaign in which he won his election, his friends made bitter complaints over the fact that various branches of that institution had favored his opponents with loans. This borrowing, of course, was a natural outcome of the fact that the anti-Jackson men were apt to be persons of greater financial reliability than those who were active in his support. Replying to an inquiry from Polk, in 1833, Jackson asserted that the draft of his Inaugural Address had given his views on the Bank, but that he had been persuaded by friends to omit the paragraph dealing with the subject; and he adds: " Every one knows that I have been always opposed to the U. States Bank, nay all Banks." [67] Whether or not this statement was colored by his recollection of the controversy that had followed, he did raise the question of the United States Bank in his First Annual Message, and suggested a bank " founded upon the credit of the Government and its revenues."

However, the President found in his own cabinet a group favorable to the Bank. Moreover, as has already been pointed out

[67] *Register of Debates*, X, Pt. II, 2263; E. I. McCormac, *James K. Polk: A Political Biography* (Berkeley, Calif., 1922), pp. 26–27; Thos. P. Abernethy, " The Early Development of Commerce and Banking in Tennessee," *Mississippi Valley Historical Review*, XIV, 321; and St. Geo. L. Sioussat, " Some Phases of Tennessee Politics in the Jackson Period," *American Historical Review*, XIV, 64–66. But see also Abernethy, " Andrew Jackson and the Rise of Southwestern Democracy," *ibid.*, XXXIII, 64–77.

in chapters on the sections,[68] New England, although strongly influenced by conservative financial interests, relied largely upon its own system of state banks; the Middle Atlantic States, at about 1830, used but one-fifth to one-fourth of the currency of the National Bank; the South Atlantic Division, one-fourth; and the Southwest of that time, one-fourth; while the Bank's branches in Kentucky, Tennessee, and Ohio had one-fourth, or almost as much as New England and the Middle Atlantic States, together; and the states that, in later years, were to become known as " the South " had over half of the circulation.[69] There were, therefore, strong reasons, also, for hesitancy in the attack upon the Bank, in this sectional need for its activities and in view of the fact that members of Congress were apt to reflect the wishes of the elements in their constituencies that felt this pressure.

Moreover, the distribution of the Bank's stock had an important bearing. Of the 4,145 stockholders (in July, 1831), 466, owning 79,159 shares, were foreigners; the United States Government held 70,000 shares; New England stockholders, 14,594 shares; Middle Atlantic, 88,206; South Atlantic, 96,415; South Central, 651; and North Central, 975.[70] More shares were held in Pennsylvania (52,638) than in any other state; there followed, in order, South Carolina (in which 40,674 shares were owned), Maryland (34,503), and New York (32,903).

There was, therefore, in the South Atlantic Division, a very strong financial interest in the Bank of the United States. Although the Western sections contained a relatively slight number of stockholders, large regions, there, were in favor of the Bank.

President Nicholas Biddle, who was himself at first a Democrat, was desirous, in the beginning of Jackson's administration, of keeping the Bank out of politics, and had written to Webster refusing a loan to Gales and Seaton, of the *National Intelligencer*, on the ground that the newspaper's services to the Bank were " considerations entirely foreign to us." After the election of 1828, he believed that " no administration would venture to set the monied concerns of the country afloat as they once were." [71]

[68] Pp. 64, 177, *ante*.

[69] On this distribution of the currency of the Bank of the United States, see Ralph C. H. Catterall, *The Second Bank of the United States* (Chicago, 1903), pp. 409–12; cf. p. 137.   [70] *Ibid.*, pp. 168, 508.

[71] *The Correspondence of Nicholas Biddle Dealing with National Affairs, 1807–1844*, ed. R. C. McGrane (Boston, 1919), pp. 58, 62.

In 1824 the entire purchase by the Bank of inland exchange bills in the West and Southwest was less than twenty-nine per cent of the total exchange bought, but by 1832 the percentage had risen to over sixty; and the purchase, there, in the later year was sixteen-fold that in the earlier.[72] In the West, therefore, the power of the Bank was marked. The Bank was in such a flourishing condition that, in 1830, its stock had gone to 122.[73]

At the close of 1827, however, P. P. Barbour, of Virginia, had proposed the sale of the federal government's holding of stock in the Bank; but the assurances given to Biddle by friends of Jackson, at that time, were that they did not mean to run their "heads against the Bank of the United States"; and, in fact, the scheme gained the support of only nine Members.[74] Yet, in December, 1828 — before the President took office — Benton had introduced resolutions to require the Bank to make compensation for the use of deposits.[75]

When, in his First Annual Message,[76] Jackson questioned the constitutionality and expediency of the United States Bank, he had already asked his friend, Felix Grundy,[77] to devise a satisfactory substitute; and soon after his message he requested J. A. Hamilton (a son of Alexander), of New York, to prepare two plans: one for a national bank to be attached to the Treasury Department and to be a bank of deposit; and the other for a mixed bank, free from Constitutional objections. From both of these men he received the desired recommendations.[78]

It was not primarily the controversy over directors of the Bank's branches that led to the President's antagonism,[79] although personal issues were always effective with him. By the summer of 1830 he had reached the conclusion that a national bank should be merely one of deposit, and not of discount, and that its profits should go to the revenue of the general government.[80]

---

[72] Catterall, *op. cit.*, pp. 142–43.

[73] *Niles' Register*, XXXVII, 359.

[74] *Register of Debates*, IV, Pt. 1, 815, 854, 858. See also *Biddle Correspondence*, pp. 44, 46.

[75] *Thirty Years' View*, I (New York, 1854), 187 ff.   [76] Dec. 8, 1829.

[77] See Sioussat, *op. cit.*, p. 65, n. 48, and S. R. Gammon, *The Presidential Campaign of 1832* (Johns Hopkins University *Studies in Historical and Political Science*, Ser. XL, No. 1; Baltimore, 1922), p. 105 — citing Jackson MSS. Library of Congress.   [78] *Jackson Correspondence*, IV, 37, 83, 111–14.

[79] Catterall (*op. cit.*, p. 173) also holds this view.

[80] *Jackson Correspondence*, IV, 161–62.

Clay informed Biddle, in September, that he believed that an application for recharter would play, for the present, into the hands of the Jackson party; and the latter answered agreeing with this view.[81] Shortly before Jackson submitted his Second Annual Message,[82] Biddle had an interview with him, from which he received the impression that the President had confidence in the administration of the Bank and was disposed to accept his (Biddle's) proposal of an arrangement, through the Bank, for paying off the national debt before the end of Jackson's present term. But Biddle also related that the President thought the power of Congress to charter a bank was limited to the District of Columbia and that he had added that he had been suspicious of all banks ever since reading the account of the South Sea Bubble.[83]

In his Second Annual Message, the President again called attention to the question of recharter of the Bank of the United States and said that nothing had occurred to lessen the fears of many citizens over that institution as at present organized, and suggested that a modified bank, as a branch of the Treasury Department, might meet the difficulty.[84]

These utterances gave Biddle, and McDuffie of South Carolina, reason for believing that the time had come for defying the President by making immediate application for recharter; [85] and the Bank began to use the press in propaganda to this end. The new Presidential organ, the *Globe,* opened fire upon McDuffie in respect to the Bank; [86] Calhoun soon afterward released the pamphlet giving the correspondence between him and the President over the Seminole affair (which, as we have seen, marked a definite break between the two) ; Biddle sent his representatives to Washington to examine the situation in the cabinet and in Congress; and the cabinet was reorganized on the tenth of March following.

---

[81] Nov. 3, 1830. (*Biddle Correspondence*, pp. 115–16.)

[82] Dec. 6, 1830.

[83] Catterall (*op. cit.*, pp. 191–92) was mistaken in regarding the document that he used, as a letter from Jackson to Biddle. See *Biddle Correspondence*, pp. 93–94.

[84] *Messages and Papers*, II, 528–29. See Benton's speech against the Bank, delivered in the Senate, February 2, 1831, in the tone of a present-day " Progressive."

[85] *Biddle Correspondence*, pp. 116–17, 119–20, 122.

[86] The New York *Courier and Enquirer*, its editors receiving a loan from Biddle, changed from an anti- to a pro-Bank attitude. (Catterall, *op. cit.*, pp. 258–64.)

This last development, together with letters from influential friends of the President, and from the Secretary of the Treasury, to Biddle, gave the impression that the administration desired to avoid the Bank issue in the coming election. In his report, which accompanied Jackson's Third Annual Message,[87] Secretary of the Treasury McLane, with the President's tolerance but on his own authority, took grounds for recharter.[88] Jackson, in his message, expressed a readiness to rely for the present upon " the investigation of an enlightened people and their representatives." The addition of " an enlightened people " quite upset the hopes of Biddle that the President intended to let the matter rest entirely in the hands of Congress. Such members of the cabinet as McLane and Secretary of State Livingston urged upon Biddle that if given time the President would acquiesce in recharter, but if defied by a demand for that action before the election he probably would not.[89]

But the National Republican convention, which met in Baltimore on December 12, 1831, declared in favor of the Bank, and nominated Henry Clay, who within a few days wrote to Biddle asking his intention regarding recharter and favoring immediate application. Also, Biddle was warned by various Senators, including Webster, that the Bank would have but a poor chance after the election. Biddle's agent wrote that some of the Clay party would be lukewarm, or perhaps hostile, if the Bank bent to administration influence, and that Webster would be cold. Clay was of the belief that a declination to ask recharter might be considered as an electioneering step against the National Republicans.[90]

Having carefully considered the matter after the receipt of reports of his agents, Biddle finally decided to make application for recharter, enlisting the services of McDuffie, of South Carolina, where there was a large number of stockholders. He was a strong nullifier and a friend of Calhoun, and was chairman of the Committee on Ways and Means in the House of Representatives. On the ninth of January, 1832, renewal of the Bank's charter was asked.[91]

[87] Dec. 6, 1831.   [88] See *Niles' Register*, XLI, 288–90, 325.
[89] Catterall, *op. cit.*, pp. 209, 219.
[90] *Ibid.*, pp. 216–18; *Biddle Correspondence*, pp. 142 ff.
[91] It is indicative of the opinion of some of the friends of the administration, that Jackson would support a bill for a modified national bank, under

Still hoping for a compromise, Biddle was ready, in February, 1832, to allow Jackson to "take the charter and make any changes he likes," noting that it would then be "his work." [92] It would appear that the president of the Bank was ready to play both parties; but it must be remembered that, through amendments in Congress, disliked details might have been modified, in the final bill, by friends of the Bank. On the Bank's side were still the Secretaries of State, the Treasury, and War, and possibly others in the cabinet. The views of Jackson, as stated by Livingston to Biddle's agent, would have made it difficult for the Bank to agree to all of the President's terms.[93]

While the question was still before Congress, a proposition was brought-in asking an investigation of the Bank on charges of violation of the charter; and McDuffie, much to the discomfort of the friends of the Bank and possibly influenced by his desire to give priority to the reduction of the tariff, yielded to this demand for an inquiry. The report (made by an anti-Bank committee) was denounced by the friends of the institution as absurd; but Jackson (who was renominated by the Democrats on May 21, 1832) and, as it proved, a majority of the people, were convinced of the truth of the accusations. Nevertheless, on the eleventh of June, 1832, the Senate passed the bill for a modified recharter, by a vote of 28 to 20, and, on the third of July, the House of Representatives assented, by a vote of 107 to 85. As shown in the accompanying map, this latter vote was largely reflective of the strength of the followers of Henry Clay in Congress. On the tenth of July, however, Jackson vetoed the bill, and there was not the necessary two-thirds in Congress to override his action.

Clay had found the issue that he had sought; and the Bank had engaged in a war that proved its ruin.

The severance of official connection between the national gov-

---

their control, that a memorial (*Senate Document 37*, 22d Cong., 1st Sess.) was presented, on January 26, 1832, from David Henshaw (the Boston administration leader) and a group of men of wealth, asking a charter for a national bank. Among the memorialists, there were also Anti-Masons and such conservatives as Henry Lee, Theodore Lyman, R. G. Shaw, and Thomas Handasyd Perkins, Jr. (See A. B. Darling, *Political Changes in Massachusetts, 1824–1848* [New Haven, 1925], p. 170.)

[92] *Biddle Correspondence*, pp. 181–82.
[93] *Ibid.*, pp. 184–85; and Catterall, *op. cit.*, pp. 226–27.

ernment and the capitalist was one of the most important steps in American history. Thenceforth, the industrial interests were obliged to act by underground methods and by the lobby. Only

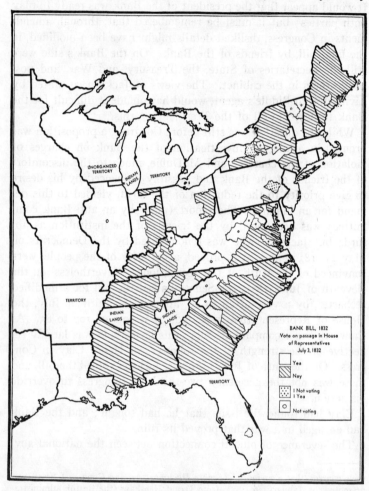

BANK BILL, 1832
Vote on passage in House
of Representatives
July 3, 1832

☐ Yea
▨ Nay
⬚ 1 Not voting
   1 Yea
○ Not voting

in very recent years have steps been taken for restoring the old relationship sanctioned by law.

Turning to the election of 1832, it will be seen that the popularity of "Old Hickory" and his denunciation of the Bank as an "engine of aristocracy" were stronger in their appeal to the people than all the influence that institution was able to exert upon the press and upon members of Congress in presenting its case. Even its financial pressure, due in part to the need of facing the problem of the expiration of the charter but in part also to its desire to win the election, proved unavailing.

Party nomenclature in this election was still unsettled, varying in different sections. Even in 1832 the followers of Jackson officially called themselves the " Republican party," while the Clay men sometimes used the same name and sometimes were dubbed by their opponents the " Federalists." But, in the Baltimore convention that nominated Clay, the designation " National Republican party " was formally used. By 1832 the press was calling the President's supporters " Democratic Republicans." Originally employed by their enemies as a term of reproach, the name " Democrat " was ultimately accepted generally by the Jacksonians. A reviewer of Francis Lieber's *Political Ethics*, in the *Southern Quarterly Review*,[94] said:

The writer of this article remembers very well when the term democrat was considered invidious at the South. The Anti-Federalist, State-rights men at the South, were called *republicans*, and they rejected the name of democrat, which had obtained at the North, and it was never until the election of 1840, that decent persons could willingly stomach the name.[95]

Writing in the fall of 1838, Calhoun declared:

In truth the word democrat better applies to the north than the South and as usually understood means those who are in favour of the government of the absolute numerical majority to which I am utterly opposed and the prevalence of which would destroy our system and destroy the South.[96]

It has been seen that the followers of Jackson in Congress had broken away, in successive steps, during his first administration.[97] The Eaton scandal had divided his cabinet; the rupture with Calhoun, and the nullification question, had alienated still another group; his signing of the tariff of 1832 had intensified Southern opposition; his Maysville veto had aroused the antagonism of

[94] Oct., 1847.
[95] See also, on this point and on the general features of the election of 1832, Gammon, *Campaign of 1832*.
[96] *Calhoun Correspondence*, pp. 399–400.
[97] Professor E. E. Robinson, of Stanford University, has in preparation a book dealing in detail with the party grouping of Jackson's administration.

important portions of the West; and his veto of the recharter of the Bank had lost friends for him among the business interests favorable to that institution. Moreover, his attitude toward the Indians had incurred the hostility of a considerable religious element, and particularly of the Quakers of Pennsylvania, where, also, was located the headquarters of the Bank, so that it became evident that this pivotal state might be regarded as doubtful territory for the Democrats. Even in Tennessee, the President had made some of the outstanding politicians his enemies, partly by his selection of Van Buren as his successor and partly by reason of state sectional rivalries in the ranks of the leaders there.

In the autumn of 1830, Jackson had suggested that Van Buren run for Vice-President in 1832 and that he himself would resign in one or two years so that his New York friend would come into the Presidency; but Van Buren had negatived the proposition.[98]

After the resignation of the first cabinet, Van Buren had been commissioned by the President [99] as minister to England, but he had not been long in that country before the news came that his nomination had been rejected in the Senate by the casting vote of Calhoun,[100] who seems to have thought that Van Buren's prospects as a candidate for the succession would thereby be destroyed. But the effect was precisely the opposite.

Meantime, the question of nominations for the campaign of 1832 had been engaging the attention of politicians in both parties.

In the spring of 1830, Crawford (who had been Secretary of the Treasury in Monroe's cabinet) had proposed that Clay should support him as a candidate for the Presidency, believing that he would then receive the votes of all the Western states, which, together with the aid of Virginia, North Carolina, Georgia, Delaware, New Jersey, and probably Maryland, would procure his election. In that case, Clay was to come to the cabinet and succeed him. He intimated that his friends might make a similar proposal to Van Buren, but that he preferred Clay. The Kentuckian characterized this letter from Crawford as a " most singular " one.[101]

[98] *Van Buren Autobiography*, pp. 505 ff. See also Jackson to Van Buren, Dec. 6, 1831 (*Jackson Correspondence*, IV, 379).

[99] Aug. 1, 1831.

[100] Jan. 25, 1832.

[101] Colton, *Clay*, IV, 271. For an estimate of the significance of the Craw-

Clay believed that the friends of Calhoun were ready to push the latter's candidacy. The election might then be thrown into the House of Representatives, where Clay rather than Jackson would be the choice.[102]

Still others were looking to the nomination. By the spring of 1831, the Anti-Masons had concluded to present a national candidate, and to that end had made overtures to various leaders.[103] Inasmuch as Clay was unwilling to come out against Masonry, the leaders of the Anti-Masons found themselves in an embarrassing position with regard to their nominee. However, the party, in its convention at Baltimore, September 26, 1831, named William Wirt, of Maryland.[104] He had once been a Mason, and he accepted the nomination as a personal honor, did not subscribe to the view that the Masons as an organization had been involved in the Morgan case,[105] and refused to adopt a policy of proscription against members of the order. Nevertheless, the convention persisted in its nomination.

The unanimous choice of Henry Clay, at the National Republican convention at Baltimore, was accompanied by the selection of John Sergeant, of Pennsylvania, as the candidate for the Vice-Presidency. This nomination, together with the convention's address criticizing the administration in respect to corruption, opposition to internal improvements, tariff attitude, the Indian question, and particularly the war on the Bank, made clear the party's hope to win Pennsylvania. In the following spring,[106] the national convention of young men, held in Washington, elaborated this address, in resolutions that emphasized the importance of the Supreme Court as the tribunal of last resort on questions arising under the Constitution and laws of the United States, and of the Senate, as the conservative branch of the federal government, upon whose fearless exercise of its Constitutional functions depended the existence of balanced powers. The President

---

ford following, see L. G. Tyler, *The Letters and Times of the Tylers*, II (Richmond, Va., 1885), 1–2.   [102] Colton, *op. cit.*, p. 382.

[103] *Adams Memoirs*, VIII, 357–58, 368, 412–13; *Calhoun Correspondence*, p. 293.

[104] Wirt is characterized in Mrs. S. H. Smith, *Forty Years of Washington Society* (ed. Gaillard Hunt; London, 1906), pp. 316–17. Also see John P. Kennedy, *Memoirs of the Life of William Wirt*, . . . (Philadelphia, 1849).

[105] See p. 119, *ante;* also his letter to McLean, Apr. 17, 1832, as quoted from McLean MSS by Gammon, *op. cit.*, p. 142.   [106] May, 1832.

was attacked for his alleged " attempts to overawe its deliberations."

The renomination of Jackson had already been demanded by
Pennsylvania and New York. A large following was opposed to
the calling of a national convention and to the nomination of
Van Buren as his running mate. Indeed, in Pennsylvania the
Democratic convention named, as its candidate for Vice-President,
William Wilkins of that state. But, through the manipulations
of members of the " kitchen cabinet," New Hampshire issued a
call for a national convention, and it met on May 21, 1832. Jackson was the unanimous choice for the Presidential nomination,
and Van Buren received more than two-thirds of the convention's votes as the candidate for the Vice-Presidency. He thus
met the requirement of the two-thirds rule, then first introduced
in a Democratic convention. In Virginia and North Carolina,
P. P. Barbour was placed in nomination for the Vice-Presidency
by conventions; but before the election he withdrew his name.[107]
At the close of 1832, Calhoun, who had definitely broken with
Jackson, resigned the Vice-Presidency, having been chosen Senator from South Carolina. He took his seat in the Upper House
at the beginning of 1833.

In the campaign, the Bank proved to be the important issue,
and Jackson's popularity was decisive. He carried the country
by 219 electoral votes against 49 for Clay, 11 for John Floyd, of
Virginia (for whom the nullifying state of South Carolina had
voted, through its legislature), and the 7 of Vermont for William
Wirt. Van Buren, with 189 electoral votes, fell behind the President, while Sergeant received the same number as Clay, Wilkins
won Pennsylvania's 31, Henry Lee, of Massachusetts (the Vice-
Presidential candidate of the South Carolina nullifiers), was
given the 11 of that state, and the 7 of Vermont went to Amos
Ellmaker, of Pennsylvania. In some of the states, a fusion
electoral ticket had been effected between the friends of Clay and
of Wirt; this, coupled with the facts that the vote of South Carolina was cast by the legislature and that no opposition to Jackson
is recorded for Georgia, Alabama, Mississippi, and Missouri,
makes it impossible to state the popular vote with exactness.[108]

---

[107] Simms, *Rise of the Whigs in Virginia*, pp. 52–58; Ambler, *Sectionalism
in Virginia*, pp. 206–9.

[108] Edward Stanwood, in his *A History of the Presidency* (Boston, 1906),

According to Benjamin Matthias,[109] the popular vote (unofficial in most cases, and here thrown into a sectional tabulation) was as follows:

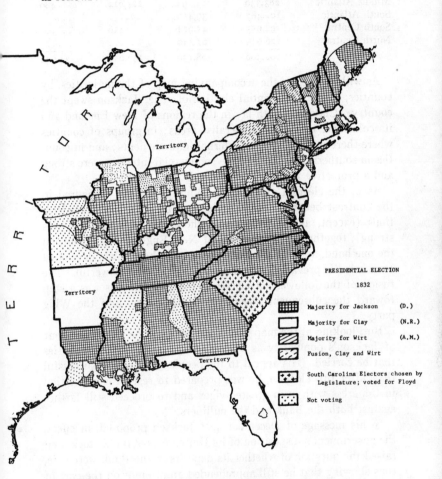

PRESIDENTIAL ELECTION

1832

▦ Majority for Jackson (D.)

☐ Majority for Clay (N.R.)

▨ Majority for Wirt (A.M.)

▧ Fusion, Clay and Wirt

⊞ South Carolina Electors chosen by Legislature; voted for Floyd

⠿ Not voting

p. 163, gives the total popular vote for Jackson as 687,502, while he puts the combined Clay and Wirt vote at only 530,189; but he seems, in some cases, to have failed to include the Wirt vote in his tabulation. See also the quite different figures in Gammon, *op. cit.*, p. 170, based chiefly on *Niles' Register*, XLIII, 135–251, *passim;* apparently the estimates in his table are based on reports prior to the more authentic figures in the tabulation that follows in the text.

[109] *Politicians Register* (Philadelphia, 1835).

	Jackson	Clay	Clay-Wirt Fusion	Wirt
New England	94,583	91,923	19,010	33,466
Middle Atlantic	283,336	23,393	221,612	480
South Atlantic	102,487	39,450	. . . . . .	. . . . . .
South Central [110]	94,955	45,924	1,436	. . . . . .
North Central	126,945	107,440	. . . . . .	. . . . . .
	702,306	308,130	242,058	33,946

As will be seen by the accompanying map of the majorities, by counties, in the Presidential election of 1832, Jackson swept the country. Clay's strength lay in the regions of New England and its colonists; in the old Federalist areas; in groups of counties where there was a desire for internal improvements; and in counties in southern Louisiana where commercial interests were strong and a protective tariff was in demand.

As in the election of 1828, the Whig party was prefigured in the contrast between regions influenced by industrial considerations (except, as in New York, where the labor interest was strong), together with the zones of New England settlement, on the one hand, and, on the other, the areas where a less developed economic life prevailed and where the masses were powerful. The fusion of the followers of Clay and the Anti-Masons was a step toward the subsequent absorption of the latter into the Whig party.

But, looking at the map as a whole, one is struck by the extent of Jackson's popularity as evidenced by the number of counties that he carried. His appeal to the people had been so successful that, after this election, he was prepared to resist the opposition in Congress with even greater vigor and to proceed still farther against both the Bank and the nullifiers.

In his message of December 4,[111] Jackson proposed, in effect, the government's disposition of its United States Bank stock, and raised the question of whether its deposits in the Bank were safe, thus showing that he still apprehended an attempt on the part of that institution to secure recharter by exerting financial pressure and that he felt he had a mandate for subjecting it to radical restraint even before the expiration of its charter in 1836. He also urged reduction of the tariff, in view of the prospective extinction

[110] On the basis of an estimate of 20,000 Alabama votes for Jackson.
[111] *Messages and Papers*, II, 591–606.

of the public debt. Probably this attitude of the President was influenced, too, by his desire, through meeting the demand of South Carolina for relief from the tariff of 1832, to avoid coming to a serious issue with her over nullification. Further, to induce the West to support his administration, he recommended the sale of the public lands to actual settlers at a reduced price and the surrender of the residue, at a convenient time, to the states in which it lay. In dealing with this question, he emphasized the importance of regarding the nation as one people and of avoiding sectionalism. Clearly, therefore, the President recognized the need of combining these outstanding issues in some measure that would bring the sections together.

We may next consider the progress of nullification in South Carolina and its reception elsewhere.

By the spring of 1831, the people of South Carolina had become sharply divided into Unionists and nullificationists, with the latter strongest in the backcountry and Charleston; but even the former grew hostile to the tariff of 1832, and in this feeling the bulk of the Southern sections shared.

It would seem to the present writer that the makers of the Constitution believed, as Madison held, that sovereignty had been divided by the action of the people of the several states.[112] In fact, as Caleb Strong wrote, on February 27, 1790,

The several States have never possessed compleat Sovereignty . . . but no one doubted of their sovereignty to certain Purposes, their Powers it is true are considerably diminished by the new Constitution, but still they are uncontrollable in the exercise of internal Legislation & the administration of Justice. . . . There is nothing absurd in the idea that a government may be sovereign to some purposes and not to all.[113]

The grant of powers by many of the colonies and states to the Continental Congress had reserved to them the control of " internal police," but had not asserted sovereign rights over such things as levying war, and foreign relations in general. Political scientists in the past have seemed to agree with Calhoun that sovereignty was indivisible; but more recently the doctrine of plural sovereignty has gained a following. What is important,

112 *Letters and Other Writings of James Madison* (Philadelphia, 1867), III, 663; IV, 6, 61, 80, 106, 293.
113 MS No. 486, examined at Libbie's " Garfield Sale," Jan. 27, 1914, in Boston.

however, is that the word " sovereignty " was loosely used at the time the Constitution was framed and that the people seem to have thought that sovereignty was capable of division and that the Constitution had so divided it by defining spheres for the operations of the federal government and of the several states. This belief of the people, rooted in their experience under the government of England, should carry greater weight than the theories of later political scientists. Behind all, was faith in the beneficence of revolution as the remedy for usurpation. The colonies had revolted against Great Britain, and even the Constitutional Convention was a revolution against the Union as formulated in the Articles of Confederation.[114] The views of the framers, however, were sufficiently varied to afford both Calhoun and Webster opportunity for appealing to contemporary utterances to support their positions with regard to the rights of the Supreme Court as the final arbiter. The question was left in sufficient uncertainty to make it necessary for the trend of events to settle the conflicting issue of overlapping powers between state and nation and to determine where the final decision lay.

However this may be, the passage of the tariff of 1832 was greeted by the South as evidence of determination to preserve the principle of protection and to make modifications only on the items where that was not involved. A popular election in South Carolina, in the fall of 1832, resulted in favor of the summoning of a constitutional convention, and an extra session of the legislature called the meeting. President Jackson had already seen in the action of the state a readiness to defy him as administrator of the federal laws, and, with his natural inclination to rely upon direct action, he had arranged to enforce the tariff and had sent agents to keep him informed of the progress of events.[115]

The South Carolina convention, meeting on November 19, issued an Ordinance of Nullification, [116] with reference to the tariff of 1832, and made provisions to prevent the payment of duties,

[114] Madison, in reply to inquiries, declared that nullification was not justified, either by the debates and outcome of the Constitutional Convention of 1787 or by the Virginia Resolutions of 1798-99. See, e.g., his *Letters and Other Writings*, IV, 87, 95-106, 204-6, 269, 354, 395-425. See also *North American Review*, XXXI, 537 ff.

[115] See, especially, Stillé, *Poinsett*.

[116] Reprinted in *State Papers on Nullification* (Massachusetts General Court *Miscellaneous Documents;* Boston, 1834), and in H. V. Ames (ed.), *State Documents on Federal Relations*, No. IV (Philadelphia, 1902), pp. 38 ff.

imposed by the act, within the state, warning that the use of force by the federal government would result in secession. Calhoun's draft of an "Address to the People of the United States" was made the basis for the further pronunciamento of South Carolina.[117] His idea that this practical application of his doctrines was a peaceful measure and that it would result in the necessity of interpretation of the Constitution by the affirmative vote of three-fourths of the states, met a rude awakening in President Jackson's Proclamation of the tenth of December following.[118] Believing that he could place forty thousand men in the state of South Carolina to put down resistance and to enforce the law, he issued this epochal document, which, in substance, bore the impress of the mind of Secretary of State Livingston. After taking extreme grounds against the view of South Carolina with regard to its rights, the Proclamation, in effect, accepted the ideas of Chief Justice Marshall and of Webster concerning the power of the general government.

This paper was "too ultra" for Clay, in its assertion of what he thought to be the theory of consolidation.[119] McDuffie, of South Carolina, asserted that, if Congress approved, "the liberties of the country were gone forever."[120] Van Buren was much concerned lest Jackson be precipitate in assuming that South Carolina's threat of force was the same as her actual use of it, and attempted, by drafting a report to the legislature of New York, to moderate what he thought to be the Federalist speculation placed in the document by Secretary Livingston. At the same time, this report antagonized the nullification doctrine and recommended a reduction of the tariff.[121]

As we have seen in Chapter V, the views of South Carolina, when presented to her sister states, were repudiated. The important state of Virginia, as pointed out, denied the correctness both of the doctrines of South Carolina and of the President's Proclamation, and sent a mediator to the nullifying state, asking for delay until Congress should close (but at the same time ex-

[117] *Calhoun Works*, VI, 193–209.

[118] *Messages and Papers*, II, 640–56.

[119] Colton, *Clay*, IV, 345.

[120] *Adams Memoirs*, VIII, 505. Cf. F. J. Turner, *Rise of the New West, 1819–1829* (*The American Nation: A History*, XIV; New York, 1906), p. 307, on McDuffie's change from his earlier views.

[121] *Van Buren Autobiography*, pp. 549–53, and *Adams Memoirs*, VIII, 510.

pressing strong objections to the existing tariff). It is significant that the former outstanding Jackson leaders in the Old Dominion opposed his Proclamation,[122] which found support in the western districts of the state, where there was marked antinullification feeling.[123]   No doubt the refusal of other South Atlantic states to uphold South Carolina's nullification doctrines was partly due to Jackson's popularity; but, even in the regions that were sympathetic with the opposition to the tariff and with the right of secession, nullification was emphatically denied support.[124]

Within a few weeks of his Proclamation, the President sent in his message asking for additional legislation to enforce the tariff laws — a recommendation that brought about the so-called " Force Bill," which passed the Senate by a vote of thirty-two against the single negative vote of John Tyler, of Virginia,[125] other followers of Calhoun having withdrawn from the chamber. In the House, the measure also passed by an overwhelming majority (149 to 48). Such anti-Jackson men as Webster and John Quincy Adams joined in the support of the bill.

But, in the meantime, the administration had shown its readiness to hold out the olive branch as well as to draw the sword. As had been indicated in his message, Jackson was willing to lower

---

[122] See citations in Simms, *Rise of the Whigs in Virginia*, pp. 69–73.

[123] See the map of a vote, in Ambler, *Sectionalism in Virginia*, p. 217, and his discussion, pp. 209–18.

[124] In his discussion of the Force Bill, Senator Forsyth, of Georgia, distinguished the attitude of his state on the Indian question from the views presented by South Carolina in asserting the right of nullification. In 1834 he succeeded Livingston and McLane as Jackson's Secretary of State. For the attitude of other Georgia leaders, see Phillips, *Georgia and State Rights*, pp. 133–35.

[125] In his speech of February 6, 1833, against the " Force Bill " (*Register of Debates*, IX, Pt. 1, 360–77), Tyler set forth the doctrine that the Constitution was a compact between sovereign states. He suggested, however, the possibility that " the decision be formally pronounced against the right of secession," and raised the question whether, in that case, " the military arm should be exerted, or other measures of a milder nature, but equally efficacious, be resorted to." He added: " I leave South Carolina to take care of herself; she rests in the hands of her able Senators on this floor. I disclaim the policy adopted by her; all here know that I did not approve of her course." L. G. Tyler (*Letters and Times of the Tylers*, I [Richmond, Va., 1884], 440 ff.) refers to Henry Clay as writing to Francis Brooke (Colton, *Clay*, IV, 348) that he understands John Tyler " opposed both to nullification and the proceedings of South Carolina." L. G. Tyler quotes a speech of 1839, in Virginia, in which John Tyler said that he differed from Calhoun in regarding nullification as a peaceable remedy, and added, " I went into no abstraction."

the tariff of 1832, urging as one reason the need of reducing the revenue but influenced no doubt by the desire to compromise. On the twenty-seventh of December, the administration's tariff bill, sponsored by Representative G. C. Verplanck, of New York, was reported.[126] The sudden drop in protection contemplated in this bill was highly alarming to the manufacturing interests. Woolens were an especial object of reduction. The measure proposed that, by 1834, duties should be lowered to around fifteen or twenty per cent.

Clay had already become convinced that some compromise was necessary in order to save the tariff system and to prevent use of force by the President against nullification, and he therefore let Webster know that he had in mind a new tariff bill. Calhoun, also, seems to have been acquainted with the movement and to have made suggestions. Webster and his friends felt that the concessions proposed by Clay would be a serious blow to the manufacturing interests and were apparently ready to fight the matter out with South Carolina rather than yield to this desire for compromise and avoidance of the issue.

As finally drafted, Clay's measure proposed a gradual reduction until 1842, when a *general* minimum of twenty per cent would be reached. It would appear that Clay privately justified his measure to the friends of protection, partly by the argument that one Congress could not bind its successors, partly by the danger that the entire protective system would be lost by insistence on the existing tariff, and partly by the need of finding a compromise to satisfy the South.[127]

The compromise tariff of 1833, introduced by Clay in the Senate, was substituted in the House for the Verplanck measure and

[126] For an indication of its character, see Stanwood, *Tariff Controversies*, I, 391–92.
[127] The question of how far Clay and Calhoun were in collusion in the framing of the bill became a matter of bitter debate. In 1838 the latter asserted that events had placed Clay "flat on his back" and that compromise was his only means of extrication — adding, "I had the mastery over him on the occasion." This called out the reply of Clay: "Sir, I would not own him as my slave. He my master!" ([Benton] *View*, II [New York, 1856], 122, 123.) On the subject, see also: Tyler, *op. cit.*, I, 457, 467; *William and Mary College Quarterly Historical Magazine*, XXI, 8; Chas. H. Ambler, *The Life and Diary of John Floyd* (Richmond, Va., 1918), p. 210; G. T. Curtis, *Life of Daniel Webster* (New York, 1870), I, 444; and *Calhoun Correspondence*, pp. 323–24.

passed there by a vote of 119 to 85. The following table gives a sectional summary:

	National Republican Yeas	National Republican Nays	Democratic Yeas	Democratic Nays	Unclassified Yeas	Unclassified Nays	Totals Yeas	Totals Nays
New England	1	18	6	5	3	5	10	28
Middle Atlantic	0	5	13	26	2	15	15	46
South Atlantic	10	1	36	1	11	0	57	2
South Central	6	0	17	0	4	1	27	1
North Central	1	4	8	3	1	1	10	8
	18	28	80	35	21	22	119	85

Thus, the two Southern sections showed an almost unanimous vote for the compromise. New England was definitely against, but exhibited divergence of attitude between its northern and southern states. In the Middle Atlantic section, New York was divided and Pennsylvania strongly opposed. The split in the North Central was indicative of its discontent with the failure of the South to support its land policy and of its desire for peace between the sections through compromise.

In the Senate, the measure passed on March 1, 1833, by a vote that exhibited similar yielding of party to sectional considerations.

Both the Force Bill and the compromise tariff came before the President and were signed on the second of March. Meanwhile, in response to the possibility of an abandonment of the protective system, the operation of the Ordinance of Nullification had been postponed in South Carolina by the recommendation of an un-official meeting at Charleston; and, on the news of the passage of the compromise act, the state rescinded her ordinance, at the same time passing a nullification of the Force Bill. Thus, South Carolina avoided the danger of encountering the fierce temper of Andrew Jackson when his authority was affronted; but she was able to claim, nevertheless, that the threat of nullification had been sufficient to bring about redress of Southern tariff grievances.

In considering Clay's readiness to lower the tariff by the act of 1833, it must be remembered that he regarded the bill for the distribution of the net proceeds of the sales of public lands (which he introduced in the Senate on December 12, 1832) as an essential part of the adjustment. Obviously, if the revenue derived by the federal government from the sales of public lands were re-duced, the need of reviving the tariff would be hastened. Although the measure passed both houses of Congress, it was given a pocket veto by the President, who stated his reasons in his message of December 4, 1833. Therefore, Clay felt bitterly that an essential

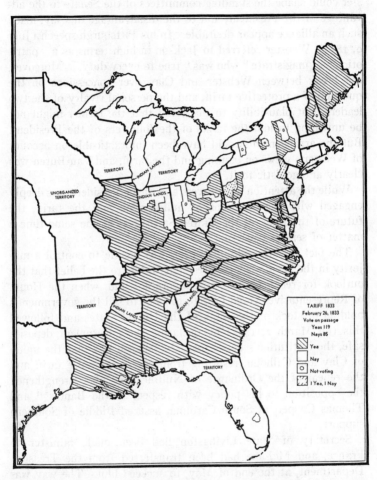

TARIFF 1833
February 26, 1833
Vote on passage
Yeas 119
Nays 85

Yea

Nay

Not voting

1 Yea, 1 Nay

part of his compromise arrangements had been refused.[128] The Charleston *Mercury,* one of Calhoun's organs, favored Clay's bill and looked to the union of the South under Calhoun and the West under Clay.

[128] On the sectional aspects of this subject, see Wellington, *Influence of the Public Lands,* pp. 43–48.

Webster's support of Jackson in the matter of nullification led to an attempt on the part of the administration to win further aid from the New England statesman. The possibility that Webster could shape the standing committees of the Senate to the advantage of the President, and to the disadvantage of Clay, made such an alliance appear desirable. In his Pittsburgh speech (July 9, 1833), Webster referred to Jackson in high terms as a " patriotic chief magistrate " who was " true to every duty." Moreover, the break between Webster and Clay over concessions on the question of a protective tariff, and the personal rivalry of the two leaders, lent plausibility to the belief that the former might not be unwilling to join the ranks of the followers of the President. But the arrangement would have been impracticable on account of Webster's views on banking and the tariff, and Van Buren was clearly antagonistic to it.[129]

While the attention of Congress and of the President was deeply engaged with the questions of nullification and the tariff, the future of the Bank of the United States was at the same time a matter of serious concern.

The fact that the administration was unable to control a majority in the Senate helped President Biddle to the belief that the outlook for recharter was still favorable; and, when the House of Representatives voted (102 to 91) not to sell the government's holding of stock of the Bank of the United States and followed this (on March 2, 1833) by declaring the government deposits safe, the institution's hopes rose.[130] Jackson felt that the union of Clay and Calhoun, resulting from the compromise tariff and the repeal of the Ordinance of Nullification, also strengthened the opposition to his policy with respect to the Bank;[131] and Thomas Cooper, of South Carolina, assured Biddle of Southern support.

Secretary of State Livingston had been made minister to France, and McLane had been transferred from the Treasury Department, at the end of May, to succeed him. The way was therefore open for the appointment to the Treasury post of Wil-

[129] For a graphic account of this episode, see *Van Buren Autobiography*, pp. 670–711. See also: *Adams Memoirs*, VIII, 90; Chas. W. March, *Reminiscences of Congress* (3d ed.; New York, 1850); and Curtis, *op. cit.*, I, 464.

[130] Catterall, *Second Bank of the United States*, p. 289.

[131] See Jackson to Rev. H. M. Cryer, Apr. 7, 1833 (*Jackson Correspondence*, V [Washington, 1931], 53), cited by Catterall (*op. cit.*, p. 287).

liam J. Duane, of Pennsylvania, who was expected to be more amenable to the administration policy with reference to the Bank. But when Jackson, a few days before leaving in early June for a visit to New England,[132] informed Duane of his intention to have the deposits removed, he found the new secretary unwilling to comply with his wishes.[133] Even Van Buren feared removal at this time, on the ground of its danger after a Congressional resolution asserting the security of the deposits. But, inasmuch as the idea of an Independent Treasury had not yet come to his attention, he supposed that banks were needed to conduct the operations of the government.

I was [he said] for having such an agency established a sufficient time before the expiration of the charter, & the future receipts of the Treasury (after a proper time) deposited with the new agents under the authority of the Secretary of the Treasury given by the charter of the Bank of the U. States, and thus to show to Congress and the Country that the government could do without a United States Bank, and secure a refusal to renew its charter.[134]

There was apprehension that so radical an attack upon the Bank as the President intended might lead those among Jackson's followers who really favored the institution, to make their opposition to the removal of the deposits the excuse for a later positive support of the Bank. Also, members of the cabinet like Cass were loath to countenance so extreme a measure. However, in his Paper to the Cabinet, of September 18, the President declared for removal, on his own responsibility,[135] and a few days later he made Taney (his Attorney-General) Secretary of the Treasury [136]

[132] See J. S. Bassett, "Notes on Jackson's Visit to New England, June, 1833," Massachusetts Historical Society *Proceedings*, LVI, 244–60; and A. McF. Davis, "Jackson's LL.D. — A Tempest in a Teapot," *ibid.*, 2d Ser., XX, 490–511.

[133] See Duane's *Narrative and Correspondence concerning the Removal of Deposits* (Philadelphia, 1838), and Jackson's letter to him, under date of June 26, 1833, printed in part in Duane's "Exposition," *Niles' Register*, XLV, 236, and more fully in the *New York Times*, Mar. 4, 1923. In this important letter, the President gave a useful résumé of his controversy with the Bank.

[134] Van Buren to F. P. Blair, Oct. 15, 1845 (Blair MSS, Library of Congress).

[135] On the whole subject, see details in: *Van Buren Autobiography* (consult Index, under " Deposits, Removal of the ") ; *Jackson Correspondence*, V, *passim;* and Bassett, *Jackson*, II, Chap. xxix.

[136] Taney served as Secretary of the Treasury until the day following the Senate's rejection (June 24, 1834) of his nomination, when he resigned. Early

in place of Duane. Jackson had now found a cabinet officer more than ready to adopt his policy in opposition to the Bank; and Taney, in his subsequent service, proved a forceful and intelligent adviser on the President's financial policy.

On September 26, 1833, the new Secretary of the Treasury ordered that government funds should thereafter be deposited in certain state banks, chosen after investigation by Kendall, that were called " pet banks " by the opposition; but the friends of the administration insisted that they had been selected without partisan purpose. This action came at a time of expansion in the purchase of cotton, slaves, and land, and of internal improvements. Many new state banks were chartered, and their issues vastly increased. In 1829 there were 329 such banks, and in 1834, 506. The circulation in the former year was less than $50,000,000, whereas by the latter it had risen to nearly $95,000,000, and by 1835, to over $100,000,000. This went on in the succeeding years, with the result that by 1837 there were 788 banks, with a circulation of almost $150,000,000. Roughly, therefore, in the period between 1829 and 1837 banks had considerably more than doubled in number and had trebled their circulation.[137] Even in New York, by the spring of 1836, bank influence was so great that apprehensions were expressed by the friends of Van Buren that the success of state banks in securing charters from the legis-

---

in 1835 Jackson appointed him an Associate Justice of the Supreme Court of the United States, but again the Senate withheld its consent. Toward the end of that year, the President named him Chief Justice to succeed Marshall, and, though once more there was opposition in the Senate, confirmation was given the middle of the following March. Biographies of Taney are: B. C. Steiner, *Life of Roger Brooke Taney* (Baltimore, 1922); and Samuel Tyler, *Memoir of Roger Brooke Taney, LL.D.* (Baltimore, 1876).

[137] Davis R. Dewey, *Financial History of the United States* (New York, 1924), p. 225. The great increase in the use of fractional currency was probably due, in part, to a law (passed June 28, 1834) changing the coinage ratio. The earlier law had led to an undervaluation of gold as compared with silver and a resultant exportation of coin and bullion of the former. But after the new law, establishing a ratio of about 16 to 1, silver proved to be undervalued and as a consequence largely disappeared from circulation. (See A. T. Huntington and R. J. Mawhinney [compilers], *Laws of the United States concerning Money, Banking, and Loans, 1778–1909* [*Senate Document 580*, 61st Cong., 2d Sess. (National Monetary Commission; Washington, 1910)], p. 496, and Dewey, *op. cit.*, p. 211. See also: Jackson to Van Buren, Aug. 16, 1834 [Van Buren MSS, Library of Congress]; Bell's speech in House of Representatives, June 23, 1836 [*Register of Debates*, XII, Pt. IV, 4429]; and [Benton] *View*, I, 469–70, also 436 ff. In addition, consult McMaster, *United States*, VI, 213–20.)

lature might, and ought to, endanger the party's control of that state.[138]

Jackson's purpose to make it impossible for the Bank to recover its power had two important results: (1) The Senate, under Clay's leadership, passed a resolution censuring the President's action as another evidence of his determination to override the wishes of Congress and denying his power under the charter to coerce his Secretary of the Treasury. Jackson retaliated with a vigorous protest against these strictures, admitting the liability of the Executive to impeachment by the House of Representatives but denying the constitutionality of the Senate's procedure.[139] The right of the President to remove members of his cabinet and replace them with others, in sympathy with his ideas, is now generally admitted. (2) The Bank, from this time forward, shaped its policy to an opposition in which loans to Congressmen and newspapers, and pressure by means of contraction of credit, paved the way for the crisis of 1834.

Some contraction by the Bank was obviously necessary in preparation for the expiration of its charter, but, going far beyond this measure of safety, it adopted a course designed to compel the restoration of deposits and the renewal of its charter. Clay's strategy was to concentrate public opposition upon Jackson's alleged usurpations and to bring in the recharter as a sequence to popular alarm over the financial suffering that followed the administration's attack upon the institution.[140] A flood of memorials

[138] C. C. Cambreleng to Van Buren, Apr. 24, 1836, A. C. Flagg to Van Buren, May 27, 1836, and J. A. Dix to Van Buren, June 7, 1836 (Van Buren MSS, Library of Congress). Even in 1834 Governor W. L. Marcy had recommended a loan of four or five million dollars' state stock to the New York banks, to compensate for the loss of the accommodations of the branch of the Bank of the United States, and suggested that, in case of necessity, a portion of this stock might be disposed of and the avails loaned to the counties. (See *Niles' Register*, XLVI, 96.) In this set of conditions may be foreseen the later split of the Democratic party into Conservative Democrats and Locofocos, and ultimately, as the slavery issue became acute, into Hunkers and Barnburners. Even in so financially conservative a state as Virginia, early in 1836 banks were also increasing in number and capital. A demand was arising for bills to incorporate banks to accommodate all parts of the state, and this involved a struggle between the different regions of Virginia over questions of the soundness of these banks, the use of funds for internal improvements, etc. Already there was prophecy of a panic. (See Richmond *Enquirer*, Feb. 7, Mar. 3, 1836; Ambler, *Sectionalism in Virginia*, pp. 220–22; and *idem, Thomas Ritchie* [Richmond, Va., 1913], pp. 177–78.)

[139] Apr. 15, 1834. (See *Messages and Papers*, III [Washington, 1896], 69 ff.)
[140] *Biddle Correspondence*, p. 220.

to Congress, from business men endangered by the fall of the Bank, poured upon this " panic session." Clay was in his element in directing and prolonging this storm of protest. It was Biddle's opinion that restriction would " ultimately lead to a restoration of the currency and the recharter of the Bank." [141] The severest contraction fell upon the South and West, but even the Middle Atlantic and New England states came to realize that the Bank was working hardships in their sections.

To the pleas of delegations for relief from the conditions that were ruining the merchants, Jackson exclaimed: " Relief, sir! . . . Come not to me, sir! — Go to the monster! — . . . It is folly, sir, to talk to Andrew Jackson — The government will not bow to the monster." [142] Biddle, on the other hand, replied, to similar appeals, that, if Congress

will do its duty, relief will come — if not, the Bank feels no vocation to redress the wrongs inflicted by these miserable people. Rely upon that. This worthy President thinks that because he has scalped Indians and imprisoned Judges, he is to have his way with the Bank. He is mistaken.[143]

Writing to T. W. Ward, the Boston agent of the English banking house, Baring Brothers, Edward Everett urged the creation of a fund to support Webster in his defense of property against numbers. " The party in power," Everett said, " would put its foot tomorrow on the neck of the Intelligence & Property of the country but for him." [144] But even Webster thought that Biddle was proceeding so persistently and ruthlessly that he was producing a reaction unfavorable to the Bank.[145] A New York committee, of which Albert Gallatin was a member, also found dissatisfaction with Biddle widely prevalent and had threatened denunciation of the unnecessary pressure upon business. A New England delegation (including Nathan Appleton, P. T. Jackson, and Henry Lee), appointed by a public meeting in Boston to

[141] With regard to the policy of Biddle, of using restriction to promote the Bank's objects, see his letter to Wm. Appleton (Jan. 27, 1834), quoted, in part, in Catterall, *Second Bank of the United States*, p. 330. See also pp. 329, 331.

[142] See *ibid.*, p. 351, and *Niles' Register*, XLVI, 9–10.

[143] *Biddle Correspondence*, p. 222. See also Catterall, *op. cit.*, pp. 329–30.

[144] Printed in *Boston Herald*, Feb. 24, 1913, and (extracts) in Darling, *Political Changes in Massachusetts*, pp. 131–32.

[145] Such a conservative magazine as *Niles' Register* (XLV, 363; XLVI, 20) conceded that the Bank possessed an excessive power that should not be continued.

memorialize Congress, met Biddle in New York, and in a private conference told him that

our community ought not and would not sustain him in further pressure, which he very well knew was not necessary for the safety of the bank, and in which his whole object was to coerce a charter through the distresses of the mercantile community.[146]

Although Biddle was noncommittal and replied in commonplaces, the effect of these representations upon him may have had some influence on his decision, after Congress adjourned, that it was no longer expedient to continue curtailment.[147]

Meantime, while Clay was pursuing his preliminary agitation against Jackson, Webster wished a modified recharter for six years and Calhoun one for twelve years; but it proved impossible for these leaders of the opposition to agree upon a unified policy. The charge of " Executive usurpation " became, therefore, the ground of attack of all the President's adversaries during the next few years.

In the elections of the spring and fall of 1834, Jackson's foes made gains in various states, including Virginia and Ohio. By autumn the use of the term " Whig "[148] had generally superseded that of " National Republicans," and the union of Anti-Masons and Whigs was being perfected. Thus, the opposition to Jackson, and to his plan to make Van Buren his successor, found a common rallying cry under a name that indicated resistance to the personal power of the President. Such a political leader as Thurlow Weed rejoiced that the Whigs no longer had to carry the Bank,[149] and Webster reached the conclusion that " public opinion . . . had decided against it."[150]

In this coalition of the opponents of Jackson on a new issue, Calhoun did not fully join; but he secured a following of the friends of state rights — a Southern group who were determined

[146] " Memoir of Hon. Nathan Appleton," Massachusetts Historical Society *Proceedings*, V, 287–88. See p. 107, *ante.*

[147] Biddle to J. W. Webb, July 9, 1834. (*Biddle Correspondence*, p. 243.)

[148] On the use of the name, see: E. M. Carroll, *Origins of the Whig Party* (Durham, N.C., 1925), pp. 123–24; Henry R. Mueller, *The Whig Party in Pennsylvania* (Columbia University *Studies in History, Economics and Public Law*, CI, No. 2; New York, 1922), pp. 15–16; and A. C. Cole, *The Whig Party in the South* (Washington, 1913), p. 18.

[149] *Autobiography of Thurlow Weed*, ed. Harriet A. Weed (Boston, 1883), p. 431.

[150] Senate speech, Feb. 26, 1835. (*Register of Debates*, XI, Pt. 1, 623–27.)

to hold the balance of power without formally connecting themselves with the Whig party.

The movement against Jackson's intention that Van Buren should follow him in the Presidency [151] found recruits among the friends of Hugh Lawson White, of Tennessee.[152] Jackson had sought to make him Secretary of War in 1831 and, as has been stated, had invited him to take up his residence at the White House. But White disapproved of Executive patronage and large appropriations, and, although he was opposed to the Bank, had desired that the deposits should remain until the expiration of the charter.[153] He had also refused, as presiding officer of the Senate, to remove J. M. Clayton, of Delaware, from the chairmanship of the Committee on the Tariff. With other Tennesseeans, he was not favorable to Van Buren's succession to Jackson.

Tennessee was showing serious divisions among the former followers of the President — partly of policy and partly of faction.[154] In 1834 [155] John Bell, of that state (previously a hesitant supporter of Jackson), defeated Polk, likewise a Tennesseean, for Speaker, after ten ballots, receiving aid from the antiadministration group and splitting the Democrats.[156] These developments made it possible for the Tennessee delegation in the House, with two important exceptions,[157] to hold a meeting, on December 23,

[151] " Believe me," wrote Van Buren to Jackson, on August 2, 1834, " that whatever you do, that can by possibility bear upon me, I always take it for granted (although I may not be able to comprehend it at the time) is intended for my benefit, and sincerely entertain the conviction that your foresight and judgement in such matters is superior to my own, I am quiet, & content." (Van Buren MSS, Library of Congress.)

[152] See pp. 234–35, ante.

[153] Senate speech, Mar. 24, 1834. See Nancy N. Scott (ed.), A Memoir of Hugh Lawson White, . . . with Selections from His Speeches and Correspondence (Philadelphia, 1856), pp. 135 ff.

[154] On politics in Tennessee, and the decline of Jackson's control in that state, see: Jas. Phelan, History of Tennessee (Boston, 1888) ; Register of Debates, XII, Pt. IV, 4401; Niles' Register, XLIX, 178–79; and the contemporary correspondence of Jackson, in the Library of Congress (which I used there, in the original, through the period it covers). Consult also: " Letters of James K. Polk to Cave Johnson, 1833–1848," ed. St. Geo. L. Sioussat, Tennessee Historical Magazine, I, 209–56 (Sept., 1915); J. W. Caldwell, " John Bell of Tennessee," American Historical Review, IV, 652–64; and Thos. P. Abernethy, " The Origin of the Whig Party in Tennessee," Mississippi Valley Historical Review, XII, 504–22.

[155] June 2.

[156] But in the succeeding session Polk defeated Bell (Dec. 7, 1835).

[157] Cave Johnson and Polk. Senator Grundy remained loyal to Jackson.

1834,[158] and to ask Senator White if he would run for the Presidency. His sturdy independence had shown that he was ready to differ with the policies of Jackson when he felt them to be inconsistent with his (Jackson's) original professions.[159] Cautiously stating his own reluctance to become a candidate, White declared, in effect, that the people were entitled to choose for themselves.[160] Within a fortnight, the legislature of Alabama nominated him,[161] and that of Tennessee followed suit in the middle of October, 1835.[162] John Tyler, of Virginia, became the candidate for Vice-President on this ticket, as well as the choice of the South Carolina legislature for the running mate of Willie P. Mangum, of North Carolina, on the state-rights issue.

A speech by White on executive patronage widened the breach with Jackson, and it was not long before the former was advocating Clay's land-distribution bill. Bell was flayed by the administration on the charge of having been a stalking-horse for White, and Jackson pointed out that whichever party made the President would control his administration. He intimated, also, that Bell looked " to ulterior objects, in building up a southern party in conjunction with Mr. Calhoun, founded exclusively on sectional feeling and prejudice, and not principle." [163] But this Tennesseean insisted that he had supported the Jacksonian party

---

[158] Scott (ed.), *op. cit.*, p. 261 *et passim*. James Walker wrote to Jackson from Tennessee, April 5, 1835, that, shortly after the action of the delegation of that state, all the newspapers there, except two, took grounds for White. It is perhaps indicative of the self-sufficient attitude of Tennessee that he proposed the nomination of William Carroll, one of its sons, for Vice-President, and spoke of the popularity of Polk.

[159] In the summer of 1836, he declared:

" Those principles are the same on which the president came into power, and if we are not now together, *the change has not been with me.*" (*Niles' Register*, LI, 44.)

" These were the great and leading principles for which we, in common with *others*, contended. The public voice sanctioned them by the election of the chief magistrate in 1828. In his inaugural address in 1829, and in his subsequent addresses, he has avowed and proclaimed several of them.

" They are the *very doctrines* on which I *have practised* from that day to this, so far as my humble capacity enabled me; and I now challenge my persecutors to put their fingers on the cases in which I have departed from them." (*Ibid.*, p. 60.)

[160] *Ibid.*, XLVIII, 39.
[161] *Ibid.*, XLVII, 378 (quoting from *Alabama Intelligencer*).
[162] *Ibid.*, XLIX, 178–79.
[163] Jackson to J. C. Guild, Apr. 24, 1835. (*Jackson Correspondence*, V, 338–40.)

even when he had been attacked himself. He denounced party spirit, in a speech at Nashville.[164] Although he came out for *a* national bank and had previously opposed the Bank of the United States as a partisan institution, he did not profess to commit White, nor did he go much farther than had Jackson in the beginning of that fight.

The excitement in the South over Northern agitation of abolition was attributed by the *Globe,* the organ of the administration, to a desire to get Southern support for White as against a Northern candidate; and it is evident that the policy of Calhoun was used to arouse the apprehension of the slaveholding sections.

A national Democratic convention met in Baltimore on the twentieth of May, 1835, and, operating under the two-thirds rule, gave Van Buren a unanimous nomination; but the candidate for the Vice-Presidency, Richard M. Johnson,[165] of Kentucky, barely obtained the necessary number of votes, and Virginia refused to accept him, preferring William Smith, who had migrated from South Carolina to Alabama after a breach with Calhoun.[166]

A Pennsylvania state convention nominated, for the Presidency, William Henry Harrison, of Ohio (the Northwestern hero in the War of 1812),[167] who relied upon a following from the pioneer democracy that had originally brought Jackson to power, as well as upon support by the Whigs and Anti-Masons; and named the Anti-Masonic Francis Granger, of New York, for the Vice-Presidency.[168] Webster was nominated for the Presidency by the Massachusetts legislature.[169]

In effect, therefore, a sectional alliance had been made, which

---

[164] *Niles' Register*, XLVIII, 330–36; cf. 263, 312.

[165] See p. 238, *ante*. For his letter of acceptance, see *Niles' Register*, XLVIII, 329–30.

[166] See the account of his political alternations, in Houston, *Nullification in South Carolina*, p. 69.

[167] See p. 330, *ante*. In view of Biddle's previous record in the shaping of Whig policies and the selection of leaders, it is worth noting that he declared (Aug. 11, 1835) that, if Harrison were taken up, it would be " on account of the past, not the future," and added: " Let him say not one single word about his principles, or his creed — let him say nothing — promise nothing. . . . Let the use of pen and ink be wholly forbidden as if he were a mad poet in Bedlam." (*Biddle Correspondence*, p. 256.) Substantially this policy was followed in 1840, also.

[168] See Chas. McCarthy, *The Antimasonic Party: A Study of Political Antimasonry in the United States, 1827–1840* (American Historical Association *Annual Report*, 1902, I, 365–574; Washington, 1903), p. 480.

[169] Feb., 1835.

leaders expected to result in throwing the election into the House. It was also suggested, by such party chiefs as Clay, that an electoral ticket should be chosen before the election, which would make it possible to combine upon the candidate most likely to win the Whig vote.[170] In view of White's popularity in the South and of his assertion that he was quite as good a representative of Jacksonian principles as the Old Hero himself, together with Harrison's contention that he exemplified pioneer democracy of this type better than Van Buren, a formidable opposition was presented. Had Webster been able to obtain any considerable support outside of Massachusetts, the case would have been still more serious for the Democrats; but as yet Van Buren had not sacrificed his following in the Southern Jacksonian Democracy.

Thus, the antiadministration forces had acquired new and important accessions, whose strength was largely in the Southern sections; and it became vital to these sections to rally to the cause of slavery.

The rise of the Garrisonian abolitionists early in the thirties, in the North, contemporaneously with the alarm of the South over such servile insurrections as that of Nat Turner,[171] had led Georgia to offer a reward of five thousand dollars for the apprehension and conviction of any of the editors or printers of the *Liberator*, and to threaten nonimportation from the North unless there was compliance with the demand of Southern legislatures for the prohibition of abolition utterances on the part of the free states. At the same time, emancipation legislation by Great Britain was stirring the whole South. Petitions for the abolition of slavery, or at least of the slave trade, in the District of Columbia had already become a question of serious concern, inasmuch as there were involved the property rights of Virginia and Maryland (which had ceded the District to the United States) and the whole problem

---

[170] Clay advised (July 14, 1835 [Colton, *Clay*, IV, 395]) joining forces on a candidate acceptable to Pennsylvania; he thought her favorite might lead over Van Buren and White. Biddle (Aug. 11, 1835 [*Correspondence*, pp. 255–56]) favored each section's running its favorite son. He would "apply local remedies" for this "disease," and finally rally under a common leader. He thought that Pennsylvania should unite on Harrison if he would run best. Benton (July 18, 1835 [*Niles' Register*, XLVIII, 462–64]) believed that the "moneyed power" planned to bring the election to the House of Representatives. The newspapers abound in evidence that this question was agitated throughout the campaign in all quarters. See also Jackson to Polk, Aug. 3, 1835 (*Jackson Correspondence*, V, 357–58).

[171] See p. 158, *ante*.

of the power of Congress so to legislate in the matter of slavery in the territories as to endanger the expansion of that system into the Western lands.

The policy of Calhoun, in this period, becomes particularly important, both because of his attempt to use a balance of power politically and because he had come to believe that only by united sectional resistance to antislavery agitation could the South find safety within the Union. This was not inconsistent with his hope to become President of the United States, for he found a sufficient antiabolition feeling in the North to give him confidence that, with a solid and threatening South behind him, he might find a large enough Northern following to reach his goal. The winning of his own section on a broader policy than that of nullification, his own convictions of the righteousness of slavery, and his desire to use that issue as a means toward the achievement of his personal ambitions and of Southern leadership, combined to influence him in a policy of aggressive agitation of this question at the time. To him it seemed that a candidate of the North would have to cater to the antislavery group, for the reason that the two parties were so evenly divided, there, that both would be obliged to yield to the need of enlisting its support. The tariff had been temporarily settled; the Bank issue was not likely to be the primary one in the next campaign; and his rival, Van Buren, would be embarrassed by the necessity of meeting the demands of both those who supported and those who opposed the system of slavery.

Excitement had arisen over the distribution through the mails of antislavery publications, in Southern states.[172] In his Annual Message of December 7, 1835, the President took notice of this, and suggested the passage of a law prohibiting, under severe penalties, postal dissemination, there, of publications calculated to arouse servile insurrection. This recommendation seemed to Calhoun, however, to grant to Congress the dangerous power of determination of whether abolition literature might, or might not, be permitted by the federal authorities to circulate within the United States. He therefore proposed a bill to make it unlawful for any postmaster to allow the distribution of such matter within a state where it was illegal. In this way he hoped to avoid the hazard of leaving decision of the point to the general government.

[172] See *Jackson Correspondence*, V, 359–61.

But he came to see that his measure was not free from inconsistencies, and finally accepted Grundy's substitute, which forbade postmasters from knowingly delivering " incendiary publications " in any state whose laws debarred them. But this latter bill was defeated in the Senate, on June 8, 1835, by a vote of 19 to 25. However, Calhoun had succeeded in compelling Van Buren to vote for the engrossment of the measure when a tie was produced.[173] By this choice, the Vice-President saved himself from loss of the South.

Petitions for the abolition of slavery, or of the slave trade, in the District of Columbia were no new thing, but at this time they rose to greater importance. The right of petition now became involved, under the leadership of John Quincy Adams. Calhoun proposed to meet the issue at the outset. " Nature," he said, " has encrusted the exterior of all organic life, for its safety. Let that be broke through, and it is all weakness within. So in the moral and political world." [174] It appeared clear to him that the criticism of slavery and the committal of the federal government to abolition in the District of Columbia constituted an attack upon the whole South, which should be met by the united opposition of the slaveholding sections. But he would act by disunion only when every avenue of defense had been exhausted; and, with prophetic insight, he later [175] wrote to his daughter that " many bleeding pours must be taken up in passing the knife of seperation through a body politick, (in order to make two of one) which has been so long bound together by so many ties, political, social and commercial." But, to cope with the situation, he seems to have urged upon his friends the project of a Southern convention that should clearly express the determination to assert the attitude of the slaveholders. He would therefore have Congress refuse to receive antislavery petitions. But in this extreme position he found himself, at the time, without support. Nevertheless, he had raised an issue disastrous to his section — the issue of the right of petition.

The compromise introduced in the House [176] by Henry L. Pinckney, of South Carolina, was carried by a large majority.

[173] See [Benton] *View*, I, 587.
[174] *Congressional Globe*, VIII, 191.
[175] Jan. 25, 1838. (*Calhoun Correspondence*, pp. 390–91.)
[176] Feb. 8, 1836.

. Under this proposal it was resolved that all petitions in regard to slavery " shall, without being either printed or referred, be laid upon the table and that no further action whatever shall be taken thereon." In the Senate it was provided that the petitions should be disposed of by laying on the table the question of reception.

Undoubtedly, in his decision to attack the circulation of abolition literature and the petitions for abolition of slavery in the District of Columbia, Calhoun was influenced by a complexity of considerations, including his desire to use these issues for campaign purposes,[177] for the union of the South, and for the advancement of his own ambitions. But none of these factors should be regarded as the controlling one ; as in so many cases, there was such a mixture of motives that an attempt to determine the relative importance of each would be impossible.

The question of Texas had become vital by this time and was being introduced in the campaign. In 1827 John Quincy Adams had been willing to pay a million dollars for well over half the present state ; and so impressed was Andrew Jackson with the importance of American possession of the province that, in the opening year of his administration, he authorized a maximum offer of five millions to Mexico for a boundary that he believed would insure " a natural seperation of the resources of the two nations." He thought that this object would be secured by a cession to the " Grand Prarie or desert west of the Nueces " and along the mountains to the forty-second parallel.[178] But in 1836 came the memorable siege at the Alamo, and on April 21 the victory of Sam Houston, at the battle of San Jacinto, and the achievement of Texan independence. So early as May 23 following, Calhoun declared himself in favor of recognition and annexation.[179] White acquiesced in a resolution for immediate recognition, passed at a meeting in Nashville in June.[180] The Mississippi House of Representatives unanimously declared for annexation.[181]   But

[177] This seemed clear to many of the friends of Van Buren in the South. Senator Rives, of Virginia, for instance, in a letter of September 20, 1836 (Van Buren MSS, Library of Congress), spoke of the Whigs' resuscitation of the " scarecrow " of abolition. P. V. Daniel also wrote him (November 27, 1836; *ibid.*) that he had " never doubted that the excitement about abolition " had " been exclusively and deliberately raised by the Whigs."

[178] *Jackson Correspondence*, IV, 58–59, 66, 79–81, 82.

[179] *Register of Debates*, XII, Pt. II, 1531.

[180] *Ibid.*, p. 1877.

[181] *Niles' Register*, LII, 258.

even so radical a statesman as McDuffie, of South Carolina, was unwilling to interfere in Texas; [182] and in this he found support among important members of the Whig cotton-planting aristocracy. On the other hand, J. Q. Adams and his followers had now come to believe that the demand for annexation was entirely due to a Southern conspiracy in behalf of slavery and the increase of the slave states.[183] Webster, also, spoke against acquisition of Texas. While the election was pending, Jackson advised that recognition should be deferred.[184]

Calhoun, having brought into prominence the issue of slavery, next turned his attention to the problem of the approaching surplus. Under the compromise tariff, it was impossible to diminish the incoming funds, except through the gradual process for which the act provided. In response to the stimulus of the state banks and the federal deposits, public lands were increasingly bringing in an apparent revenue (largely because of speculation), the reality of which would depend upon the soundness of the banks. Government receipts for public lands, which amounted to $2,409,000 in 1830, had become $16,165,000 in 1835 (after the removal of the deposits and the growth of state banks was felt), and $24,934,000 in 1836.[185] The national debt had been paid off by the beginning of 1835, and it was expected that the surplus would amount to around $9,000,000 annually for the next three years.

Clay would meet the difficulty, as we have seen, by the distribution of the net proceeds of the sales of public lands, and thereby

---

182 *Ibid.*, LI, 229–30.

183 During the same period, the Seminole Indian War was also stirring up the antislavery feeling of the North. Among these Seminole Indians, in Florida, fugitive slaves had settled and intermarried. When, therefore, in 1835 war broke out between these Indians and the government of the United States, not only was the sympathy of the Northern friends of the Indians aroused but also the charge was made that the campaign was in the service of the " slave-drivers." The contest went on until the removal of the bulk of these Indians in 1842. (See p. 147, *ante*, n.)

184 [Professor Turner left a blank space in the manuscript at this point, intending to insert the views of Van Buren and Harrison.]

185 *Review of Economic Statistics* (Harvard Economic Service), IX, 41–53 (Jan., 1927) — a paper by Arthur H. Cole (with the assistance of the authorities of the Public Land Office in Washington), on " Cyclical and Sectional Variations in the Sale of Public Lands, 1816–60." See also Professor Cole's study, " Wholesale Prices in the United States, 1825–45," in the *Review* for April, 1926 (VIII, 69–84).

secure a fund for internal improvements and education; Benton
would invest an important portion of the surplus in fortifications;
and Woodbury, in sound stocks. But Calhoun, who had attacked
the proposal of Jackson, in his First Annual Message,[186] that the
surplus be distributed among the states (with amendment of the
Constitution, if necessary, to permit this) — an idea that Jackson
had soon abandoned — had now reversed his earlier attitude, having come to the conclusion that it was to the interest of South
Carolina and Georgia to find, in the proposal to divide most of
the surplus from all sources among the states according to their
federal ratios, a means of building their railroads,[187] and at the
same time of reducing the power of the federal government derived from its employment of the revenue as a means of increasing its importance at the expense of state rights.

A bill was introduced that provided, in effect, for such a distribution of the money in the Treasury January 1, 1837, in excess
of five million dollars. This measure was finally passed, on
June 23, 1836, but only after a struggle, between the administration and those who would have made an outright gift to the
states,[188] which was compromised on the basis of making the states
the *depositories* of the surplus, in proportion to their representation in the two houses of Congress. The states, in turn, were required to transmit to the Secretary of the Treasury certificates of
indebtedness to the United States Government covering the
amounts deposited with them. These certificates were to be
subject to sale or assignment by the Secretary whenever the
Treasury's funds from other sources were inadequate; to bear
interest from the date of such sale or assignment; and to be re-
deemable by the states at their pleasure.

Jackson explained, in the *Globe,* that he signed the measure
because presented by a majority of the representatives of the
people [189] — a plea that would not have served for his action in

[186] Dec. 8, 1829. (See *Messages and Papers,* II, 452.)

[187] See p. 176, *ante.*

[188] See *Jackson Correspondence,* V, 404–11, for: Jackson's proposed veto;
Richard M. Johnson's enthusiastic letter regarding the President's acceptance of
the " deposit " amendment; and Chief Justice Taney to Jackson, differentiating
between a loan and a deposit and concluding that there was no sufficient ground
for a veto of the bill as thus amended, but regretting that Congress had passed
the bill.

[189] See Richmond *Enquirer,* July 21, 1836, and *National Intelligencer,* July
12, 1836.

respect to the National Bank or the Specie Circular; but it seemed essential to party harmony.

At the beginning of 1837, it appeared that $37,000,000 would be available for transfer to the states under the deposit act; but because of the panic of that year only about $28,000,000 could be turned over. These " deposits " were never recalled.[190]

Although President Jackson had originally supported the state banks, the insufficient provision for regulation of them and the frenzy of banking in connection with the speculation in public lands were bringing about a very dangerous situation. Therefore, on July 11, 1836, the Specie Circular [191] was issued, requiring that agents for the sale of public lands should receive payment, after August 15, only in specie and no longer in the notes issued by banks. This led to bitter discussions and to attempts to secure withdrawal of the order, but without result.

Thus, while the government surplus was in the process of redistribution and while, at this time, states were engaging in an orgy of internal improvements and state debts (as has been seen in the chapters on the various sections), an issue was presented that sharply divided the economic interests of the Whigs and their allies from the followers of Jackson and Van Buren.

In the Presidential campaign of 1836, there was persistence of Jacksonian Democracy among the masses. Also, it was important to the South to retain support in the North. Although there was much opposition to Van Buren as a Northern man who was not sound on the slavery question, and although the *Richmond*

---

[190] On the distribution of the surplus, see Edward G. Bourne, *The History of the Surplus Revenue of 1837* (New York, 1885), and Dewey, *Financial History of the United States*, p. 220.

Taney, in his correspondence with Jackson, held that, independent of the distribution clause in the act, it was open to the objection that the deposit banks lost the power of influencing their neighboring banks by balances they were accustomed to leave in their hands. He pointed out that, until the principle of giving interest was adopted, the Secretary of the Treasury had power to order deposit banks to have their money in specie when he deemed it necessary. After the banks paid interest, they could not lawfully be required to retain the deposits as specie in their vaults. But he thought that the objections would not have justified a veto. (Taney to Jackson, Jan. 3, 1837, in Jackson MSS, Library of Congress. See also the discussion in *Register of Debates*, XII, Pt. II, 1793–1845.)

[191] *Ibid.*, XIII, Pt. II, App., 107–8; reprinted in *Messages and Papers*, X (Washington, 1899), 104–5. The Circular made certain temporary exceptions, particularly with regard to Virginia land scrip and to actual settlers.

Whig [192] had declared his election would mean that " all chance of
a Southern President is gone," he stated that he regarded federal
abolition within the states where slavery existed as unconstitutional, and opposed abolition in the District of Columbia, thus
giving assurances to the slaveholding states. On the other hand,
Harrison's Northern Anti-Masonic following, and the charge that
he had been an abolitionist, worked to his disadvantage in the
South. In 1833, in a speech at Cincinnati,[193] he had stated that
he would use the surplus revenue as a fund for emancipating the
slaves, *with the sanction of the states concerned*, colonizing those
who should be freed. Nevertheless, the *Globe* continued to doubt
his safety on this question; and the Richmond *Enquirer* [194] reported that James G. Birney, the abolitionist editor, was said to
favor Harrison.[195]

White, at the beginning of 1836, was steadily turning toward
the views of Clay with respect to public lands and patronage.
He had also failed to support Jackson's bold policy in the matter
of the French spoliations and the " three-million bill."

The French spoliations had long been a bone of contention in
American history. In 1831 a treaty was signed between the
United States and France by which the latter agreed to pay five
million dollars, in six annual instalments, in return for concessions regarding the duties on French wines. But France, engaged
at the time in a struggle between friends of the then king, Louis
Philippe, and his republican opponents, did not make the promised
appropriations. In 1833 Jackson sent former Secretary of State
Livingston — able, cautious, adroit, and socially gifted — to
France as minister. The courteous John Forsyth, of Georgia, became Secretary of State about a year later. It was most fortunate that a man of Jackson's imperious will and volcanic disposition was served by three such distinguished advisers on foreign
relations as Van Buren, Livingston, and Forsyth. Forsyth suc-

---

[192] May 3, 1836 (cited by Simms, *Rise of the Whigs in Virginia*, p. 111).

[193] On " The Principles of Our National Institutions," July 4, 1833. See
also Richmond *Enquirer*, Sept. 6, 9, 1836, cited in Simms, *op. cit.*, p. 115, n. 130.

[194] Aug. 16, 1836.

[195] On the general subject of Harrison's attitude toward slavery, see *The
Tippecanoe Text Book*, compiled by W. O. Niles (Baltimore and Philadelphia,
1840), pp. 70–72, 73 (speech at Vincennes, Ind., May, 1835, and letter of Nov.
25, 1836 [from Cincinnati]); and J. P. Dunn, Jr., *Indiana* (Boston, 1888 [in
" American Commonwealths " series]), pp. 310–11.

ceeded in persuading the President to modify his contemplated warlike message on the subject, following the early failure of France to meet its obligations, but was unable to prevent his insistence, after continued delays at Paris, upon a less moderate attitude. In France and the United States alike, party rivalry had been injected into the contest. Jackson's vigorous language, however, in his Annual Message of December 1, 1834, demanding reprisals in case of the persistent refusal of France to live up to the terms of the treaty, raised intense excitement in Paris, produced what was substantially a demand for an apology, and brought about the possibility of war. The French minister, Sérurier, and, not long after, Livingston, returned to their governments. Clay, for the Whigs, offered a resolution declaring it " inexpedient at this time " to grant authority for reprisals, and encouraging France to wait " to see whether the message should be seconded by Congress." Thus, in both countries, by the close of 1834 competing parties were using the issue to promote their own interests. The struggle was complicated by the existence of an active pacifist group in the United States,[196] by the apprehension, on the part of some, of economic losses, and by the fear of others that national self-respect and honor would be sacrificed.

At this time, John Quincy Adams came forward in defense of the President, declaring that his firm stand was " high-spirited and lofty " and that it was the attitude which " the Chief Magistrate will bear before the world, and before mankind, and before posterity." Resolutions, passed on March 3, 1835, in the House, merely insisted upon the maintenance and execution of the treaty, and, while favoring " preparation " for any emergency that might arise, refused, in effect, to comply with Jackson's request for reprisals. But an amendment was added to the fortifications bill, to provide three million dollars for use at the discretion of the President (in view of the chance of French hostility before the next meeting of Congress). This led to a violent discussion that resulted in the defeat of the appropriation, and left, as a campaign issue for the election of 1836, the question of where blame lay for thus practically exposing the nation to the danger of possible attack. In his Annual Message of December 7, 1835, Jackson refused to give the " explanation " of his previous message that France had demanded as a condition to payment of its ob-

[196] See p. 78, *ante.*

ligations under the treaty; and a debate ensued as to who was at fault for the failure to vote defense funds. The spoliations question was finally adjusted through the mediation of England, and on May 10, 1836, France paid our claims against her.[197]

It is interesting, in this connection, to remember that, at the nullification crisis, Webster, of Massachusetts, so strongly supported Jackson that he was even considered as a possible ally; and now John Quincy Adams, following an attempt by Webster to fasten upon the President and the Democrats responsibility for the loss of the " three-million bill," took up the cudgels in behalf of Jackson, in a speech, on January 21, 1836, still remembered as an example of fiery response to sentiments of national honor. Himself a defeated predecessor of the President and in almost all other respects hostile to him, Adams upheld him a second time, and justified the Democratic House in its action in this matter in opposition to the Senate, controlled by Clay.

The radical objections of Calhoun to the implication that Congress could take jurisdiction on the slavery question, as involved in the petitions for abolition of slavery, or the slave trade, in the District of Columbia, were meeting response by the message [198] of Governor William L. Marcy, of New York, declaring that the legislature had powers to pass penal laws against abolition agitation in so far as it was exciting insurrection in a neighboring state.

By spring, White was taking the position that Benton's resolutions for expunging the censure of Jackson, in 1833, should be so modified as to preserve the sanctity of the Journals by framing the resolutions to read, to " rescind, reverse and annul " — thus increasing the enmity of the President, but at the same time avoiding the charge of mutilating the record.

[197] On the spoliations question, see: *Register of Debates*, for the years mentioned, important correspondence on the subject, in *Jackson Correspondence*, V; John Bassett Moore, *History and Digest of the International Arbitrations to Which the United States Has Been a Party*, . . . (Washington, 1898), V, 4447 ff.; *Messages and Papers*, III (Jackson's second term); and *Niles' Register*, XLVIII, 22–28. [Benton] *View*, I, Chaps. cxvii–cxx, cxxxii, cxxxiii, and Bowers, *Party Battles*, Chap. xiv, give the Democratic view that the Whigs proved unpatriotic. The Whig side is presented in the speeches of Clay, Webster, and others of the party, recorded in the *Register of Debates*. In the Wisconsin State Historical Society, there is an important manuscript letter (in the N. P. Tallmadge MSS) from W. C. Rives to Van Buren, January 9, 1835, commenting on the treaty with France and containing extracts from his dispatches (while minister to France [1829–32]), etc.

[198] Jan. 5, 1836.

Already, the prospect of a bank panic aroused fear; and the passage of the act, in which both parties joined, for the distribution of the surplus, had been followed by Benton's attempt to make only gold and silver the medium of payment for public lands, and by the Specie Circular in July.

The various issues were formulated through a series of interpellations to the leading candidates, in the summer and fall of the year; and their replies were, in effect, campaign platforms.[199]

In the election, Van Buren received 170 electoral votes. The South Atlantic and South Central sections gave him 57 votes, while, in these two sections, Harrison won but the 28 of Delaware, Maryland, and Kentucky, and White, only the 26 of Georgia and Tennessee. South Carolina, through its legislature, voted for Willie P. Mangum, of North Carolina. Webster was successful in Massachusetts alone. Harrison carried Vermont and New Jersey, as well as Indiana and Ohio (which he had served as an adopted son).

R. M. Johnson received but 147 electoral votes for the Vice-Presidency. Granger was successful for that office in all the states that went for Harrison, except Maryland, and he was also victorious in Massachusetts — having a total of 77 votes to his credit; John Tyler won in Maryland, South Carolina, Georgia,

---

[199] See: Van Buren to Sherrod Williams, Aug. 8, 1836 (Library of Congress; the correspondence with Williams printed as *Mr. Van Buren's Opinions. Correspondence* [Washington, 1836], and published in *Niles' Register*, LI, 25–30); Van Buren to Junius Amis and others, Jackson, N.C., Mar. 6, 1836 (*ibid.*, L, 126–28); Van Buren to Wm. W. Irwin and others (committee appointed by Anti-Masonic national convention), May 19, 1836 (*ibid.*, p. 436); Van Buren to Alex. F. Vaché and others, New York City, July 6, 1836 (*ibid.*, p. 391 [and XLIII, 125–26, for Van Buren's answers, reprinted from *Albany Argus*, Oct. 4, 1832, to questions put by Jos. H. Bryan and others, Shocco Springs, N.C., during his campaign in 1832 for the Vice-Presidency, on the issues of a protective tariff, internal improvements, the United States Bank, and nullification — answers that were used also in the campaign of 1836]); Harrison to Williams, May 1, 1836 (*ibid.*, LI, 23–25); Harrison to H. W. Doster and others, Zanesville, O., Nov. 2, 1836 (*ibid.*, p. 189); White to Williams, July 2, 1836 (*ibid.*, p. 44); White to J. B. D. Smith, Mar. 17, 1836 (*ibid.*, L, 128); extract from letter of White, Aug. 22 [1836] (*ibid.*, LI, 44); White's speech at Knoxville, [Aug.] 31, 1836 (*ibid.*, pp. 59–61); White to Col. A. A. Kincannon, Sept. 19, 1836 (*ibid.*, p. 178); and White's toast (at a dinner to Bell) to "The constitution" (*ibid.*, p. 83). For a presentation of Van Buren's case in the South, see also Richmond *Enquirer*, July 19, 1836 ("Address of the Republican Committee of Correspondence to the People of Halifax," June, 1836). See, in addition, Bell's speech, House of Representatives, June 23, 1836 (*Register of Debates*, XII, Pt. IV, 4391–4437).

and Tennessee, with 47 votes in all; and Virginia cast her ballots
for William Smith, of Alabama. Therefore, the choice for the
Vice-Presidency had to come to a decision in the Senate, where
Johnson was selected, by 33 votes to Granger's 16.

The popular vote, as given by Stanwood [200] (tabulated below,
by sections) was 762,978 for Van Buren and 735,649 for his opponents.[201]   (There was no popular vote in South Carolina, whose
electors were appointed by its legislature.)

	Van Buren	Harrison	White	Webster
New England	111,548	63,922	......	41,287
Middle Atlantic	283,882	251,791	......	......
South Atlantic	105,596	30,585	71,970	......
South Central	96,102	36,955	66,089	......
North Central	165,850	165,713	7,337	......
	762,978	548,966	145,396	41,287

In the East — North and South alike — Van Buren's vote exceeded the combined polls of his opponents; but in the two
Western sections, while he gained pluralities, he failed to achieve
majorities. Indeed, in the North Central States he barely ran
ahead of Harrison alone. However, the claim of Harrison and of
White that they represented pristine Jacksonian pioneer democracy was influential, as was the fact that both of them benefited
greatly from loyal followings in important states with which
their public careers had been associated.

The map showing the election results by counties reveals that
Van Buren's strength lay in the old Jacksonian regions. Harrison's following was chiefly in the areas of northern New England
and northeastern New York where the idealistic Anti-Masons had
been important; in Connecticut, along the Connecticut Valley
and in the northern tier of counties; in western New York; in
much of New Jersey, Delaware, and Maryland; in southern and
western counties of Pennsylvania; in the Western Reserve, the
Miami Valley, and large areas in eastern Ohio along the Ohio
River; in most of Indiana; in scattered Illinois counties; and in
the greater part of Kentucky (where some of Clay's friends were

[200] *History of the Presidency*, p. 185. A checking of his addition in the case
of the Whig votes seems to show that his total is 601 more than the sum of his
figures for the individual states. The total given above is the corrected one.

[201] The figures in *The Tribune Almanac*, I (New York, 1868), " The Politician's Register for 1841," p. 31, are somewhat different, and the footings appear to be inaccurate.

unhappy in the belief that he had supported Harrison's candidacy). White carried several groups of Virginia counties, much of northeastern and western North Carolina, Tennessee except for part of the middle of the state, and, significantly, the regions that

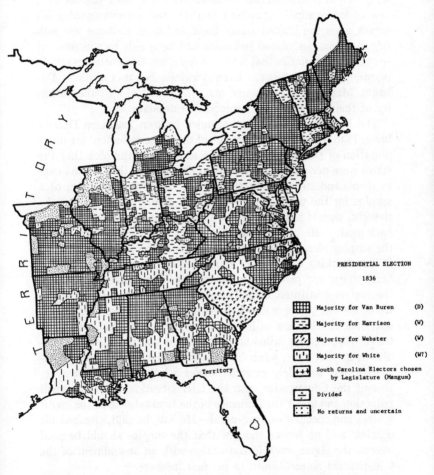

PRESIDENTIAL ELECTION

1836

Majority for Van Buren (D)

Majority for Harrison (W)

Majority for Webster (W)

Majority for White (W?)

South Carolina Electors chosen by Legislature (Mangum)

Divided

No returns and uncertain

constituted the cotton-raising aristocracy of Georgia, Alabama, Mississippi, Louisiana, and Arkansas. If we take account, also, of the probable attitude of the people of South Carolina, it is apparent that the opposition to Van Buren was most marked in the

Black Belt. This is particularly important in view of the fact that some writers have supposed that the strength of Jacksonian Democracy lay, at the beginning, in this very zone.

It had now been shown — so steadfast was the following of the General — that, in spite of the discontent of the state-rights wing of the South Atlantic States over his cabinet choices as a test of leadership in 1829 and in 1831, and notwithstanding his attack upon the United States Bank and upon Calhoun and nullification, his designated successor had been able to win most of the Southern counties that were not definitely committed to cotton planting by slave labor. Even Virginia, North Carolina, Alabama, Mississippi, Louisiana, and Arkansas had cast the majority of their votes for the Democratic candidate.

The last session of Congress under Jackson began on December 5, 1836. His Annual Message of that date reiterated his interpretation of the deposit act as not sanctioning the idea that the states were permanently entitled to the revenue thus turned over to them, and strongly objected to the future accumulation of a surplus for the purpose of distribution among them. Taxes, he thought, should not be imposed merely that they might be paid back again. He pointed out that banks were making loans upon the surplus already placed in the hands of the states, converting it into banking capital and thus, through the multiplication of bank charters, " producing a spirit of wild speculation." Under the system instituted by the deposit act, he thought, the states would be merged in a desire to secure supplies from the general government. In view of his recommendations, in 1829 and 1830, for distribution, he called attention to the contrast between conditions at that time, when internal improvements by federal authority were so widely extended under a latitudinarian construction of the Constitution, and the later situation, after the tariff reduction and under the influence of the land sales upon the credit system and speculation in general. He had, he said, changed his opinion, and no longer thought that the surplus should be paid over to the states, even in connection with an amendment of the Constitution as mentioned in his first message.[202]

---

[202] In the campaign of 1836, Van Buren expressed his opposition to the deposit act. (See Simms, *Rise of the Whigs in Virginia*, p. 112, nn. 120, 123, citing Richmond *Enquirer*, June 21, 1836, and *Richmond Whig*, June 28, 1836.) It is noteworthy that the Virginia Whigs advocated the measure.

His remarks on the currency are of interest, in view of the panic that soon followed. He laid emphasis upon the fact that it was the purpose of the Constitutional Convention to establish a currency consisting of the precious metals. On the creation of the National Bank, he pointed out, it was to the interest of its creditors that gold should be superseded by its own paper as a general currency, a value was soon attached to gold coins that made their export more profitable than their use at home as money, and, therefore, " the bank became in effect a substitute for the Mint of the United States." He accordingly urged an increase of a circulating medium of gold and silver, as a means of checking the depreciation of the currency by excessive bank issues.

In this connection, he called attention to the higher price of public lands and to the receipts of the government from their sale, but noted that these receipts amounted to nothing more than credits in banks that loaned out their notes to speculators. Under this view, he said, he had issued the Specie Circular, which he thought was checking the career of Western banks, retarding the spirit of speculation, and saving the new states from a " nonresident proprietorship." He urged a further development of the system by prohibiting sales of public lands except to actual settlers, at a reduced price and under a limitation of quantity.

In the first days of the new session, therefore, a bill was introduced [203] by the Committee on Public Lands, restricting sales of lands to bona fide settlers and providing for pre-emption.[204] Senator Thomas Ewing, of Ohio, proposed a resolution to annul the Specie Circular, and this passed to a third reading. Thereupon, Senator W. C. Rives, of Virginia, presented an amendment substituting a proposition to receive for public dues bills of banks not issuing notes under certain denominations (running from five dollars, in 1839, to twenty dollars, after 1841). The measure was supported by a speech of Rives, on the tenth of January, 1837,[205] that was a tactful attempt to retain loyalty to the President while bringing upon him the force of public opinion to secure modification of the Specie Circular in a way that would, in effect, rescind it. Here was a clear indication of the fact that a group of Democrats was forming which was favorably disposed toward state

[203] Jan. 2, 1837.
[204] *Niles' Register*, LI, 369–70 (Feb. 11, 1837), gives a résumé of the text of the bill as amended by the Committee on Public Lands.
[205] *Register of Debates*, XIII, Pt. I, 343–60.

banks (suffering from the provisions of the Circular) and, at the same time, held the opinion that specie was not sufficient to meet the needs of the currency. Many important followers of Jackson concurred in this view, so that he felt it necessary to advise his supporters to vote for Rives's measure instead of that of Ewing. Jackson made it a condition, however, that the passage of the former should be accompanied by a provision in the land bill for "restricting the sale of land to actual settlers," which he regarded as a sufficient obstruction to the land speculation that the receiving of bank notes had encouraged and that had given occasion for the Specie Circular.[206] In the outcome in the Senate, the Committee on Public Lands presented a bill that included the modification of the Circular as proposed by Rives; and he, with his friends, accepted the land bill restricting sale to actual settlers. But, before the latter measure passed the Senate, the Whigs succeeded in adding an amendment definitely rescinding the Circular; and, in the House of Representatives, Rives's bill, separate from the land bill, was passed,[207] following which the latter was killed. It was the opinion of Jackson that this had resulted from the antagonism of a combined group of Whigs and Eastern Democrats, to which the followers of Rives had not made effective opposition. In retaliation, Jackson pocket-vetoed Rives's bill.[208]

On January 16 came the memorable occasion, in the Senate, on which the censure of Jackson, for ordering the removal of the deposits, was expunged from the Journal, by a vote of 24 to 19. Thus, Benton brought to a successful close his long struggle to that end.[209]

The first half of February was a period of bitter party and sec-

[206] Wellington, *Influence of the Public Lands*, p. 55 (including n. 6), gives an able analysis of the situation.

[207] *Register of Debates*, XIII, Pt. I, 778; Pt. II, 2090.

[208] *Messages and Papers*, III, 282–83.

Blair wrote Jackson, April 14, 1839 (Jackson MSS, Library of Congress), with regard to a private letter from the President to him that desired him to hold communication with Grundy and Rives concerning a preliminary agreement for a combination of the friends of the Committee's public-land bill with rescinding of the Specie Circular by the aid of votes of Jackson's supporters. But Blair denounced Rives for having failed to carry out the agreement after the passage of the rescinding bill. (See also Wellington, *op. cit.*, pp. 54–56.)

[209] See pp. 422–26, 440, *ante;* [Benton] *View*, I, 528–50, 645–49, 717–31; and B. H. Wise, *The Life of Henry A. Wise of Virginia, 1806–1876* (New York, 1899), pp. 69–70.

tional controversy in Congress. Almost at the beginning of the month, a House committee-room was the scene of a violent attack upon R. M. Whitney, who had been a government director of the United States Bank and who was at this time acting as a representative of state banks that he apparently desired to organize into a substitute for the United States Bank. Whitney alleged that he could not appear before an investigating committee because of fear of assassination. A scowl from him, in declining to answer a question, brought from a Tennessee member of the committee a threat to " take his life upon the spot "; and Henry A. Wise, of the committee, afterwards boasted that he had moved toward Whitney in order to shoot him if he seemed about to draw a pistol. This indication of the presence of hot-headedness among Southern men in Congress was made use of in criticism of that section in the North.

On February 6 Calhoun made his famous speech in the Senate declaring slavery " a positive good." [210] Contemporaneously, a heated struggle occurred over the inquiry by John Quincy Adams, in the House, as to whether a petition that purported to come from slaves was receivable under the " gag law." This led to attempts to censure him. Never was the " Old Man Eloquent " more effective in stirring up the issue of the right of petition and, at the same time, in proving that he himself had not submitted a petition from slaves, although he declared the right of petition was a " prayer " which the lowliest might offer. Moreover, it turned out that the petition did not ask for abolition. But that week was one in which the slavery question was brought so vigorously forward that the whole country was aroused. Thomas Ritchie, the editor of the Richmond *Enquirer,* writing to Van Buren on February 11, inclosed extracts from a letter written the previous day from Washington, which declared that there was " no division among Southern men."

The South [it stated] *will not permit* petitions of that character to be entertained by any Assembly but their own State legislatures. . . . Yet the South will not continue in the Union — would freely and voluntarily, coolly and deliberately withdraw from the Confederation sooner than permit this subject to be entertained.

Ritchie himself adds that the contents of this letter startle him, and he raises the question:

[210] See p. 197, *ante.*

Is it possible there is any danger of this blessed Union coming to an end? of the noblest fabric which was ever formed for the benefit of the human race being torn to pieces by a few fanatical Priests, weak women, and some such wretches as Tappan & Garrison.

Such, he thinks, may be the consequences.[211]

On February 7 Calhoun introduced, as a substitute for the bill recommended by the Committee on Public Lands, an " amend-ment " providing for immediate relinquishment, to the states in which they lay, of all public lands that had been on the market but had remained unsold for thirty-five years or longer. Under Calhoun's proposal, it was stipulated that the states must pay to the United States, annually, one-third of the gross amounts of their sales of public lands within their borders. It was further provided that the then minimum price should continue until January 1, 1842, after which date the states were to be permitted to establish minimum prices, on a graduated scale, ranging from one dollar per acre, effective January 1, 1842, on lands that had then been on the market at least ten years, down to twenty cents an acre, effective January 1, 1862, on those that had at that date been on the market for at least thirty years — with the proviso that all other public lands remaining unsold, after having been offered for ten years, should be subject to corresponding gradua-tion in price, or to cession, after the lapse of the same periods of time, commencing at the expiration of ten years from the date placed on the market.[212] Calhoun intended, through this measure, to effect a combination between the South and the West and to diminish the power of the federal government by giving to the states a means of making their own internal improvements and of promoting their own banking enterprises.

The debate that followed has much interest to the student of sectionalism. Senator James Buchanan, of Pennsylvania, de-clared the proposal " the most splendid bribe " that had ever been offered to Congress.[213] Benton, of Missouri, opposed it, partly because graduation, under its provisions, would proceed so slowly. He declared:

[211] Van Buren MSS, Library of Congress. See also Wise's account of Adams's " hoax," in B. H. Wise, *op. cit.*, p. 55.

[212] *Register of Debates*, XIII, Pt. I, 729-30, also 705; *Calhoun Works*, II (New York, 1853), 634-52; Wellington, *op. cit.*, pp. 58-64; and Geo. M. Ste-phenson, *The Political History of the Public Lands from 1840 to 1862* (Boston, 1917), pp. 33-37.   [213] *Register of Debates*, XIII, Pt. I, 731.

We were now within less than three years of the period for taking the new census. . . . By that time we should probably have three new States: two on the Mississippi, and one on the Gulf of Mexico; while the representation of the new States already in the Union would be greatly enlarged. . . . In three years more, they [the Western states] could write their own terms, and lay them on the table of the Senate. They would be bid for, and bid deeply for, by every candidate for the presidency.[214]

To this Calhoun replied that he had no concealed purpose, and said that in four years the new states would have twenty-four Senators and would soon have the question in their own hands. He would anticipate this and break the vassalage of the new states.[215] Senator John M. Niles, of Connecticut, exclaimed that Calhoun's measure was " thrown into the Senate like the golden apple of discord." " Let not the Government become a broker," he urged, " but give up the whole domain, out and out. If the sceptre must depart from the old States, it would at least pass over to men of the same blood and of a common origin." [216]

But Calhoun's " amendment " was voted down, 28 to 7, on the day it was offered.[217] The Senate having the same day ordered the bill proposed by the Committee on Public Lands to a third reading and thus safeguarded the desire of the West to restrict sales to actual settlers and having granted pre-emption, the West was now ready to support Calhoun's cession plan, which two days later was introduced as an independent bill; but it was tabled on the eleventh, by a vote of 26 to 20.[218] Cession was supported by all the states of the North Central and South Central sections, except Ohio and Kentucky (and in each of these states one Senator did not vote). On the other hand, the only state in the North Atlantic and South Atlantic sections that gave its approval was South Carolina. The two Georgia Senators and one, each, from Pennsylvania and from Massachusetts (John Davis) did not vote. Except, then, for South Carolina's vote, all the coastal sections were opposed to cession.

Shortly before Jackson's term expired, the House provided for sending a diplomatic agent to Texas. A map of the vote reveals that, with practically no exceptions save Delaware and two Congressional districts in central Tennessee, the South Atlantic and South Central sections were in favor of this resolution, as were

214 *Ibid.*, p. 733. 217 *Ibid.*, p. 736.
215 *Ibid.*, p. 735. 218 *Ibid.*, p. 794.
216 *Ibid.*

also those portions of Indiana that voted, all of Illinois, and certain districts in central and eastern Ohio. Scattered districts in Pennsylvania, and the Democratic part of New York State, also supported it; but New England, with the exception of the seaboard corner of New Hampshire and a district in northern Maine, was opposed.[219] On the last day of his administration Jackson notified the Senate that he had concluded that the republic of Texas had established an independent government in conformity with the practice of the laws of nations and that he, therefore, recognized its independence and nominated a chargé d'affaires to represent the United States.[220]

Thus, the Presidency of Andrew Jackson came to an end. He had rested his political power upon the West and that part of the Middle Atlantic section in which Van Buren was ascendant, rather than upon the seaboard South. By his policy of securing cessions from, and removal of, the Indians,[221] he had, in the Southwest, added important areas for the cultivation of cotton, and, in the Northwest, had expanded the zone open to the wheat farmers. He had engaged in a struggle with Calhoun over the question of state sovereignty, soon to become so vital to the South as a whole and to the nation. He had checked Henry Clay's " American system " of internal improvements at federal expense, at the very time when the canals and railroads were breaking down the old agencies of transportation. The Bank of the United States had fallen before his assaults, and by its overthrow had introduced a new era in the handling of banking, finance, and currency. He had seen the state banks multiply their numbers and capital in a way that brought him great disquietude; but it was his belief that this overexpansion was due in large part to the failure of Congress to give him the legislation he desired for the regulation of those banks, and to the passage of the deposit act without due restrictions and against his own wishes but with such a country-wide demand that he did not feel warranted in attempting a veto. Thus, the destruction of the National Bank as an " engine of the money power " had led to a new phase of

[219] *House Journal*, 24th Cong., 2d Sess., pp. 546–47.

[220] *Messages and Papers*, III, 281–82.

[221] See ——— [The author intended to insert here a reference to " Benton's speech extolling Jackson for having gained so great an area for the United States by his Indian policy."] For the area of the cessions Jackson gained, see Bureau of Ethnology, 18th *Annual Report* (maps, and text regarding treaties).

the political influence of capital. The state banks passed under the influence of the Whigs; and the states themselves, anxious to create their own systems of internal improvements in place of the federal system that Jackson had brought to an end, came more and more to rely upon those sources of credit, state banks, and the Eastern and English reservoirs of capital from which they drew. Although he had not vetoed the act for the distribution of the surplus revenue, in his last message he severely criticized it and the effects that were following. The slavery issue seemed, to him and his friends, to have been raised by Calhoun with the deliberate purpose of consolidating the sectionalism of the South.[222] In foreign affairs, although his policy of trade in the West Indies had resulted in diminishing the maritime commerce of the United States, he had shown patriotic vigor, even against the reluctant Whigs, in successfully asserting the rights of the nation in the matter of French spoliations.

On the fourth of March came his Farewell Address.[223] In previous messages he had dwelt upon many of its features. But with especial solemnity he now warns his fellow citizens against " the formation of parties on geographical discriminations," and he refers, in this connection, to Washington's Farewell Address.

We behold [says Jackson] systematic efforts publicly made to sow the seeds of discord between different parts of the United States and to place party divisions directly upon geographical distinctions; to excite the *South* against the *North* and the *North* against the *South*, and to force into the controversy the most delicate and exciting topics — topics upon which it is impossible that a large portion of the Union can ever speak without strong emotion. . . . If the Union is once severed, the line of separation will grow wider and wider, and the controversies which are now debated and settled in the halls of legislation will then be tried in fields of battle and determined by the sword. Neither should you deceive yourselves with the hope that the first line of separation would be the permanent one, and that nothing but harmony and concord would be found in the new associations formed upon the dissolution of this Union. Local interests would still be found there, and unchastened ambition. . . . The first line of separation would not last for a single generation; new fragments would be torn off.

Urging sectional concessions to secure justice to every portion of the United States, he points out that the foundations

[222] See, e.g., the *Globe*, Aug. 31, 1836.
[223] He seems to have consulted various friends, including Taney and Van Buren, as to the form of this address.

of the federal government must be laid in the affections of the people.

In his observations upon banking and currency, he urges that the public interests cannot be effectually promoted unless silver and gold are restored to circulation, and cautions his countrymen that

intriguers and politicians will now resort to the States and . . . endeavor to establish in the different States one moneyed institution with over-grown capital and exclusive privileges sufficient to enable it to control the operations of the other banks.[224]

On his return to his home, " The Hermitage," he wrote to Van Buren, on the thirtieth of March,[225] of the success of his administration, declaring, " I am truly thankful to my god for this happy result," and urging a retention of his policy of executing pledges made and resisting demagogues. He warned Van Buren that there were " professed friends in whom I had great confidence who for office sake apostatised and you may meet with some judases in your ranks." He again drew attention to the dangers arising from the present state of the paper system and the deposit banks of the West and Southwest, and reported that it would take at least three successful crops to meet their debts. He went on to say that an important Mississippi bank had " already blew up." A few weeks later he wrote to a friend:

It is now plain that the war is to be carried on by the monied aristoc-racy of the few against the Democracy of numbers; the prosperous[?] to make the honest labourers hewers of wood & drawers of water to the monied aristocracy of the country thro the credit and paper system.[226]

Thus, the new President came to office with clear indications that trouble was brewing and that he must choose between the friends of the state banks and their opponents.

[224] The full text of the Farewell Address is in *Messages and Papers*, III, 292–308.
[225] Van Buren MSS, Library of Congress.
[226] To Moses Dawson, May 26, 1837 (Jackson MSS, Library of Congress).

CHAPTER X

SECTIONS AND NATION: VAN BUREN ADMINISTRATION AND THE PANIC

The coming of Van Buren into the Presidency brought to that office a man of tact, political sagacity, and initiative. Often in the wilful and volcanic administration of Andrew Jackson he had served as a restraining, and at times as a guiding, influence.[1] However, at this crucial point in his career, he chose, not perhaps without apprehensions, to follow in the footsteps of his predecessor; and almost at the beginning of his Presidency he found himself in the midst of a panic and of the threatened secession from the Democratic party of some of its most influential leaders.

The new President continued as his cabinet the men who had been serving under Jackson, with the exception that Lewis Cass (who in 1836 had gone to France as minister) was replaced as Secretary of War by Joel R. Poinsett, of South Carolina, Unionist agent of Jackson.

In Van Buren's Inaugural Address[2] no anticipation is to be found of the coming panic. Rather, he urged the fact that the United States presented "an aggregate of human prosperity surely not elsewhere to be found." He pointed out the importance of respect for the rights of the states under the Constitution, and dwelt upon the existence of separate sectional interests liable to be used for sinister purposes. He recalled the fact that the government had been "laid upon principles of reciprocal concession and equitable compromise." This he would continue; and he repeated his declaration, made in the campaign:

[1] John Quincy Adams, in his *Memoirs* (ed. C. F. Adams; IX [Philadelphia, 1876], 368–69; Sept. 9, 1837), gives a characteristic analysis of the traits of Van Buren, combining praise of his discretion and conciliatory temper with vitriolic criticism of what he regards as his duplicity and servility.

[2] Jas. D. Richardson (compiler), *Messages and Papers of the Presidents, 1789–1897*, III (Washington, 1896), 313–20.

I must go into the Presidential chair the inflexible and uncompromising opponent of every attempt on the part of Congress to abolish slavery in the District of Columbia against the wishes of the slaveholding States, and also with a determination equally decided to resist the slightest interference with it in the States where it exists.

This, of course, was not inconsistent with his later opposition to the extension of slavery into the new territories; but it was a clear indication of his desire to maintain the policy of combination of New York and Virginia, which he had made a part of his political program in 1827.[3]

Even before he had taken office as President, Van Buren was besieged by bankers, merchants, and conservative friends, demanding that he repeal the Specie Circular, which was already creating alarm.[4] Senator N. P. Tallmadge, of New York (a supporter of Jackson), wrote in the middle of March that the Treasury order was the all-engrossing topic and that the legislative branch was almost unanimous in desiring that it be superseded; and on the seventh of April a letter of Senator W. C. Rives, of Virginia (another administration man), urged its withdrawal and called attention to its injurious political effects. What, he asks, will be the position of your friends in Congress, when it reconvenes, if you do not now rescind the measure? But Van Buren had accepted the view of Jackson and those leaders of the party who took the opposite view, and he therefore decided to follow the advice of his predecessor not to repeal or suspend the Circular without consideration of the real condition of the banks.[5]

The situation had been steadily growing more and more serious. Attention has already been directed, particularly in the chapters on the South Central and North Central sections, to the overconfidence that had led to excessive bank expansion, to land speculation, and to the rage for state internal improvements by means of loans. This overconfidence of the West found a ready response on the part of Eastern capitalists, who invested their funds in paper cities [6] and who often secured the appointment

[3] See pp. 34–35, ante.

[4] Van Buren MSS (of the period), Library of Congress.

[5] Support of the Specie Circular came from such men as Silas Wright, Azariah C. Flagg, C. C. Cambreleng, and others, of New York, and from Roger B. Taney (see ibid.), as well as from numerous labor meetings.

[6] Examples of this tendency are seen in Nicholas Biddle's interest in a proposed Michigan city and in Webster's speculation in prospective cities near what is now Madison, Wisconsin. Many Senators sent their agents to engage in this

of surveyors and land-office receivers and registrars, because these
could pick the best lands for speculative purchase by their
friends. The Eastern capitalists also sent funds to their agents [7]
for investment in public lands, and were not free from responsibility for the rise of Western banks established without real
capital or adequate specie. In many cases the capital thus transferred originated in England.[8] From colonial times, English cotton factors had been active in advancing credit to the planters [9]
for the production of crops and the purchase of slaves and in
furnishing New York exporters with the means of operation.
Confidence in American securities had been increased by the
prospective extinction of the United States debt and by such
successful state ventures as the Erie Canal. Much higher interest was to be gained in the United States than in England. In
this reservoir of English capital, the firm of Baring Brothers
played an important part.[10] By the fall of 1836, bank failures
came in England, and a period of retrenchment was indicated.
The European aspect of the panic is important.[11]

Labor showed growing discontent and agitation over prices
and wages and the food supply, in this period.[12] The failure
of crops in 1835 and 1837 had an important influence upon the
financial situation. In short, it may be doubted whether the
panic that came in the latter year would not have occurred irrespective of the deposit act and the Specie Circular; but they were
important factors in hastening it. When, in January, 1837, pur-
suant to the terms of the deposit act, the banks were obliged to
pay out the first instalment of the surplus for distribution among
the several states,[13] the combination of this tying-up of funds

---

kind of operation, and some of them, like Robert J. Walker, of Mississippi,
were active in forming pools for speculation in South Central lands.

[7] Illustrations of this tendency are to be seen in the Papers of Moses M.
Strong and of Cyrus Woodman, in the Library of the Wisconsin Historical
Society.

[8] See Leland H. Jenks, *The Migration of British Capital to 1875* (New York,
1927), Chap. III, and N. S. Buck, *The Development of the Organisation of
Anglo-American Trade, 1800–1850* (New Haven, 1925).

[9] See Alfred H. Stone, " The Cotton Factorage System of the Southern
States," *American Historical Review*, XX, 557–65.

[10] Their records should constitute an important source for the history of
the period.

[11] See Davis R. Dewey, *Financial History of the United States* (New York,
1924), p. 230.   [12] See pp. 121–24, *ante*.

[13] For Van Buren's attitude toward distribution, see his letter to Sherrod
Williams, Aug. 8, 1836 (printed in *Niles' Register*, LI, 26 ff.).

in transit to the various parts of the country,[14] with the Circular's requirement that specie must be used in payment for public lands, was followed by a stringency that was increased when, in April, the turning-over of the second instalment began. On the tenth of May, specie payments were suspended by the New York banks, and similar action on the part of those in all the other large cities followed within a few days. Thus the Panic of 1837 was precipitated; and the problem was presented to the newly elected President of deciding upon the proper course to follow in view of the facts that the banks were no longer paying the specie required of them as depositories and were even liable under state laws for forfeiture of their charters because of their inability to pay specie. Accordingly, on the fifteenth of May, Van Buren called a special session of Congress for the first Monday in September following.[15]

Already, the idea of divorcing the government and its revenue from all banks had been broached. The origin of this plan is not easy to determine. Jefferson is said to have suggested it to Alexander J. Dallas, and Albert Gallatin had also referred to the possibility of such a solution.[16] In 1832 Moses Jaques, one of the Locofoco leaders, had favored a similar system, and William J. Duane has been credited with having brought forward a like scheme at the time the removal of the deposits was under consideration, but it was claimed that Jackson contemptuously rejected the proposal.[17] Again, it is asserted that in 1834 Condy Raguet [18] brought the subtreasury notion, involving the conception of divorcing the government from all banking operations, to Washington, and that he was influential in securing the intro-

[14] R. M. Whitney wrote an interesting letter to Jackson, on October 27, 1836 (Jackson MSS, Library of Congress), complaining of the situation that would result from locking up funds in transit.

[15] Jackson had written him on the twelfth of May (Van Buren MSS, Library of Congress), warning him of the critical state of affairs in the deposit banks and urging him: " be ye therefore steady, firm & unwavouring in your course and all is safe."

[16] *The Writings of Albert Gallatin*, ed. Henry Adams (Philadelphia, 1879), III, 330 (reprinting *Considerations on the Currency and Banking System of the United States*, published in Philadelphia in 1831).

[17] *Madisonian*, Oct. 27, 1837.

[18] Philadelphia merchant, editor of free-trade journals, and author of *An Inquiry into the Causes of the Present State of the Circulating Medium of the United States* (Philadelphia, 1815) and *A Treatise on the Principles of Currency and Banking* (Philadelphia, 1839).

duction by Representative W. F. Gordon,[19] of Virginia, in June of that year, of an amendment [20] to the deposit bill that would embody the plan and include a requirement that the revenue should be collected in coin. A well-known writer on banking and currency, William M. Gouge, then employed in the Treasury Department, said that he had made investigations on the subject at the time that a member of Congress, " by authority of the Secretary of the Treasury, brought in a resolution for some other mode of keeping the public money than in banks." [21] When, in December, 1834, Levi Woodbury transmitted to Congress his special report, as Secretary of the Treasury, on " the present system of keeping and disbursing the Public Money," he referred to the possibility of the government's use of agencies other than banks for its fiscal operations; but he did not sanction the idea under existing conditions. He thought, however, that a system of government control of its revenues could be devised in the event of a contingency involving the general inability of the state banks, as well as the United States Bank, to provide the machinery for adequate safeguarding of government deposits.[22] In February, 1835, Gordon presented an amendment substantially duplicating his earlier one; but it was emphatically voted down on the twelfth of that month, with only thirty-three members supporting it.[23]

Shortly after the panic began, Van Buren received a letter from

[19] See *Niles' Register*, LV, 75, for extract from letter, Raguet to W. C. Preston, May, 1834. On Gordon, see A. C. Gordon, *William Fitzhugh Gordon, a Virginian of the Old School* (Washington and New York, 1909).

[20] *Register of Debates in Congress*, X, Pt. IV, 4640–41.

[21] Gouge to Jackson, Aug. 13, 1836 (Jackson MSS, Library of Congress). In this letter, which was marked by Jackson " to be carefully perused," Gouge urges the desirability of divorcing the government from connection with banks and ceasing to use paper money in any way. He alleges that the supply of gold and silver, in every country, is equal to the effective demand and would be a convenient medium. The letter also goes on to outline the number of subtreasury offices necessary and the details of their duties, and to point out the safety of the system. The letter is important as indicating rather minutely the general lines actually followed when the Subtreasury was instituted. See his *A Short History of Paper-Money and Banking in the United States. . . . To Which Is Prefixed an Inquiry into the Principles of the System*, . . . (Philadelphia, 1833), Pt. II [abuses of local banking], and *An Inquiry into the Expediency of Dispensing with Bank Agency and Bank Paper in the Fiscal Concerns of the United States* (Philadelphia, 1837) [He notes that the second chapter is part of an article written in 1835, but not then printed.].

[22] *Register of Debates*, XI, Pt. II, App., 89.

[23] *Ibid.*, XI, Pt. II, 1281–88, 1333.

Dr. John Brockenbrough, of Richmond, President of the Bank of Virginia, which suggested views with regard to an independent treasury not unlike those of Gouge; but he believed that state banks should continue to operate for other than business of the government. Their control, he thought, should be left to the legislation of the several states. " The chimerical idea of establishing in this country a mere metallic currency is too silly for any man of sense to dwell on." In his opinion, the government should employ its own agents to collect and disburse the public funds, through the use of commissioners under the Treasury Department.[24] The influence of Gouge may be surmised from a letter of Judge Richard E. Parker to Attorney-General Benjamin F. Butler.[25] Parker states that he is reading Gouge, but that he cannot see the desirability of being opposed to all banks, although it was necessary to rally against a national bank.

Apparently Van Buren now looked upon the letter from Dr. Brockenbrough as a convenient means of drawing out the opinions of his political friends. He therefore wrote, within a few days, asking Rives's views on the subject, and he also addressed Silas Wright, Representative C. C. Cambreleng, of New York, and James Buchanan, inquiring their attitude and suggesting that they correspond with other leaders of the party to see if some agreement could be reached on the question.[26] The replies of

[24] This letter (Van Buren MSS, Library of Congress), originally written to Rives, on May 20, 1837, was inclosed by Dr. Brockenbrough in a communication to Van Buren on May 22. Its significance arises, in part, from the respect felt for its writer in Virginia, and in part from his position as an authority on banking in the Old Dominion, where state banks had always been important and highly regarded. Virginia was to be the fighting ground between friends of Van Buren, anxious to retain the state banks as depositories, and those who accepted the idea of an independent treasury.

On Dr. Brockenbrough, see *The John P. Branch Historical Papers of Randolph-Macon College*, III, No. 3, p. 253; Hugh A. Garland, *The Life of John Randolph of Roanoke* (New York, 1851), I, vi, vii, 261 ff.; John Goode, *Recollections of a Lifetime* (New York, 1906); Chas. H. Ambler, *Thomas Ritchie* (Richmond, Va., 1913) [using Index]; and Henry H. Simms, *The Rise of the Whigs in Virginia, 1824–1840* (Richmond, Va., 1929), pp. 122–23, 135.

[25] May 29, 1837 (Van Buren MSS, Library of Congress). See also the comment made by the Richmond *Enquirer*, April 21, 1837, on Gouge's foresight in his book on the banking system.

[26] The Van Buren MSS (Library of Congress) contain a draft attributed to Gouge (with corrections by Woodbury and Van Buren) of a request of the President for advice on national revenue and banks. In the *Calendar of the Papers of Martin Van Buren* (Washington, 1910), p. 302, this is dated " June [21?], 1837." See also Senator Tallmadge's statement in his speech of March 7, 1838 (*Congressional Globe*, VI, 226).

most of these men were, on the whole favorable; [27] but Rives informed the President that he still thought selected banks, with deposits adequately safeguarded, would be the best solution, and that an exclusively metallic currency was visionary.

At about this time, too, Jackson was writing to his friends that " the Government ought to seperate itself from all Banks, unless those of Deposit, & exchange." He hoped that banks would not be legalized to issue paper under $50 or at least $20, " as all have forfeighted their charters." [28] Already, the former President was fulminating against the failure of the Senate to support him in securing efficient regulation of the deposits and against the action of the deposit banks.

In New York, on the other hand, Van Buren was receiving earnest protests from the bank interests against the possibility of an independent treasury. It was evident that he would have to choose between adherence to Jackson, together with the group, led by Senator Thomas H. Benton, favorable to a metallic currency, and those who still believed in the use of regulated deposit banks. Inasmuch as the federal government was unable directly to prescribe the conduct of state banks, and in view of the tendencies that had been revealed toward overexpansion, it was dangerous to yield to the wishes of the friends of the banks; yet it was quite as perilous to his political fortunes to incur their opposition.

A letter [29] from Roger B. Taney (the former Secretary of the Treasury under Jackson, now Chief Justice) to Van Buren must have added to his worries. Taney wrote declaring strongly against the plan of keeping the public money in a subtreasury, with special officers appointed for that purpose. The reasons he gave for his objection were substantially those that were afterwards urged by Rives and by the Whigs. Instead, he would place the public money on deposit in banks, without interest but with a moderate commission for receipt and disbursement, as in the original use of deposit banks on the removal of the revenues

[27] Although, on March 21, Wright had informed Van Buren that " the great mass of the people are against the Specie Circular." (Van Buren MSS, Library of Congress.)

[28] Jackson to F. P. Blair, June 5, 1837 (Jackson MSS, Library of Congress). Cf. also his letter to Moses Dawson, May 26, 1837.

[29] July 20, 1837 (Van Buren MSS, Library of Congress). This was apparently written in reply to the draft letter referred to on p. 458 (ante), n. 26.

from the Bank of the United States, except that he would make the obligation absolute to keep the funds in specie. He did not think it advisable to repeal the law respecting the October instalment of the deposits with the states, nor to suspend its payment, holding the opinion that if the merchants paid their bonds there would be sufficient money for the expenditures of the following year. In regard to the issuance of treasury notes (which the President's letter had suggested), Taney was convinced there was enough specie in the country to make unnecessary anything like a paper currency. As a temporary measure, he would consider treasury notes, payable in twelve months with interest, receivable for government dues.

There had been a decided majority in Congress in favor of the repeal of the Specie Circular; the panic had increased the public demand for this action; and even Van Buren himself had believed that he could present the financial dilemma to Congress in a way that would remove the objections to the Circular and at the same time avoid the necessity of rescinding it. Therefore, it is not strange that a group was formed to bring pressure upon the President against the exclusive use of specie and against the possibility of the divorce of the government from all state banks. At first it was the announced purpose of this faction, which took the name of " Conservative Democrats," rather to give Van Buren information concerning the real feeling of the Democratic party than to revolt from it.

At the end of June, 1837, an interesting letter from Thomas Allen [30] to Senator Tallmadge,[31] of New York, reported the steps that had been taken with regard to the establishment of an organ for the group, but mentioned difficulty in obtaining the necessary funds to start it. However, it became increasingly apparent, in the course of the summer, that Van Buren had decided to follow the policy of Jackson and to recommend the separation of the government from banks, and reliance upon a specie currency for

[30] Tallmadge MSS, Wisconsin Historical Society Library. The *Western Journal* (St. Louis), IX (1852–53), has a portrait of Allen and a brief account of his career. Born in Pittsfield, Massachusetts, in 1813, descendant of a line of clergymen, he had entered newspaper work in New York and had been admitted to the bar. He had favored Van Buren for the Presidency.

[31] The *Albany Argus*, February 23, 1839, has a critical account of Tallmadge's career, pointing out particularly his connection with banks and his later adherence to Clay and the Whig party.

government revenues.[32] In the middle of August appeared Volume I, No. 1, of the *Madisonian* [33] (published in Washington, under the editorship of Allen), which professed to follow the conservative policy of Madison, objected to an exclusively metallic currency, and urged that the credit system should be preserved and regulated.[34] In this first number was quoted a letter of Senator Tallmadge declaring that the credit system was the distinguishing feature between despotism and liberty, and defending the deposit act.

The jealousy between the *Madisonian* and the *Globe* is evident from the former's comment: " If the Globe has an *exclusive* patent right to be the organ of the *executive* perhaps he will allow us to be the organ of the Republicans in the *legislative* department." " Are we," it asks, " to levy war upon 800 Banks with 800,000 Allies? "

By this time it was clear that Virginia was to be split, on this question, between the friends of Rives and those of the administration; and on the first page of the initial number of the *Madisonian* was printed Rives's notable speech in the Senate on January 10, 1837.[35]

The special session of Congress, which met on September 4, 1837, listened to Van Buren's message outlining the financial difficulties that the government faced; proposing the divorce of the government and banking, under an independent- or subtreasury system that would permit the government to receive, care for, and disburse its own funds, in gold and silver or their equivalent, without reliance upon banks; and recommending the withholding of the October instalment of the distribution of the surplus, and the temporary issuance of treasury notes to meet the needs of the government.

A bill, introduced in the Senate by Van Buren's friend, Wright (chairman of the Finance Committee), for the establishment of an independent treasury, without forbidding the receipt of bills of specie-paying banks, met with the objection of Senator Cal-

[32] In a letter of July 23 to Blair (printed in *Niles' Register*, LII, 370), Jackson speaks of his pleasure at having discovered, from the *Globe* of the 13th and other papers, that " the democracy " were uniting on the subtreasury plan.

[33] There is a file of this paper in the Harvard Library, presented through the courtesy of Mrs. Charles H. Haskins, herself a descendant of the editor.

[34] On the Conservative Democrats, see p. 187, *ante*.

[35] See pp. 445-46, *ante*.

houn, who offered an amendment known as the " specie clause,"
which was accepted by Senator Wright.

At this point it is important to recall the change of Calhoun
with reference to the party affiliation of himself and his friends.
As we have seen, there had been a premonition of a split between
the supporters and opponents of Van Buren within the Democratic party; now the South Carolina statesman, and those of his
followers whom he could influence, passed from an alliance with
the Whigs to one with the Democrats. It was Calhoun's purpose,
earlier as well as at this time, to keep himself and those loyal to
him, as an independent state-rights group, from formal incorporation in either party.

Even in 1834, when Gordon's proposition was submitted, Calhoun had been in favor of the " divorce " plan, but then thought
it premature.[36] When, however, the panic came, discrediting deposits in state banks, and when his personal enemy, Jackson, was
succeeded in the Presidency by Van Buren, from whom he had
no reason to expect " executive usurpation " or crushing will-
power, and who had catered to the South by his attitude with
regard to the radical abolitionists; and when he saw that continued affiliation with his former friends of the Whig party
would mean assent to Clay's doctrines of federal power in relation to internal improvements, and the possible restoration of
the protective tariff — his course seemed to him clearly marked.
Hoping to secure Southern unity [37] through the discord in the
other parties and thereby to acquire a balance of power, he decided in the summer to break his friendship with the Whigs.[38]
" If," he said, " we stand firm, the national party must become
extinct; and till it becomes so the country cannot be saved." By
the seventh of September, therefore, he had reached the conclusion that Van Buren had been " forced by his situation and

[36] *The Works of John C. Calhoun*, ed. R. K. Crallé, II (New York, 1853),
335–36, and *Niles' Register*, XLV, 54.

[37] *Correspondence of John C. Calhoun*, ed. J. Franklin Jameson (American
Historical Association *Annual Report*, 1899, II; Washington, 1900), p. 371.

[38] Calhoun to Duff Green, June 26, 1837 (*ibid.*, pp. 372–74). On July 27
he remonstrated with Green against the inference, which might be drawn from
the course recommended by the editor, that he was aiming constantly at the
Presidency. He declined to consider taking a place on the proposed Harrison
ticket, and asserted that he would have nothing to do with the convention of
the Whigs. " I am not," said he, " of the same party with Webster and others
. . . I believe the sound portion of the country, if there be one, that is left, is
to be found in the original Jackson party." (*Ibid.*, pp. 375–77.)

the terror of Jackson to play directly " into his hands,[39] and he determined to use the opportunity for breaking control by the North, " through the use of Government credit acting through the banks," of Southern industry and commerce. " I go," said he, " against the chartering of a United States bank, or any connection with Biddles, or any other bank." He expected an entirely new reorganization of parties.

Van Buren thus began his administration with the accession of recruits from his former rival in the South, but with the expected loss of a still larger group composed of the Conservative, or bank, Democrats.

It is striking evidence of the continued influence of Jackson that, although now an aged private citizen and in bad health, he had brought Van Buren to acceptance of his financial views, at the cost of a schism with the banking interests in both New York and Virginia (states on which the new President must rely for support), and that Van Buren had received Calhoun's cooperation in the policy of opposition to the National Bank and support of a metallic currency and the " divorce " system.[40]

In the special session of 1837, the administration won in the victory of Polk over John Bell for Speaker of the House of Representatives, but lost in the choice of Thomas Allen as Public Printer, by a combination of Whigs and Conservatives, over Gales and Seaton, of the *National Intelligencer*, and Blair and Rives, of the *Globe*.

The proposed Independent Treasury bill, with Calhoun's

---

[39] *Ibid.*, pp. 377–78; see also pp. 379, 380, 399, 407–10, and F. W. Moore (ed.), " Calhoun as Seen by His Political Friends: Letters of Duff Green, Dixon H. Lewis, Richard K. Cralle during the Period from 1831 to 1848," Southern History Association *Publications*, VII, 159–69, 269–91, 353–61, 419–26, *passim*. The *Baltimore Merchant* (in which, September 19–October 10, Calhoun newspapers are listed) and the *Washington Reformer* served Calhoun in this period as organs of propaganda. His notable speech in which he explained his transfer of party support was on September 18, 1837 (*Register of Debates*, XIV, Pt. I, 50–66). A typical contemporary Whig reaction to Calhoun's " defection " is in the *Autobiography of William H. Seward, from 1801 to 1834. With a Memoir of His Life and Selections from His Letters from 1831 to 1846*, by Frederick W. Seward (New York, 1877), pp. 338–39. Calhoun's speech, in Seward's opinion, " let him down at once from the proud and enviable distinction of the compatriot of Clay and Webster."

[40] As we shall see, in the critical part of the campaign of 1844 Jackson's views were probably controlling in the decision of the Democrats to prefer the nomination of James K. Polk, who favored the immediate annexation of Texas, as against Van Buren's stand in opposition to annexation.

specie amendment, passed the Senate but was defeated in the House. In successive sessions of Congress until 1840, the measure continued to fail, even though the specie clause was stricken out; but the act of (July 4) 1840 brought temporary victory to Van Buren through a compromise providing that, until June 30, 1843, a fraction (diminishing year by year) of sums due the United States might be paid in other than legal currency, but after that date only in gold and silver.[41] Throughout most of Van Buren's administration, therefore, the Treasury continued to use certain banks and also to retain some of the public moneys in the hands of its own officials.

The President's efforts to restrain the bitter antagonism between Ritchie, of the Richmond *Enquirer*, and Francis P. Blair, of the Washington *Globe*, proved unsuccessful; and by the time of the election of 1840 both Senators Rives and Tallmadge [42] were enlisted in the Whig party.

In spite of the desires of Western and Southern states, payment of the fourth instalment of the surplus, which had been due in October, was refused. This action was taken notwithstanding the view of some of Van Buren's friends that the needs of the states were such that it would have been a better political policy for the government to have borrowed money and distributed the instalment. The majority of the Whigs, under the leadership of Clay, opposed deferring payment.

The special session also authorized treasury notes in denominations of not less than fifty dollars, which bore interest and were receivable in payment of dues to the United States. In succeeding years it was found necessary to add to these issues.

Thus, the brilliant prospect that had been held out, of the extinction of the national debt — which had been the fond vision

[41] The project of an independent treasury constituted an important turning point in the relations between the capitalist and the government. Thereafter, until our own time, the so-called " money power " had to operate more or less *sub rosa* instead of being an integral part of the government. For the text of the compromise provision (Sec. 19) in the act of July 4, 1840, see A. T. Huntington and R. J. Mawhinney (compilers), *Laws of the United States concerning Money, Banking, and Loans, 1778–1909* (*Senate Document 580*, 61st Cong., 2d Sess. [National Monetary Commission; Washington, 1910]), p. 125. On the repeal of the act, following the Whig victory in the campaign of 1840, see p. 492, *post*.

[42] By the action of President Tyler, Tallmadge became governor of Wisconsin Territory in 1844.

of Jackson's administration — was shattered when the United States found itself unable to consummate the distribution of the surplus and was even obliged to borrow money.

The Panic of 1837 had at first been most violent on the Atlantic Coast, and it was not until the forties that the full effect of it spread to the interior. Thus, Van Buren's Presidency was confronted with the obstacle of hard times and discontent.[43]

The period was also one marked by the growth of antislavery sentiment in the North and corresponding apprehension in the Southern sections. It was Van Buren's desire to avoid the issue of Northern criticism of the Southern slavery system, which would be involved in the continued reception and discussion of antislavery petitions and in proposals for the abolition of slavery in the District of Columbia. On these points, in the campaign of 1836, he had aimed to satisfy his Southern supporters. But Calhoun, far from content with this negative attitude, and at the same time cognizant of the strategic advantage derived from his acquiescence in the President's fiscal policy, determined to push aggressively the insistence of the Southern sections on freedom from attack upon their social system, which rested on the institution of slavery. The murder of E. P. Lovejoy in 1837, at Alton, Illinois, by a mob opposed to his publication of an antislavery newspaper, added fuel to the flames in the North. The antislavery men divided, in their policies, into the radical wing, favored by William Lloyd Garrison, and those who recognized the Constitutional right of slaveholding within the states where it already existed, but denied its right either to expand into the territories or to retain a position of security in the District of Columbia where they felt there was a national responsibility for its continued existence. This latter wing was also recruited from those who supported the right of petition and opposed the " gag laws " that were passed at successive sessions of the House of Representatives.

On February 9, 1837, following a bitter debate in the House over the question of the right of petition, a resolution denouncing any member presenting a petition from slaves was voted down (104 to 92).[44] There is observable in this vote a distinct sec-

[43] See pp. 308–9, *ante.*
[44] *Register of Debates*, XIII, Pt. II, 1684–85 (negative vote recorded as 105, but is 104 by count).

tional alignment that overrode party affiliations. Of the votes in favor of the resolution, only fifteen were cast by Representatives (all of them Democrats) from the New England, Middle Atlantic, and North Central states — that is, the whole great area north of Mason and Dixon's line, the Ohio River, and the southern boundary of Missouri (although in these sections there was sharp division of party politics); while, in the South Atlantic and South Central states, there were but three votes given in opposition (one by a Delaware member and two by Kentucky Congressmen — all three of them of Whig connection). Here was a pattern of the geography of sentiment, on the slavery issue, that might well alarm the South.

On December 27, 1837, Calhoun, in furtherance of his design to force the Democrats to take an advanced position with respect to Southern claims, brought forward a set of resolutions [45] denying the right of Congress to receive petitions against slavery.[46] It was his opinion that, in the natural conflict in the nonslaveholding states, the Democratic party would be thrown to the Southern side and the opposition, to the Northern. " It would have been impossible to have got a single man of the latter [the Whigs], in either House, to subscribe to the principles in relation to abolition, to which the whole body of the former [the Democrats] agreed." [47]

Starting from his well-known conception that the Union was a compact between sovereign states, that the Constitution was the equivalent of a treaty embodying such a league, and that it was made in part to secure the states against domestic as well as foreign dangers, Calhoun's resolutions went on to urge that the states had the exclusive right over their own domestic institutions and that the Union would be endangered by attack upon them by any state or combination of its citizens. Going farther, he contended that it was the duty of the federal government to give increased stability and security to the domestic institutions of the states composing the Union, and that a de-

[45] *Congressional Globe*, VI, 55.

[46] " The great point," he wrote, about this time, " is to carry the war into the non slave holding states. . . . The resolutions will have a powerful tendency to bring the democratick party in these states into conflict with the abolition and consolidation parties." (*Calhoun Correspondence*, p. 388; see also pp. 389–91.)

[47] *Ibid.*, p. 409.

mand for the abolition of slavery in the District of Columbia
or in any territory would be an assault upon the institutions
of the slaveholding states. Proceeding still farther, the resolutions averred that a refusal to extend slave territory or to admit
new states on the ground that slavery was immoral or sinful, or
otherwise obnoxious, would violate the equality of the states
and tend to destroy the Union.

These resolutions embodied a policy of aggressive assertion
of Southern claims in respect to slavery, and led to an animated
debate, in the course of which important modifications were
carried. For example, the declaration that it was the duty of
the federal government to strengthen and uphold the domestic
institutions of the states was omitted; refusal to act with regard
to slavery in the District of Columbia was placed on the ground
of involving breach of faith with the ceding states, Maryland and
Virginia; and the allegation of Constitutional disability to deal
with slavery in the territories was stricken out, except that it was
conceded that slavery should not be prohibited in territories
where it already existed.[48]

These modifications met with the support of followers of both
Clay and Van Buren, and are explained by Calhoun as due to
the Presidential controversy. " One," said he, " is a Southern
man relying on the North for support, and the other a Northern
relying on the South. They of course dread all conflicting questions between the two Sections." [49]

When, in December, 1838, the problem of handling petitions
with regard to slavery again came before the House of Representatives, C. G. Atherton, of New Hampshire (a Democrat), submitted resolutions [50] (adopted on the eleventh and twelfth of the
month) declaring that, under the Constitution, Congress had no
jurisdiction over slavery in the states, and could not, with a view
to disturbing or overthrowing it, abolish it in the District of
Columbia or the territories, prohibit the removal of slaves from
state to state, or discriminate between the institutions of one
portion of the Union and another; and directing that all slavery
petitions should on presentation, " without any further action

[48] Congressional Globe, VI, 74, 80–81, 96–97, 98 (the text of the resolutions
as they were finally adopted, after the amendments by the Senate, being given
on this page) ; Calhoun Works, III (New York, 1853), 140–41.

[49] Calhoun Correspondence, p. 389.

[50] Congressional Globe, VII, 23–25, 27–28.

thereon, be laid upon the table, without being debated, printed, or referred."

These resolutions would seem to go far toward meeting the demands of Calhoun and thus satisfying his desire to commit the federal government on the important point of the procedure on slavery petitions. However, Henry A. Wise, of Virginia, insisted that the resolutions implied the right of reception of petitions by the House, asserting that " if you may receive petitions, you may refer them, and referring, you may report on them . . . you may report favorably as well as unfavorably." [51] He therefore argued that, in effect, the resolutions were a victory for the abolitionists. The decision of the chair that the resolutions disposed of the petition on presentation and that the question of reception could not be raised at that time, was upheld by an overwhelming majority.

In 1840 the so-called " 21st rule " was added to the standing rules of the House.[52] It declared against *reception* of petitions asking the abolition of slavery or of the slave trade. In the vote on this rule a striking sectional pattern was exhibited. While numerous Northern Democratic districts voted in favor of the resolution establishing this rule, and a very few Southern Whig districts voted against it, there was, on the whole, a sharp conflict between the Northern and the Southern sections over the matter.[53]

Meanwhile, as the question of Clay's attitude toward slavery became important to his future political career, and especially in Kentucky and in the campaign that was in progress in New York, he made, on February 7, 1839, his celebrated speech regarding the slavery issue.[54] It was of a somewhat compromising character and consequently lost him much support among the antislavery men of the North, while at the same time it failed to satisfy the Southern extremists. Clay had already foreseen this danger, and possibly the speech was a futile attempt to meet the situation.[55]

[51] *Ibid.*, p. 34.

[52] Jan. 28. (*Ibid.*, VIII, 150–51.)

[53] Not until December 3, 1844, was the " gag law " repealed, on motion of Adams himself. (*Ibid.*, XIV, 7. Cf. *Adams Memoirs*, XII [Philadelphia, 1877], 219.)

[54] *Congressional Globe*, VII, App., 354–59.

[55] See p. 216, *ante;* also: Clay to Francis Brooke, Nov. 3, 1838 (Calvin Colton, *The Life, Correspondence, and Speeches of Henry Clay* [New York,

In this speech Clay argued against the abolition of slavery in the District of Columbia, on the grounds that it would constitute a breach of faith with Maryland and Virginia, that it would not promote the happiness and prosperity of the people within the District, and that it was not essential to the " enjoyment of this site as a seat of the General Government." Taking up the question of Florida, he urged that, in view of the existence of slavery there when the treaty of 1819 with Spain was signed, and because, further, the territory lay to the south of the line agreed-to in the Missouri Compromise of 1820 as dividing the slave states from the free states, admission as a slave state should be granted.[56] Concerning the slave trade, he denied that the federal government had any Constitutional authority whatever to prohibit interstate commerce in slaves among the slaveholding states. He spoke at length in opposition to immediate abolition of slavery. He stressed the point that the country was faced with the *fact* of the presence of three million slaves, and declared that in the slave states the alternatives were that " the white man must govern the black, or the black govern the white." He then presented the economic argument that, on the basis of four hundred dollars a head, slave property in the Union represented a value of twelve hundred million dollars. He warned that by arousing the slave states the abolitionists were defeating their own cause, which might have succeeded in the end through " gradual emancipation." He spoke of negro competition with white labor in the North, that would follow abolition. He pictured the perils of the " unnatural amalgamation " that the abolitionists' insistence upon the freeing of the slaves, coupled with their opposition to colonization, would render inevitable; and predicted that the outcome of their course would be a " virtual

1857], IV, 431) [for Clay's apprehension regarding his position]; *Adams Memoirs*, X (Philadelphia, 1876), 116; L. G. Tyler, *The Letters and Times of the Tylers*, I (Richmond, Va., 1884), 594; *Calhoun Correspondence*, p. 424; and Wm. Birney, *James G. Birney and His Times* (New York, 1890), p. 345. In the *Albany Argus*, June 22, 1839, it is reported that Clay's proslavery speech has not been effective in gaining the South but has chilled the free states. As early as December 24, 1838, Calhoun had thought Clay's prospect overshadowed: ". . . as a man of sense, he ought to have seen that it was impossible for him to take middle ground on the abolition question." (*Calhoun Correspondence*, p. 423.)

[56] He referred to Florida as " the only remaining Territory to be admitted into the Union with the institution of domestic slavery."

dissolution of the Union," followed by a " clash of arms." As to his personal attitude toward slavery, he insisted that he was " no friend " of involuntary servitude, which he called the " one dark spot . . . on our political horizon "; but, nevertheless, he preferred the liberty of his own race to that of any other. " The liberty of the descendants of Africa in the United States," he said, " is incompatible with the safety and liberty of the European descendants."

Meantime, the controversy over the return of fugitive slaves was also proving a source of sectional controversy.[57]   Although the Constitution required the return of fugitive slaves [58] and the federal statute of 1793 provided for enforcement by state officials, the " underground railroad," [59] by which slaves escaped into the North of the United States and into Canada, became increasingly active as the opposition to slavery grew.   The personal-liberty laws of many Northern states oftentimes made impossible the use of state authorities to carry out the law.   In the dispute, originating in 1839, between Virginia and New York, over a fugitive slave, Governor W. H. Seward, on the ground that the laws of New York did not recognize property in a slave and that, therefore, the Virginia acts declaring the theft of a slave felony did not apply to his state, refused to surrender the men who had arranged the slave's escape.   In the noted Prigg case, arising over a conflict between Maryland and Pennsylvania, the Supreme Court finally (1842) held that Congress had exclusive power to legislate on the subject of fugitives from labor and that an escaped slave might be recaptured by its owner in any state, providing that his action did not involve a breach of peace; but that the states could not be required to use their officers to carry the fugitive-slave law into effect.[60]

The question of the annexation of Texas was also arousing

[57] See: Edward Channing, A. B. Hart, and F. J. Turner, *Guide to the Study and Reading of American History* (Boston, 1912), pp. 426–28 (references); H. V. Ames (ed.), *State Documents on Federal Relations*, No. v (Philadelphia, 1904), especially pp. 40–45; and J. B. McMaster, *A History of the People of the United States, from the Revolution to the Civil War*, VII (New York, 1919), 248–65.

[58] Art. IV, Sec. 2.

[59] W. H. Siebert, *The Underground Railroad from Slavery to Freedom* (New York, 1898).

[60] Richard Peters, *Reports of Cases Argued and Adjudged in the Supreme Court of the United States*, XVI, 539.

heated discussion, both in Congress and among the people of the different sections. The Antislavery Society was circulating petitions against it; state protests, particularly from New England and the states in which her colonists were strong, were pouring into Congress; and Southern elements favorable to annexation were threatening disunion in case it were not granted.

Shortly before the special session called on account of the panic, the Texan minister, Memucan Hunt, submitted to the American Secretary of State, Forsyth, a proposition for annexation; [61] and, when he found the administration unlikely to assent, he wrote to the Secretary of State of his republic, suggesting that the proposal be brought directly before the American Congress through presentation by one of its members.[62] The refusal of Forsyth to entertain Hunt's proposition was on the ground that our treaty of amity with Mexico would, in itself, forbid annexation.[63] In reply,[64] Hunt threatened an unfavorable commercial policy toward the United States and intimated that England and France might be more friendly. He wrote to his government an explanation of the American declination, attributing it to our party trammels and to treaty obligations to Mexico; furious opposition of the free states; and fear of incurring the charge of false dealings and of involving the United States in a war that might not be supported by a majority of its own citizens and that might even bring on a struggle between North and South, with the prospect of disunion.

Practically contemporaneously with the threat by Texas, at the end of 1837, that, if she had to remain independent, she would extend her boundaries to the Pacific,[65] Calhoun, as has been mentioned, introduced resolutions asserting the general right of expansion regardless of the slave question.[66] His colleague, W. C.

---

[61] Aug. 4, 1837. See Justin H. Smith, *The Annexation of Texas* (New York, 1911), pp. 63–64. In *Diplomatic Correspondence of the Republic of Texas*, Pt. 1 (American Historical Association *Annual Report*, 1907, II; Washington, 1908), p. 26, the editor, G. P. Garrison, refers (in his Calendar of correspondence already printed) to *House Documents*, 25th Cong., 1st Sess., I, No. 40, pp. 2–11, and *Senate Documents*, 28th Cong., 1st Sess., V, No. 341, pp. 103–12.

[62] Aug. 10, 1837. See *Texan Diplomatic Correspondence*, Pt. 1, p. 254.

[63] Aug. 25, 1837. *Ibid.*, p. 27, cites *House Documents*, 25th Cong., 1st Sess., I, No. 40, pp. 11–13, and *Senate Documents*, 28th Cong., 1st Sess., V, No. 341, pp. 112–14.

[64] Sept. 12, 1837. See Smith, *op. cit.*, p. 65.

[65] See p. 360, *ante*.   [66] See p. 467, *ante*.

Preston, soon proposed a resolution in favor of " reannexing "
Texas when this could be done " consistently with the faith and
treaty stipulations of the United States." [67]   This was tabled.[68]
An annexation resolution in the House, by Waddy Thompson,
of South Carolina, did not come to a vote because of a three
weeks' speech by John Quincy Adams, beginning on June 16,
1838, and consuming the morning hour until close to the end
of the session.[69]

A decision by Texas to withdraw her annexation proposition
is indicated by a letter to Webster from Nicholas Biddle,[70] who
announces the arrival of the new Texan minister, Anson Jones,
in Philadelphia, with instructions to recall the proposal. Biddle
asks Webster whether it would not be better for the United States
to protect Texas from annexation by any other nation or from
conquest, and whether a loan of five million dollars to her would
not better be taken in this country than in England. The formal
withdrawal occurred on the twelfth of October, 1838.[71]

The election of M. B. Lamar to succeed Sam Houston as president of Texas (which occurred about this time) was followed,
during the remainder of Van Buren's administration, by a policy,

[67] *Congressional Globe*, VI, 76.

[68] 24 to 14.

[69] *Congressional Globe*, VI, 454–501, *passim*. Blair wrote to Jackson, July
7, 1838 (Jackson MSS, Library of Congress):

"No confidential letter of yours having the slightest tendency to give rise to
improper constructions shall exist among my papers — but no man has less reason to apprehend injury from the violation of private correspondence than your-
self. The open honesty of every line of your most strictly confidential letters is
full security for your fame. I am led to this remark by an occurence which has
within this hour taken place in the House of Rep§ — Old Johnny Q. who has
for the last 3 weeks consumed the morning hour upon the subject of Texas produced this morning your letter to [William S.] Fulton. It was marked ' *strictly
confidential* ' which the old rouge [*sic*] laid great emphasis upon. He then read
it and you never certainly wrote a letter more distinguished for its probity,
patriotism & perfect propriety & good faith."

The Jackson manuscripts abound in further references to this episode (and to
Dr. Robert Mayo, who gave the letter to Adams).

[70] Sept. 6, 1838 (Webster MSS, Library of Congress).

[71] Smith, *op. cit.*, pp. 68–69. *Texan Diplomatic Correspondence*, Pt. I, p. 27,
cites *House Documents*, 25th Cong., 3d Sess., I, No. 2, p. 33. James Hamilton,
of South Carolina (governor during the nullification troubles), in a letter to
Van Buren (Nov. 21, 1838; Van Buren MSS, Library of Congress), claimed to
have been " somewhat instrumental " in securing this withdrawal, and pointed
out the importance of the elimination, thereby, of an irritating public question
that might have resulted in " an Era of popular agitation & violence which our
Country has never yet seen." He suggested that Van Buren speak kindly, in his
message, of Texan magnanimity.

on the part of that republic, of independence of the United States, extension of foreign free trade, and the acquisition of Santa Fe (possibly as a step toward the possession of California).

While the Texan question, involving the problem of the right of the Southern sections to extension of their slave system, was pressing upon the administration, there were also, throughout that period, controversies between the United States and England, regarding the Canadian border,[72] that threatened the peace of the two countries and brought upon Van Buren the loss, politically, of large regions of the northern frontier.

Insurrection had broken out in 1837 in Canada and was accompanied by demands, with reference to self-government, that strongly appealed to the Americans across the border. Some of these American sympathizers operated with the insurrectionists, supplying them with arms and ammunition from a Canadian island in the Niagara River, and in retaliation Canadian troops crossed to an island on the New York side and sent the American steamer, the "Caroline" (which had aided the insurgents), over Niagara Falls.[73]

In this emergency Van Buren acted with calmness, in spite of agitation by some of his friends, and issued a proclamation of neutrality, though he asked Congress for authority to use force if necessary. For about a year he refused to interfere with a court decision that W. L. Mackenzie, one of the American ringleaders in the violation of neutrality, should be imprisoned. As a result, Mackenzie's friends were alienated from the President in the election that followed.

The English government deferred action in the "Caroline" episode, in spite of earnest representations from the United States. Not until the McLeod case arose did England accept responsibility for the destruction of the steamer. This step was taken when the Canadian, Alexander McLeod, was imprisoned in New York State after he had boasted that he had participated in the seizure of the "Caroline." A grave situation arose, which threatened war; but the federal government took the position that it could not interfere because exclusive jurisdiction rested with New York. Thus, again, the serious problem of the respective relations of the United States government and the state government, in questions of foreign affairs, was involved. Settle-

[72] See p. 123 (ante), n. 58 (citations).   [73] Dec. 29, 1837.

ment of the case did not occur until the Tyler administration, when McLeod was found by a New York jury not to have taken part in the attack upon the " Caroline."

The long controversy over the Northeastern boundary, between Maine and Canada, continued during Van Buren's administration, and resulted, late in 1838, in what is called the " Aroostook War," in which Maine troops expelled Canadian intruders. Maine held that, without her consent, the United States had no power to agree to a boundary that would be considered by the state as equivalent to a cession of territory she regarded as hers. Congress [74] authorized the President to call out fifty thousand volunteers, and voted ten million dollars for the safeguarding of American interests. Van Buren, however, sent General Winfield Scott into Maine, and he secured a temporary agreement for retention by that state of the Aroostook region, " the British denying their right," and for British retention of the disputed valley of the upper St. John, " Maine denying their right." [75] Meanwhile, the President decided to submit the question to renewed arbitration.

The pacific but firm attitude of Van Buren, together with the moderation of the English authorities, had avoided the danger of a serious clash during these controversies; but, in the interval, the whole border had been in turmoil.[76]

The aged Jackson took fire at the prospect of trouble, and wrote to Van Buren: [77]

Britain is a proud & domineering nation, and the spirit breathed by Wellington & other lords in parliament, shew a hostile spirit lurking in

[74] Mar. 3, 1839.

[75] Memorandum signed Feb. 27, 1839.

[76] On these border episodes, see, in addition to the works cited on p. 123, *ante: Messages and Papers*, III (the various messages of Van Buren concerning the controversies); John Bassett Moore, *A Digest of International Law . . .* (Washington, 1906) [using Index]; [Thos. H. Benton] *Thirty Years' View*, II (New York, 1856), 276 ff.; *The Autobiography of Martin Van Buren*, ed. John C. Fitzpatrick (American Historical Association *Annual Report*, 1918, II; Washington, 1920), p. 538; John F. Sprague, *The North Eastern Boundary Controversy and the Aroostook War* (Dover, Me. [n.d.]); S. F. Bemis (ed.), *The American Secretaries of State and Their Diplomacy*, IV (New York, 1928), 330–36; Louis M. Sears, *A History of American Foreign Relations* (New York, 1927), pp. 209–12; Edward M. Shepard, *Martin Van Buren* (Boston, 1899 [in " American Statesmen " series]), pp. 350–57, 367; McMaster, *United States*, VI (New York, 1920), 429–46, 512–19; and Channing, Hart, and Turner, *Guide*, pp. 428–29 (citations).

[77] Apr. 4, 1839 (Van Buren MSS, Library of Congress).

their boosoms. The intimations against our Government in not controlling our Citizens from engaging in the Canady insurrection is both unjust & ungenerous.

He said that, if the United States were forced to war,

my feeble arm if providence permits it, shall be once more raised in defense of our government & glorious union, sustained by fifty thousand volunteers to chastise the temerity of British insolence.

In a postscript to a letter to Blair [78] he wrote:

I have been taking one bottle of the Matchless Sanative which has improved my health very much, & I feel in strength & appetite, that another will cure me — & if a British war should ensue, which god forbid, I will be able to foill their army in the field.

On no occasion does Van Buren appear in a more courageous and fair-minded light than in his dealing with these border episodes. His attitude assisted in the preservation of our peaceful relations with England and Canada, at the sacrifice of large numbers of his supporters in Maine and New York and along the boundary farther to the west. At the same time, he had insisted upon maintaining our treaty obligations with Mexico during a period in which Texas had not yet made clear her right to the position of an independent republic.

Frontier ideals had now reached the height of their influence, and the West had so grown in power that rival party leaders in the older sections — their eyes on the next Presidential campaign — were seeking to win its support. This was first made clear in the discussions regarding the disposition of the public domain.

Influenced by his desire to continue the policies of his predecessor, by the need of securing Western support for the Independent Treasury, and by the necessity of cementing his connection with the Locofocos, Van Buren, in his First Annual Message, declared in favor of the disposition of the public domain in such a manner as to promote early settlement and cultivation and to discountenance the accumulation of large tracts in the same hands.[79] To prevent the spread of migration " up the almost interminable streams of the West to occupy in groups the best spots of land, leaving immense wastes behind them," he recommended a system of graduation, with an actual valuation and classification

[78] Apr. 20 (*ibid.*).   [79] *Messages and Papers*, III, 384–89.

of lands substituted for Benton's proposal that the length of time
the lands had been on the market should determine the value.
Regarding squatters, he held that the laws to prevent intrusion
upon the public lands should either be executed, or modified or
repealed. He advised the passage of a pre-emption law and the
restriction of sales to limited quantities and for actual improvement. He thought that the time would come when the general
government should transfer all refuse and unsold lands to certain of the states. In this suggestion he aimed to meet Benton's
ideas and possibly those of Calhoun.

When, however, the Senate passed a graduation bill,[80] the
length of time the lands had been on the market was made
the basis of valuation. But the House did not take action on the
measure. A bill for temporary retroactive pre-emption passed
both houses, by a vote in which many Western Whigs joined
the Democrats. Calhoun's attempt to win Western support was
again seen in his introduction of a measure for the cession of the
public lands to the states in which they lay. This was favorably
reported from the Committee on Public Lands in the Senate. No
further action, however, was taken on it. Clay wrote, early in
1839:[81] " I can not much longer defeat the combined action of
the Administration and the new States." That his apprehension
was well founded became evident when, ten days later, graduation passed the Senate [82] by a vote in which the North Central
and South Central states gave 19 yeas and only 2 nays (those of
Clay, himself, and his colleague, J. J. Crittenden), the remaining 20 votes in opposition (including those of 8 Democrats) all
coming from the three Eastern sections. In the House of Representatives, however, the bill was tabled, by a very slight majority.[83] The vote was primarily one of party, but sectional influence was clearly in evidence.

As the election of 1840 approached, the issue of distribution
of the net proceeds of the sales of public lands, as favored by
Clay, was connected with a proposition to assume the debts of the
bankrupt states — most of them Western.[84]

In the autumn of 1839, a circular was issued by Baring
Brothers, stating that, if the states pursued their extravagant

[80] Apr. 31, 1838; 27 to 16.
[81] Jan. 7 (Colton, *Clay*, IV, 436).
[82] *Congressional Globe*, VII, 130.
[83] *Ibid.*, p. 140.
[84] See pp. 229–30, 319–20, *ante*.

projects of internal improvements, with dependence on foreign capital to finance them, it would not be possible to raise in Europe, within a short time, the large amount involved, unless the guaranties of individual states were supplemented by a national pledge.[85] The visit of Webster to England, in the summer of that year, led to the charge by Democrats that he had instigated this warning, and that he had been engaged in the sale of Western lands to English investors and had received large commissions from the Barings.[86]

Leading New York Whig newspapers approved the project of assumption and the use of the proceeds of public-land sales as a sinking fund. The desire to force the Whig party to a definite attitude on the question caused Senator Benton to introduce resolutions, on December 27, 1839, condemning any measure to authorize assumption, as establishing a dangerous precedent, as unjust to the nonindebted states, and as tending to continue unnecessary taxes that fell most heavily on the planting, grain-growing, and provision-raising states. The tendency to dependence on the federal government, that the scheme would produce, was emphasized, as was the argument that it would result in foreigners' bringing the influence of the money power to bear upon American elections. In spite of the opposition of the Whigs, these resolutions, somewhat modified, were overwhelmingly passed. Clay's friend, Senator Crittenden, proposed [87] the distribution of the proceeds of public-land sales among the several states, expressing sympathy with the commonwealths that were bankrupt and declaring that no doubt existed as to their ability or disposition to pay their debts. But this measure was defeated by a party vote.

Meantime, the campaign for the election of 1840 had been in progress almost from the beginning of Van Buren's administration. Among the Whig leaders, Clay was hopeful of securing the nomination, and he had been active, in New York and Virginia, in the plan of winning the support of Senators Tallmadge and Rives, who headed the state-bank party in those states. His speech on abolition [88] failed to satisfy the South, and at the same

---

[85] The circular is printed in *Niles' Register*, LVII, 177.

[86] See Geo. Bancroft to Van Buren, Nov. 2, 1840, Jan. 22, 1845 (Massachusetts Historical Society *Proceedings*, XLII, 387, 434).

[87] Feb. 3, 1840.

[88] See pp. 468-70, *ante*.

time was objectionable to the New York politicians, who were alarmed by the increasing power of the antislavery element and who desired to retain the vote of the Anti-Masons.[89]   Millard Fillmore reported that the western part of the state was aroused on these matters.[90]   Early in 1839 General Winfield Scott had been approached regarding his willingness to accept the Presidential nomination.[91]   In the spring Thurlow Weed called on Webster, in Washington.   Webster thought he himself should be the Whig candidate, but Weed said it looked as though William Henry Harrison was the most available man.[92]   Webster believed this not to be the case, and apparently continued his own hopes until his withdrawal in favor of Harrison, in June.[93]   When Clay, at the end of July, accepted an invitation to tour New York, he was informed by leaders that he could not carry the state; [94] and, toward the close of the summer, General Scott was openly brought forward in New York, probably as a stalking-horse for Harrison.

The national Whig convention met, at Harrisburg, Pennsylvania, December 4, 1839.[95]   Two months earlier a convention of that state had declared for the nomination of Harrison.   Scott (who was satisfactory to antislavery voters), having won the support of the New York delegation in the national Whig convention, held the balance of power; and, by a complicated scheme of voting,[96] Clay's plurality was overcome and Harrison was victorious.[97]   John Tyler, a strict-construction, state-rights Vir-

[89] E.g., *Autobiography of Thurlow Weed*, ed. Harriet A. Weed (Boston, 1883), pp. 480–81.

[90] Buffalo Historical Society *Publications*, XI (Buffalo, 1907), 183–87 (*Millard Fillmore Papers*, II).

[91] Thos. H. Clay, *Henry Clay* (Philadelphia, 1910), p. 266, n.

[92] Thurlow Weed Barnes, *Memoir of Thurlow Weed* (Boston, 1884), p. 76; and *The Writings and Speeches of Daniel Webster* ("National Edition"); Boston and New York, 1903), XVIII, 45.

[93] *Niles' Register*, LVI, 306.

[94] A meeting of the Congressional delegation of New York, on December 1, 1839, had reached the conclusion that Clay could not carry that state. (Buffalo Historical Society *Publications*, XI, 194 [*Fillmore Papers*].)

[95] See: R. S. Elliott, *Notes Taken in Sixty Years* (St. Louis, 1883), Chap. XVIII; Horace Greeley, *Recollections of a Busy Life* (New York, 1868), pp. 130–32; *Weed Autobiography*, pp. 481–82; and *Niles' Register*, LVII, 248–52.

[96] Detailed in Edward Stanwood, *A History of the Presidency* (Boston, 1906), pp. 194–95.

[97] Seward had favored continuing Harrison as a candidate (for renomination in 1840) after the election of 1836. (Frederic Bancroft, *The Life of Wil-*

ginian, was nominated for the Vice-Presidency.[98] He had been an admirer of Henry Clay, and there is reason for thinking that the nomination was in part due to a bargain that Clay had effected. For two years the contest between Rives and Tyler had continued, and during that time Virginia had had but one Senator. Rives had not sustained Van Buren's financial policy and was therefore acceptable to Clay. Under a compromise, Rives went to the Senate and Tyler, his rival, was promised the Vice-Presidential nomination. However, as has been noted, Tyler was originally a supporter of Jackson and was, therefore, in reality a representative of the desire of the Whigs to secure the adherence of the tide-water aristocracy of the South Atlantic section.[99]

The Whigs included in their motley ranks, not only followers of Clay and the old-time National Republican party, but also those Democrats (like the supporters of Hugh Lawson White and John Bell, in Tennessee) who had become alienated from Jackson; the advocates of state banks, especially the Conservative Democrats, led by Tallmadge and Rives; part of the state-sovereignty men (of whom Tyler was an example) and old W. H. Crawford men;[100] many moderate antislavery men, dissatisfied with Van Buren's attitude; the element of the Anti-Masonic party that Weed and Seward had united with the Whigs; and, in addition, a very important group of voters swayed by the fact that Harrison was regarded as a frontier hero, of the type of Andrew Jackson but free from the objection of executive usurpation that had been brought against him. In fact, "the Whigs were united only in condemning." They, therefore, refrained from the issuance of a party platform, but appealed to different sections in opposing ways; and their leaders cautiously avoided decisive utterances

---

liam H. Seward [New York, 1900], I, 59. See also *Weed Autobiography*, pp. 481–82.) At Buffalo, in the course of his New York tour, Clay had declared that, if his name created any obstacle to cordial union and harmony, it should be dropped. (*Niles' Register*, LVI, 347.)

[98] See Henry W. Hilliard, *Politics and Pen Pictures at Home and Abroad* (New York, 1892), p. 18; and *Niles' Register*, LXI, 232–33 (views of B. W. Leigh, of Virginia).

[99] Tyler, *Letters and Times of the Tylers*, I, 591, and Henry A. Wise, *Seven Decades of the Union* (Philadelphia, 1872), p. 158. See also pp. 34, 186, *ante*. The significance of the Tyler wing of the Whigs at this time is presented in Tyler, *op. cit.*, II (Richmond, Va., 1885), 2–3.

[100] *Ibid.*, pp. 1–2.

concerning the Bank, the protective tariff, the public lands — indeed, all the former Whig policies.[101]

On April 1, 1840, following a convention at Warsaw, New York, in the autumn of 1839, a wing of the abolitionist group [102] met in national convention at Albany and nominated James G. Birney, of New York, for President, and Thomas Earle, of Pennsylvania, for Vice-President.[103] The significance of this convention is emphasized by a letter of Clay, in the fall of 1838,[104] in which he calls attention to the new element of abolition in elections, which was creating solicitude because the abolitionists were sufficiently numerous in several states to turn the scale, and the contagion might spread.

Not until May 4 did the Democratic convention meet (in Baltimore). There was no opposition to Van Buren (even Tennessee and South Carolina now supporting him) ; but, on the question of the Vice-Presidency, the name of R. M. Johnson encountered the violent objection of many Southern states.[105] James K. Polk, who had been elected governor of Tennessee in 1839 and had thus temporarily restored Democratic rule in that state, was urged by prominent leaders for second place on the ticket.[106] Indeed, Jackson had indicated to Blair and to Van Buren his belief that Polk should be the nominee.[107] In view of these divergent ideas,

[101] See, e.g., the analyses of the result, in *Niles' Register*, LVI, 250; LVII, 125–27, 249–52, 379; LVIII, 5–10; LIX, 201–7.

[102] *William Lloyd Garrison, 1805–1879: The Story of His Life Told by His Children*, II (New York, 1885), 319, 339–42.

[103] See: Birney, *Birney*, p. 350; T. C. Smith, *The Liberty and Free Soil Parties in the Northwest* (*Harvard Historical Studies*, VI; New York, 1897), pp. 37–39; and *The Liberty Party: Its Origin, Principles, and Measures* (tract [Boston? 1847?]), pp. 5–6.

[104] Clay to Brooke, Nov. 3 (Colton, *Clay*, IV, 430–31). Cf. Francis Granger to Weed, Mar. 14, May 1, 1838 (*Weed Memoir*, pp. 57–58).

[105] See p. 238, *ante*.

[106] E. I. McCormac, *James K. Polk: A Political Biography* (Berkeley, Calif., 1922), pp. 159–63.

[107] Jackson to Blair, Nov. 8, 1839 (Jackson MSS, Library of Congress), Feb. 15, 1840 [*Correspondence of Andrew Jackson*, ed. J. S. Bassett, VI (Carnegie Institution of Washington, 1933), 50–51], Feb. 17, 1840 (Jackson MSS, Library of Congress) ; Jackson to Van Buren, Apr. 3, 1840 (Van Buren MSS, Library of Congress). So early as January 4, 1838, Justice John Catron, of Tennessee, in a letter to Jackson, had urged the extent of that state's migration into others (see n. 45, p. 230, *ante*) and that it followed men, " is clanish, has no very strongly fixed creeds, and to a certainty can only be carried by the means of a local candidate." He therefore recommended the nomination of Polk for the Vice-Presidency, instead of Johnson, whom he thought not a proper candidate.

the Democrats made no national nomination for the Vice-Presidency, hoping that a decision would be reached by nominations of the separate states or by Congressional election. The convention therefore resolved " not to choose between the individuals in nomination [for Vice-President], but to leave the decision to their Republican fellow-citizens in the several States." The platform was a clearcut declaration of the Democratic principles that had been exemplified by the administrations of Jackson and Van Buren and was in sharp contrast with the lack of definiteness of the Whig campaign.

Even before his nomination it had been urged upon Van Buren that there was need of excitement to carry the election.[108]   But, though this would seem to have been the natural course for the successor of Jackson, in whose campaigns the " hurrah " element was so prominent, it was, in fact, the followers of Harrison who took advantage of that kind of tactics.   A characterization of Harrison as one who, if given an annual pension of two thousand dollars, a log cabin, and plenty of hard cider, would be content without aspiring to the Presidency, was explained by the administration organ, the *Globe*, as having been originally used by a Clay man and quoted by Democratic papers.[109]   But the Whigs assailed it as a Democratic slur upon their candidate and appealed to the people to repudiate such an attempt to stigmatize the common man.   On the other hand, Van Buren was denounced for an alleged reckless expenditure of public money, and for having made the White House into a President's palace, in which he slept on French bedsteads, sat on French tabourets, and ate *pâté de foie gras* from silver plates, with gold forks.[110]   A popular song ran:

> Let Van from his coolers of silver drink wine,
> And lounge on his cushioned settee;
> Our man on his buckeye bench can recline
> Content with hard cider is he!

In fact, the Whigs sang their way through the campaign, with verses, set to tunes then in vogue, in which " Tippecanoe and

---

Jackson replied (Jan. 23) that the subject was premature, but that, when the time came, Polk should be brought out by some other state.   (Jackson MSS, Library of Congress.)

[108] Geo. Sullivan to Levi Woodbury, Mar. 4, 1840 (Van Buren MSS, Library of Congress).

[109] McMaster, *United States*, VI, 561–62.

[110] Speech of Chas. Ogle, House of Representatives, Apr. 16, 1840.

Tyler too" was the refrain. "The campaign," wrote George W. Julian, "was set to music."[111]   "We have taught them how to conquer us!" declared a prominent Democratic organ.[112]   Huge processions, with floats of log cabins, coonskins, canoes, etc., and gatherings of thousands of supporters, were features of Harrison's campaign.[113]   This "mummery" aroused the indignation of Jackson and his friends.   One of them wrote to him [114] that the United States had become worshipers of the most imbecile animals of the forest; and he himself, forgetful of the emotional aspect of his own contests, virtuously contrasted the decorum of the Democratic campaign with the Whig mode of electioneering.

To understand the frontier and camp-meeting type of this campaign, we must recall that in 1840 most of the states of the North and South Central sections were still in process of settlement, that the men of that generation could look back to the time when these commonwealths were raw wildernesses, that the western counties of many of the Atlantic states were still in a pioneer stage of society, and that, indeed, the old men of the seaboard could remember the crossing of the Alleghenies by Daniel Boone and the first opening of Kentucky and Tennessee.   The frontier was no legend, but an actual experience of all sections; and at this time the frontier West reached its height in American politics.

A second suspension, in 1839, of specie payments by banks, and the hard times that followed, throughout the Union but particularly in those Western states that had recklessly engaged in expenditures for internal improvements and for banks, served to arouse hope in the West, and America in general, for a new régime under another "hero."

---

[111] *Political Recollections, 1840 to 1872* (Chicago, 1884), p. 17.

[112] *The United States Magazine and Democratic Review* (New York), VII, 486 (June, 1840).

[113] J. J. Crittenden wrote to Webster, October 27, 1840 (Webster MSS, Library of Congress): "Since the World began there was never before in the West such a glorious excitement & uproar among the people. It is a sort of popular Insurrection, in which patriotism, intelligence & good order, have governed & prevailed in a most exemplary manner." On the other hand, John Quincy Adams (*Memoirs*, X, 352) was apprehensive of the effect of these gatherings of thousands of people to hear inflammatory harangues. He wondered where this "revolution in the habits and manners of the people" would end. He feared that such meetings would result in "deeper tragedies." "Their manifest tendency is to civil war."

[114] I. G. Harris to Jackson, June 13, 1840 (Jackson MSS, Library of Congress).

Harrison counted largely on the appeal he believed he could make to the pioneer followers of Andrew Jackson.

I am acknowledged [he said in a letter to J. R. Giddings [115]] the oldest and most extensively known of the Veteran Pioneers. . . . Now it so happens that almost all of the pioneers and old soldiers of the west were on the side of the Administration, brought over to that side by their attachment to Genl. Jackson, and that attachment produced by his being himself one of the class to which it was their boast to belong. He, out of the way, is there any difficulty in believing that they might be willing again to give their support to another of the same class although of inferior pretensions, than to any one whose pursuits and course of life had no resemblance to their own.

In similar vein, he wrote to Tallmadge [116] that he was confident that he would secure the vote of this element in Kentucky and throughout the Northwestern states. Said he:

We have also many recruits in our ranks from the pressure of the times. Most of them however "will not be Whigs" but vote for me as they say upon the same grounds as they supported Gen'l. Jackson.

This analysis of the situation proved to be substantially correct. In his speeches during the campaign,[117] Harrison refrained from any very definite statement of principles. Indeed, he was apparently checked in his public utterances by a committee of his party.[118]

The speeches and letters of the Whig leaders avoided specific support of the Bank.[119] After some hesitation as to whether he

---

[115] Dec. 15, 1838.

[116] Feb. 22, 1840 (Tallmadge MSS, Wisconsin Historical Society).

[117] See, for example, an interesting report, in the Van Buren Papers, of a speech of General Harrison at the Old Hamilton Convention, on October 1, 1840; among other speeches were those at Columbus, Fort Meigs (*Ohio Archaeological and Historical Quarterly*, XVII, 200–206), Carthage, and Dayton. See also *Catalogue of the Torrence Papers* (Aug. 4, 20, 1840) (Historical and Philosophical Society of Ohio, Cincinnati, 1887), and A. B. Norton, *The Great Revolution of 1840: Reminiscences of the Log Cabin and Hard Cider Campaign* (Mount Vernon, O., 1888). See, in addition, Stanwood, *History of the Presidency*, pp. 196, 202.

[118] In *Niles' Register* (LVIII, 247), there is a letter from him referring to his "*conscience keeping committee*," and soon afterward (*ibid.*, p. 265) he humorously alluded, in a speech, to the story that he had a " CONFIDENTIAL COMMITTEE."

[119] Tyler, *Letters and Times of the Tylers*, I, 597–627, quotes various utterances of Whig leaders on this point; see, particularly, Clay's address at Taylorsville, Va. (Colton, *Clay*, VI, 197–214, and *Niles' Register*, LVIII, 322 ff.; see also *ibid.*, LXI, 95).

should promulgate a definite plan of measures for an expected Whig administration,[120] Clay yielded to his party's program of general opposition to the Democrats, without definite issues of its own. However, in his speeches he continued his advocacy of distribution of the net proceeds of public-land sales, without proposing in a formal way the assumption of state debts; but he held that the protective tariff should be interpreted in the spirit of his compromise of 1833.[121]

The Democrats were convinced that the campaigning machinery of the Whigs in the election of 1840 was more satisfactory than their own. Before the close of the contest, Whigs and Democrats, alike, had developed formal organizations in Congress, the wide distribution of keynotes by newspaper organs, the dissemination of speeches, and the fostering of young men's conventions. From ward meetings, with lectures and libraries, and ward vigilance committees, up to the formation of state central committees, both parties had elaborate arrangements, particularly in New York and Massachusetts. Thus, with all the appeal to popular emotions, neither party neglected the factor of organization.

In the election, Van Buren carried only New Hampshire, Virginia, South Carolina, Alabama, Missouri, Arkansas, and Illinois, with an electoral vote of 60 against Harrison's 234. Tyler won the Vice-Presidency by the same Whig vote. In spite of the apparent overwhelming plurality for the Whigs, the popular vote gave Harrison less than 150,000 over Van Buren. Birney's vote was about 7,000. The following tabulation of the popular vote [122] shows that, whereas in 1836 Van Buren had a plurality in all sections, in 1840 he carried none of them (even losing his own state of New York):

	Harrison	Van Buren	Birney
New England	214,968	177,521	2,476
Middle Atlantic	403,189	387,233	3,220
South Atlantic	168,633	143,222	....
South Central	183,325	146,273	....
North Central	304,901	274,753	1,373
	1,275,016	1,129,002	7,069

[120] He sent such a list to J. M. Clayton, in a letter of May 29, 1840 (Clayton MSS, Library of Congress).

[121] Taylorsville address (cited in n. 119, above).

[122] Based on the figures given by Stanwood (*op. cit.*, p. 203), but with correction of his footing for the Van Buren vote.

The map of the election reveals that the Whig preponderance lay in the same regions as in 1836, but that the areas of opposition to Van Buren were considerably enlarged. Particularly was this

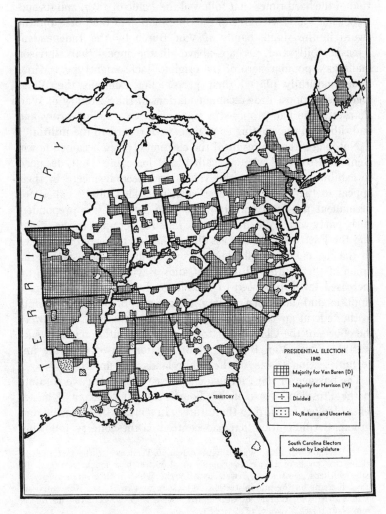

PRESIDENTIAL ELECTION
1840

Majority for Van Buren (D)

Majority for Harrison (W)

Divided

No Returns and Uncertain

TERRITORY

South Carolina Electors
chosen by Legislature

the case in Kentucky, in New York, and in the parts of Michigan and northern Illinois recently settled by the New York-New England stock. The force of Harrison's appeal to the older pioneer element was exhibited, not only by the large number of additional counties that he carried in states responsive to this appeal, but also by the increase of the Whig vote in Democratic areas.

On the whole, the result of the election was due to the continuation of the hard times that followed the Panic of 1837, and its successor in 1839; the charge of the combination of the purse and the sword in the single hands of Van Buren by the Independent Treasury bill; and, perhaps above all, the appeal that Harrison made as a popular hero of the original Jacksonian type. Minor issues naturally played their parts. For example, the Whigs vigorously opposed the recommendations of the Secretary of War, Poinsett, who had proposed a more effective standing army and had ridiculed the existing conditions with regard to the militia.[123]

Not long after the result of the election of 1840 became known, Benton introduced what he called his " log cabin " bill, designed to exhibit the fact that the Whigs had been insincere in their appeal to the Western pioneer element. This bill[124] called for permanent pre-emption. It passed the Senate by a preponderantly party vote. When the House failed to act upon it, the Whigs and the East were bitterly assailed as having preferred the palace to the log cabin. Calhoun, desirous of finding a basis for the union of the South and the West and of avoiding the need of an increased tariff, proposed to include graduation, permanent pre-emption, and the return of sixty-five per cent of the gross receipts to the federal government.[125] But this also was lost. Nor were the efforts of the Clay Whigs to enact a distribution measure successful. Thus, Van Buren's administration closed with the important sectional issue of the public lands still unsettled.

The passage of the Independent Treasury bill[126] gave comfort to the President when, in his Fourth Annual Message,[127] he serenely looked forward to the future. In spite of the financial and diplomatic difficulties that had confronted the country following

---

[123] Jackson attributed Van Buren's defeat in Tennessee to the fact that, in taking the census of 1840, " the foolish questions, of how much crop[?], how many chickens, geese &c &c," were used by the Whigs with great dexterity to bring discredit on the administration. (Jackson to Van Buren, Nov. 24, 1840 [Van Buren MSS, Library of Congress].) See also G. D. Wall to Van Buren, from New Jersey, Nov. 5, 1840 (*ibid.*).

[124] Presented Dec. 14, 1840.

[125] R. G. Wellington, *The Political and Sectional Influence of the Public Lands, 1828–1842* (Cambridge, Mass., 1914), p. 89 *et passim*.

[126] July 4, 1840.

[127] Dec. 5, 1840 (*Messages and Papers*, III, 602–20).

Jackson's administration, he felt that he had kept the Democratic faith and had met the trying situations with equanimity and a desire to hold the sections together in common support of the Constitution and the Union.

Van Buren had been trained in the school of the New York politician; but the charge of the opposition that he was merely the " Little Magician " who handled his problems as a wily politician, was not justified by his course as President. Moderation and a desire to hold together the Northern and Southern wings of his party were manifest in his administration. Although he drafted, modified, and redrafted replies to letters designed to embarrass him on such issues as slavery, his messages and state papers reveal a powerful and courageous mind in the many exigencies that pressed upon him. Even after his failure to secure re-election in 1840, he continued to hope that the " sober second thought " of the American people would give him another term as President.

CHAPTER XI

SECTIONALISM AND THE WHIG DISSENSIONS UNDER TYLER

As we have seen,[1] the Whigs had conducted their campaign in the spirit of a general attack upon the Executive power as illustrated by Van Buren and the Subtreasury, but at the same time had appealed to the pioneer element that had supported Jackson. Clay had been dissuaded from presenting definite recommendations for a National Bank, protective tariff, etc.; and Harrison came into power without a platform, more than hesitant on the question of a Bank,[2] and with Tyler as his running mate. The reluctance of the latter to an increase of the tariff beyond the basis of the compromise of 1833, his Constitutional objections to a United States Bank, and his extreme state-sovereignty views were well known. In short, he was a representative of the tidewater planters of Virginia, with their ultraconservative ideas as to Constitutional restrictions. Webster had said, in a speech to a Whig convention at Richmond, Virginia, in the course of the campaign, that " family controversies " were to be adjourned in the presence of the common enemy, leaving differences to be settled if the Democrats were defeated.

Obviously, the situation was not an easy one. Early in 1841 Clay expressed " strong fears ";[3] and the difficulties were hardly diminished when Harrison, apprehensive of the effect of the charge that Clay was the mentor of his administration, requested him to communicate in writing rather than by frequent personal interviews. Indeed, Clay found it advisable to address a letter to Harrison, a few days after the latter's inauguration, repelling the

[1] Pp. 479, 481–84.
[2] See *Niles' Register*, LXI, 95.
[3] Clay to J. M. Clayton, Feb. 12, 1841 (Clayton MSS, Library of Congress).

allegation of dictation to the President.[4] Nevertheless, there was a general expectation that Clay would determine the policies of the administration.[5] Before long the underlying sectional differences on public policy, which had been concealed in the campaign by means of the combination of " Tippecanoe and Tyler too," were to appear violently.

Harrison chose the following cabinet: Secretary of State, Daniel Webster, of Massachusetts; Secretary of the Treasury, Thomas Ewing, of Ohio (a warm friend of Clay); Secretary of War, John Bell, of Tennessee; Attorney-General, John J. Crittenden, of Kentucky (another of Clay's friends); Postmaster-General, Francis Granger, of New York (one-time Anti-Masonic leader); and Secretary of the Navy, George E. Badger, of North Carolina. The strength of the cabinet rested upon the Clay wing, and the only representative of the South Atlantic section was the North Carolina member.

In his Inaugural Address,[6] Harrison pledged himself not to consent to a second term; and he urged the importance of the separation of powers, which he thought might be jeopardized by Executive vetoes made on the theory that the President was given legislative powers, although he supported the veto when made on Constitutional grounds. The variety of the sections, leading to the danger that the rights of a minority might be sacrificed even under a Constitutional law not subject to the jurisdiction of the Supreme Court, was also declared to be a proper reason for the incorporation of the veto power in the Constitution.

He urged forbearance of the sections with regard to the domestic institutions of the different states, and declared his opposition to the spoils system and the Subtreasury. He objected to an exclusively metallic currency, but, without making a specific recommendation concerning a National Bank, left to Congress the duty of devising revenue schemes and the mode of keeping the public treasure. Induced by Clay, on March 17 he called an extra session of Congress to meet on May 31.

[4] Calvin Colton, *The Life, Correspondence, and Speeches of Henry Clay* (New York, 1857), IV, 452–53; L. G. Tyler, *The Letters and Times of the Tylers*, II (Richmond, Va., 1885), 10–11; and Nathan Sargent, *Public Men and Events from . . . 1817, to . . . 1853* (Philadelphia, 1875), II, 116.

[5] *Correspondence of John C. Calhoun*, ed. J. Franklin Jameson (American Historical Association *Annual Report*, 1899, II; Washington, 1900), p. 468.

[6] Jas. D. Richardson (compiler), *The Messages and Papers of the Presidents, 1789–1897*, IV (Washington, 1897), 5–21.

In spite of his attitude on the patronage, he had been subjected, from the time of his election, to the pressure of office seekers. This, together with his failing health, was probably the cause of his death, on April 4 — a month after his inauguration.

Thus, Tyler was brought to the Presidency, with all of his Virginian Constitutional scruples and with ideas that ran counter to Clay's on the essentials of Whig policy. In view of Harrison's deference to his alleged " conscience committee " during the campaign,[7] it cannot be said positively that he would not have submitted to the domination of Clay; but, with the accession of the Virginian, there was certain to be both a personal and a sectional contest.

Asserting, in spite of objection, his right to the title and authority of President even though the accident of Harrison's death had brought him (without historical precedent) to the Executive chair, Tyler made known that he was determined to use the full powers of the office. In his Inaugural Address,[8] however, he showed a desire to compromise with the Clay wing of the Whig party, and he retained the cabinet of his predecessor, in spite of the fact that most of its members were partisans of Clay.

Although Whig historians have tended to view Tyler in the worst light, there seems to be sufficient reason to think that he was not only honest and courageous but also a man of ability, of ingratiating personality, charm of manner, and tact.[9] But Tyler's conception of proper legislation and his possible continuance in office through election in 1844 strengthened the determination of Clay to be the ruler of the Whig party and himself become the next President. Harrison's pledge not to accept a second term would have left the way open for Clay, but Tyler, who had contemplated a similar declaration, was, he says, dissuaded by his cabinet from incorporating it in his Inaugural. In his observations, in that address, relating to his accession to the Presidential office by the contingency of Harrison's death, he said: " The spirit of faction, which is directly opposed to the spirit of a lofty patriotism, may find in this occasion for assaults upon my Adminis-

---

[7] See p. 483, *ante*.

[8] Apr. 9, 1841. (*Messages and Papers*, IV, 36–39.)

[9] Anne Royall, *Letters from Alabama on Various Subjects* (Washington, 1830), p. 178; Chas. Dickens, *American Notes for General Circulation* (London, 1842), I, 301–2; and Henry W. Hilliard, *Politics and Pen Pictures at Home and Abroad* (New York, 1892), pp. 4, 17–18, 115–16.

tration"; and he placed his reliance upon "the intelligence and patriotism of the people." In view of his later actions, his determination "to carry out the principles of that Constitution which I have sworn 'to protect, preserve, and defend,'" had a special significance. He denounced the Subtreasury, pledged himself against the misuse of the patronage, demanded rigid economy in appropriations, and promised to sanction "any constitutional measure which, originating in Congress, shall have for its object the restoration of a sound circulating medium"; and he added that he would "resort to the fathers of the great republican school for advice and instruction" as to the constitutionality of measures proposed to that end. On the same date he wrote Senator W. C. Rives: "I shall act upon the principles which I have all along espoused, and which you and myself have derived from the teachings of Jefferson and Madison, and other of our distinguished countrymen." [10]

Tyler himself would probably not have called a special session, for he needed time to consider some acceptable project in lieu of a National Bank; but, having the session on his hands, he gracefully congratulated himself on finding that he was so soon "surrounded by the immediate representatives of the States and people." [11] Adverting, in his Special Session Message,[12] to the needs of the Treasury, he asked for some temporary provision to meet a probable deficit. He held that the compromise act of 1833 should not be altered except under necessities not then existent; but he intimated that discriminating duties for revenue might be required at the expiration of that tariff. He believed that a "fiscal agent" for the collection and disbursement of the revenues was essential, and mentioned the alternatives of a Bank of the United States, the use of state banks as depositories, and the Subtreasury system. Expressing his own sympathy with Jackson's veto of the National Bank and interpreting the recent election as condemning the Subtreasury, he submitted the question to Congress, reserving to himself "the ultimate power of rejecting any measure which may, in my view of it, conflict with the Constitution or otherwise jeopardize the prosperity of the country." He suggested a compact among the states to curb their

---

[10] Tyler, *Letters and Times of the Tylers*, II, 20.

[11] *Messages and Papers*, IV, 40.

[12] June 1, 1841. (*Ibid.*, pp. 40–51.)

unrestricted creation of banks; and he favored distribution of the proceeds of the land sales, with the important proviso that this should not impose heavier burdens upon commerce than contemplated by the act of 1833. Opposing assumption of the state debts, he looked to distribution as a means of meeting the necessities of the states.

Tyler had already received, from his friend Judge N. Beverley Tucker, of Virginia, a project [13] of a bank based upon a compact between the states, with consent of Congress; but, when it was shown to Clay, the latter had argued that Virginia should yield her Constitutional scruples to the precedent of Madison's signature of the old National Bank. Moreover, he felt that the failure of the Old Dominion to give a Whig majority in the election had absolved that party from the obligation to consider these scruples. However, in asking Clay to submit a plan, Tyler had warned him that it must avoid all Constitutional objection and had opposed any premature presentation of the question. [14] Thus, a sectional warfare between Clay, the leader of the Ohio Valley, and Tyler, spokesman for the Southern seaboard, was clearly presaged.

Rushing to reap the fruits of victory, Clay introduced a bill on June 4, 1841, to repeal the Independent Treasury, and five days later it passed the Senate. Thereby the impetuous Whig leader had initiated a movement that would place the Treasury under unregulated control of the Executive if there should be delay or failure in immediately passing his favorite measure of a National Bank. [15] To Senator Rives, he " seemed to desire not only to put down the Sub-Treasury law, but by the same blow to prostrate the State banks, and any other fiscal agent; so that nothing should remain to be adopted but a Bank of the United States." [16]

---

[13] Tyler, *op. cit.*, II, 29–30, 34, 37–38; III (Williamsburg, Va., 1896), 93–94.

[14] *Ibid.*, III, 93–94.

[15] [Thomas H. Benton] *Thirty Years' View*, II (New York, 1856), 219–28. The repeal was not signed until August 13, 1841. The use of state banks as depositories (operative under R. B. Taney in Jackson's administration) was revived; but banking ethics had improved and consequently the safety of the public funds had increased. In fact, the revenues were well cared for during the Tyler administration, in spite of the previous apprehension of the Whigs. (See David Kinley, *The Independent Treasury of the United States and Its Relations to the Banks of the Country* [*Senate Document 587*, 61st Cong., 2d Sess. (National Monetary Commission; Washington, 1910)], p. 43.)

[16] *Congressional Globe*, X, 25.

On June 7 had come the celebrated resolutions of Clay outlining a Congressional program which assumed that the election had resulted in a mandate to carry out his own ideas of the proper Whig policy — ideas most of which had been concealed or subordinated in the campaign. These resolutions included the repeal of the Subtreasury; the incorporation of a Bank; adequate revenue duties and a temporary loan; and distribution of the proceeds of sales of the public lands.[17]

Describing the Secretary of the Treasury as the "servant of Congress" (referring to Jackson's contrary view), Clay called for a report by this officer on a National Bank — afterwards modified, however, into a call for a report on such a Bank, or fiscal agent, free of Constitutional objections. Secretary Ewing presented a report to Congress on a Fiscal Bank, which, as he himself later admitted, had not received Tyler's express or implied assent. He had rather hoped for than expected the President's approval.[18] This report, received in the Senate on the twelfth of June, seems to have been shaped by a proposal made by Senator Hugh Lawson White when the question of a National Bank was pending in Jackson's administration.[19] It attempted to avoid the Constitutional difficulty by providing for the incorporation of the institution in the District of Columbia (which was admittedly under the jurisdiction of Congress) and by restricting Bank branches to those states that should assent. But, in addition, the report provided for a bill that would permit the operations of discount and deposit — things obnoxious to Tyler. Clay promptly showed his unwillingness to accept the Ewing bill, but finally agreed to a so-called compromise by which a state gave implied assent to the establishment of Bank branches, if its legislature did not object at its first session thereafter. Thus amended, the bill finally passed the Senate, by a vote of 26 to 23. Not until the sixth of August, however, did the House give it a majority (128 to 97). Through the defection of the Tyler Whigs, the normal Whig majority had fallen by some thirteen votes.

---

[17] *Ibid.*, p. 22.

[18] *Niles' Register*, LXI, 33. Ewing, who was Clay's friend, had also admitted that the Bank was not an issue in the campaign of 1840. (*Ibid.*, p. 95.)

[19] See Tyler, *op. cit.*, II, 37; and *The Autobiography of Martin Van Buren*, ed. John C. Fitzpatrick (American Historical Association *Annual Report*, 1918, II; Washington, 1920), p. 595. Cf. Jackson's annual messages of 1829, 1830, and 1831 (*Messages and Papers*, II [Washington, 1896], 462, 528–29, 558).

Tyler's veto of this Fiscal Bank of the United States [20] referred to the knowledge of the country that he had been elected Vice-President while holding the belief that a National Bank operating over the Union was unconstitutional. He called especial attention to the provision of the bill which assumed the assent of states to the establishment of branches in their midst in case they did not refuse at the first session. This issue had not been involved in state elections held during the pendency of the measure; moreover, assent would be assumed in cases where the two houses differed or the governor vetoed adverse action. These facts, together with the provision that assent was not withdrawable and that the Bank had discount privileges — not a "necessary means" — all combined to convince the President that the bill implied a superior power in Congress to establish a country-wide National Bank and to prescribe terms to any state. Having clearly warned Congress that the bill was not one that he could sign, Tyler felt that, in spite of his desire to unify the Whigs by the Ewing bill, his overtures had been rejected. The veto was sustained in the Senate.

Meantime, logrolling and bargaining had gone on over a land bill. Western new-state Whigs, representing constituencies that were heavily in debt, were won by the combination of pre-emption with distribution; and the manufacturing Whigs in the Eastern sections saw in the proposal to sacrifice the revenue arising from the public lands, at a time when there was a deficit in the Treasury, the pleasing prospect that a higher tariff would result. However, the bill met with the opposition of Southern Whigs for the very reason of its bearing on the tariff, and not until it was modified by an amendment, proposed by J. M. Berrien, of Georgia, suspending distribution when the rate of the tariff should exceed that of the compromise act of 1833, did the measure pass the Senate, by a party vote (August 26, 1841); and later, in the House, by 108 to 94. As a part of the series of bargainings, a bankruptcy bill was forced by Senator John Henderson, of Mississippi.

The land bill provided that ten per cent of the proceeds of the sales of public lands within Ohio, Indiana, Illinois, Michigan, Missouri, Arkansas, Louisiana, Mississippi, and Alabama should be given to those states, together with a grant to each of 500,000

[20] *Messages and Papers*, IV, 63–68.

acres of public lands within its limits.[21]   Thus, an important
inducement was offered to the North Central and South Central
sections — the West of the period — to vote for the bill.   The re-

LAND BILL 1841
Vote in House of Representatives
July 6, 1841

Affirmative Whig
Negative Whig
Affirmative Democrat
Negative Democrat
Affirmative Tyler Whig
Negative Tyler Whig
Whig not voting
Democrat not voting

maining proceeds were to be divided among the states and territories according to their respective federal representative populations.

[21] The act provided that the same quantity (including whatever acreage had
been received during territorial status) should be given to each new state thereafter admitted.   (Thos. Donaldson, *The Public Domain* [Washington, 1884],
pp. 255, 256.)

Distribution was to cease whenever the duties levied should exceed twenty per cent ad valorem. By insisting upon this provision, the Southern Whigs, with the aid of the Democrats, had, in effect, brought about a situation that merely enabled the Clay Whigs to " save their face " and hope for a later repeal of the restriction, because almost immediately the duties were so increased as to render distribution inoperative.

More important, in the long run, was the permanent and prospective grant of pre-emption of public land, not exceeding 160 acres, to heads of families, widows, and single men over twenty-one years of age (who were, or had declared their intention of becoming, citizens), on condition of erecting a dwelling and cultivating the land. This was, in fact, a recognition of the customs of the settlers of the Western sections, as developed in the era of squatter sovereignty and by the passage of successive acts of Congress from year to year legalizing the pre-emptive right to the lands thus occupied. The Homestead Act of 1862 was a natural extension of the pre-emption acts and was illustrative of the growing power of the North Central section.

Thus, Bank, tariff, pre-emption, and distribution of the proceeds of the public lands (involving a substitute for assumption of the debts of the bankrupt states) had all been under consideration at the same time; sectionalism and party control were clearly marked, and each modified the other.[22] Clay's leadership and Whig discipline had been obliged to make important sectional concessions, but still remained powerful.

There followed discussions of a new bank bill, between Tyler and Whig Congressional leaders and between Tyler and his cabinet.[23] The reader may accept the statement of Secretary Bell that Tyler had wished (in vain) to see the bill before it went to the House, and that of Webster that, for his part, he had not committed the President, who, therefore, was free to exercise his opinion of the constitutionality of the measure. However, in the

[22] On the relations of the land bill to sectional bargaining, see: R. G. Wellington, *The Political and Sectional Influence of the Public Lands, 1828–1842* (Cambridge, Mass., 1914), pp. 97–104; Geo. M. Stephenson, *The Political History of the Public Lands from 1840 to 1862* (Boston, 1917), Chap. III; and B. H. Hibbard, *A History of the Public Land Policies* (New York, 1924), pp. 156–64, 184–87.

[23] " Diary of Thomas Ewing, August and September, 1841," *American Historical Review*, XVIII, 99–103; and Tyler, *Letters and Times of the Tylers*, II, 81 *et passim*.

course of these various discussions, serious misunderstandings arose between Tyler and members of his cabinet as well as Congressmen.[24] No doubt politics played an important part in those misunderstandings; and Clay's ambitions, together with his resentment toward Tyler, led him to force a break with the President. But Tyler himself must share some of the criticism, because in his desire for Whig harmony he had not made his position unmistakable to his enemies.

After these conferences, the new bill was submitted, providing for a " Fiscal Corporation of the United States." Partly because the President was represented as having favored the measure and partly because of Clay's Whig influence, Tyler was supported in the Senate by only Rives and the Democrats, and in the House by only the few Tyler Whigs and Democrats. However, the President again sent in a veto,[25] on the ground that the Fiscal Corporation

was, in fact, a charter for a national bank, with power to deal in exchanges; and the only provision which connected it with the District of Columbia was the fact that the parent board was to be located at Washington instead of Philadelphia. It limited ostensibly the power to dealing in exchanges, and yet it was, in fact, a bank of local discount.[26]

The President had made clear his opposition to local discounts in any bill to replace the old National Bank, but he believed that, in the course of the formulation of the Fiscal Corporation bill, such discounts had been surreptitiously included.

Either members of his cabinet had failed to understand his scruples on this point because he had not made them sufficiently clear, or the Clay wing, disgruntled by a second veto, had determined to bring the issue to a climax. The essential point was,

[24] On the bitter controversy, involving the question of veracity, between Tyler and John M. Botts, Representative from Virginia and a one-time friend, see Tyler, op. cit., pp. 105–6 (n.) et passim. In spite of the opinion of H. von Holst (The Constitutional and Political History of the United States . . . 1828–1846 [Chicago, 1881], p. 422), the " complete honesty " of Botts in his recollection of his interviews with Tyler cannot be regarded as established. Botts later became a bankrupt and was confined for debt. (See Brock Papers, Huntington Library, Feb. 12, 1846.)

[25] Sept. 9, 1841.

[26] This is Tyler's summary of the reasons for his veto. (Tyler, op. cit., p. 99; see also pp. 86–98. The text of the veto is in Messages and Papers, IV, 68–72.)

in Tyler's opinion, that the bill provided for " a corporation
created by Congress to operate over the Union by the naked authority of Congress." [27]

An " Exchequer Bank " recommended by Tyler, in his Annual
Message of December 7, 1841,[28] aimed at safeguarding the public
moneys, furnishing a paper circulation equivalent to gold and
silver, and providing for exchange in commerce between the states.
A board of control in Washington, with agencies in the states,
was to be set up. Although the plan was explained and supported
by Webster, who thought that it would prove to be " the most
beneficial institution ever established, the Constitution only excepted," it was rejected.

Meanwhile, the President's veto of the Fiscal Corporation had
aroused a storm of indignation among the Clay Whigs.[29] Secretary Ewing claimed that Tyler had failed to support a bill to
which he had, in effect, previously assented; Ewing, together with
Secretaries Bell, Badger, and Crittenden, giving varying reasons,
resigned from the cabinet, on September 11, 1841, and Granger
soon followed.[30] Webster alone remained. He saw no sufficient
reason for the voluntary dissolution of the cabinet and thought
that its members had been precipitate in any case.[31] Of course
the fundamental fact was that the Clay partisans had concluded
that Tyler must be discredited and that Webster was a rival of
Clay. According to Tyler's son, John Tyler, Jr. (who was his
secretary), Webster replied to the President's statement that he
must decide for himself the question of remaining: " If you leave

[27] Tyler, *op. cit.*, p. 99.

[28] *Messages and Papers*, IV, 84–87.

[29] Clay's proposed amendments to the Constitution, introduced in the Senate early in the succeeding session (including a provision to restrict the veto
power by allowing a majority of the membership of both houses to overrule the
veto), were manifestations of this indignation. Although unsuccessful in this
attempt, Clay returned to the attack on January 24, 1842. His speech at that
time met with a long and able reply by Calhoun, who showed clearly that the
government was not based on majority rule, and pointed out how, under the
Constitutional system, minorities often controlled. (For these opposing views,
see *Congressional Globe*, XI, 69 and 164–67 [Clay]; 266 and [App.] 164–68
[Calhoun].)

[30] See their views, conflicting with each other and with those of the President, in their letters of resignation, published in *Niles' Register*, LXI, 33–34, 53,
and in Ewing's " Diary " (cited *ante*).

[31] See *The Writings and Speeches of Daniel Webster* (" National Edition ";
Boston and New York, 1903), XV, 137–39, and Webster's letters of Sept. 11, 13,
1841, reprinted in *Niles' Register*, LXI, 34–35.

it to me, Mr. President, I will stay where I am." Thereupon, Tyler answered, " Give me your hand on that, and now I will say to you that Henry Clay is a doomed man from this hour." [32]

The cabinet resignations were followed by party passion, and on the day of adjournment of the special session was issued the Whig manifesto reading Tyler out of the party for his failure to conform to the Clay proposals.[33] The President had promptly sent to the Senate nominations to fill the positions of the cabinet members who had resigned. To succeed Ewing, he named Walter Forward (Pennsylvania) Secretary of the Treasury; John McLean (Ohio) declining, John C. Spencer (New York) was chosen in place of Bell as Secretary of War; Abel P. Upshur (Virginia) followed Badger as Secretary of the Navy; Hugh S. Legaré (South Carolina), Crittenden as Attorney-General; and Charles A. Wickliffe (Kentucky), Granger as Postmaster-General. Tyler pointed out that they, like himself, were all original Jackson men, and meant to act upon " Republican " principles.[34] The President still had, perhaps, some hope of winning the Whig party, for all of these men had voted for Harrison, and, along with Webster, could act as mediators; but from this time forward Tyler, " a man without a party," felt himself obliged either to rally a Whig following for himself as a prospective Presidential candidate or to look for support among the Democrats. The latter, however, were so firmly attached to Van Buren and their other leaders that he could not hope for a party-following there. Where they might support him in resistance to the Clay Whigs, they would not favor him as a candidate to succeed himself.

To Calhoun, influential in the Southern sections, it seemed that Tyler would steer a middle course, as indicated by his choice of Forward, who represented the Pennsylvania interest in the tariff, as a member of his cabinet. Believing that such a policy would ultimately result also in a Bank, Calhoun proposed for his group an independent position in order to hold the balance of power, which he hoped would force Tyler to join them.[35] This proved to be the outcome.

At about this time, also, it became clearly the policy of Tyler

[32] Tyler, *op. cit.*, p. 122, n.
[33] The manifesto is printed in *Niles' Register*, LXI, 35–36.
[34] Tyler, *op. cit.*, p. 125.
[35] *Calhoun Correspondence*, pp. 487–89.

and his friends to proceed regardless of party support. Judge Upshur wrote: [36]

> We came in against all parties, and of course without any support except what our measures would win for us. . . . Of course it became necessary that we should create a party. On this subject we have consulted together freely and without reserve. We have all agreed, without a single exception, that our only course was to administer the government for the best interests of the country, and to trust to the moderates of all parties to sustain us.

The Whigs had suffered losses in the election that preceded the resumption of Congress, and there were reasons for believing that, in spite of the discipline of Van Buren over the Democrats and of Clay over the Whigs, a Tyler party might be formed.

Whether Tyler saw the bearing of the Texan question in building up support for him among Democrats and Southern Whigs at this time, cannot be definitely determined. His friend Henry A. Wise asserts, in his not altogether dependable *Seven Decades of the Union*,[37] that Tyler, in the beginning of his administration, agreed that Texas should be annexed as soon as possible. Within a month of the cabinet resignations, Tyler had hinted to Webster the probability of acquiring Texas by treaty, and had urged that the shipping interests of the North would be advanced and that slavery should not be an obstacle, since it already existed and, he argued, " a rigid enforcement of the laws against the slave-trade would in time make as many free States south as the acquisition of Texas would add of slave States." [38] When, later, Webster returned to the Whig party, he declared that the determination of Tyler to build up a party of his own, and the attitude of the Executive toward the acquisition of Texas, were among the things which made it undesirable for him to continue in the cabinet. As yet, however, Webster was a loyal supporter of the President and a champion of his measures in the *Madisonian*, the administration organ.[39] Nevertheless, the Presidential policy in respect

---

[36] Dec. 23, 1841. (Tyler, *op. cit.*, p. 154.)

[37] Philadelphia, 1881; pp. 181–82.

[38] Tyler, *op. cit.*, p. 126.

[39] See, e.g., the file of the *Madisonian* (given by Mrs. C. H. Haskins, and others of the Allen family, to the Library of Harvard University), which contains indications of Webster's contributions; and see *The Letters of Daniel Webster*, ed. C. H. Van Tyne (New York, 1902), pp. 249–52, and Tyler, *op. cit.*, p. 154, n. 1.

to Texas foresaw the difficulties of retaining him as Secretary of State.

The problem of sectional relations in the field of diplomacy became critical in the years immediately following 1830. Was slavery purely a domestic interest, in which the United States Government had no concern in diplomatic affairs; or was our Department of State under obligations to consider that the slave interest was entitled to protection when threatened? The interstate carrying trade had not only raised the question of the status of free negroes arriving by Northern vessels in Southern ports and there subjected to local restraints, but in foreign relations the problem had presented itself in serious ways. Accidents of shipwreck or weather had sometimes, by "unavoidable cause," brought American slaves within English jurisdiction in the free West Indies, and, for one reason or another, the question of the applicability, to such slaves, of the English emancipation law had become a subject of diplomatic controversy. There was also the problem of the English assertion of the right of search to determine whether a vessel on the high seas, carrying slaves, lawfully bore the flag of the United States.[40]

The "Creole" case arose when slaves en route from Virginia to New Orleans mutinied and carried the ship to Nassau, where they were declared free by the English authority. Secretary Webster held that the recognition of slaves as property in the states in which slavery existed, under the Constitution of the United States, extended to the high seas. Not only was his legal mind operative here, but no doubt his associations with the Tyler cabinet influenced him in a way that suggested the line of reasoning he adopted in his 1850 seventh-of-March speech.

Probably the most important phase of Webster's public activity in this administration, however, was his negotiation of the Ashburton Treaty,[41] which was signed on the ninth of August, 1842.

---

[40] See John Bassett Moore, *History and Digest of the International Arbitrations to Which the United States Has Been a Party*, . . . (Washington, 1898), I, Chaps. XI, XII. Von Holst, *United States, 1828–1846*, pp. 312–29, 538–40, has a survey of these questions from the point of view of the North.

[41] See: Moore, *op. cit.*, Chaps. I–VI; W. M. Malloy (compiler), *Treaties, Conventions, International Acts, Protocols and Agreements between the United States of America and Other Powers, 1776–1909* (Senate Document 357, 61st Cong., 2d Sess.; Washington, 1910), I, 650–56; *Messages and Papers*, IV, 112–50, 162–77; Edward Channing, *A History of the United States*, V (New York, 1921), 536–41; J. S. Reeves, *American Diplomacy under Tyler and Polk* (Balti-

The controversy with England over the Northeastern boundary-line was thereby compromised on a somewhat less favorable basis than that proposed in the former arbitration by the King of the Netherlands. Maine and Massachusetts participated in the negotiations, under the contention that their rights to the boundaries that they claimed, might not be within the jurisdiction of the United States.[42] Although the Ashburton Treaty left unsettled the important Northwestern boundary, it did procure an adjustment of our differences with England in many other respects and is one of the important stages of the long continued peace between the two countries.

On the question of prevention of the slave trade, it was stipulated, in the Ashburton Treaty, that England and the United States should each furnish a squadron to be stationed off the coast of Africa, and that these two naval forces should co-operate in the suppression of this trade. This was designed to meet the opposition to the English claim of the right of search. The " Creole " case was dealt with by an exchange of notes between Ashburton and Webster, in which the former made an " apology for the necessity of the act." Thus, Webster had responded to the sectional feeling of the South in the " Creole " case, and to the New England antagonism to the slave trade and to the right of search.

As a whole, the country seemed to recognize that Ashburton was a fortunate selection for this mission. Judge Upshur, of Virginia, characterized him as

a plain, common sense, man, who understands our institutions, and correctly estimates our character. He will, therefore, ask nothing which the government has not the power to grant, and nothing which the people will not be likely to approve.[43]

---

more, 1907), Chaps. I, II; E. D. Adams, " Lord Ashburton and the Treaty of Washington," *American Historical Review*, XVII, 764–82; and S. F. Bemis (ed.), *The American Secretaries of State and Their Diplomacy*, V (New York, 1928), pp. 12–53.

[42] Probably the final amenability of Maine was influenced by Mr. Webster's having revealed to her representatives the theretofore unknown " Red Line Map," found in the archives of our Department of State, which had been prepared at the time of the treaty of peace that recognized our independence. This line would have given England more territory in Maine than she was contending for. (For a discussion of the differing " red line " maps in English and American archives, see Channing, *op. cit.*, pp. 540–41.)

[43] Tyler, *op. cit.*, p. 198.

As a member of the firm of Baring Brothers, Ashburton had come to know Webster and the United States; and perhaps the influence of his American wife contributed toward his friendly and conciliatory attitude in the face of hampering instructions. Tyler's gracious and tactful participation at critical periods of the negotiations was acknowledged by Webster.

The Oregon-boundary question was postponed. Neither Ashburton nor Webster, apparently, realized how soon it was to become the occasion of a diplomatic crisis.

While Lord Ashburton was complaining of the Washington heat [44] and the delay in the negotiations, Congress was struggling with the problem of a tariff that would provide adequately for the Treasury needs but not antagonize the free-trade South. Even historians who favor the protective-tariff policy agree that Clay's proposal to continue to distribute the net proceeds of the sales of public lands, involving the loss of federal revenue at a time when Congress was obliged to authorize a loan to meet the existing deficit, was unwise; but still more to be deprecated was his policy of combining distribution with a bill for a protective tariff.[45] The political purpose was to win the friendship of the states that had so recklessly entered upon internal improvements and whose stocks were seriously falling: continued distribution would be welcomed by those states. Moreover, distribution would make such inroads upon the federal income as to necessitate the higher tariff demanded by the North Atlantic sections.

To prevent the loss of revenue that would result from making the final reduction of duties that was called for by the tariff of 1833, a provisional tariff — the so-called " little tariff " — was passed and sent to the President. By its terms, the twenty per cent limit, which under the tariff of 1833 was to become effective on the thirtieth of June, 1842, would not go into effect until the first of August. But distribution would be continued, in contravention of the stipulation in the land act of 1841 that it should cease whenever the duties rose above the twenty per cent maximum of the tariff of 1833.

[44] Ashburton wrote to Webster (July 1, 1842): " I continue to crawl about in these heats by day & pass my nights in a sleepless fever. In short I shall positively not outlive this affair if it is to be much prolonged." (Webster MSS, Library of Congress.)

[45] See, e.g., Edward Stanwood, *American Tariff Controversies in the Nineteenth Century* (Boston, 1903), II, 25.

The President vetoed the bill.[46]　He recognized that it was an emergency measure and for a limited period, and he realized that, because of the fiscal requirements, the tariff rate must be increased beyond the twenty per cent provided by the act of 1833. He was even willing to assent to a tariff that would give incidental protection to manufacture. But he felt that to increase the tariff while retaining distribution was in violation of the spirit of the compromise act. Congress sustained his veto, and the government continued to collect duties under the act of 1833.

A general tariff bill was presented to Tyler early in August. It also contained a clause to repeal the provisions of the land act of 1841 requiring distribution to cease when the tariff exceeded twenty per cent. In the contest over this bill, sectional divisions between the Northern and the Southern Whigs were influential upon the votes by which the measure passed [47] and were a factor in the fate of the party. Courageously meeting the situation, the President also declined to sign this tariff bill — a bill that because of its distribution feature was declared by one of his supporters to be " designed to create a vacuum, that it may be filled by increased taxation." [48]　In spite of the obvious impropriety of coupling a measure that would sacrifice revenue with one designed to raise revenue, it would have been impossible to preserve Whig unity except for Clay's insistence upon the combination of distribution and the tariff. The failure of the combination resulted in the loss to Tyler of Whig voters in the West and South, and particularly in those states that had hoped for this means of relieving their heavy indebtedness.[49]　Tyler's veto message [50] precipitated a report violently denouncing him; and the House refused to enter his formal protest [51] on the Journal. In the end a tariff bill continuing the requirement of the cessation of distribution passed Congress, and received the approval of the President on August 30, 1842.

This act abandoned home valuation, required cash payment of

[46] June 29, 1842. (See *Messages and Papers*, IV, 180–83.)

[47] Wellington, *Influence of the Public Lands*, pp. 108–13, and Stephenson, *Political History of the Public Lands*, Chap. v.

[48] Minority Protest of Thomas W. Gilmer. (See *Congressional Globe*, XI, 898.)

[49] A separate bill for continued distribution was passed in the closing days of the session; but it was pocket-vetoed by the President. See his message of December 14, 1842 (*Messages and Papers*, IV, 255–56).

[50] Aug. 9, 1842. (*Ibid.*, pp. 183–89.)　　　　[51] *Ibid.*, pp. 190–93.

duties, gave preferential rates to goods imported in American vessels, and in its rates was not unlike the tariff of 1832. However, heavier duties were laid on wool, cotton, and glass, specific duties were applied more extensively than in the tariff of 1832, and in general the act was highly protective.[52] Yet it met with the favor of President Tyler, primarily because of the needs of the Treasury. As a revenue law it proved satisfactory: the public debt was reduced and the expenses of the government were brought within its income. The revival of manufacture in New England — and, later, elsewhere — contrasted with the depressed condition of agriculture. Writing some seventeen years afterwards,[53] Tyler asserted that

after two vetoes I securd the Bill of 1842. Pennsylvania ought to know that when I took office her stock was down to 50. In 12 months afterwards or thereabout it attaind par value and repudiation was a possibility of the past, with her and other states. The Country ought to know that Industry was paralized and Commerce nearly dead — and that new vitallity was imparted to them and new sails furnished. All should know that Maine and New Brunswick were armd to the teeth, and that a word hastily spoken would have been followed by war.

Sectionalism was strikingly evident in the final vote (104 to 103) on the passage of the tariff of 1842 (August 22) in the House of Representatives. New England gave 26 affirmative votes (one cast by a Democrat) and only 7 in the negative (including that of John Quincy Adams, a Whig).[54] The Middle Atlantic States gave 49 votes for, and only 9 against. The section's votes in the affirmative included those of 9 Democrats in New York (more than the number of Democrats who voted against this tariff in that state) and all 10 Democrats in Pennsylvania. In fact, in the combined area of Vermont, Massachusetts, Connecticut, Rhode Island, Pennsylvania, New Jersey, and Delaware, only the vote of John Quincy Adams was cast in the negative, and that not from opposition to a protective tariff. On the other hand, no

---

[52] For the text of the tariff, see Robt. G. Proctor (compiler), *Tariff Acts Passed by the Congress of the United States from 1789 to 1897* (*House Document 562*, 55th Cong., 2d Sess.; Washington, 1898), pp. 102–20.

[53] Oct. 6, 1859. (Copied from the original manuscript of the letter, in the Huntington Library. L. G. Tyler printed a portion of the letter, in his *Letters and Times of the Tylers*, II, 553.)

[54] Adams thus registered a protest against Tyler's insistence upon the elimination of distribution and against the President's conception of the veto power.

Democratic vote in favor of the tariff came from the South Atlantic, South Central, and North Central sections. Of the total of 87 Democratic votes cast, nearly one-fourth were in favor of the tariff and were almost entirely from the Middle Atlantic States.

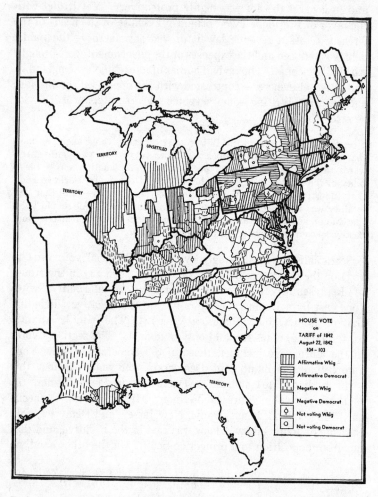

It is noteworthy, also, that 3 Democratic Representatives from New England failed to vote, as did 10 from the Middle Atlantic section. Possibly most of these were in favor of the tariff but desired not to go on record. One-third of the Whigs (almost entirely from the South Atlantic and South Central sections) had voted sectionally against the tariff espoused by their party.[55]

These votes, so little reflective of traditional party attitude and so strongly sectional, suggest the subsequent pattern of the Free Soil party and that of the later Republican party. But even in these cases the Northern zone showed, not a homogeneous area, but an alliance of Eastern and Western wings, with different emphasis by each upon the relative importance of the various issues; and in the Western wing there was always a cleavage between the Southern-upland stock of the Ohio Valley and the New England stock in the Great Lakes Basin.[56]

The Senate's vote (24 to 23), like that of the House, showed a majority of only one.[57] The Senate *bloc* of Whigs who voted against the tariff included the two from Virginia, the two from North Carolina, and one, each, from South Carolina, Georgia, and Mississippi. The Senate Democrats who voted for it included the one from Maine, the one from New York, and both those from Pennsylvania. In the Senate as a whole, only the single negative New Hampshire vote prevented the New England and Middle Atlantic sections from presenting a united front in favor of the tariff. The opposition vote included all but one of the South Atlantic Senators (and he was from Delaware) and all but four of the South Central Senators (those from Louisiana and Kentucky).[58] The North Central section was divided. The two Democrats from Ohio, the two from Missouri, and one from Illinois voted against the tariff.

It was, in short, a combination of the Northeastern sections against the Southern sections, with the North Central Division in a state of unstable equilibrium. The attitude of that section on the tariff of 1846 was to be significant and important.

The enactment of the tariff of 1842 led to violent, but on the whole unsupported, efforts by South Carolina to bring about a renewal of nullification or to call a Southern convention with a

[55] Kentucky's vote of 6 against, to 4 for, the tariff, was probably due to terms of the bill affecting that state. All but one of Tennessee's Whigs voted against their party's measure.

[56] See maps of Interstate Migration and of the elections of 1848, 1852, and 1856 (at end of volume), and text, pp. 255–56, 261–74 (*ante*).

[57] The vote on the third reading was recorded by ayes and nays.

[58] The sugar interests of Louisiana and the power of Clay in Kentucky explain these exceptions to sectional unity. Tennessee's seats were vacant.

view to resistance. The radical Robert Barnwell Rhett was a leader in this movement, and a dinner was given to him at Bluffton, South Carolina, at the end of July, 1844, to foster it.[59] At that time the question of Texas had inflamed the South Carolina mind to such an extent that opposition to the tariff of 1842 was joined with support of the annexation of Texas even at the cost of disunion. However, the restraining influence of Calhoun and of Langdon Cheves prevailed over the extremists. The prospect of a Democratic victory in the coming election was too good to be sacrificed by the proposals of the hot-heads. Nevertheless, the Bluffton episode is interesting as showing the failure of Calhoun to apply his nullification doctrine to a tariff that was probably as obnoxious to the South as had been that of 1832. Indeed, James H. Hammond, a former nullificationist, had now reached the conclusion that nullification was not a *" peaceful & constitutional remedy."* [60] But the specter of disunion endured.

Shortly after the termination of the Ashburton negotiations, Webster faced the problem of adjusting our relations in respect to the Pacific Coast and Texas. It is quite as necessary to understand the apprehensions of the United States, and the proposals of British, French, and American explorers and representatives, as to know the official intentions of the several governments. For some years England had been urged to occupy California as well as to control Texas. In 1839 Alexander Forbes, in his history, *California*, published in London, set forth the importance of California and the danger that " the northern American tide of population " would overwhelm California. He pointed out the opportunity it afforded for English colonization and suggested that its cession be brought about by exchanging the debt of fifty million dollars, due England by Mexico, for a transfer of California to the creditors.[61] Various American newspapers sounded an alarm over his proposals. Shortly after the publication of Forbes's book, Richard Pakenham, the British minister at Washington, advised an increase of naval strength in the Pacific.[62]

[59] W. M. Meigs, *The Life of John Caldwell Calhoun* (New York, 1917), II, 250 ff., and R. R. Russel, *Economic Aspects of Southern Sectionalism, 1840–1861* (University of Illinois *Studies in the Social Sciences*, XI, Nos. 1, 2; Urbana, 1924).

[60] Meigs, *op. cit.*, p. 257, citing Hammond's diary (Oct. 25, 1844), in Library of Congress.   [61] P. 152 and Chap. VIII.

[62] E. D. Adams, *British In rests and Activities in Texas, 1838–1846* (Baltimore, 1910), pp. 236 ff.

In 1841–42 Eugène Duflot de Mofras (an agent of the French government), Governor George Simpson (of the Hudson's Bay Company), and Lieutenant Charles Wilkes (who was engaged in an exploring expedition for the United States) were all cruising along the Pacific coast and reporting their conclusions. They were agreed that California, where revolution had succeeded revolution, was lost to Mexico and open to occupation by some other power. As Duflot de Mofras put it, " It is the lot of this Province to be conquered." Simpson declared that Mexico did not " attempt to exercise any dominion over it, its remote situation, together with the disturbed state of the mother country admitting of little intercourse or communication between them." Wilkes " found a total absence of all government in California."

Duflot de Mofras, in his report to François P. G. Guizot, held that California would be more contented under French control than that of either England or the United States, and saw potential French colonists in the French Canadians employed on the Willamette by the Hudson's Bay Company. He believed that France should supplement her holding of the Marquesas and Tahiti by possession of one of the Sandwich Islands, and acquire San Francisco as the " key to the Pacific Ocean." [63] Mariano Guadalupe Vallejo thought France was intriguing for California. Simpson advocated that Great Britain should acquire it (which he felt could easily be done),[64] and called San Francisco " the finest harbor in the Northern Pacific." Wilkes, in turn, was enthusiastic over the future of California and believed that it would separate from Mexico (from which it was cut off by a barren waste) and join Oregon to control the destiny of the Pacific.[65]

Webster, although strongly antagonistic to incorporating a slaveholding Texas in the Union, was not unwilling to add a portion of the Pacific Coast, so long the field of operation of New England trading vessels; he was ready to accept the line of the Columbia River for our Oregon-country limits and to acquire

[63] A. P. Nasatir, " French Activities in California before Statehood," and G. V. Blue, " Unpublished Portions of the Memoires of Duflot de Mofras," both in *Proceedings* of Pacific Coast Branch of American Historical Association, 1928 (pp. 76–102).

[64] " Letters of Sir George Simpson, 1841–1843," *American Historical Review*, XIV, 70–94.

[65] Chas. Wilkes, *Narrative of the United States Exploring Expedition* [1838–42] (Philadelphia, 1845), V, 171.

California. It was hoped that Great Britain, in return for our conceding to her the territory north of the Columbia,[66] would induce Mexico to part with California. The fact that England's bondholders owned several millions of Mexican securities was believed to give her a leverage to this end.[67] Lord Ashburton thought that England would not object to Mexico's cession to the United States of part of California, including San Francisco and Monterey.[68] Tyler desired to unite the acquisition of Texas with that of California and with the fixing of a restricted Oregon boundary. In approving a letter of Webster to Edward Everett, our minister in England, the President, perhaps following a suggestion of Waddy Thompson, declared that, if merely the issue of the annexation of Texas were gone into, it would have the effect

of separating the question from California, and stirring up all the agitations which you anticipate, whereas introduced into the same treaty, the three interests would be united, and would satisfy all sections of the country. Texas might not stand alone, nor would the line proposed for Oregon. Texas would reconcile all to the line, while California would reconcile or pacify all to Oregon.[69]

In respect to this scheme of sectional compromise on territorial annexations, it cannot be said that Webster was ready to yield with regard to Texas; but Tyler attempted to arrange for him to undertake a mission to England, and this plan may have had for its object the clearing of the way for the accomplishment of such an adjustment. However, the refusal of the House Committee of Foreign Affairs to support Adams in his effort to secure

[66] Webster believed Oregon "a poor country . . . and of very little consequence to the United States. The ownership of the whole country is very likely to follow the greater settlement, and larger amount of population, proceeding, hereafter, from whichsoever of the two countries." (*Writings and Speeches*, XVIII, 179–80.)

[67] On January 30, 1843, Waddy Thompson wrote to Webster from Mexico, saying that England had made a treaty with Mexico securing to British creditors the right to the lands in California in payment of their debts; and he prophesied that in ten years England would own the country. (Webster MSS, Library of Congress. But see Adams, *British Interests and Activities in Texas*, Chap. XI.)

[68] *Memoirs of John Quincy Adams*, ed. C. F. Adams, XI (Philadelphia, 1876), 347 (Mar. 27, 1843).

[69] Tyler, *Letters and Times of the Tylers*, II, 260–61. See also: Waddy Thompson to Tyler, May 9, 1842, cited by Reeves, *Diplomacy under Tyler and Polk*, p. 101 (cf. p. 110); Justin H. Smith, *The Annexation of Texas* (New York, 1911), p. 109; *Writings and Speeches of Webster*, XIV, 611; and R. G. Cleland, in *Southwestern Historical Quarterly*, XVIII, 32–33.

an appropriation for this special mission,[70] and the unwillingness of Everett to be transferred to China,[71] left Webster still in the cabinet.

But both he and Tyler were becoming convinced that his continuance as Secretary of State was undesirable. The question of the annexation of Texas was developing into a bitter public issue.[72] In a speech in the House (April 13, 1842), Tyler's friend, Henry A. Wise, had favored annexation and looked to the expansion of Texas throughout the entire Southwest to the Pacific Ocean, with a view to extending slavery. John Quincy Adams, in September of that year, warned his constituents of an annexation "conspiracy." [73] Wise, however, was notoriously reckless in speech, and more than once placed the President in a position that he himself would not have taken. When, however, in January of 1843, former Governor Thomas W. Gilmer, of Virginia, published in the administration organ, the *Madisonian*, a plea for annexation, it attracted widespread attention. It was sent by A. V. Brown, of Tennessee, to Jackson, who replied in his celebrated letter [74] urging the importance of immediate action. But Jackson's letter was not published for over a year.

On the closing day of the session of Congress,[75] a manifesto was

[70] *Adams Memoirs*, XI, 327–28, 329–30.

[71] The increase of commerce with China, and the conditions resulting from England's opium war with that country, led Tyler to recommend to Congress, on December 30, 1842 (*Messages and Papers*, IV, 211–14), an appropriation for sending a Commissioner to China. The administration's interest in trade on the Pacific Ocean and with the Far East was stimulated when Admiral George Paulet took possession of the Hawaiian Islands for England (February 25, 1843), although this act was afterwards disavowed by that country. (See John Bassett Moore, *A Digest of International Law* . . . [Washington, 1906], I, 478.) As has been seen in Chapter III, American trade was important in both the Hawaiian Islands and in China. On the day of Webster's resignation as Secretary of State, Caleb Cushing was designated Commissioner to China. His mission resulted in a treaty, which he concluded on July 3, 1844, granting commercial privileges to the United States and providing for extraterritoriality. Tyler's fruitful interest in the Pacific and Far East was an important phase of his administration. (See: J. W. Foster, *American Diplomacy in the Orient* [Boston, 1903]; J. M. Callahan, *American Relations in the Pacific and the Far East, 1784–1900* [Johns Hopkins University *Studies in Historical and Political Science*, Ser. XIX, Nos. 1–3; Baltimore, 1901]; Claude M. Fuess, *The Life of Caleb Cushing* [New York, 1923], I, Chap. X; and Tyler, *op. cit.*, pp. 262–63.)

[72] See *ibid.*, p. 270, and von Holst, *United States, 1828–1846*, pp. 625–26.

[73] Smith, *op. cit.*, p. 131.

[74] Feb. 12, 1843. The Washington *Globe* of March 20, 1844 (not 1843 [misprinted " 1483 "], as Tyler, *op. cit.*, III, 122, has it), published the letter with its correct date.   [75] Mar. 3, 1843.

issued by thirteen Members (most, or all, of them of New England birth or ancestry), headed by John Quincy Adams, declaring that the annexation of Texas would be in itself a dissolution of the Union and placing in the worst possible light, as parts of a slaveholders' conspiracy, the movements in progress for annexation.[76]

Although Adams had been very critical of the New England Federalist disunion movement [77] that eventuated in the resolutions of the Hartford Convention, his antagonism to the incorporation of a slaveholding Texas within the United States had now brought him to the disunion position of his former enemies. While there is abundant evidence that extremists of the Southern states thought they saw, in annexation, political and economic advantage to those states, and some of them were even considering the possibility of secession were it not effected, there was no " plot of the slavocracy," such as Adams and much of New England imagined.[78] But Adams, as we have seen, had long waged a vigorous campaign in behalf of the right of petition, rendered nugatory by the " 21st rule " of the House (commonly known as the " gag law "). He had declared that, if this were retained as

[76] *Niles' Register*, LXIV, 173-75. The document was apparently written by S. M. Gates, one of the Congressional signers, and not by Adams himself. See the latter's *Memoirs*, XI, 41, and Annie H. Abel and F. J. Klingberg (eds.), *A Side-light on Anglo-American Relations, 1839-1858* (published by The Association for the Study of Negro Life and History, Inc., 1927; printed by Lancaster Press, Inc.; Lancaster, Pa.), p. 132. *Appletons' Cyclopaedia of American Biography* (II [New York, 1888], 616) attributes its authorship to Gates, and says that the correspondence between him and Adams is still in the possession of the Gates family. The fact that only thirteen Members signed this radical protest is significant, since it had been desired to include signatures of all the Members who were opposed to annexation.

[77] His *Documents Relating to New-England Federalism, 1800-1815*, ed. Henry Adams (Boston, 1877), were issued to prove these disunion projects.

[78] This is my conclusion after a careful study of the evidence. For example, Representative Gilmer, of Virginia, writes, on December 13, 1843, to Calhoun (see *Calhoun Correspondence*, pp. 904-6, reprinting Tyler, *op. cit.*, III, 130-32), inquiring about his position on the annexation of Texas; and Senator George McDuffie, of South Carolina, in a letter of January 3, 1844, to Calhoun (see American Historical Association *Annual Report*, 1929 [Washington, 1930], p. 198), says: " There is an impression here that the administration are negotiating for the annexation of Texas, but nothing certain or definite has transpired." He adds that " It would be *ipso facto* making war on Mexico " and that " there would be hazard that Great Britain would take part with Mexico." Such letters are inconsistent with the idea of a " conspiracy," as charged by Adams in March, 1843. Benton, in his *View*, is also unwarrantedly suspicious of a " plot."

a settled rule, three-fourths of the states would be absolved from their allegiance to the Union. His defense of the right of petition included the presentation of petitions for disunion as well as against slavery. The South not unnaturally saw in him the hated and able leader of a movement, by New England and her Middle Atlantic and North Central settlements, aimed at its security and power,[79] and sectional animosity increased.

Nicholas Biddle had advised Webster not to leave the cabinet,[80] and shortly afterward had urged upon Tyler that the Secretary of State, having " no political party, no body of political adherents. . . . no political aspirations," should be retained.[81] But, at about that time,[82] a friend (H. Shaw) had written to Webster, from Pennsylvania, of an interview with Tyler, who, he said, had no faith in securing control of the Whig party. " I will be frank with you," Shaw continued. " In my opinion he would feel relieved if you should resign your place, and I am much mistaken if you do not find it impracticable to stay." In his reply to Biddle, Webster explained [83] that Tyler was determined to try the chance of an election in 1844 (a movement in which he himself could not concur) ; that the President was disposed to " throw himself altogether into the arms of the loco foco [Democratic] party " ; and that every appointment he made raised the question of its political effects.[84]

By the middle of March, Isaac Van Zandt, the Texan minister at Washington, had informed his government that Webster was to resign and that, although friendly, he was " very much in the way at present," being timid and " fearful of his abolition constituents in Massachusetts." [85]

[79] See, for example, the bitter speech of Wise (Jan. 25–26, 1842) on resolutions of censure of Adams (*Congressional Globe*, XI, 171–72, 173–76).

[80] Feb. 27, 1843. See Webster MSS, Library of Congress (Vol. III, p. 179), and *The Correspondence of Nicholas Biddle Dealing with National Affairs, 1807–1844*, ed. R. C. McGrane (Boston, 1919), p. 344.

[81] *Ibid.*, pp. 346–48.

[82] Feb. 28. See Webster MSS (III, 181). In these manuscripts (III, 199), there is a letter of A. Taft to Webster (Cincinnati, April 7, 1843), which may perhaps indicate that there was another consideration in Webster's mind. This letter assured Webster that the people disliked the ultra-Whig politics, that Clay could not get the vote of Ohio, and that, were he out of the way, Webster could combine the Whigs.

[83] Mar. 11.   [84] *Biddle Correspondence*, p. 345.

[85] Anson Jones, *Memoranda and Official Correspondence Relating to the Republic of Texas* (New York, 1859), p. 213.

The simple explanation by Webster's friends, and at times by himself, that he had remained in the cabinet solely to complete the negotiations with England, is untenable. Not only had he continued after the cabinet break-up and actively assisted the administration in its fiscal measures; not only had he retained the confidence of Tyler at that time and later; but he had unquestionably been influenced by his rivalry with Clay and by his hope to bring about new leadership in the Whig party.

When Webster finally submitted his formal resignation as Secretary of State,[86] he apparently followed the course recommended by Biddle, who had written him, over a month before,[87] advising him to part from the President with good will and retire to private life. He also advised him to declare, at some meeting, that he was an unchangeable Whig; that the party had separated from him, not he from it; and that he had remained in the cabinet to make the English treaty, but had found that he could not " do the good " he had proposed. When, in the fall of 1843, Webster made a speech at a Whig convention at Andover, Massachusetts,[88] he declared that he was not a candidate for any office; protested against attacks made upon him; and explained that he had continued in the cabinet because of his desire to accomplish a settlement with England and had retired when it became clear that Tyler had broken with the Whigs. " I am," said he, " a Whig, a Massachusetts Whig, a Faneuil Hall Whig." He was welcomed back to the Whig fold.

The relation of Texas to the struggle between the sections now becomes so vital as to warrant a restatement. To the South, the issue was one that involved the question of its own safety. The possibility that Texas, allied or friendly with England and France, might continue as an independent nation on its borders, alarmed it. There was a fear that, under the influence of these powers, Texas would declare for emancipation, in return for financial assistance and protection against Mexico and the United States. Moreover, in that case it would become a refuge for escaping slaves. Unsatisfactory as the Constitutional provision for a fugitive-slave law had proved, it was at least more effective than would be a condition under which a neighboring nation might invite the fugi-

[86] May 8, 1843.
[87] *Biddle Correspondence*, pp. 348-50.
[88] *Writings and Speeches*, III, 185.

tive. The example of an independent country, free from slavery, on the borders of the Southern sections, would menace the stability of their social structure, as well as block their further expansion. With the aid of France and England, such a separate nation might extend itself to include the vast territory westward to the Pacific Ocean.

Quite as important was the positive advantage of the annexation of Texas as a means of preserving the sectional equilibrium of South and North. Several states might be made of Texas, and thus the power of the South in the Union be increased and its equality in the Senate be preserved. This would enable it to render less menacing the increasing number from the North in the House and in the electoral college.

On the other hand, New England (always apprehensive of a loss of power by expansion of rival sections) and the Middle Atlantic States were growing more responsive to antislavery sentiment and resentful of the refusal of the South to accept their tariff policy.

But the North Central States were still swayed by a passion for westward expansion. In this section, also, apprehension of the increase of the power of the slaveholding South existed; but the section's devotion to expansion was so strong that it was ready to bargain with the South over equivalent territorial gains.

Thenceforward, until the Civil War and Reconstruction, the issues of tariff, internal improvements, banking and currency, and public lands became subordinate to the issues of expansion and slavery.

During the administration of President M. B. Lamar, the new Texan republic was brought to extreme exhaustion. Not only was the attempted capture of Santa Fe in 1841 a total failure, but there was no money in the treasury and there was a heavy public debt. Depression and fear of bankruptcy were still prevalent in 1843,[89] under the presidency of Sam Houston.

At that time negotiations (fostered by English mediation, but ultimately unsuccessful) for an armistice with Mexico were in progress. There were serious reasons for fearing control of an independent Texas by foreign nations.[90] Commercial motives played their part, for Texas would be a consumer of English manufactures, a producer of cotton for the English market, and

[89] Smith, *Annexation of Texas*, pp. 39–42.
[90] Adams, *British Interests and Activities in Texas*, pp. 106 ff.

an avenue of smuggling. Also, as a barrier to encroachments of the United States upon Mexico, it would promote the wishes of England.[91]

From the time of her own abolition of slavery in her colonies, in the previous decade, she had been desirous of emancipation throughout the world.[92] As she found in the United States itself, particularly on the part of leaders in New England and the North in general, strong opposition to the annexation of Texas, she was encouraged to advise Mexico to combine recognition of Texas with a requirement for the abolition of slavery there.[93] Various means for securing this were proposed to the British government, including a loan to Texas to enable it to buy the slaves and provide for permanent emancipation, or, to achieve the same end, British purchase of Texan lands conditioned on the application of the proceeds to the reimbursement of the owners of freed slaves.[94]

Although Lord Aberdeen declined to do more in this matter than advise Mexico to consent to the independence of Texas on condition that the new republic abolish slavery, reports of these connections between the English government and American antislavery leaders reached the United States in letters by such men as Duff Green and Ashbel Smith, as well as in the steady stream of correspondence between the American and English groups of abolitionists favoring an independent, nonslaveholding Texas.[95] John Quincy Adams notes, in his *Memoirs*,[96] at the end of May, 1843, that, when visited by a delegate to the London antislavery convention, he told him he " believed the freedom of this country and of all mankind depended upon the direct, formal, open, and avowed interference of Great Britain to accomplish the abolition of slavery in Texas." [97] Still earlier, William Ellery Channing,

---

[91] At least so thought the Texan agent, Ashbel Smith. See *Diplomatic Correspondence of the Republic of Texas*, ed. G. P. Garrison, Pt. III (American Historical Association *Annual Report*, 1908, II [2]; Washington, 1911), p. 1105.

[92] See St. Geo. L. Sioussat, *Duff Green's " England and the United States ": With an Introductory Study of American Opposition to the Quintuple Treaty of 1841* (American Antiquarian Society *Proceedings*, N.S., XL, 175–276), p. 182, n. 2 (references).

[93] E. D. Adams, *op. cit.*, Chap. VI, especially pp. 138–47, quoting Aberdeen's letters.

[94] *Texan Diplomatic Correspondence*, Pt. III, pp. 1100–1101.

[95] See Abel and Klingberg (eds.), *Side-light on Anglo-American Relations*, *passim*.

[96] XI, 380.

[97] He added, with characteristic skepticism: " but that I distrusted the sin-

in his private correspondence with a member of the English Parliament, had urged that England " join with all the powers holding islands in the Gulph of Mexico in protesting " against American annexation of Texas.[98]

England's agent, Charles Elliot, was actively encouraging Texas to continue her separate existence, and President Houston, whether sincerely or not, labored to secure Elliot's support for Texan independence by means of English aid.[99] Houston ultimately rejected the proposed armistice, because Mexico insisted on calling Texas a " department," in spite of the persuasions of the English minister to Mexico against this. But, while the prospects of peace were still bright, Houston expressed his appreciation to England and his desire not to expose his country to renewed attack if annexation were discussed without the promise of effective protection by the United States.

Opinions on Houston's policy will always differ. His attitude may have been due to a desire to arouse the fears and jealousies of the United States to such a degree that she would support annexation because of the prospect of a separate Texas bound by ties of gratitude and interest to England. On the other hand, personal ambition, the prospect that independence would insure peace to Texas and give her prosperity through her cotton trade with England, and the vision of extending her borders to the Pacific, may have brought him to a decision against annexation. Perhaps both alternatives still occupied his mind and led him to seek to safeguard Texas in either event.[100]

In the middle of October, 1843, Upshur, of Virginia, Webster's successor as Secretary of State,[101] alarmed by the reports that a

---

cerity of the present British Administration in the anti-slavery cause." Cf. *ibid.*, p. 374. See the letter (in Abel and Klingberg [eds.], *op. cit.*, p. 240) of Lewis Tappan, giving his version of Adams's efforts to have England intervene against slavery in Texas.

[98] MS letter of Channing to Thos. Thornely, M.P., Dec. 31, 1841, in Harvard University Library. (My attention was called to this item by Professor Frederick Merk.)

[99] E. D. Adams, *op. cit.*, pp. 106 ff., 126.

[100] Smith, *op. cit.*, pp. 163–69.

[101] Upshur had been transferred from the Navy secretaryship. Thomas W. Gilmer, also of Virginia, had been named to that post following the service there of David Henshaw, of Massachusetts, whose recess appointment had failed of confirmation. On the relations of Henshaw and Calhoun in this period, see A. B. Darling, *Political Changes in Massachusetts, 1824–1848* (New Haven, 1925), pp. 284, 301–14.

separate Texan nation might mean dependence upon European influence and a possible menace to Southern slavery, proposed a treaty of annexation to the Texan minister at Washington.[102] That Upshur's fears were not unwarranted appears from the correspondence of Edward Everett (our minister to England) with him, which declared that England had connected emancipation in Texas with a proposal that Mexico acknowledge her independence. In spite of Aberdeen's later denial of such a formal proposal, the information undoubtedly affected the attitude of Upshur.

The Mexican minister at Washington, becoming aware that a movement for annexation was in progress, officially declared that, if Texas were annexed, his government was " resolved to declare war." [103]

When Congress opened, in December, 1843, Tyler's message denounced Mexico for not having recognized Texas after her eight years of successful assertion of independence and after recognition by the important powers. He declared that Mexican hostilities against Texas must cease: they were merely weakening Texas and Mexico, alike, and rendering both nations liable to interference by more powerful countries, to our disadvantage. Clearly, the administration was considering a treaty of annexation.

By the middle of December, American interest in annexation was given impetus by the message of President Houston reciting the prosperous condition of Texas under suspension of arms while discussion of a formal armistice was in progress and giving thanks, especially, to the English government for its representations to Mexico.

At this point, the administration encountered the difficulty of a demand by Houston that during treaty negotiations the United States should defend Texas against Mexican attack.[104] This was obviously beyond the powers of the President, and, in fact, a demand for a declaration of war, which under the Constitution could be made only by Congress. Houston gave Elliot to understand that the stipulation would prevent the United States from accepting the proposed treaty.

Under all the circumstances, it is not strange that Aberdeen

[102] *Niles' Register*, LXVI, 169.

[103] Smith, *op. cit.*, pp. 135–36, citing *Senate Document 1*, 28th Cong., 1st Sess.

[104] Tyler, *Letters and Times of the Tylers*, II, 286, and Smith, *op. cit.*, pp. 163–69.

thought that a firm stand by France and England might defeat annexation. This resulted in his letter [105] to the English minister in France, proposing joint action to that end. The project was cordially and quickly agreed to by France.

Meanwhile, Secretary Upshur had sounded the Senators and had concluded that the necessary two-thirds majority for ratification of a treaty of annexation of Texas could be secured.[106] Even leading opponents of such a treaty feared that it might win.[107] So far, the question had, on the whole, been presented to members of both parties as a national one, in which America's safety from foreign interference on her borders, the commerce between the Mississippi Valley and Texas, the gains from our cotton export, the nation's possession of a monopoly of that crop, and, in general, the traditional attitude of the country toward westward expansion, had been operative upon the Senatorial mind. Of course, the South's fear of a free Texas immediately to the west of her would have been very influential upon the attitude of the Senators from the slaveholding sections, but the administration [108] had not made annexation officially the leading issue.

At this juncture, two important factors entered to affect the question. One of them was the death of Secretaries Upshur and Gilmer, in an explosion on board the " Princeton "; [109] the other was the Presidential campaign of 1844, which resulted in making the annexation of Texas an important party issue.

The problem of a successor to Upshur was solved by the selection of John C. Calhoun. Apparently Tyler had considered a different appointment, but his hand was forced by an interview which Representative Wise, so often his spokesman, had with Senator George McDuffie, of South Carolina. Wise designedly gave McDuffie the impression that he was speaking for Tyler and that the President had already selected Calhoun and desired a conversation with him.[110] Fearful, perhaps, of the break that would follow a disclaimer of Wise's action, Tyler offered the posi-

[105] Jan. 12, 1844.

[106] Tyler, *op. cit.*, pp. 283–85; *Calhoun Correspondence*, p. 934; and Mrs. Chapman Coleman (ed.), *The Life of John J. Crittenden, with Selections from His Correspondence and Speeches* (Philadelphia, 1871), I, 216.

[107] Abel and Klingberg (eds.), *op. cit.*, p. 177.

[108] Tyler, *op. cit.*, pp. 422 ff.

[109] Feb. 28, 1844.

[110] Wise, *Seven Decades*, pp. 221–22; Tyler, *op. cit.*, pp. 291 ff.; and *Calhoun Correspondence*, pp. 934, 938–39.

tion to Calhoun — an offer that was made easier by the President's stating in his invitation that Calhoun's friends had withdrawn his name from the canvass for the Presidency.[111]

Toward the close of December, 1843, Calhoun,[112] replying to an inquiry by Gilmer[113] regarding his position on the annexation of Texas, had shown how thoroughly Southern he was on the question. At that time, he declared that annexation was necessary both for Texas and the South, and that, if Texas became a bone of contention between the United States and England, Mexico would join with England, and Texas would be subjugated. He — rather incidentally — mentioned the advantage to the North and Northwest in the opening of a market, and called attention to the fact that the proposed extension of the nonslaveholding states to the Pacific " on the line of the Oregon " warranted the adding of Texas to the South. He then grappled outright with the question of slavery. " The objection," he said, " that it would extend our domestic institutions of the South, must be met as a direct attack on the compromise of the Constitution, and the highest ground ought to be taken in opposition to it on our part." He referred to his resolutions of December, " '38 or '39 " (really 1837),[114] on the subject of abolition, as applicable now. One of these asserted the right of annexation of new territory regardless of the effect upon slavery extension; but it had been refused passage by the Senate.

On taking office as Secretary of State, Calhoun found on his desk the diplomatic correspondence regarding Texas and the general lines of the proposed treaty of annexation. He seized the opportunity afforded by the so-called " Pakenham correspondence "[115] to make slavery the controlling issue in connection with the Texas-annexation treaty. Lord Aberdeen, in a letter to Pakenham, admitted[116] that Great Britain desired to see slavery abolished in Texas and throughout the world, but by open means.

[111] Mar. 6. (*Ibid.*, p. 939.) His withdrawal was rather as an active candidate before the Democratic convention than as a possible recipient of the nomination. See, e.g., *ibid.*, pp. 554, 557.

[112] *Ibid.*, pp. 559–60.

[113] See p. 512 (*ante*), n. 78.

[114] See pp. 466–67, *ante*.

[115] Printed in *The Works of John C. Calhoun*, ed. R. K. Crallé, V (New York, 1855), 330–47. See also pp. 311 ff., and, for interpretations, Smith, *op. cit.*, pp. 200–220 (with citations), and E. D. Adams, *op. cit.*, pp. 156 ff.

[116] Dec. 26, 1843. (See *Niles' Register*, LXVI, 171.)

" We should rejoice," he said, " if the recognition of that country by the Mexican government should be accompanied by an engagement on the part of Texas to abolish slavery eventually and under proper condition throughout the republic." He added : " We shall counsel, but we shall not seek to compel, or unduly control either party." But, aside from the disturbing suggestion that England would " counsel " the abolition of slavery in Texas, the " purely commercial " objects which he ascribed to England would have included the desire for the independence of Texas as a cotton-producing country, with free trade with England and under her influence. Irrespective of the direct question of slavery, therefore, this professed disavowal on the part of Aberdeen, together with Mexico's instability and her feeble hold upon California and the Southwest, and England's claims in the Oregon country, would have awakened national apprehensions.

While admitting Great Britain's right to abolish slavery in her own possessions, Calhoun declared it the duty of other countries, whose safety or prosperity might be endangered, to adopt measures for protection. In view of the difficulty that Texas as an independent nation would experience in resisting English desires, he held that the abolition of slavery, there, would imperil the safety and prosperity of the Union and that it must annex Texas in self-defense. He insisted that countries that had put an end to slavery had left the African race in a worse condition than those that had not. In short, Calhoun made the Texan issue the occasion for a thoroughgoing defense of slavery. He may have thought this the opportunity decisively to compel the Northern sections to accept his view of the right of slavery expansion.

In reply to the demand of Texas for protection, he said that a strong naval force had been ordered to concentrate in the Gulf of Mexico and that similar instructions had been given to move disposable military forces on the Southwestern frontier; and he gave assurance that, during the pendency of the treaty of annexation, the President would use all Constitutional means to protect Texas from foreign invasion.[117] In view of Mexico's threat of war, this was not an unreasonable precaution.

As finally signed and submitted to the Senate, the treaty[118]

[117] *Ibid.*, p. 232.
[118] Concluded April 12, 1844, and communicated to the Senate April 22. The text is in *Calhoun Works*, V, 322–27.

recited the desire of Texas to join the Union and provided for the
annexation of that republic as a territory (with statehood to follow as soon as consistent with the Constitution). Texas was to
yield to the United States her sovereignty and public property,
while the United States was to assume the public debt and liabilities of Texas in return for her public lands and a certain amount
of Texan securities.

Although diplomatic correspondence, raising the slavery issue
to decisive importance, was placed before the Senate along with
the treaty, the President, in his message of transmittal,[119] spoke
of the treaty rather from the points of view of the rights of American colonists already in Texas, the navigating interests of the
" Eastern and Middle States," and the opening of a market for the
" Western States "; and then, as a part of his proposed adjustment
of sectional interests, he mentioned the protection and security
of the " Southern and Southeastern States."

From the outlook of later years, which revealed factors leading to
the defeat of the treaty, Tyler came to criticize both Upshur and
Calhoun for the primary emphasis they had placed upon the defense of slavery as the reason for pressing annexation, and for
their elaborate arguments on that subject.[120] In fact, far from
advancing the movement for annexation, the slavery issue proved
to be the most serious obstacle to its consummation. In view of
Northern suspicions of a slaveholders' " conspiracy," Calhoun's
assertion that slavery was a national interest and his plea for the
annexation of Texas as a means of safeguarding that interest, were
ill advised and of themselves might have defeated the treaty.

The efforts of Tyler to build up a following of his own had but
feeble results. The popularity of Clay as the probable Whig
candidate and the strength of Van Buren and his supporters in
the Democratic ranks, led to the decision of James Buchanan to
withdraw and that of Calhoun not to allow his name to go before
the Democratic convention. Tyler no doubt expected that the
Texan issue would work to his advantage, but he hoped in vain.

Clay and Van Buren both published letters, on the same day,
opposing the treaty of annexation. The former's " Raleigh letter " had been written on the seventeenth of April, 1844,[121] and

119 *Messages and Papers*, IV, 307–13.

120 Tyler, *op. cit.*, pp. 299, 483.

121 On April 16, George Bancroft wrote to Van Buren that " today Webster

forwarded to Crittenden. On the nineteenth Clay urged haste in its publication, and two days later asserted that Van Buren and he stood on common ground against the treaty.[122] Clay's Raleigh letter appeared in the *National Intelligencer* the morning of the twenty-seventh, and was an argument that the measure would compromise the national character, would involve us in war with Mexico, was financially inexpedient, and was uncalled for by general public opinion. He thought it would be dangerous to the Union, and, far from aiding the South, would probably (because of the inapplicability of slavery to the regions west and north of San Antonio) add three free states and only two slave states. He looked forward to a future independent Canadian republic, on the one side, and an independent Texan republic, on the other, as more desirable than Texan annexation. They would be natural allies, ready to repel European attacks and friendly to the United States. In the afternoon of the twenty-seventh appeared Van Buren's letter (dated April 20) to Representative W. H. Hammet, of Mississippi. Silas Wright, who received the letter on the twenty-sixth for approval and transmittal, held an evening consultation with some of Van Buren's friends, and, even before the letter was seen by Hammet, decided to publish it in the afternoon edition of the Washington *Globe*. In view of the action of these intimate friends of Clay and Van Buren, respectively, it is evident that both desired their announcements against annexation to appear on the same date. Van Buren believed that he could count on a clear two-thirds majority of the coming Democratic convention, and Clay was sure of the Whig nomination, so that the Tyler plan of injecting the Texan issue would be frustrated.

Van Buren's cautiously worded letter asserted the constitutionality of the treaty, but questioned its expediency. He believed it would bring on a war with Mexico, that immediate action was not called for, and that there was no danger of foreign interference. But he added that, if Mexico went so far in her efforts to reconquer Texas as to convince a majority of the people of the United States that annexation should be effected, whatever the

---

asserted that he had letters from Washington to this effect: Clay had sent to some person there a letter twenty pages long, saying this is not the time for annexing Texas (i.e. let me humbug the Northern Abolitionists and after that humor the South)." (Massachusetts Historical Society *Proceedings*, XLII, 424.)

[122] Smith, *op. cit.*, p. 240, citing Crittenden Papers, Library of Congress.

consequences, he would be guided by the will of that majority, as expressed in a Congress elected after mature consideration of the issue.[123]

Both Clay and Van Buren, who while Secretaries of State had negotiated with Mexico for the annexation of Texas, made it clear that they thought the honor of the United States, under present circumstances, was in jeopardy and that annexation would mean war with Mexico.

The Whig convention, which met on the first of May, at Baltimore, unanimously nominated Clay for President and chose Theodore Frelinghuysen, of New Jersey, as its Vice-Presidential candidate. Reasserting Whig principles, the convention seems to have been completely under the domination of Clay. Although he had thought at Raleigh [124] that the people would demand a Bank of the United States and although the Whigs had broken with President Tyler on this very question, it is noteworthy that no specific recommendation with regard to it was made in the convention's resolutions. The "well-regulated currency" demanded, there, was certainly a feeble expression, after the importance the party had given to the issue of a National Bank.

At the time, perhaps, the Whigs did not realize the significance of a convention of abolitionists that had met in Buffalo in August of the previous year and nominated James G. Birney, of New York, for President. Demanding the divorce of the federal government from slavery, these abolitionists denied that they were a sectional party.

When Van Buren's letter, opposing Texan annexation under the existing conditions, appeared, it stunned his Southern friends. Jackson, in spite of his affection for Van Buren, quickly came to the conclusion that this letter would prevent his nomination or, if he were nominated, deprive him of the Southern electoral votes. Determined that nothing should stand in the way of immediate annexation, Jackson, in an interview with Polk, urged him to seek the Presidential nomination, as a compromise candidate. Polk still desired the support of the Van Buren delegates, for the Vice-Presidential nomination; but, after this conversation, he wrote a

---

[123] On the letters of Clay and Van Buren, see: *Niles' Register*, LXVI, 152–57; p. 522 (*ante*), n. 121; E. I. McCormac, *James K. Polk: A Political Biography* (Berkeley, Calif., 1922), pp. 223–26; and Smith, *op. cit.*, pp. 239–45 (with citations).

[124] See *Niles' Register*, LXVI, 299.

letter to his political ally, Cave Johnson, reporting Jackson's attitude, and in another letter, marked " Highly Confidential," authorized Johnson to show this report to Van Buren's close friend, Silas Wright, who had already declared to Johnson that Polk was " the only man he thought the Northern Democrats would support if Van Buren was set aside "; and Polk added that Jackson had previously expressed the same thing to others. Clearly foreseeing the possibilities of the situation, Polk suggested a plan for consultation of delegates as they arrived, in order to secure harmony in the convention; and he stressed the importance of not antagonizing the Van Buren men.[125]

On the twenty-seventh of May, 1844, the Democratic convention met at Baltimore.[126] Van Buren had a clear majority of the delegates, but not the two-thirds necessary, under its rules, for nomination. On the first ballot he received 146 votes against the 83 for his nearest competitor, Lewis Cass, of Michigan. On the fifth ballot the vote for Cass (who was an advocate of annexation) surpassed that for Van Buren, whose friends attempted in vain to repeal the two-thirds rule. The evening of the second day of the convention, the conferences urged by Polk bore fruit. Both George Bancroft, of Massachusetts, and Gideon J. Pillow, of Tennessee, claimed the credit for the final result;[127] but clearly Polk's unanimous nomination for the Presidency was due to conditions that had been foreseen by both Jackson and Polk himself. His nomination could not have been effected without the support of friends of Van Buren, and it was not desirable that he should be placed in the position of being the candidate of the South. Nor was the nomination that of an unknown man. He was a tried exponent of the fundamental principles of the Democratic party. He had been the lieutenant of Jackson in his historic political fights, and twice an efficient Speaker of the House of Representatives; and, by his election as governor of Tennessee, had temporarily wrested that state from Whig control. He was

---

[125] The *Tennessee Historical Magazine*, Sept., 1915, contains the Polk-Johnson letters. See also: " Letters of Gideon J. Pillow to James K. Polk, 1844," *American Historical Review*, XI, 832–43; Bancroft letters, in Massachusetts Historical Society *Proceedings*, XLII, 428–30; and McCormac, *op. cit.*, pp. 231–36.

[126] The proceedings are reported in *Niles' Register*, LXVI, 211–13.

[127] See M. A. De W. Howe, *Life and Letters of George Bancroft* (New York, 1908), I, 253; and " Pillow-Polk Letters," *op. cit.*, p. 841, n. 1.

an embodiment of the far-flung Western and Southern influence of Tennessee.[128] Above all other things, perhaps, as the protégé of Jackson he stood for the continuation of that westward expansion which had begun with the earliest colonization on the Atlantic Coast and of which his own family record was a part. In short, he was the natural choice of the convention after the rejection of Van Buren.

Silas Wright having refused the nomination for Vice-President, because of his relations to Van Buren, George M. Dallas, of Pennsylvania, was selected. The convention's resolutions favored "the re-occupation of Oregon and the re-annexation of Texas at the earliest practicable period."[129] The principles adopted in 1840, including the resolution against fostering one branch of industry to the detriment of another or cherishing the interest of one portion to the injury of another portion of our common country, were repeated; and tribute was paid to the Presidency of Van Buren.

A convention that nominated Tyler had met at Baltimore at the same time as the Democratic convention. But the President was desirous of insuring the defeat of Clay, and, having converted the Democrats to support of Texan annexation and having (as he understood) assurances that his political friends would be taken care of, he withdrew his candidacy on the twentieth of August.

The injection of the Texan issue into the campaign for the Presidency, together with the violent Northern opposition that had been aroused by the tone of Calhoun's Pakenham correspondence, made certain the defeat of the treaty of annexation when, a few days after Polk's nomination,[130] it came to a vote. Instead of the expected two-thirds majority for the treaty, the ballot stood 16 yeas to 35 nays. Every Senator from New England, with the exception of the Democrat, Levi Woodbury, of New Hampshire, voted against annexation; and of the seven Democratic Senators who voted nay in opposition to their party platform, three were

---

[128] See pp. 230, 233, *ante*.

[129] Influenced, perhaps, by the argument of Senator R. J. Walker, of Mississippi, in his "Letter [of Jan. 8, 1844] . . . Relative to the Reannexation of Texas: in Reply to the Call of the People of Carroll County, Kentucky, to Communicate His Views on That Subject" (various printings, including Washington, 1844).

[130] June 8.

from New England, two from Ohio, one from New York, and one from Missouri. Of these seven, five were of New England birth. On the other hand, only one Whig (Henderson, of Mississippi) voted for annexation.

After the Texan issue had risen to prominence as a campaign issue, the English and French ambassadors to the United States warned their governments against disclosing, before the election, their plan of joint interference to forestall annexation, on the ground that knowledge of it would harm Clay's cause and that the United States would occupy Texas, " leaving it to the Guaranteeing Powers to carry out the objects of the agreement as best they might." France accordingly agreed with England to postpone any intervention.[131] But the apprehensions that had been aroused by the menace of European interference continued to influence the voters. Letters from both candidates were used to cloud the Texan issue. In Clay's " Alabama letters," responding to requests that he make clearer his attitude on annexation, he did not really modify his Raleigh letter giving his reasons for opposition, but reframed them to conciliate Southern voters. He said that, " far from having any personal objection to the annexation of Texas," he " should be glad to see it, without dishonor — without war, with the common consent of the Union, and upon just and fair terms." " I do not think," he added, " that the subject of slavery ought to affect the question, one way or the other."[132] These Alabama letters did not satisfy the South (the vote of the Whigs in some of their most important regions, there, was seriously diminished), and they lost Clay many votes in the pivotal state of New York. The phrase, " should be glad to see it," withdrawn from its context, was used by the abolitionists against Clay, as was his statement that it " would be unwise to refuse a permanent acquisition, which will exist as long as the globe remains, on account of a temporary institution." He wrote that he should be governed by the state of public opinion at the time he might be called upon to act, and, above all, by the duty of preserving the Union. But threats had been made in New England and the South that the decision regarding Texas would determine their continuance in the Union.

The strongly protectionist state of Pennsylvania was won to

[131] Adams, *British Interests and Activities in Texas*, pp. 178–83.
[132] *Niles' Register*, LXVI, 439; see also p. 372.

Polk by his " Kane letter,"[133] declaring in favor of a tariff for revenue, but with such moderate discriminating duties as would afford incidental protection to home industry. " I am," he wrote, " opposed to a tariff for protection *merely*, and not for revenue." Calling attention to his votes on tariff bills, he declared it

the duty of the Government, to extend as far as it may be practicable to do so, by its revenue laws & all other means within its power, fair and just protection to all the great interests of the whole Union, embracing agriculture, commerce and navigation.

This statement did not go beyond the resolution of the Democratic convention and was clearly limited by the citation of his votes on tariff bills; but " Polk, Dallas, and the Tariff of 1842 " became a protectionist slogan of the Democrats of Pennsylvania, where the Kane letter helped to bring victory for the party.[134]

Polk's election can hardly be said to be due to the issue of Texas and Oregon: many other factors were involved.[135] But his popular vote of 1,337,243, as against Clay's 1,299,062 and Birney's 62,300, showed that, although his expansion policy was clearly understood, he won over Clay by more than 38,000. On the other hand, the combined Clay-and-Birney vote exceeded his by upwards of 24,000.

The following table gives the popular vote by sections:[136]

	Polk	Clay	Birney
New England	178,474	186,586	25,861
Middle Atlantic	442,618	432,003	19,081
South Atlantic	171,706	171,271	.....
South Central	198,099	185,162	.....
North Central	346,346	324,040	17,358
	1,337,243	1,299,062	62,300

From this it will be seen that New England's combined Clay-and-Birney vote was nearly 34,000 against Polk, while that of the Middle Atlantic States was less than 8,500 against him. In the latter section, the supporters of Birney were an important factor

[133] To J. K. Kane, of Philadelphia, June 19, 1844.

[134] McCormac, *op. cit.*, pp. 260–61.

[135] This has been clearly shown by Smith, in his *Annexation of Texas*, Chap. xv.

[136] Compiled from the figures in Edward Stanwood, *A History of the Presidency* (Boston, 1906), p. 223. The totals given in the *Whig Almanac*, for 1845 (New York), p. 53, vary slightly from Stanwood's (even after correction of the former's apparent errors in addition).

in giving Polk the decisive electoral vote of New York. But it is possible that many Whigs in favor of annexation had supported Clay (whose letters were conflicting on this issue), and that other annexationists had voted for him out of personal loyalty or on

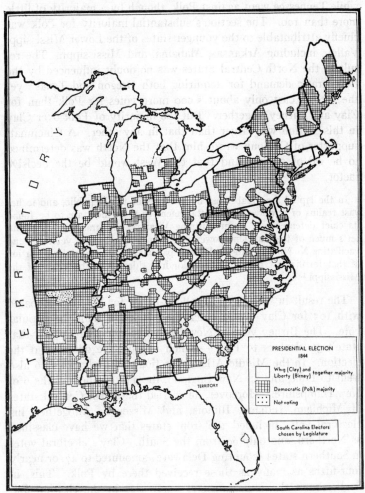

PRESIDENTIAL ELECTION
1844

Whig (Clay) and Liberty (Birney) together majority

Democratic (Polk) majority

Not voting

South Carolina Electors chosen by Legislature

purely Whig principles. Irrespective of the Texan issue, established party habit and Democratic discontent over the failure to renominate Van Buren may account for more votes than Birney received. The misrepresentation of Polk's protectionist attitude was probably responsible for his large vote in Pennsylvania. The South Atlantic section was nearly evenly divided between Clay and Polk. In the South Central, however, Polk led by almost 13,000. Kentucky gave her favorite son a majority of over 9,000, while Tennessee went against Polk, though by a majority of little more than 100. The section's substantial majority for Polk was chiefly attributable to the younger states of the Lower Mississippi Valley, including Arkansas, Alabama, and Mississippi. The result in the North Central States was no doubt influenced by the Democratic demand for acquiring both Oregon and Texas; yet the section cast only about 5,000 more votes for Polk than for Clay and Birney, together. But the majority of Polk over Clay in this section was larger than that in any other. A Cincinnati supporter of Calhoun wrote him that the North was determined to be rid of slavery and that the West would be the decisive factor.

In the lap of the great West lie the keys of the Republic, and in her vast realms of power, and her attachment to the Union, are to be found its chief defense. . . . From usurping Virginia, and grasping Massachusetts much of their ancient power is gone never to return, yet they, and vacillating N. York absorb the Federal patronage: henceforth let a portion of that fertilizing stream flow with kindred tides down the valley of the Mississippi.[137]

The result in the electoral college — 170 for Polk as compared with 105 for Clay — was much more decisive than the popular vote. The Birney vote in New York was sufficient to turn that state's 36 electors to Polk — which would have determined the election. In the Middle Atlantic section, Pennsylvania's 26 also went to Polk, and, in New England, the 9 of Maine and the 6 of New Hampshire. Moreover, he carried the North Central states of Michigan, Indiana, Illinois, and Missouri. Altogether, his electoral votes included 110 from states that we have classified as Northern, and only 60 from the South. Clay's electoral votes in Southern states (counting Delaware) amounted to 47, or nearly four-fifths as many as those received there by Polk. This, in itself, shows the importance of party ties in the election and throws doubts upon the Northern idea of an intrigue by the "slavocracy."

Although the Texan issue was not the only important one in

[137] American Historical Association *Annual Report*, 1929, pp. 281–82.

the election, the discussion and the results tended to strengthen the demand for annexation. Tyler regarded the outcome of the election as a mandate to press the issue. In his last Annual Message,[138] he denounced the Mexican utterances "preparatory to the commencement of hostilities, full of threats revolting to humanity," and urged that Congress annex Texas by joint resolution. Reversing the Calhoun policy, he presented the argument for annexation as a national rather than a sectional interest.[139]

Various proposals were offered in Congress during the succeeding months. The difficulty of uniting the Van Buren and Benton factions, on the one side, and the Calhoun followers, on the other, was very great. The House had passed a joint resolution [140] for annexation of Texas as a state. Such a joint resolution would have substituted approval by merely a majority in each house for the two-thirds necessary to ratify a treaty. In the Senate, Benton, partly responsive to public opinion in Missouri but also desirous of delay and possible defeat of a project urged by his enemy, Calhoun, had proposed a measure that would have required further negotiations and perhaps a treaty with Texas; but the attitude of the Senate had shown that a treaty could not pass that body. A compromise proposed by Senator R. J. Walker, of Mississippi, left the choice between the alternatives to the President of the United States. On February 27, 1845, this compromise passed the Senate (27 to 25), and was adopted by the House (132 to 76), the next day, by substantially a party vote. It seems that the expectation was that the " President of the United States " who would decide between the two alternatives would be Polk. But Tyler, urged by Calhoun and fearing the consequences of delay, construed the phrase as authorizing him to proceed, and, on the last day of his term, after vainly attempting to procure Polk's advice, offered annexation, with statehood, to Texas. Polk accepted Tyler's action.[141]

[138] Dec. 3, 1844. (*Messages and Papers*, IV, 341–45.)

[139] The *United States Magazine, and Democratic Review*, for January, 1845 (XVI, 3–9), in an article entitled " The Abolitionists," criticizes Calhoun for the proslavery tone he had given, in the Pakenham correspondence, to the question of annexation.

[140] See map of the vote, Jan. 25, 1845.

[141] Tyler's account of these events is in *Letters and Times of the Tylers*, II, 364–65. See also Smith, *Annexation of Texas*, pp. 351–55 (with citations). The charge that Polk had expressed a preference for Benton's alternative requiring further negotiation, as presented in von Holst, *United States, 1846–1850* (Chi-

By the terms of the joint resolution's alternative chosen by Tyler, Texas, with rightful boundaries, was to be admitted into the Union as a state, after the adoption of a republican form of

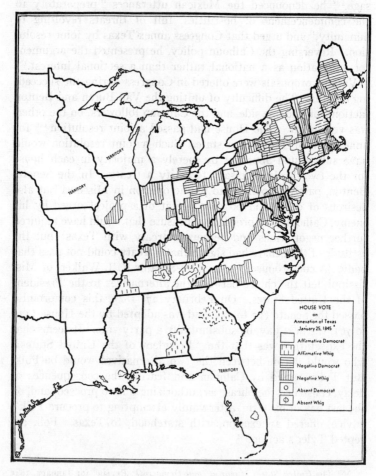

HOUSE VOTE
on
Annexation of Texas
January 25, 1845

☐ Affirmative Democrat

▥ Affirmative Whig

▤ Negative Democrat

▦ Negative Whig

○ Absent Democrat

◌ Absent Whig

government, with the consent of the existing government. Questions of boundary arising with other governments were to be

cago, 1881), pp. 61–66 (with citations), seems to be overborne by the evidence presented in McCormac, *Polk*, pp. 315–18, and by *The Diary of James K. Polk during His Presidency, 1845 to 1849*, ed. M. M. Quaife (Chicago, 1910), II, 84, IV, 38–47, 49, 51–52, and Smith, *op. cit.*, pp. 347–48.

adjusted by the United States, and the state's constitution was to be submitted to Congress by January 1, 1846. Texas was to retain its lands and to be responsible for its own debts. There was a provision that, with its consent, four additional states might be formed out of its territory; and it was stipulated that such of these new states as lay south of the Missouri Compromise line of 36° 30′ should be admitted " with or without slavery, as the people of each State asking admission may desire," but that, north of that line, slavery was to be prohibited.[142]

Thus, the fate of annexation was transferred to Texas; but the final decision on statehood was still to be made by the Congress of the United States. In the spring of 1845, neither President Houston, nor his successor President Anson Jones, publicly favored annexation; and, after the action of the United States Congress, Mexico threatened war and sought to persuade Texas to prefer independence.[143] Had the alternative of continued negotiation been chosen by Tyler and Polk, annexation might have failed.

Looking at the Tyler administration as a whole, one cannot but feel that it exhibited the least satisfactory pages in the history of Henry Clay. Under the spur of ambition and the delusion that the election of 1840 had constituted a mandate to carry out his own ideas of Whig policy, Clay had gone to the extreme in attempting to eliminate Tyler as a possible rival and to discredit him because of his refusal to submit to dictation. Even the friends of Clay realized that he had overreached discretion in his desire to triumph over the President.[144] Later writers are disposed to regard Tyler's vetoes as for the best interests of the country, in spite of the torrent of Whig protest with which they were greeted at the time. Tyler's realization that he had been read out of the Whig party and his knowledge that the Democracy was in the control of his opponents, so far as his political fortunes were concerned, led him to consider the possibility of building up a party of his own — a possibility that no doubt seemed to him like noth-

142 *Congressional Globe*, XIV, 362–63.

143 Adams, *British Interests and Activities in Texas*, pp. 203–18, and Smith, *op. cit.*, Chaps. XVIII, XIX.

144 E.g., see: *Adams Memoirs,* X (Philadelphia, 1876), 387; Carl Schurz, *Henry Clay* (Boston, 1899 [in " American Statesmen " series]), II, 210–12; von Holst, *United States, 1828–1846*, pp. 410, 418–19, 426, 427–28, 455–57; " Ewing Diary," *American Historical Review*, XVIII, 105–6; and Coleman (ed.), *Crittenden*, I, 159.

ing more than the acquisition of a following in support of measures which in themselves were for the nation's good and free from party enmities. His Virginian scruples appeared to some of his Whig critics to be sheer refusal to accept bills to which he had already committed himself. A careful survey, however, points toward the conclusion that his views were sufficiently known to leaders like Clay and his friends to indicate that their bills had been so shaped as to appear to meet his scruples while in reality maintaining their own policy.

CHAPTER XII

[POLK ADMINISTRATION: EXPANSION
AND SLAVERY] *

The administration of James K. Polk was in many ways a continuation of the era of Jacksonian Democracy. He had been the trusted spokesman for Jackson in Congress, and was the beneficiary of the latter's reaction against Benton's Texan letter — a reaction that was probably responsible for Polk's nomination — and the inheritor of the belligerent expansionist policy of the fiery Tennessee leader.

Looking back through the years already covered in this survey, one sees that the popularity of Andrew Jackson clearly marked him out as the expression of the contemporary United States — a country dominated by its rural democracy. He may not have been a man of profound insight into the issues of his time,[1] but those issues were deeply affected by the way he led the public mind in the direction of breaking with the established order. He had won in his contests with most of the leading statesmen who opposed him. Even so violent an enemy as John Quincy Adams came to his support in the crisis of the French-spoliation question, when war threatened.[2] Webster fully recognized his invincible popularity, praised his Nullification Proclamation, and even considered a union with his administration at the time; later, this statesman abandoned the issue of the National Bank and lauded President Tyler's exchequer recommendation, which was in many ways not unlike proposals seriously considered by Jackson during the war on the Bank.[3] His old friend, Hugh Lawson

---

* [This chapter was evidently in an early stage of composition, and no title had been given to it.]

[1] J. Franklin Jameson, in Preface to *Correspondence of Andrew Jackson*, ed. J. S. Bassett, V (Carnegie Institution of Washington, 1931), vi.

[2] See pp. 439, 440, *ante*.   [3] See pp. 422, 498, *ante*.

White, who had been induced to become a Presidential candidate in 1836 against Jackson's favorite, Van Buren, met defeat.[4] Calhoun accepted the Independent Treasury policy of Van Buren — a policy that was the natural outcome of Jackson's victory over the National Bank.[5] Members of Jackson's cabinet had differed with him in his program of destroying this institution, only to be overruled by him and by the people.[6] Far from being plastic in the hands of the " Little Magician," Jackson ignored Van Buren on such vital questions as the composition of his first cabinet, the terms of the Nullification Proclamation, and the time and method of removal of the deposits; and, finally, when Van Buren would not yield to his demand for the annexation of Texas, successfully blocked his nomination and proposed in his stead his new favorite, Polk.[7] William Henry Harrison had been brought to the Presidency in 1840 by the kind of " hurrah " campaign that had led to Jackson's own election; " Tippecanoe " had appealed to the pioneer element, professing, indeed, to be more truly Jacksonian than Jackson himself.[8] Tyler, who alone among the Senators had opposed the Force Bill, acted substantially in the Jacksonian spirit when, as President, he signed the tariff of 1842. When the Whigs, under Henry Clay, brought forward a program that had not been announced during the campaign of 1840, Tyler not only wielded his veto against the National Bank but even administered the Treasury under the system that followed Jackson's overthrow of the " monster." [9] He received Jackson's decisive support in the matter of the annexation of Texas, and, when Tyler finally decided to withdraw his name in the Presidential campaign of 1844, it was Jackson, perhaps, who exercised the determining influence.

In short, this volcanic son of the South Central section represented the dominant forces of his time, and his capacity for the achievement of his ends makes him the outstanding figure of the era.

When Polk became President, he was confronted by serious sectional and party problems. Calhoun's management of the Texan controversy with England had placed annexation primarily on the basis of the menace of a free Texas to slavery, and thus

[4] See pp. 428-30, 438, 440-43, *ante.*   [7] See pp. 383, 417, 423, 524-25, *ante.*
[5] See pp. 461-63, *ante.*   [8] See pp. 479, 481-83, *ante.*
[6] See pp. 405-6, 422-27, *ante.*   [9] See pp. 503-5, 491-94, 496-98, *ante.*

had increased the opposition of many in the Northern sections to annexation as a means of promoting the interests of the South. The Democratic party was threatened by dissensions between the followers and opponents of Van Buren, antislavery sentiment in the North had steadily grown, and the Van Buren wing, angry at the Southern withdrawal of support from their leader, were the more ready to fall into line with this sentiment. Increasing sectionalism was gravely compromising the success of the administration. New England and its migrated sons were responsive to the antislavery movement, and the parent section did not share in the passion of the time for expansion. Moreover, this section and the neighboring Middle Atlantic States were becoming dominantly industrial and keenly interested in the protective tariff. In all these things, the Northeastern states were finding common ground, at the same time that the South, more and more convinced of the importance of slavery in its social organization and fearful of a loss of political power unless territorial expansion were accompanied by slavery, now constituted a potential field for party break-up in behalf of sectional unity. Although conditions were thus shaping to form a sectionalism of North against South, the Border States still played a part of their own, the Mississippi Valley still held a distinct position, and both the North Central and South Central sections, influenced by the hard times that had followed the Panic of 1837, were the sections most eager for expansion into Texas and the Far West.

Determined to be master in his own house and wishing to put an end to the rivalries of the prominent Democratic statesmen, Polk declined to accede to Southern demands to retain Calhoun as Secretary of State; and, in inviting men to serve in his cabinet, he required assurances that they would retire if they became aspirants for the Presidency. " I desire," he wrote James Buchanan, " to select gentlemen who agree with me in opinion, and who will cordially co-operate with me." [10] Although he decided to retire at the end of one term and not to take part in the selection of a successor,[11] his aim was to unify the Democrats under his own leadership.

[10] Feb. 17, 1845. (*The Works of James Buchanan*, ed. John Bassett Moore, VI [Philadelphia, 1909], 110; see also E. I. McCormac, *James K. Polk: A Political Biography* [Berkeley, Calif., 1922], pp. 325–26.)

[11] *The Diary of James K. Polk during His Presidency, 1845 to 1849*, ed. M. M. Quaife (Chicago, 1910), I, 98, 142, 280.

For Secretary of State, he chose Buchanan, of Pennsylvania; for Secretary of the Treasury, Robert J. Walker, of Mississippi; for Secretary of War, William L. Marcy, of New York; for Secretary of the Navy, George Bancroft, of Massachusetts; for Attorney-General, a personal friend, John Y. Mason, of Virginia; and for Postmaster-General, his political confidant, Cave Johnson, of Tennessee. Although this cabinet recognized the influence of the lower half of the Mississippi Valley, it will be noted that the North Central States had, at first, no representative.

The appointment of Buchanan was a concession to Pennsylvania. He was cautious to the verge of timidity, and often the President rejected his diplomatic proposals.[12] In his *Diary*, Polk criticizes Buchanan's habit of softening the President's language, " making the paper less firm and bold than I had prepared [proposed?]." At times, also, Polk had to remind him of his promises regarding Presidential ambitions and to recall to him Secretary William H. Crawford's experience in Monroe's cabinet.[13]

Walker's influence in the nomination of Polk for the Presidency and in urging the advantages of the combination of " the re-occupation of Oregon and the re-annexation of Texas," and the facts that he was a family connection of Vice-President Dallas and was in harmony with the President's tariff views — all contributed to Polk's decision to place him in the Treasury. Although Walker was suspected of corrupt connections regarding the public lands and dealing with Texan scrip, and although Jackson later warned Polk against him [14] and his aspirations for the succession, Polk continued to give him his confidence.

The selection of Marcy [15] as the New York member of the cabinet was made only after Polk had sought to conciliate the Van Buren group by vainly offering portfolios to two warm friends of the former President (the Treasury post to Silas Wright and

---

[12] E.g., see *ibid.*, pp. 17–20, 66–67, 73–77, 99–100, *et passim*. " Mr. Polk," said Buchanan, " was a wise man, and after deliberation he had determined that all important questions with foreign nations should be settled in Washington, under his own immediate supervision." (McCormac, *op. cit.*, p. 330, citing G. T. Curtis, *Life of James Buchanan* [New York, 1883], II, 76, also 72.)

[13] F. J. Turner, *Rise of the New West, 1819–1829* (*The American Nation: A History*, XIV; New York, 1906), pp. 195–98.

[14] *Polk Diary*, I, 67, and McCormac, *op. cit.*, p. 335. On Walker's career, see p. 240, *ante*.

[15] See John Bassett Moore, " A Great Secretary of State: William L. Marcy," *Political Science Quarterly*, XXX, 377–96 (Sept., 1915).

that of War to B. F. Butler) and had finally despaired of satisfying him.[16] The choice of Marcy was a momentous one. For some years he had antagonized Van Buren in New York politics, and became a conservative " Hunker." [17]

On the whole, it was an able cabinet, expected by some to dominate the President. Nevertheless, there is ample testimony to his own control of it.[18] Further evidence of his independence is seen in his replacing Jackson's spokesman, Francis P. Blair, the editor of the Washington *Globe*, by Thomas Ritchie, the veteran editor of the Richmond *Enquirer*. Polk believed that Blair was more interested in the political fortunes of candidates for the succession than in sustaining his administration for its own sake.[19] The first issue of Ritchie's Washington *Union* appeared on May 1, 1845. Although Ritchie desired to support the President's harmonizing policy, his vigorous, but sometimes unwisely irritating, editorials renewed the factional fights within the party and justified the apprehensions which Jackson, moved by his own experience with the Virginia editor, expressed in his correspondence with Polk. In spite of Jackson's efforts to protect Major W. B. Lewis, one of his political advisers, Polk, doubting his loyalty, removed him from the office of Second Auditor of the Treasury. But Jackson remained the President's friend,[20] and apparently admired his courage as a chip of the " Old Hickory " block.

In this era of the triumphant spoils system, Polk was a party man, but he did not think of himself as " proscriptive," and he asserted that he was free from pledges. His failure to give the Tyler faction the Democratic recognition that had been expected was resented by that group. During his administration, somewhat over three hundred removals were made; but his Whig successor, Taylor, removed over five hundred Presidential appointees. Even Webster, recognizing Polk's devotion to party, wrote that he appeared to him " to make rather good selections from among his own friends." [21]

[16] On the relations of President Polk and Van Buren, see McCormac, *op. cit.*, pp. 295–98, and *Polk Diary*, I, 103–5.   [17] See pp. 108–9, *ante*.

[18] See quotations in McCormac, *op. cit.*, pp. 324–30.

[19] See the quotations from correspondence, *ibid.*, pp. 332–33. See also Chas. H. Ambler, *Thomas Ritchie* (Richmond, Va., 1913), pp. 251 ff.

[20] See Jackson's letter of June 6, 1845 (two days before his death) to Polk, who referred to it in his *Diary* (I, 67) as " a highly prized memorial " of the unbroken friendship of Jackson.

[21] See C. R. Fish, *The Civil Service and the Patronage* (*Harvard Historical Studies*, XI; New York, 1905), pp. 158–61, and McCormac, *op. cit.*, pp. 335–49.

Secretary Bancroft, over forty years later, reported that, " soon after he had taken the oath of office," Polk told him that his four great measures would be: reduction of the tariff; an Independent Treasury; the settlement of the Oregon boundary; and the acquisition of California.[22] In the course of forty years, Bancroft may have confused the *results* of Polk's Presidency with a *program* set forth by him at the beginning of his administration. Whether or not Bancroft's memory was correct, all of the objectives with which he credited Polk were achieved by his administration, and some of them were made known in his First Annual Message.[23] No President, perhaps, left a deeper impression than Polk upon the immediate future of the country and upon its destiny largely viewed. Fortune, rather than the man's inherent ability, played a large part in the result, but his own qualities and relentless determination to achieve the goals that he had set for himself, and his willingness to take the chances of war — even against the advice of his Secretary of State — were at least equally potent.

The attitude of Southern statesmen like Calhoun and Tyler, and that shown in the writings and correspondence of Duff Green,[24] had aroused a real conviction on the part of the South, and perhaps of Americans in general, that Great Britain's position on the slavery question and on Texas was primarily determined by the self-interest of her economic policy — the desire for finding a reciprocal exchange, under free trade, between her manufactures and the cotton supply, and of excluding from competition with her the cotton and sugar areas that were given an advantage by their slave economy. Coupled with the resentment of the Mississippi Valley and the South Atlantic States, especially, over any interference by a European rival with the historic movement of American expansion, was, of course, the apprehension with regard to slavery in the neighborhood of a free Texas and with regard to the future of American commerce by way of the Mississippi River and the Gulf of Mexico. Fortunately for the United States, the European situation, the domestic need of food supply,

[22] Jas. Schouler, *History of the United States of America, under the Constitution*, IV (New York [copyright, 1889]), 498 (Bancroft to Schouler, Feb., 1887).

[23] Dec. 2, 1845. (Jas. D. Richardson [compiler], *Messages and Papers of the Presidents, 1789–1897*, IV [Washington, 1897], 385–416.)

[24] See, e.g., St. Geo. L. Sioussat, *Duff Green's " England and the United States": With an Introductory Study of American Opposition to the Quintuple Treaty of 1841* (American Antiquarian Society *Proceedings*, N.S., XL, 175–276).

and the conciliatory attitude of the responsible English statesmen, rendered the solution by war less inevitable.

In his Inaugural Address, Polk sustained his campaign pledge by asserting that the title to the Oregon country was " clear and unquestionable," and he recommended that the laws of the United States be extended over the settlers there.[25] Lord Aberdeen, the English Foreign Secretary, regarded the address as made for the American public rather than as an " official message," but was prepared to support what he called the " clear and unquestionable " rights of England.

After consulting his cabinet, Polk decided to approve Tyler's invitation to Texas, under the general resolution of Congress; and A. J. Donelson, nephew and former secretary of Jackson, was allowed to continue on his way to Texas as chargé d'affaires. He proved a fortunate choice, both because of his natural ability and his relationship to Jackson, which enabled him to deal intimately with ex-President Sam Houston,[26] whose advice was to be so influential toward Texan action on the American offer and who was believed now to be either hesitant or hostile regarding acceptance.

Both France and England were desirous of persuading Texas to remain independent and were exerting their influence on Mexico to bring about such a solution.[27] Neither France nor England, however, wished to press the issue to the point of war. France finally definitely determined not to take such action, and, without her co-operation, England was reluctant to proceed. The Oregon situation rendered England's course still less certain, and proverbial Mexican delay finally incurred the bitter criticisms of both countries.

Meantime, intrigue was still rife in Texas, and the existing government hesitated over the terms of the joint resolution and perhaps even desired independence by some friendly arrangement with Mexico (through French and English intervention). But the Texan public were showing unmistakable preferences for annexation. In May,[28] Houston was induced to visit Jackson at " The Hermitage," and by the latter's persuasion was made more

---

[25] Mar. 4, 1845. (*Messages and Papers*, IV, 381.)

[26] His successor, Anson Jones, a native of western Massachusetts, had been inaugurated December 9, 1844. (Justin H. Smith, *The Annexation of Texas* [New York, 1911], p. 373.)

[27] *Ibid.*, pp. 390–463 (*passim*).

[28] McCormac, *Polk*, pp. 357–58.

friendly to annexation. Polk [29] agreed to protect Texas to the extent of her claim, up to the Rio Grande. President Anson Jones, who was not favorable to annexation and who had scruples regarding his constitutional authority, reluctantly summoned the Texan congress; and, when it met in the middle of June, submitted both a proposal [30] for conditional recognition of independence by Mexico, and annexation by the United States under the terms of the joint resolution. By unanimous vote, it preferred the United States' offer and rejected the Mexican treaty. When the convention, recommended by President Jones, met on July 4, it voted in favor of annexation, followed by the making of a new constitution for the state of Texas; by November 10 President Jones announced that both annexation and the new Texan constitution had been approved by popular vote; and, in his First Annual Message, Polk announced this action and urged the admission of Texas as a state. [31]

Meanwhile, Secretary Buchanan had assured Donelson that the United States would use the army to defend Texas as soon as she accepted the American proposal, [32] and Secretary Marcy had given confidential instructions to General Zachary Taylor. [33] Donelson, in correspondence with Taylor, [34] advised occupation of Corpus Christi (near the mouth of the Nueces), then the farthest point actually held by Texas, as a healthful place and convenient for supplies. Mexico, he admitted, held Santiago, not far from the mouth of the Rio Grande. The ownership of the intervening country, he said, was a disputed question. [35]

At this time, Polk seems to have intended the United States

[29] June 15, 1845. (*Ibid.*, p. 363, citing " Polk-Donelson Letters.")

[30] As signed by the authorities of the two countries, on Mar. 29 and May 19, 1845. (G. P. Garrison, *Westward Extension, 1841–1850* [*The American Nation: A History*, XVII; New York, 1906], p. 155.) It had been worked out chiefly by English influence.

[31] *Messages and Papers*, IV, 386–88.

[32] May 23, 1845. (McCormac, *op. cit.*, pp. 358–59.)

[33] *Ibid.*, p. 364.

[34] June 28, 1845. (*Ibid.*)

[35] But, as McCormac notes (*ibid.*, p. 365), the location of Taylor's troops was suggested by reasons of health and convenience rather than because of the disputed question of possession. The comments of von Holst on Taylor's letter of July 8, 1845, speaking of San Antonio as on the " western boundary " (" *Grenze*," in von Holst) of Texas, may well have been due to a mistaken translation of Taylor's words, the " western frontier." On this point, see the interesting suggestion of McCormac (*ibid.*, pp. 365–66, citing *House Executive Document 60*, 30th Cong., 1st Sess., p. 802).

forces on the frontier of Texas only for defensive purposes.[36] Secretary Marcy had, on July 8, instructed Taylor not to molest the posts of Mexico on the east side of the Rio Grande unless war actually existed. Secretary Bancroft had informed the naval authorities "that while the annexation of Texas extends our boundary to the Del Norte, the President reserves the vindication of our boundary, if possible, to methods of peace."[37] Nevertheless, it would seem that Polk was determined to make use of the boundary demands of Texas, and of our claims against Mexico (which will be considered later), to bring about a military situation that would compel that nation to meet the terms of settlement which he was to propose.[38]

Not only the fate of Texas and its boundary lay in the hands of Polk, but the destiny of the whole Pacific Coast was at stake. California, evidently a region over which Mexico had no real control and torn by its own internal strife, was exposed to acquisition by some other nation.[39] This the administration was determined to prevent.

In the fall of 1845, Lord Aberdeen, in response to a request by Tomás Murphy, the Mexican minister to England, for naval aid against an expected seizure of California by the United States, informed him that he would not commit himself to go to war alone, but that, if war should result from the Oregon question, Mexican offers of co-operation and a land grant in California should be accepted. Murphy added that, were France to join England in opposing the aggressive policy of the United States, the danger that the proposed grant might result in war might not deter England. The suggested land grant by Mexico was to be in satisfaction of the holdings of British owners of Mexican bonds.[40]

Not long after this, Buchanan sent instructions [41] to our consul, Thomas O. Larkin, at Monterey, to discover and defeat attempts

[36] *Ibid.*, p. 376.

[37] *Ibid.*, p. 375.

[38] By the close of August, he had decided that, if Mexico crossed the Rio Grande, Taylor should be instructed to regard this as an act of war against the United States and to drive her back. (*Polk Diary*, I, 8–9.)

[39] See pp. 509–10, *ante.*

[40] G. L. Rives, in *American Historical Review*, XVIII, 289–94 (including a citation of Gordon, *Aberdeen*, pp. 183–84), and *idem*, *United States and Mexico, 1821–1848* (New York, 1913).

[41] Oct. 17, 1845. (*Buchanan Works*, VI, 275–78.)

of foreign governments to establish themselves in California, but to take no part in contests between Mexico and California unless the former commenced hostilities against the United States. He added, however, that, if California asserted and maintained independence, the United States would " render her all the kind offices in our power, as a sister Republic," but that we did not desire more territory " unless by the free and spontaneous wish " of its people. Although this was qualified by the statement that California would be received into the Union when it could be done " without affording Mexico just cause of complaint," the instructions as a whole constituted an indirect invitation to California ultimately to join the United States. Coincident with this letter, Secretary Bancroft issued instructions to our Pacific fleet looking more in detail to the seizure of Californian ports in case Mexico declared war.

Meanwhile, in the Oregon country, England's diplomatic action had been largely shaped by the influence of the Hudson's Bay Company. An expedition of Lieutenants H. J. Warre and M. Vavasour was chiefly instigated by Sir George Simpson, governor of the Hudson's Bay Company. Their first report on Oregon was made toward the close of October, 1845.[42] They had found the river route leading to the passes of the Rocky Mountains impracticable for the support of troops, whereas the route to the Columbia followed by the American pioneer was entirely possible. They mention the fact that, in the summer of 1845, the employees of the Hudson's Bay Company had entered into a compact with the American settlers in Oregon to form a provisional government acceptable to both.[43] Doubtless this arrangement was due to the fear that frontier lawlessness might result in the capture of the company's stores at Vancouver, on the Columbia. As a result, the company transferred its headquarters to Vancouver Island.

Prime Minister Peel, doubtful whether the Hudson's Bay Company or the American settlers held the preponderance of power in the Oregon country, sent to the Northwest coast the frigate " America," whose captain was a brother of Lord Aberdeen and

[42] " Documents Relative to Warre and Vavasour's Military Reconnoissance in Oregon, 1845–6," ed. Jos. Schafer, in Oregon Historical Society *Quarterly*, X, 10, 39 ff.

[43] See R. C. Clark, " The Last Step in the Formation of a Provisional Government for Oregon in 1845," *ibid.*, XVI, 313–29, and Frederick Merk, in *American Historical Review*, XXIX, 689.

aboard which was the son of Peel as a young officer instructed to report on conditions.

In spite of the assertions of his Inaugural Address, Polk felt compelled by the action of his predecessors to offer to England a compromise on the basis of the forty-ninth parallel as the boundary — an offer that Richard Pakenham, the British minister to the United States, brusquely, and much to the regret of his government, declined to consider.[44] Thereupon, Polk withdrew the proposal. Before the close of October, 1845, he was aware, through dispatches from our minister in England, that Lord Aberdeen had condemned Pakenham's actions and had raised the question of whether the United States would renew the compromise proffer. But, when this suggestion was brought before Polk, he decided to let England take her own course rather than to repeat our offer. Knowing that country's attitude and having informed both Buchanan and our minister in London that if England herself should submit a compromise on the basis of 49° he would refer it to the Senate for advice but without approval,[45] he was in a position to press England to action by procuring the abrogation of the existing treaty for joint occupation of Oregon, and at the same time to save his own political consistency by deferring to the Senate. The administration lacked a majority in this body. Whatever of bluff there may have been in his course, the facts that he knew England's reluctance to force the issue to war and her desire for a compromise and that he had formulated his own program, must be borne in mind. When, therefore, in the midst of the contest that soon followed over the proposal to terminate joint occupation, Polk informed a Member of Congress that " the only way to treat John Bull was to look him straight in the eye," [46] he was far from speaking with the recklessness attributed to him by his opponents.

With regard to the part that California played in this program, it may be significant that Polk had a confidential talk with Senator Thomas H. Benton [47] (who for a time now came to support the administration), and that in less than a week thereafter the President held a confidential conversation with Lieutenant A. H.

[44] *Buchanan Works*, VI, 212–20.

[45] *Polk Diary*, I, 62–66 (Oct. 21–23, 1845), 73–83, 134–36, 141, 191–92, and *Buchanan Works*, VI, 366–68 (Buchanan to Louis McLane, Jan. 29, 1846).

[46] Jan. 4, 1846. (*Polk Diary*, I, 155.)

[47] Oct. 24, 1845. (*Ibid.*, pp. 71–72.)

Gillespie,[48] who was to bear Buchanan's instructions regarding California to Larkin,[49] and who was also to give verbal information to John C. Frémont, Benton's son-in-law (then in California).

Oregon, also, received his attention at this time. Pakenham refused to transmit, as official, a note from his government until he learned what its reception by the United States would be, and, since Polk had declined to receive it on those terms, the President had evidently made up his mind to force England to take the initiative in proposals regarding the Northwest,[50] failing which he was determined so to shape his policy concerning the whole Pacific Coast that the entire area would fall within the United States.

Engaged in November in writing his message to Congress, Polk notes the timidity of Buchanan, who feared the Oregon question would lead to war and who continually attempted to soften the President's language regarding Mexico and Oregon.[51] Contemporaneously, Polk had reason for thinking his New York appointments (particularly that of Marcy) had made it likely that Van Buren was discontented and looking to the Presidency.[52] In both of the powerful states of the Middle Atlantic section, the President saw a rising opposition to his administration and to his policy as a representative of the South Central section. He had already been reported as saying that he relied upon the South and West for support and would lead the way for their measures.[53]

Meantime, Polk had been informed by his confidential agent (W. S. Parrott) that Mexico desired to receive a " commissioner " from the United States.[54] The President took this to be a suggestion that a *minister* would be received.[55] However, news from Mexico left him in doubt whether Parrott's report might not have been mistaken, and on September 17, 1845, he and his cabinet agreed to defer sending a minister until it was ascertained officially that he would be accepted.[56] After Parrott reached Washing-

---

[48] Oct. 30, 1845. (*Ibid.*, pp. 83–84.)

[49] See pp. 543–44, *ante.*

[50] Oct. 21–27, 1845. (*Polk Diary*, I, 62–75 [*passim*].)

[51] *Ibid.*, pp. 99, 107–8.

[52] *Ibid.*, pp. 103–4.

[53] American Historical Association *Annual Report*, 1929 (Washington, 1930), pp. 300–302.

[54] Aug. 26, 1845. (McCormac, *Polk*, p. 384.)

[55] *Ibid.*, pp. 389, 392–93, and *Polk Diary*, I, 33–36.

[56] *Ibid.*, pp. 35–36.

ton (November 9), bearing the Mexican note, the President continued to speak of sending a minister. Two days before this, he and Buchanan had settled upon the terms of the instructions to John Slidell (who was chosen as minister to Mexico); after amendment, they were agreed to; and, on the day following Parrott's arrival, when Polk " had a full conversation " with him, the President signed Slidell's commission as *minister*.[57]

For some time, it had been known by the Department of State that any government in Mexico would be endangered by negotiating with a minister from the United States rather than with a commissioner.[58] The question of whether Slidell's commission as minister was due to misrepresentations on the part of Parrott or to Polk's wilful determination to send such an official, is one of the unsolved problems of history. Later, Mexico refused to receive Slidell, on the ground that he was a minister and not a commissioner. This has been explained as arising from a desire of Mexico to resort to technicalities at a time when a revolution threatened the government's downfall.

Slidell's instructions [59] made the question of our claims [60] against Mexico a basis for an adjustment of the boundary quarrel. These claims, extending over many years, were for various acts, against American citizens, in violation of international law. By a treaty of arbitration in 1839,[61] Mexico was held liable for some of these claims, but before long she defaulted in her payments. Again, by the convention of 1843,[62] she agreed to pay the adjusted award, with interest, in instalments, but by 1844 it became clear that she could not meet her obligations, and the Texan issue made her still more unwilling. Instead of using force to collect our claims, as France had done in 1838, Polk now proposed to make use of the

[57] *Ibid.*, p. 93.

[58] McCormac, *op. cit.*, pp. 392–93.

[59] Nov. 10, 1845. (*Senate Documents*, 30th Cong., 1st Sess., VII, No. 52, pp. 71–80; see also *Polk Diary*, I, 91–94.)

[60] John Bassett Moore, *History and Digest of the International Arbitrations to Which the United States Has Been a Party*, . . . (Washington, 1898), II, Chap. xxvi; Justin H. Smith, *The War with Mexico* (New York, 1919), I, 74–81; and C. H. Owen, *The Justice of the Mexican War* (New York, 1908), Chap. x.

[61] W. M. Malloy (compiler), *Treaties, Conventions, International Acts, Protocols and Agreements between the United States of America and Other Powers, 1776–1909* (*Senate Document 357*, 61st Cong., 2d Sess.; Washington, 1910), I, 1101–4.

[62] *Ibid.*, pp. 1105–6.

only means of payment that Mexico possessed — the giving up of her ineffective assertion of ownership of Texas and the granting of the desired boundary to the United States.

To Mexico, the crossing of the Sabine by the United States would have been an act of war. At each stage of the negotiations leading to the annexation of Texas, Mexico had warned us that annexation would be a declaration of hostilities. Historically, Mexico's claim to the territory between the Nueces and the Rio Grande was superior; and constantly recurring revolutions in Mexico would in all likelihood have overthrown any government that might have agreed to Texan annexation. Already, England and France had recognized Texas and later warned Mexico of the dangers arising from her course.

Under modern international practice, the boundary might well have been made a subject for further negotiations; but, in view of conditions in Mexico, of the demands of Texas regarding her boundary (to which Polk had yielded in his negotiations with her), in view of our long patience in regard to the unpaid claims against Mexico, and in view of the fact that the annexation of Texas to the Union as a state was not yet fully accomplished and that foreign influence was still feared, the charge, by the Whigs and other enemies of the administration, that the United States was deliberately preparing a war of aggression, can hardly be sustained. But Polk undoubtedly intended to make such use of Mexico's attitude regarding Texan annexation and our claims against her as would not only result in bringing to the Union all the area that Texas insisted on as embraced within her boundaries, but would also add New Mexico and California. He believed that, if Mexico refused to accept his proposals, she would be responsible for the consequences.

Slidell's instructions proposed that, in satisfaction of our claims against her, Mexico should accept the Rio Grande boundary. If she would also cede New Mexico, in order to " obviate the danger of future collisions," the United States would assume the claims and in addition pay $5,000,000. Slidell was authorized to make a treaty with Mexico on either basis.[63] For New Mexico, together

---

[63] As McCormac (*Polk*, p. 391) points out, the acquisition of California by the United States was not an essential condition of the proposed treaty. In any case, California would not have been prevented from revolting and joining the Union, since no guaranty of Mexican territory was to be offered.

with California northward from San Francisco, he was empowered to offer assumption of the claims, plus $20,000,000, or $25,000,000 if the grant included Monterey.

Reaching the city of Mexico on December 6, 1845, Slidell found the government embarrassed by his early arrival and by his commission as minister, and shortly after the middle of the month Mexico refused to receive him.[64] At the end of the year, a new revolution brought about the downfall of the Mexican government, and the government that followed was even more hostile to negotiations. As a result, the United States felt that its cup of forbearance was full.

While these events were in progress in Mexico, important developments had occurred in the United States. In his First Annual Message,[65] Polk reiterated his campaign pledges; and he urged that Texas, having complied with the conditions of the joint resolution, should be admitted as a state. By the end of the year,[66] this had been done. In his message, the President also referred to the mission undertaken by Slidell. Concerning the Oregon country, he proposed that England should be given notice of the termination of joint occupancy, that measures should be taken for extending the laws of the United States over our settlers there, and that forts should be established along the route thither. Clearly, his words might indicate that he was ready to take the chance of a war in which England and Mexico might both be involved; but he still hoped for a peaceful solution of the difficulties. His recommendation of a reduction of the tariff and his inclination to consider, and refer to the Senate for advice, any new proposition by England regarding Oregon,[67] were soon followed by a favorable attitude, concerning both the Corn Laws and the Oregon question, on the part of leading English statesmen.[68]

Polk's desire for a peaceful solution of the problems that confronted the United States was also shown in his unfortunate dealings with Colonel A. J. Atocha. About a month after it became clear that Slidell's mission would be unsuccessful, this friend of

[64] *Ibid.*, pp. 394–95.

[65] *Messages and Papers*, IV, 385–416.

[66] Dec. 29, 1845. (Smith, *Annexation of Texas*, p. 468, and McCormac, *op. cit.*, pp. 371–72.)

[67] *Polk Diary*, I, 135, 141, and *Buchanan Works*, VI, 366–68.

[68] *Sir Robert Peel . . . From His Private Correspondence*, ed. C. S. Parker, III (London, 1899), 323–24, and Frederick Merk, in *American Historical Review*, XXXVII, 653–77.

the former Mexican dictator, Antonio López de Santa Anna (who was then in exile in Havana), gave Polk to understand that Santa Anna desired to regain power, and that he was favorable to granting our desired boundary (including California from San Francisco northward) in return for some thirty million dollars, and thought that Mexico should appear to be forced to agree to our demands, by naval and military demonstrations which should include the occupation of the Rio Grande.[69] Meantime, Polk was given to understand that to arrange matters with the opposition would require a preliminary sum of money. Beguiled by these considerations, Polk discussed the possibility of an appropriation to facilitate negotiations, and, when war with the United States actually broke out, permitted the wily Santa Anna to return to Mexico, where he became the leader of the Mexican armies and the determined opponent of the American advance. It was to facilitate Santa Anna's supposed scheme that Polk, in a message of August 8, 1846, asked Congress for two million dollars to secure peace.[70] To this request, David Wilmot, a Pennsylvania Democrat, proposed his proviso that slavery should not be permitted in whatever territory might be acquired from Mexico.[71] In different forms, this " Wilmot Proviso " appeared again and again and aggravated the sectionalism of North against South.

Already,[72] Taylor had been ordered to move his forces to the left bank of the Rio Grande, as the boundary of Texas, threatened by invasion. Moreover, the position was thought to be a healthful one and permitted the reception of supplies by sea through the mouth of the river.[73] Not until two months later, however, did Taylor advance to the Rio Grande, against the warnings of Mexico, and occupy Fort Brown (opposite Matamoros), where, April 25, 1846, he was fired on by the Mexicans. The news reached Washington on May 9. On the same day, before its receipt and following an interview on the previous day with Slidell (who had just returned with his story of Mexican conditions), Polk told his cabinet that he had decided on war.[74] Word of the outbreak of hostilities arrived in time, however, to permit him to send a mes-

[69] *Polk Diary*, I, 222–25.
[70] *Messages and Papers*, IV, 459–60.
[71] *Congressional Globe*, 29th Cong., 1st Sess., p. 1217.
[72] *Messages and Papers*, IV, 440–41.
[73] McCormac, *op. cit.*, p. 412.
[74] *Polk Diary*, I, 384–85.

sage to Congress, May 11, 1846,[75] saying that Mexico had "shed American blood upon the American soil." Congress (by votes of 174 to 14 in the House and of 40 to 2 in the Senate) promptly declared that war existed "by the act of the Republic of Mexico." [76]

Deferring, until later, brief consideration of the military campaigns that followed, we may next consider the solution of the Oregon question and the passage of the tariff of 1846,[77] which, together, rendered it more than probable that Great Britain would not participate in the war. In both of these issues, the sectional aspect was clearly in evidence.

The discussion in Congress of the question of giving the prescribed twelve months' notice of the termination of the treaty of joint occupation of Oregon began soon after the President had recommended such action in his message of December 2, 1845. Characterized by Ritchie, the editor of the administration's newspaper organ, as the "monster debate," it continued until well into April of the next year. To Polk it seemed that the debate was shaped rather by party considerations and Presidential aspirations than by the merits of the case.[78] Confusion existed as to the President's intentions — whether or not Great Britain was to be forced to war — and the sectional aspect of the controversy was unmistakable.

Imperialists in the North Central States, led by Senators E. A. Hannegan, of Indiana, Lewis Cass, of Michigan, and William Allen, of Ohio, and Representative Stephen A. Douglas, of Illinois,[79] were ready for war to secure all of Oregon to 54° 40'; and Hannegan, especially, charged that the Southern Democrats, having secured Texas, were ready to violate the pledges of the campaign of 1844 combining Oregon and Texas.[80] This charge of

[75] *Messages and Papers*, IV, 437–43.

[76] *Congressional Globe*, 29th Cong., 1st Sess., pp. 795, 804.

[77] See pp. 554–60, *post.*

[78] *Polk Diary*, I, 280, 297, 345.

[79] Calhoun's correspondence seems to show that they were supported by the popular opinion of their section. E.g., see *Correspondence of John C. Calhoun*, ed. J. Franklin Jameson (American Historical Association *Annual Report*, 1899, II; Washington, 1900), Index (under "Oregon question"); and the letters to Calhoun, for the period, in American Historical Association *Annual Report*, 1929. See also [Thos. H. Benton] *Thirty Years' View*, II (New York, 1856), Chap. CLVII.

[80] Speech of Dec. 30, 1845. (*Congressional Globe*, 29th Cong., 1st Sess., pp. 109–12 [*passim*]. See also p. 379. C. E. Persinger, in *American Historical*

" Punic faith " on the part of Southern Democrats was the more serious because, in the same period, antislavery sentiment was gaining strength in both parties in the North Central section. Even Joshua R. Giddings, the abolitionist, of Ohio, declared himself in favor of the annexation of all of Oregon, now that the South had annexed Texas.[81] The ranks of Northern Whigs and Democrats, alike, were so honeycombed with this sentiment that its strength can by no means be measured by the strictly abolitionist vote.[82]

In the South Atlantic section, the leadership in favor of continued negotiations rather than a decisive break with England over Oregon was taken by Calhoun. Already,[83] he had indicated his belief that the forty-ninth parallel would be a fair compromise, and, March 16, 1846, he made his famous speech on the question of giving notice of the termination of joint occupation.[84] If notice were to be given, he thought, it should include the words of the amendment offered by Senator W. T. Colquitt, of Georgia: " unless the President, in his discretion, shall consider it expedient to defer it to a later period." [85] Calhoun reiterated his belief that a policy of " wise and masterly inactivity " would bring Oregon to us without the danger of war. Through his correspondence with our minister in London, Louis McLane, he had been informed of the English desire for a compromise arrangement.[86] His speech met with the approval of such New England leaders as Edward Everett and Abbott Lawrence. From many states of both of the Southern sections came enthusiastic support.[87] Even the Whig leader, Representative Robert Toombs, of Georgia, who believed that notice of the termination of joint occupation would force an agreement on the basis of the forty-ninth parallel, ad-

Review, XVII, 455–56, and, more fully, in Oregon Historical Society *Quarterly*, XV, 137–46, emphasizes this split, which is minimized by McCormac [*op. cit.*, p. 593].)

[81] *Congressional Globe*, 29th Cong., 1st Sess., pp. 139–40.

[82] See, e.g., T. C. Smith, *The Liberty and Free Soil Parties in the Northwest* (*Harvard Historical Studies*, VI; New York, 1897), and A. B. Darling, *Political Changes in Massachusetts, 1824–1848* (New Haven, 1925), pp. 334 ff.

[83] *The Works of John C. Calhoun*, ed. R. K. Crallé, IV (New York, 1854), 238–58, and *Calhoun Correspondence*, pp. 574–76, 653–54, 656, 660–61, 678–79, 680–81.   [84] *Calhoun Works*, IV, 258–90.

[85] *Congressional Globe*, 29th Cong., 1st Sess., p. 430.

[86] See American Historical Association *Annual Report*, 1929, p. 313.

[87] E.g., *ibid.*, pp. 338–39, 341–42, 343.

mitted: " I don't [care] a fig about *any* of Oregon, and would gladly get ridd of the controversy by giving it all to anybody else but the British if I could with honor. The country is too large now, and I don't want a foot of Oregon or an acre of any other country, especially without ' niggers.' " [88]

Finally (April 16, 1846), the Senate passed the House resolution directing the President to notify England of the termination of the joint-occupation convention, with the important amendment authorizing the President to give the notice " at his discretion." [89] The Senate vote on this amendment (by Reverdy Johnson, of Maryland) was 30 in favor to 24 against.[90] It showed New England in favor of the amendment (8 Whigs to 4 Democrats) and the Middle Atlantic States opposed (2 Whigs to 4 Democrats), by strictly party votes; in the South Atlantic section, the sole vote cast in the negative was that of one Democrat from Virginia; in the South Central section, only two Democratic Senators (one from Alabama and one from Mississippi) supported the amendment, and the others (seven) opposed, while the entire Whig vote was in the affirmative, and, as a whole, the section was evenly divided; the North Central States gave but two Whig votes for the amendment, and all of the eight Democratic votes were against it.

This analysis reveals that, in general, the vote was a party vote, not a single Whig being recorded among the nays, but, also, that the opposition to leaving the question to the discretion of the President, and thus suggesting the possibility of compromise, was strongly concentrated in the West, made up of the South Central and North Central sections. The House, after conference, accepted the amendment (April 23).[91] Nearly a month later, Polk sent the notification to England.

But, in the meantime, England, aware of Congressional sentiment, had decided to offer a compromise yielding the jurisdiction of Oregon up to the forty-ninth parallel, from the Rocky Mountains, through the Strait of Juan de Fuca, to the sea (thus retaining Vancouver Island) — at the same time reserving the title of

[88] *The Correspondence of Robert Toombs, Alexander H. Stephens, and Howell Cobb*, ed. U. B. Phillips (*American Historical Association Annual Report*, 1911, II; Washington, 1913), p. 74.

[89] *Congressional Globe*, 29th Cong., 1st Sess., p. 683.

[90] *Ibid.*, p. 680.

[91] *Ibid.*, p. 721.

the Hudson's Bay Company, and of the British occupants, to hold-ings south of 49°, subject to the jurisdiction of the United States. The important part that the Hudson's Bay Company had played in the whole question was further illustrated by the grant to it of free navigation of the Columbia until the expiration of its charter in 1859. Reiterating his former adverse views, Polk submitted the treaty to the Senate, June 10, for advice, and, after two days' deliberation, that body advised the acceptance of the treaty, which was signed on June 15. Thus, the " bold & firm course " of Polk had resulted in the settlement of the Oregon question with-out war. Incidentally, the refusal of Buchanan to draft the Presi-dent's message submitting the treaty, gave Polk still further grounds for believing that his attitude was dictated by a desire to curry the favor of the Democrats.[92]

While these events were occurring, Congress had also been en-gaged upon the formulation of the tariff of 1846.

On December 3, 1845, Secretary Walker, an avowed freetrader, presented a Report [93] that is one of the outstanding public papers in the history of the tariff, and the lines of which were followed, in the main, by the tariff of 1846. So early as September 13 of that year, the British minister to the United States had informed his government of a conversation with Walker on the terms of the new tariff. The hopes aroused by this prospect of a wider mar-ket for English manufactures and an adequate supply of food-stuffs, at a time when England was in need of both, may have in-fluenced the stand of both Sir Robert Peel and Lord John Russell, in November of 1845, which indicated the probable repeal of the Corn Laws and a conciliatory attitude on the Oregon boundary.[94]

[92] See: *Calhoun Correspondence*, pp. 1081–83 (McLane to Calhoun, May 18, 1846); *Polk Diary*, I, 444–56 (*passim*), 467, 470–71; *Messages and Papers*, IV, 449–50; and Malloy, *Treaties, Conventions*, . . . , I, 656–58.

[93] Printed in *Finance Reports*, V, 4–16, and *Senate Documents*, 29th Cong., 1st Sess., II (Washington, 1846), Doc. 2; reprinted in F. W. Taussig (compiler), *State Papers and Speeches on the Tariff* (Cambridge, Mass., 1892), pp. 214–51, and, in part, in Edward Stanwood, *American Tariff Controversies in the Nine-teenth Century* (Boston, 1903), II, 45–57. Stanwood says that it was reprinted in England by order of the House of Lords.

[94] See American Historical Association *Annual Report*, 1929, pp. 311–15 (McLane to Calhoun, Jan. 3, 1846). See also Donald G. Barnes, *A History of the English Corn Laws from 1660–1846* (New York, 1930), p. 284, n. 29. This book (especially Chap. XII) gives an account of conditions leading to the repeal, with some suggestions as to its influence on the attitude of the various sections of the United States toward the tariff of 1846.

Walker, in his Report, discussed the Constitutional and economic questions arising from protective tariffs. He alleged that

while the profit of agriculture varies from 1% to 8%, that of manufactures is more than double. The reason is, that whilst the high duties secure nearly a monopoly of the home market to the manufacturer, the farmer and planter are deprived to a great extent of the foreign market by these duties. The farmer and planter are, to a great extent, forbidden to buy in the foreign market, and confined to the domestic articles enhanced in price by the duties.[95]

Inasmuch as he realized that the home market was wholly inadequate for the products of the fertile lands of the United States, he declared that they must have a foreign outlet, or the surplus would result in depression of prices. Ohio, Indiana, and Illinois, he said, if cultivated to their fullest extent, could of themselves raise more than sufficient food to supply the entire home market, and Mississippi could meet the nation's cotton requirements. He believed that the repeal of the English Corn Laws would follow reduction of our duties. Famine conditions, particularly the Irish potato-crop failure of 1846, and the general shortage in the food supply, brought victory, toward the close of June of that year, to the school of Richard Cobden, which had worked so effectively for repeal; and, almost contemporaneously, the American tariff of 1846 passed the House.

In accordance with Walker's recommendations, there were several schedules. Luxuries, particularly spirituous liquors, were placed in Schedule A, at 100%; Schedule C, at 30%, included iron and other metals, their manufactures, wool and woolens, and manufactures of leather, paper, glass, and wood — in short, most of the articles under dispute in tariff bills. Cottons were to pay 25%. Against the wishes of Walker, the act finally left tea and coffee free. By this tariff, all specific duties and all minimums were to be abolished; duties were to be levied ad valorem in all cases.

The proposed tariff was a moderation, for revenue purposes, of the act of 1842, rather than strictly a free-trade measure. The need of increased federal funds on account of the Mexican War was clearly one of the reasons for its passage.

The probability of war with Mexico and the discussion of the possibility of war with England over the Oregon boundary, perhaps explain why the Committee on Ways and Means did not

[95] Taussig (compiler), *op. cit.*, p. 235.

report the tariff bill until the middle of April, 1846, and why debate on the measure did not begin until two months later.

It should be observed, however, that the compromise treaty on Oregon was submitted by Polk to the Senate on June 10; that the English repeal of the Corn Laws had for some time been fairly certain; [96] and that on July 3 the tariff won in the House, and, passing the Senate with amendments, was repassed by the House and on July 30 signed by the President.

Because of the adjustment of party to sections in the Presidential election of 1844, sectionalism and party became measurably coincident. In a speech in the Senate,[97] George McDuffie had declared that, on the supposition

that the Union were now peaceably dissolved, and that three separate confederacies were formed — one consisting of the Middle and Eastern States, another of the Western and Northwestern States, and the third of the Southern and Southwestern States — denominated respectively the manufacturing, the farming, and the planting confederacies,

the Northeast, or the industrial " confederacy," deprived of revenue from a high protective tariff, would have to resort to internal taxes and would lose its disproportionate share of appropriations from the federal treasury; that the South and Southwest, under a revenue tariff instead of the high bounty exacted by duties now levied, would prosper through the free interchange of their products and foreign manufactures; and that the West and Northwest would find in the planting states vastly extended markets, at high prices, and would obtain manufactures cheaply. This ominous suggestion of McDuffie was reflected in the sectional votes on the tariff.

The following table shows the House vote of July 3:

	Democrats and Native Americans		Whigs		Totals	
	Affirmative	Negative	Affirmative	Negative	Affirmative	Negative
New England	9	0	0	19	9	19
Middle Atlantic	17	18	0	26	17	44
South Atlantic	34	1	0	8	34	9
South Central	23	0	1	13	24	13
North Central	30	0	0	10	30	10
	113	19	1	76	114	95

[96] Queen Victoria assented on June 26 to the bill of repeal.

[97] Jan. 29, 1844. (*Congressional Globe*, XIII, 201; App., p. 144.) Calhoun, in his South Carolina Exposition of 1828, had considered the effects of a separate customhouse for the South. (See Turner, *Rise of the New West*, p. 327.)

Except for New York, New Hampshire, and the nonindustrial state of Maine, where party lines prevailed, the Northeastern sections (New England and the Middle Atlantic) were strongly opposed to the measure, regardless of party. In Pennsylvania the

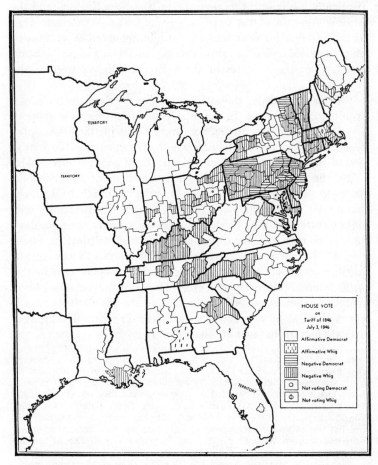

only member in favor of the tariff was David Wilmot, a Democrat from the "northern tier" of counties.[98]   Massachusetts, Connecti-

[98] The former Democratic governor, D. R. Porter, was alleged to have said that, in Wilmot's district, "the only thing the people manufactured were shingles, and they stole the lumber to make them, and the only *protection* they wanted was protection from the officers of justice." (Henry R. Mueller, *The Whig Party in Pennsylvania* [Columbia University *Studies in History, Eco-*

cut, Rhode Island, and New Jersey cast not a single vote for it; and, in New York, the northeastern and western districts (constituting the " Greater New England " parts of that state) opposed it. The South Atlantic and South Central sections were as emphatically in favor of this revenue tariff as New England and the Middle Atlantic States were against it. The Democratic vote of the two Southern sections on the bill amounted to 57 ayes to only 1 nay (Maryland). However, all but 1 (that of an Alabama member) of the 22 votes of Whig Representatives were in the negative.

But, in the Senate, the attitude of the Southern sections was even more influential. In the final vote, of 28 to 27, the support given the bill by the two Senators from Texas justified the apprehensions of Joshua R. Giddings, who had warned that the admission of that state would place the balance of power in her hands. " Are," he asked, " the liberty-loving democrats of Pennsylvania ready to give up the tariff . . . in order to purchase a slave-market for their neighbors . . . ? . . . are the mechanics and manufacturers of the North prepared to abandon their employments, in order that slave-markets may be established in Texas . . . ? " [99] The speech showed clearly that the North was uniting hostility to slavery with the fear of Southern opposition to the tariff, internal improvements, etc. That Pennsylvania had been mistaken in her support of " Polk, Dallas, and the Tariff of 1842," was made clear by the casting vote of Vice-President Dallas, at a critical juncture, in favor of the tariff of 1846.[100]

---

nomics and Public Law, CI, No. 2; New York, 1922], p. 133, n. 1, quoting from Philadelphia North American, Nov. 18, 1846.) In defying the protectionist sentiments of Pennsylvania, Wilmot relied upon the loyalty of his district, which evidently still reflected its frontier traits. (See pp. 96-99, ante.) Wilmot's own attitude is presented in C. B. Going, David Wilmot, Free-Soiler (New York, 1924), pp. 84-93 and Chap. x. He had desired a higher tariff on iron, but was opposed to the act of 1842. There was apparently little or no connection between Wilmot's Proviso and his district's re-election of him in 1846 on the tariff issue.

[99] Joshua R. Giddings, Speeches in Congress (Boston, 1853), pp. 104-6, quoted by Carter G. Woodson, The Negro in Our History (Washington, 1922), p. 355. There is a letter (John Connell to W[illiam] D[avid] Lewis, Mar. 21, 1846) in the manuscripts of the Huntington Library, intimating that the attention of Senator Sam Houston would be drawn to the fact that, if he came out in favor of the [former protective] tariff, " it would soften down nearly all the hostility against Texas " and assist in enabling that state to carry out her views and interests. (William David Lewis had been secretary to Henry Clay.)

[100] On his action, see Stanwood, Tariff Controversies, II, 79-81.

The North Central States turned the balance between the sections. Their affirmative vote in the House, on July 3, was three times their negative, and was on party lines, the section having shown, in the election of 1844, its preference for the policies of Polk and the Democratic party. It was reported to Calhoun [101] that Hannegan, the influential Indiana Senator, had said, before the meeting of Congress, that " the West will be united and will demand funds for the improvements of their harbours, rivers and the Cumberland road, and the graduation of the price of the public land, and that if the South will give these to the West the West will go with the South on the tariff." This is a clear indication of the sectional bargaining that was in progress. The North Central States shifted from their tariff alliance with the Northeast to an alliance with the South, and the change was decisive until the Civil War. The importance of the attitude of the section appears from the fact that, in the House vote of July 3, the majority cast by the South Atlantic States in favor of the tariff of 1846 was only slightly less than that of the Middle Atlantic States against it. New England's negative majority of 10 was overborne by the affirmative majority (11) of the South Central States. Therefore, the North Central section's majority of 20 in support of the tariff was decisive in the result.

The reason for the shift of this section was dominantly political; but the facts that, with an agricultural surplus demanding export and with the passion for Oregon expansion, she should come into agreement with the South on the tariff would, in themselves, go far to explain the section's attitude. While it is true that the restrictions of the English Corn Laws had been mitigated by the North Central States' outlet for their wheat through Canada (which was given preferential treatment), and while they thus, to some extent, had an advantage over northern Europe, yet the prospect of a free and extensive market in England for their surplus food supplies, at a time of famine conditions there, must have been influential upon the section. Moreover, it had come to look more favorably upon England as a result of the compromise treaty on the Oregon boundary, which Polk had submitted to the Senate several weeks before the House voted on the tariff.

This tariff did not produce the dire results expected by the

[101] Duff Green to Calhoun, Sept. 24, 1845. (*Calhoun Correspondence*, p. 1055.)

Whigs. Cotton manufacturers were not harmed; but the woolen manufacturers suffered from the thirty per cent duty on wool, although a raw material, and this protection to wool growers may have contributed to the North Central section's support of the tariff. The lead industry complained bitterly. But, on the whole, the great increase of American trade, both exports and imports, with Europe; the success of the tariff as a revenue producer; and the return of prosperity, after the late panic — prosperity that reached its height with the gold discoveries in California — resulted in the persistence of the revenue type of tariff until the Civil War.

For our purposes, the important facts are that Polk's policy had now, not only brought England and the North Central section closer together over the settlement of the Oregon question, but, also, had changed that section's long-held views upon the tariff and had led it to unite with the South in the enactment of a revenue measure that endured, in principle, until hostilities broke out between North and South, and that won the favor of England.

In the course of the Mexican War, Polk showed himself fundamentally a Democratic politician desiring to redeem his pledges, to unify his party, to mitigate sectional animosities, and, at the same time, to carry out his policy of expansion in the spirit of Andrew Jackson and in accordance with the traditional attitude of the Mississippi Valley. It was not Calhoun and the " slavocracy " that guided his official conduct — a belief that has led historians, influenced by the charges of the Whig and some of the Democratic chieftains, to criticize the administration with unwarranted severity for its course in dealing with Mexico. Many of them wrote in the period when political conflict over the issues that were uppermost during Polk's Presidency was still rife and were affected by their sectional and party prejudices following the Civil War. Some of the most able of these historians were from New England and were still responsive to the section's interpretation of the policies of Jackson, Tyler, and Polk as those of an " aggressive slavocracy." John Quincy Adams's views cast a lengthened shadow over historical writing. Moreover, historians have been affected by the bitter denunciation of his course, with regard to Mexico, by such Democratic leaders as Calhoun and Benton. It must be remembered, however, that the years of Jackson's Presidency had brought Calhoun and Polk to the parting of the ways and that Polk had refused to make him a member of his cabinet and had believed that he was more concerned with the cause of slavery than with that of the Union. The South Central section's ambition for expansion to the Pacific, as voiced by Polk, met with the opposition of Calhoun, who was apprehensive that a war might add to the United States regions from which slavery was already excluded by Mexican law or from which Congress might attempt to exclude it. A victorious war, attaching new areas to the nation, might result in the loss to the South of the increased political power gained by the annexation of Texas and would even add to the number of free states.

Benton, also, came to be as severe in his version of Polk's course as were the Whig critics; but here, again, it must be recalled that, although for a time he and Polk were on friendly terms, yet after the President's failure to secure for him the supreme command in the war and more particularly when the administration found itself constrained to favor the court-martialing of his son-in-law, Frémont (because of his activities in California), Benton broke with Polk and, in his *Thirty Years' View*, turned upon him the vials of his wrath.

In determining to risk a war with Mexico in order to procure territorial cessions in exchange for our claims against her, President Polk was faced with serious situations. Mexico, although warned by England and France, failed to realize the potential military strength of the United States. She was aware of the bitter party and sectional divisions within the United States regarding the Texan question. The vain and proud-spirited people of the Mexican republic, overconfident of their own prowess, would revolt against any administration which would relinquish considerable parts of the territory that she claimed, even though Texas was already effectually lost and California was only nominally a part of her domain. Nevertheless, Polk persisted in his obsession that he could purchase a peace with hardly more than the threat of hostilities.

For a real war, the President was confronted with many obstacles. There was a lack of effective military preparation and organization. The New England section was in opposition. It was swayed by the fear of slavery extension and by the same attitude toward the increase of our territory that it had shown in connection with the Louisiana Purchase. It also feared for the

safety of its manufacturing enterprises, menaced by the increase
of the area opposed to a protective tariff, and was influenced by
the contemporaneous movement of its peace societies.[102]

This sectional attitude was violently expressed, not only by
New England's statesmen, like Webster and John Quincy Adams,
but even more extremely by her poets. In his *Biglow Papers*,
James Russell Lowell declared:

> But *my* narves it kind o' grates,
> Wen I see the overreachin'
> O' them nigger-drivin' States.
>
> .   .   .   .
>
> Ez fer war, I call it murder.

The soldiers' uniforms he characterized as "darned like them
wore in the state prison." [103]   And yet, some years later, writing of
the war, he admitted: "We had as just ground for it as a strong
nation ever has against a weak one." [104]   Although Lowell's was
perhaps the most caustic arraignment of the war, the utterances
of other leading poets, newspaper editorials, and even resolutions
of legislatures, showed a similar sectional opposition. The Massachusetts legislature declared the war one of conquest, "hateful
in its objects," "wanton, unjust and unconstitutional." [105]   Nor
was this opposition limited to New England: in many other parts
of the North, particularly where the sons of New England had migrated, there were like outbursts, notably the speech of Senator
"Tom" Corwin, the Ohio Whig orator, who said that, if he were
a Mexican, he would greet the Americans "with bloody hands"
and welcome them "to hospitable graves." [106]

This attitude was strengthened by the fact that Polk had fully
accepted the Rio Grande as the boundary of Texas (and consequently of the United States), although he might have negotiated
regarding the comparatively worthless disputed region between
the Nueces and the Rio Grande. The Presidential messages asserting that Mexico had shed American blood upon American

[102] See p. 78, *ante*.

[103] Justin H. Smith, "The Biglow Papers as an Argument against the
Mexican War," Massachusetts Historical Society *Proceedings*, XLV, 602–11.

[104] Horace E. Scudder, *James Russell Lowell* (Boston, 1901), I, 257.

[105] Apr. 26, 1847. (H. V. Ames [ed.], *State Documents on Federal Relations*, No. VI [Philadelphia, 1906], p. 2.)

[106] *Congressional Globe*, 29th Cong., 2d Sess., App., p. 217. See also J. B.
McMaster, *A History of the People of the United States, from the Revolution
to the Civil War*, VII (New York, 1919), Chap. LXXXI.

soil led, early in the next Congress, to the celebrated " spot resolutions " of the young Whig Representative, Lincoln, of Illinois, demanding that Polk should indicate the spot on which this occurred.[107] The President's desire to acquire California, New Mexico, and possibly part of northern Mexico itself, doubtless influenced his action in ordering Taylor to the Rio Grande.

When Congress responded to Polk's message, on the outbreak of hostilities, by a bill whose preamble declared that, " by the act of the Republic of Mexico, a state of war exists between that Government and the United States," Calhoun passionately exclaimed that " it was just as impossible for him to vote for that preamble as it was for him to plunge a dagger into his own heart, and more so." [108] The bill preceded by a month the submission of the Oregon compromise treaty to the Senate, and Calhoun was desirous that the Oregon question should be settled before a war with Mexico was begun. It may be that he also had in mind the possibility of an alliance, such as had been suggested by his speech in the Memphis Convention, between the West and the South over tariff and appropriations for internal improvements: [109] these hopes a war would destroy. His Constitutional scruples were also opposed to the preamble. His opposition awakened much criticism in the South, and possibly ruined his hopes for the Presidential nomination.

In the selection of his generals, Polk prepared the way for later political trouble for himself. Both Taylor and Winfield Scott were Whigs. Even at the time of his early victories, Taylor, apparently forgetting the slowness of communication, resented what he thought to be the administration's failure to give approval; " perfectly disgusted " with the inefficiency at Washington,[110] he also criticized the " ambitious views of conquest & agrandisement " of the United States, and soon came to believe Polk's purpose to take California an " outrageous " piece of land-grabbing. Almost from the first, Scott, who was given command of the army, declared that he could not go until September, and wrote insultingly that he feared " a fire upon my rear from Washington and the fire in front from the Mexicans." [111]

[107] *Congressional Globe*, 30th Cong., 1st Sess., p. 64. See also Albert J. Beveridge, *Abraham Lincoln, 1809–1858* (Boston, 1928), I, *passim*.

[108] *Congressional Globe*, 29th Cong., 1st Sess., p. 796.

[109] See pp. 225–27, *ante*.   [110] McCormac, *Polk*, pp. 431 ff.

[111] *Polk Diary*, I, 413–16, 419–21.

As the brilliant victories of Taylor and Scott were reported, the politicians came to see in these men timber for the Whig nomination in 1848 — a fact which was not pleasing to the Democratic President and which led the generals to believe that his supposed failure to support them was due to this.

For the purposes of this work, it is not necessary to enter into the details of the campaigns and battles of the Mexican War.[112]

Early in May, 1846, Taylor defeated the Mexicans at Palo Alto and at Resaca de la Palma, and, shortly after the middle of the month, crossed the Rio Grande and occupied Matamoros (which the Mexicans abandoned); but not until September did he advance to the capture of Monterey. The armistice deemed necessary by him to secure a proper force and equipment for further operations angered Polk, who set it aside. Taylor next took possession of Saltillo, and by the close of the year had seized Victoria, in Tamaulipas. His indignation grew strong when he was deprived of half of his troops to reinforce Scott at Vera Cruz. Without awaiting attack from that port, Santa Anna, who was now in power, rushed a vastly superior force against Taylor at Buena Vista (near Saltillo), where, on February 23, 1847, Taylor, with an army chiefly of volunteers,[113] won a surprising victory, which made him, in the public mind, the hero of the war. He returned to the Rio Grande, where the American troops that had served under him remained unmolested during the rest of the war. His preference for the occupation of only northern Mexico having been frustrated, he himself went home on leave of absence and watched the growing sentiment in his favor as a Presidential possibility.

While Taylor's campaigns were in progress, Polk was setting in motion an army of the West for the purpose of securing New Mexico and California. Believing that a policy of friendly assurance to the discontented Mexicans, there, would make it easy to bring about incorporation of those regions in the Union, the President relied upon a small force.

Early in June, 1846, General Stephen W. Kearny left Fort Leavenworth. The governor of Missouri was asked to furnish a thousand mounted volunteers. Kearny was not to wait for them,

---

[112] The detailed account by Justin H. Smith, in his *War with Mexico*, is a work of sound scholarship.

[113] Edward Channing, *A History of the United States*, V (New York, 1921), 596-97, discusses the misunderstandings between regulars and volunteers.

however, but was instructed to enlist a few hundred Mormons, then en route under Brigham Young to what was supposed to be California. The President desired, not only to have their military aid, but, if possible, to prevent them from establishing an independent nation in the Far West.[114]

This Mormon battalion, numbering some five hundred, was recruited at Council Bluffs, Iowa, the Mormon leaders seeing in the arrangement a means of getting supplies and pay for the men — as well, perhaps, as protection for their westward trek.

Reaching Santa Fe in the middle of August, Kearny easily gained possession, and, before the end of September, had established a civil government for New Mexico. The organic law, based upon the statutes of Missouri, that he drew up, promised territorial status; but, when this caused violent reactions in Congress, Polk decided that Kearny had exceeded his instructions.

Leaving orders for the Mormons to follow him, and for Colonel A. W. Doniphan, with the Missouri volunteers, to join the forces of the United States at Chihuahua, Kearny set out for California. The main body of the Mormon battalion arrived there at the beginning of 1847; and, at the end of their period of enlistment, some of the men returned to settle with their fellow-religionists at Great Salt Lake.

The story of Doniphan's expedition gives, likewise, an example of the quality of the men of the frontier. Not unlike the Kentuckians in the War of 1812 — roughly clad, unshorn, insubordinate, and profane — they took their way across forbidding deserts, through El Paso, defeating some four times their own number in a battle; occupied Chihuahua (a city of perhaps 14,000) in the spring of 1847; and at length returned to Matamoros, whence they passed by sea to New Orleans and thence marched home to Missouri. William Cullen Bryant compared the expedition to Xenophon's *Anabasis*, in the distances covered and the spirit of adventure.

While Kearny was proceeding to California, he met Kit Carson with the news that the country was already conquered. Retaining but one hundred dragoons, he continued, only to be met by word that a fresh uprising had occurred. Early in December of 1846, he was forced to give battle to the Californians, but finally succeeded in reaching the coast, at San Diego. Shortly

[114] *Polk Diary*, I, 445–46, 449–50.

after the close of the year, he took part in a victorious engagement near Los Angeles, which ended the Mexican resistance.

To understand the situation that Kearny had to face on his arrival in California, it is necessary to recall the episode of the Bear Flag insurrection.[115]

Early in 1846, Frémont, instead of going to Oregon as he had told the Mexican authorities at Monterey that he would, returned to San Jose, and was ordered by José Castro, the Mexican *comandante*, to leave. In the spring he retired to Sutter's Fort, and thence went northward until he received the dispatches and verbal information that had been sent him through Lieutenant Gillespie.[116] Although the dispatches merely reiterated the government's desire to conciliate the Californians, with a view to a possible connection with the Union, he later professed that the information borne by Gillespie, read in the light of what he knew of the policy of Polk and Benton, justified his precipitation of war. His actions that followed were, however, rather the result of his own wilful nature than expressive of the wishes of the administration.[117] Gillespie's interview with Frémont occurred on the very day that news reached Washington of the outbreak of hostilities with Mexico and that Taylor won the victory of Resaca de la Palma. But knowledge that Mexico and the United States were at war was not received in California until considerably later.

However, on June 14, 1846, before this news arrived, a party of Americans, apprehending that Castro was about to attack them, raised the "bear flag" and declared California an independent republic. Frémont brought his force to their assistance.[118] But the "Bear Flag republic" was of brief duration.

While off the coast of Mexico, Commodore John D. Sloat learned, as early as the middle of May, that war had broken out; but it was not until the seventh of July that he raised the American flag at Monterey. Two days later, on his orders, the posts on San Francisco Bay were occupied. He was superseded

[115] See pp. 374–75, *ante*.
[116] See pp. 545–46, *ante*.
[117] Smith, *War with Mexico*, I, 331–33; Josiah Royce, *California, from the Conquest in 1846 to the Second Vigilance Committee in San Francisco* [1856] (Boston, 1886 [in "American Commonwealths" series]), Chap. II; and McCormac, *Polk*, pp. 425 ff.
[118] See p. 375, *ante*.

in the command of the Pacific squadron by Commodore R. F. Stockton, who established a government over the conquered Californians. This action did not meet with local approval. Instead of the friends that the American government had hoped to secure, it found itself opposed by a rebellious people.

Thus, in the course of the year 1846, the United States had made good its claim to Oregon south of the forty-ninth parallel, by peaceful adjustment, and had won California and New Mexico, by war. With Texas already a state, a vast new section, the Far West, had been added to the Union. Altogether, it amounted to over 1,200,000 square miles — an area nearly fifty per cent greater than that of the Louisiana Purchase. It was a section made up of lofty mountain ranges (treasure houses of precious metals), towering forests, fertile valleys, and the coasts of the western sea. Occupation of this vast province would demand the adaptation of the American to different conditions from those he had met on his previous advances. The passion for fulfilling the " manifest destiny " of the United States had won the enthusiasm of " Young America "; and a new future for the nation had opened on the Pacific.

Turning, now, to consider the military operations, from the east coast of Mexico, against the capital city, we find that Polk had to deal with the problems arising from the selection of the commanding general and with the question of whether, under the spirit of " manifest destiny," we should acquire all of Mexico.

Discontented with Taylor and perhaps influenced by his growing popularity as a possible nominee for the Presidency, Polk decided to supersede him by the appointment of General Scott. He was reluctant to make this appointment of a man " hostile to the administration," but yielded to the advice of his cabinet on the ground that Scott was " the highest officer in command in the army." On November 19, 1846, he informed the General he had been selected.[119] Apparently Scott, after conversations with the President, temporarily abandoned his previous critical attitude. He soon left to take charge of the operations from the east against the city of Mexico, and wrote praising Taylor but informing him that he would have to take a large part of his (Taylor's) army for his own operations.[120]

But, even before Polk was thus replacing Taylor by Scott, an-

[119] *Polk Diary*, II, 241–45.   [120] McCormac, *op. cit.*, pp. 477–78.

other Whig, he was holding conversations with the Democratic Senator Benton, who suggested [121] that he himself be made Lieutenant General, with diplomatic powers and the rank of commander in chief, and who, according to his own account, persuaded Polk to substitute, for the plan of a " sedentary " occupation of the conquered part of the north of Mexico (until that nation came to terms), a plan of operations, with " a large and overpowering force," designed to push an advance against the Mexican capital by co-operative armies from the north and from the eastern seaboard.[122]

The day before Polk had informed Scott of his appointment, he had assured Benton that, if he could induce Congress to create the office of Lieutenant General, he would name him " to command the whole forces." [123] This promise he repeated a fortnight after Scott had accepted the command of the expedition, by way of Vera Cruz, against the city of Mexico.[124] On December 29, he sent a message to Congress recommending the appointment of such a general officer; [125] but the Senate tabled the proposal — a fact that Benton attributed to the covert influence of Marcy, Walker, and Buchanan, members of Polk's cabinet.[126]

When Scott learned of this unexpected attempt to place Benton over him, his dislike and suspicions of the President were naturally revived. His anger was further inflamed when Polk, still hopeful of securing a peace by financial negotiations and by providing the necessary money to win-over Santa Anna (who, from representations of Colonel Atocha, he believed willing to come to an agreement), sent N. P. Trist, the chief clerk of the Department of State, as an agent to negotiate with the enemy while Scott was advancing. He bore a draft of a treaty providing for the acceptance of the Rio Grande boundary and the cession of New Mexico and California in return for our assumption of the claims and the payment of from fifteen to thirty million dollars, depending upon the terms to be made and the territory to be acquired.[127]

Early in March, 1847, Scott landed at Vera Cruz, took the castle

[121] Nov. 10, 1846. (*Polk Diary*, II, 227.)
[122] [Benton] *View*, II, 678, 693–94. Cf. *Polk Diary*, II, 232–33.
[123] *Ibid.*, p. 243.
[124] *Ibid.*, pp. 261–62. See also pp. 268–70.
[125] *Messages and Papers*, IV, 508.
[126] [Benton] *View*, pp. 678–79; *Polk Diary*, II, 419–20.
[127] *Ibid.*, pp. 466–68, 471–75.

of San Juan de Ulúa from the rear, and, by the rapidity of his advance, surprised the Mexicans and avoided the dangers of the fever-infested coast. Santa Anna, relying upon the obstacles at Vera Cruz to Scott's progress, had left the port exposed while he rushed to attack Taylor at Buena Vista. Hurriedly returning from his defeat there, he showed great energy in rallying his forces for the defense of the capital. Scott, after his victory at Cerro Gordo in the middle of April, refused to forward Trist's letters to the Mexican authorities, and the administration's agent was obliged to send them through Charles Bankhead, the English minister to Mexico. Before long, however, Scott and Trist ceased their misunderstandings, and became fast friends in their common criticism of Polk.[128] Scott's little army succeeded in forcing its way toward the " Hall of the Montezumas," partly because of its own daring, partly because the General himself was an able commander, who had with him men, such as R. E. Lee, G. B. McClellan, and G. G. Meade,[129] afterwards famous as officers in the Civil War, but also because the American superiority in cannon was effective here, as it had been in the campaigns of Taylor.

In the course of the summer, the Americans won the victory of Churubusco, followed by a brief armistice to permit Trist and the Mexicans to negotiate; but when the latter refused the American terms and were taking advantage of the opportunity to improve their defenses, Scott resumed the offensive, and, at Molino del Rey and Chapultepec, won victories that enabled him, by the middle of September, to occupy the city of Mexico.

But, early in October, Polk, unaware of this, directed the recall of Trist.[130] Nevertheless, the latter, believing it to be the last chance, took matters into his own hands, and, while writing insulting dispatches to the government,[131] continued to negotiate, and finally secured the treaty of Guadalupe Hidalgo, signed February 2, 1848. The Rio Grande boundary was established, and New Mexico and California (not including Lower California) were ceded to the United States, which, in turn, agreed, in addition to assuming the claims of American citizens, to pay Mexico $15,000,000.

The treaty, reaching Washington on February 19, placed the President in an awkward position. As his *Diary* shows, its terms

[128] McCormac, *op. cit.*, pp. 509–12.
[129] Channing, *United States*, V, 601.
[130] *Polk Diary*, III, 185.
[131] *Ibid.*, p. 367.

were within the instructions given to Trist when he left for Mexico; and Polk, in spite of resentment over his agent's insubordination, concluded to submit the treaty to the Senate, fearing the consequences of its rejection by himself. Made on his own terms, if it were not now accepted he apprehended that Congress, influenced by the charges that conquest of Mexico was the purpose of the war, would refuse him men and money for its continuation, the army would waste away, and he might lose New Mexico and California through victory of the Whigs in the Presidential election. In coming to this decision not to demand additional Mexican territory, he had to antagonize those of his cabinet who were in favor of still greater annexations.[132]

Early in 1847 Calhoun had declared that " Mexico is to us the forbidden fruit; the penalty of eating it would be to subject our institutions to political death." [133] But the spirit of " manifest destiny " had now gone so far that Secretary Walker [134] and Senator Hannegan of Indiana were demanding the whole of Mexico. Even Buchanan, in a proposed draft of the President's message of December 7, 1847, would have him say that, if the Mexicans did not come to terms, the United States " must fulfill that destiny which Providence may have in store for both countries." But Polk did not contemplate the conquest of Mexico, and retained his own language rather than throw upon Providence the responsibility for acquiring Mexico. Yet, earlier, even he had contemplated the acquisition of part of northern Mexico, if necessary for indemnity.[135]

On February 22, 1848, the President submitted the treaty for the Senate's consideration,[136] and it was accepted by that body on March 10 (38 to 14).

Although Polk showed a prudent attitude toward the acquisition of all Mexico, his objections to the possible transfer of Texas, Oregon, or California to any European power, and his desire to acquire Cuba and Hawaii, so enlarged the Monroe Doctrine that his declarations have been dubbed the " Polk Doctrine." [137]

---

[132] *Ibid.*, pp. 346–50.
[133] Feb. 9, 1847. (*Congressional Globe*, 29th Cong., 2d Sess., App., p. 324.) [Professor Turner intended to add a statement of Webster's attitude.]
[134] *Polk Diary*, III, 229.
[135] *Ibid.*, I, 496–97; II, 16; III, 161, 164.
[136] *Messages and Papers*, IV, 573–74.
[137] McCormac, *op. cit.*, Chap. XXIV.

In the spring of 1848, the President, in a message to Congress,[138] reported an offer from Yucatan, a department of Mexico, to transfer its sovereignty to the United States. His *Diary* shows [139] that he was ready to annex the department in preference to allowing it to pass to Great Britain. He left the matter of measures to Congress. In the debate Senator Cass declared: " The Gulf of Mexico, sir, must be practically an American lake for the great purpose of security." [140]   However, the episode served only as a means for exhibiting jingo sentiment, for Yucatan soon settled its own difficulties.

The day the President's message transmitting the treaty of Guadalupe Hidalgo was received by the Senate, John Quincy Adams died. Stricken while at work at his desk in the House of Representatives two days earlier, his career ended, as he would have wished, while he was still serving the nation. His devotion to duty as he saw it, his ardent support of his country's foreign interests, his courage, and his skill in argumentation, were recognized even by those who hated the venerable statesman and who abhorred his sectional attitude toward Texas, the right of petition, and slavery. His death closed one chapter in the history of the slavery struggle and opened another, fraught with grave peril to the Union.

In the course of the war with Mexico, the sectionalism of North and South had greatly increased. The North Central States were increasingly finding bonds of connection with the Middle Atlantic and New England. The South Central section, likewise, was gradually losing its individuality, and merging with the South Atlantic under the developing menace to slavery. But these transformations were still incomplete. The sections of the Mississippi Valley were still swayed by influences that separated them from the East and carried them on in a course of their own. The border states remained a distinct zone between the North and the South, belonging entirely to neither. It is misleading to write of the struggle of North against South, without recognition of the fact that both North and South were composed of Eastern and Western wings and that the nationalism of the two great parties continued to render collision between the slaveholding and the free states

138 *Messages and Papers*, IV, 581–83.
139 III, 444–45.
140 *Congressional Globe*, 30th Cong., 1st Sess., App., p. 616.

difficult. These parties were still responsive to the peculiarities of the sections and the ambitions of their leaders.

To trace the events that led to the Presidential campaign of 1848 and to the crisis that was postponed by the Compromise of 1850, we must return to consider how the Wilmot Proviso and the territorial organization of the newly acquired lands occasioned bitter struggles, at the same time that economic and social developments were preparing the way for a new era.

The Wilmot Proviso ———

[At this point the narrative was cut short by Professor Turner's death. He had made, in December, 1931, an outline for the then unwritten portions of the chapter. Of these, the following topics had not been covered:

" Wilmot Proviso and sectional reactions."
" ' Manifest destiny ' and efforts to extend slave territory."
" Campaign of 1848 — include Memphis and Chicago conventions; split in Mississippi Valley."
" Problem of organization of acquired territories, to end of Polk's administration."

He had, moreover, prepared the following résumé to conclude this chapter:]

Thus Polk closed his Presidency, having added to the nation a vast new area. He had seen the triumph of that movement of the Southwestern pioneers which Theodore Roosevelt has described in the words:

In obedience to the instincts working half blindly within their breasts, spurred ever onwards by the fierce desires of their eager hearts, they made in the wilderness homes for their children, and by so doing wrought out the destinies of a continental nation. They warred and settled from the high hill-valleys of the French Broad and the upper Cumberland to the half-tropical basin of the Rio Grande, and to where the Golden Gate lets through the long-heaving waters of the Pacific. The story of how this was done forms a compact and continuous whole.[141]

The militant and expansive South Central section was as clearly represented by Polk as by Andrew Jackson; but, in the course of the administration just ended, its cotton-raising portion was in-

[141] *Winning of the West*, I, Chap. I.

creasingly aware of its common destiny with the South Atlantic as the slavery issue grew acute.

Although a strict party Democrat, Polk found himself at odds with such Jacksonian leaders as Van Buren, Benton, and Buchanan, in dealing with the problems arising from expansion. He antagonized the demand of Walker, of his own section, for all of Mexico, and the proposals of Cass and Douglas, of the North Central section, to apply to the new acquisitions the time-honored Western insistence upon local self-government,[142] couched in terms of "squatter sovereignty."

His break with Calhoun, who had temporarily carried his group to the side of Van Buren and then of Tyler, and who had thought of himself as a possible member of Polk's cabinet, was not unnatural, in view of the enmity that had arisen between Calhoun and Jackson in the period when Congressman Polk was a stout defender of "Old Hickory"; but it also illustrated the different points of view of Calhoun, the South Carolinian, as a representative of the South Atlantic, primarily interested in the power of the slaveholding South, and Polk, the Tennesseean, chiefly bent upon carrying forward the traditional westward advance of the pioneer, so richly exemplified in the history of his South Central section. More and more, however, Calhoun — now convinced that the slavery issue must be fought to a finish, even at the probable cost of Southern secession — was making converts in that part of the South Central States that lay within the Lower South. More and more, it was becoming evident that neither the extension of the Missouri Compromise line to the Pacific nor the application of squatter sovereignty to the newly won territory, would satisfy both North and South. The expansion of the nation to the Pacific raised the cleavage between North and South over the issue of slavery to predominant importance. The old pattern of sectional differences was not effaced, but for a time it was to be overshadowed by the pattern of North against South.

[142] F. J. Turner, "Western State-Making in the Revolutionary Era," *American Historical Review*, I, 70–87, 251–69 [reprinted in Turner, *The Significance of Sections in American History* (New York, 1932), as Chap. IV].

CHAPTER XIII

[TAYLOR ADMINISTRATION AND
THE COMPROMISE OF 1850]

[This chapter was never written.]

CHAPTER XIV

[THE PERIOD IN REVIEW] [1]

Looking back upon the years that we have been considering, it is evident that the thirties and forties were a definite period in American development; and this fact will become the clearer from a comparison of conditions in 1830 with those in 1850, from the point of view of the general movement of the history of the United States.

In 1830 the slavery struggle was still in its infancy. Immediate abolition was supported by William Lloyd Garrison in his Boston *Liberator*, which appeared in 1831. Two years later the American Anti-Slavery Society was organized. At this time, the border states of the North were still in doubt about the permanence of the system. The legislatures of Virginia and North Carolina were earnestly debating the advisability of gradual emancipation, and Kentucky passed an act against the importation of slaves for sale. But none of these states contemplated the retention of the freed negro in their midst, and the attacks of Northern abolitionists hardened and unified the resistance of all the slaveholding states. The Cotton Kingdom demanded more slaves for its plantations, and the rise of slave values created an increased economic interest in the institution, even in the border states. The South, as a whole, came to the conviction that the economic interests, the social institutions, and the political power of the section were de-

[1] [The substance of this chapter was written before much of the book had been worked out. It is therefore to be regarded as a rough draft of the author's conception of the whole, not as a finished product. As originally written it was intended to be a part of the introductory chapter, but the author became convinced that it was more suitable for a conclusion. In transferring it he had as yet made no change except for the insertion of a short opening paragraph. Consequently, it is not in conformity with the chapters which now precede it but which were expected to follow it. The fact that it was written at an earlier time also produces some inconsistencies — for example, with regard to the use of the words " section " and " South."]

pendent upon the defense of slavery, and in this defense the cotton-raising Lower South gradually came to replace Virginia as the leader of sectional policy.

Nor were occasions lacking for this defense. The opposition of large parts of the North to the annexation of Texas, and the general Northern support of the Wilmot Proviso to exclude slavery from the new acquisitions, were convincing evidence of a real danger. The formation of the Free Soil party in 1848 was followed by Southern addresses and conventions until, by 1850, a crisis was reached: secession was threatened. For the time, this was averted by the Compromise of 1850, and one phase of the slavery struggle was ended.

The period is also clearly marked, in the field of politics, by the organization of both Democratic and Whig parties in the earlier thirties and the disruption of the Whigs around 1850. Between these years, cross currents of political opinion had led to the formation of temporary parties like the Anti-Masonic, the Locofoco, the Conservative Democrats, the Liberty, the Free Soil, and the Native American. It was an era of political ferment. Even the Democratic party, which persisted after the disintegration of the Whigs, had, in these twenty years, suffered various vicissitudes. From the days of triumphant Jacksonian Democracy, the party had been losing successive fragments. Almost at the outset, Calhoun had withdrawn the nullification wing, strongest in South Carolina. Then a Tennessee group, led by Hugh Lawson White and John Bell, had broken with Jackson when he determined to transfer the Presidential succession to Van Buren, of New York. Senators W. C. Rives, of Virginia, and N. P. Tallmadge, of New York, had organized the Conservative Democrats in revolt when President Van Buren broke with the state banks; and, finally, Van Buren himself, perhaps the most influential figure in the political management of the Democratic party, withdrew his Northern followers into the Free Soil party. The years between 1830 and 1850, therefore, constitute an epoch in party history.

These years were also distinguished by the passing away of one generation of statesmen and the rise of a notable group of younger men, strongest in the Senate, who were dominant during the era and who died towards its close. Jefferson and John Adams died in 1826, De Witt Clinton, in 1828, Monroe, in 1831, John Randolph, in 1833, William H. Crawford, in 1834, John Marshall, in 1835, and Madison, in 1836. With the exception of Adams, Clinton, and Crawford, these were all Virginians, and Crawford was of Virginia birth. With their death the power of the Virginia dynasty ended. These leaders had grown up in the Revolutionary era which gave birth to the Union and which shaped the experimental years of its infancy. The generation which succeeded them came to leadership in the period of the War of 1812 and reflected the nationalizing spirit of the years that immediately followed. They would gladly have continued this spirit had their sections permitted, and, even when the home pressure swayed them into new courses and when they championed their own sections' interests, both their past tendencies and their hope of gaining a national following in their ambitions for the Presidency, led them to seek means of accommodating sectional divergencies. A brilliant Senatorial galaxy shone in these years. But Calhoun, the South Carolinian, died in 1850, and Webster, of Massachusetts, and Clay, of Kentucky, in 1852. Thomas H. Benton, of Missouri, after his defeat for re-election to the Senate in 1850, lost his former influence, and the public career of Van Buren practically closed with his defeat for the Presidency in 1848. James K. Polk, of Tennessee, who carried on the Jacksonian tradition of expansion and added the Far West to the Union, died in 1849. John Quincy Adams was stricken at his post in the House of Representatives in 1848, after a career in Congress, running from 1831, which outshone his Presidency.

The new generation which took the lead around 1850 were more concerned with the rights and power of their particular sections than with the menace to union which the insistence upon these rights involved. While, in general, they believed that their opponents would not press the issue to disunion, they did not hesitate to make extreme demands. Although Eastern and Western wings persisted, the North and South became, for the time, the significant sections. Having won their ascendancy in state politics, such leaders as William H. Seward, of New York, Charles Sumner, of Massachusetts, John P. Hale, of New Hampshire, and Joshua R. Giddings and Salmon P. Chase, of Ohio, on the one side, and Jefferson Davis, of Mississippi, Alexander H. Stephens, Robert Toombs, and Howell Cobb, of Georgia, and Robert Barnwell Rhett, of South Carolina, on the other, brought a new aggressiveness and a new spirit into the great debate. North Central Democrats who sought a compromise position, like Lewis Cass, of

Michigan, and Stephen A. Douglas, of Illinois, were unable to win the confidence of the South, nor did they convince their own section.

A change in American social and political ideals likewise took place between 1830 and 1850. Slavery was far from being the only leading issue of ideals in those years. Jacksonian Democracy implied a fuller trust in the common people and in their right and capacity to rule. A stronger note of optimism, as well as of innovation, came into American life with the confident new forces that formed in the rural communities and especially in the West. Organized labor in the Eastern cities also awoke to self-conscious activity and found in Jacksonian doctrines a support for its desire to reshape society in accordance with the gospel of " equal rights," in opposition to " special privilege," " vested interests," and monopolies. Social theorists, mingling with Locofoco leaders and land reformers like George H. Evans and Horace Greeley, introduced the new humanitarian and radical movements which characterized the forties and found clear expression in the new state constitutional conventions at the close of the period. Greeley's *New York Tribune* carried the gospel from East to West. These were the years when the public-school system was revolutionized, foreign and domestic missionary movements flourished, and temperance agitation, nativism, Fourierism, woman's rights, relief of the debtor class, an elective judiciary, homestead exemption, mechanic's-lien laws, reforms in penology, and many similar movements for ameliorating the conditions of life in America, were active.

It was not until our own time that a like social unrest appeared again. The slavery issue, the Civil War, Reconstruction, and the industrialism that followed, turned agitation into new channels. The thirties and forties were also a period of European radical philosophies and revolutions. Even conservative England had its Chartist agitation and its Reform Bill. In America the transportation net was not yet so developed as to bring the cheap Western lands within the reach of the poorer workmen, or to afford an adequate outlet for the farmers' surplus products. Hard times characterized the major portion of the period. Even the flush times preceding the Crisis of 1837 brought prosperity to the speculator rather than to the pioneer or the workingman. The soil of discontent was ready for the growth of social-reform movements, planted and tended by philosophic minds and watered by European philosophies. In a sense they were the urban analogues of Jacksonian Democracy, which in itself was not philosophically self-conscious, not in the least given to general ideas.

Many of the reforms sprang indirectly from foreign immigration, which began in renewed volume after 1830 and reached a new high-water mark by 1850. The Irish famine, the failure of German crops, the distress of small craftsmen driven out by factory labor, and the effects of the European revolutions of 1830 and 1848, all played their parts in bringing to our shores a tide of poor and unfortunate immigrants, the poorest of whom were forced to remain in the greater Eastern ports, where they swelled the ranks of cheap labor, brought-in the problem of the slums, and contributed disproportionately to the pauper and criminal classes. The humane leaders of the cities established agencies of relief and studied the problem of prisons. This immigration led, likewise, to an agitation against the foreigner, which took the form of nativistic opposition to his possession of the franchise and to alarm over the increase in the membership of the Roman Catholic churches. In New England, especially, the Irish immigration marked the beginning of a social, economic, and political revolution.

Even in the eighteenth century, there had been, particularly in the middle colonies and the interior of the South, a very important immigration of non-English elements, which had called out alarm and demands for restraint; but this had spent its force with the Revolution, and a breathing space of more than a generation had promoted assimilation.[2] But there was a special significance in the immigration during the decades with which we are concerned, for it was in the forties (as General Francis A. Walker once pointed out [3]) that a far-reaching change occurred. No longer did the native-born increase by a definite mathematical ratio decade after decade, as earlier. It was only by the sudden rise in the influx of the foreigners that the population of the United States continued its former rate of increase. Before long the new labor class changed the conditions of manufacturing, accentuated the tendency to class-consciousness, and formed the basis on which rested a larger leisure class, with domestic service, refinements, and less

[2] Max Farrand, in *The New Republic*, IX, 209.
[3] "Growth of the Nation" (a Phi Beta Kappa address at Brown University), in *Providence Journal*, June 19, 1889.

simple standards of comfort. Between 1830 and 1850, there was, therefore, a cycle of change in American ideals and in the composition of the people.

Less than one per cent of the population of the United States in 1830 were unnaturalized foreign-born; by 1850 the foreign-born had risen to nearly two and a quarter millions, or nearly ten per cent. In 1830 the negroes constituted about eighteen per cent of the population; by 1850 they were less than sixteen per cent. By the latter date the negroes numbered 3,638,000, and the foreign-born, 2,210,000. Thus, rising from a negligible amount in 1830, the foreign-born, of whom the overwhelming majority were in the North, gained rapidly upon the negroes of the South and exerted a pronounced influence upon all the aspects of American life.

Prior to the establishment of steam navigation on the Great Lakes and the extension of the railway lines into the North Central States, the poverty of the immigrants, the preference of many for industrial centers, and the taking-up of the cheap lands of the North Atlantic states, resulted in a congestion of the immigrant wage-laborers in the larger Eastern cities and along the lines of newly constructed canals and railroads. Thus, remoteness of the vacant cheap lands of the West prevented their direct influence, and the status of labor was unfavorably affected.

But, from the middle forties to the end of this period, there was an increase in emigration to the farms of the interior. This corresponded to the cheaper transportation and to the changing sources and resources of the immigrant stock. By the middle fifties, immigration in proportion to the population had reached its high-water mark.[4]

In the field of religion and church organization, likewise, there were marked changes. The coming of the immigrants, both Irish and large numbers of Germans, increased the strength of the Roman Catholic church. From five hundred thousand communicants in 1830, they rose to a million and a half in 1840 and to three millions in 1850. This rapid increase startled the older sects. At the same time, the trend of population to the Mississippi Valley convinced the Northeast, in particular, that power was passing to those new lands and that, if the East was to preserve its influence and its ideals, it must impress its culture upon the West.

[4] Norman Ware, *The Industrial Worker, 1840-1860* (Boston, 1924), p. 11, and P. F. Hall, *Immigration and Its Effects upon the United States* (New York, 1906), p. 11.

This was the era when rival denominations strove with each other for ascendancy in this new field. Home-missionary societies, building upon earlier foundations, sent band after band of New England missionaries into the West, concerned over the possible ascendancy of the Church of Rome and anxious to spread their faith among the pioneers. But it was a time of division as well as expansion. Doctrinal differences, and especially dissensions over the compatibility of slavery and Christianity, by the close of the era, had caused sectional disruption in several of the larger Protestant sects. The downfall of the established church in Congregational New England was accomplished, by the beginning of the period. New faiths arose and developed. Of these the Mormon church was the most striking. Beginning in western New York early in the thirties, it migrated to the Middle West and, at the close of the forties, founded its new commonwealth in the Great Salt Lake basin. Modern spiritualism likewise began with the " spirit rappings " at the home of the Fox family in western New York, about the same time that the Mormons settled in Utah.

The thirties and forties have a special significance in the history of American literature. It was at the beginning of these decades that Emerson and Hawthorne, Whittier and Longfellow, opened the classic era of New England writers and strongly reflected the section's quality. Thoreau and Lowell, also, did much of their most creative work at this time, and it was then that transcendentalism flourished and the famous Unitarian preachers, like William Ellery Channing and Theodore Parker, gained their place. William Cullen Bryant, who overlaps the period, had already shown an American quality, both in scene and spirit, in his verse. Perhaps the most original of the American writers of this generation was Poe, whose work was done between 1827 and 1849; but he was an individual genius, less expressive of his country and his period than some of the writers not so great in fame. In the early thirties, the colonial and Revolutionary frontier life and adventure were used to give a native quality to American literature, by such writers as James Fenimore Cooper, of New York, William Gilmore Simms, of South Carolina, John Pendleton Kennedy, of Maryland, and Daniel Pierce Thompson, of Vermont. At its close, Francis Parkman had begun to publish the volumes that make up his history of France and England in America — the epic of the American forest — and, significantly, his preliminary study appeared in the form of the *Oregon Trail*, when a new frontier was pushing into the Indian country. Irving's *Astoria* (1836) and his other works descriptive of the life of the Great Plains and the Rocky Mountains marked the tendency to find a new American scene and new native material in this remoter frontier, and Cooper, in his *Oak Openings* (1848), showed the same tendency.[5] Charles Sealsfield, a German writer living in the new Southwest, portrayed the pioneer life of that region, in his *Cabin* books. While such writers followed the advancing frontier, others depicted the contemporaneous great adventure of New England sailors and whalers on the Seven Seas. A new freedom, a new and native quality, found expression in such themes.

This was the classic age of American oratory, when the stately periods of Clay, Calhoun, and Webster sounded in the Senate chamber. It was also the time in which historians of distinction turned to their own country as their theme. In 1834 George Bancroft published the first volume of his *History of the United States*, saturated with the spirit of Jacksonian Democracy; and Parkman's *Conspiracy of Pontiac* appeared in 1851. To William H. Prescott and Irving, the golden age of Spain offered greater attractions. Joseph Story published his *Commentaries on the Constitution* in 1833. Foreign travelers, like Alexis de Tocqueville, Michel Chevalier, F. J. Grund, Francis Lieber, Harriet Martineau, Frances Trollope, Dickens, and a host of lesser writers, discussed American society and estimated the meaning of this new democracy for their countrymen.[6]

American newspapers took on a new form and a new spirit in this epoch. At its beginning, the daily penny press was established in Boston, Philadelphia, and New York, changing the newspaper from the special organ of well-to-do subscribers to the journal of the masses reached by newsboys. It catered to the tastes of the crowd, and at the same time competed for news with a vigor

[5] See pp. 140–41, *ante*.

[6] On the interchange of American and European literary ideas and amenities in these years, see: W. B. Cairns, *British Criticisms of American Writings, 1815–1833* (University of Wisconsin *Studies in Language and Literature*, No. 14; Madison, 1922); S. H. Goodnight, *German Literature in American Magazines Prior to 1846* (University of Wisconsin *Bulletin*, No. 188; Madison, 1907); and B. A. Uhlendorf, *Charles Sealsfield* (Chicago, 1922; reprinted from *Deutsch-Amerikanische Geschichtsblätter*, XX–XXI). For American authors and travelers in the United States, consult *The Cambridge History of American Literature* (New York), I (1917) and II (1918), using also the bibliographies.

that gave a new tempo to journalism. In many ways, the modern newspaper began in 1835 with the *New York Herald*, edited by James Gordon Bennett. The *Man*, a labor organ, appeared in 1834. By 1841 Greeley's *New York Tribune* was founded, with the aim of laying stress upon the " Moral, Social, and Political well-being " of the people. It became the most influential journal throughout the zone of New York-New England settlement that extended into the West. This was the era of the party organ at Washington, where Gales and Seaton's *National Intelligencer* gave the keynote to the followers of Henry Clay, and Francis P. Blair's *Globe* defended the measures of Jackson and his successor. From them the country press took its cue. By the close of the period, Richard M. Hoe's rotary press had made it possible to meet the increasing demands of circulation among the masses; and, in the middle forties, the telegraph revolutionized the rapid gathering of news. Periodical journalism also took on new life between 1830 and 1850. Magazines grew like mushrooms, and the leading periodicals became the vehicles of expression for the sections in which they were edited, and also gained a national circulation.[7]

But, however striking the changes in such matters as those which we have considered, it is doubtful if these decades were so strongly marked by them as by the economic and social transformations. The period was clearly defined and notable in the history of communication.[8] The Erie Canal had just been opened

[7] For a popular presentation of the main changes in the newspapers, see Jas. M. Lee, *History of American Journalism* (Boston, 1917). See also, both on the newspapers and on the periodicals, the discussions in the chapters, *ante*, dealing with the various sections.

[8] On the subject in general, see B. H. Meyer [ed.], *History of Transportation in the United States before 1860* (Carnegie Institution of Washington, 1917), and H. V. Poor, *Sketch of the Rise and Progress of the Internal Improvements, and of the Internal Commerce, of the United States, . . .* (in *Manual of the Railroads of the United States*, 1881) and *Manual of the Railroads of the United States*, 1868–69. On the South, the following give an insight into the transportation developments of the period: U. B. Phillips, *A History of Transportation in the Eastern Cotton Belt to 1860* (New York, 1908); T. D. Jervey, *Robert Y. Hayne and His Times* (New York, 1909); W. M. Meigs, *The Life of John Caldwell Calhoun* (New York, 1917), II, 354–74; *Correspondence of John C. Calhoun*, ed. J. Franklin Jameson (American Historical Association *Annual Report*, 1899, II; Washington, 1900), pp. 347, 349–51, 411–15; R. S. Cotterill, " Southern Railroads and Western Trade, 1840–1850," *Mississippi Valley Historical Review*, III, 427–41, and " The Beginnings of Railroads in the Southwest," *ibid.*, VIII, 318–26; and St. Geo. L. Sioussat, " Memphis as a Gateway to the West," *Tennessee Historical Magazine*, III,

(1825) and was followed, early in the thirties, by the epidemic of canal building which brought many states to the verge of bankruptcy in the forties. By 1850 the canal fever was at an end. Railroad building practically began with the opening of the period. In 1830 there were only twenty-three miles of railroad. By 1850 the mileage was nine thousand. By about the middle of the century, Boston, New York, Philadelphia, and Baltimore had rail connections with the Great Lakes and the waters of the Mississippi. This connection of the Great Lakes Basin and the Ohio Valley with the Northeast changed the current of trade and transportation of the interior. The monopoly of flatboat and steamboat over the Mississippi Valley was broken, and its northern half was served by New York rather than New Orleans. The economic unity of the Mississippi Valley was split in two. By 1853 Chicago was united by rail with the Atlantic Coast, and, within two years thereafter, the northern half of the Mississippi River had been reached at many points. Beginning with 1850, in a grant to the Illinois Central, designed to connect the Gulf and the Great Lakes, the federal government made lavish donations of public lands to the states, to be assigned to railroads, and the era of railroad influence upon federal and state legislatures was begun. The new gold of California furnished the basis for astonishing expansion of credit, the railroad net was woven across the North Central States, and the new sectional relations were emphasized.

In the South, the rivalry of the leading cities to tap the Cotton Belt led to railroad projects at an early date. The roads tended to supplement river navigation rather than to replace it. So late as 1860, the only through east-and-west line south of the Ohio and Potomac was that connecting Memphis and Southern-coast cities. Thus, the development of the transportation system worked to the advantage of the Northern sections, in spite of the large designs of Southern statesmen, and much of the trade of the upper half of the Mississippi Valley, as well as of the Great Lakes, was diverted to the Northeast. These were weighty facts in the history of the United States, as well as in the history of transportation and internal commerce.

Distances were shrinking, when measured by time of transit and

1–27, 77–114 (Mar., June, 1917). For the Northwest, see Frederic L. Paxson, "The Railroads of the 'Old Northwest' before the Civil War," Wisconsin Academy of Sciences, Arts, and Letters *Transactions*, XVII, 243–74.

cost of freightage. The canal and steamboat had worked one revolution at the beginning of the period; by its end, the railroad had worked a greater revolution. Even though astonishing progress had been made in railroad building in the nation during the hard times of the forties, the period as a whole was but the preparation for the era that followed.

The beginning of strictly steam navigation between Europe and the United States was marked by the advent at New York, in 1838, of the " Sirius " from Cork and the " Great Western " from Bristol, after voyages of eighteen and fifteen days, respectively. This was hardly better than the best (but exceptional) record of the sailing vessel, but it meant a revolution; and, by 1850, the screw propeller (invented between 1836 and 1838) had been utilized by the greater English lines and the American navy. The American Collins line, subsidized by Congress, increased the importance of New York in trans-Atlantic trade after 1850. But the sailing vessels served to transport the masses of the immigrants in the forties and fifties, as well as the freight — a voyage often lasting more than six weeks. This era had its brilliant sunset in the beautiful clipper ships which began in the forties and reached their glory in such creations of Donald McKay as the " Flying Cloud " and the " Glory of the Seas," stimulated by the demand for swift ocean passage in the Chinese, and then the California, trade.

With the opening of the Erie Canal, New York had leaped to the front, among the Eastern cities, in value of both exports and imports; but New Orleans, as the emporium of the Mississippi Valley and the outlet for cotton, held the lead in exports until 1845. While Boston and Philadelphia remained stationary in the value of their exports from 1835 to 1850, New York raised her export values from about $29,000,000 to over $47,000,000, and her imports from over $87,000,000 to over $116,000,000. Thus, though Boston increased its import values by a large amount and Baltimore nearly doubled its export values, New York's share, derived from the growth of the surplus of the interior (with which she was in closest touch), was that of the lion. New Orleans raised its exports relatively little in value from 1835 to 1850, and lost heavily in imports. During this period, the whaling industry reached its height, and the ships of Yankee merchants plowed every sea and visited the byways of the Orient and South America.

But gradually the profits of direct Chinese trade declined, the interest of New England in the Pacific diminished, and New York took over its tea trade and outstripped it in number of ships. Boston merchants turned their capital into factories and railroads; Philadelphia merchants invested in mines. After 1830, ports like Salem, Massachusetts, and Charleston, South Carolina, sank rapidly in rank among American cities. New York, the Atlantic gateway to the interior of the nation, was reaping the full fruit of its favorable location. Wealth and population accumulated on Manhattan Island. The opportunities furnished by the markets of the agricultural West and the cotton-raising South became the magnet, rather than the old colonial intercourse with Europe.

The domestic commerce of the United States rose rapidly and enormously. The combined tonnage of the American coastwise and lake-and-river trade trebled between 1830 and 1850.[9] The tonnage on the Great Lakes rose from less than 6,000, in 1829, to over 184,000, in 1850; that on the rivers of the Mississippi Valley, from about 28,000, in 1827, to 275,000, in 1850.

The surplus of the West was feeding the industrial Northeast and finding an urgent demand in Europe. In 1830, breadstuffs to the value of only $7,000,000 were exported; but, in 1847, they had risen to over $50,000,000. This was exceptional, due to the European crop failures and the opening of English ports, and the figures dropped in 1848 and 1849 to $22,000,000. But the capacity to supply such a relatively large surplus of breadstuffs indicated the new resources of the West, and its need of a market. Even the lower figures represent threefold the export of 1830.[10]

Cotton [11] had risen from a production of less than 800,000 bales, around 1830, to over 2,000,000 bales, in 1850. As over two-thirds of the crop was exported, this furnished the most important single factor in our foreign exchange and an essential basis for the use of bank credit in domestic business. The value of the cotton export was, by the close of the period, over three times the value of the exports of foodstuffs. In short, during these two decades an enormous and transforming increase took place in the agricultural

[9] The figures cannot be trusted in detail; see E. R. Johnson [and others], *History of Domestic and Foreign Commerce of the United States* (Carnegie Institution of Washington, 1915), I, 341–42.

[10] See the discussion in Chapter VII, *ante*.

[11] *Atlas of American Agriculture*, Pt. v, Sec. A, " Cotton " (U.S. Dept. of Agriculture; Washington, 1918).

production of the interior of the United States, due to the opening of virgin soils in regions equal in size to European countries, and furnished new exports, new markets, new supplies to the manufacturing cities, and new fields for investment to the capitalists of the coast.

After the Panic of 1837, hard times, and overproduction in consequence of the restricted export market, brought an era of low prices in agriculture, lasting through most of the forties. This had a pronounced effect, both upon domestic politics and upon the readiness of the whole West to press to new adventures in Oregon and the outlying possessions of Mexico. The cotton planter suffered in the decade of the thirties, for, while the Northern pioneer then found a home market for his surplus crops, due to the rapid influx of new settlers, the planter was dependent, for his sales, upon the foreign market, and the rise in slave values, as the new cotton lands were entered, increased his cost of production. The era of antitariff agitation and nullification coincides with years of low cotton prices.

In spite of the hard times, the ascendancy in the production of wheat, corn, and live stock, as well as cotton, was passing from the Middle Atlantic States and the Southeast to the West. The prairies and oak openings were revealing their value. A new Wheat Kingdom was founded as well as a new Cotton Kingdom. By the close of the period, as we have seen, the development of the railroad routes to reach the Great Lakes and the Ohio Valley had given an outlet to this section, whereas, before the Western supply was made available, grain had to be imported from Europe to supply the deficiency of the North Atlantic states. In 1846 the English government was forced by fear of famine to begin the repeal of the Corn Laws, and the price of wheat leaped upward. The revolutionary age of farm machinery began. Early in the fifties, the railroads had fairly entered upon their work of gridironing the open prairies. The foundations were thus laid for a new era in agriculture.

In the history of manufactures, naturally there were no sharp lines of division marking off the period; but it stands out as an era in which household manufacture gave way to the factory system — slowly in the remoter counties in the hills and mountains, and rapidly in the areas near the cities. The per capita value of household industries in the United States was $1.70 in 1840,

$1.18 in 1850, and but $.78 in 1860. The age of homespun was succeeded by the age of ready-made clothing, and the farmers' daughters were released from much drudgery and attracted to the factories. The markets widened under transportation changes; the farm needed no longer to remain a self-sufficing economic unit, for it was more profitable to sell and buy. These developments involved spiritual changes as well. The great mills on the Merrimac developed textile production, while Pennsylvania corporations made that state the leader in the production of iron. The combined ownership of coal lands, limestone, coke, and railway, with blast furnace, foundry, and rolling mill, had been achieved by certain companies, just as the various elements of textile manufacture had been earlier put together in Waltham and Lowell. Automatic machinery and interchangeable parts were being developed and applied to firearms, the sewing machine, the printing press, and the reaper. In 1851 American exhibits at the World Fair in London taught England that a new and creative competitor had arisen.

The larger factories tended to absorb or destroy the little mills that had dotted the countryside. Closely connected family groups of bankers, great mill owners, and merchants made the beginnings of a new élite, especially in Boston. The time when the workers furnished the capital and the manufacturer worked in his mill with his men and took part of his profits or losses in his wages, gradually gave way to the time when the capitalist managed a co-ordinated industry and bought and sold where he could in a wide market, using labor as a commodity.[12] As these changes became evident, labor showed an increasing tendency to organize and to strike. But, as yet, it was largely native-born and recruited from the nearby rural communities. Nevertheless, economic classes were in process of formation. Travelers, who were impressed by America's contrast with the Old World in this respect, dwelt upon our relative general equality, but in the early thirties the French observer, De Tocqueville, sensed the possibility of change with the development of industrial forces.[13]

[12] I have made particular use of the valuable data in Victor S. Clark, *History of Manufactures in the United States* (New York, 1929), I, and R. M. Tryon, *Household Manufactures in the United States, 1640–1860* (Chicago, 1917).

[13] *Democracy in America* (New York, 1898), II, 193–97. He wrote:

" I am of opinion, upon the whole, that the manufacturing aristocracy which is growing up under our eyes is one of the harshest which ever existed in the

About the time of triumphant Jacksonian Democracy, around 1830, labor became increasingly self-conscious and strikes were more frequently in evidence. Labor papers and radical labor theorists marked a new era. By 1850 the influence of the labor-reforming philosophers had receded with the general decline of idealistic movements. The opportunities of the West, opening freely as the railroads reached its unexploited riches; the influence of California gold upon wages and upon the conception of " the self-made man "; and the diversion of the reformers to the abolition issue — all helped to end " the Prophetic Age " of " the roaring forties." [14]

In financial history, the period from 1830 to 1850 begins with a time when the Bank of the United States, in its home in Philadelphia, was the master of the country's credit and its regulating center. Jackson's successful war on " the monster," as a monopoly and an " engine of aristocracy," opened the era. The efforts of a number of states to outlaw banks and the entire credit system, marked its close. Between these events, lay a series of struggles and changes in the field of finance and currency, the relations of government and business. The growing surplus in the federal treasury, fed by the tariff and by land sales, brought about the extinction of the national debt in 1835. The approach of this event affected party and sectional struggles over the proper policy of disposing of the public domain, and modified the tariff measures and the policy of the government toward internal improvements. The credit of the federal government was so high and European confidence in the soundness of investment in state canals was so great, that even the individual states were able to borrow lavishly to support their public works and banking enterprises. In 1830 state borrowings are estimated at thirteen million dollars, and, in 1843, at over two hundred and thirty million. In the " flush times " preceding the Panic of 1837, many states had plunged into reckless expenditures; when the lean years followed, some of them repudiated, and all of them were forced to abandon the field of transportation to the corporations. The new state constitutions with which the epoch ended, rigidly limited the power of the state to borrow and to engage in internal improvements, and often legis-

---

world; . . . if ever a permanent inequality of conditions and aristocracy again penetrate into the world, it may be predicted that this is the gate by which they will enter." (P. 197.)

[14] Ware, *Industrial Worker*, p. 25.

lation to that end required a favorable popular vote. The state as an economic agency lost power which the railroad corporation gained, and this was at the very time when the influence of the latter was increased by the opening of the era of railroad land grants.[15]

As a whole, the period was one of financial experiment, resulting disastrously to both state and federal governments and increasing the economic and political power of the banking and transportation corporations, although it had begun in attacks upon the entire credit system and in attempts to replace this with hard money. But advances had been made by the substitution, in New York, of a general banking law for special legislative franchises — a device which was adopted by other states. In all these events, there was clear evidence of sectional contests, as well as of divisions by regions within the states and by the economic interests of different elements in each community. As never before, political discussion among the people was concerned with problems of finance and currency.

In other fields of legislation, the era has a unity. In the tariff, it began with the high protection of the " tariff of abominations " in 1828 and ended with the tariff for revenue, in 1846. The years between were filled with sectional threats and sectional bargainings, out of which emerged the tariffs of 1832, 1833, and 1842. In the course of these years, the North Central States passed from the support of the protectionist party of the manufacturing Northeast, influenced by the need of a home market, to the support of the antiprotectionist South.

In federal land legislation, the period extends from the years when Clay urged the policy of distribution of the net proceeds of the sales of public lands among the states in proportion to their federal ratios; when Benton pressed his policy of graduation, preemption, and reduction of the price of lands to settlers; when

[15] Horace Secrist, *An Economic Analysis of the Constitutional Restrictions upon Public Indebtedness in the United States* (University of Wisconsin *Bulletin*, No. 637; Madison, 1914); Henry C. Adams, *Public Debts* (New York, 1887); *A Memoir of Benjamin Robbins Curtis, LL.D., with Some of His Professional and Miscellaneous Writings* (Boston, 1879), II, 93–148; and Davis R. Dewey, *Financial History of the United States* (New York, 1924). There are excellent illustrative details in J. B. McMaster, *A History of the People of the United States, from the Revolution to the Civil War*, VI (New York, 1920), Chaps. LXIII, LXV, LXVIII. On the Bank of the United States, see Ralph C. H. Catterall, *The Second Bank of the United States* (Chicago, 1903).

Calhoun urged the cession of the lands to the states in which they lay; and when John Quincy Adams supported the use of the lands as a great national resource for federal internal improvements — to the triumph of pre-emption in 1841, under the demands of the Western settlers. This was followed by the more radical demands of the land reformers of the labor group and the pioneers, in conjunction, that the lands should be donated, in homesteads, to the actual settlers. The issue thus raised became so involved in sectional jealousies that it was not until the Civil War that the Homestead Act — the natural culmination of the tendency of the period toward free lands — was passed. The land question showed itself to be intimately connected with American social ideals, as well as with the economic and political interests of the rival sections.

It is clear that all these legislative questions interplayed with each other and with the changing conditions of the times. Looking at the country and the era as a whole, whether we consider politics, inventions, industrial processes, social changes, journalism, or even literature and religion, the outstanding fact is that, in these years, the common man grew in power and confidence, the peculiarly American conditions and ideals gained strength and recognition. An optimistic and creative nation was forming and dealing with democracy and with things, in vast new spaces, in an original, practical, and determined way and on a grand scale. Not even in the South, where the slaveholding planter doubted the doctrines of the Declaration of Independence and looked with fear upon the tendencies of democracy, nor in the industrial centers, where class struggles between capital and labor began to emerge, could these forces be overlooked or defeated.

INDEX

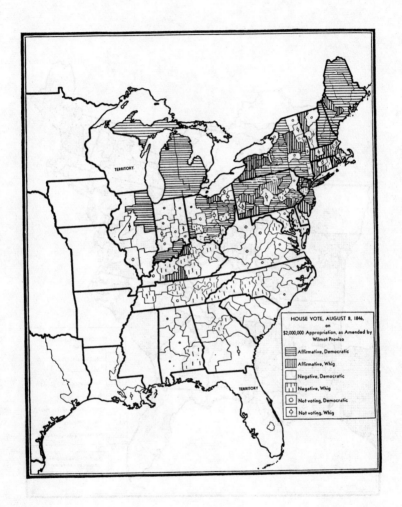

HOUSE VOTE, AUGUST 8, 1846,
on
$2,000,000 Appropriation, as Amended by
Wilmot Proviso

Affirmative, Democratic

Affirmative, Whig

Negative, Democratic

Negative, Whig

○ Not voting, Democratic

⊕ Not voting, Whig

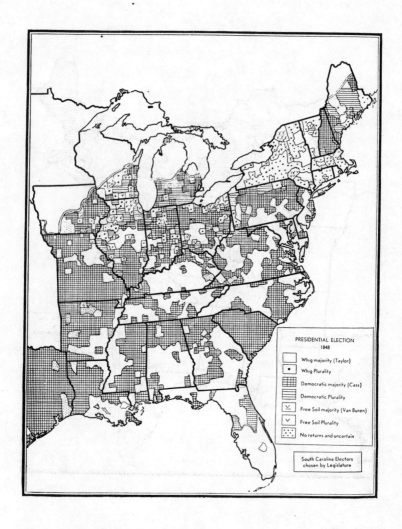

PRESIDENTIAL ELECTION
1848

☐ Whig majority (Taylor)

· Whig Plurality

▦ Democratic majority (Cass)

▤ Democratic Plurality

⌄ Free Soil majority (Van Buren)

⌄ Free Soil Plurality

∴ No returns and uncertain

South Carolina Electors
chosen by Legislature

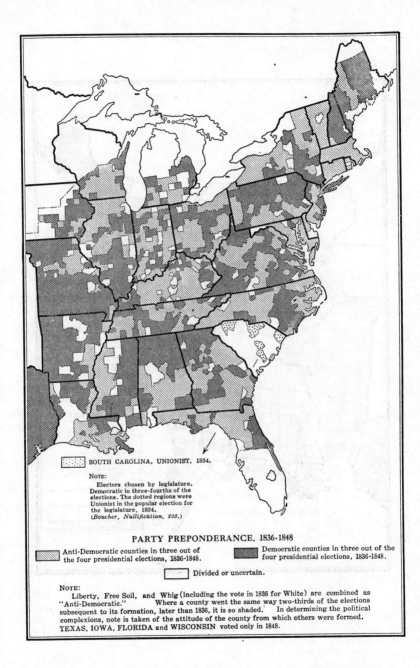

SOUTH CAROLINA, UNIONIST, 1834.

NOTE:
Electors chosen by legislature.
Democratic in three-fourths of the
elections. The dotted regions were
Unionist in the popular election for
the legislature, 1834.
(*Boucher, Nullification, 203.*)

PARTY PREPONDERANCE, 1836-1848

Anti-Democratic counties in three out of
the four presidential elections, 1836-1848.

Democratic counties in three out of the
four presidential elections, 1836-1848.

Divided or uncertain.

NOTE:
    Liberty, Free Soil, and Whig (including the vote in 1836 for White) are combined as
"Anti-Democratic."   Where a county went the same way two-thirds of the elections
subsequent to its formation, later than 1836, it is so shaded.   In determining the political
complexions, note is taken of the attitude of the county from which others were formed.
TEXAS, IOWA, FLORIDA and WISCONSIN voted only in 1848.

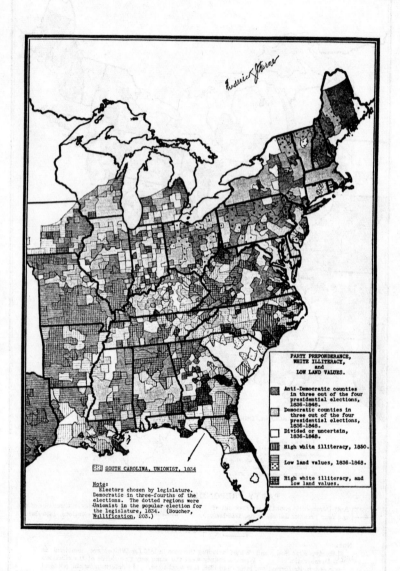

Frederick J. Turner

PARTY PREPONDERANCE,
WHITE ILLITERACY,
and
LOW LAND VALUES.

Anti-Democratic counties
in three out of the four
presidential elections,
1836-1848.

Democratic counties in
three out of the four
presidential elections,
1836-1848.

Divided or uncertain,
1836-1848.

High white illiteracy, 1850.

Low land values, 1836-1848.

High white illiteracy, and
low land values.

SOUTH CAROLINA, UNIONIST, 1834

Note:
  Electors chosen by legislature.
Democratic in three-fourths of the
elections. The dotted regions were
Unionist in the popular election for
the legislature, 1834. (Boucher,
Nullification, 203.)

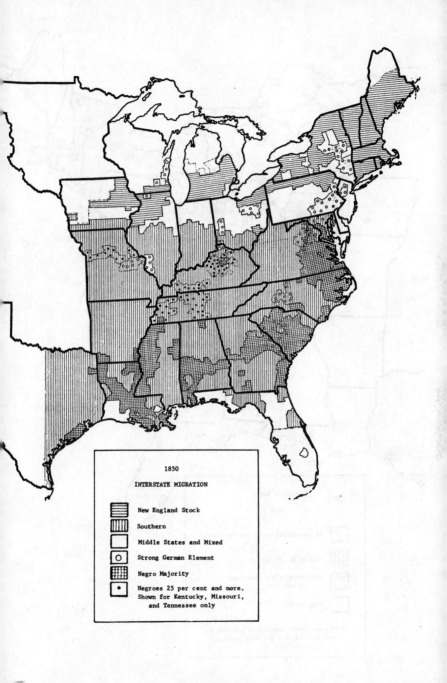

1850

INTERSTATE MIGRATION

New England Stock

Southern

Middle States and Mixed

○ Strong German Element

Negro Majority

• Negroes 25 per cent and more.
Shown for Kentucky, Missouri,
and Tennessee only

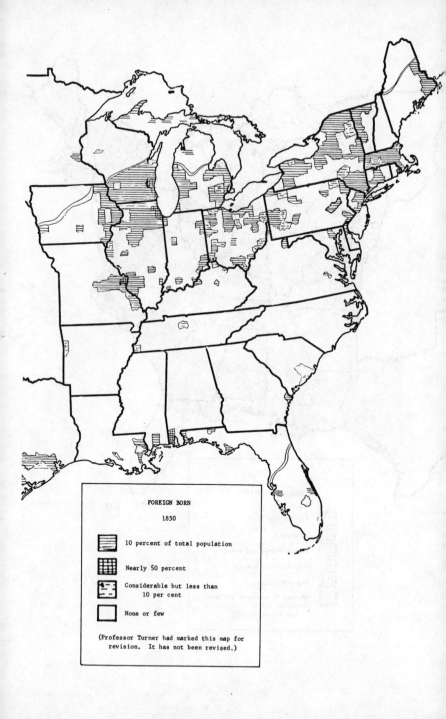

FOREIGN BORN

1850

10 percent of total population

Nearly 50 percent

Considerable but less than
10 per cent

None or few

(Professor Turner had marked this map for
revision. It has not been revised.)

CROPS, 1850.

| | WHEAT over 300,000 bu. per co. | | CORN over 600,000 bu. per co. | | COTTON over 100,000 bales (400 lbs.) per co. |

| T | TOBACCO " 900,000 lbs. per co. | | R | RICE " 500,000 lbs. per co. | | ● | HEMP " 500 tons per co. |

| ⊖ | C. SUGAR over 7,000 hhd. per county |

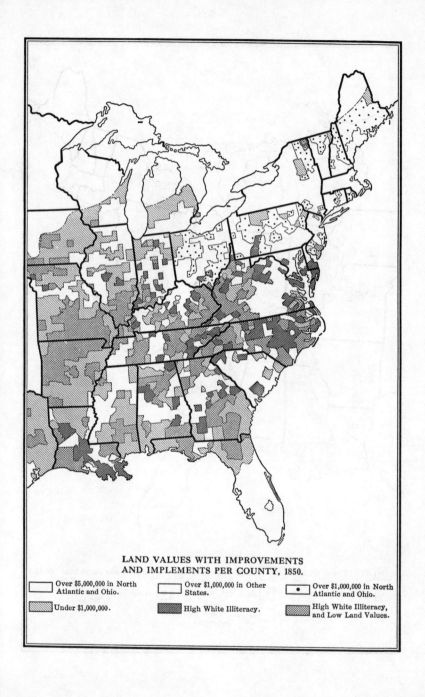

LAND VALUES WITH IMPROVEMENTS
AND IMPLEMENTS PER COUNTY, 1850.

Over $5,000,000 in North Atlantic and Ohio.

Over $1,000,000 in Other States.

Over $1,000,000 in North Atlantic and Ohio.

Under $1,000,000.

High White Illiteracy.

High White Illiteracy, and Low Land Values.

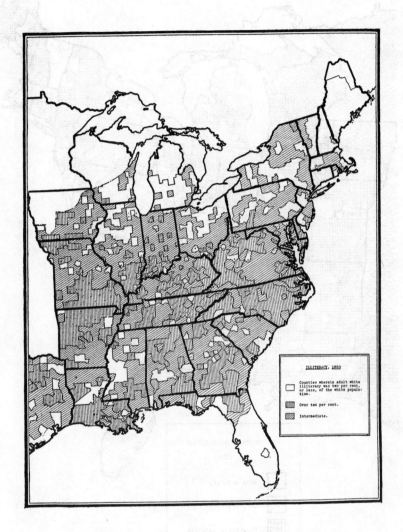

ILLITERACY, 1850

☐ Counties wherein adult white
  illiteracy was two per cent,
  or less, of the white population.

▨ Over ten per cent.

▧ Intermediate.

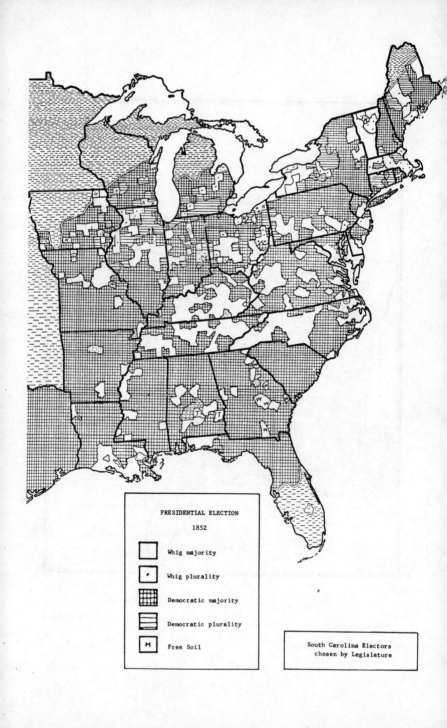

PRESIDENTIAL ELECTION

1852

Whig majority

Whig plurality

Democratic majority

Democratic plurality

Free Soil

South Carolina Electors
chosen by Legislature

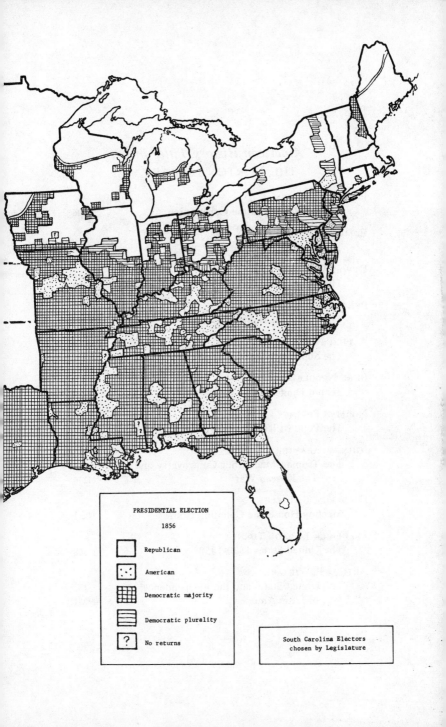

PRESIDENTIAL ELECTION

1856

Republican

American

Democratic majority

Democratic plurality

? No returns

South Carolina Electors
chosen by Legislature

American History Titles in
THE NORTON LIBRARY

IN THE NORTON LIBRARY